Underwriting

Principles & Practices

Third Edition

Robert B. Holtom, CPCU

National Underwriter

A National Underwriter Publication

Third Edition

Library of Congress Catalog Card Number 87-63160
International Standard Book Number 0-87218-337-8

Printed in the United States of America

To My Three Sons—
Paul, John and Mark

Contents

II DECISION MAKING IN UNDERWRITING

III BASIC FUNCTIONS OF UNDERWRITING

VI UNDERWRITING PACKAGE POLICIES

VII AUXILIARY DUTIES OF UNDERWRITERS

Preface

The insurance business has changed dramatically since this book was first written. This third edition has been substantially revised to reflect those changes.

The underwriting cycle was in a severe downward trend during the first half of the 1980's. Attempts at recovery are causing serious repercussions throughout the industry. These cyclical fluctuations have required more flexibility than ever on the part of underwriters, and demanded a better knowledge of the principles of underwriting. Practices must change to conform to current requirements and situations, and these changes are made much more effectively by those underwriters who understand the principles involved.

The Insurance Institute of America has introduced a diploma program on Underwriting, correcting the absence of such a program which was lamented in the preface to the first edition. The four books written for that program, along with my two books published by The National Underwriter Company, now offer underwriters the necessary literature by which they can secure education in the principles upon which their craft is based.

New policy forms, new court decisions, and new laws have caused changes in the practices followed by underwriters. The most significant of those changes are reflected in revisions in this edition. A major development has been the introduction by the Insurance Services Office (ISO) of a completely new commercial lines program in simplified language. While this book is not intended to be a definitive text on coverages, brief discussions of policy coverages are included so that the reader will know the frame of reference used in discussing specific underwriting practices. The commercial forms are handled by brief discussions of the new forms, but the prior material is also retained, since much of it will continue to be used for some time.

One of the major innovations in forms is the introduction of claims-made liability coverage in the program used for all commercial businesses, as an alternative to occurrence forms. Since this approach will require new knowledge on the part of underwriters, a section has been added to explain how to underwrite claims-made policies. I am indebted to Jonathan Owens for his valuable help in writing this material.

It is my hope that this new edition will continue to give the assistance to underwriters which this book has provided in the past, and to supply more current information on the practices of underwriters.

November, 1987
Whittier, California

R. B. Holtom, CPCU

Preface to First Edition

Underwriting has been the very heart of insurance since earliest times. This great industry of insurance, which has grown so large and affects every person so closely, has depended completely upon the ability of underwriters to handle their operations in ways which benefit all parties.

Perhaps it is because of this pervasive nature of underwriting that it becomes the object of good-natured ridicule. Perhaps it is even a touch of envy of the central position of underwriters in insurance that causes others to poke fun at the craft. Whatever the reason, insurance folklore contains poems, stories, and sayings about underwriting, more so than any other position in this huge industry.

One of the best examples of this — in my opinion — is the following description. Its author is unknown, but it was printed in The National Underwriter on March 5, 1965.

> "A typical underwriter is a man past middle age, spare, wrinkled, intelligent and cold; passive, noncommittal, with eyes like a codfish, polite in contact but at the same time unresponsive—cruel, calm, and as damnably composed as a concrete post. Happily, underwriters never reproduce, and all of them finally go to hell."

Underwriters have their own answers to slurs like these, as might be expected. One of these illustrates the trials and tribulations of underwriters, not singling out any one group of tormentors but rather encompassing all of them. Its author, likewise, is unknown.

An underwriter knocked at the pearly gates,
His face was scarred and old.
He stood before the man of fate
For admittance to the fold.
"What have you done," St. Peter asked,

"To gain admission here?"
"I've been an underwriter, Sir," he said,
"Many and many a year."
The pearly gates swung wide and St. Peter touched the bell.
"Come in," he said, "and choose your harp,
You've had your taste of hell."

These humorous examples illustrate the esteem in which underwriting is held, for one does not take the time to deride that which one does not respect. They also illustrate the cohesiveness and unity which exists among underwriters, regardless of the line of insurance which they handle; you will note that they refer to underwriters as a class, not to any particular type of underwriter.

In the face of these indications of importance and position, it is difficult to comprehend why underwriting in the property-casualty insurance business has been such an ignored stepchild, so far as any attempt to reduce its principles to writing is concerned. Although honored as the very essence of insurance, underwriting has been taught by word of mouth and by example, rather than by written principles.

Other areas of insurance have fared better in recent years. Claims adjusting is the subject of a number of text books and study classes. Electronic data processors are flooded with written material. There are classes in coding, rating, and other aspects of the clerical and technical handling of insurance. Producers are offered courses in "how to sell" and "how to manage an agency." Even company management has been reduced to a science and is taught as a study program.

Why, then, has underwriting been slighted? Why do underwriters continue to teach new underwriting trainees by example, by having the trainee sit at the elbow of the experienced underwriter? Why not use books which explain the *principles* of underwriting and tell *why* underwriting is practiced as it is?

I asked this question of many underwriters over the past few years as this book took shape. The answers were interesting.

Most of the answers appear to result from the approach used by underwriters in training neophytes over many years. This approach is a carry over from the guild system used in medieval days to train craftsmen. The apprentice observed the master, learning by observation and by listening to the instructions of the teacher. This method of imparting the principles and practices of underwriting to trainees is still favored by many experienced underwriters. They learned in this fashion and are convinced that nothing else can do the job as well.

Many old-time underwriters honestly believe that the principles which they follow cannot be reduced to writing. They believe that these principles can be learned only by a type of osmosis, a process by which the new underwriters absorb the principles as they learn how to underwrite from their mentors.

Other underwriters seem to feel that underwriting should be learned only at the side of an experienced underwriter. They appear to fear some loss of their own prestige or importance if some aspects of underwriting could be learned from a book.

Still other underwriters who were questioned gave the rather surprising response that there was not enough substance to underwriting to warrant a book or a study program. They feel that parts of an underwriter's knowledge must come from studies of insurance principles (which is true) and from detailed studies of contracts and rating methods on specific lines of insurance (also true). Apparently they feel that the remaining part, the underwriting function itself, has so little substance or body that it does not require formal study. Some of them even seem to feel that underwriting principles do not exist. Since they never have taken the time to reduce to words the principles which they follow, they feel that there are no principles used by underwriters. The group which answered this way appears to believe that *insurance* principles are the basis of their work, not *underwriting* principles.

None of these viewpoints is realistic to me. Underwriting principles *can* be reduced to writing. They *should* be made available to students and to those who want to learn about underwriting. The insurance industry and the people in it will benefit in the long run from using reference material which presents the principles of underwriting.

It is important to the future development of the insurance industry that more of its people be taught the "why" of insurance and of underwriting. There are many people who know "how" to underwrite or carry out their duties; they have been *trained* well. The industry needs more people who are *educated* to know "why" certain things are done. This education will prepare these people for the problems of tomorrow as well as of today. At the same time, the basic practices followed by underwriters for each line of insurance likewise can be written in a book, to give general background and reference material.

This book will not replace experienced underwriters as teachers of new underwriters. Examples from actual cases will help to explain the principles, and repetition will assist in fixing them in the minds of the neophytes. Many details of underwriting practices can be taught only at the underwriting desk. Different company practices, if nothing else, rule out a general text book which explains all of the practices of underwriting.

This book is an attempt to fill those needs which can be met by written material. It states the principles followed by all underwriters, and contains information about the practices followed generally by underwriters of individual lines of insurance.

Insurance is a dynamic business. Its principles do not change, but revisions continually occur in coverages and approaches used. The underwriting practices explained in this book are correct at the time of writing, so far as can be determined. Students are cautioned, however, that they can keep up to date only by reading current periodicals and by attending specific educational courses in various fields.

This book is dedicated to all persons who want to know more about the underwriting process. Students, as well as practicing underwriters should benefit from its material whether they are experienced in underwriting or not, and regardless of age. The material is intended to be an explanation of the underwriting process, not a recital of phrases couched in academic language.

Many people have helped in the preparation of this material. I am particularly indebted to J. Folger Allen, CPCU; Jack Gamboa; George Head, CPCU; Gerald Isom; Stan Manning; Bruce McBirney, CPCU; Allen Nixon; Ralph Peters; Henry Sanguinetti, CPCU; Les Stern; and T.J. Sullivan. While these people have rendered valuable advice and assistance, any errors or inaccuracies are my responsibility alone.

September, 1973 R.B. Holtom, CPCU
Los Angeles, California

INTRODUCTION TO PART I

ORGANIZATION AND PERSONNEL

The first step in understanding the principles and practices of underwriting is to know the meaning of the term "underwriting." The first chapter, therefore, explains the background and fundamental nature of underwriting.

The second chapter contains definitions of a number of terms which are used by property and casualty underwriters. Some of these terms are used differently by underwriters than by laymen. Some are even used in several different ways by underwriters. It is vitally important to learn to speak the language before being able to understand the functions of underwriting and to converse with underwriters. These definitions are everyday, practical definitions of terms used by practicing underwriters, and they do not necessarily coincide with textbook definitions.

The importance and position of underwriting in the business of insurance is discussed in Chapter 3. Included are such subjects as the changes that have occurred, the purposes of underwriting and the opportunities for the future.

The organization of underwriting departments and their position in insurance companies are the last subjects contained in this part. There are many types of organizational structures used in underwriting departments, and many different approaches to the actual scope of activities assigned to underwriters. These alternative types are explained in Chapter 4. Finally, the position of an underwriting department, and its underwriters is studied in Chapter 5. There are not only many types of organizational structures used in companies, but there are also many different relative relationships between underwriters and other employees. The relative importance of each function is explained as it relates to underwriting. This part focuses on a discussion of the basic question: Who has the final authority when the underwriter wants to follow one course of action in opposition to another department, such as Claims, Service, or Sales?

1

The Nature of Underwriting

Underwriting is not a part of insurance; underwriting *is* insurance. There are many other essential elements in insurance, such as sales, accounting, investments, legal, and clerical operations; all of these are also functions of many other industries. Only underwriting and claims are unique to insurance — underwriting before the insurance policy is effective, and claims after a loss has occurred.

When insurance first began, it was a very personal matter. A property owner and another party discussed the problems and values which would be involved in a commercial enterprise, and they would then agree on the terms under which the other party would insure the property. Together they would draft a contract, with the property owner's name placed at the top as owner of the property and beneficiary of the contract if the property was subsequently damaged by a specified peril. The other party would, as guarantor, sign at the bottom; literally writing a name under the contract, or *underwriting* it.

An early development of marine insurance involved the practice of persons desiring to secure insurance, and those desiring to write it, to meet in a coffeehouse. The person seeking insurance would bring a paper that described the ship and its cargo, crew and destination. This paper circulated among those persons who wished to assume such obligations. All of the people who wished to do so merely wrote their names and the amounts of exposures they were willing to assume at the bottom of this paper. The agreed rate and terms were also indicated on the paper. These persons, because they wrote their names under the description of the risk, became known as *underwriters.*

As the years passed and insurance matured, the personal contact became lost. Intermediaries arranged the insurance between the parties. Contracts became standardized with fairly stable terms and rates. The insurers continued to sign their names under the contracts but as insurers changed from individuals to companies, the signatures became those of the company officers rather than the individuals who actually accepted the risk. The term "underwriter" continued to be used but only applied to the person who performed the process of selecting risks and determining the terms of insurance. These duties — risk selection and determination of policy terms — are basically the same today as they were for the early underwriters.

Today, underwriting is only a part of the insurance mechanism, although it comprises the very heart of the operation. There are many other indispensable functions of a modern insurance operation: selling the insurance, preparing an application, typing the policy, printing the policy and other forms, billing and accounting, investing the funds, settling claims and performing legal duties, to mention only the major functions.

Insurance is now divided into two major classes: (1) life insurance, and (2) property and casualty insurance. The number of people involved is roughly the same for each class. There are major differences in terminology and approaches between these two lines. Only property and casualty insurance is covered in this book; any references to life insurance are incidental, given for purposes of comparison, and are labeled as such.

The total number of people directly employed in the insurance industry in the United States was estimated to be almost 1,900,000 in 1981. More than 525,000 of these worked in property/casualty companies, and 845,000 in life, health and title companies. Agencies, brokers, and service organizations accounted for about 525,000. In the property/casualty companies, perhaps 10 to 15% of company office employees are in underwriting departments, including supervisors, managers and staff people, as well as line underwriters. While no actual count seems to exist, it appears that about 65,000 people are employed in the vital function of underwriting — a class of insurance which accounted for more than $140 billion of direct premium annually by the mid-1980's.[1]

CLASSIFICATION OF UNDERWRITING

Underwriting is an occupation. Underwriters work for business firms. They are employees; in some cases, they are also supervisors, managers, executives, or even officers, although the two latter classifications are usually reserved for those in staff positions rather than line underwriting. The work which they perform is called underwriting. There are several possible classifications of underwriting.

Field Underwriting

In the life insurance business, a producer is called a "field underwriter" or sometimes just an "underwriter." The studies toward the designation of Chartered Life

---

1. The employment figures are from "Insurance Industry Employment 1981," published by the Alliance of American Insurers in 1984. The premium figure is from "Review and Preview," *Best's Review, Property/Casualty Insurance Edition* (January, 1986), p. 14.

Underwriter contain a great deal of information concerning the selling of life insurance and most C.L.U.s are, or have been, engaged in some aspect of sales.[2]

In the property-casualty insurance business, the producer is expected to perform some "field underwriting." This does not mean that the producer will bind every prospect that is encountered but, instead, will apply a degree of screening. This screening operation is designed to eliminate those risks that the insurer does not want. The producer is given a manual containing lists showing the types of risks that the insurer considers eligible or ineligible, or is told otherwise about such risks. Many producers use employees, who are called "underwriters," whose function is to select the insurer to which the application is to be submitted, apply its underwriting criteria to the application, and supply the rates for the risk.

This screening operation by a property-casualty producer is not underwriting. Most producers do not consider themselves as underwriters, and less than half of the persons who have qualified for the Chartered Property and Casualty Underwriter designation are producers. The C.P.C.U. study program contains relatively little material about the needs of prospects and the best means of meeting those needs. Although producers are not underwriters, they do perform a part of the underwriting function by supplying information to underwriters, as do other entities who furnish facts which underwriters use in making their decisions.

Another use of the term "field underwriting" in the property-casualty insurance business is to apply it to the function performed by company employees who work with producers and who have a specified degree of underwriting authority. A common example is the "special agent" classification of employees. They often combine the duties of encouraging sales, helping to write the more complicated risks, maintaining good relations with producers and performing some underwriting functions. The degree of underwriting authority that they carry differs by insurer. A few may have unlimited authority to bind any risk and to determine the rate and cover age to be used; others many be given no authority at all; the rest may be given limited authority up to certain limits of liability or amount of coverage. Rarely is final underwriting authority given to these people.

Still another concept practiced by some insurers is to have an underwriter visit producers on a scheduled basis, helping the producers with specific risks. Such a "traveling underwriter" or "field underwriter" would normally have the same degree of authority as an underwriter in the company office. This approach is not really "field underwriting" as the term is usually understood; it is, instead, regular underwriting performed in the field rather than at a desk. This concept is not used very commonly because it is difficult for underwriters to maintain objectivity if they spend

---

2. "The large majority of C.L.U.s were engaged in life insurance sales or sales management during most—if not all—of their careers." Rahmlow, Harold F.; Staines, Jeanne M.; Bowers, John J. *C.L.U. Profile 1979;* Bryn Mawr: American College of Life Underwriters, 1980, p. 20. At the time this survey was done in 1979, only 10% of CLU's indicated they had no such experience or that the question was not applicable, and over 65% were in positions normally defined as "production" in the property and casualty insurance industry.

most of their time with producers. There are advantages to having a person in the field who can guide and help producers, but most companies find that such a person should not have the final authority. It is better to keep the real underwriters in their offices most of the time.

Finally, some underwriters travel among producers on an infrequent schedule, discussing mutual problems and offering help and advice. This type of "field travel" by underwriters might be considered as being close to "field underwriting" but it is not really considered in that light. The underwriter, whether a desk underwriter or a supervisor, may make some decisions while in the field, but this function is incidental to the primary purposes of these trips: education, training, discussion, exchange of ideas and improved relations.

In summary, there is very little 'field underwriting" in the property and casualty industry, as the term "underwriting" is used in this book.[3]

Underwriting As a Profession

Underwriting is such a specialized, unique field that consideration might well be given to whether it is a profession.

A number of studies have been made of the term "profession." These studies have developed a set of components that are held in common by the recognized professions. Some of these include a degree of altruistic behavior, a code of personal ethics, a unified body of specialized knowledge and a broad educational background containing generalized knowledge.

Measured against these criteria, underwriting is not a profession. While a degree of altruism is evident in some decisions of an underwriter, most actions are taken in an attempt to make a profit for the insurer — not to serve the welfare of others. While many underwriters possess a personal code of ethics and conduct themselves accordingly, the practice of underwriting does not appear to require such a code.

Presently, there is only a sparse body of knowledge about underwriting, but it is increasing. The program of the Insurance Institute of America which leads to the Associate in Underwriting designation, is the first organized effort in this direction. This program, along with a few underwriting books now available, will help to increase the knowledge of specialized underwriting activities.

Also, there is a considerable amount of knowledge about insurance in general. Underwriters must be familiar with it in order to perform their duties successfully. At the least, they must be familiar with the line of insurance with which they are working.

Only the last criterion seems to apply; successful underwriting requires broad educational background in order to comprehend various factors involved in decision-making and the ability to picture the relationship between those factors. Generalized knowledge is extremely important in underwriting; without it, it is doubtful that an underwriter can be truly competent.

---

3. See Chapter 49 for developments which might result in changes in the relationship between producers and underwriters.

Underwriting, itself, appears not to be a profession, measured against the accepted criteria. A different answer might be given to those underwriters who have achieved the Chartered Property and Casualty Underwriter designation.[4] Without judging the merits of the latter position, there is no question but that an underwriter does not need to have the C.P.C.U designation in order to be a true underwriter.[5]

Underwriting As a Science

A science is generally considered to be a body of knowledge which is attained through study or practice. It refers to a technique that may be studied or learned, particularly through the means of systematized knowledge.

Most fields of science are quite precise, with an exactness that is measurable and standardized. Underwriting does not fit within that category. Much of the underwriting function is quite inexact and imprecise; it varies by so many subjective factors that it is not easily measured. At best, underwriting could be considered as "inexact science."

Science usually includes more than exactness; it also requires a body of systematized knowledge. There is no such system for underwriting. The closest that an underwriter can come is to study insurance; it is not possible to study the technique of underwriting through existing programs. Consideration is being given toward establishing such a system, but it does not exist now. When it is available, underwriting might qualify as a science, albeit an inexact one.

Underwriting As an Art

An art is a skill in performance that is acquired by experience, observation and study. It may be an occupation that requires knowledge and includes a personal creative power.

A common application of the term "art" is to apply it to the creation of aesthetic objects. Underwriting does not produce any object; it is more the application of knowledge in performing a function. The final result of underwriting may be the issuance of an insurance policy, but the mind boggles at the very thought that an insurance policy might be considered to be an "aesthetic object." Few objects are less beautiful or enjoyable than an insurance policy.

In a more general sense, an art is any skill or occupation requiring knowledge which may be acquired by experience and study. Underwriting is an occupation and it may also be considered to be a skill. It requires knowledge for proper performance. This knowledge may be gained by experience; the accepted method of learning underwriting has been, for many years. to practice at the elbow of a senior underwriter and to learn by experience. Underwriting knowledge also may be gained by observation; this includes the observation of the world and people in general, as well as

4. For a convincing analysis of this position, see the monograph by Edwin S. Overman, *The Professional Concept and Business Ethics.* Bryn Mawr: The American Institute for Property and Liability Underwriters, Incorporated. Published about 1964.

5. By the mid-1980's, more than 20,000 people had received the C.P.C.U. designation, and less than half of these were underwriters. Thus, perhaps 10,000 of the 65,000 people engaged in underwriting hold the professional designation, or barely over 15%.

observation of the activities of more experienced underwriters. Underwriting knowledge is even available by study; not in a precise manner but by studying insurance, psychology and other fields which may have an effect on the knowledge that is applied to the characteristics of a specific risk.

Underwriting is an art, as the term is generally used. It does require knowledge, experience and creative power. Now two risks are precisely alike, and a considerable degree of these qualities is required in analyzing the peculiarities of each risk.

Many people might consider underwriting to be an esoteric art, one that is understood only by the specially initiated. It is true that the underwriting function is a mystery to most buyers of insurance, as well as to many producers and company employees. Because underwriting is an art and not a science, it does not use mathematical models by which to judge a risk. Underwriters cannot point to precise rules that determine which risks are acceptable and which are not. Without proper experience and study, people cannot practice the art; they cannot even understand it. In many cases, because the underwriting process is performed within the brain of an underwriter, the end result is a decision, not an object.

This esoteric quality of the art of underwriting does not mean that a person of normal intelligence cannot master it nor understand it. Efforts should be made to teach the basic principles of underwriting to other insurance practitioners and purchasers so that they may understand better the workings of the insurance system. Efforts also should be made to teach insurance principles and practices to new and older underwriters so that they will be able to perform their functions in an effective manner.

Underwriting As a State of Mind

It is possible to think of underwriting as a state of mind — a mental approach to a situation. An underwriter tends to think along certain lines, looking for objective or subjective factors that might separate an individual risk from others in the group, but still trying to find a means of writing insurance for that risk.

A person who approaches individual risks from such a standpoint does indeed have a necessary qualification of an underwriter. This mental attitude must include such characteristics as curiosity, skepticism, thoroughness, perception, discernment, discrimination, judgment and diplomacy. Every successful underwriter has this state of mind. It is not conceivable that a person could truly underwrite risks without this attitude.

Underwriters are not the only people possessing this "underwriting state of mind." Many persons in other aspects of the insurance industry approach risks with this same attitude. Some producers, claims adjusters, loss prevention specialists, and executives are imbued with this basic insurance approach which aims at a separation of acceptable risks from unacceptable risks. This is a healthy situation and one which benefits the entire insurance operation. At the same time, it must be recognized that this particular state of mind is not essential to the performance of those other functions. An underwriting approach is helpful in other fields but it is essential only in the actual underwriting process.

Thus, this underwriting state of mind is a necessary attribute of an underwriter, but is not exclusive. The underwriting process includes many additional skills and much knowledge and experience. The state of mind with which an underwriter approaches this task is exceedingly important but it is only part of the picture. Attitude, knowledge, experience, creativity, skill in performing the underwriting functions — all of these are essential to an underwriter.

QUESTIONS FOR DISCUSSION

1. Why is the role of underwriting considered to be one of the primary and indispensable functions of an insurance operation?
2. Contrast "field underwriting," as that term is commonly used to denote the work of agents, special agents or marketing representatives, and underwriting, per se.
3. What reasons may be given in support of the statement that underwriting is *not* a profession nor a science, but possibly an art.
4. Describe three ways in which underwriting skill can be developed.
5. List five mental characteristics which an underwriter must possess, and explain the value of each.

2

Definitions

Underwriters use a number of terms that are not readily comprehensible to a layman. Some of these terms are peculiar to insurance, while others are common words with special meanings. Underwriters tend to use these terms somewhat loosely. The meaning often given to them in actual practice is somewhat different from that used in classical texts.

Every new underwriter should have a general knowledge of the most common terms employed in underwriting. The following definitions may be helpful as guides. No attempt is made to be super-technical because words tend to mean different things to different people, and some terms may be used in various ways by the variety of underwriters who work in the insurance industry. The meanings given here are those used in this book. It is believed, however, that they are correct for most underwriting usage.

Insurance

Insurance is a contractual arrangement under which one party agrees to indemnify another against loss or damage arising from an unknown event. Under this arrangement, insurance is purchased in order to transfer the risk to a professional risk bearer by means of the underwriting process.

Underwriting

Underwriting is the function of securing and evaluating information, and making decisions to accept or reject risks. It also involves determining the terms under which the insurance will be written if the risk is acceptable. In its original usage, underwriting referred to the operation of the insurance business; insurance and underwriting, in this case, were synonymous. Today a more restricted meaning is intended.

Underwriting is a systematic technique for evaluating risks which are offered by prospective insureds. The function of underwriting involves evaluating, selecting, classifying and rating each risk, and establishing the standards of coverage and amount of protection to be offered to each acceptable risk. The purpose of underwriting is to secure a safe and profitable distribution of risks. A secondary purpose of underwriting is to formulate and administer the rules and procedures which are used to assure that predetermined standards are met by underwriters.

Underwriters

Underwriters are those persons who secure and evaluate information, and then select, classify, and rate risks and who determine the standards and practices of acceptability. This is the meaning intended in this book unless specifically stated to the contrary.

In this meaning of the term, underwriters perform the basic function of accepting or rejecting risks. Along with this selection process, they also determine the contract to be issued, the premiums to be charged and the amount of the company's retention. In addition, underwriters must consider their relationship with producers, claims adjusters and loss prevention specialists, as well as with inspection programs and with competition. The underwriter attempts to select the better risks out of each class but, at the same time, other factors are weighed, too, in an attempt to write every risk that has a reasonable chance of making a profit. Rejection of a risk is the last resort of an underwriter. It occurs only when an agreement cannot be reached with the applicant upon acceptable terms.

Underwriters also try to select the better risks out of a large number of risks. Within each class, some risks are better than others, when such factors are taken into account as expected loss frequency and severity, rates and policy forms. The underwriter must attempt to select those better risks; often this includes the acceptance of a risk that is somewhat unusual for its class. This selection is accomplished by securing information, analyzing it and making a decision. Knowledge is required for proper analysis, along with a good background, good sense, and the ability to analyze, to think and to reason.

The principal responsibility of an underwriter is to make a profit for the company. This is accomplished this by the practical application of knowledge to the various factors of the risk which are submitted. The underwriter takes the steps necessary to reduce the chances of unexpected losses which are inherent in any program of risk selection.

The term 'underwriters" is sometimes used in a broader sense to include all those persons who are involved in the insurance function. A better practice is to limit the term to those who are engaged in the underwriting function. The term "underwriting process" can then be used to apply to all persons who contribute directly to underwriting. In addition to underwriters, this includes producers, inspectors, loss prevention specialists, persons in Departments of Motor Vehicles, authors of technical books used by underwriters, and all others who secure information which is used in underwriting. Obviously, most of these people also perform tasks which are not related to underwriting, but when they, or their work product, contribute to the function of underwriting, they are said to be a part of the underwriting process. In an insurance company, the term "underwriting process" refers only to those who actually contribute to underwriting, and not to all employees of insurers.

Insurers

Insurers are also known are carriers, insurance companies, or just companies (in an insurance text book). The term "insurer" refers to the person, corporation, or entity that guarantees to provide indemnity to another. All types of insurers are included in this term, whether stock, mutual, reciprocal, or Lloyds-type. The insurer is the entity that furnishes the insurance and evidences this fact by issuing a policy.

Policy

The term "policy" is also called the insurance policy or the contract. Several meanings can be given to this term.

First the written contract of insurance is called the policy. This is the most common meaning and is the one used unless the context implies otherwise. It includes the entire contract as endorsed and issued, unless otherwise specified.

Second, "policy" or "company policy" refers to a settled course of action or method of operation which has been adopted by management. This is not an insurance term but is applicable to insurance organization, as well as to others.

Finally, the term "policy" refers in some instances only to the basic part of the contract. In order to be a complete contract, it must be supplemented by endorsements.

Endorsements

Endorsements are forms added to insurance contracts to modify coverage. They may be printed and used automatically on certain lines; printed with spaces or check boxes for tailoring specific contracts; or manuscripted to meet the special requirements of some risks.

Coverage

Also called "protection," coverage is the specific protection which is provided by the policy against the results of the perils insured against up to the limit of liability.

Limit of Liability

The limit of liability is the maximum sum of money which the insurance company agrees to pay under the policy in the event of a covered loss involving the subject.

Subject

The subject, or the subject of insurance, is the object to which the perils can cause loss. It is often referred to as "the risk." It is important that the policy specify the subject, as well as the perils. This rule is applicable for each major group.

Major Groups

There are two major groups or classes of coverages written, plus a combination of the two. One is property insurance. This group includes protection against loss or damage to real and personal property. The major property lines are fire, inland marine, and ocean marine.

Casualty insurance is the group which includes insurance against liability claims, generally; that is, protection of the insured against claims of others from specified causes. This term includes more than liability insurance, because 'casualty" has been used for years to include specific other types of coverage. Many types of crime insurance are classified as casualty insurance, although the coverage is closely akin to that afforded by some property policies. Automobile insurance is classified as casualty insurance, but a substantial portion of the premium is assigned to coverages which protect against loss or damage to the vehicle itself. At the present time, the general terms "casualty insurance" and "liability insurance" are used somewhat interchangeably, when not referring to a specific type of coverage, and the industry has not yet settled on which of these terms will be used more commonly.

Multiple line insurance is a combination, in one policy, of coverages from each of the two major groups. At least one coverage from each of these groups must be included automatically in order that a policy qualify as multiple line. Such a policy, however, may contain any number of lines.

Lines

A line may mean one of several things in insurance:

First, the type of policy which a company issues is called a line. The name usually is taken from the major perils, such as fire line, casualty line and inland marine line.

Second, the classes of business which a company writes are called lines. There are only two of these in general use: personal lines and commercial lines.

Third, a given set of exposures is called a line. In this context, the term "line" is synonymous with "account." An underwriter may agree to accept "50% of the line," or may say that the company "will write the fire insurance for the Johnson line" when is talking to the producer.

Producer

The person who sells insurance is called the producer. This term includes all persons who are engaged in selling insurance, although they vary greatly in their mode of operation. The major types are as follows:

Independent agents. The largest single group of producers is the independent agent, a term which is used to designate members of the American Agency System. As a group, they control about 45% of the property and liability insurance in the United States.[1]

Agents represent insurance companies and are given specific authority to bind insurance, collect premium, etc. An independent agent represents two or more companies.

Brokers. Insurance brokers represent the applicant, not the insurance company. This theoretical distinction is sometimes lost in practice, for a majority of the agents also hold brokers licenses.

Exclusive Agents. Some agents represent only one company or group, rather than many companies. These are called exclusive agents. They have the same authori-

---

1. "Insurance Premium Distribution 1981," *Best's Review, Property/Casualty Insurance Edition*, (July, 1982), p. 12.

ty to act as agents for a company, but they place all of their business with only that one company. Sometimes exclusive agents act as agents for other companies when some lines are not offered by their regular company.

Company Employees. Some insurance companies write business through employees rather than through agents or brokers. Sometimes these employees appear to be similar to agents, operating out of local offices. In other cases, they obviously are employees working out of the company branch or home office. Those insurers which solicit insurance through the mail might consider those employees who prepare the mailings, and handle the applications and money that are sent to the company as "producers," too.

Solicitors. Some states permit employees of agents or brokers to be licensed as solicitors. As such, they may not be licensed as agents or brokers at the same time. Employees of agents or brokers are sometimes licensed as agents or brokers themselves but, if not, they may be solicitors where permitted.

A solicitor can be considered as an intermediary, serving the function of bringing together those who desire to sell insurance and those who wish to purchase it; that is, the insurer and the applicant.

Excess and Surplus Lines Brokers. Some brokers specialize in handling risks which cannot be written in the normal markets. Every state has regulations as to the way that this can be handled. Generally, these brokers can place the insurance in a nonadmitted carrier, but must keep records on each applicant.

Applicant

An applicant is also known as a client, customer, policyholder, assured or insured. This is the person who owns property, who has potential liability exposures, or who desires insurance for any reason. This is the person who is indemnified in case of loss or liability; the person in whose name the policy is issued — the "first party" in the insurance contract. (The insurer is the "second party" and the "third party" is the person claiming liability damages.) Applicants are usually considered as clients or customers of the producer during the entire insurance transaction. Before a policy is issued, they are known as applicants because they have submitted their requests to a company for insurance by means of an application. After a policy is issued, they are policyholders or insureds.

Application

The form upon which the applicant presents a request for insurance is called the application. The basic part of the application contains the essential elements of the insurance requested, such as the applicant's name and address, the type and amount of coverage desired, and the proposed effective date. The application almost always includes another section which is a questionnaire or a producer's report. It is designed to elicit information which will help the underwriter determine if the applicant appears to meet the eligibility requirements of the company. The application ordinarily is printed by the insurer and completed by the producer on behalf of the applicant. It may or may not include a binder.

Binder

A binder is also called a binding slip. Some producers are authorized to bind insurance with certain companies — that is, they can give temporary protection to the applicant until such time as the underwriter can see the application and take action upon it. The actual binder or binding slip is a written memorandum of important terms of coverage which is temporarily provided.

An agent has authority to bind the company, either verbally or in writing, on risks and on coverages which are within his or her authority. No written form is needed, but applicants, understandably, sometimes request written confirmation. For this purpose, a separate binder form is available. Some companies print the binder as part of the application in order to save the need for a second form.

A binder is effective for a stated period, such as 30 days. Ordinarily it is replaced by a policy that has the same effective date. If the underwriter does not wish to write the insurance, the binder can simply be left to expire. However, it is customary in most lines to take affirmative action to cancel the coverage. This action ordinarily involves an advance notice of cancellation, in accordance with the terms of the policy which would have been issued if the application had been accepted. In spite of this type of handling, common usage within the insurance industry requires the client to remain an "applicant" rather than a "policyholder," and any adverse underwriting action is a 'decline" instead of a "cancellation." An underwriter has two choices when a binder is issued, the same as under a non-bound application: accept the risk and issue a policy that supersedes the binder or decline to write the risk.

Risk

Two separate and completely different meanings are given to the word "risk" as it is used by underwriters.

First, the term "risk" is used most commonly to denote the subject matter of insurance, i.e., the object of an underwriter's attention. Thus, a home, a commercial building, a business or the driver of a car may be referred to as a risk.

Second, the term "risk" is used in an academic sense, and also by practicing underwriters, to mean "uncertainty of financial loss." In this sense, risk is the uncertainty of the happening of an unfavorable contingency or the possibility of an unfortunate occurrence.

An important concept inherent in the reduction of loss uncertainty is the operation of the so-called "law of large numbers." This refers to the natural law that, given enough similar exposures to the happening of an event, specified results will be obtained. If a coin is tossed into the air often enough, for example, it will come up heads approximately as often as it comes up tails. Similarly, if a company insured all of the dwellings in the world, it would know with almost absolute certainty how many of them would be damaged by fire within a given period of time. If all of the houses were of the same value, the company would know the amount of its aggregate loss. No one would know which houses would burn, of course, but a close estimate of the total number that would burn could be determined. This principle is the basis for insurance. By its operation, a company can determine, in advance, approximately how much premium it will need, during a specified period, to pay losses. A major duty of underwriters is to write policies in such a manner that the aggregate losses will not exceed those which are expected — that is, to select applicants who will have an average or better than average distribution of losses.

No one individual knows if he or she will have a loss. It may be possible to predict that 10 out of 1,000 homes will be damaged or destroyed by fire, but no one can say which 10 they will be. Each home owner purchases insurance, paying a small premium, with the assurance that if this property is the one to have a loss, reimbursement will be made for that loss.

The uncertainty of loss is transferred to the insurer. The insurer does not have a comparable uncertainty, for by insuring a large number of similar homes, it is able to foretell with some accuracy the aggregate amount of its losses.

Risk, the uncertainty of loss, is thus converted into relative certainty by means of the insurance process and the operation of the law of large numbers. If these processes worked perfectly, underwriting would be a dull routine of accepting a large enough volume of similar risks. However, insurance involves people, and they are not always predictable; sometimes they interfere with the process. This type of interference is called a hazard.

Hazard

A hazard is a condition prevailing in a risk or a class of risks which increases the likelihood that loss will occur. There are so many hazards that they are grouped by types. If a property owner is dishonest and deliberately sets fire to his own property, this increases the chance that loss will occur. The term "moral hazard" is used to describe these cases when there is an increased likelihood of loss because of deliberate or dishonest acts of a person. When a person is careless or indifferent to the chance of loss because insurance has been purchased, this will also increase the chance of loss and is called "morale hazard." Other types of hazards include 'physical hazard," the increase caused by deficiencies in construction, and "legal hazard," the conditions caused by laws or court interpretations which increase the likelihood of loss. The intention is that all hazards can be assigned to one or more of these types, and some overlap may exist.

The term "hazard" is sometimes used by underwriters to denote various factors contributing to uncertainty. In this connotation, the many factors which contribute to the possibility of loss of any particular object or person are called hazards. Since no object or person is free from the chance of loss, a hazard thus exists in every risk.

There is really no basic difference between these definitions of hazards. The first definition deals with the conditions which increase the likelihood of loss and emphasizes the unusual nature of these hazards; in effect, it infers that few risks have hazards. The second definition recognizes that every risk has some hazards, because each one has some factors which contribute to uncertainty. The difference is one of degree. It is true that every object and person furnishes some degree of uncertainty, but most of these are common enough in their total result that they are included in the basic rating. The problem comes when too many hazards are present, or when more severe hazards exist.

An underwriter who insures many risks with too many hazards, or with severe hazards, will find that the law of large numbers does not work. These policies will more than likely be required to pay out more in losses than he anticipated. This will be caused by the acceptance of applicants who have too many conditions, or too severe conditions, which increase or create the chance that losses will occur from a given peril.

Peril

A peril is a cause of loss. Examples of perils are fire, windstorm, explosion, collision, sickness, premature death, dishonesty and negligence. A person faces loss by various perils by owning property, driving a car, or interacting with other people. To clarify the distinction, a 'hazard" is a condition which increases the likelihood of loss, while a "peril" is the actual cause of loss.

Loss

A loss is a condition or circumstance which results in the unintentional reduction in the value of owned property. In insurance terminology, it is more common to refer to a loss as a valid claim for recovery under a policy. Almost synonymous with the term "loss" are the terms "damage," "claim," or "occurrence"; slight difference in usage are present in different lines. In all cases, these are events or incidents which happen without being intended or expected. Protection against loss is the reason for buying insurance, but if too many losses occur under a specific policy, the underwriter might decide to cancel it.

Cancel

The one who terminates an insurance policy before its expiration date in effect cancels it. Most policies provide that the policyholder may cancel at any time, but the company can cancel only with advance notice of a specified time, such as 10 days. Statutes sometimes restrict the right of the company to cancel except for specified reasons. In common usage, an underwriter can cancel a policy after it has been issued, but when a new application is not acceptable, it is not necessary to issue a cancellation notice, but merely to decline the applicant for insurance.

Decline

When an underwriter rejects a new application for insurance, he or she, in effect, declines it. This term is used for any rejection based on the investigation that is normally conducted with a new application, although the actual policy may have been issued and may have been in force for several weeks. In most cases, the declination actually involves a cancellation with advance notice; if notice is not given, the underwriter, in effect, rescinds the application.

Rescind

Occasionally an application contains information which is at variance with the facts developed by investigation. Some of these cases will reveal that the applicant is not eligible or acceptable, and the underwriter declines it. In a few cases, a material misrepresentation is made on the application. When a misstatement of important information is made, and the underwriter relies on it to his or her possible detriment pending completion of the investigation, this can be grounds for cancelling the policy back to its inception; this is called rescission of a policy.

A policy rescission is a serious step for an underwriter to take. It should be taken only when misrepresentation is of a serious nature, i.e., when it is obviously deliberate, and when the true facts can not be discovered without investigation. An example of the problem and possible effects may clarify this. Assume that a producer completes an application and binds the coverage on March 1, for personal automobile insurance. The application, which is signed by the applicant, shows the applicant's driving record for the past three years to be free of accidents and traffic citations. The application is tentatively accepted and a policy is issued on March 10, based on the information contained in the application. The underwriter seeks more information, and receives a motor vehicle report from the state which shows that the applicant had been involved in four negligent accidents and has been given six speeding citations, all within the past year. This report is received by the underwriter on March 20.

If the underwriter does not wish to continue insurance in view of the driving record, there are two choices. The policy can be cancelled by giving the required notice. If the notice requirement is 10 days plus mailing time, cancellation cannot become effective before April 2. This means that the company is exposed to loss on an undesirable, perhaps unacceptable, risk for more than a month. The other alternative is to rescind coverage. This requires the prompt mailing of a letter to inform the applicant that the contract is void from its inception because of the material misrepresentation. The seriousness of the action is now evident. The applicant receives a letter on about March 24, informing him that there has been no coverage since March 1, the date of the application. This action is in accord with contract law and is reasonable from the standpoint of this underwriter. It is vital to remember, however, that under rescission, the coverage is void from the proposed effective date.

Effective Date

The time at which the insurance contract becomes effective is called the effective date. A producer who has authority to bind coverage can set the effective date at a time before the underwriter sees the application. However, most companies prohibit the use of an effective date prior to the time the coverage is applied for, without approval of the underwriter. "Back dating" of coverage may be done for valid reasons, but since the practice may include the coverage of a loss which has already occurred, the underwriter will insist upon an opportunity to review all pertinent facts before giving approval.

If a producer does not bind coverage, the underwriter determines the effective date, usually giving consideration to the date specified by the applicant. In any case, the effective date is the point in time from which the applicant is expected to pay the premium.

Premium

The consideration for the insurance contract is called the premium. It is not used in the common sense, where "premium" means an extra benefit, or a sum paid in addition to the normal price of something. Rather, it simply means the amount of payment required to continue the policy during its term.

Term

The term of an insurance policy is the period of time during which coverage is effective. It starts with the effective date and ends with the expiration date.

Expiration Date

The time at which an insurance contract ceases is called the expiration date. Every policy has an expiration date, except for some perpetual or continuous policies; a few of these are single-payment policies and continue for the life of the property, but most are billed for successive periods and cancelled if payment is not made for a certain period. Some policies are extended beyond the expiration date by renewal certificates. Most types of policies terminate on the expiration date and are continued only by rewriting a new policy, which is called renewing. The underwriter has the option to renew or nonrenew the policy.

Nonrenew

One of the duties of an underwriter is to maintain a profitable book of business. It is not enough to select and classify new applicants with care, because some risks will develop worse experience than anticipated; some will deteriorate. The underwriter must review files, continually screening those that should not be retained. Some of them should be cancelled as soon as a problem is discovered. However, the underwriter may be prevented from doing this, in many cases, because of the noncancellation laws in existence. Furthermore, good public relations dictate that a policy be continued throughout its term if at all possible. Most terminations on existing policies, therefore, are accomplished at the renewal date, although this, too, has been prohibited on specified lines in some states. When an underwriter does decline to renew a policy, this is said to be a nonrenewal. Such action is the result of a reunderwriting program.

Reunderwriting

The action of the underwriter in reviewing policies that are in force is called reunderwriting. The underwriting process is not merely a single event accomplished at the time the application is submitted, and then forgotten. It is, instead, the steps an underwriter takes many times in reviewing risks with the intent of improving the book of business. Reunderwriting can be accomplished when a change is reported on a policy, when a claim is presented, or at any other time the file comes to the attention of the underwriter. Sometimes a special reunderwriting program is instituted at which time the underwriter reviews a number of risks of specified types; these may be all of one class, in one territory, all of one producer's business, or some other grouping. After reunderwriting, some files will remain undisturbed, some will be cancelled or nonrenewed and still others will receive new deductibles or other restrictions. The entire reunderwriting process is an integral part of the program of the underwriter in the attempt to secure a profit.

Profit

Insurance companies can show several different types of profits on their accounting reports. Underwriting profit is the gain realized from the insurance operations and is computed by deducting losses and expenses from premium. Investment profit is the sum of the return received from investments and the statutory reevaluation of investments at the end of the year. Net profit is the sum of underwriting and investment profits. Each of these can be losses as well as profits, of course.

Underwriters have some degree of control over underwriting profits and so do those in departments which control rates, policy forms, claims payments and expenses. Underwriters contribute to profits by carefully selecting applicants who have no more losses than are expected for their group, or whose losses are less severe because of such underwriting requirements as restrictions in coverage or deductibles.

Deductibles

Some policies require the insured to pay the first portion of every loss. The amount which the insured pays is called a deductible. It may be applied only to specified perils or coverages, or it may apply "across the board," i.e., to every loss. There are several types of deductibles. One is a disappearing or diminishing deductible, under which the deductible amount decreases as the loss increases, and the deductible amount disappears entirely if the loss increases, and the deductible amount disappears entirely if the loss exceeds a specified amount. A franchise deductible is somewhat similar, except that it does not diminish; the deductible amount applies to losses up to a certain amount, and no deductible applies above that amount. The flat deductible is the most common type. The amount of the deductible is applied to each loss, regardless of its loss size.

Some deductibles are mandatory, with the applicant being required to use them on specified risks or coverages. More often, optional deductibles are offered with choices on the amount of the deductible. Usually, but not always, there is a choice whether a deductible should apply or not. Applicants may elect to purchase higher deductibles in order to reduce the cost of the insurance. Carriers offer deductibles in order to reduce the number of small claims, because the cost to pay most minor losses is out of proportion to their size. Underwriters, on the other hand, sometimes require deductibles or higher deductibles in order to avoid small losses. More underwriting profits result from higher deductibles because of the reduction in claims expenses in most cases. Also, underwriters find that applicants who are inclined to present many small losses will be reluctant to accept deductibles. The underwriter's insistence on a deductible, therefore, tends to discourage applicants from buying the coverage, leaving a larger book of preferred risks.

Preferred Risks

Applicants who are expected to have a better loss experience than the average are considered to be preferred risks. Those are risks who are offered the lowest rates.

Some companies attempt to write only preferred risks, so their rates are generally lower than those used by most companies. Underwriters try to accept as many preferred risks as possible, on the assumption that loss experience will be better than for standard risks, in spite of lower rates. The percentage of preferred risks varies by line of insurance, but there are fewer of them than there are of standard risks.

Standard Risks

The term, standard risks, is used to identify the large group of applicants who are "average," neither good nor bad. Most risks fall within this category. So-called "bureau" rates are used by most companies to write these risks. Loss frequency and severity generally develop in a middle-ground, average-type of pattern. Standard risks are the largest group; they are neither as good as preferred risks nor as bad as substandard risks.

Substandard Risks

Applicants with the poorest loss experience are called substandard risks. These are the applicants whose history of losses, along with other factors, indicates that the future loss experience will be worse than average. This is not to say that these risks are undesirable; with the proper rate, they may be profitable. However, most companies find them difficult to handle because their rating structures are not established to include substandard risks. For this reason, they try to avoid them. In most lines, companies attempt to refine and avoid substandard risks by placing them on ineligible lists.

Unacceptable Lists

The types of risks that a company does not wish to insure are specified in an unacceptable list, sometimes called a prohibited list. These risks may not be bound by a producer nor accepted by an underwriter. Some risks are unacceptable because reinsurance treaties exclude them; without reinsurance, most risks cannot be written. Other risks are unacceptable by company policy, which means that the company has decided that it does not wish to insure them. Risks on the unacceptable list usually can be accepted by someone with enough authority, such as the officer in charge of underwriting, but as far as producers and underwriters are concerned, the risks are prohibited. Also placed on this list, by some companies, are risks which are acceptable but not desirable. However, a better, and more common, practice is to place them on a non-binder list.

Non-binder List

The types of risks which a company wishes to write only with extreme caution are specified in a non-binder list. These risks are not to be bound by the producer. Rather, the information about the risk must first be submitted to the underwriter; some companies use the term "submit-for-approval list." Underwriters have the authority to accept these risks, although they are taught to secure complete information and make exceptions only for the best risks in the class.

QUESTIONS FOR DISCUSSION

1. Define underwriting. Give two purposes of underwriting.
2. Contrast a narrow definition of underwriters with a broad definition.
3. Explain the two types of forms used with insurance policies.
4. Explain the differences between independent agents, exclusive agents, brokers, company employees, and solicitors.
5. Explain the differences between "hazards" and "perils." Give an example of each.
6. Under what circumstances is a policy cancelled, declined, rescinded, or nonrenewed?
7. How is an underwriting profit computed?

3

The Importance of Underwriting

Underwriting has changed over the years, but it remains an essential part of insurance. Originally underwriters performed all of the insurance operations. Now, only the selection process, along with related functions, is their responsibility. Although this is only a part of the process, it is still a major key in achieving profitability.

HISTORICAL PROGRESSION OF CHANGE

Other changes have taken place in the lines of insurance handled by underwriters. For many years, each underwriter handled only one line: ocean marine, fire, etc, becoming an expert in that one line. Then package policies were introduced in the mid-1950's, and suddenly several lines were combined into one policy. This produced multiple line underwriters, capable of handling all lines of insurance that can be combined into one policy. The division was changed to utilize two groups: personal lines and commercial lines. After a time, difficulties arose with these divisions, causing companies to experiment with still other types of organizations, such as committees of individual experts to handle the more complicated package policies.

Another type of specialization was developed over the years. Some underwriters concentrated on handling individual risks. Others moved into staff work, helping to prepare rules, underwriting programs, reports and similar projects. The separation between line and staff positions opened new opportunities for underwriters. These new jobs, along with supervisory and management positions in underwriting, added to the complexity of work performed by the underwriting departments.

As insurance progressed from a complete identity with underwriting into a departmentalized operation, a high degree of interdependence developed among departments. This close relationship is particularly strong among the three departments that are peculiar to insurance companies: *actuarial, claims,* and *underwriting*. The actuarial department is primarily responsible for rates. Rating structures and classifications are the joint responsibilities of the actuarial and underwriting departments in most companies. The claims department, on the other hand, settles claims and pays losses; its members sometimes advise underwriters about individual risks, as well as economic trends, and underwriters help to interpret coverage in return.

CONFLICTS IN UNDERWRITING

Underwriters accept or reject individual risks, applying rates, rating classifications and certain policy terms. A high degree of skill is required in these operations. A rating structure may be developed carefully, but if it is applied with undue liberalism, the rates soon will become inadequate.

The fundamental position of underwriting is recognized by the common term of "underwriting profit" (or "underwriting loss") to measure the financial operation of an insurance company, other than investments and taxes. This term tends to obscure the relationship among the three "insurance" departments. Underwriting acceptability needs to take into account the adequacy of rating structures, the broadness of the policy contracts and the liberality of the claims practices. If any one of these falters or deteriorates, adjustments must be made in one or more of the others. These adjustments require careful coordination among departments.

The purpose of underwriting is to help the company achieve a profitable operation. One method of achieving this goal is to select risks which are average or better than average for the rate charged and the coverage provided. Another method requires that the underwriting function be conducted in as efficient a manner as possible. Conflicts sometimes arise between these two methods; in order to reduce claims, more money may need to be spent in investigating risks. Underwriters must strike a balance between these methods and achieve profitability without incurring unnecessary expense.

Another type of conflict sometimes involves underwriters and other departments, particularly the sales department. For example, the producer may want a borderline risk to be written, while the underwriter feels that the facts do not warrant acceptance. Skill in handling such situations must be exercised by underwriters, in interests of harmony and profitability.

TRAINING, EDUCATION AND OPPORTUNITIES

An underwriter's job requires careful training and education. Selection of risks, application of rates, determination of contract provisions and cooperation with other departments are all subjects which must be learned. The time-honored method of learning by observing an experienced underwriter is inadequate in today's changing world. The luxury of slow, tedious learning cannot be afforded in this era of small underwriting profits, intense competition, rapidly changing technology and emerging social concepts. An intensified, structured program of training and education is needed by underwriters.

Those who are underwriters in today's insurance operations enjoy unlimited opportunities for promotion. If they are trained, educated and experienced, they are invaluable to companies. Such underwriters are not limited to one class of insurance. They may work in line or staff positions and may move up into supervisory or managerial positions in underwriting. Alternatively, they may transfer into other departments and make valuable contributions while enjoying rapid progress.

The promotional opportunities for underwriters are infinite. Many of them rise to high positions within the insurance industry. Most of the potential for advancement lies with the individual; it depends upon his or her ability and determination. The basic secret consists of learning the principles of underwriting well — for they comprise the essence of insurance.

QUESTIONS FOR DISCUSSION

1. Why did multiple line underwriting develop, and how did it differ from the prior system?
2. Name the three departments which are peculiar to insurance companies, and briefly explain the function of each.
3. Explain the conflict that can arise between the two methods of achieving the purpose of underwriting.
4. Why is it inadequate to learn underwriting by observation of an experienced underwriter?

4

Organization of Underwriting Departments

Underwriting departments, like departments of other businesses, must be organized in order to function effectively. Every company that has more than one underwriter has to establish some type of organization in order to divide work and provide lines of authority and responsibility. No established pattern for the organization of underwriting departments has ever been promulgated, nor is one necessary or even desirable. Each company establishes its own organization based upon size, type of operation, corporate philosophy and abilities of employees. Furthermore, most companies constantly study the organization and seek new arrangements which offer such benefits as improved communications, better supervision, new lines for promotion and development, and enhanced utilization of specialized knowledge.

A surprising degree of similarity exists among the underwriting departments of various companies in spite of those differences. The same general trends seem to affect all companies. One company may be somewhat different from another, but a brief analysis will reveal that one or both of them have changed recently and that the patterns are really quite similar.

These similarities exist in both major organizational categories of underwriting departments. One of these categories is the type of work handled by each underwriter or underwriting section, whether by line, by geographical area, or otherwise. The other category is the identification of operating and supervisory jobs within the department, ranging from vice president to neophyte. Each of these categories is discussed in this chapter.

TYPES OF WORK

Some degree of specialization or separation of work is present in the underwriting departments of virtually every company. The only exception might be the small company which writes only one line of insurance. Many combinations are possible because the division may be by line of insurance, by type of policy, by class of risk, by geographic distribution or by several combinations of these categories.

The principal patterns of separation by type of work are explained subsequently.

Line of Insurance

Traditionally, the insurance business has been divided into many lines. The major divisions are property and casualty, but the actual lines are much smaller, including such lines as liability, automobile, fire, inland marine, workers' compensation, surety, and the like. These divisions are not only traditional, they are statutory in many states as well. The separation among lines was so severe at one time that the policies could not contain more than one line of insurance until the middle of the twentieth century; what are now known as multiple line policies with indivisible rating were still prohibited in some states as recently as the 1960s.

It was natural for underwriters to handle only one line of insurance under this system; most companies wrote only one line. If a company, or a group of companies wrote several line, the underwriting was kept separate. This division existed in all aspects of insurance: rating bureaus were separate by line, different sections of the insurance laws applied to different lines, and organizations of companies or their employees were segregated by line. This division of underwriting departments by line of insurance was logical during its time, perhaps even necessary.

Many advantages were realized by this division of underwriting into separate lines of insurance. Specialization resulted in a high degree of proficiency; many underwriters spent all of their working careers in one line and became true experts. Since producers generally handled all lines, they were able to secure expert help in each line by contacting an underwriter in that field of specialty. A body of specialized knowledge was developed because of the number of years that many people spent in a fairly narrow field. Associations and other insurance organizations were able to call upon a group of underwriters who were knowledgeable in each line, thus aiding in the development of industry approaches to new problems. An advantage from the standpoint of the underwriters, themselves, was the psychological benefit which they received from becoming experts in their fields; they felt secure and confident because they were thoroughly acquainted with the various ramifications and unique situations in the specialized lines.

The disadvantages of separating underwriting into individual lines did not become apparent until the advent of the multiple line policies. When companies prepared to issue policies which included two or more lines of insurance, they realized that they had few, if any, underwriters who were knowledgeable in more than one line. The system of separation by line had developed a corps of underwriters who were experts in their own lines but were quite ignorant of other lines. The major disadvantage of the line approach to underwriting was the apparent inability to adapt to the multiple line concept. Producers were required to contact several underwriters for answers on just one policy. The relative weights of each line became items of contention, and the former confidence and expert knowledge vanished before the new breed of contracts.

Other disadvantages to the line concept of underwriting had appeared earlier, of course. They had been ignored because no alternative appeared available. When the multiple line concept was accepted, these disadvantages of the separate line approach became evident. One of these disadvantages concerned lack of flexibility. A young underwriter, for example, who had become expert in one line might be confronted with a more experienced underwriter who was only a few years older. The younger person in this situation would be doomed to a second-level position, unless a change in companies was made. Very few opportunities for promotion were available, because each underwriting section was fairly small and was narrow in its breadth of business handled. The path of progression from underwriter trainee to superintendent or manager was within one line only, severely limiting the opportunities for an individual to progress and restricting the available personnel who could be appointed by management to supervisory positions. A related disadvantage was the lack of replacements for vacancies in the ranks of underwriters. An underwriting manager was limited to promoting the best available person within the line, rather than selecting the most capable person in the entire underwriting department.

This traditional structure of separation by line of insurance encountered major problems when multiple line policies were introduced in the 1950s. Suddenly, for the first time in United States insurance history, major lines were combined in one policy. As underwriting departments tried to adjust to this new concept, they realized that the old organization of the departments was inadequate. A multiple line policy needed to be referred to several underwriters, each handling one special line. This was enough of a problem by its time-consuming nature, but larger problems soon arose. It became apparent that if each underwriter tried to impose judgment concerning the acceptability of the risk and the conditions precedent to acceptance, serious conflict would arise. An underwriter handling a small portion of a multiple line policy might want to decline the risk, while the underwriters for the major lines found the risk acceptable. Questions soon arose about the ultimate authority, the weight to be given each line, the relationship among the various recommendations for improvement of the risk, and the ability to make a prompt decision on the entire policy.

Underwriting by line of insurance was inadequate for the new concept. A change appeared to be necessary.

Multiple line

The logical answer to the inadequacies of underwriting by line, when handling multiple line policies, was to train underwriters to handle multiple lines. This was the approach adopted by most companies in the 1950s. All underwriters learned enough about the underwriting of all lines contained in the packages to enable them to underwrite the entire policies.

A modification of the multiple line approach was made in most companies from inception. Since multiple line policies were designed either for personal lines or commercial lines, but never both, it was natural to separate underwriters on the same basis. A personal lines underwriter handled all lines which fell within the personal lines field; a commercial lines underwriter did likewise for that field. In this way, an underwriter did not need to learn how to handle all lines. A personal lines underwriter did not handle workers' compensation insurance, for example, nor did a commercial line underwriter handle dwelling fire coverages. Within each of the categories of personal and commercial, underwriters were true multiple line underwriters, handling all lines within that category.

A number of advantages became evident to the multiple line underwriting approach. A package policy now could be handled by just one underwriter who was familiar with all lines, who knew the proper weight to give all component parts and who could make a decision on the entire policy. A producer needed to talk to only one underwriter in order to get answers to all questions on a policy. Responsibility for results on package policies could be fixed more precisely, for only one underwriter handled the file.

In addition to these advantages in the handling of multiple line policies, some advantages in the relationship of underwriting personnel were also realized. Morale tended to improve as underwriters learned new coverages and broadened out from the old limitations imposed by handling just one line. Promotional possibilities were improved, for all underwriters were trained in all lines, permitting the best workers to rise to the top — limited only by the differences between personal and commercial lines.

Disadvantages to the multiple line approach to underwriting soon became evident, however. In time, supervisors realized that an underwriter does not become expert in all lines merely by reading the rules and receiving a title of "multiple line underwriter." Too many policies were being handled with no recognition of potential problems. Too many losses were occurring which might have been prevented by proper handling on the part of a fully trained underwriter. Even if older underwriters could have grasped the fundamentals of lines, other than their specialties, on the basis of the general insurance education which they had received, it was obviously impossible to train new underwriters in all lines.

Other areas besides underwriting also were helped less than had appeared at first glance. Producers found that the benefit of talking over a file with one underwriter was more than offset by the problems which were caused when that underwriter was not really an expert on the subject. Producers realized that it was better, in some cases, to talk with two or more underwriters, if each one could render expert help on an aspect of the problem. Even the promotional possibilities were less than anticipated. The barrier between personal and commercial lines became greater than before because of the complexities of the policies used by each line. Supervisors found that they were less expert on certain aspects of policies than were some of the underwriters, and it was realized that this condition was inherent in the system. Morale tended to decline as underwriters struggled with unfamiliar situations and as they recognized the difficulties in becoming expert in all lines.

Multiple line underwriting became discredited after a few years. Loss results deteriorated and insurers searched for a better alignment of underwriting duties.

Combination Organization

The next development involved an attempt to combine the best features of line underwriting with those of multiple line underwriting. This was accomplished by separating policies into two groups. One group required expert knowledge of each of several lines in a package policy, each line having significant weight. The other group consisted of those policies in which one line predominated and others were relatively insignificant. Expertise, therefore, was needed only on the major lines.

It so happened that, to a considerable degree, the more evenly-weighted policies were commercial, while the uneven policies were personal. For example, a commercial package policy contained substantial exposures in each of the fire, crime and liability fields. By contrast, the most popular personal lines package was mainly comprised of a fire-type policy, plus the closely related crime coverages, while the liability portion was so slight that it required little attention from underwriters. Accordingly, many companies returned to line underwriting in the commercial section, with package policies being handled by several underwriters. In the personal section, multiple line underwriters are used for package policies; fire lines may be handled alone or by the multiple line underwriters, while automobile policies are handled by separate underwriters who handle only that line.

The coverage combinations vary by company but generally follow the practices previously outlined. It appears that this approach offers the largest number of advantages and the least number of disadvantages. Each is, of course, carried forward from the separate approaches. An advantage is the flexibility which the combination system introduces, because underwriters and policies can be changed from one approach to another with a minimum of disruption. A disadvantage is the confusion of organization which results, and the danger of some underwriters feeling that they are being denied as many opportunities as others. In the latter case, it is not certain whether multiple line underwriters feel slighted because they cannot become expert in one line, or vice versa.

This combination approach appears to have gained favor with a large number of companies. It seems to be the best approach for existing conditions. As conditions change, and as new concepts of insurance are introduced, the organization of underwriting departments will undoubtedly change.

Geographic Separation

One remaining type of organization of underwriting departments concerns the separation of underwriters by geographic factors. This type of treatment can be used with any of the other types: line of insurance, multiple line, or combination.

Many variations of this approach are used. Most large companies use some type of separation. If two states are handled by a branch office, for example, it is not unusual to divide the underwriters into two groups, each handling a state. The efficiency of this system depends upon the size of operation because there are minimum and maximum numbers of underwriters which a company wishes to place under one supervisor.

Several reasons are used for adopting this system. One is for efficiency — having an underwriting section contain not more than a stated number of underwriters. When size requires a split, the most logical split in many cases is only along geographical lines. However, another reason is equally compelling. This is the desire for underwriters to specialize in a particular territory. For many lines of insurance, conditions differ among states: laws, court conditions, driving enforcement, employment conditions and many more. There are obvious advantages to having underwriters specialize by states.

Another reason often given by companies for separating underwriters along geographical lines is the increased ability that comes with knowing the producers more thoroughly. As an underwriter and a producer become more familiar with one another, the underwriter usually can help the producer more; by knowing weak points and problem areas, the underwriter may be able to be of substantial benefit to the producer. At the same time, the underwriter learns which producers are thorough in the information that they submit and which ones require more investigation of their risks. Many companies feel that underwriters should "underwrite the producer" to some degree, making more exceptions for profitable producers and adhering stricly to the rules for unprofitable producers. This type of underwriting requires thorough knowledge of the producers and their records. Obviously, it is much easier to know a few producers in a small area than to attempt to know all of the producers who are served by the office.

The principal advantage of geographic separation within the underwriting department is one of efficiency. While the first division of underwriters in an office may be by line or by a separation between personal and commercial, the second split often is geographical. This permits better knowledge of the area and reduces travel expense when the underwriters visit in the field. A secondary advantage, but almost as important, is the improvement that comes in the relationship between underwriters and producers following the assignment of one group of producers to a small group of underwriters.

In spite of the advantages and the widespread use of this divisional type work, there are some disadvantages. One is, the underwriters might become too familiar with producers through prolonged close contact. This might result in becoming overly concerned with the problems of the producer. This tendency, to blend the objectives of underwriters and producers, might further result in decreasing the emphasis on the basic concern of underwriting, which is to classify and rate risks in such a fashion that they will be profitable. Many companies do not feel that this condition is of much concern, because underwriters can maintain their objectivity regardless of their familiarity with producers. Others recognize the possibilities of problems and attempt to avoid them either by not dividing the underwriters into groups which are too small, or by frequently rotating the underwriters. Both of these precautionary methods tend to destroy some of the advantages of geographical separation, but they are attempts to balance good and bad points.

Other disadvantages of geographical separation of underwriters are less severe but still important. For example, all mail needs to be sorted into more sections as the number of geographic groups increase; this is not serious, nor of much concern to underwriters, but it does raise costs. Morale may decrease if the geographic units are too small, too. Some members may be incompatible, and find that the close working relationship of small units increases the chances for discord. Small units destroy flexibility; if one member of a three-man section is absent, and the other two cannot handle the volume, a substitute must be used. The substitute may not have the familiarity with the area or the producers that the regular underwriters have. He or she may not even have the familiarity that an underwriter in a large unit would have. This lack of flexibility also tends to limit promotions, at least in the minds of the underwriters, because each person is familiar with only a limited section of the work.

These difficulties may restrict the spread of geographical separation in the underwriting departments of some companies, but they certainly do not prevent it. Most insurers divide underwriters on some sort of a geographical basis. There is no pattern to the types of separation which are used by companies. In fact, some insurers use one system for personal lines and another for commercial lines. Perhaps the most common separation involving underwriters in the personal or commercial lines sections in an office is to divide them into two to four units, each handling a state or a portion of a state. The size of each unit depends on the company and on the number of its producers. A large unit might contain 20 or 25 underwriters. Smaller units, down to three or four underwriters, are not uncommon. At the extreme, in geographical separation, is the practice of some large companies to assign each underwriter with all of the personal or commercial business of a few producers, perhaps 10 or 12, or even to handle *all* of the business of these producers.

Trends in Organization

The organization of underwriting departments by types of work has changed drastically over the past few decades and will probably change again in the future. The traditional separation by line of insurance served the needs of the industry when mono-line policies were used. The advent of multiple line policies led to an immediate change whereby almost every underwriter handled all lines. The futility of this approach for all lines soon became evident and led to sort of a compromise which kept single line experts where they were needed, and permitted multiple line underwriting where it could be handled without too much difficulty. Threading through all of these systems was a concept of separating underwriters by geographical areas.

Over the years no clear-cut pattern emerged for use by all companies, or even by most of them. Experimentation continued as each insurer searched for the best combination for its operation. At one extreme, specialists still handled single lines for some companies, sometimes working with all of the producers served by that office. At the other extreme, underwriters were assigned small groups of producers and handled all lines of insurance written by their company.

Most insurers used systems which fell between those extremes. Most separated underwriters between personal and commercial lines. Commercial underwriters tended to handle only one line, or perhaps two lines which were closely related. Personal lines underwriters tended to be multiple line, depending upon the relative volume of the lines written. Geographical separation depended upon the size of the office, with the most common pattern providing for about 10 underwriters to form a unit handling a distinct geographical area.

The future will contain further changes but their general outlines are predictable now. It appears likely that multiple line underwriting will become more common as more coverages are packaged and underwriters become more knowledgeable. The trends toward more packaging appear to be fixed. Increased knowlege of underwriters is inevitable as more educational courses are made available, along with training courses which are better designed. The belated recognition of underwriting as a subject which can be studied and taught, as a field of endeavor apart from the general insurance picture, leads to the conclusion that the underwriters of the future will be more knowledgeable than their predecessors. Increased study of the principles and practices of underwriting will result in a group of underwriters who are well equipped to handle the problems they will face in a changing world. Certainly they will be able to adapt better than the specialty underwriter of the past who owed all underwriting knowledge to the teachings of an older, experienced person. The education and training which future underwriters receive will give them a better foundation for the conditions which will exist, and it will also enable them to handle more and varied lines. Thus, the underwriter of the future is likely to be a true multiple line underwriter, handling all of the policies of a rather small number of producers.

LINES OF AUTHORITY

The lines of authority in underwriting departments, as shown by organizational charts, are relatively standard among companies. Differences occur partly because of the personnel available and partly because of philosophies of management, as evidenced by the entire organization. Size plays an important role in determining the precise organization, too. Still, all of these variations are somewhat minor, and they do not conceal the similarities which exist.

Every insurance company, except for the very smallest, is divided into two major classes: line and staff. Underwriting departments follow the same pattern. Staff is basically the home office, setting policy standards and watching the over-all operations. Line is the group that carries out the underwriting duties, usually in the branch offices, working with files and producers.

Within each of these two major groups, the organization of all companies is similar enough that an analysis can be helpful in understanding the underwriting function.

Underwriting Staff

The members of the underwriting staff ordinarily are situated only in the home office. Large companies may place some staff members in regional or zone offices in order to get them closer to operations. There is some value, at least for some companies and some lines, in dividing staff personnel by territory, in order to handle better the regional differences which may occur. Some insurers divide the staff in the home office into territorial groups, while others place the staff members in the territory with which they work. It should be emphasized, however, that most companies keep all of the staff in the home office, and provide for specialization by line of insurance or by function rather than by geographical areas.

The underwriting vice president is the top officer in the underwriting department, in most companies. The title varies by company, but the importance of underwriting is recognized generally by establishing it as one of the major departments headed by a full vice president. The full vice president, in turn, reports to the executive vice president or the president, which is on a level with other functional officers.

The underwriting vice president establishes underwriting policy for the entire company, subject to the overall policies of the company. This person is in direct charge of the staff, but the responsibility for line underwriting varies by company. The underwriting vice president directs staff members in their work, presents recommendations for changes in policy to top management, and cooperates with other officers in establishing general programs and recommendations for the company as a whole. Because underwriting is such a basic function to an insurance company, the underwriting vice president becomes involved in a large share of the discussions among the officers of the company. In some companies, the officer who is in charge of underwriting may even be given the title of a senior vice president or some other designation which recognizes the importance of underwriting to an insurance company.

The first level below the underwriting vice president consists of one or more persons who may be assigned various functions depending upon the company. It is at this point that the type of division used by the company in its underwriting becomes evident. The people at this level may be in charge of one major line, such as commercial or personal, or they may divide the work along such traditional lines as property and casualty. Some companies prefer to separate responsibilities to a greater extent at this level, having people in charge of automobile, fire, marine, etc.

Still another division may be along geographical boundaries, with each person having responsibility for all underwriting within a region or zone. Many other separations of duties are possible and, of course, many combinations of these divisions are used. The people at this level may be called managers, directors, supervisors, etc; they may or may not be officers at the vice president or assistant vice president level. In some companies, they are vice presidents who report directly to the executive vice president, with the latter then assuming the duties of the top officer for all underwriting.

At this level of reporting to the underwriting officer in charge, some companies implement other types of staff functions. Examples are statistics, training, education, procedures, personnel research, loss prevention, and many others. Where these functions are not placed under separate sections, they are combined within the sections which are used, or the functions are assigned to another department.

The next level of authority below that of the people reporting to the underwriting officer is even more diversified. Probably no two insurers use the same organization because it not only depends upon the division at the next highest level, but also upon the major points of each company's emphasis. An insurer which is strong in workers' compensation insurance may have a specialist in charge of that line, while another company may include that line within the responsibilities of a commercial liability specialist.

Examples of possible divisions at this level will illustrate the complexity in organization of insurance underwriting. If the next higher level is divided into commercial and personal lines, the specialists may represent, within the commercial line, such fields as liability, workers' compensation, fire, crime and bonds. If the major division is by property and casualty insurance, the property specialists may represent personal fire, commercial fire, inland marine and marine. If a geographic division if used at the higher level, each specialist may handle one or more of the major lines handled by the company, or may handle a smaller geographical area, perhaps directing all underwriting activity in a few branch offices.

Titles at this level are varied, again depending upon the pattern used by the company. Some may be called specialists, managers or directors. Also, other related functions may be divided here if not at the higher level, or further subdivided if the second level in the department is divided by function. Thus, specialists may be used for training, education, procedures, etc.

Below the level of specialists, the division becomes so varied that no general discussion is meaningful. The number of workers, their titles and their duties are so dependent upon the organization and its needs that there is no industry pattern. There may be few, if any, people at these levels, if a company prefers to use a small staff. On the other hand, a company may choose to use a sizeable staff consisting of specialists, analysts, technicians, clerks and many others.

Together, these people comprise the underwriting staff. They prepare, recommend, and disseminate matters of company policy relating to underwriting. They may have some authority over the line underwriting, or they may carry only the traditional staff authority of advice but no authority. Staff members may travel extensively among the branch offices, among producers, or they may do little or no traveling. They may have an audit responsibility over line underwriting or their duties may be restricted to publishing rules and answering questions. Staff members may work in teams on problems and during visits to branch offices; or they may operate alone, each within his own specialty.

Staff underwriting departments may perform many functions. Their primary duty is to prepare and disseminate broad policy decisions. A secondary duty is to prepare underwriting programs for the guidance of producers and desk underwriters; such programs will define the eligible and ineligible risks, as well as the acceptable and unacceptable ones. Other duties include the preparation, or assistance in preparation, of policy forms and rating structures, as well as reinsurance arrangements. An important duty involves checking to see that programs and rules are being followed and that the desired results are being obtained; constant reviews of statistics and reports are necessary. Finally, staff underwriting personnel work towards coordinating departments to verify that uniformity is maintained and that each underwriting department keeps a close relationship with others; the latter necessary to avoid cancelling a policy of a large and profitable account.

Staff underwriters also perform many miscellaneous functions which are not directly related to underwriting. They work with other departments of the company in the preparation of new or revised programs for sales, rating and others. They serve on boards and committees composed of representatives from many companies in the administration of industry educational programs, rating bureaus and pools. Staff underwriters concern themselves with proposed legislation either through trade associations or on behalf of their own companies. They support the prosecution activities of the various law enforcement agencies. In general, through their various contacts and activities, staff underwriters perform a sizeable share of the work needed in maintaining good relationships among insurers, as well as between insurers and their public.

In spite of the differences among staff underwriting departments, the basic organization is the same. Staff is usually in the home office, it promulgates and disseminates underwriting policy, and it has little or no direct authority over line underwriting. The work performed by staff is analytical, detailed and exacting; some people enjoy the type of work performed at the staff level, while others prefer line underwriting. Both functions are essential to an insurance company.

Staff members work much less with the *practices* of underwriting than line underwriters. The details of handling the underwriting on individual risks are not of daily concern to staff but they are the major concern to line. Still, staff members must know the practices in order to be able to perform their duties and advise the line underwriters. For this reason, staff members often are selected from among line underwriters who appear to have a talent along staff lines. Most companies feel that this is preferable to hiring new employees, other than clerical, directly into staff, or transferring employees from other departments into staff positions.

The principles of underwriting must be familiar to staff members, if they are to perform their functions in an adequate fashion. Principles are essential to line underwriters, too. It is obvious, therefore, that all underwriters, at whatever level and in whatever office, must be familiar with underwriting principles, if they are to underwrite successfully.

Staff work in underwriting can be stimulating and challenging. It may be a necessary stepping stone to higher positions in the company. It is different from line underwriting, yet staff members should know the duties of line underwriters. The staff function is an essential part of underwriting.

Line Underwriting

Line underwriters may be either in the home office or in a branch office, depending upon the degree of centralization of the company. A centralized operation is used when the company is too small to have branches or because management chooses to keep some or all of the line functions within the home office. This centralization has some advantages, permitting staff to work closely with line operations and thus to be aware of problems which arise. It also permits line personnel to have ready access to the help or staff. Sometimes staff and line operations are combined in one underwriting department but the *functions* are still separate.

A decentralized operation requires the establishment of branch offices in major cities or within major geographical areas. Line personnel are placed in the branches to handle underwriting, sales, claims, and office services for the risks located within the territory served by the branch. Among the advantages of a decentralized operation are shorter lines of communications to producers and policyholders, and greater familiarity with the local conditions and problems. Underwriting, in particular, requires knowledge of local conditions and this in itself may benefit greatly from a decentralized operation.

Line Underwriting In Decentralized Operations

It is less confusing to picture the staff operation being performed in home office and the line operations in the branches. For this reason the balance of this discussion on line underwriting is based on decentralization of an organization.

A branch underwriting manager is usually the top underwriting official in the line operation. This person usually reports directly to the branch manager, although he or she may report to an assistant branch manager or even to a division manager of some type. Company organizations vary greatly in this regard. However, underwriting is recognized as a prime function in most companies and managers report to the top person within the branch or territory. The title of the top underwriting manager also varies by company but is seldom held by an officer in the company.

Branch underwriting managers have overall responsibility for underwriting and underwriting personnel within their branches. They supervise several people directly, in most cases. They report to staff on various matters as instructed. They represent the underwriting position during meetings with other managers in the branch and with the branch manager. They have an underwriting background in one or more categories — an experience which is invaluable in view of the responsibilities assigned to them not only for underwriting results in general but also as the highest authority in the department for decisions on individual cases.

Two or more assistants may report to a branch underwriting manager. Sometimes they are called managers for their own specialities: commercial lines, personal lines, property, casualty, automobile, fire, etc. These assistants may be in charge of their specialties for the entire branch, or for divisions along geographic lines. These people are responsible for the management of their functions in whatever manner they may be assigned by the company. This responsibility includes the enforcement of the standards of acceptability used by the company, the preparation of reports, the management of investigation sources and the like. These assistants to the branch underwriting manager are responsible for the people under them: recruitment, salary review, training, development and appraisals. They are assisted in these duties by supervisory people.

Superintendents comprise the next level of authority in line underwriting of decentralized organizations. They bear a varied assortment of titles, such as underwriting superintendent, underwriting supervisor, chief underwriter or lead underwriter. Their principle function is to supervise a group of underwriters frequently composed of about 10 to 20 people as a general pattern. Superintendents usually represent a further refinement of the division used for their superiors. If the superior is a commercial assistant underwriting manager, the supervisors may handle liability, property, crime and workers' compensation coverages.

In other companies, superintendents may represent only geographic divisions, with each one handling all of the lines under the control of a superior. Thus, an automobile assistant manager may have four superintendents reporting to him or her, each one handling a different territory.

Superintendents work more closely with the actual underwriters, but they seldom engage in underwriting on individual risks. Their duties are to train and develop underwriters, to supervise their activities and to direct their underwriting. In some companies, they are the highest ranked working underwriters but, generally, their responsibilities are limited to supervising others.

Desk underwriters, those who actually perform the underwriting on individual risks, comprise the largest single group of underwriting personnel. Many different titles are used for them, depending upon company. Some of these are: underwriter, special underwriter, multiple line underwriter, underwriting analyst, junior underwriter, or fire, automobile, or crime underwriter. New underwriters often are called underwriting trainees. There is no apparent pattern of titles above the trainee state, so it is common to use the term "underwriter' to include all of them.

Underwriters perform the day-to-day operations of underwriting risks. They do not have supervisory authority, although some may be used to train others. Their underwriting authority varies with their experience and ability, as well as with company policy. Commonly, new underwriters handle only simple or routine risks, or perhaps changes on existing policies rather than with the acceptance or rejection of new applications. New or junior underwriters follow specific instructions on handling applications and policies; their work is a rather mechanical operation under the instructions prepared by more experienced underwriters. As the underwriters gain knowledge, they are given more authority for more complex risks, larger risks, and more authority to give higher limits of insurance. It may take years before an underwriter is given full authority on all risks which he or she is authorized to handle. Such authority may include the use of special classifications, manuscript endorsements or policies, judgment rating, and all of the other underwriting functions which must be performed.

These underwriters who actually perform the underwriting on individual risks are the ones about whom reference is made when discussing underwriting in most aspects. Whenever the term "underwriter," "line underwriter" or "desk underwriter" is used without other qualification, it refers to these people. They are the ones who make the specific underwriting decisions.

Clerks are also used in some underwriting departments. They may be able to relieve the underwriters of many clerical duties, thereby permitting underwriters to send more time on judgment matters. Some of the clerical duties may include assembling files, completing form requests and notices to producers and bureaus, securing information from other files, delivering and removing files and correspondence to and from the underwriters' desks, recording statistical information and preparing reports. Clerks may do the rating and coding or these tasks may be assigned to others in the underwriting department or other departments.

The line underwriting department is composed of those who are "on the firing line." They work closely with producers and policyholders, as well as with other employees of the company. Their work requires attention to detail and knowledge of both insurance and company rules and, yet, they must temper their decisions with understanding. They bear heavy responsibilities, but their work is exciting and they are given substantial authority.

Line underwriting may lead to higher positions in the branch office or in staff work. Underwriting staff members ordinarily benefit from line experience, even though the reverse is also true. A good line underwriter is valuable to any company and is the foundation upon which a book of business is built.

QUESTIONS FOR DISCUSSION

1. What is meant by the term "line of insurance," and what is the derivation of that term?
2. Give four advantages of underwriting specialization by line.
3. What was it about the advent of the multiple line concept that made underwriting by line disadvantageous?
4. Describe some of the advantages and disadvantages of multiple line underwriting.
5. What prompted the need, among some insurers, to convert their underwriting organization to combinations or coverage combinations.
6. Why might an insurer set up its underwriting department by geographical separation? For what reasons might an insurer decide against that system?
7. Who usually comprises the underwriting staff of a company? What are their primary functions?
8. Describe some of the functions of staff underwriters which are not directly related to underwriting but nonetheless are important.
9. Differentiate between the roles of the underwriting manager, superintendent and desk underwriter.
10. What is the rationale for the statement that: Line underwriters are those who are "on the firing line"?

5

The Relationship of Underwriting To Others

Underwriting is one of many functions which is necessary in an insurance company. In early days, underwriting *was* insurance; that is, the underwriter performed all of the functions connected with the insurance. Today specialization is practiced, with each of the major functions performed by a separate department.

The underwriting department must operate within an organizational structure which is composed of many departments and many people. The relative importance of these departments and people is important to underwriters. They cannot operate effectively unless they know the position of underwriting in the company. In addition, they can operate more efficiently when they know the relationship of their duties to those of other people in the company.

INSURANCE COMPANY ORGANIZATION

Insurance companies are all organized along the same general lines. There are many individual differences, of course. These differences may be brought about by size, by number of lines handled, by the philosophies of those who own or control the company or by the personal ties of members of management. The ultimate control is in the hands of a board of directors in a stock company, and a similar group in a mutual company and a reciprocal. The top executive officer is usually the president. The company may also have one or more executive vice presidents. These positions and their functions are not dissimilar from those of other businesses.

The next level is composed of numerous departments, each headed by an officer who is usually a vice president or its equivalent. Some of those are similar to other businesses: accounting, investments, personnel, purchasing and sales, along with a secretary and a treasurer. Others are unique to the insurance business: actuarial, claims and underwriting.

In general, these departments are approximately on the same level, although some of them may be combined under one person who might be called a senior vice president. Sometimes a single important department might be headed by a person with a similar title: usually this is more a matter of personality than organization.

The departments which are peculiar to insurance companies are interrelated in their functions.

Actuarial

The promulgation of rates, rating structures and classifications, and the preparation of policy forms and endorsements are the primary functions of the actuarial department. Statistics are used extensively, too. Rates are determined from past experience as projected into the future, so they necessarily reflect the claims which are paid and the quality of risks which are accepted. Rating structures and classifications are the joint responsibility of the actuarial and underwriting departments in most companies; they are determined by joint efforts but are controlled by the actuarial department. Policy contracts and endorsements may be controlled either by the actuarial or underwriting departments, and are the result of management decisions in which the claims department also plays an important role. The practices of the insurance industry and leading competition are important factors which are taken into consideration in rates and contracts. Many companies satisfy these vital requirements through rating bureaus that prepare rates, rating structures, classifications and contracts for use by their members and subscribers. When bureaus are used, the actuarial function in the company is limited, but since most companies use some nonstandard forms or plans, there is an actuarial function performed by almost every insurer.

Claims

The settlement of claims is the function of the claims department. Many companies that employ their own claims adjusters are involved in the entire process of selecting, hiring, training and supervising adjusters. Other companies are outside adjusters, either independent or in organizations; their company staffs are reduced correspondingly. All types of claims departments assist the actuarial and underwriting departments in preparing contracts and in revising them as needed. They often operate in an advisory capacity on classifications and other areas where they can supply their expert knowledge. In return, underwriters often assist the claims department in interpreting coverages; the underwriting intent sometimes is the determining factor on questionable claims.

Underwriting

The acceptance or rejection of risks, and the application of classifications and rates, are functions of the underwriting department. Its members also cooperate with the actuarial department in establishing rating structures, rates, classification systems, and contracts. The underwriting department assists the claims department in decisions on borderline claims and in establishing company policy on settlement of claims.

Underwriting requires a high degree of technical skill and detailed knowledge of the relationship with other major departments. A rate structure may be developed carefully, with a projected underwriting profit when used in conjunction with an approved underwriting program. If underwriters become unduly liberal in the acceptance of risks or become careless in the assignment of rate classes, the rate structure can become inadequate within a very short time. This can result in underwriting losses and financial disaster.

None of the insurance functions can be omitted by a company. However, it is not uncommon to delegate outside organizations with some functions, such as promulgation of rates, preparation of policy contracts and the settlement of claims. On the other hand, an insurer rarely delegates the underwriting function to an outside company. The underwriter is so closely related to management philosophy — reflecting its views of the position within the insurance industry which the company intends to occupy — that almost every insurer uses its own underwriters.

THE POSITION OF UNDERWRITING

The position of the underwriting department in a company is unique as it relates to other departments. The primary purpose of underwriting is to accept risks which will, as a class, result in a profit to the company. In performing this function, underwriting is inextricably involved with the other major functions of the insurer.

Relationship to Insurance Departments

The acceptability of an individual risk is a complicated matter. Most risks are acceptable to one company or another but few companies accept every risk. An applicant presents certain characteristics which place it at a fixed point in the classification system. If the rate for that risk is inadequate, the application must be declined. Also to be considered is the contract; if it is too broad for the rate, a profit cannot be realized. The claims adjustment practices are also important; if they are more liberal than contemplated by the rate and the contract, a loss is inevitable.

Thus, underwriting must involve the functions of the actuarial, contract writing, and claims departments, and underwriters must work closely with those departments. Every action which is taken by those other departments will have a potential effect on underwriting. Acceptance of risks must be tightened if rates are lowered, contracts are broadened, or claims are settled more liberally. The underwriter must adjust the acceptance of risks to situations which prevail in related fields. If a state insurance department refuses a needed rate increase, or a court in one state interprets a policy provision more liberally than the company intended, the underwriter must consider restrictions on acceptability.

This inter-relationship among the four insurance company departments is illustrated in Figure 1.

FIGURE 1

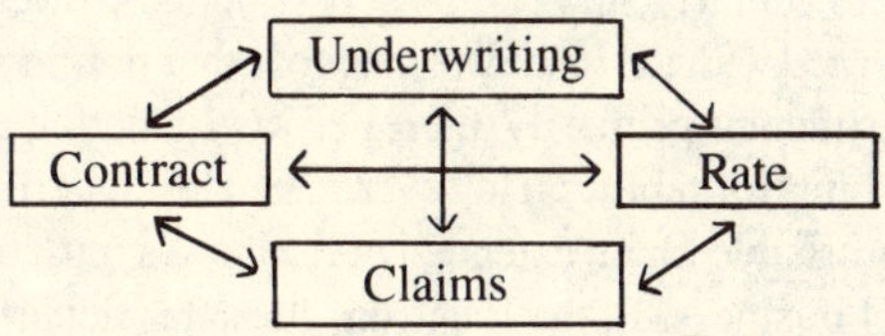

The relationship of the four departments — actuarial, contract writing, claims, and underwriting — is not always understood by underwriters. The financial operation of an insurance company, other than investments and taxes, results in an "underwriting profit" or an "underwriting loss." These terms — underwriting profit or underwriting loss — recognize the fundamental position of underwriting in the insurance system. At the same time, they tend to obscure the role played by rates, contracts and claims practices.

An underwriter may establish a consistent and profitable pattern of acceptability only to have underwriting profits turn into underwriting losses because rates are reduced, contracts are broadened, or claims practices are liberalized. Since this can happen, and since underwriting is supposed to consider these factors, the underwriter must be flexible enough to adjust the acceptability of risks in order to meet changes in those other fields.

Adjustments in underwriting, to meet changing factors, involve careful coordination among departments. Consistency is a virtue in underwriting, to a considerable degree, in order to avoid confusion on the part of producers and to assure a fairly uniform book of business for the insurer which gives stable loss results. An underwriter, therefore, should not tighten the acceptability requirements for a few weeks while a rate increase is delayed temporarily. An underwriter should look, instead, at long range trends, such as a pattern of inadequate rates caused by refusal of insurance departments to grant increases; an industry trend toward broadened contracts without offsetting rate increases; or a company decision to change claims practices, such as requiring only one bid or estimate of damages on some types of losses, or the settlement of certain claims by telephone instead of by a personal contact.

As changes occur in these areas, and as they appear to be of long duration, the underwriter must adjust the acceptability to compensate for these changes. Another alternative, of course, is that offsetting changes may be made in other departments, e.g., a contract may be broadened and rates increased accordingly. Where these conditions exist, underwriting may be able to remain constant.

This relationship among the actuarial, claims and underwriting departments must be recognized in company organization structure. Heads of these departments must work together in order to coordinate changes. The inter-relationship of these departments must be made clear to everyone in the company, in the same fashion that all underwriters must be familiar with the effects that rates, contracts and claims practices have upon underwriting.

Relationship to Non-Insurance Departments

Underwriters must work just as closely with some of the non-insurance departments as they do with actuarial and claims departments. However, the underwriter usually is less concerned with the inner workings of other non-insurance departments.

The sales department is primarily interested in production and thus would seem to be less interested in profitability. However, the sales department is aware that if the company is unprofitable for an extended period, rates must be raised or the company must go out of business. In the long run, the sales department is just as anxious to show a profit in the total operation as is the underwriting department.

Some conflict may arise on individual cases, but basically there is little problem between these departments. In fact, there is a close working arrangement in most insurers between the sales and underwriting departments; each pursues its own goal of increasing sales or profitable underwriting results, while working together achieving the company's goal. An important goal of many companies is "growth with profit." Here, both the sales and underwriting departments must be oriented toward increased production and profitable operations.

The policy service departments, sometimes called by such titles as administration department, service department or processing department, handle the functions of issuing policies, collecting premiums, maintaining files and other necessary detail work involved with insurance. Some of this work is peculiar to insurance, but most of it is similar to functions performed by companies in other financial or service-type businesses. The people in this department are essential to underwriting because they conduct the necessary details of the business. Underwriters work closely wtih some of these people, particularly in the policy issuance and rating sections.

Underwriters also may be hampered in performing their tasks if mail is handled improperly or files are often misplaced. These inter-relationships emphasize the close harmony needed in any business office. No portion of the underwriting function is involved here, so underwriters need be concerned only in working with the policy service department in getting the work out — not in the underwriting itself.

The loss control department is a separate department in many large companies, although it is a part of the underwriting department in others. It has two separate functions. One is to inspect risks and report findings to the underwriters. The other is to provide a loss control service to policyholders, helping them to improve their premises or operations in order to reduce losses. Both of these services can be very helpful to underwriters and insurance companies.[1]

Other departments in the company are even less closely associated with underwriting, however essential they may be to the company. An insurer needs departments to handle accounting, investments, purchasing and other vital functions. An underwriter is involved with these departments only incidentally. A working relationship with them, therefore, is not essential to the underwriting function.

AUTHORITY OF UNDERWRITING

The two basic purposes of underwriting — profit and efficiency — carry a common goal: to reduce expenses. When expenses are reduced, the break-even point is improved. In insurance, the break-even point is that point at which no profit or loss is realized; expenses equal income. The measure is the loss and expense ratio,

[1]. For more information on the loss control function of engineers, see Rollin H. Simonds and John V. Grimaldi, *Safety Management,* Richard D. Irwin, Inc., Homewood, IL, 1963; *Industrial Safety,* edited by Roland P. Blake, Prentice Hall, Inc., Englewood Cliffs, NJ, 1963 and *Readings in Loss Control Management,* Insurance Institute, Malvern, PA, 1980.

which is a comparison of loss costs (the amount paid out in claims plus the cost of settling those losses) plus expense costs of all types, to premium income. A high loss ratio can result in an operating loss; a high expense ratio can do likewise. If one is high and the other is low, the relative importance and amount of differentiation will determine the profit or loss.

Conflicts of Interests

A basic problem in underwriting is that those two purposes may be diametrically opposed. In order to reduce claims, the underwriter may need to spend more money to investigate the risks. If everything is in balance and the company decides to reduce expenses by allowing less time for underwriting, the claim costs will probably increase.

Underwriting is a fairly delicate balance between claim costs and operating expenses. Underwriters, particularly the managers and staff people, are fully aware of the problems caused by these conflicting items. On a relatively low premium policy, an underwriter cannot afford to conduct a thorough investigation. Still, if this is not done, a sizeable loss could occur which might have been avoided.

A conflict of this type may be internal within the underwriting department or it may involve other departments. It is internal if the only consideration is in underwriting costs, such as investigations; the underwriting department must determine the degree of investigation needed. The conflict may involve the policy service department if the problem is in maintenance of certain records or speed in securing files. These conflicts are seldom of great significance and can be settled quite easily by the department managers involved.

Much more critical are problems involving the ultimate authority to accept or reject risks. These cases usually involve only the selectivity to reduce losses, although they may involve the degree of investigation which will be conducted. Since these situations strike at the very heart of underwriting, they must be resolved. Some of these cases are fairly easy to settle. The head of the investment department may urge the underwriter to accept more business so that there will be more money to invest. If the management of the company supports the investment department, it has really decided not to underwrite, regardless of what titles it uses. Such a company will soon be bankrupt.

Another fairly simple, yet not uncommon, conflict arises between the claims and underwriting departments. Claims personnel may inform underwriters that a certain class of risk should not be accepted because losses in that class are excessive. The answer, of course, is that if the rate is adequate for those losses, the underwriting appears to be proper. The claims department can be a valuable ally of an underwriter, suggesting where problems are developing and suggesting a remedial course of action. These recommendations may be on individual risks or on classes of risks. In any event, they must be received as recommendations only, and taken into consideration but with the final authority resting with the underwriters. A few problems may arise, but these can be resolved quite easily, as soon as all parties understand the function of each department.

A much more serious problem exists when conflicts develop between the underwriting departments and the sales or marketing departments. The difficulties arise most often with borderline risks which are submitted by certain producers who may be profitable, influential or have a large volume of business. The underwriter may evaluate all of the information available concerning a specific risk and then decide to decline to write the coverage. The producer might appeal to the sales department and then a real problem of authority arises.

The underwriting department feels that it must make its decisions on the basis of the available facts, only. If it starts making exceptions for certain producers, the underwriting function becomes inferior to the sales function and losses increase. The sales department feels that it has a duty to promote production, and that the strict standards of the underwriting department must be superseded by the necessity to increase sales. If this risk is declined, the producer and all of that business might be lost, it is argued.

In most companies, these conflicts are settled on a case basis by the highest line person available, usually the branch manager. Sometimes the line managers of the sales and underwriting departments can settle the question, one or the other recognizing the weakness of a position. Some companies establish committees to settle such conflicts. When agreement cannot be reached otherwise, the case can be referred to the branch manager for a decision.

Some underwriters feel quite strongly that their decisions should be final and not subject to review by others outside of the underwriting department. They maintain that they, alone, are trained to recognize charcteristics which may result in losses. They question the wisdom of training a person in underwriting if the resulting decisions are to be vetoed by persons who are not trained in underwriting. On the other hand, sales people feel that the critical problem is to maintain good relations with influential producers and to produce business. They point out that most underwriting decisions stand and only the borderline ones are challenged. Furthermore, they point out, no underwriter knows exactly which applicants will suffer losses and which ones will not.

The decision is wisely placed in the hands of the person who has responsibilities in all areas, the branch manager. This person should have had enough basic training in underwriting to recognize an obviously bad risk from one that is borderline. He or she should know whether the producer is serious or merely pushing to determine the limits of influence. The branch manager represents management, and balancing conflicting viewpoints is a function of management.

The solution is the same for general problems which may involve staff members. The underwriting department may recommend withdrawal from a certain market or discontinuance of a certain line. Such action may be resisted by the sales department. The officers in charge of the departments may need to resolve the question or perhaps refer it to the president of the company.

The good of the company must prevail. Underwriting is but one facet of the company operation and must be weighed along with other factors. An underwriter at the desk is taught to make decisions on underwriting factors alone, letting superiors resolve conflicts with other departments. This is not to say that an underwriter does not consider the producer; this is done as one of the factors evaluated. The underwriter may have received instructions to allow for the experience of the producer, but even in the absence of such instructions, this experience should still be taken into account. The point is that an underwriter must make decisions on underwriting factors alone. Any exceptions must be made by management people on the basis of management factors, not just on underwriting factors.

Underwriting Freedom

Underwriting policy is established by management; it is implemented by the underwriting department. Within the framework of that policy, underwriters must be free to underwrite each risk; to exercise their own judgment. Wise management will give a considerable degree of autonomy to underwriters, in the sense that their decisions should stand in most cases. Underwriting results are the desired end, not the specific manner of underwriting each separate risk, and if this freedom is denied to underwriting, the department cannot be held accountable for results. When accountability and responsibility are removed from the underwriting department, an insurance company has taken a long step toward financial ruin.

The preparation of the general underwriting policy must be coordinated among all departments. When business is profitable, a liberal underwriting attitude may be adopted. This must be changed to a more conservative position if expenses increase, investment returns decline, or other factors threaten the surplus of the company. Not only may the pattern be changed concerning the selection of risks but also concerning such items as the coverages offererd, commission rates, retention limits, and amount of rate deviation may have to be revised.

RELATIONSHIP OF DUTIES

For the most part, the primary duties of underwriting are unique; no other department has similar duties. However, the basic duties of underwriting may be supplemented by several subsidiary duties. These might include coding, maintenance of statistics, reinsurance placement, or other clerical duties, none of which are really considered as underwriting.

Assignment of these subsidiary duties to underwriters is usually made at the level of company policy and ordinarily involves costs and efficiency. If someone needs to look up a code to use, it is less expensive for a clerk to do this than an underwriter. However, the underwriter may have the codes available as an aid in determining the classification to place on the risk. There is no reason for the underwriter to write a note of instruction about the proper code to use, if it can merely be indicated on the application or coding form. Similarly, the underwriter may be able to write a memorandum to a producer with the same amount of effort that is required to write a note to a clerk, informing that person to tell the producer. Sometimes it is less expensive and quicker, for an underwriter to perform a clerical function than to instruct a coder or clerk to do it.

Effect of Subsidiary Duties on Underwriters

These subsidiary duties can become problems if they are not controlled carefully. There is a tendency to assign more clerical functions to the underwriter, because he or she must know almost everything about the risk before making a decision. This increase in clerical duties can interfere seriously with the time that an underwriter can devote to basic duties.

Even more important is the psychological effect on the underwriters if they are required to perform a number of clerical duties. Underwriters need to exercise judgment on every risk. They must have the authority to make decisions which may involve large sums of the company's money. They need to feel that this is their basic purpose, that the acceptability of risk is their private area of authority. If they are encumbered with a myriad of duties which could be performed just as effectively by clerks, underwriters will lose some of their self-esteem and confidence. It is important, therefore, that underwriters be free to underwrite, rather than be tied down by clerical duties, to the extent that this is practical.

Aside from the basic functions which are unique, underwriters carry on a close relationship with other employees. Many of the functions of underwriting are closely related to those of other departments, as was mentioned previously involving subsidiary duties which could be performed either by underwriters or by employees in other departments. Most of the company rules and employee practices apply to underwriters just as to other employees.

One basic difference between underwriters and clerical employees is in the area of work measurement. Clerical workers often are assigned quotas of work which they are expected to perform within a stated period of time. A typist may be expected to type 100 policies a day, a coder to code 150 files, and so forth. Quality is important, but a determination can be made of the number of files which normally can be handled by each clerical employee and each person is expected to complete that assignment. The quantity of work produced is most important and errors seldom cost more than a small amount to correct.

Underwriting does not lend itself to a rigid quota of files to be handled. If an underwriter encounters a difficult case, he or she is expected to review it carefully and thoroughly. A superficial evaluation of the available information could lead to an erroneous decision — one which is quite costly to the company. Quality, therefore, is the supreme goal in underwriting, with volume of work being secondary.

At the same time, efficiency of operation requires that a certain amount of work emanate from the underwriting department each day. Few companies could afford a group of underwriters who handle one or two files per day on most lines of insurance. The answer lies in the complexity of the underwriting operation. At one end of the scale, an underwriter might spend several days with one large commercial account, and the operation of the company is designed with that in mind. At the other extreme, an underwriter who handles only simple, standardized coverages can average a large number of cases in a day. Some of these cases may take longer than others, but the average over a number of cases is quite uniform. Companies writing the more standardized lines, therefore, such as personal automobile and personal fire, customarily set quotas for underwriters; it is not a question of quality versus quantity; a good underwriter can produce both.

Most underwriters handle lines of insurance that are fairly uniform in their requirements. Because of this, most companies establish some types of work measurement and quotas for underwriters. This does not in any way detract from the importance nor the complexity of underwriting decisions, it merely recognizes the realities of any business, under which efficiency of operation and predictability of work flow are essential to a profitable operation.

The result of these work practices is to provide a degree of uniformity among underwriters and among insurance company employees. The differences among underwriters of various lines is gradual, with the complexity of handling increasing slowly from the standardized lines to the individualized lines. Most underwriters within a company will have the same general types of duties and functions. As a result, underwriters can move with relative ease from one underwriting section to another; they may also move from one company to another. The similarity in work permits an easy exchange of information between underwriters within a company and with those of other companies. The latter fact is demonstrated by the many associations of underwriters composed of those from a number of companies in an area, each sharing principles and practices and learning more about the business from one another.

Promotional Opportunities

This uniformity in the principles of insurance, coupled with the many contacts which underwriters must make with other departments, results in unlimited opportunities for the promotion of underwriters. They are not limited to just one line. Rather, they can be promoted into other lines with relative ease because acquiring the practices of underwriting each line is a fairly simple matter after the principles are learned. Contacts with other departments promotes familiarity with other functions, thereby permitting promotions to take place quite often.

The promotional opportunities for underwriters are unlimited. Many of them rise to high positions within the insurance industry. Most of the potential for advancement lies with the individual; it depends upon abilities and determination. The basic secret consists of learning the principles of underwriting well, for they comprise the basis of insurance.

QUESTIONS FOR DISCUSSION

1. What are the primary functions of the actuarial department, and why is its relationship to underwriting important?
2. In what ways can a claims department aid the underwriting department? How can the underwriting department be of help to the claims department?
3. If an insurance company makes a profit or sustains a loss, overall, is it solely because of the underwriting department? Explain.
4. To what extent do other departments of a company have an effect on underwriting flexibility?

5. What is the role of the following departments, and to what extent are they an asset to underwriters:
   (a) Sales or marketing department.
   (b) Policy service department.
   (c) Loss prevention department.
6. Explain why profit and efficiency can sometimes be a source of conflict to the underwriter.
7. If a claims representative recommends the cancellation of an individual risk because of problems involved in the settlement of a claim, should the underwriter automatically proceed with cancellation? Why or why not?
8. On an individual risk, the underwriter may want to decline the risk, but the sales department may want to accept it in order to help an outstanding producer. Outline the steps which could be taken to resolve the conflict.
9. Sometimes, underwriters must perform so-called subsidiary duties which do not have any direct application to underwriting, but nonetheless are important. What are some of these duties and why can they sometimes create problems?

INTRODUCTION TO PART II

PRINCIPLES OF DECISION MAKING IN UNDERWRITING

Underwriting is a decision-making process. The underwriter makes decisions on every risk, not only when it is newly submitted but also at periodic stages while the policy is in force.

Underwriters must be able to make decisions. They must also know the steps to follow in arriving at their decisions. Without an organized, scientific approach to the process of making decisions, they may overlook vital steps or disregard important alternatives.

A common misunderstanding of underwriters is that they must choose between two alternatives: accept or reject each risk. The common folklore then assumes that the underwriters have a "crystal ball" in which they can see whether the risk will have a loss or not, and make decisions accordingly. Some unbelievers are under the assumption, too, that an underwriter "flips a coin" to decide whether to accept or reject the risk.

Nothing could be further from the truth. Underwriters reject risks only as a last resort. This course is taken only when they cannot devise a course of action which will let them write the risks. In an attempt to find a means of accepting risks, the underwriters will seek further information and develop various alternatives for action.

At the same time, the underwriters seek a means of making a profit. Their performance is measured, to a large degree, on the loss ratio of their business. The loss ratio is determined from premiums and losses. Losses depend upon the contract used and the selection standards employed. Thus underwriters need to balance all three factors: premium, contract and selection practices. In addition, losses are limited by the maximum exposure of the company, so retention and reinsurance are important. All of these factors are kept in mind throughout the decision-making process. This process may be studied in many ways, but a common way is to separate underwriting into five steps. These steps, each of which are discussed in separate chapters are:

1. Secure information
2. Develop alternative courses of action.
3. Decide on the best course and take action.
4. Evaluate the selected course of action.
5. Make corrections that are indicated.

Each chapter describes the important facets that an underwriter observes. These steps are performed on every application and policy and on every line of insurance; they are basic steps to all underwriting.

Some authorities would say that the first step is to "Define the problem." Such a definition is assumed here. There is no problem if it is obvious that the application should be accepted or declined. The only problem is with borderline risks. The factors which make the risk borderline must be identified before the underwriter starts to analyze the application in detail. For this reason, this step is not included here as one of the steps in the decision-making process.

Most of this discussion is concerned with handling individual risks. The final section of Chapter 10 explains the relationship of the last two steps, evaluation and correction, as they relate to the control function of underwriting management. These are the steps that a manager follows in auditing and correcting work of underwriters.

6

Secure Information

The first step in underwriting any risk is to secure information about the risk. Underwriters need to secure basic information which describes and identifies each specific applicant. They also need to secure as much related information as is needed to make a decision within the bounds of reasonableness.

"Get the facts!" This is the battle cry of underwriters. Every underwriting action must start with this admonition. Every discussion about the underwriting decision to be made on an application must be based upon facts that have been secured. Every new underwriter must learn this cardinal rule of underwriting: get the facts before attempting to arrive at a decision.

Underwriters need to know the factors which must be considered in securing information, such as why they really need to secure facts, how much information should be gathererd and what types of information may be secured. The following pages explain these factors and then illustrate the sources of information available to underwriters.

FACTORS TO CONSIDER

As an underwriter contemplates securing information a number of questions will be asked:

- — Why is it essential to get information about every risk?
- — What type of information is needed?
- — How much information is reasonable?
- — When is the information needed?
- — Where is the information found?

Why is it essential to secure information about each risk?

An understanding of the reasons will make an underwriter's assignments more reasonable; he or she will know the purpose of the admonition to "get the facts." There are three major reasons for securing information about each risk.

First, a policy cannot be issued without certain basic information, nor can any evaluation of an applicant even start without these underlying facts. This basic information varies somewhat by line of insurance but usually includes the name and address of the applicant, the type of information requested, the limits of the coverage desired, the proposed effective date and whether there are any additional interests or loss payees. An underwriter cannot begin evaluating any applicant without these facts; they must be secured, therefore, as the starting point in the underwriting process.

Second, some applicants have a greater chance of loss than the average. A major part of the underwriting process involves the control of these increased chances of loss. Some of these hazards, as increased chances of loss are called, are in the nature of physical factors, such as construction of a building. Others are called moral hazards, referring to the tendency of some persons to deliberately cause loss or damage, such as arson. Morale hazards are still another type; these are the increased chances of loss because of the indifference or carelessness of people. A fourth type of hazard is that caused by legal conditions, whether by law, by regulations, or by court decisions.[1]

These hazards can be recognized only by securing information, often a great deal of information. An underwriter must get the facts — upon which to base decisions — about the existence of hazards, and if they do exist, how to control them. A large amount of the information that an underwriter secures is pointed toward identification of possible hazards.

The third reason for securing information is to determine whether there is any adverse selection; it is a continual problem of underwriters. This is a condition based upon the fact that those persons to whom insurance is the easiest to sell are the ones most likely to have a loss. Most people are inherently optimistic, feeling that they will not have a loss; this condition changes when factors are present which tend to increase the possibilities of loss. When the latter condition exists, people are more likely to be sold insurance and might even seek to buy it. If they already are insured when less favorable circumstances arise, they are less likely to drop the insurance than those who do not feel that they have a great chance of loss. Because of this tendency, the poorer risks in each class are the easiest to write and to keep.

A different but related tendency of people is to secure the best possible terms when purchasing insurance. To the extent that people are aware of the competitive position, they will choose the coverage which seems to be most favorable. If one company offers unusually broad coverage in one part of the contract, those persons who feel that they have a particular exposure in that area will tend to buy the insurance from that company. If one company decides to use an average rate for risks which bear different rates with competitors, those risks which are more exposed to loss and thus have higher rates with other companies will tend to buy from the company with the average rate. In each of these cases, the risks which are more likely to have

---

1. See Chapters 15 through 18.

losses in relation to the premium will tend to insure with the company offering a different program.

An important part of underwriting is to secure the necessary information about applications, to identify and control any special hazards, and to overcome the bad effect of adverse selection.

What type of information is needed?

There are tremendous amounts of information that can be secured about each applicant. Some of it is essential for every applicant, but much of it is not relevant to many risks. In order for the underwriter to determine the type of information to seek, he or she must consider the coverage being requested, the chances of loss facing the applicant and the past record of similar risks. Each item of information may answer the needs of the underwriter or may indicate the need for more information.

The most important types of information are these.

1. Policy issuance information. These are the details needed to issue the policy and are required on every risk.

2. Psychological factors. Moral attitudes of the applicant are of vital concern for most kinds of insurance. Included in this category are such qualities as honesty, dependability, diligence, ethical behavior and attitude toward citizenship.

3. Housekeeping and living habits. An indication of the type of business or individual who is applying for insurance is secured from information about the manner in which the person maintains the premises or property and the conditions under which a family lives.

4. Physical condition. Property and persons have good or bad physical conditions. Some poor conditions can be improved while others must be tolerated. The underwriter needs information upon which to base an evaluation of these conditions. Related factors are the size of buildings, the age of buildings or people, the degree of fire or police protection available and other physical characteristics.

5. Financial and business reputation. The financial reputation and condition of every applicant is important to many kinds of insurance. The business reputation is vital to certain types of commercial coverages. These related factors may be crucial in the underwriting decisions.

6. Past experience. Past experience of the applicant in those areas which are relevant is highly important under certain conditions. This experience may concern the number of losses that have occurred in the applicant's driving record: the number of times that other companies have cancelled insurance policies, and so forth.

How much information is reasonable?

Underwriters must determine how much information they want, out of the great wealth of potential facts. They should never feel that they need more information in order to make a decision but are denied it because of relatively unimportant reasons. On the other hand, they should never seek information simply because it is available. The only proper answer to the question of how much information is reasonable must be this: "As much as is required to make a decision." No more nor no less than this is reasonable. Sometimes, however, underwriters must compromise and accept somewhat less information than they would like to receive. In deciding whether to seek more facts or make a decision on the material already received, the following factors must be considered.

Cost. The greatest obstacle to securing complete information involves cost. The amount of money expended should bear some logical relationship to the value of the information, the exposure under the policy, and the chances that the information will reveal new circumstances. In addition, most companies assign budgets for the costs of securing information, just as for other items of expense; this must be kept in mind when considering whether to request more information.

Trouble. Some information can be secured at minimum cost to an underwriter, but at an exorbitant cost in time or money to someone else. For example, producers can supply valuable information, but underwriters should refrain from requesting nonessential material or that which will consume too much of the producer's time. The same is true of other sources, such as underwriters in other companies. In addition, the underwriter should not ask one source, particularly one to whom direct payment is not made, for information which is readily available elsewhere or which may be secured in conjunction with a request for other information. Finally, the underwriter should not ask someone to secure facts if the search might involve an unusual danger of physical harm.

Relevancy. Much available information is irrelevant to the underwriters of most insurance lines: an automobile underwriter does not have to know the age of the applicant's dwelling, nor does the fire underwriter have to know the driving record of a client. Facts not relevant to underwriting the coverage requested are not reasonable.

Time. Some information can be secured only after a considerable period of time. If it would take months to secure all pertinent data about the past financial transactions of an applicant, it is seldom reasonable to request such material. The underwriter should limit the search for information to that which can be furnished within a relatively short time.

When is the information needed?

The securing of information requires time. It is useless to request certain data if it cannot be used because too much time will elapse before it can be received. There are two factors to consider in this regard.

First, time is of the essence in underwriting transactions. The applicant usually wants coverage in the very near future; in fact, much insurance is already bound before the underwriter ever knows of its existence. The applicant and producer want an early answer. The underwriter needs to make a prompt decision in order to avoid a lengthy exposure on an undesirable risk. Mortgagees may have established deadlines when coverage is required. Since every party to the transaction wants an early decision, only that information which can be secured within a relatively short time should be requested.

The second factor to consider is that noncancellation laws usually provide a "discovery period" during which time a policy may be declined or cancelled but not thereafter. The period usually covers about 45 to 60 days. During this brief period, the underwriter must conclude the investigation and make a decision. Information which arrives too late to permit action within the period is worthless, at least insofar as the initial term of the policy is concerned. There is no reason to request information that cannot possibly be received and processed before the end of the discovery period, and there is little reason to request it if its receipt is unlikely within that time.

The underwriter often makes simultaneous requests for information, if the need for such material is likely, in order to avoid this problem. For example, consider automobile insurance, the line most often regulated by noncancellation laws. The underwriter might request the driving record of the applicant from the motor vehicle department and then decide, on the basis of that information whether to secure an investigation report. If the underwriter suspects at the beginning that an order might be requested from both sources, both types of information are often requested at the same time. Some of the material may be irrelevant and unncessary, but the extra expense may be more than offset by the ability to take action within the discovery period when unfavorable information is received.

Where is the information found?

Many sources of information are available to the underwriter. Each of these must be considered and those which are most practical must be selected. The balance of this chapter explains these sources.

INFORMATION FROM PRODUCERS

Producers are valuable sources of information for most lines of insurance. Sometimes they are the only source used. If information supplied by the producer appears to be complete and appears to indicate no problems, the underwriter may accept the applicant with no further investigation. On the other hand, a risk may be unacceptable on the basis of the facts furnished by the producer. In this case the underwriter may decline the application immediately.

For a few lines, such as boiler and machinery, only the limited information needed to conduct further investigation is requested from the producer. The company will secure its own facts through other sources. The producer is expected to supply only the name and address of the applicant, the type of coverage desired and the proposed effective date. These situations are not common, and producers usually are requested to furnish somewhat more infomration on most risks.

Forms Which Supply Information

Producers may furnish information to underwriters in four different forms.

1. Application. The producer completes the application for most lines of insurance. The application contains the basic information needed to issue the policy. Included are such items as name and address of the applicant, name of the business, location of the property, type of business or occupancy and whether the business is an individual, partnership, or corporation. Also specified is the type of insurance and coverage requested, limits of liabilty or coverage, and special clauses or provisions, rate and amount of premium and proposed effective date and term.

Some producers are called upon less often than others to furnish certain information. For example, companies writing commercial crime coverages through brokers often expect to receive no information from them on the physical aspects of the applicant's business. In these cases, other sources must be used.

Various lines of insurance require special information. Property insurance applications may ask for construction of the building, type of roof, a description of other occupancies in the building, and the fire or police protection that is available. Liability insurance applications may require a complete description of the business pursuits, listings of any special agreements that might affect liability, and details concerning such exposures as elevators and parking lots. Many applications call for name and address of any mortgagees, loss payees or additional interests to be shown on the policy. The signature of the applicant is required on most applications and the producer is also expected to sign them.

2. *Producer's report.* A report is requested from the producer on most lines. It is furnished with the application and is customarily printed on the same form. In fact, the application and producer's report are really considered as being the application for most lines, with the producer's report being merely a separate item. The discussion of the two are separated only because the sources and uses are separate. The first part of the application is supplied by the applicant and is used primarily for the issuance of the policy, although it is of obvious interest to the underwriter. The producer's portion of the report contains information that is supplied by the producer as an aid to the underwriter, and thus is part of the underwriting function.

The producer's report contains many items of underwriting information. The extent of the questions vary by company and by line. In each case, the data relates to the underwriting rules of the company and each item is considered to be important to the underwriter. For this reason, producers are expected to complete all sections and to answer all questions. Any failure to do so may result in a request from the underwriter for the missing information since a complete job of underwriting cannot be performed without all of the relevant facts. Sometimes an underwriter's suspicion increases when a question is not answered; perhaps the lack of information indicates that a condition exists which is being kept quiet. For these reasons, complete answers are requested and producers may be censured for failure to complete all items.

The type of information requested on property lines may include the size and age of buildings, value of the property, protective devices in use, types of records that are kept, and so forth. Liability underwriters will ask for answers on additional premises or businesses, the experience of the owner and special exposures to loss — to give just a few examples. General questions for all lines might include the length of time an applicant has been at the present location in the present occupation, the details of any previous losses and information about the previous insurer, as well as other present insurers.

The producers usually are asked for recommendations, either specifically or by implication. The underwriter will, of course, consider each item of information. However, the producers are expected to perform a preliminary screening, a type of field underwriting. They see the applicant and the property which is an advantage seldom available to an underwriter; they are, therefore, in a good position to recommend the risk. The producers are expected to furnish, in addition to answers to the questions, any comments or remarks which might be helpful to the underwriter, whether good or bad. The quality of these remaks, as of the entire report, depends greatly upon the producer. An underwriter is expected to become familiar with the reliance that can be placed upon the reports from each producer. Regardless of the degree of confidence brought about by the information, producers are expected to complete the applications and to forward them with recommendations.

3. Answers to specific questions. Underwriters occasionally need answers to specific questions which producers are requested to furnish. Sometimes questions are raised because of suspicions aroused from the information furnished in the application. Other times, questions are raised because the information is not asked for on the application. (There are just so many questions that can be placed on the application.) The underwriter, therefore, requires answers only upon request.

The most common situation involving these specific questions arises when additional information is secured from other sources. Sometimes information will conflict; such a case may arise when an investigation reveals that a youth in the family does indeed drive the automobile. Other times the information will indicate unrevealed conditions, such as a second location operated by the applicant about which the producer may have been uninformed. In these cases, the underwriter may choose to verify the new data by asking the producer for answers. The degree to which this is done and the reliance given to answers which may conflict, depend upon the producer, the company, the line, the underwriter and the type of information involved.

4. Photographs. Producers furnish photographs on certain risks or certain lines as guides for the underwriter. Sometimes these are required as part of the application. Other times, they are requested by special communication from the underwriter in an attempt to clarify a particular condition or situation. In still other cases, the producer may volunteer photographs in order to better help the underwriter understand the applicant.

Regardless of how or why photographs are supplied, they can be valuable tools to the underwriter. Some insurers have recognized this by requiring photographs on specified applicants, such as personal or commercial fire and automobile risks; these companies usually furnish cameras to their producers. Much of the value of photographs depends upon the quality of the picture: the angle from which the picture was taken, the distance from the object, the exposure and the lighting.

INFORMATION FROM INSPECTION REPORTS

Inspection companies furnish reports upon requests of underwriters. The reports are often called "credit reports" because the original use of reports was to assist financial institutions and merchants whose primary interest was the credit standing of the subject. Credit reporting companies still furnish credit information to many clients, although much of their business, and all of it for some companies, is devoted to inspection reports for insurance underwriters.

Many types of reports are available. New types are prepared frequently. These are short-form, long-form, narrative, drive-by, telephone, driver information, and many others which may be used by underwriters. Each has a particular purpose or usage and costs vary by type of report. Many inspection companies which furnish reports for insurance are private enterprises. Some are nationwide while others are local or regional. All of them employ and train inspectors to gather information and prepare reports. Some of the material is secured from the files of the inspection company, either from prior reports or from clippings which they maintain. Much information is gained from personal contact with the applicant or with neighbors and associates. The inspectors may also secure other types of information which underwriters use and which are described elsewhere in this chapter, such as motor vehicle reports. Reports may or may not contain recommendations of inspectors about the desirability of the risk; it depends upon the underwriter's instructions.

Types of Inspection Reports

The many types of inspection reports used by underwriters may be grouped into four classifications.

1. Moral/Morale. Reports on subjective factors such as attitude, housekeeping and reputation can be very helpful to underwriters of many lines. They indicate those factors which may lead to losses because of the living conditions or personal attitudes of applications.

Reports with information that is gathered by visits to applicants' homes and conversations with neighbors and associates may contain comments about unfavorable or questionable conditions that are discovered. Some of the areas covered include housekeeping, personal and business reputation, neighborhood environment, cooperative attitude, stability, types of associates, police records, and personal characteristics. Almost every report will contain comments on questionable conditions, regardless of the type of insurance involved.

Special reports contain specific information on pertinent data in addition to general areas. For example, an automobile report may also give information on where the car is garaged, the driving record of the applicant and the use of the car. The underwriter ordinarily may indicate items to which special attention should be made.

2. Physical. Reports on objective factors such as construction and condition of property indicate factors which may lead to losses because of poor physical characteristics of property. Various types of these reports are used by underwriters.

Physical reports are based on visits to the premises of the applicant. Ordinarily a rather complete survey of the premises is required in order to give all helpful information to the underwriter. Some risks may require only an external report while some may need only a cursory look to determine the general facts upon which information is needed.

Commercial property and liability lines usually require complete reports containing details about the physical characteristics of the premises. Construction, devices to prevent or control losses, neighboring premises, and types of materials used in processing are among the items upon which reports are expected to comment. Most of these reports contain comments only on unfavorable factors but others report both favorable and unfavorable items.

Personal property and liability underwriters require less detailed reports, as a general rule. The type of construction and maintenance of a home or the condition of an automobile will suffice in most cases. The inspector ordinarily walks around the home or car, although he may inspect the interior. Some underwriters, on certain lines, may require only a "drive-by" report which gives only basic construction and maintenance data. Physical reports are used when the only concern of the underwriter is the physical aspect of the risk. Sometimes both the physical and moral/morale aspects may be questionable, and these two types of reports may be combined upon request.

3. Classification. Reports may be requested that aid the underwriter in determining the proper classification and rate. They contain factual information about the factors upon which classifications are based.

Classification reports are used by underwriters for those lines where rating information is not otherwise available or for information which seems to require additional checking. A common use for these reports is in automobile insurance, when rates are based upon various factors, such as use of the car, number of miles driven, ages of all operators and percentage of driving by each operator. All of this information could be revealed on the application but it sometimes is omitted. Other times, the underwriter wishes to verify that the information on the application is correct and complete. Profitability in many lines depends upon establishing proper rate classes — a fact that leads underwriters to investigate by whatever means is available.

Classification reports accomplish somewhat the same purpose as physical reports, since both report factual information. A physical report contains data about the physical risk itself, while the classification report reveals details about how rating factors should apply, particularly on the use of property. Classification reports may be combined with moral/morale and physical reports, if various types of information are desired.

4. Financial. Reports on financial conditions of applicants are called financial reports. They include the reporting of all types of financial information which is essential to the underwriting of some lines. Financial reports are based on data that is secured from many sources. The books of the applicant are a primary source. Others are the books or reports of banks and other lending institutions, customers and suppliers of the applicant and the reports of companies which furnish financial ratings. A financial report will also indicate to an underwriter if an applicant company is solvent, if it is making a profit and if it can be expected to perform in the future. The acceptability of many commercial risks is based upon such information.

Financial reports often are a combination of facts and unprovable allegations. As such, they are closer in content to moral/morale reports than to physical or classification reports. Any of these four types may be combined with others to furnish a picture as complete as the underwriter needs.

Effects of Fair Credit Report Act

In 1971 a significant change was made in handling investigation reports. The Fair Credit Reporting Act became effective in the United States as a consumer protection measure. It provides that all reports made on individuals are subject to certain procedures. If the report concerns the subject's character, general reputation or mode of living, the subject must be notified in writing, not later than three days after the report is ordered, that a report will be made and that additional information may be secured about the scope of the report. A consumer who requests this information in writing, is entitled to receive an explanation about the type of investigation that will be made.

Under the Fair Credit Reporting Act, an underwriter may still cancel or reduce coverage or increase premium. However, if this action is based, in whole or in part, on the information received from the report, the consumer must be notified of this fact. The name and address of the reporting agency must also be given. The agency must disclose the nature and substance of all file information to the consumer, upon proper identification. If the consumer disputes the accuracy of the information, the inspection company must make an appropriate investigation and send corrections if inaccuracies are discovered. The consumer also has a right to prepare a statement that must be sent to previous and future recipients of reports.

Early concerns about the negative effects of this law have generally disappeared. Underwriters still order reports, and consumers are able to verify the information, although few of them do so.

On the other hand, underwriters now use few of the "moral/morale" types of reports, as discussed in the previous part of this section. Concerns about the reactions of consumers, coupled with the often-inaccurate nature of subjective information, have generally reduced the volume of these reports. On automobile applications, most reports are of the classification type. On homeowners and residential fire business, physical reports are most commonly used. On commerical lines, physical and financial reports are favored, as the need arises. Some insurance and reporting companies treat all of these reports, including Motor Vehicle Reports (MVR's) on automobile risks, as being consumer reports, subject to the provisions of the Fair Credit Reporting Act. Other companies feel that factual material, such as MVR's does not fall under the requirements of the Act.

INFORMATION FROM LOCAL SOURCES

Many local sources are able to furnish information to insurance companies about applicants. These sources may be used by others in developing their data; inspection companies may use them in many cases. Companies may secure the information directly, however, through employee contacts. These contacts may be made in person, by telephone or through correspondence. Valuable, specific information may thus be gained without the necessity of using intermediaries. Direct contact by the insurer may be preferable in some cases.

Some Important Sources

The most important of these local sources are these.

Banks — Financial information may be obtained through the bank where the applicant transacts business. The size of a bank account may not be revealed, of course, but even more important facts may be available, such as how carefully the firm's books are kept, whether the account is over-drawn, whether loans are paid on time, and the like.

Creditors — Those to whom the applicant owes money may reveal the promptness with which bills are paid. The largest group of creditors is usually suppliers, and they maintain good payment records on their clients. This information can be a valuable indicator on the financial condition of the applicant.

Customers — The record of keeping promises about deliveries and the financial terms offered to customers are clues to the financial condition of the applicant. This data may also indicate the quality of management. Satisfied customers tend to lead to a successful future, while dissatisfied customers can cause financial ruin within a short time.

Competitors — Most lines of business are highly competitive, and the competitors usually know a great deal about each other. The owner of a business may fool inspectors, suppliers, even bankers but can seldom fool competitors. Valuable information about an applicant may be secured from competitors. This includes such items as the firm's future in the industry, its competitive position, its pricing practices, and the quality of management and personnel.

Neighbors — People who know a person or a business through contacts because of proximity are in a position to supply a wealth of information. An uninitiated observer is always surprised at the extent of neighbors' knowledge and their willingness, even their eagerness, to share that knowledge. Whether in personal or commercial lines, neighbors and associates can be sources of much information not readily available elsewhere. One problem with this source is its comparative unreliability; some information is biased, prejudiced, even untruthful. People tend to apply their own interpretations to the actions of others and they also seek opportunities to damage the reputations of those with whom they have had difficulties. Neighbors can be an important clue about problem areas, but their information usually should be verified from other sources before it is used.

Police and fire departments — The records of police departments and fire departments are usually available to responsible seekers of information. These records can give reliable data about arrest and conviction histories and fire experience of applicants. When indications of difficulties are revealed by other sources, these departments may be able to confirm or deny the allegations.

Court houses — The records contained in court houses and similar public recording institutions may reveal critical information about applicants. Details about bankruptcies which were filed, deeds which were recorded, and applications for licenses or permits may change the entire picture from an underwriting standpoint. When unverified information is received from another source, these public records can be used to determine if the information is true or false.

School officials — Personal lines underwriters may seek information concerning youthful applicants from school officials. The data may include such items as the grade level achieved, scholastic accomplishments, special honors indicating stability and any recorded trouble with authorities. Some automobile underwriters regularly receive the most recent grades of specified persons from school officials in order to determine if those persons qualify for the discount applied to good students under certain rating plans.

INFORMATION FROM BUREAUS

A number of bureaus and associations have a wealth of information available which may be used by underwriters. Some of these bureaus are connected with the insurance industry, but others are not. Much of the data available from these sources is not available elsewhere, making contacts with them even more valuable. Membership or subscribership is required before information is released by many of these organizations, but not all of them.

Important Bureaus and Associations

The most important of these bureaus and associations are these.

Insurance Rating Bureaus. Many state or regional rating bureaus are able to furnish valuable underwriting information in addition to rating material. Others, such as automobile rating bureaus, supply only classification and rate information. Fire rating bureaus are the leading source of this type of material that can be helpful to underwriters. Commercial fire risks are usually inspected, graded, classified and rated by the bureaus. Skeleton information is published in conjunction with rates, in many cases. More detailed information may be secured upon request; this could include a copy of the entire inspection report. From such sources, an underwriter can determine construction, occupancy, exposures and many other pertinent details about each risk. Rating bureaus also publish reports about catastrophic losses, both individual-risk and multiple-risk. Important information can be gleaned from these reports to help in future decisions.

Arson and Theft Bureaus. Several bureaus have been established to aid in the identification of dishonest claimants. Losses of questionable legitimacy may be recorded by such bureaus and reported, upon request, to member or subscriber companies. These bureaus are established by insurance companies in order to assist in the prosecution of dishonest persons and in the avoidance of future claims. The avowed purpose of such bureaus is to help the claims departments, but the information that they are able to supply could be of importance to underwriters, too.

Clipping Bureaus. A number of bureaus and associations have been established to act as clearning houses for newspaper clippings that contain information of potential value of underwriters. These bureaus are sometimes established by insurance companies and are sometimes operated by independent enterprises. These bureaus ordinarily receive their clippings from professional clipping services but they may perform this function themselves. Underwriters inquire about specific applicants and receive all clippings on file for those persons.

A great deal of material that is reported in the public press can be helpful to underwriters when it can be matched with applications for insurance. Articles may describe such activities as bankruptcies, arrests for alcohol or drug possession, accounts of fights and attacks, detailed descriptions of automobile accidents and divorce actions. The problem has always been to match the clippings with the applicants; and it is this function which is performed by the clipping bureaus.

Trade Associations. Many industries have established trade associations that are able to supply certain types of information. While they may not reveal all of the facts about a member, they are usually pleased to report favorable information. From these associations, an underwriter may be able to determine that an applicant is considered to have a good reputation, has not been known to engage in unethical conduct, has not been criticized by customers to any unusual extent, and that creditors are not complaining. In addition, the association may reveal hitherto unknown branches or related activities of the applicant and perhaps may disclose partners or officers about whom the underwriter had no knowledge. All of this information can be helpful as the underwriter seeks facts upon which to base decisions.

INFORMATION FROM GOVERNMENTAL AGENCIES

Federal and state governments also publish a great deal of information that can be valuable to businesses. Insurance underwriters can secure booklets, pamphlets and other material on a variety of subjects from federal agencies. Some of these, such as data on past tornadoes or earthquakes, can be of immediate value in establishing programs for writing certain types of insurance. Other material is helpful in developing background in certain lines, since these booklets are designed more specifically for industries which are served by insurance. There is no limit to the knowledge which can be gained by studying such publications, but there is little immediate or practical benefit to be gained from most of them.

The Census Bureau publishes a wealth of information that is derived from the census figures. Underwriters may be able to determine the economic or property value patterns of various areas, and may be able to design underwriting programs which take these facts into account. Individual applicants may also be checked against this information; an example is an applicant whose property values appear to be unusual for the general area. This information could be verified for the immediate neighborhood.

At the state level, the greatest help can be secured from the Departments of Motor Vehicles. These departments are maintained in every state to accumulate data about the driving record of each licensed driver in the state. Their principal purpose is to serve law enforcement agencies. However, the data is sold to various other institutions, and insurance companies generally are able to purchase this information. Pressures arise frequently to deny this data to such outsiders as insurance companies. Some states may take such action at any time but potential loss of revenue restrains most states from doing so.

Insurers secure a motor vehicle record (called an MVR) on each driver under many circumstances. Some automobile companies use the conviction record as a part of the rating process, so they secure MVRs on every risk. Other companies use the driving record, both convictions and accidents, in the selection process. Actually, MVRs permit insurers to qualify preferred risks and to charge a higher rate for those who have had driving problems. This permits lower rates for better drivers, supplying still another reason why most citizens of a state will benefit from the continued access of insurers to these motor vehicle records.

The quality and cost of motor vehicle records vary considerably by state. Some localities report every citation to the state, while others report only serious convictions and accidents. The records in some states are available from many years back while others are only recent. The cost of the report bears little relationship to the quality, with some of the larger states supplying good information at reasonable costs and some of the less efficient states charging several times more. Each underwriter must determine the quality of these reports in states of operation and must compare this with the allowable budget for securing this type of information.

A few states also have printed studies that have been conducted on driving records and trends. Some good material is available indicating the relationship of driving records and the predictability of future accidents. Such information is of obvious benefit to automobile underwriters, since a large portion of their job is to select those applicants whose experience will be no worse than the average for their classes.

INFORMATION FROM SPECIAL SOURCES

Four separate types of sources are available for furnishing information to underwriters. They are unrelated to each other and to other sources, but each represents a business which serves the insurance industry by supplying data that may be helpful in the underwriting process.

Each of these special sources is explained in detail.

Companies Supplying Financial Ratings and Data

There are companies that analyze and publish financial data concerning most business enterprises in the country. Since these publications are divided into geographical areas, an underwriter who purchases these books may check any business applicant. In addition to the financial data itself, the publishing company rates each business on such factors as its stability, its net worth and its ability to pay. Such information can be very helpful to underwriters of many commercial lines.

These companies also supply more detailed information upon individual companies when requested to do so. By this means, a commercial underwriter who detects possible difficulties from the entries in the books may secure a more detailed description of the financial status of the applicant. These individual reports are usually available along with a subscription to the regular publications or they may be purchased separately.

Engineers

Various types of engineers who work for other concerns are able to furnish information to underwriters. These people are experts within their limited fields; the reports they make, therefore, are quite authoritative.

Safety engineers are trained to recognize situations in which improvements may be made in order to reduce injuries to workers or others. They are valuable to workers' compensation underwriters but they may also supply help to those who handle liability insurance on stores and other locations to which the public has access.

Fleet engineers are specialists in the loss exposures of automobile and truck fleets. They can furnish information concerning capabilities of drivers, physical condition of equipment, maintenance and route schedules. They may conduct training sessions for drivers, plan safe driving campaigns and help in scheduling. Fleet engineers may also patrol the highways to observe driving habits and equipment condition of vehicles operated by drivers of the insured.

Loss prevention specialists (formerly called engineers) are those who inspect premises and recommend improvements that will help avoid losses. Most of their activities lie within the property field, with comments directed toward such areas as housekeeping, fire and crime prevention and detection devices, construction or alterations, and heating. They also may analyze production activities to find methods of preventing loss to material upon which work is being performed, of preventing errors in production that may lead to injury to users of the product, and similar activities.

Some of these loss prevention specialists work for companies which supply their services to insurance companies for a fee, much like inspection companies. Others operate as loss prevention consultants to policyholders. In any case, their reports ordinarily contain recommendations for improvement and give considerable information about the details of the risk. (Loss prevention specialists who are employed by insurance companies are described in a later section of this chapter.)

Marine Surveyors

Special companies and individuals are available for furnishing marine surveys to underwriters. Boats and ships have peculiar characteristics which require considerable training before they can be identified properly. Marine surveyors supply their services to underwriters, as well as to the ship owners for a fee. They furnish reports upon request, much like inspection companies. Their reporting forms are highly specialized, identifying the unique features of marine objects. These reports are specifically aimed at reporting the facts as they exist. Ordinarily the reports also contain recommendations for improvements, if any can be made.

Ocean marine underwriters also depend heavily upon marine surveyors. Some inland marine underwriters may also use their services for large boats, but the principal activity of these surveyors is concerned with yachts and larger ships.

Psychological Testing Laboratories

A few psychologists have developed attitude tests used by underwriters of certain lines, particularly automobile. These psychologists have established laboratories for testing or for grading.

Automobile underwriters have believed for years that the attitude of a driver is a strong factor in an inclination toward having accidents. Many attempts have been made to develop tests that contain reliable indicators of attitude. Psychologists eventually became interested and devoted considerable research to the preparation of such tests. Those that have been developed and have proven to be reliable are offered to insurance companies for a fee, usually a modest fee for each test taken by an applicant.

Some of these tests are administered in the testing laboratories under controlled conditions. Much more practical to the ordinary underwriter are tests that can be given by the producer or company personnel, or can even be completed by the applicant at home. When the tests are administered by other than the psychologists who developed them, the grading keys are retained by the psychologist as protection against unauthorized (or uncompensated) use. The tests are graded and a summary of results is sent to the underwriters. These results are shown to be reliable within certain parameters of reliability. The underwriter, therefore, may need to apply considerable judgment in interpreting and applying the results.

INFORMATION FROM OTHER INSURERS

The actual record of a policy holder is much more reliable as an indicator of future performance than most other items. Underwriters depend heavily upon the principle of predicting the future by an analysis of the past. The problem, when an underwriter is considering a new applicant, is to find out the previous experience. It may not be available through any other source; even the application may contain errors or misrepresentations to facts of previous losses.

The books of the previous insurer are sometimes made available to the underwriter, giving access to this valuable information. The reporting of experience may be made by means of a telephone call or a written inquiry from the underwriter to whom application has been made, to the underwriter of the previous insurer. The latter is expected to reveal all of the pertinent facts about the loss experience while the applicant was insured by his company.

No fees are charged for this exchange of information; rather, reciprocity is practiced. Each underwriter who participates in such an exchange is expected to reveal the information contained in the company's files in return for the receipt of experience from other underwriters. Any company that feels it does not benefit by such an arrangement is free to discontinue the exchange at any time, with or without notice to other insurers.

Probably the most important information which can be received from previous insurers concerns losses. The date of loss, amount paid, who was driving the car if an automobile policy, and similar facts may be secured. These facts can probably be secured elsewhere but it is quicker and easier to obtain them from the previous insurer. In addition, it may be helpful to learn how the other company rated the risk, in order to discover any hidden exposures such as youthful drivers, and to ascertain the coverages carried and the premium paid. Finally, the reason the client changed companies may be important to the underwriter. Did the other company cancel, reduce coverage or request a voluntary cancellation? Or would they welcome the client back? This information can be helpful to an underwriter in determining the facts about the applicant.

INFORMATION FROM COMPANY EMPLOYEES

Insurance companies employ people in many different tasks. As these employees perform their duties, they may encounter information that can be helpful to underwriters. A well-organized company makes provisions by which this information is made available to the underwriters.

Employee Sources

Three types of positions contain functions which permit employees to secure underwriting information. (Not included in this section are employees who may be producers; they were included with other producers in a previous section.)

1. Engineers[2] Some companies employ their own engineers, rather than hire the services of outside concerns. These engineers are comparable in their functions to other engineers, and may be safety engineers, fleet engineers or loss prevention specialists. The reports and duties are similar insofar as the technical parts of the reports are concerned. In many cases, engineers employed by insurers perform a valuable loss control service to policyholders, as well as supply information to underwriters.

Engineers who are employees of insurance companies may furnish an additional service: opinions about the insurability and desirability of risks. In some ways, engineers are in a unique position of supplying information to insurers. In the first place, they are technical experts and can give specific, factual reports; they see so many risks that they can recommend those that are average or better. In the second place, their position permits them to give a disinterested, unbiased report. Producers tend to be influenced by the prospect of commissions and the existence of competition. Company management is often sales minded, too. Since underwriters seldom see specific risks, engineers who are employees are in an excellent position to report the facts to them.

Most companies encourage their engineers to include recommendations in their reports. Engineers are expected to report first on the technical findings and recommendations and then to report on the attitude of management toward loss prevention, the spirit of cooperation on the part of employees, the catastrophe potential and any other problems which they see or sense. These matters may be requested on the engineering report form, or they may be requested in the remarks section. The findings may be in the form of reporting facts which involve these factors or they may be specific recommendations concerning the desirability of the risk.

2. Claims adjusters. Most companies use outside adjusters, but some companies employ their own. An advantage of using company employees is that they can be encouraged to furnish recommendations to underwriters. In some ways, adjusters are similar to engineers; being employees, they know what the company wants and they are in an excellent position to give recommendations. Claims adjusters, like engineers, also are able to give disinterested information based on personal contact and their recommendations can be valuable to underwriters.

It has been stated, somewhat facetiously, that an adjuster is a person who stands between a man and immediate wealth. There is a grain of truth in that remark, for the duty of the adjuster is to protect the assets of the company by giving a claimant no more and no less than that claimant is entitled to receive; this is the principal duty. A secondary duty is to help the company by warning the underwriter of

---

2. Terminology is changing, and the current trend is toward calling all of these types of employees by the title of "loss prevention specialists." However, since some of them handle only specific functions, such as fleets of trucks, the name "engineer" seems to still be correct as a general name used in the industry.

problems that are discovered.

Most insurers who employ claims adjusters require them to submit underwriting information only when specific facts or opinions appear to be worth mentioning. Others require comments on every loss report. In either case, adusters are encouraged to report facts which may be important to underwriters, along with their personal recommendations. Adjuster reports concerning the insurability and desirability of risks may be received on any line of insurance. To this extent, those reports may be of more value to underwriters, as a whole, than engineer reports because engineers are used only on certain commercial risks.

3. Auditors. Auditors are employed to furnish specific rating information to the companies. Those who perform their duties in the offices of policyhodlers may be able to supply valuable information to underwriters.

Auditors visit policyholders in order to verify reported figures or to secure the figures. They check records to determine amount of gross sales, number of products produced or sold, number of employees on the payroll, number of vehicles owned and a description of each, and similar data. Many commercial policies are issued under which the premium is determined after the expiration of the policy, based upon the number of units of exposure of a type specified. An error or misrepresentation could affect the premium to a large enough extent that it is worthwhile for insurers to employ auditors to verify or secure the figures.

Auditors do not report their routine findings to underwriters. Most reports contain only the specific information required, and this is important only in determining the premium. Occasionally, however, an auditor encounters a situation which should be brought to the attention of the underwriter. Perhaps this is evidence of an impending bankruptcy, a shortage of cash with which to maintain equipment, evidence of an illegal activity or some other factor of importance. Auditors should be encouraged to be alert for any such conditions and to report them to the underwriters immediately. Since this information is factual and disinterested, it is usually valuable to underwriters.

Auditors are seldom asked to submit recommendations. It is sufficient for them to furnish factual information only; underwriters can interpret it themselves. Like engineers, auditors are used only on certain commercial accounts. For that reason, they are helpful to a limited number of underwriters.

INFORMATION FROM COMPANY RECORDS

Insurers maintain many records which are valuable sources of underwriting information. Sometimes overlooked by underwriters is the fact that company records are exact, relevant and inexpensive to obtain.

It is probably more common than not, that a person or firm will insure more than one exposure with the same company. A homeowner tends to place insurance for home and contents, valuable articles, and automobiles in one company. A businessman often insists that fire insurance, business liability coverage and vehicle protection be written in one company or group of companies. These policies can be cross-referenced to be sure that important information received on one policy is referred to the underwriters of other lines.

Insurance companies receive and retain a great deal of information about their policyholders. The data which is received from any of the sources previously described is kept in the files. When claims are reported, the facts are recorded in the policy files. A considerable body of information may be stored over a period of a few years even if only one policy is written.

When an application is received for a new coverage, the underwriter is foolish not to review all of the information already in the company's files. It costs nothing to secure beyond the clerical expense of locating and forwarding the files. The data is factual and indisputable. This is such a valuable source that many companies have established procedures under which each new applicant is checked to see if other policies are in the company. If so, they are referred with the application to the underwriter. Thereafter, the files are marked so that any pertinent data which comes to the attention of one underwriter will be referred to other underwriters.

A considerable degree of valuable information may accumulate rapidly even on just one policy. Correspondence with a policyholder, asking or answering questions can be quite revealing. The regularity with which an insured pays premiums or submits reports of values gives a clue about dependability. Finally, the loss record on the policy is another excellent source of indisputable information about the policyholder and the risk. These items in the policy file are not available on a new application, of course. This portion of the discussion is concerned primarily with new applications. The underwriting practices that are followed in maintaining policies on the books and in underwriting renewals are discussed in Section VII. However, this material in the policy file itself is an excellent source of underwriting information and should not be overlooked.

QUESTIONS FOR DISCUSSION

1. What are some of the basic types of information which an underwriter must have before deciding whether sufficient information is available for decision-making or whether additional information is necessary?
2. Define "adverse selection" and explain why it is a problem to underwriters.
3. Describe, briefly, four factors which an underwriter should consider before deciding to pursue additional sources of information.
4. Give two reasons why time is an important factor in securing and making underwriting decisions.
5. Aside from the application, what are some of the other ways producers can be of assistance to underwriters in securing information?
6. Why is the Fair Credit Reporting Act important for an underwriter to understand?
7. Besides the application and inspection report, what are some of the other outside sources which can be of benefit to the underwriter in securing information?
8. Briefly describe the inter-company sources for securing additional underwriting information.

7

Develop Alternatives

The second step in underwriting decision-making is to develop alternative courses of action. It is not enough to secure large quantities of information; these facts are worthless until some use is made of them.

"Weigh the facts!" This is the necessary second phase of underwriting. As the facts are weighed and evaluated, alternative courses will become apparent. These alternatives must be developed from vague ideas into specific possibilities for action.

There are two general types of information available: objective and subjective. Underwriters must know the difference if they hope to evaluate the facts with any degree of benefit. Next they must analyze the reliability of the sources of information from which they get their facts. At this point, underwriters can organize the facts which they have obtained, and survey any budget and time limitations to see if more material can or should be requested. The final step in the evaluation process is in applying judgment to the facts to be certain that they are reliable and relevant.

As the underwriters complete their evaluation of the available information, they can start to develop some alternatives. They will encounter some hazards that must be controlled. Three major variables must be considered in preparing alternatives: premium rates, policy conditions and reinsurance, along with the selection process itself. (Each of these phases is discussed in this chapter.)

OBJECTIVE INFORMATION

Pertinent facts that can be proved constitute objective information. These facts are the greatest benefit to an underwriter since they are irrefutable and easily recognized by others.

Property insurance depends heavily upon objective information. Much of the basic underwriting handling depends upon these facts, whether they are rates, forms, or matters of retention. Some facts used in property lines are these.

1. Construction of the building.
2. Occupancy of the premises.

3. Protection available, whether police, fire or private.
4. Exposures from surrounding structures, from other occupancies in the building, or from neighboring premises.
5. Past record of losses.

Liability insurance underwriting also uses objective information to a considerable degree. Classification, rating, and forms are dependent upon some of these facts. Examples are the following.

1. Maintenance of premises.
2. Type of operations performed.
3. Safety measures used and steps taken to prevent losses.
4. The driving records and the types of vehicles to be insured, in automobile lines.
5. The age, physical condition, and mental stability of the insured, particularly on vehicle coverages.
6. Marital status.
7. Past record of losses.

In many respects, the most important of these items is the past record of losses. A basic tenet of underwriting is that the past is the best indicator of the future. This is particularly true on such lines as personal automobile with a high loss frequency. Underwriters know that people can change their habits and that such changes are rather unusual and almost always gradual, not sudden. A pattern of past losses, therefore, can be expected to continue in the future, unless some important change can be proved.

SUBJECTIVE INFORMATION

Relevant facts which are difficult or impossible to prove are considered subjective information. Sometimes these facts are very important to an underwriter because they reveal facets of an applicant's character which may not otherwise be evident. This information often is not known to the producer, so underwriters must be doubly vigilant when they encounter this material.

Under any line, the same types of information are important. These facts relate to the general living habits and reputation of the applicant. If such conditions are poor, losses can be heavy in any line of insurance. Illustrations of some of the more common types of subjective information are these.

1. Business and personal reputation.
2. Stability and dependability.
3. Social behavior.
4. Types of associates.
5. Housekeeping practices.
6. Neighborhood environment.

These subjective factors are important to every underwriter. Persons who are not familiar with the principles and practices of insurance underwriting sometimes question the use of subjective information. For example, they may ask the reason an automobile underwriter is concerned about the housekeeping of the applicant's home. After all, they reason the automobile may be clean and the applicant may be a good driver.

Underwriters know the relationship between living habits and general behavior. It has been said that, "As a man lives, so he drives." Automobile studies have proved that people who are problem drinkers, whose moral conduct is poor or who have criminal records almost invariably have high accident frequencies. On the other hand, according to the studies, a person who lives a stable and respected life and takes an active interest in church and community affairs almost invariably enjoys an accident-free record. Underwriters know that these relationships exist and have learned by experience that they cannot ignore these subjective indications of trouble and still achieve profitable business.

RELIABILITY OF SOURCES

No information is better than its source. The most startling, revealing, or apparently-proven facts are worthless if the source is unreliable. An important step to be followed by underwriters as they evaluate information is to check on the reliability of the source. This does not mean that every source must be absolutely identified and checked. Sometimes vague hints from unrevealed sources may lead an underwriter to discover important facts. The important thing is to use unreliable sources only as guides to other data, not as proven facts in themselves. When considered in that light, an underwriter will never discard any fact which might be relevant but will use it as a starting point. The underwriter will secure confirmation from a reliable source, if at all possible.

The consideration of the informant's reliability is performed concurrently with an evaluation of the information itself. Underwriters do not evaluate all facts, then weigh the reliability of the source. Rather they consider the reliability along with the information, balancing the two at each step.

Indications of Reliability

Some indications of reliabilty that underwriters can expect from their major sources are discussed next.

1. Producers. Most producers honestly try to present the true facts to underwriters. A few may attempt to misrepresent certain facts, and they can, of course, cause trouble for underwriters until they are discovered. Almost all producers are, by nature, salesmen. As such, they are more inclined to look on the positive side than the negative — to be more optimistic than pessimistic. Even more important, most producers are paid a commission based on the business that they write, not on business they turn away. A common feeling is that some producers have dollar signs in front of their eyes, blurring their vision of unpleasant circumstances. Some producers are eligible for bonuses based on their loss ratio, which helps a little; still many producers are more inclined to take the commission today and worry about the loss ratio tomorrow.

These comments are not intended to be critical of producers. If they did not approach selling on that basis, they would not be successful. The entire insurance mechanism depends too heavily on their selling ability to want to attempt to change it. The point is that an underwriter must not overlook the fact that producers are not underwriters nor impartial fact-gatherers. They are involved too closely in the transaction to always be able to furnish unvarnished facts. Recognizing this, underwriters should not depend too heavily upon the information of producers until they feel secure in such dependence.

2. *Applicants.* Most applicants are reasonably honest in the information they furnish to producers and insurers. In fact, many people feel that insurers are much more omniscient than they really are. Furthermore, many members of the public fear their policies will be void if they do not reveal every fact that might be pertinent. Unfortunately for underwriters, this feeling does not guarantee that all applications are completed in absolute honesty. In the first place, some people do not share those feelings; rather, they attempt to conceal or misrepresent unpleasant facts. Secondly, producers sometimes dissuade people from revealing all of the facts and even refuse or neglect to enter all answers to questions on the application. Finally, the producer may ask questions in such a manner that an honest answer is almost impossible. A typical question might be: "You haven't had any accidents lately, have you?'

For these reasons, underwriters do not accept statements on applications as being "the whole truth and nothing but the truth." Even if the application is signed, it may be questionable to some degree.

3. *Inspection reports.* The information given on reports from inspection companies or other outside reporting companies is generally reliable. Their existence depends upon their ability to furnish complete and correct information to insurers. They try hard, in most cases, and are quite reliable. However, they are far from infallible. Their inspectors may be inexperienced or poorly trained. They may even be incompetent, lazy, or dishonest; being human, some of them will be less than perfect and no inspection company can avoid the hiring of some such workers. Thus, reports may contain information that belongs to a different subject, is secured only by telephone, or is fabricated in the mind of the inspector and is woefully incomplete.

Another problem with inspection reports is the reporting technique used. Some neighbors are vicious, vengeful or slanderous and may enjoy relating untrue or exaggerated stories about a subject. Almost as serious is the fact that different people have different standards; a teetotaling neighbor may consider a man to be a drunkard if he is seen on Saturday afternoons in his back yard with a beer in his hand. A reliable report will emphasize that only one person alleges this situation, if further verification is impossible, but some reports may overlook this detail.

Underwriters generally rely quite heavily on outside inspection reports, particularly if reliable information has been received from the company in the past. Still, they must attempt to verify the information if it appears to be questionable. Most inspection companies will reopen reports if requested to do so because someone, such as the producer, has challenged the statements. Too many such requests should cause underwriters to consider ordering reports from a different company.

4. *Local sources.* Banks, stores, customers, suppliers and similar sources are usually quite reliable, but it may be difficult to secure anyting more than basic objective information from them. Of course, a desire for revenge or a dislike for someone may cause some slanted material. Caution must be exercised, therefore, and the

underwriter should double check if the facts appear to be distorted.

5. Bureaus. Rating bureaus, credit bureaus and similar organizations are generally objective and reliable. They have nothing to gain by furnishing incorrect or inaccurate information. Unfortunately, they are not infallible. Their material depends upon clerical employees, some of whom may be poorly trained and underpaid. When an entry is made on the wrong card, figures are transposed or the wrong address is used, the information is useless. When the facts are challenged, perhaps by a producer, the underwriter must find a means of checking further to verify the accuracy of statements.

6. Governmental agencies. The most common information received from governmental agencies are motor vehicle reports from state departments of motor vehicles. This information is factual and reliable, generally speaking. The problem sometimes encountered is lack of accuracy by clerical personnel. Since errors can occur, the underwriter may need to recheck the data when it is challenged. Barring these errors, these reports are objective and factual.

7. Engineers. Company engineers and loss prevention specialists, or those working for outside companies, are quite reliable in the information they furnish. Most are conscientious and try to render factual, honest reports. One problem is that engineers may be so technical that they do not speak the same language as the underwriter. Engineering reports should tell the underwriter about existing conditions and problems and should contain recommendations. The underwriter must evaluate the information contained in the report, weighing the reliability of the report. Ordinarily, engineering reports are more reliable than other sources, especially when the engineers are employees who are interested in helping the underwriter and are proud of their work and their reputation.

8. Other outside sources. The information received from such sources as financial reporting companies, marine surveyors and psychological testing laboratories is quite reliable. The reputation of the source must be verified, of course. The major problem to underwriters is sorting out material that they can use. If the report is understandable and is relevant, such a report can be very reliable and helpful.

9. Other insurers. The information received from insurance companies is one of the most reliable sources. Errors can occur, of course, and untrained employees may furnish the wrong information or use the wrong file. But, most companies do not want other insurers to catch them in errors, and most of them desire reciprocation in kind. For this reason, they use trained employees to complete the forms, in fact, underwriters often complete the forms themselves. This source is particularly valuable because it contains information not available elsewhere, such as the rate that was charged and the real reason for cancellation. The answers from the prior insurer as to which party initiated the cancellation are usually more reliable than those received from the applicant.

10. Company employee. Underwriting information sometimes is furnished by such employees as claims adjusters and auditors. This information is very reliable and may be depended upon by underwriters. Occasionally, of course, an employee may have had a personality conflict with a client and may try to get revenge for alleged wrongs by furnishing a damaging report. An underwriter must recognize that such events can happen, and be ready to secure confirming information if challenged.

11. Company records. Perhaps the most reliable source of all is the record that the client has built on other policies. This is why many underwriters like to have every other policy file made available for review during the underwriting process. Except for the occasional error which can occur on any type of record, the experience in the files is absolutely reliable.

ORGANIZE THE INFORMATION

The organization of information into a useful form is a very important part of the process of evaluating data and preparing alternatives. A great deal of actual and potential material is available and the underwriter must organize it as it is used.

During the evaluation process an underwriter must decide upon what additional information is needed. For example as the answers on the application are analyzed, it may be decided to secure confirmation of certain items and request further details on those that arouse suspicion. This process continues during the evaluation of each item of information.

The underwriter must be careful not to accept all data submitted; some material will be irrelevant and some will merely duplicate facts already received. Part of the organizing process includes discarding unimportant material. This permits a more complete evaluation of facts which can be used.

Some important information may be missing, in many cases. Perhaps certain questions are unanswered on the application. Perhaps a motor vehicle department report has no record on the driver's license number that was given. As the underwriter analyzes and organizes the information, these omissions will be discovered.

Underwriting requires an orderly process of decision making. Only disorder and confusion will result without some system of organizing material. Whatever method is adopted, the underwriter should follow the same general pattern on each case. A check list is used by some underwriters. Under this system, each important item is checked on a form when it is identified. Such a system must permit consideration of items that usually are not significant but may cause problems in a few cases. Another problem to watch for is the case where several relatively minor points, each no worse than borderline, may combine to form a major problem. Under any system, the underwriter must watch for circumstances or peculiarities that appear to be insignificant upon a quick glance but may present real problems when all of the facts are known.

As the material is organized and the underwriter discovers needs for further information, two choices are available. One is to return to the original source and the other is to employ a new source. The original source is used in most cases when information is missing. If a producer omits an answer to a question, the normal process is to request the information. If an inspector or an engineer fails to comment upon an important point, the underwriter usually requests the data from the same person. New sources are used when the underwriter is suspicious about one aspect of the risk and desires further information. It is the feeling of some that the original source would have explained the situation if it was known, so it is wasteful to ask that same person. These are merely general guides, of course. Perhaps some insurers, on some lines, prefer to return to the producer for answers on any questions. Others may prefer to use outside sources for each item, even those the producer should have answered in the first place. Each underwriter must be guided by the practices of his company.

BUDGET LIMITATIONS

Budgets control the information underwriters can secure. There is such a wealth of potential information available that without some checks, underwriters might spend exorbitant sums in securing more data. Most insurers assign budget amounts to information that must be secured. This may be a combined sum for all sources or it may be segregated by type, such as inspection reports and motor vehicle reports. When the budgeted amount for a month or a quarter is exceeded, each underwriter must explain this because the company expects the underwriters to operate within a budget.

This limitation requires underwriters to select risks upon which they will request more information. They know that on any one case they *might* secure some helpful data, but at the same time, they should know how to separate the risks upon which they are *likely* to learn something from those where the chances are slight. Underwriters must learn to identify risks with potential problems and to investigate them, while acting upon information at hand on others. There are three methods by which underwriters can avoid the limitations imposed by budgets.

Determine exactly what information is needed. If only the driving record is needed, a motor vehicle report is preferable to a more expensive inspection report. If moral problems are suspected, an engineering report will seldom produce satisfactory results.

Request the information in advance. Underwriters should anticipate the data which they need and insert questions on the application or producers' report which will give the answers. If age or occupation of the applicant is a factor in underwriting in many cases, it is foolish to pay for an inspection report in order to get the information. There is a limit, naturally, on the questions that can be asked of the producer, so the underwriter must consider carefully those questions to ask.

Use less expensive sources. Some sources cost more than others. The accident record of a driver can be secured by an inspection report but a motor vehicle report is usually less expensive. A letter to the prior insurer is even less costly — needing only a form letter, a stamp and handling costs. The record on another policy in the company, if one exists, is still less expensive.

The underwriters must decide what information is needed and must secure it in the least expensive manner possible, within practical limits. Often they must act on imcomplete data. Seldom, in fact, are all of the relevant facts known. An important part of underwriting training is to learn when to act on the available information and when to secure more facts. An important part of underwriting is to make the proper decision after evaluating the facts. An equally important part is to know when the facts at hand are sufficient for decision making and when more information is needed.

TIME LIMITATIONS

Underwriters do not have unlimited time in which to develop alternatives. Where there are specific limitations, they act as absolute limits on the underwriter. Even where limitations do not exist, the nature of insurance requires that the applicant be told within a reasonable time if he or she is acceptable or not.

Even though some producers have binding authority, a producer may still choose to submit facts about an individual risk for advance approval of the underwriter. This may occur because the producer is not clear about some of the underwriting requirements; feels uncertain about the quality of the risk; or wants the underwriter to gather more information than the producer can secure. Whatever the reason, producers may submit risks for approval, even though they have the authority to bind the coverage. In addition, most companies specify certain types of risks that must be submitted before binding. In such cases, the underwriter has a duty to complete the examination as quickly as possible and to notify the producer.

As mentioned earlier, cancellation laws have been enacted in many states. Under them, policies in specified lines may not be cancelled during the term. Some laws even prohibit non-renewal. All such laws contain a "discovery period," a certain number of days during which the underwriter may conduct his investigation, discover any problems and decline the coverage if necessary. The period is about 45 to 60 days, although some laws vary. Since these laws place tight limitations on the time available to an underwriter, there may not be enough time to investigate all aspects of a risk and to develop alternatives.

Since time is a limiting factor, the underwriter must consider the length of time needed before reports are ordered. Sometimes two or more reports may be ordered at the same time, even though there is a chance that the answers will be duplicates, just because there may not be time for sucessive investigations.

EVALUATE THE INFORMATION

Having secured the necessary or available information, it must then be evaluated. All material in the world is useless without an evaluation. The basis of the evaluation may differ by types of data.

Objective information may be evaluated by statistical means. For instance, the number of accidents that have been incurred, the degree of fire protection available, the burglary protective devices in use and similar facts may be counted and measured. Sometimes the answer will make a risk unacceptable. Other times, the answer is used by the underwriter in determining acceptability, although it may also play a part in classification, rating and reinsurance.

Subjective information must be evaluated by judgment. Underwriters use their background, training and experience to determine the desirability of a risk. These factors are the most difficult to analyze and their handling represents the principal reason for using trained underwriters in writing insurance. Seldom are these factors either black or white; rather, they are usually in shades of gray, requiring underwriting knowledge to determine acceptability of risks.

In every case, the purpose of evaluation is the same. Underwriters are attempting to learn if the facts indicate an increased susceptibility to future losses. Underwriters are not moralists; they do not care about what happened yesterday, and they are unconcerned about other activities of the applicant, *unless* these factors tend to indicate an increased chance of loss in the future. The underwriter is interested in *every* fact about an applicant that may have an effect on future losses. This is the purpose of evaluation and ultimately of underwriting itself.

FIND ALTERNATIVES

At this point, all pertinent information has been received and evaluated. The next step is to develop alternative courses of action. Underwriting alternatives seldom are simple or obvious. Almost always, several courses of action are possible. The duty of an underwriter is to find each of the alternatives that is available before a decision is made. If all alternatives are not considered, underwriting duties are not being properly performed for the company, the producer, the client, or the public.

An important step in training and developing an underwriter is in teaching methods of finding alternative courses of action. It takes little training to say "yes" or "no." It requires years of training to see that many other answers are possible, most of them preferable to the simple answer. A good underwriter always tries to find alternative courses before arriving at a decision.

Alternatives can be divided into *four* major groups, each containing a multitude of options. These four are:

1. Acceptability
2. Policy conditions
3. Premium rates
4. Reinsurance

Acceptability

The first set of alternatives deals with acceptability of risk, based on hazards that are present. To some degree, all alternatives may be concerned with acceptability. The difference is that those listed in this group are the alternatievs based upon inherent conditions in the risk, while other groups contain alternatives which may be used if the risk is accepted.

1. Decline or cancel. If a risk is totally unacceptable, it must be declined or cancelled. In some cases, this is the simplest alternative: no other conditions need be considered in conjunction with it. At the same time, it should be the last alternative — considered only after all other alternatives have been discarded. The job of the underwriter is to write business, not reject it. An underwriter should try to write every risk if there is a profitable means of doing so.

2. Rescind coverage. An action which is even more serious than declination or cancellation is rescission. This is the act of voiding coverage or, in other words, of considering that no contract existed because of material misrepresentations made in securing insurance. Sometimes an underwriter discovers facts that are at variance with those shown on the application for coverage bound by a producer. Some of these are serious, such as undisclosed physical infirmities or major citations received. When these are so serious that the coverage would have been completely ineligible if the true facts were revealed, the underwriter may choose to rescind. The policy is thus declared void as of its inception.

3. Accept as requested. Underwriters often accept risks with no changes in coverages for which application is made. If the producer has done a good job of submitting the application in conformity with the rules of the company and if no adverse information is developed, the risk will be accepted as requested.

4. Accept with reservations. Many times an underwriter will find a risk acceptable provided certain changes are made from the conditions requested on the application. These changes may be in policy conditions or premium rates. Each of these has several alternatives that are discussed under the next two points. Changes might also be required in the risk itself. Protective devices may be required, housekeeping improvements might be demanded, changes in oeprations might be needed or other basic changes in the risk itself might be specified by the underwriter. In these cases, the underwriter is saying that the risk is acceptable provided certain physical changes are made; this alternative is used quite commonly in commercial lines.

Policy Conditions

A risk may be acceptable provided certain changes are made in the policy contract that is issued. Some of the more common alternatives are these.

1. Deductibles. Property contracts usually contain deductibles. In some lines certain size deductibles are mandatory while in others several choices are offered. Ordinarily, the applicant is permitted to select the deductible desired from among those available. Occasionally an underwriter will insist upon a higher deductible in order to control an expected loss frequency, particularly small losses. In those cares, the underwriter may require a deductible as an alternative to declination or cancellation.

2. Perils covered. Many policies offer choices of perils and coverages, with the applicant selecting those desired. Sometimes the underwriter feels that a particular risk should not be written to cover certain types of losses and selects the alternative of writing the policy under a more limited kind of coverage, or cancelling it.

3. Coinsurance and similar clauses. An underwriter has many clauses that may be used to limit amounts of loss, usually by making the policyholder a coinsured to some extent. Other clauses distribute the coverage in specified ways or require the insured to carry certain amounts of protection. Applicants often request these clauses, usually as a means of reducing the premium. When they do not do so, the underwriter has the alternative of requiring one of the clauses, as the need is indicated, rather than cancelling the entire contract.

4. Warranties. These are special policy provisions requiring the policyholder to meet specified conditions. If they are not met, the loss will not be paid. Under some warranties, the entire contract may be void. Examples are warranties that specify that protective devices will be maintained in good operating order; that only certain solvents or fluids will be used; or that a stated amount of clear space will be maintained between piles of material. A warranty may be required by an underwriter as an alternative to cancelling some risks.

5. Coverage suspension. Some clauses provide that the entire coverage is suspended during the occurrence of a particular event. These may be acts of omission, such as lack of building occupancy. These may also be acts of commission, such as increasing the hazard by a means within the control of the insured. One example is starting a hazardous manufacturing operation in a previously innocuous business. An underwriter who suspects that such acts may occur may require a suspension clause or may cancel the policy.

6. Restrictions. Endorsements may be used to restrict or exclude certain persons, property, or perils. If only one aspect of the risk appears to be a problem, the underwriter might wish to remove that item as a condition of accepting the risk.

Premium Rates

Underwriters are somewhat limited in their alternatives on premium rates by rating laws that prohibit unfair discrimination, but in many cases it is not unfair to use rate adjustments as alternatives. The three major areas are these:

1. Change rate classes. Under many lines, rate class definitions permit some degree of judgment. Where this occurs, underwriters who feel that the premium is inadequate for the risk, as requested by the producer, may require a higher rate class as an alternative to other action. Sometimes an underwriter may have information which indicates that a different rate class is justified. Other times the underwriter simply may not believe the statements in the application, such as a statement that a 19 year old son in the household will never drive the family car. Where those conditions exist, and the underwriter does not wish to accept the risk at the requested rate, a different rate class may be used as an alternative.

2. Use individual rate programs. In some commercial lines, underwriters have access to several optional rate programs. For example, a retrospective rate plan may be used on large risks under which the final premium is determined by the actual experience of the risk itself. If a normal fixed rate structure is unacceptable, the underwriter may require a variable type as one alternative.

3. Adjust rating factors. Some commercial rate structures provide for debits and credits based on such factors as quality of supervision and type of management. Where these are available, they offer excellent alternatives to the underwriter. Judgment may also be applied to the rating factors, giving a greater number of choices.

Reinsurance

An underwriter may limit the company's retention by securing reinsurance under some conditions. There are two such areas where this is possible.

1. Single risks. Certain risks offer exposures that exceed the desired limits of retention of an underwriter. In these cases an underwriter would have to decline the application if the alternative of reinsuring a portion of the risk was not available.

2. Multiple risks. Catastrophes are a threat under many lines. The exposure of multiple risks can easily cause the retention limits of the company to be exceeded. The underwriter would need to limit the acceptance of risks if the alternative of purchasing catastrophe reinsurance was not available. When such reinsurance is secured, the underwriting alternatives are increased permitting the acceptance of many more risks.

QUESTIONS FOR DISCUSSION

1. What is meant by "objective information," and why can it be of benefit to the underwriter?
2. What examples of objective information are essential to property insurance? To liability insurance?
3. What is meant by "subjective information"? What relationship might there be between a person's neighborhood and that person's auto?
4. Why must an underwriter exercise caution in the information acquired from:
   (a) applicants
   (b) inspection reports
   (c) other outside sources
5. Briefly describe three ways by which an underwriter can avoid limitations imposed by budgets while developing alternatives.
6. Briefly describe the alternatives available to underwriters involving:
   (a) Acceptability
   (b) Policy conditions
   (c) Rates
   (d) Reinsurance

8

Decide and Take Action

The third step in underwriting decision-making is to decide upon a course of action and to act upon it. The list of alternative courses is useless until a decision is made from among them and action is taken.

"Make a decision!" This is the first phase of this step. "Take action!" is the second part of it. The two are inseparable. These must follow after securing information and developing alternatives. This step is the action step — the one which puts into effect the background work that the underwriter has done.

The underwriter often develops a number of alternatives and must select from those alternatives. It will be evident that there are certain principles to be followed and certain viewpoints to be considered in the selection process. It will also be evident that a tentative position may be taken, and that a tentative choice may be made. Still the underwriter cannot delay in making the decision; action must be taken. These are the aspects of the decision-making process that are explained in this chapter.

SELECT FROM THE ALTERNATIVES

Many alternative courses of action are available to an underwriter. Some are easy to choose and perhaps are almost automatic. Others are difficult, requiring the underwriter to evaluate them carefully.

Cancellation, declination or rescission are the easiest. No future losses can occur under policies and no problems can emerge later. On the other hand, no premium is received in the future and no insurance is written. The aim of underwriting is to write business; this goal cannot be accomplished by cancelling risks. At the same time, another aim is to make a profit and this cannot be achieved by accepting risks that have a high loss expectancy. The underwriter should try to find another alternative, no matter how distasteful it might be to the applicant and producer. The refusal to write coverage should be chosen after all other alternatives have been considered and discarded.

Acceptance without qualification is almost as easy. This is a preferable alternative from the standpoint of producer and applicant. It should be the first choice of the underwriter, if possible. Acceptance with qualification comprises the rest of the alternatives. If unqualified acceptance is not possible, a qualification should be considered. The type to be used will depend upon the risk. Some require physical changes while others need contract changes, rate adjustments or reinsurance arrangements. Some risks may require several of these types of alternatives. The underwriter should try to find one or more of these to use before a decision to cancel is made. The basic principles of insurance must be followed when deciding upon the alternative to select. The following are some of the most important ones.

Spread of Risk

A broad spread of risk is essential to the operation of the insurance mechanism. The underwriter should be careful not to accept a large number of risks of one type or risks located only in one area, while others are rejected.

Homogeneity

A group of risks with the same probability of occurrence and loss severity are necessary to achieve accuracy in predicting future loss experience. The underwriter can achieve this goal by selecting alternatives that maintain homogeneity and requiring the same conditions for all risks of the same class.

Avoid Small Losses

The insurance system is designed to protect against serious losses, not against every minor, maintenance-type loss. This principle may be furthered by selecting alternatives that require deductibles or the use of other policy conditions.

Loss Must Be Accidental and Definite

Insurance cannot be written to protect against deliberate acts or those where the amount of the loss is undeterminable. Policy conditions should be used where needed to assure that this principle is followed.

Catastrophe Hazard Must Be Small

The chance of a major catastrophic loss must be avoided if insurance is to operate correctly. The underwriter should consider this principle as decisions are made from among alternatives. Risks should be accepted with an eye toward geographic distribution and policy conditions and reinsurance should be used to assure that the catastrophe exposure is not too great.

Premium Must Be Commensurate With Exposure

An important principle of insurance is that the premium should be in direct relationship to the loss exposure. Where alternatives to premium rates exist, the underwriter must attempt to comply with this principle.

Law of Large Numbers

Insurance is based on the theory of probability. In effect, this theory states that in predicting the number of occurrences, the larger the number of events, the greater the probability that the actual number and the predicted number will agree. An underwriter will base many decisions on this principle, recognizing that if enough risks are written, their experience will come close to that predicted. Of course, statistical data is necessary in determining the probability of loss for each class and this data must be accumulated over a period of time. The selection process, therefore, must take into account the law of large numbers and the statistical data supporting it.

Viewpoints To Consider

Various viewpoints must be considered when deciding upon alternatives to use. The principal ones are these.

Profitability to the Company. The underwriter is an employee of the company with the major purpose of achieving a profitable book of business. The first consideration must be the expected profitability of the risk.

Related Business. Applicants who have other policies in the company may move all of their insurance to another company if they do not like the alternative that an underwriter offers on one policy. The effect on other business cannot be ignored.

Producer. Commissions on premiums written are the life-blood of the producer. An alternative which does not permit the producer to write the policy will pay no commission on that policy. Since producers are essential, an underwriter must consider the possible impact on the producer if certain alternatives are selected.

Social Problems. Society has taken an interest in the alternatives underwriters use. Rejections based on the age, sex or racial origin of the applicant have been declared illegal in some states; such actions are frowned upon by many legislators and others. The use of geographical boundaries for acceptance and rejection are likewise prohibited or restricted. Insurance is deeply involved in social problems such as racial discrimination, segregation, economic restrictions and the rights of individuals and groups. These problems must be considered when selecting an alternative course of action.

All of these principles and all of these viewpoints must be considered in the decision. Their complexity indicates the problems involved in making decisions. These factors demonstrate the necessity of using trained underwriters to make decisions with the best course of action being selected. Experience is more important than book learning in guiding the underwriter into the best decision but it is also essential to know the principles upon which the decision is based.

TAKE ACTION

The underwriter is now ready to take the best course of action from the alternatives available. The action to be taken may be based on complex factors. Sometimes an underwriter will accept risks that are less than desirable. Such action may be best in the long run: to act otherwise might result in loss of future business because of loss of loyalty and confidence on the part of producer and public.

Actually, it is difficult and dangerous to take action on the basis of arbitrary definitions the underwriter has adopted. Many of these definitions regarding economic groups, geographical areas or other classifications are based on the prejudices and hopes of the underwriter and the company and should be looked upon as guides only.

"Substandard" is a term that is often misused. Most underwriters consider a substandard risk to be one that is not acceptable from the standpoint of their companies. The problem is that other companies might accept these risks because of different rate structures, contracts or philosophy.

An underwriter should always consider making exceptions to the rules. The action taken should not blindly conform to written rules; otherwise, there is no need for underwriters. Rules are meant to be guides to underwriters, with only a few exceptions. Some lines of insurance use more rules than others. In any case, the action should be based on an intelligent application of the rules, with exceptions made as warranted.

The proper action taken can be illustrated by a risk that is considered to be highly hazardous. It is unacceptable under the rules of most companies. Perhaps it is uninsurable at standard rates and coverages, but an intelligent, experienced underwriter may find that the risk is acceptable under a limited policy form with adequate rates, after securing sufficient reinsurance.

The proper action under such conditions is to offer the insurance under those terms. The applicant may accept them. If the applicant will not accept those terms an area of negotiation can usually be found. Perhaps competition will force the underwriter to modify the original position, too. If this cannot be done, at least the offer to write the insurance has been made.

It is important many times to be able to offer coverage, even if the terms appear to be exorbitant. There are political and social reasons why it is preferable to offer insurance under modified terms rather than to refuse to write it. This is the reason that underwriters are encouraged to find alternatives, using cancellation only as a last resort.

The action taken will depend somewhat upon the producer. Different action might be exercised for a regular producer than otherwise. A regular producer is one who uses the company as the regular market for this class of business; who shares profitable business at least equally among the companies; or who cooperates with the underwriter in maintaining a satisfactory level of quality on a book of business. Many underwriters may also include the clientele of a producer in this list who is at least average for the territory in which the producer operates, provided rate levels are established.

"Taking action" means conveying the decision which the underwriter has made to the proper parties. It might include the following.

Acceptance as submitted. — Ordinarily, the policy is issued without prior notification to the producer. However, such notification might be sent if the producer requests it, if the application was submitted on approval or if more time is needed to secure forms or information necessary to issue the policy. Without such notification being required, the underwriter customarily requests the proper clerical personnel to proceed with the policy issuance.

Acceptance with modifications. — The usual procedure is to notify the producer. This route is used whether modifications are in the physical structure or operations, in the contract, in the rates, or in the retention. In some companies, a direct contact is made with the applicant, but this is relatively rare. Most companies stipulate that the underwriter communicate with the producer, explaining the necessary modifications. The means of communications are details handled under the company procedure — whether by letter, form letter, telephone, or otherwise.

Declination or cancellation. — When a risk must be terminated, legal notification must be sent to the applicant or policyholder under most state laws. It is customary to give advance notification to the producer, too. This permits the producer to warn the client before the cancellation letter arrives and perhaps arrange for replacement coverage before the cancellation letter is mailed. The amount of advance notification to the producer varies. Company policy usually specifies how this is to be handled. Ordinarily, companies like to give considerable time to the producer in order to permit a chance to rebut the decision, to warn the client, and to try to arrange substitute coverage. Underwriters sometimes give somewhat less notification under certain conditions. State cancellation laws limit the time that an underwriter can act on a new application; if the deadline is approaching, not much time can be given.

Sometimes underwriters discover factors that indicate such a high probability of loss that they feel unsafe in allowing any more time than is absolutely necessary. Usually underwriters try to send notification to the producer at least a day or two in advance of the cancellation notice to the client, but even this is not always possible. Underwriters must weigh their obligations to the producer against their obligations to the company and act accordingly.

Rebuttal of underwriting action is not uncommon among producers. Cancellations bring the most rebuttals, but modifications may also be challenged. When rebuttals are received, the underwriter needs to reconsider the case. This is especially necessary if the producer has submitted new facts about the risk. The underwriter needs to start again through the process of evaluating the facts, determining the alternatives, making a decision, and taking action. Whether the decision will be the same or different will depend upon the result of this second underwriting process.

TAKE A TENTATIVE POSITION

No clear division is evident between taking a firm action and then receiving rebuttals, and taking a tentative position until a rebuttal is received. In the minds of underwriters, the distinction involves the feeling that a rebuttal will or will not be made. An underwriter often feels that the producer will argue with the decision. The underwriter even suspects that the producer has further information which will be submitted if it is needed. In such cases, the action of the underwriter might be considered to be a tentative decision. Perhaps every notice of action to be taken, with advance notification to the producer, could be considered in that light. Since an important reason for sending advance notice is to permit a rebuttal, perhaps every one of these is a form of tentative decision.

The terminology is not important; the handling is. If the underwriter suspects that the producer has additional information that would be relevant, it should be requested. This request can either be a direct request of a tentative action with a notice telling the producer, in effect, that this is the contemplated action, unless other facts are submitted. In the latter case, as those where rebuttal is permitted but not encouraged, it is essential that the underwriter take a firm action. The notice must state that this is the action which will be taken, whether rebuttal is encouraged or not.

Challenges to underwriting action can come from sources other than producers, too. Clients may write directly to the company, often to the chief executive officer. Others will complain to the state insurance department, which, in turn, relays the complaint to the company and requires an answer. In some states, laws have been enacted specifying the procedures for handling complaints.

Underwriters do not take tentative positions pending complaints. However, they may be called upon to justify their action and if justification is not acceptable, a reversal might be required. Sometimes an underwriter's supervisor or superior will insist that the decision be reversed; insurance departments might make a similar demand. When these situations occur, the underwriter has to review the alternatives and the reasons for making the decision. It helps if the underwriter has acted judiciously. It also helps if the reasons for the action were placed in the file.

A new course of action may be required following a rebuttal. The underwriter who has prepared alternatives properly may be able to try a different one, if necessary. At least, the preparation has been done to try a different course of action.

THE DANGERS OF INACTION

The least desirable course for an underwriter to take is one of inaction. If there is a delay before any action is taken, an underwriter is not performing properly. Many excuses can be given for inaction. A common one is lack of complete information. Seldom does an underwriter have all of the information that may be desired. Rather than making a decision and taking action on that information which is available, an underwriter may postpone a decision. Another reason often used is the inability to secure all related files in the company. Sometimes files are difficult to locate and the lack of ability to review every file can furnish an excuse for inaction. Still another reason is the fear that an adverse decision will upset the producer. Perhaps the underwriter is contemplating the use of a deductible but is not sure that this will be acceptable to the producer or the client. Instead of making a decision and taking action which, in turn, may cause a rebuttal, the underwriter may, instead, start an exchange of correspondence with the producer. The decision is, of course, delayed while letters are sent and received.

At least five dangers of inaction can be identified.

1. The "discovery period" under a noncancellation law may expire. Those lines which are subject to these laws may suffer irreparable financial loss through inaction since the underwriter must remain on the risk for the balance of the term if action is not taken within the period, usually 45 to 60 days. States with guaranteed renewable laws, require the underwriter to remain on the risk forever! Both types of laws have specified reasons which may be used to retire from a risk, but these are few and limited to serious circumstances, such as nonpayment of premium and loss of driver's license.

These laws impose a definite time limit within which action can be taken. An underwriter who delays making his decision may find that it is too late. Timely action must be taken even if information which appears to be critical to the decision has not been received.

2. An unexpected loss may occur, if a risk has been bound. The producer might have indicated no deductible, perhaps been in violation of underwriting rules, while a substantial deductible may be desired by the underwriter. If there is a delay in making the decision and in taking action, a loss may occur before notification of the deductible. The loss would be adjusted without the deductible, of course, and this puts a dollar value on this type of delay.

3. A valued client may be lost, if the risk is not bound. Producers often submit applications for the approval of the underwriter. Ordinarily the submission is made well in advance of the expiration date of the present policy. An underwriter who fails to make a decision and take action on accepting the risk will find that the eventual decision is moot. On or before the renewal date, the client will renew the old policy or will purchase a new one from another company. Many times it is the more complicated and costly policies which are submitted for approval, so a sizeable account may be lost by inaction. Again, a dollar amount can be attributed to this lack of action.

4. Producers lose confidence in underwriters who cannot make decisions. They have to write insurance in order to survive; they cannot stay in business long if underwriters delay in making decisions and they lose sales. Producers may well start placing business elsewhere. Even if they remain, they will have lost confidence in their underwriters which can also result in many future problems. If producers leave, the loss in income to the company may be considerable. If they remain, the intangible loss from shaken confidence and loss of respect cannot be measured, but it is present, nevertheless.

5. Indecisive underwriters are not performing as true underwriters.Since underwriting is a decision-making process, it follows that true underwriters must make decisions. Those who fail to make decisions or who delay them for too long are not operating as underwriters. The self-respect and confidence of these underwriters will be shaken; fellow underwriters will shun them; and producers will by-pass them. In addition, their superiors will soon terminate their services, if they cannot change.

It is absolutely essential that underwriters make decisions and take action after evaluating the alternatives. Inaction and indecision have no place in the underwriting process.

QUESTIONS FOR DISCUSSION

1. Discuss the reasons why each of the following basic principles must be considered when deciding upon an alternative course of underwriting action:
   (a) Spread of risk
   (b) Homogeneity
   (c) Avoidance of small losses

(d) Loss must be accidental and definite
(e) Catastrophe potential must be small
(f) Premium must be commensurate with exposure
(g) Law of large numbers

2. Why is it so important, when deciding upon alternative courses of action, to take the following into consideration:
(a) Profitability of the company
(b) Related business
(c) The producer of such business
(d) Social problems
3. Is a substandard risk one which should be avoided by all underwriters? Explain.
4. What is the difference between an underwriting rule and an underwriting guide.
5. Aside from the characteristics of the risk itself, what other factors might be taken into consideration before deciding upon a course of action?
6. Why is the action of an underwriter sometimes considered to be a tentative one? Why is it absolutely important that an underwriter maintain a file containing the reasons for actions taken?
7. Briefly describe five dangers of an underwriter's inaction on a risk.

9

Evaluate the Action

After underwriting action has been taken, an evaluation must be made. No decision making process is complete until results of the decision and the action are analyzed.

"Check results!" This is the next step which the underwriter must take. This action will indicate if the proper decision has been made. Two completely different approaches to evaluation may be taken. One is the evaluation of individual risks, and checking the results of decisions taken separately by underwriters. The other is to observe the results of a total class of business, measuring the cumulative results of all actions taken.

Before analyzing each of these two approaches, it is helpful to determine the relative importance of each. Should there be a profit on most or all of the individual risks, on the assumption that the total effect will then be profitable? Or is the individual profitabilty of little concern so long as the class is profitable?

To approach these questions from a different standpoint, should the goal be to make a small profit on each unit of a large risk volume? Or would it be better to make a larger profit on each unit of a small risk volume?

The answers are not easy; they must reflect the policy of the company to a considerable extent. However, a few general statements can be made.

1. Underwriters can exercise only a limited control on any one risk. Chance will always play a part in individual results.
2. If sufficient volume is written in a class and if the underwriter has proper statistics, enough controls can be used to almost assure a profit on a class.
3. Low-rated individual policies offer little opportunity for assured profits. So few dollars are available for profit that one small loss can make the risk unprofitable.
4. High-rated risks offer a much better chance for individual profit since controls can be exercised and some losses can be tolerated without destroying the profitability.
5. Pressures do not permit most underwriters to write only average or above average risks. These pressures may come from producers, politicians, social reformers and others. The result is that the underwriter will be required to accept some individual risks that are be-

low average. This fact does not necessarily change the profitability of the class, so long as good risks offset the poor ones in the class, a profit on the class can be achieved.

Based on these statements, it is evident that the usual goal of an underwriter should be to make a profit on the class, not on an individual risk. A few unprofitable individual risks may be tolerated, provided they do not constitute a disproportionate share of the total. The aim then becomes twofold: (1) attempt to keep each individual risk from becoming too unprofitable, and (2) attempt to permit as few unprofitable risks in each class as possible. Both the majority of individual risks, and the class in total, should be profitable. Each of these aspects requires separate analysis.

INDIVIDUAL RISKS

An underwriter has many opportunities to check the results on individual risks in most lines. If these opportunities are taken, the underwriter can evaluate the action taken and any changes that have occurred in the risk.

When Reviews May Be Taken

Underwriting review is possible at the following times.

When a claim is presented. The underwriter should be notified of each claim, with the possible exception of minor, infrequent claims with no evidence of fault on the part of the insured. Whether these are referred to the underwriter when the claim is presented or when it is paid or at some other time is relatively immaterial; it depends somewhat upon the line of insurance and policy of the company.

When a change is made on the policy. Each change has some potential effect on a risk. Many changes are serious — virtually constituting a new set of circumstances while others may have a negligible effect on the chance of loss. Each change, however, affords a new opportunity to review the decision that was made.

When the renewal date approaches. Almost every property and casualty policy is renewed regularly, usually semi-annually or annually. This permits an underwriter an excellent chance to review the action originally taken in view of changes in the risk that may have occurred.

When new facts are presented. Occasionally some new information about a risk will be sent to an underwriter. Some investigation services and clipping bureaus follow the practice of sending new information to supplement a previous report. A loss prevention specialist or producer might also develop new facts and send them to the underwriter. Each new item of information can permit review of the original action.

When an underwriting review program is instituted. Underwriters sometimes undertake reviews of specified policies that have been written and are in force. These reviews may be on the basis of risk type, geographic area, producer, or on other factors. Possibly the review will include all risks within a subclass or even an entire class. Each such review includes an evaluation of the prior decision.

Standpoints of Analyzing Information

Many factors can be analyzed at the time of such reviews. All of the information previously secured is still available, supplemented by the company's own experience. This new information may be analyzed from several standpoints.

Has there been a frequency of loss? If so, are these losses within the control of the insured? When a loss frequency does develop, the underwriter should check why the original action permitted this situation. Maybe a different contract or a deductible should have been used. Some lines are expected to have a greater frequency of loss than others. During observation of the losses that have occurred, the underwriter can recheck the prior action.

Has there been a severity of losses? If so, could the severity have been controlled by the insured? When large losses occur, the underwriter has to examine the choices originally considered, evaluating the one selected.

Was the insured at fault in these losses? Evaluating the prior decision depends upon this consideration, in many lines. The underwriter has to review the situation to see if these events should have been foreseen and could have been controlled. The type of control may differ by degree of fault which occurs on losses that develop.

Have conditions changed? Not only losses, but all other opportunities for review of the file permit an analysis of this factor. If conditions have not changed, the underwriter must review why the situation was not foreseen if losses or other problems have arisen. If conditions have changed, the review must include an analysis of the reasons the underwriter did not foresee these changes. Next, of course, the underwriter must reevaluate the risk as it now exists.

TOTAL CLASS OF BUSINESS

An underwriter uses a different approach for checking results on a *class* of business from those used on *individual* risks. The class can be reviewed at various times and different standpoints may be reviewed. Reviewing classes of business is usually conducted at these times.

At the end of a period, such as a year. It is customary in business to review results for a period just closed and underwriting is no exception. As soon as reports are available, an underwriter should review the experience of the class. The period to be evaluated will differ by line and by company; common periods are monthly, quarterly, semi-annually and annually. Longer periods may be used to supply trend patterns but in most lines, experience beyond a year is too old to help in checking the results of underwriting action.

When a problem becomes evident. Sometimes sources other than regular reports will indicate that an evaluation of underwriting action is needed. Examples are comments from other departments, complaints from producers, passage of new legislation and indications from financial statements. When such sources reveal possible problems, evaluation is needed.

When revisions in programs are planned. All changes in existing programs or plans for introduction of new programs, require reevaluation of underwriting decisions. The previous decisions are analyzed to see how they relate to the new program and to see if changes are needed.

A number of sources are available in supplying information needed to conduct evaluation of prior underwriting action. The most common are these.

1. Statistical reports published for use by the company.

2. Audits conducted by the auditing or accounting departments.
3. Claims reports, giving summaries of conditions.
4. Inspection reports, containing summaries of conditions found or indications of trends in risks which are inspected.

Factors for Evaluation

A number of factors may be evaluated as the underwriter reviews the prior action as it affects a class of business.

Profitability. — This is the most common and the most universal of all indicators. It is also the most easily understood by other than underwriters. Whether computed in terms of dollars gained or lost, or in percentages as related to a tolerance, the underwriting results can be measured in terms of profit. Each class of insurance, as well as each line and the total all lines is evaluated.

Loss frequency. — The number of losses for each group of policies for a stated period can be expressed as a loss frequency ratio. It is much more accurate to measure frequencies and their trends for a class rather than for individual risks. Underwriters are ordinarily held accountable for frequencies. Proper underwriting action will result in pre-determined frequency ratios within broad limits. When frequencies and trends are poor, it is an indication that underwriting action was deficient.

Loss severity. — The average size of loss for each group of policies for a stated period is expressed as the loss severity ratio. Although the severity of individual risks may not be controllable, the severity of a class usually can be controlled within limits. The types of action taken by underwriters will have a direct effect on severity, particularly those lines over which underwriters have substantial control or can use reinsurance. External factors also affect severity; examples are hospital rates, repair costs, labor costs and weather conditions. Underwriters cannot be held responsible for all factors that affect severity, but underwriting action should be evaluated if severity trends are adverse.

Retention ratio. — The number of applications actually accepted by underwriters from among those submitted by producers can be compared to the number submitted in order to secure a retention ratio. To some degree, the retention ratio is affected by ability, knoweldge and understanding of the producers. As such, the responsibility falls lightly on underwriters, if at all; the degree depends upon the responsibility placed on underwriters to train producers and to write rules which are easy to comprehend. However, the underwriting action also affects the retention ratio. If underwriting decisions are too restrictive, the retention ratio will be too low, resulting in lost income and wasted effort on the part of producers. If the underwriting action is too liberal, the retention ratio will be too high, perhaps resulting in the acceptance of too many borderline risks. Goals should be established, with deviations from them giving cause for evaluation of prior underwriting action.

Protective ratio. — The number of cases in which new information is received from investigative sources may be compared to the number of reports requested in order to develop a protective ratio. The ratio may measure an entire group of reports or may be separate by type of report. The underwriter makes a decision in obtaining a report because a feeling is present that information might be received which will help protect against losses; hence the name "protective information." The protective ratio helps measure efficiency and value of various sources of information. It also helps measure decisions which the underwriter has made in ordering reports. If the protective ratio is low, either the source is poor or the underwriter wasted money by poor selection of cases. If the ratio is high, indications are that the underwriter probably took proper action in selecting cases for investigation; that is, of course, unless the quality of total applications was so poor that every risk would have developed protective information. This latter qualification indicates the need of using these ratios carefully, comparing them with other factors as well.

FACTORS AFFECTING RESULTS

As the results of underwriting action are evaluated, it is helpful to know the factors that affect those results. Good or bad results can be caused by a number of factors acting separately or in combinations. The most important of these factors is the next subject of discussion.

Rates. The rates which are charged for the coverages have a direct effect on underwriting results. Rates that are inadequate can prevent profits regardless of the care the underwriter exercises in selecting risks. For this reason, the underwriter has great interest in rates and will try to secure adequate rates or adequate rate levels.

Coverages. The provisions of policies and forms also have direct and immediate effects on results. Coverages that are too broad will create more losses. Underwriters have deep desire to control the contracts, both in individual cases and for total classes.

Retention. Retention and reinsurance programs will affect results. Losses are bound to occur and underwriting profits may depend upon the degree to which retention is limited. Underwriters attempt to control retentions on individual risks and on reinsurance programs of the company.

Claims proficiency. The abilities of the claims department have a direct effect on underwriting results. If adjusters do not know the contract provisions, do not know how to settle losses at fair figures or if they are not well versed in legal and repair matters, they are almost certain to overpay claims. Even expert adjusters must follow the claims policy of the company which may be more liberal than is contemplated in the rate and the policy provisions. Seldom do underwriters have direct control over these factors but they may exercise indirect influence through education and correspondence.

Expenses. If too great a portion of the premium income is paid in expenses, the underwriting results will be affected adversely. Companies that do not control their expenses can cause underwriting losses in spite of the best efforts of underwriters and others. Underwriters have some control over their share of the expenses but little influence over other portions.

Social, legal, and political climate. Underwriting results may be affected by the climate in which insurance operates. Social pressures may prevent the underwriter from taking certain actions which are desirable from an underwriting viewpoint. Legal decisions may broaden coverages beyond the intent of the writers.

Politicians may, through pressure or legislation, require companies to share in risks that are unprofitable. The underwriter has little control over these factors.

Underwriting proficiency. The abilities of underwriters are important factors affecting the results. Poorly trained underwriters may accept risks that are not contemplated by rates and coverages. Incorrect decisions about investigations, limitations and other underwriting factors can have immediate repercussions in the results.

STEPS IN EVALUATION

Underwriters must evaluate actions they have taken. This evaluation is a continuing process not limited to a specific period of time. Individual risks are evaluated when new information is received and when renewal of the policy is approaching. Classes of risks are evaluated when reports are received or problems arise.

Adverse underwriting results must be evaluated from several different aspects. One of these is to find the reasons for losses. It is essential to find the real reasons behind those that are more apparent. For instance, rates may be too low, but this situation may be caused by competition or pressures from regulatory authorities. Further, unacceptable risks may have been written because producers did not screen applicants properly or report facts correctly; pressures may also be exerted by producers to secure approval of borderline risks, as well as competitive rates, and coverages.

Another method of evaluating adverse underwriting results is to compare the related factors. Those which the underwriter can control, at least to some degree, are acceptability, rates, coverages and retention. If any one of these is out of balance, the results will be affected. The factors over which the underwriter has little control are claims, expenses and the climate from social, legal and political standpoints. These latter factors are relatively uncontrollable by the underwriter, but must be taken into account. Each of these steps must be considered since they furnish a basis for evaluating action that was previously taken by the underwriters.

QUESTIONS FOR DISCUSSION

1. Why is it necessary for an underwriter to evaluate the courses of action taken? What are two appraoches to evaluation?
2. Explain why evaluation of action by total class is more appropriate when considering profitability than by individual risk.
3. Briefly describe the circumstances when evaluation of individual risks may be appropriate.
4. What are some of the points underwriters should consider when there is a frequency and/or severity of loss?
5. Why is an underwriter usually held accountable for frequency of loss and not severity of loss?
6. Discuss the approaches for checking results on a class of business. What are some of the types of information that are available to evaluate classes of risk?
7. What is the so-called "retention ratio," and what purpose does it serve?

8. What is the so-called "protective ratio," and what is its purpose?
9. How do the following affect underwriting results:
   (a) rates
   (b) expenses
   (c) socio-economic and political climate
10. Explain the steps to evaluation in general.

10

Make Corrections

The final step in the underwriting decision-making process is concerned with corrections that are indicated. After evaluating underwriting actions, the underwriter is able to see those areas to improve for the future. The next step, therefore, is to make these corrections.

"Correct the action!." This is the last duty an underwriter performs on a risk or a class of business. The last, that is until the entire cycle is started again under new circumstances. Corrections cannot be made until the previous steps have been taken and analyzed. Then the correction process must logically follow the same steps because correction means underwriting, underwriting means decision-making, and decision-making requires the steps discussed in the previous chapters in order to be successful.

Corrective action includes the following steps, each of which is discussed in this chapter.

1. Secure information.
2. Develop alternatives
3. Decide and take action.
4. Evaluate the action.

After these steps, more corrections may be indicated, starting the cycle again. All of the above steps are involved in underwriting individual and class risks. This is the meaning of underwriting, of course. However, there is another phase of work performed by an underwriting department. This is the supervision of underwriters, including the control of the underwriting process. In the last section of this final chapter on the decision-making function of underwriting, the methods of this control are discussed. They involve making corrections on policies and classes—a function vitally important and an integral part of the underwriting process.

SECURE INFORMATION

Problems cannot be corrected without adequate information. Data available during the original underwriting analysis, if inadequate, can obviously lead to incorrect action. Possibly, the underwriting analysis of that data was faulty, but the assumption has to be that the data was insufficient.

New information is available in virtually every case. No correction is needed unless evaluation of previous action indicates that a problem exists, and information had to be available in order to permit the underwriter to arrive at that conclusion. This type of information may consist of a record of losses, an indication of a changed risk, or some other allegation of a problem.

The underwriter often needs to secure additional information before starting to determine the necessary corrections. The same pattern will be followed as on the first evaluation. The type of problem which has arisen will indicate the kind of information that is needed and will lead the underwriter to the proper source. Most of the sources available on new risks are able to furnish additional information. The producer may be requested to furnish some data, reports may be requested from inspection companies, engineers, bureaus and other sources, too. Other policies may be rechecked for additional information that may have developed since the original review. The only sources not available are another completed application and the previous insurer.

The underwriter may be selective on this request for further information. On most cases, the nature of the problem will be known to the underwriter. He or she should, therefore, request answers only on these problems. For example, if an accident occurred involving the automobile policy in which drinking was the cause, the investigation may be limited to drink habits. The underwriter may wish to know if this appears to be an isolated case or if there is a pattern of drinking which would indicate that future losses can be expected.

Other cases may call for complete investigation. Perhaps no inspection report was ordered during the first evaluation because the underwriter did not suspect a problem. Later, a loss indicates an instability or other factor that requires additional checking. In this case, a complete inspection might be needed in order to secure facts on all aspects of the risk. As with the original underwriting, the underwriter will obtain as much additional information as is needed and, when combined with data already in the file, will permit corrective action.

DEVELOP ALTERNATIVES

After securing as much new information as is necessary and feasible, the underwriter is ready to develop another set of alternatives. These may be the same alternatives as those previously developed or they may be different ones.

A few of the alternatives used on new applications are not ordinarily available for corrective action. Recission may not be exercised after the policy has been in force for a very long period, under most cases. Cancellation may be prohibited under state laws for some lines. Even nonrenewal is unavailable for specified lines in a few states. Most of the other alternatives are available at the time correction is being considered, just as on new applications. Improvements in the risk may be required as a condition of continuing coverage. Policy conditions may have to be changed, including the imposition of new or larger deductibles, a reduction in perils covered, or a requirement for limiting clauses. Premium rates, rating programs or classifications may also be changed, and retentions may be adjusted.

The types of alternatives developed will depend on the problem of the individual risk. If one driver has caused the difficulty, that driver might be restricted from coverage. If a new location or operation has been added, it might have to be removed from the policy. When the problem is caused by losses, alternatives will depend upon the nature of losses. A frequency problem may call for the imposition of deductibles or a limitation on perils. A severity problem might require such action as a reduction in the limits, or changes in retention.

Ordinarily, fewer alternatives need be developed at the time corrective action is indicated than on new applications. Since the underwriter has identified the problem areas better one existing policies, he or she should be able to develop fewer but more precise alternatives from which to choose corrective actions.

Total classes of risks may also need correction and alternatives will then need to be developed for them. Those classes or subclasses that are profitable should be separated from those that are unprofitable and different alternatives developed for each. Rates might be adjusted, deductibles changed, coverages amended or retentions revised. The same types of alternatives are available as on individual risks, except that these may be applied to all risks in the group or class.

DECIDE AND TAKE ACTION

A decision must be made and an action taken, if reevaluation and corrections are to be of any use. As on new applications, the underwriter must comply with the principles of insurance and must consider various viewpoints as the decision is made. The action, however, may be handled differently.

Corrective action often requires more careful handling than new business. Existing policyholders, rather than applicants, are involved here and somewhat more tact and notification must be used in many cases. Producers often are given extensive notification of contemplated action, well in advance of the effective date. If the change is to be made at the renewal date, adequate time is available in almost every case to permit advance notification. This practice permits the producer to tell the policyholder about the impending action or to send a rebuttal to the underwriter. Good relations with producers are maintained by allowing adequate opportunity for discussion before action is taken. A different alternative might even be selected after the producer has sent comments, with new information, to the underwriter. Advance notification, with a complete explanation, should always be given to producers when corrective action on an entire class or group of policies is to be taken.

Corrective action may be placed into effect at any time, unless state laws require otherwise. Some laws permit certain types of action, such as cancellation, only at the renewal date. Even though most action may be taken at any time, it usually is preferable to withhold action until renewal. When policyholders have purchased coverage for a specified period, they will resent any adverse changes during that period. It is much more acceptable to insureds, producers, and politicians alike, for changes to be imposed only at the time of renewal.

Sometimes the underwriter cannot wait until the renewal date to take corrective action. Perhaps the frequency of losses has been so great that the underwriter feels that action cannot be delayed. Perhaps new conditions have made the risk undesirable without changes. In such cases, corrective action may be taken at any time, subject to applicable laws and policy provisions. Ordinarily, advance notice of any restrictive changes must be given to the policyholder. Relations with producers can be improved or maintained, however, if they are given advance notification before changes are mailed to the policyholder.

EVALUATE THE ACTION

Finally, the underwriter must again evaluate the new action that has been taken. As before, the evaluation may be either on an individual policy basis or a class basis. No consistency is required; one basis may be used now and the other one next year; the underwriter may evaluate on any basis at any time. Further corrective action may be taken following each evaluation. This will start the entire cycle again.

The decision-making process of underwriting is a continual process. Once an application is received, the process continues as long as the risk remains on the books. The frequency and timing of each step may vary, and long delays may occur after each action is taken until an evaluation is made. However, the risk will remain within the underwriting cycle until it is terminated.

Figure 2 illustrates the entire underwriting cycle in graphic fashion. An application is received and the underwriting process is applied: information is secured, alternatives are developed, an underwriter makes a decision, and takes action. For those policies written, an evaluation must be conducted at a later date. If there are no problems, the file is replaced without any further action until the next evaluation is conducted. If correction is needed, the same decision-making steps are taken, resulting in corrective action. This, too, is evaluated later and either the file is closed for awhile or further correction is made. Evaluation is a never ending process. Repeated corrective action may be taken as conditions change. So long as the policy remains in force, evaluation and correction need to be made periodically.

Figure 2

Cycle of Underwriting

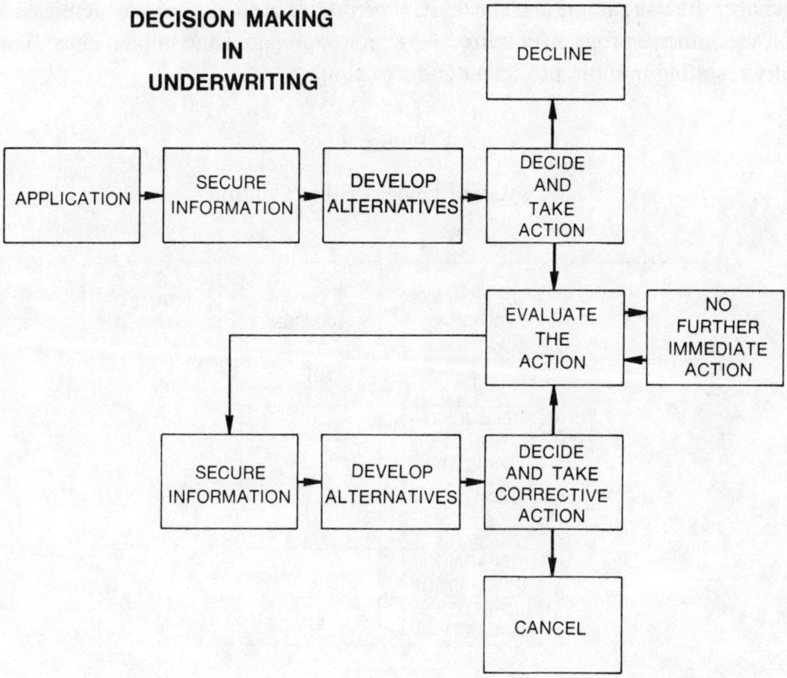

The previous discussion is concerned with underwriting individual risks or groups of risks. Another important phase of underwriting concerns the control, by management, of the underwriting process. Underwriting supervisors or managers must evaluate underwriting that is performed and see that needed corrections are made.

This phase of the underwriting process is different in most respects. When a manager finds an error, he or she is more interested in correcting the thinking or the handling of the underwriter than in correcting the individual file. Most phases of underwriting management are similar to the management of other operations and this is no exception. It is, however, an important phase of the underwriting process. For this reason it deserves mention.

The technique of underwriting control is to sample items of work and determine from these samples if the handling is correct. If errors are found, corrections must be made and the entire process is repeated. In this respect, the control of underwriting follows the same pattern as underwriting itself: evaluate results, take corrective action and repeat the process at intervals.

Figure 3 shows the cycle of underwriting control. The input may be an application for new business, but it may also be a file coming to the attention of the underwriter for changes, claims and for other reasons. The underwriting process includes the steps discussed in this Part II. From the work produced by the underwriter, the manager draws a sample and checks it. If errors are present, they are identified and analyzed, then a program of corrective action is prepared and implemented, hopefully resulting in more proficient underwriting.

Figure 3

Cycle of Underwriting Control

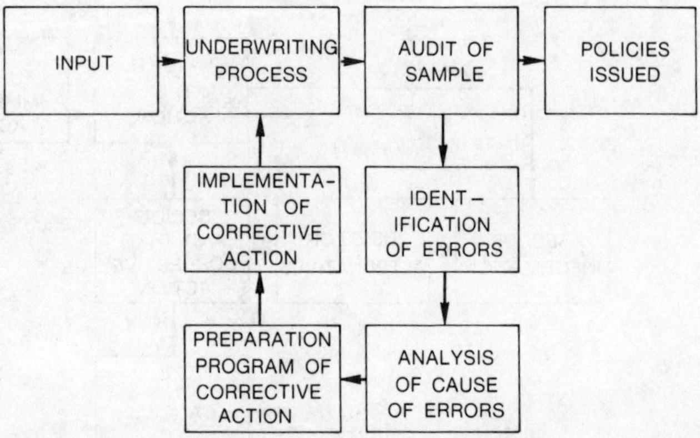

The sample for audit may be secured in many ways. The manager may sit with the underwriter, discovering errors as they occur, or may take some files as they leave the underwriter's desk. Sample files may even be pulled after the entire transaction is completed, perhaps after filing is made. The latter practice requires that the underwriter's signature or stamp be placed on all transactions that are completed; it is common practice to use identification for purposes of showing that action has been approved and for purposes of identifying the underwriter who approved it.

There is no "correct" number of transactions that must be audited. The manager will make this decision, based upon such factors as the experience of the underwriter, the complexity of the line, the statistical results, and the time the manager can devote to audits of transactions.

Corrective action may consist of many types of programs. Simple errors need only be pointed out to the underwriter. More serious errors may require further training or education of the underwriter. Sometimes changes in assignments need to be made. Finally, if corrections cannot be accomplished in any other fashion, the underwriter must be released.

The entire control process requires much more than an audit of transactions with an identification and correction of errors. The manager must establish standards of performance against which results are measured. Performance must be measured carefully and objectively, a task which is not simple when a complex operation like underwriting is involved. Errors or deviations must be corrected in a predetermined manner and may include major changes in direction, in re-organization of the department or in the leadership demonstrated by the manager. All controls and corrections should be objective, flexible and forward-looking.

These facets of management are more of a subject for management study than underwriting study. Still, it is vital that underwriting managers practice the proper techniques of scientific management the same as any other manager. In addition, of course, the underwriting manager must establish and practice programs of controlling the underwriting process. Only in this way will a company know that its underwriting practices comply with the programs prepared by management.

QUESTIONS FOR DISCUSSION

1. If an underwriter feels that some corrections are necessary after evaluating prior underwriting decisions on a risk, (a) why might fewer alternatives have to be developed, and (b) under what circumstances may an underwriter be unable to exercise some alternatives?
2. Why might corrective action require more careful handling than is the case with new business?
3. Explain briefly what is involved in underwriting control by management, including its purpose.
4. Why are standards of performance considered to be essential with any underwriting control system by management?

INTRODUCTION TO PART III

BASIC FUNCTIONS OF UNDERWRITING

The process of underwriting involves four basic functions for any line of insurance and every underwriter must perform each of these four functions.

1. *Selection of risks. This is the starting point of underwriting. It includes securing factual information, evaluating that information and deciding upon a course of action. The selection process is aided by the use of acceptable and prohibited lists of risks. However, these are only guides to an underwriter who must use many sources to develop information that will help in making decisions to accept or reject risks.*
2. *Classifications and rating. Having decided to accept a given risk, an underwriter must then determine the proper classification and rate. Many lines of insurance use complex classification systems and a multitude of rating plans. The classifications and rates must be established carefully in order to comply with legal requirements and to avoid the possibility of substantial underwriting losses because of inadequate premiums. Determining the proper classifications and rates, therefore, is an indispensable function of underwriting.*
3. *Policy forms. An integral part of the process, one which is handled with classifying and rating, is in determining policy forms to be used. Insurance policies are constructed in various ways from a mechanical standpoint. Regardless of the format used, the underwriter must know the contract that will be issued and be able to change it when necessary to meet the needs of the applicant, as well as the insurance company's own requirements.*

These three functions are inter-related to such a degree that it is difficult to separate them. An underwriter accepts a certain risk under the condition that specified rates and forms will be used; if they cannot be used or are unacceptable, the risk must be declined. If the rate is inadequate or the role must be reduced, the coverage must be limited in order for the risk to be acceptable. If the coverage is required to be broadened, such as by law or by business operations of the applicant, the rate must be increased or the risk must be declined.

These three functions are essential and inseparable in the underwriting process. When the underwriter has completed them, the primary functions of underwriting are completed. However, there is one more function that must be performed on every risk before the underwriting is completed:

4. *Retention and reinsurance. Every risk not only presents a possibility of loss but also a possibility of loss which will at least equal the policy limits. If this were not so, some policies would not be sole, or low limits would be requested. Furthermore, there is always a possibility that one or more risks, perhaps a great number, will be involved in one loss. It is up to the underwriter to take necessary steps to prevent the company from sustaining undue financial strain if such losses should occur. This can be accomplished by retaining only a portion of certain risks, and by securing reinsurance to protect against losses exceeding the amount the company can safely lose. At the same time, the underwriter must retain as much of the risk as is reasonably possible, because reinsurance costs money, and little or no profit can be realized on business that is placed elsewhere. The underwriter, therefore, must balance these two objectives, thereby realizing maximum profits commensurate with safety.*

These four basic functions are required on every risk that an underwriter handles. With them, the principle purpose of underwriting can be achieved, which is to secure safe and profitable distribution of risks. If any of these functions are omitted, the possibility of an unprofitable operation is substantially increased.

The degree to which an underwriter exercises absolute control over these factors varies by line of insurance. Rates and classifications for the mass lines, such as automobile, are established by the company — leaving little flexibility in the hands of the underwriter; policies for these lines are also fairly standard with little opportunity for changing coverage. In these mass lines, the underwriter must classify applicants according to strict rules; the risks which fit within the categories must be selected. At the other extreme, such uncontrolled lines of some inland marine classes permit the underwriter to develop or adjust rates to fit the circumstances of each case, and to write contracts which contain precisely the proper coverages. In between these extremes lie the bulk of the lines, particularly commercial insurance, where the rates are fairly-well established but can be adjusted by the underwriter, and contracts which are quite standard but can be tailored to fit many situations.

Insurance companies are in the business of writing insurance, not rejecting it. The underwriter's job is trying to write each risk and taking those actions that will result in overall profits for the company. This is accomplished by determining if a risk is acceptable by its very nature — that is, if the risk is insurable and fits within the pattern of risks written by the company. If it is, the underwriter must then seek to balance the rates and coverages to arrive at a balance which appears to offer at least an average chance of being profitable. Then catastrophic losses must be avoided by limiting retention or otherwise reducing exposure.

In Part III, each of these four basic functions is discussed in a separate chapter. Each function is viewed in a general sense, including its application to all lines of insurance. In Part V, each separate line of insurance is explained in a separate chapter. Each such line contains an analysis of these four basic functions.

11

Selection of Risks

An underwriter, through experience and judgment, selects risks in order to determine which of those within a given class offers a probability of loss below that for the average of the class. The underlying purpose in making such selections — an inherent part of every insurance transaction — is to achieve profitable distribution of insurance written. This is what "underwriting selectivity" is all about.

While underwriters usually do the selecting, there are some cases when applicants do the selecting. An extreme example of this is when an insurer agrees to accept all applicants for accident insurance without selectivity during a certain enrollment period. Generally, those applicants who consider themselves most likely to suffer losses will purchase the coverage offered. From an insurance company standpoint, it is what is commonly referred to as "adverse selection."

There is a degree of adverse seletion in every insurance transaction, but the tendency is greater in some lines than others. For example, a home buyer must carry a fire policy to satisfy the requirements of the mortgagor; an automobile owner finds insurance the best means of meeting the financial responsibility law of the state; and an employer may be required to purchase workers' compensation insurance in order to meet the legal requirements of protection for employees against job-related injuries. But there is usually no compulsion to buy theft or public liability insurance, so a greater degree of adverse selection faces the insurer on these lines than others.

Even the producer is in a position to select adversely against an insurer merely by sending one insurer — among many reprsented — only the least desirable of the applications. An underwriter unaware of this practice may be under the impression that the better risks within a preferred class are being selected while, in reality, only the better of those within a nonpreferred group of risks are being selected. It is extremely important, therefore, for an underwriter to utilize experience and judgment in selecting risks which will produce losses fewer than the average for a given group.

Of course, no one knows with any certainty which risks will have losses. If there were any such certainty, those with no chance of suffering losses would not purchase insurance, while those who were certain to sustain losses would be faced with prohibitive premiums because insurers need premiums to pay losses and expenses. In any event, uncertainty of loss is the very basis of insurance, i.e., substituting a known small loss (premium) for an unknown large loss.

The underwriter also must be able to predict, with some degree of certainty, the frequency and severity of loss for a general class. Then judgment is applied in selecting the individual risks that will, as a group, have lower frequency or severity, or both, than the average of the class. At the same time, those risks in the class who appear to be less desirable than the average must be refused.

For an example of this process of selection, consider personal automobile insurance. It is the largest in premium volume of all lines in the property-casualty insurance business, and affects almost every person. Some classes of drivers will tend to have few accidents; these risks can be identified by age, driving record, use of the automobile, stability of living habits, marital status and other factors. An underwriter would accept such risks, ordinarily, even though knowing that any one of those drivers may have a serious negligent accident the next day. On the other hand, experience has taught underwriters that other classes of drivers include a high percentage of risks who are expected to have accidents. The underwriter would tend to reject such applicants, unless a higher rate can be secured, even though some individuals in those classes may never have accidents.

It is apparent that the underwriter must know the general characteristics of the line that he is handling in order to know those factors that make a risk one that falls within the category of "average." Then, as each item of information available on a particular applicant is evaluated, each factor must be compared with the average. If the factor does not measure up to the average, the underwriter must question why this is true, how serious the failure might be and what, if any, corrections can be made. If proper underwriting is to be performed, this evaluation must be made on each item, no matter how insignificant it might appear.

For another example, does it make any difference to the underwriter if the car is registered in the name of the wife, rather than the husband or jointly? Certainly the registered owner is not one of the major factors in automobile underwriting; indeed, it is seldom even considered. But the underwriter must evaluate this fact and find out why the registration does not include the husband. It may be revealed that the husband has a poor driving record or has no driver's license or was cancelled by a prior insurer. The underwriter must take each item into account when selecting risks.

This selection process demonstrates the *positive* nature of underwriting. Many persons, particularly producers, picture underwriting as a *negative* function: a process of declining or cancelling risks not meeting the criteria established by the underwriter (who is usually accused of acting in a capricious manner in establishing those criteria). In actuality, underwriting is a positive, forward-looking approach to writing insurance. It is through the application of ability, knowledge, experience and courage that risks can be selected properly and produce a profit for the insurer.

This approach is in the best interests of all parties: applicant, producer and insurer.

ELIGIBLE RISKS

The first step in selecting a risk is to establish its eligibility. If a particular applicant does not fit within the eligibility rules, no further consideration is needed.

Every insurance plan or program contains rules as to the types of exposures which may be included. These rules often are filed with insurance departments when approval is requested to write the program.

For example, a private passenger car program may be designed only for four-wheeled vehicles owned by a family. A motorcycle, then, would not be eligible, nor would a passenger car owned by a corporation.

Another example is a homeowners policy. If the eligibility rules include only one and two-family dwellings, a three or four-unit dwelling would not be eligible, nor would a larger apartment house.

This factor says nothing about the *desirability* of these classes. They may be excellent risks. However, they are not *eligible* for a specific program, because of the rules of eligibility established by the insurer.

ACCEPTABLE RISKS

The next step is to determine if the applicant is acceptable. Even though a risk may be *eligible* under the rules, it may not be *acceptable* to the insurer. At this point, again, if a particular applicant does not fit within the category of risk that the underwriter considers to be acceptable, there is no reason to proceed further into the other aspects of risk selection.

Every insurer aims at a particular segment of the market. After a company has decided to write a particular line of insurance, and has established its eligibility rules, the next step is to specify the general class of acceptable risks that the insurer wants to attract by relative rate levels. Parameters are established which specify, usually in broad terms, the types of risks which are expected to be written. There are three general classes within this grouping.

Preferred Risks. These are usually considered to have relatively low loss expectancies. They are the lowest-rated risks and are considered to be the "clean" risks from the standpoint of past losses.

Substandard Risks. These are the risks with the highest loss expectancies. They are often the "problem" risks; those that most insurers do not want.

Standard Risks. These are the average risks, neither good nor bad. They are the large bulk of the prospects, with loss records that are between the other two groups.

There is no automatic selection which results from the decision on which of these three groups an insurer will try to write. Each group can be profitable with proper coverages at proper rates. Thus, the next step is to establish details of the risks which will fit within the selected group. (Selection is needed in order to reach the desired market and achieve a profit, regardless of which group is written.)

The task of determining details of acceptable risks within a selected group is given to the underwriter. Ordinarily, this is a function of the underwriting department as a whole, with staff underwriters establishing the broad outlines and line underwriters guiding the decision and refining them in actual practice.

One of the problems in establishing broad outlines of acceptable risks is that an insurer will always be happy to write business that is of a higher quality than its average. A substandard automobile insurer will use relatively high rates designed to handle applicants with poor driving records. Such an insurer obviously would like to write risks with good driving records, since such practice can improve the experience and permit the insurer to make more profit, or permit the insurer to reduce rates and attract more business. This situation is seldom possible, however, in an industry as competitive as insurance. Few prospects will pay rates which are noticeably higher than they can secure elsewhere. The only conclusion is that an insurer must select the market segment it intends to reach, and not indulge in wishful thinking about better risks which naively apply for coverage.

The previously mentioned comments imply a greater mobility of policyholders than is actually the case. In most lines of insurance, there is undoubtedly an immobility that does permit some insurers to write risks which could secure coverage at lower rates. Why then would a policyholder pay more for insurance than is required? There are many reasons. Insurance is a service, not a commodity; some people will pay more just to receive more service, whether real or fancied. There is a degree of "brand loyalty" among many policyholders, keeping them with the same insurer even if they have improved to the point where they could save money elsewhere. There is also a loyalty to the producer in many cases; this even extends to the point where some clients will continue to pay more even if the producer has a better-rated insurer available but does not offer it to the client. There are policyholders who cherish their longevity with a particular insurer, too, and feel that this will assure better treatment if loss problems should arise. All of these situations, therefore, deter free movement and tend to blur the lines dividing the three groups. To the extent that this exists, it improves the experience of standard and substandard insurers (but not, of course, the preferred risk companies). These comments about immobility in some lines refer primarily to exiting policyholders, especially long-time policyholders; new applicants will seldom pay very much more for their insurance than is necessary.

The size of the market available to each of the three groups will vary by line of insurance. As a very rough estimate, perhaps 15 to 20% of the risks can be called preferred, maybe 10% are substandard and the balance are standard. In personal fire insurance, perhaps no more than five percent are so deteriorated that they can be called substandard; the preferred-risk category might be as high as 50 or 75% of all dwellings. There are no easily defined breaks between groups in any line of insurance, so general comments cannot be more specific on percentages. In personal automobile insurance, for example, one insurer might consider preferred risks to be those with not more than two accidents and two citations during the past five years. Another preferred-risk insurer may consider only those applicants eligible who are between the ages of 30 and 65, married and living with their spouses, working on the same job at least one year, and having no more than one accident and one citation in the past five years. It is obvious that the share of the market available to each of these insurers will differ considerably.

Regardless of the exact share of the market available, there are a great number of risks available to most insurers. A list of the acceptable risks for commercial liability insurance in a standard-rated company would be almost as large as the yellow pages of the telephone directory. Such a list would be so long that it would be practically worthless. For this reason, most insurers, rather than attempting to publish actual lists of acceptable risks, make general statements about defining, in broad terms, the segment of the market that the insurer intends to approach. Thus, it is generally a misnomer to refer to an acceptable list for insurers.

Some insurers, nevertheless, do use acceptable lists. These are companies which are aiming at a rather limited share of the market — one which can be described quite precisely. An automobile insurer might list nondrinkers as an acceptable class. Another insurer might list all prospects with no claims in the past three years as acceptable, or all those who have been at their present address for at least five years. It is apparent that these criteria are merely the opposite way of saying "all drinkers are unacceptable." Some people may feel that there is value in the more positive approach, but regardless of these attempts at applied psychology, the facts remains that while few insurers use acceptable lists, virtually all insurers use unacceptable lists.

UNACCEPTABLE LISTS

As previously mentioned, underwriters tend to use unacceptable lists much more than they use acceptable lists. There are several reasons for this.

1. Since most risks are acceptable, an unacceptable list is much shorter.
2. It is easier to be more specific on risks taht are unacceptable. A list of acceptable risks is quite general and inexact, while an unacceptable list can be more precise for most lines of insurance.
3. Producers are inclined to consider all prospects as being acceptable. They try to fit all prospects within the bounds of an acceptable list. Thus, they need an unacceptable list in order to arrive at a meaningful separation of risks.
4. Producers generally prefer to be told of the risks which an underwriter will not accept. They say to the underwriter, "If you don't want this type of risk, why didn't you say so?

Although not a problem, one argument against an unacceptable list is that is it inherently negative. Since producers tend to consider all prospects as being acceptable, the underwriter must select those desired from those submitted. It seems sensible and easier for all parties if those the underwriter does not want are specified on a list. In effect, an unacceptable list is an agreement between the underwriter and the producer concerning those risks the producer cannot expect the underwriter to accept.

Factors Determining Size of Lists

The size of an unacceptable list is determined by five different factors for each line of insurance.

The first of these is the segment of the market at which the insurer is aiming.

If a broad segment is desired, the unacceptable list will ordinarily be shorter than if a rather restricted share of the market is desired. The more tightly the insurer circumscribes the type of risk it wants, the more detailed must be the unacceptable list. The opposite would hold true if the insurer were to publish an acceptable list. For example, if it was said that an insurer desired to insure only bowling alleys, its unacceptable list would be shorter than that of an insurer who published a list showing all commercial risks as acceptable. However, acceptable lists are seldom published for producers, and an insurer offering to write commercial risks would require a longer unacceptable list if it wanted only a small segment of the market. By using a long unacceptable list, therefore, an insurer can standardize the risks it writes and achieve a high degree of homogeneity.

The facilities of the insurer to supply needed services is the second factor. Many classes of risks need specialized services for loss prevention activities, claims handling, help in placement of coverages on unique exposures, and the like. An insurer that is not in a position to furnish such services will specify this fact by placing, on its unacceptable list, those risks which need such services.

The third factor concerns knowledge of producers in classes of risks. If producers are well-trained, a shorter unacceptable list can be used, but if a producer is a specialist in a particular class, the unacceptable list may be extremely brief.

The fourth factor concerns the knowledge of underwriters in the classes of risks. If underwriters are somewhat limited in their knowledge, management may choose to limit their scope of authority by means of lengthy and detailed unacceptable lists. Thus, unacceptable lists can be used as guides to underwriters, as well as to producers. An underwriter may make exceptions to most unacceptable lists, as is explained subsequently, but an unacceptable list can be a guide to an inexperienced underwriter.

The fifth factor deals with reinsurance requirements. Since most reinsurance treaties exclude certain risks or classes of risks, the insurer's unacceptable list must necessarily show these excluded risks or classes. This means that if the treaty contains a long list of these exclusions, the insurer's unacceptable list will also be longer.

Origination of Lists

While lists of unacceptable risks originate in high levels of management, they are not necessarily developed by top management, at least not in detail. The general outlines are set by the chief executive officer, as are the generalities of acceptable lists.

The details of unacceptable lists are prepared by the top underwriting officer, often in conjunction with general management. However, there must be coordination with other functional departments, because unacceptable lists are one of the basic elements of selection. They must, therefore, balance with rates and other factors if profitability is to be achieved. The actual wording and other details of the unacceptable list, on the other hand, are prepared by the underwriting staff, while application of lists to specific cases is made by line underwriters.

Every unacceptable list is modified from time to time, as conditions change, underwriters and producers gain more experience and new facts become available. Unacceptable lists, therefore, are not fixed static rules.

Producer and Underwriter Uses of Lists

Publication of an unacceptable list is for the benefit of producers and underwriters. It is a precise and specific in its terminology as its writers can make it, within the needs of its users. While the same list is given to producers and underwriters, its use is completely different for those two groups.

Producers are expected to follow an unacceptable list without modification. For example, they are not permitted to bind an application for a risk shown on the unacceptable list, unless prior approval has been obtained from an underwriter. Of course, some exceptions may be made for certain producers or for certain classes of risks. However, these exceptions can destroy the concept of an unacceptable list and turn it, so far as the areas of exception are concerned, into a caution list, as will be explained. As long as the list remains a true unacceptable list, producers may not violate it without facing the possibility of serious consequences, such as termination of their relationship with the insurer.

Underwriters on the other hand, are expected to use an unacceptable list as a guide. They recognize the unacceptable lists as representing the type of risks the insurer does not want to cover, under normal circumstances; hence, they start by assuming that such risks are not to be accepted. However, as underwriters gather more information about a risk, they may decide that it is acceptable provided it carries a deductible.

This difference in the applicability of an unacceptable list between producers and underwriters is extremely important; it lies at the very heart of the insurance business. Underwriters *must* have the authority to make exceptions to the unacceptable list, otherwise they are not underwriters. If an insurer were to decide that the unacceptable list must be followed exactly, it would not have to hire underwriters; it would need only clerical employees to check the classifications of applicants to be sure that they do not fall within the scope of unacceptable risks shown on the list.

Some insurers employ junior underwriters or screeners to separate the obviously acceptable risks from those that appear to be unacceptable or questionable. This is done only on simple risks in mass lines and, perhaps, on changes in existing policies. For example, consider an automobile policy on which a change is made to replace one car with another because the policyholder had sold the old car and bought a new one. If the new car had no problem characteristics and there were no unfavorable aspects to the policy, such as loss frequency, a clerical employee might have authority to make the policy change. This is not underwriting; it is merely approval of a routine clerical transaction. Any other action must be approved by the underwriter. Thus, if the new car has performance characteristics which places it on the unacceptable list, the underwriter must decide whether to make the change or to cancel the policy.

Although producers are not supposed to bind coverage for any risk shown on the unacceptable list, they do so every day. Sometimes this is caused by their ignorance of the list, and at other times by misclassification of the applicant or misunderstanding of the rule. In such cases, an underwriter is asked to consider a risk that is unacceptable by the company's standards. However, no underwriter should cancel an applicant simply because the producer bound the risk in violation of the rule. Rather, the underwriter should perform all the usual functions of underwriting, perhaps with more speed than usual but without malice or bias just because the applicant is unacceptable according to the list. The producer should be told about the error, of course, in order to avoid repetition, but this is not part of the underwriting function. The case should be referred to the proper department for discipline or education, depending upon the structure of the insurer and the assignment of duties.

There is one exception to the principle that an underwriter has authority to accept any risk on the unacceptable list. Some items may be on the list because a reinsurance treaty excludes them, and an underwriter should never approve writing a risk that has no reinsurance. Sometimes special reinsurance or other protection can be arranged for the exposure. But, in the absence of such arrangements, the underwriter has no authority to write risks that are unacceptable because of reinsurance provisions.

One other exception may apply in certain instances. There may be risks on the unacceptable lists that management has determined shall not be written. Management has a right to determine this, and may make such a decision on the grounds of inadequate rates, poor experience with the class, market problems and others. Even in these classes, there are few, if any, individual applicants who could not be written by someone in the company. Perhaps the line underwriter does not have authority to write such unacceptable risks, but this authority may be given to someone of higher rank; underwriting supervisor or manager, branch manager, or underwriting vice president.

Many steps should be taken before an underwriter accepts risks that are on the unacceptable list. In the first place, it is obvious that sufficient facts upon which to make an intelligent decision are needed. Next, underwriting judgment must be applied, based on all the facts at hand. Of course, these are the starting points for all underwriting, but these are even more important when handling applications for unacceptable risks by the company's rules. A higher degree of care is required on these risks, and the normal factors must rate higher in order to warrant acceptance than for risks not on the unacceptable list.

Various factors must be considered by the underwriter. One of these is the producer; many underwriters give heavy weight to loss ratio, volume and cooperation of the producer. Probably all underwriters tend to consider the producer as an inherent part of underwriting and not needing to be specifically defined. However, this consideration is a more important factor on unacceptable risks. In addition, some insurers may follow a practice of giving special consideration to certain producers, with underwriters instructed to follow that practice.

In like manner, the underwriter will consider size of the entire account. The specific application at hand may be unacceptable but the balance of the account could be acceptable. For example, an unprotected restaurant may be on the fire unacceptable list but considered to be an excellent risk for liability and workers' compensation. The underwriter's judgment must then be applied in determining the relative advantages and disadvantages of each line, and in determining if the expected profits from the good lines may reasonably be expected to offset the expected losses from the poor lines.

Still another factor to consider is loss history. Previous losses ordinarily indicate the pattern of future losses. Sometimes loss history is part of the unacceptable list — that is, a certain class of risks may be unacceptable if an applicant has suffered more than a specified number of losses during a period. Whether loss history is part of the unacceptable list or not, it is a factor to be considered on every risk, and it will receive more careful scrutiny on risks that are on the unacceptable list. The underwriter, therefore, must apply judgment in considering whether the expected loss pattern of the future will outweigh other factors.

The entire matter of unacceptable lists is handled differently by various insurers, of course. Some insurers refer to them as "prohibited risks," which appears to have no real difference in meaning. Certain insurers use non-binder lists instead of, or in addition to, their unacceptable lists. These non-binder lists may be called "caution lists" or "submit-for-approval risks." Whatever term is used, the intent is to prohibit the producers from binding coverage on such risks, and requiring instead, that they submit all such applicants to the underwriter for approval before insurance is made effective. In contrast, then, an unacceptable list includes those risks that the producer should not even consider because they will not be accepted under any circumstances. The distinction is more apparent than real because, as was pointed out previously, the underwriter must have the authority to accept any risk, limited only by reinsurance requirements and the level of authority the underwriter holds.

Purposes Served by Unacceptable Lists

Unacceptable or caution lists serve several purposes. They indicate those risks that the insurer cannot write because of reinsurance considerations. They also point out the risks that the insurer does not wish to write because of management decisions: experience has shown that such risks present a greater exposure to loss than the average; the proper facilities to service the risks properly are not available; or those risks simply do not fit within the marketing pattern of the insurer. These lists guide the producer away from unwanted risks, thus saving valuable time and sparing the applicant the disappointment of possible declination; the producer may try other insurers without even submitting the risk to this insurer. Finally, these lists serve as guides to the underwriter of those risks that are inclined to have more undesirable charcteristics than the average. For these reasons, these risks must be handled with extreme care.

A clearly written, properly administered unacceptable list can serve all parties to an insurance transaction. It can be of inestimable help in guiding producers to submit a balanced book of business. With such a book, underwriters are in a good position to develop a profitable book of business.

SECURING INFORMATION

An underwriter cannot determine risk eligibility or acceptability without careful analysis of factual information. A prerequisite to such an analysis obviously is the securing of information. This is a fairly simple process for some lines but it can be quite complex and time consuming (as well as expensive) for other lines.

Sources of Information

Several sources of information are available to the underwriter. The following are some of the more important ones.[1]

Producers. They are required to submit applications for almost every type of insurance; the application is the primary, and sometimes the only, source of information about most risks. In addition, producers may be asked to submit other material such as photographs of buildings or the latest financial statements of an applicant's.

Reporting Companies. A number of companies exist for the sole purpose of supplying information to clients, and insurance companies are among their largest users. Credit reporting companies furnish reports about the financial condition of applicants, and also inspect risks in order to supply reports on other information, such as the condition of the property and the use of a vehicle. Other companies publish financial data for most businesses and supply these publications to clients. Still other companies furnish loss prevention services under contract, giving underwriters authoritative information about applicants, as well as attempting to reduce losses.

Bureaus. An underwriter can secure considerable information about applicants from bureaus. The prime example of this source is the fire rating bureau information; not only does the rate book or card shown the construction and rate for the risk being considered, but it also gives important facts about an adjoining structure which may be an exposure to loss.

Governmental Agencies. Various levels of government furnish information that may be helpful to an underwriter. The principal use of this source is the motor vehicle reports that helps to determine the past driving record of applicants. Other sources used less often but vital occasionally are court records and census reports.

Other Insurers. Most applicants have been insured before, and an underwriter is usually anxious not only to ascertain why the applicant changes insurers but also to determine the loss experience of the prior insurer. It is common in some lines for insurers to reciprocate in supplying the claims record of specific risks upon request. When this source is available, it can be extremely valuable to an underwriter because these reports show facts, not opinion, and indicate the actual loss experience that can be expected.

Insurers' Employees and Records. Much information can be secured from within the insurer itself. Company engineers or inspectors may be utilized; their information is expected to be factual and unbiased. Sometimes these employees can supply photographis of property to be insured which underwriters often find helpful. An excellent additional source is the records on file for other policies carried by the applicant with the insurer. Many applicants are already insured by the company for other lines, and the loss record on those other lines can be a good indica-

1. See Chapter 6 for further details about securing information.

tion of the moral and other hazards which may be present.

Most of the information supplied to an underwriter must be evaluated carefully. There are always possibilities of error in identifying a specific risk, transposing policy numbers, bias on the part of the person supplying the information, and even lax supervision permitting faked reports. Fraud, misrepresentation, and error in supplying information can be damaging but can usually be rectified. An underwriter must be constantly alert for apparent discrepancies, and must take all reasonable steps to resolve any uncertainties.

As regards false or misleading information, the application is in a class by itself. The application is ordinarily completed by the producer, but it is considered to contain the statements and representations of the applicant. Indeed, the applicant must sign the application for most lines and if material misrepresentations are discovered, such as material misstatement of a risk's age, driving record or loss record, the underwriter may rescind the coverage. This means that the policy is void as of its inception and no coverage is ever considered to have been in force. It is obvious that rescinding coverage is a serious step for an underwriter to take, so there must be certainty of the grounds before taking such action. On the other hand, material misrepresentation or fraud is ground for voiding a contract, and an underwriter must consider the insurance policy to be a contract, one based upon mutual trust and good faith. The underwriter, therefore, must take action when facts provide that action is indicated.

Applications for some lines of insurance contain "declarations," which are statements of facts about important elements of the risk. When they are used, the declarations usually are made a part of the policy. This practice tends to strengthen the position of the insurer in cases of misrepresentation since the policy is issued in reliance upon the declarations, and the declarations are stated in the same manner as they are answered by the applicant. Some authorities consider the declarations to be the application, but it is more common to use the term "application" to include both declarations and other information of interest to the underwriter. Thus, the application performs three functions: (1) it may contain declarations which are made a part of the policy, (2) it includes a detailed description of the risk (that is, as detailed as the underwriter requests), and (3) it makes an offer for insurance protection.

ACCEPTANCE AND REJECTION

The first and most important function of underwriting is in properly selecting risks. This selection is accomplished by accepting or rejecting those applicants who are submitted by the producer.

The underwriter considers many factors in arriving at the decision to accept or reject a risk. One of these is the identification of hazardous conditions which are not measured adequately by the premium. Every class of business includes a large number of risks, and a successful underwriter is able to separate those specific risks that have hazardous conditions that are most likely to produce adverse underwriting results.

The underwriter of a specific class of insurance becomes quite familiar with its characteristics. With this knowledge, steps can be taken to minimize expenses, both as to claims and to the handling of them. The underwriter will know the hazardous conditions which are reflected in the definition of the class: those which are expected average risks. Then hazardous conditions which are not expected and those which are likely to produce adverse underwriting results can be determined. Any one of these conditions, or any combination of them, is sufficient grounds for rejection of the risk by the underwriter. Rejecting a risk with a greater chance of loss than is expected for its class will help minimize claims costs.

Having determined those characteristics which may result in rejection, the underwriter is then in a position to publish a list containing those characteristics, or perhaps publish a list of classes that usually contain a high percentage of individual risks having one or more of the undesirable characteristics. This unacceptable list helps to reduce the expense of handling these risks because producers are expected not to bind coverage on unacceptable risks, and to submit to the underwriter only those applicants on the list who have unusual circumstances or conditions which merit special consideration. In addition to minimizing expenses, this method of telling producers in advance which risks are likely to be rejected reduces friction between producers and underwriters.

In actual practice, there are few risks which are absolutely unacceptable. Someone in the company has authority to accept them; if not the line underwriter, then one of the superiors. An unacceptable list establishes the types of risks where care is required to a greater degree than for the average risk, and puts the underwriter on notice to be particularly careful. By application of judgment, the underwriter decides whether to write the risk or not.

A risk does not have to be on the unacceptable list, or even on a caution list, in order for the underwriter to decline it, nor does absence from such a list mean that a particular applicant is acceptable. While a risk is *eligible* if it is permitted by the company's filings, a risk is *acceptable* only when the underwriter applies judgment and says that it is acceptable. In the final analysis, a risk can be accepted even if it is on an unacceptable list; and it can be declined even when it is not on such a list. This is what underwriting is all about.

QUESTIONS FOR DISCUSSION

1. Define the term "adverse selection" and cite one example. What effect can adverse selection have on the role of underwriting?
2. If an underwriter is to group homogeneous risks, he or she must give consideration to certain individual characteristics of risks. Using personal auto insurance, as the line, how can these individual characteristics be identified?
3. Does the fact that a risk is eligible under the rules for a particular line of insurance mean that it also is acceptable? Explain.
4. The size of unacceptable lists concerning each line of insurance depends upon certain factors. What are they?
5. For what reasons is there a tendency, during the selection process, for an un-

derwriter to rely more upon unacceptable, rather than acceptable, lists?

6. Compare the uses of unacceptable lists for underwriters and producers.
7. Give two exceptions when an underwriter may accept a risk despite the fact that it appears on an unacceptable list. Give two examples of when an unacceptable risk may not be accepted even though the facts make the risk acceptable.
8. Discuss some of the factors that an underwriter must consider before accepting risks that are on the unacceptable list.
9. Explain the purpose of unacceptable lists.
10. Why is the experience of an underwriter considered to be a plus when it comes to the selection process?

12

Classification and Rating

When an underwriter decides to accept a particular risk offered, the work on that risk is by no means finished. The next step is to classify and rate the policy. In actual practice, these functions of an underwriter are not performed in any chronological order. The underwriter often classifies the risk as the information is gathered, and as the information is evaluated, the underwriter considers the classification which will apply to the risk.

This tentative classification process may be formal or informal. A *formal* way would be one in which the underwriter indicates, in the proper place on the application or other form, the tentative classification decided upon. For example, if the underwriter determines that a personal automobile appears to be operated about 25% of the time by an 18 year old driver, the underwriter could enter the appropriate class in the space for classification. An *informal* way would be one in which the underwriter would either keep a mental note of the classification or make a notation someplace on the application for formal handling later.

It is important to note that the classification is *tentative* at that point. As more information reaches the underwriter, the classification may be changed. For example, if it is learned from another source that the youthful driver actually operates the automobile about 10% of the time, or is actually 22 years old rather than the age previously indicated, the classification would be changed under many rating plans because of these additional facts.

A revision in the classification of a risk can even be made later on, such as when the underwriter is at the point of making the underwriting decision. For example, information may be received indicating that this 22 year old driver has had such a poor driving record that the individual would be a problem to any insurer. One of the alternative courses of action may be to transfer the entire risk to another insurer, if the underwriter works for a fleet of companies and can move business to another insurer. In this case, the second insurer may have a completely different classification system. Another alternative may be to exclude the 22 year old driver from the policy, leaving coverage only for the parents. This may be the decision if the underwriter feels that the rate is inadequate to cover the poor driving record of the youth. If this were the decision, a different classification would probably be used.

The *final* decision on classifying risks cannot be made until all available information has been received and evaluated, and the underwriting decision on acceptability has been made. When the underwriter decides to accept a risk, the classification which is to be used must be known. The two functions are inseparable, because the decision to accept the risk must be accompanied by a decision on the proper classification which is to apply. In effect, the underwriter is saying, "This risk is acceptable under this classification." The classification can be changed, of course. Additional information may reach the underwriter later which causes a reclassification of the risk. It could perhaps simply involve an error, such as the age of the driver or a change in exposure, such as a poor driving record of one driver. No matter what type of a change is involved, the underwriter must approve the new classification, but must reevaluate the risk before doing so.

WHY CLASSIFICATIONS ARE USED

The purpose of using classifications in insurance is to separate risks into homogeneous groups. The heart of the insurance mechanism is in the sharing of exposures by similar risks, and the most equitable means of accomplishing this is to separate all of the risks into smaller, homogeneous groups. Classification is the technique by which this separation is achieved.

Many risks are *heterogeneous*, which means that they are different in important characteristics. Being made up of unlike elements or parts, they cannot be grouped together for insurance purposes. Insurance requires the grouping of *homogeneous* risks, which means those which are composed of similar elements or parts.

Since every line of insurance contains risks which are similar in some respects but dissimilar in others, a broad range of characteristics is present in each line. For example, dwelling fire insurance is written only for buildings and contents of residential occupancies, with a further requirement in many states that not more than four family units may be present in the building; in this respect, all such risks are similar. However, there is a great degree of dissimilarity between a 100 year old rundown shack containing three rooms and located in an isolated forest area, and a 30 room mansion built last year and located in an area having the finest fire-fighting facilities available. These extreme risks are not homogeneous, and the underwriter would put them in different classifications.

There are several types of classifications which are automatic and inherent in the system. The first separation is by line of insurance: a commercial liability applicant is automatically placed in a different category than a commercial fire applicant. Another separation occurs within some lines because of the coverages desired. For example, an applicant for dwelling fire and extended coverage insurance is classified separately from one selecting broad form coverage. These extreme risks are heterogeneous, not homogeneous, and the underwriter would put them in different classifications. Other classifications also are made by the underwriter in order to refine the groups. To do this, the parameters of each group must be established. These will vary by line, but can include such factors as age, construction, use and past experience. The underwriter must be thoroughly familiar with the precise characteristics of each group because misclassification can cause more problems than not attempting any classification whatsoever. If homogeneity is to be achieved, therefore, it must be based on precise, easily determined characteristics. The last step, of course, is to classify each applicant into its proper group.

One danger in the classification process is when groups are too small because the parameters are too tightly drawn. Insurance requires a large number of similar risks sharing exposures, and this basic requirement is violated if the groups are too small in number. Thus, an automobile insurer may place in one group, all drivers between 30 and 65 years of age who drive only for pleasure and not over 10,000 miles per year. It would be possible to refine the group much farther, for example, by placing into one group all 32 year old school teachers with blue eyes and blonde hair and who drive black cars between 6,000 and 7,000 miles per year. Such a refinement violates the classification principle that groups be easily determined. It also would be prohibitively expensive to attempt to classify in such a manner. In addition, such a group would undoubtedly be too small to constitute insurance.

An important reason for classifying risks is to be able to apply rates in a discriminate manner. A liquor store should probably pay more for crime insurance than a dairy store, so this is a logical classification difference. Each factor in classification should be based on rate differences which are measurable. That is why the color of an applicant's eyes, hair, and car are not used — there is no statistical proof that these factors have the slightest effect on loss experience, and, thus, on rates. Classifications, therefore, should separate similar risks, and this implies that the differences are significant, as well as measurable.

ESTABLISHING AND APPLYING CLASSIFICATIONS

Rates and classifications are inextricably related; each is dependent upon the other. There can be no rate without defining the classification to which it applies, and an important purpose of the classification is to determine the applicable rate.

Some insurers secure their classification and rating systems from rating bureaus. In those cases, insurers need only apply classifications and rates to individual risks. Some insurers, however, establish their own classification and rating systems. (This is a staff function, ordinarily performed in the home office.) In most companies, the actuarial department is responsible for establishing the rates and thus the classifications to which they apply. The staff underwriting department, on the other hand, is usually involved in determining the definitions of classifications, because there are more factors to consider than just rates. Staff underwriters ordinarily can contribute valuable opinions and facts upon particular classifications being proposed or studied. The actuarial department, in turn, can determine the proper rate to charge for a specific classification, but it requires the combined knowledge of the actuarial and underwriting departments to determine if the classification itself is proper.

Factors To Consider

There are many factors to consider in establishing classifications. Simplicity and understandability are important; misclassifications are possible, unless definitions of classifications are easy for the producer, for the underwriter and for the rater to apply. Competition is always a vital factor, too. A specific classification may be different from that used by competitors, and some pricing advantages may be gained in this way, but an insurer must be aware that competitive disadvantages may also result because another insurer's classification system may attract the better risks. For example, if competitors use 10 classifications for service stations, based on construction and fire protection, and one insurer uses one classification for all service stations, the latter insurer will have to use an average rate in order to achieve a normal profit. (This probably will be near the competitor's rate for about a class five risk, using a grading of one through 10.) That one insurer will gain by its simplicity but to the degree that price is a factor in buying insurance for service stations, that one company will get very few of the low-rated risks and most of the high-rated risks. Soon its average rate will be inadequate, and to avoid an underwriting loss, that one insurer will have to raise its single rate to a point which is close to the highest rate used by competitors. As a result, it will attract very little business. It is certainly not impossible nor impractical to use a system of classification which is different from that used by competitors; many insurers have profited from doing this, but the consequences must be considered carefully.

The classification system should be fair, stable and responsive to changes, too. Each classification should be mutually exclusive so that there is no overlapping between classifications; each risk must fit within only one classification. More important, however, is the requirement that the classification system achieve homogeneity by grouping similar risks within one classification; hence primary consideration is given to the similarities of risks.

Staff members prepare the classification system. Working together, the actuarial and underwriting departments are also considered: The marketing department may have comments about the expected impact on producers and on competition. The accounting or rating department will want to be sure that clerical employees are able to apply classifications and that classifications are compatible with the requirements of insurance departments concerning how premium writings are to be reported. Finally, the data processing department will insist that classifications be compatible with the other operations of the company. After all of these factors and viewpoints are considered and balanced, classifications are established, adopted and published.

Line underwriters are the ones who apply the classifications. Each applicant is assigned by an underwriter into a classification. The underwriter may exercise judgment in some cases involving proper classification for a specific risk. For example, authority may exist to decide whether a homemade fire extinguishing system in a restaurant is adequate for a preferred classification instead of a standard classification. However, the underwriter does not have the authority to change classifications. If bakery trucks are assigned to class five, a bakery truck applicant may not be assigned to class six. Even in those classes when classifications are not filed with an insurance department, such as some inland marine lines, the underwriter must be consistent in applying classifications in order to avoid unfair discrimination.

In some lines, the underwriter may not know the exact classification for each risk. In dwelling fire insurance, for example, it may not be known on which side of a rate class boundary the applicant's house is located. (A rater or clerk may determine the exact classification later.) However, the underwriter must know the approximate classification, at least. The expected profitability of an applicant cannot be evaluated unless the rate level within rather narrow boundaries is known, and it is determined by the classification. If there is uncertainty in dwelling fire coverage insurance, whether the applicant's house is in class five or class 10 location, the underwriter must determine the proper classification because the disparity in rates and underwriting considerations would be too great to ignore. The difference between class five and six, on the other hand, is probably small enough for the underwriter to disregard.

In addition, the underwriter has to know the approximate classification, if a rater or clerk performs the actual classification. The underwriter must also know the characteristics of each class and must verify that each applicant has those characteristics. Only in this way can he be reasonably certain of homogeneity and profitability.

The line underwriter can also be helpful to the staff in the development and revision of classifications by observing the manner in which classifications are applied in actual practice. An underwriter may sometimes find that the actual application of the classification system gives a different result than was intended. In other cases, areas where homogeneity can be improved or the competitive situation improved by a change in the classification system may be found. Areas may even be discovered where more classes should be created in order to secure a lower rate for a better risk within a class or a higher rate for a less desirable risk.

While homogeneity is considered to be the prime purpose of using classifications, it is not really achieved in actual practice. No matter how small the class, there will be differences among the risks within it. In automobile insurance, drivers under 25 years of age could form a class, but those who are 21 and over have better driving records than those under 21, and females have better records than males at all youthful ages. Several classifications, therefore, might well be made out of the "under 25" class of drivers. The most that can be expected is that all of the risks within a class are relatively homogeneous, and that any further division would result in such small classes, or classes with such few differences, that subclassification is impractical. However, it is always true that subclassification is possible and that such refinement might prove to be profitable.

The line underwriter is expected to watch for areas susceptible to further refinement in classifications. Perhaps, in reviewing claims, it will be noticed that persons of a certain age or a certain occupation appear to have fewer accidents or perhaps less severe accidents. These findings should be reported to staff, along with any precise data that may be acquired.

While line underwriters apply classifications to specific risks, they can also be helpful in establishing and revising classifications. Their experience with actual cases can blend well with the theories and statistics of staff underwriters and actuaries. For this reason, a well-organized company uses both groups in establishing its classifications system.

ESTABLISHING RATES

Classifications and rates are inseparable. The value of classifications is to separate risks into homogeneous groups and the sharing of exposures among homogeneous risks is accomplished through the use of rates. Rates are established for each classification and cannot be stated without reference to the classifications upon which they are based. The common practice is to place a risk within its classification and, then, to ascertain the rate which is applicable.

The rate is the price that a policyholder pays for the privilege of transferring a unit of the risk to an insurer. These units of exposure to risk differ by types of insurance. For this reason, the rate is quoted on different bases. For example, fire rates are usually stated for each $100 of insurance purchased, while the rate for workers' compensation is given for each $100 of the policyholder's payroll.

The policy premium, in turn, is determined by applying the rate to exposure units. If a fire rate is 20 cents and the amount of insurance is $30,000, the premium is $60.

The likelihood of loss is measured by the rate, too. An employer who furnishes a sale place to work and requires nonhazardous types of work will have a lower workers' compensation rate than one with hazardous working conditions. In the same manner, a fire rate depends upon such factors as fire protection, building construction and type of occupancy.

Severity of potential loss is measured by the number of exposure units. Since exposure units are the dollars of insurance carried for insurance, a total fire loss, for example, on a $100,000 building will be more severe than a total fire loss involving a $30,000 building. Both the likelihood of loss and the potential severity are measured by the premium. The combination of a low rate and a small amount of insurance results in a low fire premium.

The understanding and use of all of these terms and relativities are important to an underwriter since they are the starting points for understanding rating. There are many additional facts and concepts to be known in order to underwrite properly, such as the types of rate structures and rate plans, the methods of establishing rates, and the systems by which rates are applied to risks.

During most of this discussion, the emphasis is upon *rates*. The importance of *premiums* is explained at the end of this chapter.

Types Of Rates

One important difference in rates is found between the major coverages under casualty and property insurance. Generally speaking, liability coverages are rated for each $1,000 or $5,000 of liability exposure, and reduce as limits increase. For ease of handling, it is customary to apply rates to liability limits so that the manual shows the premium, not the rate. These practices can be illustrated by a hypothetical table showing premiums of $30 for a $25,000 limit, and $33 for a $50,000 limit. Another common practice is to show the premium for a basic amount, such as $25,000, and to give percentage increases for higher amounts. Fire insurance, in contrast, is rated for each $100 of insurance purchased. The rate is the same for the first $100 as it is for the last $100, (although some modification of this has been made in residential rates over the years).

These rules do not apply to all classes within these insurance lines because of the diverse coverages written. Under casualty insurance, burglary coverage is rated per $1,000; glass coverage on the basis of size of glass or per pane; and vehicle material damage (damage to the vehicle) is made on the basis of cost new of the vehicle or by rating symbol and age. Under property insurance, inland marine rates often are reduced as the amount of insurance increases.

There also are rate differences among the general types of risks insurers write: preferred, standard, or substandard. Most lines of insurance can be divided into those three major types, although the dividing lines seldom are that precise.

Preferred risks are those considered to be least likely to have losses. The prediction for future losses may be based on past experience (automobile), construction and occupancy (fire), neighborhood (crime), safety measures used (workers' compensation), and so on. Preferred risks carry the lowest rates for risks within any general classification, but, since premiums would then be lower, underwriters have fewer dollars with which to pay losses which are inevitable for all risks combined, even though they may be relatively few in number. Since there will be losses, and since severity is often impossible to estimate in advance, the question could be raised whether these risks are really the most desirable. It would appear that they are, for most insurers seem to try to attract them more than any other. The answer is that these risks incur the least expenses and have the greatest predictability of future losses; hence, underwriters prefer them. Too, expenses are lower because they require less investigation and they sustain fewer losses. Predictability of losses is easier if fewer losses are expected; the more losses that are predicted, the harder it is to accurately predict future experience. The reasons may differ by line, but the general statement is true for most, if not all, lines; that is, rates are lower for preferred risks and underwriters want to write them.

Standard risks are those which are neither the best nor the worst. In most lines, they are the average, run-of-the-mill risks. Most rates are set for these risks, and the other types are moved upward or downward from them. Most insurance is written at these rates, and most insurers consider that the bulk of their prospects lie in this area. Underwriters may *want* preferred risks, but they *write* more standard risks, with the exception of some selective companies that only accept preferred risks.

Substandard risks are the least desirable — those most likely to have losses. They may consist of the automobile drivers with poor driving records, property owners with run-down buildings, or employers with unsafe premises. Rates are highest for these risks on a relative basis within each classification. In spite of the higher premiums developed, most underwriters tend to reject these risks, feeling that the rates may not be adequate. Many underwriters feel, furthermore, that it is more difficult to predict losses with as much certainty as the other types of risks. In addition, many of these risks have other problems which cause them to be considered less desirable. Finally, many of these applicants may be in an economic class which finds it difficult to pay the higher premiums which the class requires, and are undesirable for that reason, too.

Theoretically, rates can be set so that each risk — whether preferred, standard or substandard — is profitable. It can be said: "There is no such thing as a substandard policyholder, only a substandard risk." Some insurers have been consistently profitable by writing substandard automobile risks, for example. Based on usual underwriting standards, these risks present problems, so the only profitable method of writing them is to use unorthodox underwriting practices, including rating systems. An insurer that specializes in writing substandard risks and has developed an underwriting department trained in that class, may be able to show good results. Equally important is a rating structure that allows for peculiarities of these risks, not just from the standpoint of statistics but from the standpoint of unusual characteristics which underwriters can uncover. Most insurers are not prepared to allow for these various peculiarities and do not attempt to write substandard risks. As a matter of fact, substandard classifications are not commonly used in property and casualty insurance, other than personal automobile and sometimes fire insurance; risks are so different that it is better, in most cases, to use separate rate classes than to try to up-rate a risk from standard to substandard. A risk which is substandard in one class may be standard in another. The approach used in most lines, therefore, is this: Do not consider a risk as being substandard, but place it instead, in a different class — one which has characteristics and rates more suited to the risk.

The bureau versus independent approach presents yet another difference in rating structures. A majority of insurers in most lines are bureau members or subscribers; their classifications and rates are established by a rating bureau. All members and subscribers agree to follow the bureau classes and rates, at least in most states and for specified lines. However, deviations from bureau rates are permitted under the laws of most states. These deviations are usually percentage deviations and apply to the specified classes; for example, a company may use rates which are 15% below bureau rates for all protected dwelling fire policies. Additionally, some insurers may subscribe only for some classes and file independently for others.

Independent classifications and rates are used by some insurers for some or all classes. This approach is rarely used in such lines as commercial fire. However, they are used by a number of companies writing personal automobile insurance; while these are a minority of companies, they write a majority of automobile insurance in some states. In fact, some of the largest insurers in the United States are independent companies.

Both bureau and independent companies use the same techniques in promulgating rates. Their actuaries accumulate a large body of statistics and prepare classifications and rates in conjunction with underwriting personnel. The details are explained later in this chapter. It is important to note here that the same functions must be performed, whether the company is a bureau or an independent one.

Objectives Of Rating Plans

There are four general objectives of all classification and rating plans.

1. Solvency of the insurer must be maintained. This is the first and most important objective. No matter how attractive or competitive a rate may be, it is useless if its continued use threatens the solvency of an insurer.

2. Competition must be considered. A rate which is high enough to guarantee the solvency of an insurer will be worthless if it is so far above the rate used by competitors that prospects will not pay it. A rate must be reasonably competitive. This does not mean that it needs to be equal to or below the rate of competitors; it only need be within a reasonable range of competitors' rates. This range can vary by line, because some people have a high degree of insurer loyalty while others do not.

3. Simplicity and objectivity are highly desirable. Producers, underwriters and clerks must be able to apply rates easily and quickly. A complicated rate structure leads to many errors in classification, thus destroying the basis of the system, and it can be very inefficient. Objectivity is related to this and is equally important, because everyone who handles the risk must know the specific rating items. Some items upon which rate structures could be constructed are so subjective that they are difficult to ascertain precisely. For example, it is poor practice to adopt a classification for automobile insurance that applies to "drivers with poor driving records." Each person handling the transaction would have a different interpretation of that phrase. However, the rule is objective if it applies to "drivers who have two or more chargeable liability accidents within the past two years."

4. Significant criteria must be employed. Every item in the classification and rating system must be relevant in order to have a proper plan. Examples of irrelevant items are color of the applicant's eyes, the number of trees on the applicant's property or the number of stockholders in an applicant's business. Illustrations of significant, relevant items in actual use are the age of a driver, the type of roof on a home, and the number of employees in a business.

There are, in addition, three specific objectives which must be followed in order to comply with the rating laws in most states.

1. Rates must not be inadequate. Every rate must be adequate for the exposure, within reasonable limits. This factor is closely related to the general objective of maintaining solvency; in fact, some state laws define an inadequate rate as one that threatens the solvency of the insurer. Rate adequacy also relates to the second general objective, because it prohibits unfair competition by requiring that a rate be adequate. Without this criteria, an insurer could use an inadequate rate to attract a large volume of business, and then raise rates substantially, thus achieving a degree of monopoly.[1]

2. Rates must not be excessive. These are circumstances under which an applicant might be required to pay any rate demanded by the insurer. This criteria provides that a rate may not be so high as to result in excessive profits for the insurer. Every rate must be based on experience and projections, and must anticipate no more than a reasonable profit.[2]

3. Rates must not be unfairly discriminatory. This means that all risks which are similar must be charged the same rate. No discrimination may be made on factors which are unfair; that is, on factors which are not significant in rating. This relates closely to the general objective of significant criteria, and illustrates that it would be unfair to discriminate on irrelevant items listed, such as the color of one's eyes. It is important to note that when it is stated that rates must not be unfairly discriminatory, this implies that they may be fairly discriminatory. In other words, rates should be different for risks having different and measurable factors which are significant; an insurer should discriminate (that is, differentiate or select) on the basis of factors which are significant and fair. On this basis, rates are different by age of drivers, type of roofs, etc.[3]

Finally, there are three subsidiary objectives which are not necessary in any rating plan but which are desirable objectives to attain.

1. Rates should be responsive to changes. It is helpful, if not essential, that rates be adjusted to allow for changes in the cost of settling claims, in the expenses of doing business, in the hazards presented by the policyholders, in the techniques and products used by businesses, in long-range economic trends, etc. These rate adjustments will help to maintain equity among policyholders and help to guarantee a good competitive position.

2. Rates should be stable. To some degree, this is the opposite of the objective of responsiveness to change. The conflict is deliberate; while rates should respond to change, they should not fluctuate continually with every minor shift in cost factors. Insurance is based on the trust and confidence of the buying public, and rate stability nurtures those feelings. If buyers find that rates are different every few months, or even every few years in some lines, they tend to lose confidence in the

---

1. A few states define the term of "inadequate" rates. California, for example, provides that 'No rate shall be held to be inadequate unless (1) such rate is unreasonably low for the insurance provided and (2) the continued use of such rate endangers the solvency of the insurer using the same, or unless (3) such rate is unreasonably low for the insurance provided and the use of such rate by the insurer using same has, or if continued will have, the effect of destroying competition or creating a monopoly." *Insurance Code 1983, State of California, Department of General Services, Documents and Publications Section, North Highlands, California, Section 1852. (a).*

2. The California code provides that "No rate shall be held to be excessive unless (1) such rate is unreasonably high for the coverage provided and (2) a reasonable degree of competition does not exist in the area with respect to the classification for which such rate is applicable."

3. The generally accepted definitions of the term "unfair discrimination" are used, rather than defining this term in the state laws.

financial steadiness of the insurer. It is good public relations to maintain a steady rate, so long as this can be done without violating the other objectives.

3. Rates should encourage loss reduction. A rate is generally better received by buyers if it rewards policyholders who have had no losses, or if it penalizes those who have had losses. In a large line with a relatively high frequency, such as personal automobile insurance, policyholders who are claim-free tend to resent paying the same premium as that charged policyholders who have suffered losses. In other lines, such as workers' compensation and commercial crime, policyholders can take positive steps to improve loss experience by installing safety or protective devices, and businesses which have done so are inclined to seek rate reductions in return. Rates, therefore, should encourage those who take steps to reduce losses, provided other rating objectives are not violated because of such rate refinements.

These objectives seldom can be entirely accomplished in any rating plan. There are so many diverse considerations that compromise is necessary. An insurer wants to attract a large share of desirable business, and can do so only by excluding less desirable risks from a preferred-rate class; only in this way can competitive rates be maintained. On the other hand, rates for less desirable risks should not be prohibitive, partly because the insurer may wish to write some of these risks, and partly because of social pressures, if rates are too high. Every applicant presents some hazards, and most of them present a degree of moral hazard. The rate structure should reflect these factors, charging more where the hazard is greater. At the same time, the underwriter cannot check every detail of every risk because the cost would be prohibitive. The solution is to use broad groupings, placing in each class those applicants who appear to present approximately the same chance of loss.

Other objectives must also be subordinated to the necessity of securing approval of rates by regulatory authorities, in most states. These authorities usually require statistical justification of each rating plan, and this is impossible when the plan includes a relatively small number of risks. A successful rating plan must use fairly broad classifications for this reason, destroying some of the perfection of a plan designed to meet the states objectives. In fact, the classes are often so broad that there may well be more difference between the extremes which fit within a classification than between risks which fall easily within different classifications. Each of these rating plan objectives must be kept in mind at all times.

Factors In Establishing Rates

Rates are established by taking statistical and nonstatistical factors into consideration. (The nonstatistical factors are explained elsewhere.) Statistical factors are used in many ways by those who practice the actuarial science of promulgating rates. Underwriters do not have to know the intricacies of rate computations, but they should be familiar with the general principles and terms that are employed. Furthermore, underwriters should have knowledge of those major factors which are considered in ratemaking, the types of ratios that may be developed, the use of these ratios in ratemaking, and how such ratios can affect these results.

The factors which are used in establishing rates are shown in Figure 4, and are explained next.

Premium—The price the policyholder pays for insurance is called the premium. This corresponds to "income" or "revenue" in other types of businesses, and represents the amount received by the insurer for the protection given.

FIGURE 4

Pro-Forma "Desired" Distribution
Of Property/Casualty Premium

6%	CONTINGENCIES AND PROFIT
4%	TAXES AND FEES
10%	OVERHEAD EXPENSE
10%	ACQUISITION EXPENSE
9%	LOSS ADJUSTMENT EXPENSE
61%	LOSSES

Losses — Predictions must be made on losses which are expected during the period insurance is in force. These predictions cannot be made from any one risk, of course, but must be made for all risks within a classification. This is the largest single item of expense for almost all insurance, amounting to about 70% of the total premium for most major lines.[4]

Loss Adjustment Expense — There is an expense involved in paying every loss, whether an insurer uses its own claims adjusters or outside firms. This expense varies considerably by line of insurance, but must be approximated before rates can be calculated. While the adjustment expense is more closely related to losses than to premiums, it must be estimated as a percentage of premiums in order to compute rates; a rough general estimate is 10% of premiums for adjustment expense.

Acquisition Expense — Every insurer incurs some expense in acquiring or writing insurance. This represents commissions to producers, in most companies. Most commissions are a percentage of the premium for the policy, and while the percentage varies greatly among insurers and lines of insurance, a rough general average is about 13%.

Overhead Expense — This category includes a large number of expense items considered to be in various accounts by insurers, and may be identified by many names. A major item is salaries of underwriters, typists, clerks, raters, accountants, supervisors, executives and all other costs, advertising, postage, travel and so on. All expenses not otherwise listed are included here, even including such items as the cost of examinations by insurance departments. There is wide variance between insurers and lines of insurance, but an estimate of 15% is roughly correct as an average. Some items of overhead expense are fixed while others vary with the amount of insurance or the number of policies written. It is important to note that this is the main area where an insurer may realize a profit which is greater than average, other than selection by underwriters of those risks which have loss frequency or severity below average.

Taxes and Fees — It is not difficult to estimate insurance taxes for any one state because they are established as a percentage of premium and are in lieu of most other taxes. An average of three percent appears to be correct for taxes. Fees may include many items, but the major one is the cost of membership or subscribership in bureaus, i.e., rating, forms, statistical, etc. About one percent may be assigned to fees making a rough total of four percent for taxes and fees.

Contingencies and Profit — A margin should always be allowed for contingencies. Since it is impossible to predict catastrophes or other unusual occurrences, as well as adverse loss experience from too many "usual" losses, a small allowance should be made for these contingencies; one percent is a common figure. Finally, an allowance should be made for a profit to the insurer, if it is a stock company. Mutual

---

4. All percentages used in this section are approximations derived from "Best's Aggregates and Averages, Property Liability," 1985. *A.M. Best Company,* Morristown, New Jersey. These figures differ from the "Pro Forma 'Desired' Distribution" shown in Figure 4 because these are actual figure during the most extreme "soft market" ever known.

and reciprocal companies do not make a profit as such, but ordinarily try to allow for a contribution to surplus in order to finance future growth and to provide for increased financial stability. The usual percentage for profit or surplus contribution is five percent; some state laws even specify this amount for some lines. The total for contingencies and profit is six percent.

Investment Income — A great amount of controversy surrounds the use of investment income in ratemaking. Investment income is not ordinarily included, and is not shown in Figure 4. However, this subject cannot be ignored.

Every insurer has to build reserves against future contingencies in order to assure future solvency. In insurance accounting practices, income from investments and appreciation (or depreciation) in the value of investments are taken on the books as separate items after premium income and expenses have been computed. Thus, this income is not considered directly in rate computations. However, some critics of the industry feel that this income should be combined with the premium income before rate adjustments are made. In fact, some states have taken steps to require this handling. Such an approach overlooks two problems: (1) the reevaluation of investments, and (2) it is much more difficult to predict investment income than other factors because the gyrations of the stock market play a large part in investments. These problems make it difficult and inaccurate to base rate computations on such uncertain grounds.

On the other hand, most insurers do consider investment income, although not formally, in establishing rates. This is demonstrated by the fact that some companies continue to use rates which result in losses from the insurance operation, year after year, obviously depending upon the income from investments to maintain solvency and finance growth.[5]

UNDERWRITING CONTRIBUTIONS TO PROFIT

Since underwriters can affect some of the income and expense factors, and can affect the final results of the company, they play an important role in producing profit. It is vital, therefore, for underwriters to understand the relationship of these income and expense factors and how underwriting actions can change them.

Key functions of all types of businesses have their effects on the final profitability of operations. Manufacturing concerns have no functions which are comparable to insurance underwriting, but the persons responsible for profits in noninsurance organizations must understand how they can contribute to profit. Insurance underwriters, on the other hand, should be aware of the basic differences between manufacturing and insurance operations, and should be familiar with ways in which underwriting can help the company achieve a profitable position.

5. The "soft market' of the early 1980's vividly demonstrated how this can work in practice. The five items of expense actually incurred, as shown in this section, total 112%. Obviously, companies depended upon investment income to offset the underwriting losses and for contributions to contingencies and profits.

One of the basic differences between manufacturing enterprises and insurance companies is in determining costs of products. A manufacturer may determine, quite accurately, the costs of producing its product; these costs are known because the product is completely manufactured before is is sold. Therefore, it can set a price which will guarantee a profit after production is completed. On the other hand, insurance is sold before its costs are known because losses develop after the policy is placed into effect, not before. This difference underlies all aspects of insurance and is of vital concern to actuaries, as well as underwriters.

Another difference is found in the area of fixed expenses. Manufacturers normally have high fixed expenses. Because of this, they need a substantial volume of sales in order to break even. After the break-even point is reached, profit tends to increase as the volume of sales increases. Figure 5 demonstrates this relationship in simplified form, assuming that fixed expenses do not change. Figure 5 also shows that a loss is suffered at any sales volume below the break-even point, and a profit is made above that point.

Insurance companies have relatively low fixed expenses. There is some fixed expense in buildings, equipment and managerial salaries, but these are relatively minor. Figure 6 demonstrates, in the same simplified form as Figure 5, that the volume of sales has little effect on profit. A break-even point is shown but this is relatively unimportant in this type of situation because almost all expenses increase in direct proportion to sales, and the fixed expenses are small.

Insurance company expense is approached from a different viewpoint. Since most expense bears a direct relationship to sales, an increase in profit cannot be achieved by an increase in sales. The only means of getting more profit is by reducing expenses. In order to find a means of reducing expenses, it is first necessary to determine their relative relationships. Figure 4 shows the premium distribution of a typical average insurer, using the percentages previously specified for each of the factors.

An underwriter can use Figure 4 to determine the areas in which it is possible to contribute to the profitability of the company. It is obvious that if expenses increase, the percentage for profit will decrease. Conversely, decreasing any expense factor, without offsetting increases in other factors, will increase the profit. Since the goal of an underwriter is to help the company in achieving and maintaining a profitable position, the objective should be to reduce the expense factors.

First, of course, the underwriter must recognize those expense factors which cannot be affected. Two such items in this category are items shown on Figure 4.

1. *Taxes and fees.* Taxes are completely beyond the control of the underwriter. Perhaps a small savings in fees can be realized in some cases, by such means as withdrawing from a rating bureau and promulgating rates independently. Such an action would transfer at least a portion of the expense to the company payroll, and could actually cause an increase in total expense. For purposes of this evaluation, it is assumed that company management has decided to maintain bureau membership or subscribership, so this expense is beyond the control of the underwriter.

FIGURE 5
Relationship of Expenses
And Profit
(Assured Figures)
Manufacturing Enterprise

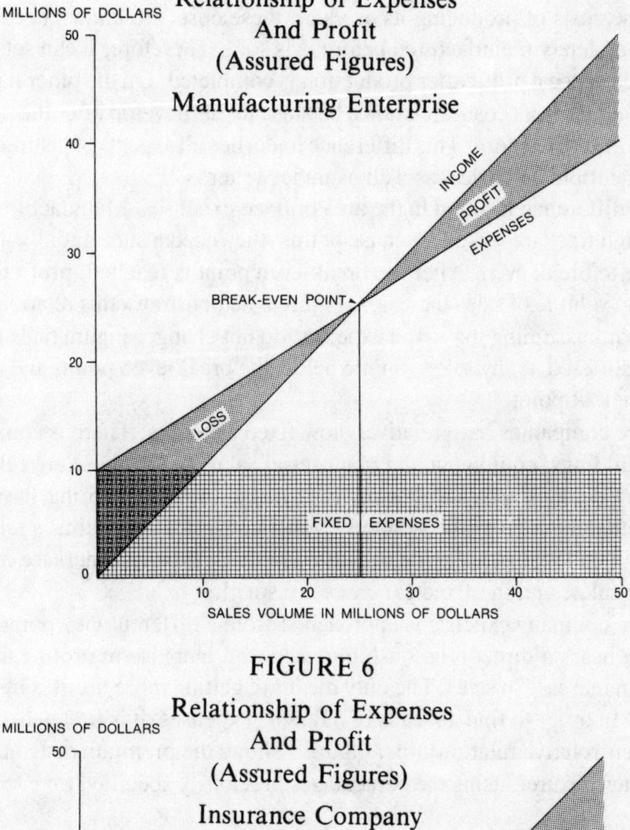

FIGURE 6
Relationship of Expenses
And Profit
(Assured Figures)
Insurance Company

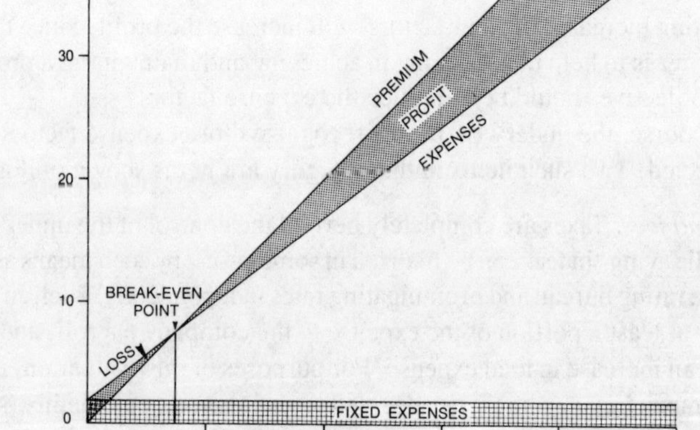

2. *Acquisition expense.* The percentage of commission is a management decision. It may vary by line and it may change from time to time, but the underwriter has no effect on it at any given point.

Next, there are two factors over which the underwriter has little control:

1. *Loss adjustment expense.* The percentage of each claims dollar which is charged to the adjustment of losses is determined by the claims department. However, when the percentage of the premium dollar is considered, as in Figure 4, part of the computation must be on the amount of losses paid. To the extent that underwriters have some effect on the latter, as will be explained, underwriting can have a small effect on loss adjustment expense. Ordinarily, however, this is not considered to be an item under the control of underwriters.

2. *Overhead expense.* Most overhead expense is completely beyond the control of underwriters. Some control is possible over such items as investigation reports; if the underwriter orders fewer reports, overhead expenses will be reduced. Underwriters may also help in achieving a more efficient operation, as may any employee, and thus reduce overhead expenses. Finally, underwriting managers and supervisors have some control over these expenses by the type of underwriters they hire and the efficiency of their operation. However, these items, although important, are minor in relation to a company's total overhead expense.

This leaves only losses as an expense item over which an underwriter has any noticeable degree of control. This is the primary purpose of underwriting, of course: to select risks in such a manner that losses will be reduced and profits will be increased. At the same time, the underwriter must not overlook the relationship of this item with other factors.

Consider a theoretical situation under which an underwriter decides to secure information from every source at his disposal, in an attempt to secure every shred of evidence that an applicant is indeed "preferred." Losses may be reduced, but overhead expenses would undoubtedly increase, perhaps more than enough to offset the reduction in losses; the total effect would be lower profits. However, an increase in profits by reductions in losses can be dramatic, particularly if the underwriter has not incurred large offsetting expenses.

Frequency Versus Severity

Losses actually consist of two components: frequency and severity. Since the underwriter has some control over each of these, the difference between them should be known.

1. Frequency of loss is the ration of losses to the number of exposure units. If 1000 losses are sustained over a stated period of time, and 100,000 automobiles are insured, the frequency is one percent. Frequency can also be computed by using the number of policies, the number of drivers, the number of locations on a fire policy and so forth. If the size of the losses remains constant, it is apparent that a higher frequency means that more money will be paid in claims.

An underwriter also can reduce losses by selecting only risks which can be expected to have a low frequency. This is an important part of the selection process and furnishes a method of measuring the performance of underwriters on some lines.

Of course, the desire to achieve a low frequency of loss must be balanced against the company's goals of writing business. An underwriter who declines every risk that appears to have any chance of loss would accept very little business and would not serve the company well. The goal should be to select those risks whose loss frequencies will be average or better for the class which the company intends to write, and this is keyed to the rate which is charged.

2. Severity of loss is the average size of losses. If 1000 losses are suffered and the aggregate which is paid on those losses is $200,000, the severity is $200. Severity depends upon many factors, such as the number of people injured in automobile accidents, the amounts to repair burned buildings, or the value of merchandise taken by burglars. If the frequency of losses remains constant but the severity increases, the total dollar amount of losses will increase.

An underwriter has only limited control over severity. In other words, there is no way to determine which applicant will have a serious accident and which will have only a minor one. Moreover, an underwriter cannot cannot control inflation, the cost of repairs, the size of jury awards or similar factors. However, large liability losses can be avoided by accepting only low limits of liability. This may restrict sales, but this depends upon the marketing plans of the company.

The underwriter may retain only a small amount of the exposure and reinsure the balance, as is explained in a later chapter in this part. He or she may also require that protective devices be installed to prevent large losses; examples are automatic sprinkler systems and burglar alarms. The methods by which underwriters control losses are many. They constitute a major goal of underwriting, and are woven throughout many facets of underwriting. It is important only at this point to recognize that this is the expense item upon which an underwriter exerts the most control, and that both frequency and severity are elements of loss expense.

RATES AND THEIR USES

All of the statistical factors can be related for easy use in ratemaking and analysis. It is common in the insurance business, particularly among underwriters, to use various ratios. Before they can be understood, however, a few definitions are necessary, along with examples as shown in Table 1.

Definitions

Premiums Written. The gross amount of premium income is called the premiums written. It corresponds with gross sales in a manufacturing or retail business. As an example, $100,000 would be the premiums written for a company for a stated period if its total income from new policies, renewals, and additions to existing policies amounted to that sum. Premiums written can be divided in many ways: by line, by geographic area, by period of time or by producer, to name the more common ones.

Premiums Earned. An insurance company cannot use all of the premiums written as soon as the money is received. Policies may be cancelled either by the policyholder or by the company at any time.[6]

The premiums written are placed in an unearned premium reserve, indicating that this money is not earned by the company until insurance protection is provided for a given period. As each period expires, a portion of the premiums is removed from this reserve and is considered to be earned. The sum of the amounts so removed over a period of time is referred to as earned premiums.

Several different methods are used to compute premiums earned. A common type for an annual policy is to consider one-twelfth to be earned each month. However, only one-half of the first month's premium is earned at the end of the first month.

TABLE 1

Ratios of Expenses and Premiums with Illustrative Figures

WRITTEN — PAID			EARNED — INCURRED		
ITEM	AMOUNT	RATIO TO WRITTEN PREMIUMS	ITEM	AMOUNT	RATIO TO EARNED PREMIUMS
Premiums Written	$100,000	100.0	Premiums Earned	$90,000	100.0
Losses Paid	45,000	45.0	Losses Incurred	50,000	55.6
Loss Adjustment Expenses Paid	9,000	9.0	Loss Adjustment Expenses Incurred	10,000	11.1
Combined Loss & Adjustment Expenses Paid	54,000	54.0	Combined Loss & Adjustment Expenses Incurred	60,000	66.7
Other Expenses Paid	30,000	30.0	Other Expenses Incurred	30,000	33.3
Combined Expenses Paid	84,000	84.0	Combined Expenses Incurred	90,000	100.0

TRADING RATIO

Loss and Loss Adjustment Expense Incurred to Premium Earned	66.7
Other Expense Paid to Premium Written	30.0
TRADING RATIO	96.7

6. When the policyholder cancels a policy, there is no full pro rata return. Rather, a portion is retained by the company to help cover its costs of writing the policy. The return is based on established short rate tables. When the company cancels, a full pro rata return must be made. Recent laws have restricted the right of companies to cancel policies in many lines, but cancellation is still permitted for extreme situations, so companies are required to maintain reserves on the pro rata amount of all policies. Also, some state laws require a pro rata return of all cancellations.

To illustrate, assume that January is the first month in a given period and policies are written uniformly throughout the month. At the end of January, only one-half of the month's premium is earned on the average. Therefore, the common practice is to earn 1/24 the first month, 1/12 during each of the following 10 months, and 3/24 during the last month. Thus, the premium is fully earned at the end of the annual policy.

Ordinarily, earned premiums are less than written premiums, partly because there are cancellations, and partly because most companies tend to increase their writings by rate increases and expanded volume of business. For example, a company with premiums written of $100,000 might have premiums earned of $90,000 for the same period. The premiums earned, like the premiums written, can be divided in many ways, such as geographically or by line of insurance.

Losses Paid. The actual amount of money paid out in claims is called the losses paid. This is the money actually paid, regardless when loss occurs or when claim is presented. This figure is a cash transaction only, useful to determine the cash position and to secure a quick statistic on the immediate picture of the operation.

Losses paid are most often related to premiums written because both are direct cash items and both can be computed quickly. The use of the ratio of these items will be discussed next; for purposes of illustration, a loss paid figure of $45,000 is used. Again, this could be for an entire company for a stated period, or for a segment of the company.[7]

Losses Incurred. Claims that a company becomes liable to pay, or subject to pay, are called losses incurred. This factor includes three separate items. The first item consists of those losses reported as occuring during the policy period and the company is thus obligated to pay, whether or not actual payment is made during the period being studied. The second item is the sum of all losses estimated to have occurred but are not yet reported as of the close of the period; these are called Incurred But Not Reported losses (IBNR). The third item consists of reserves on losses which occurred in previous periods, but have not yet been paid, these reserves may flucuate as new information is received.

Most losses incurred within a period of one year are paid within the same period, but many are not. The incurred loss figure tends to be larger than paid losses because most paid losses are also incurred in that period, and incurred losses also include estimates of unreported losses and reserves on known losses. Conservative accounting requires rather generous estimates of unreported losses and reserves, particularly since reserves are generally on the larger claims. In our example, when losses paid are assumed to be $45,000, it is reasonable to use $50,000 as the figure for losses incurred, applicable to the same line or period of time.

Loss Adjustment Expense. The expense involved in paying losses is called the

7. The figures used in this discussion, and in Table 1 differ somewhat from Figure 4. The reason is that Figure 4 is an example of typical average expense items over a period, while Table 1 is strictly an example based on theoretical statistics for purposes of illustrating the two methods of comparing various factors.

loss adjustment expense. Obviously, it varies in accordance with losses. However, it may then be related to premiums, and must be so related if the various expense items are to be compared to income. Loss adjustment expenses vary considerably by line; they depend upon the amount of work and time needed to pay losses or claims. This expense item is relatively high on liability lines and low on property lines; a fair average is 20% of losses.

On a paid basis, if losses are assumed to be $45,000, the loss adjustment expense at 20% would amount to $9,000. This is nine percent of the assumed written premiums ($100,000). On an incurred basis, assuming losses at $50,000, the loss adjustment expense is $10,000, or 11.1% of the $90,000 earned premiums.

Combined Losses and Loss Adjustment Expense. Losses paid or incurred and adjustment expenses related to them are so closely allied that it is often common to combine them for purposes of analysis. In a manner of speaking, they are a single item, related to any losses which may occur. Table 1 illustrates the effect of combining these items.

Other Expenses. All expenses, other than losses and adjustment expenses, may be combined for purposes of analysis. Major categories of these expenses are (1) commissions and other aquisition costs, (2) salaries and other expense involved in issuing policies, collecting premium, and other overhead items, and (3) taxes and fees. Most of these expenses are related directly to premiums written because they are paid as policies are written. However, they can also be compared to premiums earned if this type of ratio were desired, and some minor changes could be made if expenses incurred were computed instead of expenses paid. For purposes of the example, 30% of the premiums written is assumed to apply to these other expenses, whether paid or incurred.

Combined Expenses. All expenses may be combined for purposes of relating outgo to income. This is the sum of the previous expense items: losses, loss adjustment expenses and other expenses. Either paid or incurred figures can be used for each item, too.

Types of Ratios

Ratios can be developed in many different ways. The most common are as follows.

Combined Written-Paid Ratio. When combined expenses paid are divided by premiums written, the result is a written-paid ratio. This is a ratio relatively easy to compute and it can be prepared rather quickly, giving a rapid picture of results. It can also be valuable in developing ratios by small units, such as for each major line of each producer. A written-paid ratio can be quite accurate for a company or line which has been quite stable for a considerable period of time.

On the other hand, a written-paid ratio can be very misleading under certain circumstances. A company or line which is growing will find that its premiums written are considerably more than the premiums earned, because premiums written are counted as soon as policies are written, while premiums earned develop over the entire term of a policy. At the same time, losses paid tend to lag behind losses incurred as the number of policies are increasing, because there is always some delay in paying claims after they are reported. Furthermore, at any point in time, losses are incurred which are not yet reported, much less paid. These factors of not paying claims immediately and delays in reporting claims are more prevalent in liability than property lines. Thus, a written-paid ratio will be less realistic in liability insurance than in property insurance.

Table 1 shows the ratio of combined expenses paid to written premiums as 84%. This indicates that 16% remains for contingencies and profit. Such profits are almost too much and reflect the fact that either underwriting has been too severe or rates have been too high. Based on these figures alone, either rates should be reduced or underwriting should be relaxed, provided these figures are felt to be large enough to be credible. Before any changes are considered, however, the underwriter and actuary should analyze other types of ratios.

Combined Earned-Incurred Ratio. A more realistic picture of actual results is obtained by dividing incurred expenses by premiums earned. This ratio which shows the actual calculated, long-term results of the insurance operation is most often used to measure performance and to compare companies. However, it is quite complicated to compute and calculation of earned and unearned premiums is time-consuming. The estimation of losses incurred, including reserves and IBNR, takes considerable time and knowledge, too. Estimates of losses incurred can also be quite inaccurate for small volume figures, such as the experience of one producer or one line in a small geographical area. For these reasons, the earned-incurred ratio is used most for company and large-area, long-range results — not for small volumes nor quick indications.

Table 1 illustrates the effect of relating premiums earned to expenses incurred. In this example, the combined ratio is 100 — leaving nothing for contingencies or profits. Based on these figures, the underwriter should tighten the underwriting, or the actuary should increase rates.

The earned-incurred ratio has its weaknesses, however. The $30,000 included for other expenses is really related much more closely to premiums written than to earned premiums. Almost all of the other expense items relate directly to premiums written; therfore, it is misleading to relate this expense factor to premiums earned. Before an underwriter or an actuary takes action on the basis of the earned-incurred ratio, the use of one more ratio should be considered.

Trading Ratio. A consolidation of the most relevant relationships of each of the previously discussed ratios produces the trading ratio. Losses and loss adjustment expenses incurred are related to premiums earned, while other expenses are related to premiums written.

This ratio is not easy to compute either. Actually, it requires computing most of the other figures. It is not designed to produce quick statistics, nor is it used very often for separate lines or for geographical areas. Its advantage is in its logic; each item is compared to the premiums to which it is more nearly related. The trading ratio is often used to judge actual operating results and financial positions of a company because it gives less distortion than either of the other ratios. It may also be used by underwriters who are interested in actual results of their efforts.

In the example shown in Table 1, the trading ratio is 96.7. This is a reasonable ratio which allows for some profit and contingencies, but not quite as much as the desired six percent. The value of this ratio is seen by comparing it with the others. The written-paid ratio is too low and might lead to rate reductions or other steps which are really not justified by actual conditions. The earned-incurred ratio is too high, possibly causing rate increases or other actions which likewise are not really indicated over a longer period of time. The trading ratio is helpful for some purposes, but is not used as commonly as the other ratios, and is not accepted in the annual reports of the companies. However, it is used in comparisons of the financial strengths of companies.

Loss Ratio. All of the previous ratios relate total expenses to premiums, but a loss ratio relates only losses to premiums. An underwriter seldom is concerned about total expenses; as was explained previously, since little control may be exerted over most of them. Primary concern is with the one item of outgo over which some control exists: losses. The underwriter is not solely responsible for losses, but this is the area of greatest concern.

A loss ratio may or may not include loss adjustment expenses. Some companies, or some tabulations, include loss adjustment expenses because they are inseparably related to losses. On the other hand, underwriters have no control over loss adjustment expenses, other than a degree of control over the losses which demand adjustment expenses. For most underwriting purposes, and in this discussion, the term loss ratio means only losses divided by premiums, without including loss adjustment expenses.

Loss ratios can be computed in two ways: A paid loss ratio relates losses paid to premiums written. An incurred loss ratio relates losses incurred to premiums written. An incurred loss ratio relates losses incurred to premiums earned. (These ratios are shown in Table 1, where the paid loss ratio is shown as 45.0 and the incurred loss ratio is shown as 55.6.) The advantages and disadvantages of each type are the same as were given for combined ratios. The earned loss ratio is generally considered to be the most accurate for most underwriting and rating purposes, but the paid loss ratio if often used where a quick approximation of results is needed.

Whenever loss ratios are used, it is important to ascertain the type of ratio. The user must first determine if loss adjustment expenses are included, and then find out if it is a paid or earned loss ratio. Everyone who uses loss ratios must recognize that these ratios depend upon premiums and losses. If premiums are constant while losses increase, the loss ratio will be higher. It is apparent, therefore, that since underwriters have little control over rates, they must depend upon their ability to reduce losses if they are to achieve lower loss ratios.

UNDERWRITING GAIN OR LOSS

In judging the performance of underwriters and in promulgating rates, it is essential to know if an underwriting gain or an underwriting loss has resulted from past performance. (These gain or loss statistics are developed by comparing loss ratios with break-even or tolerance figures.)

A loss ratio by itself is meaningless. If all that were known in Table 1 was an earned loss ratio of 55.6, neither underwriter nor actuary would know if the results had been profitable or unprofitable. If the loss ratio is 100 or more, it is obvious that there have been losses, since nothing remains for expenses or profits. Any ratio which is less than 100, therefore, must be compared with a break-even or tolerance figure in order to determine if there is a profit.

Break-even points are established by computing the reciprocal of combined expenses exclusive of losses. Those other expenses are deducted from 100, and the resulting break-even point indicates the loss ratio at which there will be no profit and no loss. Using the earned-incurred amounts in Table 1, as an example, all expenses except losses are seen to be $40,000, or 44.4 of premiums earned. Deducting this percentage from 100 leaves 55.6, which is the break-even point. If the loss ratio is 50.6, a five percent underwriting profit will be realized. If the loss ratio is 60.6, a five percent underwriting loss will be suffered. The break-even point, therefore, indicates the ratio at which there is no underwriting profit or loss.

Tolerance points are established by deducting from the break-even points, an amount equal to the desired profit and the contingency cushion. If the goal is five percent profit and one percent cushion for contingencies, the break-even point is reduced by six percent in order to determine the tolerance point.[8] When the break-even point is 55.6 as in the previous example, the tolerance would then be 49.6. An actual loss ration of 49.6 would produce the desired profit. A loss ratio which is higher than 49.6 will produce less profit, up to the break-even point of 55.6, at which there is no profit. A loss ratio below 49.6 will produce more than the projected six percent.

Underwriting gain or loss is determined by the break-even point. Either dollars or percentages may be used, and the determination may be made by any desired division of the business of a company, as well as for the entire company. The amount by which actual results are below the break-even point is referred to as underwriting profit; above the break-even point, it is called underwriting loss. The tolerance point indicates the desired underwriting gain, or the goal of the company. If the break-even point is 55.6 and the tolerance is 49.6, an actual loss ratio of 53.6 will produce an underwriting gain of two percent, but will not produce the desired results.

The performance of underwriters is measured partly by underwriting gain or loss. Sometimes performance is measured entirely by this yardstick, but such an approach is unrealistic. Underwriters have some control over frequency and severity of losses by the degree to which they select risks properly. However, underwriters have little or no control over the premiums, and this is very important in determinin loss ratios. Apparently the term "underwriting gain or loss" originated in the early concept which held underwriting and insurance to be synonymous. Perhaps

8. The contingency cushion is actually a part of profit. It is customary in many lines to consider it as a separate amount, in order to achieve a rate level which will produce the desired profit after any catastrophes or other unusual events. This amount may be placed in a contingency reserve, but not necessarily. It is, therefore, more realistic to include it in profit, producing a profit margin of six percent in this example. This item is considered in that manner for balance of this discussion.

the term has endured because the word "underwriting" is sometimes used as a generic term today, as including all persons involved in the insurance mechanism (excluding buyers), whether they be producers, underwriters, actuaries, claims adjusters or managers. Whatever the source or justification of the term, underwriting gain or loss is one measure of the proficiency of underwriters, but more so of the entire company. It is sometimes referred to as a measure of insurance operation, since it disregards the investment operations.

Rates for insurance are determined partially by underwriting gain or loss. The actuary measures the adequacy or correctness of past rates by results, and underwriting gain or loss is one means of measurement. Again, other factors besides rates contribute to underwriting results. On the other hand, the quickest means of correcting an underwriting loss situation is to increase rates. Such increases may bring other undesired results, such as loss of competitive position, but it usually can improve underwriting results for the immediate future. For these reasons, the actuary will adjust rates based in part on underwriting gain or loss. The latter is based on the break-even point, as explained previously, but the goal of the actuary should be to promulgate rates which will produce a loss ratio approximately equal to the tolerance. This will guarantee the desired profits — if all other factors remain equal.

A major problem of insurance is that few factors remain equal or stable, but future protection must be provided at present rates. An inherent weakness of loss ratios and underwriting results is that they are based on past performance. They measure, in part, the ability of underwriters to have selected risks with characteristics which are average or better, and they measure, in part, the abilities of claims adjusters to settle losses, the costs of ratios and the adequacy of rates. All of these relate to the past. Projections must, therefore, be made in order to determine the expected results in the future.

Actuaries project these ratios and expectations as guides in establishing rates; trend factors are important, too. In some lines, a mere comparison of actual and expected results will indicate needed rate modifications. In other lines, more details are needed, such as the number of claims and units of exposure. The use of these statistics comprises the highly specialized function of the actuarial department.

While underwriters are not required to know the details of these statistics or computations, it is helpful for them to use loss ratios, breakeven points, tolerances, and underwriting gain or loss when evaluating the quality of the policies written. Underwriters are not required to understand how statistics are used by actuaries in the promulgation of rates either; knowledge of the basic composition of loss ratios and the underwriting gain or loss is ordinarily sufficient for the underwriting department.

TYPES OF RATING PLANS

The types of rating plans are few in number but there are a myraid of detailed differences among them and underwriters should know at least the generalities of them.

While statistics are used in the preparation of all rating plans, the availability and reliability of statistics vary extensively among them. However, there are never enough reliable statistics to enable an actuary to be certain about the adequacy and correctness of rates. Complicating matters is the rapidity of changes and the fact that while statistics are based upon past experience, rates are predicated on the future. Insurance ratemaking is thus the best estimate of experts on what should be changed; but it is not an exact science.

Class rates are used for large groups of homogeneous risks — that is, risks having similar characteristics. Automobile insurance, with its high frequency and low severity of losses is an example of this type of rating plan. Each class of risk carries a uniform rate and losses and expenses are apportioned over all of the exposure units which comprise a given class. Dwelling fire insurance is also class rated. While its frequency of losses is lower and its severity of losses is higher than in automobile insurance, both factors are still within the requisites of class rating.

Class rates, when used, are an excellent method of sharing losses and expenses among large numbers of policy holders, and are also the most reliable method of predicting future losses. On the other hand, they do not recognize individual differences, which might be significant. The boundaries of the classes also must be set by judgment and this can result in inequities and competitive disadvantages where inaccuracies occur.

Class rates are normally published in tables for the use of producers, underwriters and raters. These tables may be extensive, with every final rate specified. The difference is only one of editorial arrangement; the rates themselves are the same under any system of printing rates.

Individual rates are used for risks which do not fit within a class of homogeneous risks, i.e., there are so many individual rating characteristics that a class rate cannot account for the variables in an equitable fashion. A rate which is designed for an individual risk is able to reflect better its actual loss experience, such as a large risk which has enough exposure units to reflect its losses in the premium. Most commercial risks fall within this category, although some smaller commercial risks may be class rated for some coverages. Generally speaking, risks having low premiums are class rated while high premium risks require individual rating. As a result, more policies are written at class rates, but more total premium volume is generated from individually rated risks.

The advantages of individual rating plans are obvious. They result in rates which are fairer to large risks, encourage safety programs and other means of loss reduction, because reduced losses are reflected directly in the premium, and they provide a competitive weapon in securing better risks. Of course, there are disadvantages. and one of them is that it is easy to give too much of a rate reduction. An improperly written rate provision, on the other hand, can result in substantial losses if conditions worsen. On an overall basis, however, individual rating plans are not only here to stay, they are growing steadily.

There are many rating plans that come within the general category of individual rates. The following are among the most common.

Schedule rates are developed by comparing each risk with a predetermined list containing the average characteristics of all risks of the same general type. Each risk has its rate adjusted by the degree to which it varies from the standard. If a risk is better in some categories, it gets a plus or credit; if worse in others, it gets a minus or debit. The total of the variances determines the extent of modification made for the individual risk from the rate for all risks of that type.

Schedule rating is commonly used with commercial fire risks rather than class rating because frequency of loss is low but severity of loss is high. Each risk is compared on a number of factors, all of them physical, in order to determine the modification to be made in the rate. Rates for each individual risk are then published or otherwise made available.

Two major weaknesses of schedule rating are: (1) its dependence upon the judgment of the person making the inspection and (2) its emphasis on physical factors alone. Both of these shortcomings indicate that rates are not exactly equitable in all cases; underwriting, therefore, can play a large part in developing a profit or a loss because it can take these factors into account.

Experience rates are developed like schedule rates except that modifications are based upon past loss experience of the policyholder rather than on physical characteristics. Obviously, such a plan requires a fairly large risk and a reasonable loss frequency. These rates are used on larger commercial risks for such coverages as liability, burglary, and workers' compensation. Since an experience rating plan assumes that past loss experience will continue in the future, it is considered a prospective rating plan. There are many types of these rating plans, but most of them give reductions in basic rates for good loss experience. They also assume that expenses will remain at a stated percentage of the net rate rather than change with the actual experience under the policy.

Retrospective rates use the experience of the current period to determine the rate for that period — not for some future period. The insurer collects a deposit premium when the policy is written, and at the end of the period, calculations are made to determine if the policyholder will get a partial return of the deposit or whether additional premium is due. A maximum premium must be set; otherwise, the policyholder would simply pay all the losses plus a service charge to the insurer. In practice, the policyholder has an insurance policy if losses exceed a stated amount, but the policy, otherwise, is more like a service contract. This type of rating is the closest plan yet devised to self-rating, yet still retaining elements of insurance. It is apparent that the insurer must charge enough to cover the insurance exposure for large losses, as well as to cover expenses; hence even this rating plan does not guarantee a profit to the insurer.

Premium modification rating plans — used primarily with the large commercial risks — are a combination of judgment rating and schedule rating. Basic rates are calculated from a schedule, with modifications applied by the underwriter on a judgment basis. Rate regulatory laws do not permit indiscriminate modification; they must be applied to predetermined factors in a specific fashion. For example, a commercial liability rate on a factory may be subject to debits (increases) or credits (reductions) based upon such factors as housekeeping, safety programs and quality of management. Each rating plan may permit variations, such as five percent credit for better-than-average management and a 10% credit for superior management.

It is readily apparent that a degree of judgment must be applied in determining the quality of these factors. Most states permit such modifications if they are based upon factors that are reasonably objective, and if modifications are applied as fairly and uniformly as possible. Underwriters are expected to put enough details into the file about the modifications to verify that a uniform, objective approach is being used.

Controversy has arisen over attempts to modify rates on the basis of expenses, such as commissions. A producer may offer to accept a lower commission in return for a rate reduction which will give a competitive advantage. Most insurers feel that this practice is legal, since one of the component factors in determining a rate is commission expense. However, there are those who claim that this is rebating — an illegal practice under which a producer returns a portion of commission to the policyholder.[9]

Judgment rates are used in a few classes of risks when there is considerable dissimilarity among them. Ocean marine and some types of inland marine are the major lines using rates based on the judgment of the underwriter rather than on a body of statistics.

There is, of course, a degree of judgment in all rating, but most classes apply this judgment to statistics in order to arrive at a manual or stable rate for the class, or to the physical facts in order to arrive at schedule rates. A greater degree of judgment is applied to experience and retrospective rates than to other rates, but even these are based on sound starting rates.

True judgment rates are based entirely on the knowledge and judgment of the underwriter. Naturally, every decision is grounded in experience and familiarity, however informal, with past performance of risks which are somewhat similar. Almost every risk has precedence in a related risk, and experience gives an underwriter a "feel" for the right rate. There are not many risks in the United States rated on the basis of judgment; most rates are promulgated and usually filed as a starting point, at least. Naturally, a beginning underwriter would not be expected to handle such rating problems.

APPLYING RATES

When line underwriters apply rates to individual risks, their first step is to apply the classifications, as was explained previously. The next step is to apply the rates. Ordinarily, the rate is determined by the classification, but modifications by the underwriter are possible. When a producer submits an application, the underwriter often considers the rate while the appropriate category into which to place the risk is being determined, because there is often room for judgement in applying classifications and rates. Regardless of the mechanics of the system used by an

9. The insurance laws in most states prohibit rebating, but these laws are being attacked because they are viewed as a means of preventing lower insurance premiums. The prohibition against rebating may be removed in the future.

insurer, the application of rates is a function of underwriting.

A working knowledge of a rating system is essential to an underwriter. At least a rudimentary knowledge of how rates are promulgated for the lines being underwritten is needed, especially on lines involving individual rating rather than on mass lines which use class rates. Moreover, thorough knowledge of rating is essential before an underwriter can apply a restrospective rating plan on a premium modification, and even more critical, of course, is the knowledge of rates on lines when judgement rating is used.

An underwriter must have some general idea of the rate on mass lines although, in some cases, it is not necessary to know the exact rate applicable to each risk. For example, there is very little difference in rates for dwelling fire risks located in protection classes 3 and 4. If an underwriter knows that a specific applicant is located near the border of those two classes, usually it will not be of concern which one is correct and a rating clerk can determine the applicable rate.

However, an underwriter must know the rate for each risk, at least the approximate rate, and an integral part of underwriting is matching the premium to the exposure. As the loss exposures of an applicant are being measured, the underwriter must determine if an adequate rate will be developed. To do this, the degree of exposure the rate is intended to include must be known, before a decision can be made to accept an application, accept if subject to modifications, or decline it.

In a few lines, such as personal automobile insurance, the parameters of each class may be so tightly drawn that the underwriter is expected only to fit applicants within proper classifications. A rating clerk will then apply the correct rate. Even in these situations, the underwriter should be aware of the approximate rate so that income can be compared with the estimated average expected losses.

An underwriter is almost always expected to assign the classification or the rate, or both, and must determine at least one of these in order to make a decision on acceptability. Since the underwriter has to determine the classification and rate, the proper one to use might as well be indicated in the file. Because an underwriter ordinarily assigns codes and perhaps rates, it may appear that this is a clerical function. Such a conclusion is exactly opposite from the truth; determining classifications and rates are essential parts of the underwriting function, and the underwriter must indicate the decision on these items, as on others, in the file for the guidance of other employees.

The line underwriter computes rates only on certain large lines. Usually there is no authority to modify rates, once the classification and the contract are established. However, either the classification or the contract may be modified in most cases, and thus the rate is determined. In every case, the rate applying to each risk, or at least the approximate rate, must be known so that proper underwriting may occur.

tion must be analyzed to ascertain all of the pertinent facts that will enable the determination of the best combination of coverage, classification, and rates to assure the most equitable treatment for all parties. Additionally, whether to use deductibles or otherwise modify the contract, or whether to apply a classification different from that suggested by the producer must be decided. An underwriter must also apply a rate that is adequate and equitable.

Determining the proper rate is an essential part of underwriting. A good risk placed in the wrong classification, or charged the wrong rate, may be a worse risk for the insurer than one on its unacceptable list. Rating is even related closely to the social problems underwriters face, particularly with respect to large lines, such as personal automobile insurance. Insurers select preferred automobile risks by establishing classifications that furnish a competitive edge for those risks. As the process develops, more classifications are established, leaving less desirable risks to be placed in fewer classes with higher rates. These less desirable risks are so classified because of their driving records, but it is not uncommon for a majority of these risks to be in the low income classes. These drivers complain about high rates they are charged because of the classification system, and politicians tend to believe that insurers are "underwriting through the rate structure," by employing rates for nonpreferred risks that are so high that many persons cannot afford to buy the insurance. In this manner, it is alleged, an underwriter can honestly say that the coverage was offered, while using a rate that is prohibitively high. The classification and rating systems are inextricably involved, therefore, in every aspect of an underwriter's operation, social and political, as well as economic and financial.

RATE TERMINOLOGY

Although most of the discussion in this chapter is about rates, an underwriter must know more than that in order to be able to underwrite risks properly; the relationship of the rate, the amount of insurance and the premium must be known.

Rate measures the likelihood of loss. A risk more likely to have a loss than the average for its class should have a higher rate. One of the principal functions of an underwriter is to determine the likelihood of loss for each risk submitted, based on all of the information available. Then the underwriter is in a position to apply a classification to the risk, but to do that the parameters of each classification must be known so that proper classification can be assigned. If a risk does not fit within its classification (that is, if it has a likelihood of loss that is greater than contemplated within the classification), the underwriter must take some action: a different classification can be assigned, the risk may be modified by requiring such measures as protection devices, the coverage can be reduced by such means as deductibles or exclusions, or the insurance can be declined. In some lines, the rate can be modified.

Whatever steps need to be taken, the underwriter must receive an adequate rate. This is the reason that the rate to be charged must be known and compared with the likelihood of loss.

Amount of insurance measures the potential severity of loss. Every property insurance policy has a limit of insurance, such as the amount of fire insurance on a building. Liability insurance policies carry limits of liability, such as the maximum amount of protection available for any one occurrence. The underwriter must take the amount of insurance into consideration to control the severity of losses. (A few large losses can cost an insurer more than a multitude of small losses.) While an underwriter is not expected to know which applicants will have large losses, it is expected that the amount of insurance will be kept within reasonable limits, as related to the characteristics of the risk. Since any risk can incur a loss which is equal to its amount of insurance, the underwriter has the responsibility of keeping limits on liability insurance within reasonable bounds, and keeping the amount of property insurance within the maximum the company can afford to lose in one loss.

Premium is the combination of rate and amount of insurance. It represents the total amount of money the policyholder pays. It is, therefore, the total of the funds available to pay losses and expenses. By applying the likelihood of loss to the potential severity of loss, the underwriter arrives at a premium that gives an indication whether there is a good chance of making a profit on the risk. The underwriter can then compare the premium with the average expected loss for the class, and relate this to the characteristics of the risk and the class. In this manner, an underwriter has a measurable comparison of each risk with the average of its class. Since many of the factors comprising an underwriter's decision are somewhat intangible and subjective, it is helpful to be able to reduce these factors to a dollar premium amount — one which can be handled and compared. In many respects, this is the final step in underwriting an application that is submitted, i.e., determining the actual premium and comparing it with other known factors, such as average loss amounts and average frequencies of loss.

Each of these steps is an integral part of underwriting: The risk must be classified properly, the rate must measure the actual likelihood of loss, and the amount of insurance must indicate the potential severity of a loss. Finally, the premium combines all of these factors into a specific, measurable amount of money that indicates the possibility of making a profit on the risk. An underwriter cannot hope to perform other functions without taking these primary components of insurance into consideration.

QUESTIONS FOR DISCUSSION

1. What purposes are served by classifying risks?
2. Compare the importance of heterogeneous and homogeneous risks and give an example of each.
3. Explain some of the factors that have to be considered in establishing classifications.
4. Describe a possible pitfall to establishing classification based upon the competition factor of other insurers.
5. Compare the role of rates and classifications for a given line of insurance.
6. Why would a rate be different for preferred, standard, and nonstandard risks?
7. Explain the four general objectives for all classification and rating plans.
8. By laws in most states, rates must meet certain criteria. What are they and give an example of each.
9. Compare the advantages of a rate that is responsive with one that is stable.
10. How can a rate serve as an incentive for possible loss reduction?

11. Explain the components of every rate and why an underwriter should be familiar with them.
12. Of what importance is investment income to an insurer? To an underwriter?
13. When it comes to determining costs of products or services how do insurance companies and noninsurance companies differ? Of what significance is the difference?
14. Can an insurance company increase its profits by increasing its sales?
15. What are some of the factors of costs over which underwriters have no control?
16. To what extent do underwriters have control over loss adjustment and overhead expenses?
17. Distinguish between frequency and severity of loss. Why are they both important?
18. What are the differences between:
    (a) Premiums written and premiums earned;
    (b) Losses paid and losses incurred;
    (c) Loss adjustment expense and other expenses.
19. Why is the combined earned-incurred ratio more advantageous than the combined written-paid ratio?
20. What purpose do the trading ratio and loss ratio serve?
21. Given a combined earned-incurred ratio of 60, what other information must the underwriter have in order to determine the significance of that ratio?
22. Distinguish between an individual and schedule rating plan, giving one use for each.
23. When might it be more practical to use judgment rates on a risk?
24. Why might a retrospective rate be more responsive than an experience rate?
25. What components make up the premium?

13

Policy Contracts

An underwriter is ready to issue a policy after determining the acceptability of an applicant and applying the proper classification and rating. Issuance is accomplished by an instruction to the clerical department as to the proper policy contract to use. These three functions of classification, rating, and the determination of the proper policy form are interdependent; that is, each must be considered at all points in the underwriting process.

A policy contract may consist of both the printed policy plus any applicable endorsements. Each of these two parts requires additional comment. Also, the decision to use bureau or independent forms needs analysis.

POLICY FORMATION

The traditional formation of policy contracts involved combining a foundation policy or skeleton policy, containing the basic provisions applicable to all policies of the same type, to other policy forms that identified the policyholder, the property or exposure protected, the conditions and any special extensions and exclusions. The classic example of this type of contract was the standard fire insurance policy. State laws specified the content of the policy itself, as a means of guaranteeing to policyholders that the contract contained at least a minimum specified degree of protection. A policy form was then attached to tailor the contract to a building, or other property.

The standard fire policy was adopted by the states because some companies issued contracts which contained unexpected exclusions or requirements. For many years, the states required that all fire insurance policies contain the standard fire policy, verbatim. The advent of the plain language policies in the late 1970's caused a modification in this requirement, because the standard fire policy was not very "readable" (readable policies are discussed later in this chapter), with its stilted language and numbered lines. All states have now enacted laws which permit these provisions to be written in any other form, provided that no protection to the policyholder is taken away.

Self-Contained Policy

Some insurance policies are self-contained contracts with all the necessary coverage provisions and conditions included in one form. If modifications are needed, endorsements are used (as explained in the next section), not other policy forms. Examples of self-contained policies are homeowners and businessowners policies.

Modular Policies

A recent trend in the arrangement of policies is the use of a modular format. Traditional forms and endorsements are replaced by modules which can be used on monoline (single coverage) or multiple-line (two or more coverage) policies.

The 1986 commercial lines program of ISO (Insurance Services Office, a large rate and form bureau) is an example of the modular arrangement. Common policy declarations and common policy conditions are used; these contain all of the provisions which are common to all commercial lines of insurance. Each line, such as property or liability, then uses a conditions form which contains those policy conditions which are applicable to that line. Next, one or more coverage forms are used to describe what is covered, such as the building and personal property coverage form. Finally, one or more causes of loss forms are used to describe the perils insured against, such as basic, broad, or special (on property lines).

This modular approach reduces the number of forms, because the same forms can be used for monoline and multiple-line policies. The arrangement is logical for a person who is trained in the language of insurance, separating coverages from perils, from conditions. Whether this arrangement is logical or understandable to policyholders could be debated. At any rate, this appears to be the policy arrangement which will be used in the future.

Underwriters need to know the component parts of policies, and to be able to identify these parts regardless of the arrangement of the policy. The legal structure does not change, but the format looks different under various policy arrangements.

Bureau of Independent Forms

Most companies use bureau forms, rather than preparing independent forms. For smaller companies, this is virtually a necessity. Larger companies have the staff and the experience which permit the use of independent forms on many lines.

Bureau forms have a number of advantages. Standardization is a major benefit: producers who represent more than one company need learn only one contract. Training material need not be duplicated. Another advantage regards the concurrency requirement—where, every policy covering specific property must read exactly the same or the policyholder may be penalized on some losses. When bureau forms are used, no problem of concurrency arises when two or more companies insure the same risk. From the company standpoint, a contract-writing staff is not needed when bureau forms are used, and changes can be implemented quickly and easily.

Independent forms have advantages for those companies which are large enough to use them. Competitive advantages can be gained through coverage differences.

Revisions in contracts can be made when the need becomes apparent, without the necessity of waiting for bureau action. Individual company preferences can be incorporated into contracts.

There is room in the industry for both bureau and independent policies and forms. The competitive nature of the insurance business is demonstrated by the existence of both approaches.

ENDORSEMENTS

Endorsements, used with any type of insurance policy, modify printed documents. Endorsements may be prescribed for certain risks, may be optional with the underwriter, or may be tailor-made for specific cases.

An endorsement may be defined as an optional amendment to an insurance contract in order to modify the terms of the contract. An endorsement may be prescribed by the bureau or company, or it may be applied by the underwriter for the purpose of amending the coverage, waiving certain policy provisions, or permitting additional privileges.

There are literally hundreds of printed endorsements available to multiple line underwriters, some of which are quite complex, while others are quite simple. Some printed endorsements are complete in themselves while others require the addition of information. An example of the latter is an endorsement that "excludes the following property." The underwriter must specify the exact wording to be used. Another example is when check boxes are used. In order to achieve economics in handling, several related amendments may be printed on one page, and the underwriter must specify the box or boxes to be checked. There are innumerable combinations that are made available to the underwriter.

Tailor-made endorsements may be used and, of course, there is no limit to their use. An underwriter may write almost any endorsement for any policy even though restricted to some degree by statues, regulations, bureau rules, company policy and competition. If a risk is acceptable only with a particular endorsement and that endorsement cannot be used, the underwriter has no choice but to decline the insurance. On the other hand, use of the endorsement is preferable to declining the risk. An underwriter should always try to tailor an unacceptable risk by using an endorsement to change it into an acceptable risk. Sometimes this can be accomplished by using a printed endorsement; other times the underwriter must write a special endorsement for attachment to a policy.

Endorsements attached to policies when they are issued become part of such policies; the entire contract is the policy as endorsed. Endorsements on exising policies are a different matter. They may be applied by the underwriter when new information is received or when the risk changes. A contract may also be amended by mutual consent. The underwriter and the policyholder, therefore, can agree that an endorsement is applicable; in such cases, the written acceptance of the policyholder should always be obtained in order to avoid future controversy. The underwriter may also, in most cases, amend an existing contract by a change in consideration. Thus, specified property may be excluded if the premium is reduced accordingly, but the underwriter cannot merely send the policyholder a restrictive endorsement that is to apply to an existing policy, unless some provision is made for reducing the premium, or otherwise giving up some right which is granted to the insurer by the contract.

Categories of Endorsements

Many types of endorsements are used by insurance underwriters and they can be classified within the following six categories.

1. Conformance to state laws and regulations. Policies which are printed for use in all states, or in most states, sometimes need endorsements in order to conform provision to laws or regulations in some states. An endorsement is ordinarily less expensive than printing a separate policy for each state and can be applied by a clerk rather than by the underwriter on specific risks. Examples of such endorsements are those amending cancellations provisions, those changing time limitations and method of filing suits, and those providing uninsured motorists coverage (which often varies by state).

2. Exclusions or restrictions for certain types of risks. Underwriters sometimes may decide to apply blanket exclusions or restrictions to specified classes of risks within a line. Since these changes apply only to some risks, they cannot be printed in the contract. A few of these endorsements can be applied by clerks because they are automatic for all risks in a class, but most are specifically applied by the underwriter. Examples of this type of endorsement are: under personal automobile, an exclusion of damage caused by wind-driven sand for risks located in specified geographical areas. Under commercial vehicles, mileage restrictions on the use of the vehicle for some rating classes, under personal crime insurance, an exclusion of personal property taken on business trips, for such occupations as traveling salesmen.

3. Exclusions or restrictions for specific risks. Underwriters often encounter applicants who are desirable except for one factor. If that one factor is sufficiently important, so that the risk cannot be written while it remains, the underwriter has only two alternatives: decline the business (sometimes this is the only practical solution); or endorse the policy to exclude or restrict the offending factor. Ordinarily no rate credit is given for such endorsements because the risk is not acceptable without them. Examples of these endorsements are: 1) under personal or commercial automobile insurance, an exclusion of specified drivers, either by name or by class (such as all drivers under 25 years of age), or an exclusion of previous damage to the vehicle which has not been repaired; and 2) under personal crime insurance, entirely excluding (or limiting to certain specified perils) certain property, such as valuable jewelry, which the owner refuses to insure specifically under a schedule, but that the underwriter is not willing to insure under blanket coverage.

4. *Broadening coverage.* Producers sometimes request that coverage be broadened on certain policies, in order to meet unusual conditions. Underwriters who approve such changes must endorse policies to include the changes. An example dealing with property coverage is the underwriter who changes a policy to provide that specified property is covered for replacement cost rather than just actual cash value.

Another example deals with the permits clause that is broadened to permit the use of the premises for an exposure not contemplated in the base rate, such as occasional repair of automobiles in a storage garage. Examples in casualty lines include extensions of mileage limitations under specified conditions, and permission for some insureds to settle certain small claims directly with claimants.

5. Application or removal of deductibles. Underwriters will accept certain risks only if deductibles apply. In some cases, the rates are reduced because of the deductibles; in others, the change is considered to be an underwriting deductible, without which the coverage would not have been written. For this reason, no rate adjustment is made. Some types of insurance are rated with an automatic deductible, and the underwriter may choose to reduce or remove it upon request. All of these changes must be made by endorsement. Deductibles are quite common in property insurance but are rare in liability insurance. Underwriters of property lines may insist upon deductibles to meet such cases as school buildings that are unusually subject to vandalism damage.

6. Amendment of premium payment basis. Many types of premium payment and premium adjustment plans are available in the property and casualty insurance business. The applicable type for each policy is specified within that policy. However, changes are sometimes made, and an endorsement is required to effect such a change. An annual payment policy may be changed to a monthly payment basis; dividends may be made available; or a gross receipts or retrospective rating plan may be applied, with the details specified in the endorsement.

PREPARING POLICIES

Policy wording is prepared by a bureau for most types of property-casualty insurance. The staff of the bureau determines the content of the policy in conjunction with industry representatives who serve on the committees of the bureau, and companies use these policies without making changes. The advantage of this practice is standardization: legal interpretations and decisions apply to all of these policies alike; reference books explain one contract for each line which assists many companies that use this material; and producers who represent many insurers can learn one contract and know that it applies to all, or most, of the companies represented. These advantages of standardization, therefore are persuasive.

However, some insurers prepare independent policies with wording and coverages following the bureau policies rather closely, but this is not universal and there are exceptions. An advantage of the independent approach is that a company can offer extra coverages or extensions and, thereby, gain sales or competitive advantages. Too, coverages can be reduced when a problem arises without having to wait for a bureau to change its language through committee action. Thus, an independent company can respond more quickly to adverse legal decisions, statue amendments or sociological changes.

Independent policies are written by the staffs of the insurers. Some companies place the contract writing function in the underwriting department, some in the actuarial department, and some in the legal department. Wherever the responsibility lies, the cooperation of all departments must be involved in writing or revising policies.

Policies and forms are handled in much the same fashion as rates. Staff departments determine the content of the documents and arrange for their printing, and line underwriters apply policies and forms to specific cases. When a line underwriter suggests a type of policy or a revision in a policy, these recommendations are always considered carefully because the underwriter is closer to policyholders and producers than are the staff members. However, a line underwriter has no authority to change the contracts, other than by endorsements and, as with rates, many policies must be filed with state insurance departments and may not be changed without prior approval.

Unusual, one-of-a-kind type policies are manuscripted. Underwriters authorized to write these special policies are highly trained specialists. In other words, no underwriter of the more common lines is permitted to write a manuscript policy. Some persons may consider manuscript policies to be essential to true underwriting — writing a policy to fit the needs of the applicant and the decisions of the underwriter — but there is no reason to believe that any line, even a mass line where standard policies are used, is any less vital; the underwriter still selects risks to fit the contract, and may tailor the policy by means of endorsements to fit the needs of any situation. The important factor is not the person who writes the contract, it is the knowledge and understanding of the person who uses it.

A number of factors must be considered in preparing policies and forms. Being legal documents, laws must be studied for one thing, and help of the legal departments is essential for another. Being a regulated industry, insurance must conform to the regulations of regulatory bodies which means submitting most forms for approval. Here the assistance of legal and other personnel who handle filings is needed. Being a business, insurance is controlled by its executives who determine corporate policy. All forms that are written and used, therefore, must conform to such policy. Being in a competitive business from the standpoint of its costs, an insurance company must achieve economies in the issuance of policies.

PREPARING FORMS AND ENDORSEMENTS

Forms are prepared by many different persons or organizations. State legislatures and insurance departments specify the content of some forms, rate and form bureaus promulgate others, mortgagees or other additional interests demand specific forms, policyholders insist upon certain provisions, and insurers prepare still other forms.

The states are becoming more active in insisting upon the contents of some forms that must be used; that is, they are requiring certain provisions in policies, and the most efficient means of meeting these requirements is by using endorsements. The only alternative is to print separate policies for each state, but this becomes quite expensive and cumbersome to handle. One example of a state requirement is that concerning specific provisions which must be included in coverages. Uninsured motorists coverage is a good illustration of this under automobile policies. Since states usually specify the minimum requirement of such coverages, various state uninsured motorists forms are used, as well as endorsements to modify the provisions of uninsured motorists clauses which may be printed in the policy. Another example of a state requirement deals with the time within which suit may be filed or the number of days notice of cancellation that may be required. As an illustration, in some states the insurer may cancel the policy upon 10 days notice, but some states require that this notice be extended to 20 or even 30 days. Changes of these types must be endorsed on policies by means of forms, unless insurers revise the printed contracts.

Rate and form bureaus often specify special provisions which must be attached to policies in order to qualify for certain rates, or in order to meet the rule requirements of certain situations. An example of a rate qualification is the use of cleaning fluid clauses, attached to policies covering dry cleaning establishments, limiting the types of fluids that may be used under the applied rate. An example of the rule requirement is the necessity of adding a clause permitting a building to be vacant without coverage being excluded. Since these provisions apply only to special situations, the use of endorsements is the only practical means of placing them on the policies.

Mortgagees and other parties who have interests in insured property must be recognized in contracts. Policy forms usually contain loss payable or mortgagee interest provisions, but many special forms are demanded. Some of these special forms provide for additional advance notice of cancellation even beyond the period of notice given to the policyholder. Other special clauses limit or waive deductibles, as regards the interest of the mortgagee. Still other clauses provide that on all loss settlements over a specified amount, the loss payee must be named on the claim draft, along with the policyholder. There are standard mortgagee or additional interest endorsements available for most lines of insurance. However, many special forms are used by mortgagees, lending institutions, leasing firms and other parties with interest in the proceeds of policies. Insurers must stock and use these special forms if they wish to write insurance on property in which these parties have an interest.

Policyholders sometimes insist upon having certain provisions attached to policies as a condition to retaining insurance. An example, in a commercial liability line, is the policyholder who occasionally uses the truck for pleasure, perhaps to take the family on a camping trip. This policyholder may accept a mileage limit as an integral part of the policy for commercial operations, but will insist upon a special clause that voids the limit while the truck is used for pleasure purposes. An example in the personal automobile line is the policyholder who accepts an exclusion of unrepaired damage on the car; when the damage is repaired, the policyholder applies for an endorsement removing that exclusion. Such situations obviously can be handled only by endorsements.

On occasion, underwriters prepare some forms to meet specific situations. An underwriter may agree to extend replacement cost coverage to certain equipment. Another may want to exclude named persons from coverage under a liability policy. An automobile underwriter may choose to exclude damage by winddriven sand, or theft of stereo equipment. A crime underwriter may accept a certain risk only if an exclusion endorsement is attached to the policy, precluding theft coverage while the policyholder is on a business trip. Underwriters even use endorsements to change other endorsements on policies, as well as to effect other changes in policies.

Some of those who require special endorsements will specify the exact wording to be used; this is particularly true of some state and mortgagee forms. Bureaus often specify the wording and may even supply the printed forms. However, many endorsements must be written by the insurer. These, like the policies themselves, are written by staff personnel, usually the underwriting or actuarial departments in conjunction with the legal department. Line underwriters may suggest or request certain forms, and have authority to prepare them for individual risks, too. Forms which are to apply to many risks are prepared by staff. One reason for this is to assure that company policy and legal requirements are met and another reason is to assure the proper relationship between the contract and the rate.

Regardless of the party originating the endorsement, the underwriter must arrange to have it in a prepared form, ready for application to the policy. Insurers must print or type the endorsements with exceptions in the following cases: standard forms printed and distributed by bureaus; special mortgagee forms printed by mortgagees; and state forms. Since insurers must bear costs of printing and handling, in most cases, they endeavor to achieve as many economics as possible. For this reason, some endorsements have check boxes indicating which of several options are applicable; some are complete except for a blank to be completed; others are printed such as the ones required by state laws. Finally, of course, some are blank endorsements that are used to accomodate endorsements written by underwriters, or used so seldom that it is more economical to fill them out individually rather than to have them specially printed.

READABLE POLICIES

A recent trend is toward the writing of insurance policies in simplified language. This is in contrast to the traditional legal wording which evolved over many years, and which often resulted in a long series of clauses connected by commas and semicolons, making comprehension by a layperson very difficult indeed.

Many states have passed laws which require that policies be written in readable form. Personal lines policies, particularly automobile and homeowners forms, have been the principal targets of these laws. Commercial lines policies may well be made subject to similar laws in the future, so bureaus and companies are anticipating this by using simplified wording when major revisions are made in the policies.

The measure of readability, as used in most laws, is a specified score on a "reading ease" chart developed by Rudolph Flesch.[1] A "Flesch scale" of 40 or 45 is common. These scores are in the "fairly difficult" to "difficult" range, which means that these

1. Rudolph Flesch, *The Art of Readable Writing* (New York: Harper & Row Publishers, Inc., 1974). The score is developed by selecting a text sample, counting the number of words and computing an average sentence length, then counting the number of syllables and applying the formula given in the book. Some insurance companies have eased this tedious counting task by the use of computer programs.

policies are not as easy to read as a child's book, but they are a vast improvement over the Flesch scores of older policies.

Arguments have raged over the benefit of the "readable policies." Some critics say that readability and understandability are two different traits, and that a policy which is readable enough to get a good score on the Flesch scale is not necessarily capable of being understood by typical policyholders. While this is true, most people feel that it is somehat easier to read a document containing short words and simple sentences, than one with long words and complex structures. The average person can at least read and comprehend the words that are read when looking at a "readable policy." The content of the text may not be fully understood, but this reflects largely the complex nature of insurance and the strict construction placed by the courts on all policies. The drafters dare not use common, imprecise language in writing insurance policies. The wording may not be as simple as some would like, but improvements are being made, and will continue in the future.

APPLYING FORMS AND ENDORSEMENTS

Line underwriters specify the forms to be used on a policy. Even on lines when the policy is incomplete without a standard form, there are a number of options that can be used, so the underwriter must designate the proper form to be applied in each case.

The underwriter provides instructions for the policy assembly in a manner which varies by company. Sometimes the policy form number is shown on the application, sometimes on an underwriting ticket and sometimes on other documents, depending upon the procedures of the insurer. In those companies with electronic equipment for underwriters to use in entering the information needed for insurance, the underwriter can designate the form number on the terminal. In all cases, the underwriter must specify the form number for standard forms. On other forms, the underwriter must indicate the number or type of form, the box to check on forms using this device, or indicate the insertions to make when blanks are used. On manuscript forms, those written by the underwriter, the entire wording must be furnished to the typist.

In some states and for specified lines, an audit bureau is used to verify whether proper forms have been applied. This is principally employed in property insurance, where the rating bureau specifies the precise forms to be used for every risk and every rate. The function of the audit bureau is to verify that the rates and the forms are correct and compatible on every policy. The audit bureau is optional with insurers in most states, but mandatory for bureau members and subscribers in others.

Producers issue policies complete with forms and rates in some instances. This practice is usually restricted to the mass lines, such as automobile. When a producer issues a policy, a copy is sent to the insurer for its records. Since it is more efficient for insurers to check those policies for accuracy on forms and rates by having a copy sent to a central audit bureau, this is the practice that has flourished. Fewer policies are issued now by producers, because it is more economical for insurers to issue policies, but audit bureaus still fill a need for some companies.

When producers issue policies, it may appear that they, rather than the underwriter, have the authority to specify forms. This is not at all the case. The underwriter must handle every risk, whether the policy is issued or not, and must make decisions on acceptability, rate and policy forms. If the risk is not acceptable, the policy must be cancelled. If an improper rate or form is used, or a form omitted, the underwriter must endorse the policy to correct this. In any event, the final decision rests with the underwriter.

An underwriter who applies any restrictive or limiting endorsement to a policy must be careful of its legality. Such an endorsement, on a newly issued policy, is generally no problem. The applicant who accepts the policy is considered to have accepted all of its terms. However, the producer should be notified of any such endorsement, so that it can be called to the attention of the new policyholder. It is always better for all parties to arrive at a complete understanding when the policy is issued, rather than discovering areas of misunderstanding after a loss occurs.

Restrictive endorsements are much more of a problem when they are applied after a policy has been issued. The underwriter may insist upon applying such endorsements, either on new policies which producers have issued, or when new conditions are discovered on policies which are in force. These conditions may come to the attention of the underwriter either through the investigation of a risk or because of a claim. There are other circumstances, too. Legal conditions are different since one party is attempting to amend a contract. The underwriter should always request a signed acceptance from the policyholder for the change, and if there is a premium reduction because of a restriction, this may be held to constitute proper consideration; however, the underwriter is usually on better grounds when the signed acceptance of the policyholder can be obtained. Again, it is better to settle disagreements before a claim is presented.

The decision to apply a restrictive endorsement to a policy, whether it is a new or an existing policy, must not be made lightly. The underwriter must realize that the applicant or policyholder might become bitter about receiving such an endorsement, because by its nature it results in coverage that is narrower in scope than was sought; or is more limited than what is being sold to other applicants. The underwriter must also recognize that the endorsement might be refused; a new policy might be refused by the applicant, and an existing policyholder might refuse to accept and sign an endorsement. On new policies, the underwriter will weigh, in advance, the possibilities of a policy being refused, and will issue an endorsement only when the risk cannot be accepted without it. If these are the terms for writing the policy, that decision must be made.

Applying a restrictive endorsement to an existing policy is a different matter. The underwriter might decide to use such an endorsement on the policy because of information developed from an investigation or a claim. The question is: What does the underwriter do if the policyholder refuses to accept it? The underwriter must reevaluate the risk following the regular pattern of decision-making. More information might be needed, although presumably a sufficient amount was secured before the decision was made to apply the endorsement. The underwriter must also weigh the premium against the risk, recognizing that the policy will not have the desired restriction. If the underwriter can tolerate the exposure, and would accept another applicant on similar grounds, the proposed endorsement should be withdrawn, and the policy retained. Otherwise, the policy should be cancelled.

A general rule becomes evident when considering the consequences of failing to receive acceptance for use of a restrictive endorsement. An underwriter should never apply such an endorsement, unless these are the only terms desired for retaining the risk. In other words, the underwriter should consider the alternatives in advance. If the risk is acceptable without the restriction there is the risk of alienating the applicant or policyholder, as well as the producer, by attempting to apply it. But, if it is not acceptable, that decision should be made before applying the restriction, and time should not be wasted reconsidering it later. Of course, if new facts are presented, it is a different situation, and could cause reconsideration at any time.

Importance of Underwriters' Knowledge

The proper education and training of underwriters is essential in handling policy forms. The underwriter must know, thoroughly, the coverages which are given under a policy, including all of the forms attached, and this applies even on mass lines where the underwriter may not see the actual policy delivered to an applicant. It is impossible to select risks intelligently unless the underwriter knows what the policy covers. If an automobile underwriter is told that a neighbor of the applicant occasionally borrows the car for a vacation trip, the underwriter should know if that person is covered under the policy. If a fire underwriter learns of an old tool shed on the rear of the property, it is essential to know if it is insured under the policy issued. Endorsements cannot be added to policies, with any degree of intelligence, unless the underwriter knows the content of the policy to which it is attached and the endorsement, itself.

The intentions of the underwriter are of little importance if the proper policy is not furnished. An insurance policy is a legal document and is ordinarily governed by the written form. If a mutual mistake occurs, it can be corrected, but, if an underwriter erroneously attaches the wrong form to a policy, or neglects to add a clause, the insurer is usually held to the contract that is issued. Furthermore, since the underwriter prepares the policy form, the courts have held that it must be interpreted against the insurer and in favor of the policyholder, in case of ambiguities. Insurance is a transaction closely involved with law. The person writing the contract, meaning the underwriter in an insurance transaction, must understand what is in that contract and must know actually what coverage is intended.

Underwriting skills generally are acquired only through experience rather than through classroom training. However, the content of policy forms can be taught in the classroom. Since the insurance contract is an integral part of underwriting, this is an area where time must be spent before a person can be considered a qualified underwriter. Education in the content of policy forms is essential to good underwriting, along with training in the proper use of these forms.

UNDERWRITING THROUGH THE CONTRACT

Every applicant presents many potential exposures to loss and every underwriter must evaluate these exposures in relation to the premium. In this evaluation, it is essential that the contract be understood so that the coverage provided is completely understood by the underwriter.

An underwriter need not be too concerned, ordinarily, with exposures that are excluded by standard contracts. For example, if an automobile underwriter learns that a policyholder owns a go-cart or similar miniature, motor-propelled recreation vehicle and knows that the standard automobile policy excludes coverge for such vehicles, it is not necessary for him to make a decision on the degree of exposure; the contract removes the problem with no action on the part of the underwriter.

Examples

An exception to the previous example could involve a case where the producer reports an exposure to the underwriter with the obvious expectation of obtaining coverage. Using the previous example, assume the producer informs the underwriter, by letter, that the policyholder — under an existing automobile policy — has purchased a go-cart. The underwriter could ignore the letter, since the policy does not extend coverage; but this is the worst possible solution, since the producer obviously expects coverage. The underwriter may choose to extend coverage to the go-cart. If such is the decision, the policy should be endorsed to remove the exclusion or otherwise cover the exposure. On the other hand, the underwriter may not wish to extend coverage; in this case, the producer should immediately be notified that there is no coverage under the contract even though such notification is more of an educational than an underwriting function.

Quite a different situation exists when the contract does indeed cover the exposure, but there is a serious question whether the underwriter wishes to assume it. Suppose that the standard automobile policy used by an insurer does not exclude go-carts, and the underwriter learns that a policyholder has just purchased such a vehicle. There is no problem if the underwriter is willing to accept the additional exposure, with or without an increase in premium. But what is the underwriter to do if there is no desire to cover the exposure brought about by the go-cart in this particular case? The underwriter may cancel the entire policy (subject, of course, to the noncancellation laws in this state), or may issue an endorsement excluding coverage for the go-cart. The latter is usually the preferable course, assuming that the balance of the risk is desirable. In effect, the underwriter is adapting the contract to fit the underwriting decision.

There are many cases when the underwriter tailors the contract to conform to situations presented by the applicant or to the underwriting decision. If a risk is good otherwise, it is preferable to adjust the contract and retain it, rather than to cancel it. This is one purpose of underwriting through the contract — changing the policy provisions to conform to the underwriter's decision.

Limitations or exclusions added to standard policies must conform to the laws, of course. Some states prohibit an exclusion of certain drivers under automobile policies, and it is generally unwise in any state to exclude a named insured (one who is defined in the policy as being "named insured"), because the courts might well consider such an exclusion as being contrary to public policy. Many policy forms must be filed with state regulatory officials, and there are limits beyond which these policies may not be restricted, at least not without giving reductions in premium.

Reducing Moral Hazard

Another purpose of underwriting through the contract is to reduce the moral hazard. Some provisions are placed in the contract by its writers, but others are added by the underwriter to fit specific cases. Certain rights of the insurer are specified in some of these provisions, such as the right to cancel the policy or to reduce the coverage; and the right to repair or replace property damaged or destroyed rather than to pay for it in cash. Other provisions are intended to prevent over-insurance. Examples are clauses that provide that the policyholder will, after recovering under the policy, assign all rights of recovery to the insurer against negligent third parties; provisions stating that the policy will pay no more than its proportionate share of each loss, or that the policy is excess over other policies. Yet another example is that provision which limits the policyholder's recovery to the insurable interest in the property at the time of loss. Other policy provisions that reduce moral hazards are those that include certain perils or property, such as mysterious disappearance under a crime policy, because it is difficult to detect a fraudulent claim under such a peril; also, property that may be excluded are items of value or even items that are difficult to establish, such as accounts, bills, currency, deeds, evidences of debt, money and securities.

Applying Deductibles

Another effective means of underwriting through the contract is to employ deductibles. All types of property insurance may bear deductibles. Some are chosen by applicants to reduce insurance costs. However, others are applied by underwriters to avoid small nuisance claims; to make the applicant a co-insurer on each loss; or to remove the cause of frequent claims and thus to avoid the necessity of cancelling the policy. Traditionally, liability insurance has seldom used deductibles, but their value in underwriting and in insurance cost reductions are leading many insurers to using them.

Questionable Practices

It is important to note at this point that the expression "underwriting through the contract" is sometimes used to refer to a practice that is not considered good underwriting. This practice involves using policy restrictions and limitations for the sole purpose of keeping costs down and thus to encourage sales. Insurers that follow this practice are those that are more anxious to sell insurance than to serve the buying public. Through means which are not illegal, but are unethical, policies are offered containing less coverage than those of other insurers. In other words, insurers do not fully reveal the extent of the reduced coverage. Such practice is poor underwriting because it reduces coverage for the preferred risks, as well as the nonpreferred risks, and it is poor selling because it leads buyers to believe that they are getting more protection than the policy really provides. This practice is also poor public relations for insurers because it complicates claims settlements and results in misunderstandings with producers and policyholders.

Legitimate Uses

There is a legitimate place for limited contracts. When applicants cannot afford to buy broad coverages, or when applicants do not feel a need for comprehensive coverage, limited or "stripped down" policies should be offered at reduced premiums. There is nothing wrong with this approach, as long as the restricted nature of the contract is revealed. Some insurers go so far as to print — in bold letters on the outside of these policies, or on stickers to be attached to them — such cautionary remarks as, "This is a limited policy — read it," or "This policy contains a deductible clause." An underwriter cannot be criticized for offering an inexpensive, limited policy to those applicants who do not want or who cannot afford broad coverages, nor for developing less expensive means of handling insurance and thus reducing the cost of the product. The criticism which is justified is directed at those insurers that use subterfuge in selling restricted policies under the guise of reduced-rate broad policies; such practices have no place in an insurance business that is run by ethical people.

QUESTIONS FOR DISCUSSION

1. What are the basic and necessary components of a complete policy?
2. Of what general purpose does a form serve when attached to a policy?
3. Under what circumstances might an insurer decide to use bureau or standard policies? Nonstandard or independently-filed policies?
4. Explain the uses for endorsements.
5. Why must an underwriter exercise caution when issuing an endorsement after the policy has been issued?
6. Why is knowledge of coverages essential to the underwriting function?
7. Explain with some examples how underwriting can be performed through the contract.
8. After a policy is issued, what can an underwriter do to reduce the frequency of small claims sustained by an insured?

14

Retention and Reinsurance

The final step in underwriting any risk is to make a decision on the amount of exposure to loss that is to be retained. This decision can be made only after an underwriter has selected the risk, has classified it, has rated it and has determined and designated the policy forms to be used. These functions lead to the decision of writing a risk at specified terms, but the underwriting process must not end at that point — the underwriter also must consider the catastrophic loss aspect of the risk; otherwise, the insurer can find itself confronted with a larger loss than it is financially able to handle.

An essential underwriting function, therefore, is to determine the proper retention and to secure adequate reinsurance, if necessary. The reason for this is, no matter how carefully an underwriter selects risks, some of them will have losses and some of the losses may be catastrophic in nature.

An underwriter who lacks confidence and who reinsures every risk which is not absolutely "clean" will soon find that so much of the premium has been given away that there will be difficulty in making a profit, because underwriting profit is only possible by keeping more premiums than are paid out in losses and expenses. Even if losses are small, expenses might be large, and sufficient premiums still must be available to pay them. Thus, it is not enough to just reduce losses; it is also essential to retain as much premium as is practical.

To be kept in mind, too, is the fact that the aim of the underwriter is not only to retain as much premium as possible but to limit the retention of exposure to amounts the insurer can afford. There are three methods of achieving this aim and each is discussed in detail.

—Limit the amount of exposure written on any one risk.

—Write the entire risk and place a portion of it with a reinsurer.

—Protect against multiple losses with catastrophe reinsurance.

LIMIT THE WRITINGS

The most obvious method of avoiding a large loss on any single risk is by writing only a limited amount of insurance on such risk. If an insurer feels that it cannot tolerate any single loss in excess of $10,000, then it can be perfectly safe if it writes no more than $10,000 insurance on any one risk.[1] But there are several reasons this is not a practical solution for all cases. Some applicants may insist that all of their protection be written in one company which is particularly true in personal liability coverages, such as automobile and premises liability. In addition, it is extremely rare for any applicant, except those desiring liability limits of $500,000 or more, to purchase more than one policy; most applicants expect an insurer to write the entire exposure and do not want to buy two or more policies. Furthermore, some producers are prevented from using more than one insurer. Those who are employees of the insurer, or who are exclusive agents, have no other outlet in which to place the balance of a risk if the insurer accepts only a portion of it. This is not to infer that these producers are less able to handle risks, but only to say that they are not in a position to use more than one insurer. Therefore, an underwriter for an insurer that has such producers must employ other means of limiting exposures.

In spite of these difficulties, the method of limiting exposures is a common one. Commercial liability insurance, for example, often requires high limits of liability, more than many insurers wish to write. This means that when an underwriter writes a policy for the maximum limit, it is up to the producer to find another company which will write the remainder. Since liability insurance is written with reduced rates for higher limits, it is customary for the first policy to be "primary" and the second to be "excess." This means that the insurer of the primary policy pays the entire loss until its limits are exhausted, and then the insurer of the excess policy pays any remainder up to its limits.

The maximum amount a liability underwriter may write is called the "liability limit" which may be a fixed amount for all risks or a flexible amount varying by type of risk. Thus, the limit may be $500,000 on a hardware store and $100,000 on a petroleum trucker. This method of reducing the exposure to individual losses is commonly used in fire insurance. The underwriter issues a policy for the approved limit, with the producer writing policies with one or more other insurers in order to secure the desired amount of insurance. (Fire insurance is rated by even amounts, with the last $100 of insurance costing the same as the first $100.) There is no deterrent, therfore, in having several insurers share in a risk; and these policies are written on a pro rata basis which means that each insurer gets a stated percentage of the premium, and each pays the same percentage of every loss, up to its maximum amount of coverage.

The maximum amount a fire underwriter may write is called a "line limit." Many fire insurers use "line limit tables' that specify line limits by various factors. The line limit, for example, may be higher for risks having better fire protection, better

---

1. A loss could involve several risks, thus presenting a new problem. This facet is covered later in this chapter.

construction and preferred occupancies. However, there is no standard line limit table as such. Each insurer adopts one which fits its particular needs. For example, the limit could differ by National Board Class, or could be consolidated into protection groups, perhaps as few as two: protected and unprotected; construction could be ignored or could be separated by frame, masonry, fire resistive and others; the presence of sprinklers could be a factor; and occupancies may be combined in many different ways, too. As an indication of the type of information which could be used, see Table 2.

TABLE 2
Hypothetical Line Guide
Commercial Fire Insurance
(All dollar figures in thousands of dollars)

Type of Risks	**Construction**	**National Board Protection Class**		
		1–6	**7–8**	**9–10**
A. Offices, apartments	Frame	$200	$100	$ 50
	Other	300	250	200
B. Churches, museums	Frame	100	75	40
	Other	200	175	150
C. Mercantile, motels	Frame	75	50	35
	Other	175	150	135
D. Machine shop, printers, miscellaneous manufacturing	Frame	50	35	25
	Other	150	135	125
E. Bars, restaurants, supermarkets, lumber yards, sawmills, feed stores	Frame	40	25	20
	Other	125	100	75

The retention amounts shown in a line guide are not necessarily the total amount of insurance written. In the first place, the amount includes only the exposure at one location, although it does include coverage on all property at the location which could be involved in one loss. Thus, the first step is to determine the "amount subject" to one loss. If considerable distance separates two buildings, the underwriter must decide whether both buildings are subject to one loss or not. In doing so, consideration must be given to such factors as construction, occupancy, type of material between the buildings, direction of prevailing winds, distance between the buildings and so forth.

The second step for the underwriter is to determine the amount which could *possibly* be incurred in one loss, and the amount which *probably* will be so incurred. This is done by establishing the "probable maximum loss" (PML) on the basis of the same factors that are used to establish the "amount subject" (A/S), except that the PML may even involve dividing one building into two or more divisions.

For example, assume that the total amount of fire insurance on a risk is $1,000,000. If the underwriter estimates that $800,000 of this is subject to one loss, the retention and reinsurance might be handled as shown in Table 3. After analyzing all of the factors, the underwriter may conclude that the probable maximum loss (PML) is 50%. Based on these estimates, a fire would involve a loss of $400,000 (50% of $800,000). Assuming that the maximum retention, as determined by the underwriter or the line guide, is $100,000, the underwriter for Company A can accept only one-fourth of the risk, since the maximum retention is 25% of the largest expected loss. The balance of the risk, for purposes of this example, is placed with Company B. (The exposure of each company is shown in the lower part of Table 3.) This illustrates that while Company A issues a policy of $250,000, its largest expected loss ($100,000) is no larger than its maximum retention.

Line guides are not absolute limits, ordinarily, but are published only for the guidance of the fire underwriter. While an inexperienced underwriter ordinarily will not accept more than the limits shown, an experienced underwriter usually has the authority to exceed the limits if this is justified. While most underwriters accept the limits and conform to them with little thought, it is obvious that the preparation of such guides requires considerable analysis of probable maximum losses.

TABLE 3
Example of Retention
Fire Insurance

Total amount of insurance	$1,000,000
Amount subject to one loss	$ 800,000
PML	50%
Largest expected loss	$ 400,000
Maximum retention, Company A	$ 100,000

	Company A	**Company B**
Amount of insurance	$250,000	$750,000
Amount subject to one loss	$200,000	$600,000
PML	50%	50%
Largest expected loss	$100,000	$300,000

TYPES OF REINSURANCE

When it is not possible for an underwriter to limit the amount of insurance written, especially if the underwriter wishes to write the business, the problem can be solved by writing the entire risk and reinsuring the amount above the desired retention. Such reinsurance is usually placed with a reinsurance company, but arrangements are sometimes made by placing a portion of the insurance with another insurer. The types of reinsurance available are shown on Table 4. The balance of this chapter is devoted to explaining each of these types and explaining the actual practices of underwriters in using various forms of reinsurance.

Underwriters should first understand the principal types of reinsurance and then should study the reinsurance programs of their own companies, finding not only differences among them but also determining how to blend their own underwriting with reinsurance that is available.

First, clarification of terms is required: reinsurers use underwriters who employ the same principles of selection as are explained in this book for other underwriters. To avoid confusion, however, a reinsurer is referred to as a "reinsurer" or "reinsurance company." Every reference to "company" or "underwriter" refers to the company issuing the original policy to the customer. In reinsurance terms, the "company" may also be called the "primary company," the "primary insurer," or the "reinsured." The importance of this distinction becomes apparent in the discussion because, while most reinsurers have contracts only with companies, some may issue policies directly to customers.[2]

Pro Rata Reinsurance

Pro rata reinsurance is used almost exclusively on property lines. Its concept is understood most easily by considering it as a replacement for the time-honored practice of fire companies accepting only portions of large risks. Under this practice, the underwriter accepts as much of the risk as desired, with the producer then placing the balance of the risk with one or more other companies until the amount has been assumed in full. As a result, each of the companies gets its share of the premium and pays its share of the losses. Pro rata reinsurance, therefore, permits a company to issue a policy for the entire risk with the amount above the company's desired retention placed with a reinsurer.

Quota share reinsurance is one method by which pro rata reinsurance is handled. This is a form of automatic reinsurance treaty under which the reinsurer accepts a stated percentage of *each exposure* written by the ceding company on a defined class of business, or on all of the business written by the company. The primary purpose of quota share reinsurance is to give financial support to a company which enters a new field or starts writing a new class of business. This type of reinsurance limits the potential loss in an unknown area, and entices a reinsurer to accept a share of the exposure until the line is established. Another type of financial support is the "surplus relief" given to a smaller or weaker company in a group of companies. Having a limited amount of surplus, the small company is restricted in the amount of business which it can write because of the necessity for maintaining a reasonable balance between surplus and written premium. By reinsuring a percentage of its entire writings, the company transfers that share of its writings of the reinsurer, thus per-

---

2. Whether the latter is true reinsurance is irrelevant here. From the standpoint of the underwriter, it is reinsurance and is considered as such in this text.

TABLE 4
Outline of Principal Reinsurance Provisions

	Pro Rata		Excess	
	Facultative	**Surplus Treaty**	**Individual**	**Catastrophe**
Names of typical Arrangements	Facultative agreements	1st Surplus Treaty, 2nd Surplus Treaty, etc.	Facultative Excess arrangements. Specific Excess arrangements	Catastrophe Excess Treaties
Lines usually applicable	Property	Property	Liability, some Property	All lines
Risks involved	Individual	Individual	Individual	Individual or Multiple
Obligatory upon Reinsurer	No	Yes	No	Yes
Premium	Pro rata of entire premium	Pro rata of entire premium	Specified rate or premium	Specified rate or premium
Contingency arrangements	Possible	Usually	No	Possible
Losses shared	Pro rata	Pro rata	Reinsurer pays only after retention is exceeded	Reinsurer pays only after retention is exceeded
Reinsurer pays its entire share of loss	Yes	Yes, but may use a deductible	Yes	No, usually pays only a stated percentage
Limitation on amount of reinsurer	None	Yes, usually stated as percentage of retention	None	Yes, as provided in treaties

mitting it to write more business. It should be noted that quota share reinsurance is considerably more profitable to the reinsurer than other types of pro rata reinsurance.

An underwriter is not concerned with quota share reinsurance because this is a type of treaty which is arranged by the reinsurance department, usually in cooperation with the financial executives of the company. Since the reinsurer shares in every risk, the process of reinsurance is handled by the accounting department with no reference to underwriters. (The latter may not even be aware of its existence.) As a matter of fact, the major reason quota share reinsurance is so profitable is that there is no possibility of selection against the reinsurer. The latter shares proportionately in a small residential contents policy or in the company's retention of a large commercial building.

Since there is no underwriting involvement with quota share reinsurance, it is not to be discussed further in this book. The following sections describe the other types of pro rata reinsurance, sometimes called participating reinsurance, which are an integral part of underwriting.

Types of Pro Rata Reinsurance

Two types of reinsurance arrangements are utilized: facultative and surplus treaties.

1. Facultative arrangements. When an underwriter wants to write a policy with an exposure larger than the desired retention, that underwriter can "shop around" for another underwriter who is willing to accept a portion of the risk. The first underwriter may offer a pro rata share of the risk to another company or to a reinsurer, which is not an uncommon practice. This is so informal a procedure that it may not even carry a title, but it is usually called "facultative reinsurance." More commonly, "facultative" refers to pre-arranged agreements about the general terms to which parties agree. This term is used most often with reinsurers, although facultative arrangements may be made among primary companies, too.

Although general agreements often are made, they are only in general terms. The word "facultative" means "optional." Each individual risk is offered by the primary company to the reinsurer, and may be accepted or not. Thus, a "facultative placement" is arranged on an individual basis for each risk. The primary company cannot bind the reinsurer. There is no limit to the maximum or minimum amount a reinsurer will accept, but the nature of the arrangement usually requires that the reinsurer accepts the entire risk above the company's retention if it accepts any. However, if the company customarily places portions of the risk with several companies and reinsurers (with several companies, several reinsurers, or an combination of them), and if it calls this "facultative," then the other party may limit the amount it will accept. The most important principle is that the reinsurer (or other company) always has the option of accepting or rejecting the risk and specifying its terms. The amount of coverage placed with the reinsurer is called the "ceded" amount, and the process of placing reinsurance is referred to as "cession."

The terms specified by the reinsurer on facultative placements always include the amount of commission given by the reinsurer to the primary company. Since the company will pay the entire amount of taxes and commission to the producer, and will incur all of the policywriting and premium collection expense, the reinsurer ordinarily will reimburse the compay for its pro rata share of these expenses; this reimbursement is called "reinsurance commission." If the reinsurer is not willing to pay that much, the company must (1) absorb the difference, (2) reduce its expenses, (3) seek another reinsurer, or (4) decline to write the risk. Sometimes the volume of placements becomes large enough that the reinsurer agrees to pay a contingent commission, meaning that it will pay additional amounts of reinsurance commission if the loss ratio on the reinsured portion falls below specified limits. A sliding scale of loss ratio contingent commissions may be employed.

The reinsurance commission may be large enough to allow for an additional amount above the company's actual expenses. In such a case, the company may be able to make a profit on the cession. The amount of the reinsurance commission depends upon the merits of the individual risk, so a company can make more profit on cessions if it offers good risks. The company may also make a profit on the cessions if its expenses are low.

2. Surplus Treaty. A surplus treaty accomplishes the same purpose as a facultative arrangement, but enables an underwriter to place reinsurance more quickly and with fewer complications. Surplus treaties are used when the volume of facultative placements becomes so large that individual discussion of each case becomes tedious, or when speed is needed in placing coverage.

A surplus treaty differs from a facultative arrangement in several respects. A formal treaty is used under surplus types, while a facultative arrangement seldom is formalized beyond informal agreements. The reinsurer under a surplus treaty is bound to accept each risk placed under the treaty, in contrast to a facultative reinsurer that has the option of acceptance or rejection under each case. Because of this mandatory provision, the surplus reinsurer receives only sketchy information about each risk, usually on a monthly list called "bordereau," while a facultative reinsurer is furnished many details about each risk before it is placed. A surplus treaty usually has a limitation on the amount of coverage that may be placed under it, often shown in realtionship to the company's retention, such as "ten times the retention but not more than $500,000." In contrast, the only limit on the amount of coverage under a facultative arrangement is the amount the reinsurer will accept. Finally, several surplus treaties may be used by a company: the first surplus treaty may accept up to $500,000, the second surplus treaty may accept up to $1,000,000, and so forth. Each treaty usually requires that the previous treaty be used to its limit before a placement is made under it. Once placed, however, each treaty is on a pro rata basis. Facultative arrangements may be placed in layers but this is uncommon.

In other ways, surplus treaties are similar to facultative arrangements. Both share the entire risk on a pro rata basis, after the reinsurance is placed. Neither requires the primary company to share in the reinsurer's portion of the loss, although surplus treaties occasionally use a deductible to avoid handling small losses where the handling expense is out of porportion to the size of the loss. Finally, both surplus treaties and facultative arrangements apply only to individual risks and almost exclusively to property lines.

Excess Reinsurance

Excess reinsurance may be used on any line of insurance, but it is the only type used on liability lines, generally. On property lines, it has long been used for catastrophe coverage, and it is becoming increasingly popular for individual lines.

Excess reinsurance pays only in the event loss exceeds a specified amount. Thus, it is the opposite of pro rata reinsurance. An excess reinsurance program provides that the primary company will pay each and every loss up to the limit of its retention; above that limit, and only then, does the excess reinsurance pay.

Types of Excess Reinsurance — Differences

Two types of excess reinsurance are used, as shown in Table 4. One applies only to individual risks. The other applies to multiple risks, which are defined as being catastrophes, although this type may also apply to some individual risks. While they are generally the same, there are differences:

1. Individual excess reinsurance. Some risks are larger or have higher limits of liability than an underwriter wishes to retain. The underwriter may seek another company to write the exposure above the retention, or the underwriter may use some type of agreement with a reinsurer under which the reinsurer will write the excess amount.

Two types of individual arrangements are used for excess placements. The first is *facultative.* It is similar to pro rata facultative, with the only difference being in the participation of the reinsurer: it shares proportionally in the entire risk under pro rata, and pays only when the loss exceeds the retention under excess arrangements. The primary insurer issues a policy to the insured for the entire amount requested, and the reinsurer agrees to pay the insurer all amounts above that retention. The insured may not even know about the existence of reinsurance, but looks to the primary company for the total amount.

This first type of arrangement may be used on property lines, instead of pro rata facultative. The handling is similar, with the major difference being in the participation of the reinsurer and, of course, the premium paid to the reinsurer. Its use is relatively rare on property lines, but is becoming more common; some reinsurers prefer this approach on certain risks. This type of reinsurance is commonly used on liability lines. Insureds generally prefer receiving only one policy and prefer looking to one company for reimbursement of losses, and they are quite unconcerned how the insurer handles its exposure.

The second type of excess reinsurance on individual risks is *specific excess.* Under this arrangement, the reinsurer actually issues a policy to the insured for the excess amount. The insured gets two policies: a primary policy for the first layer, and a secondary policy for the excess layer. Thus, this is not true reinsurance, but it is considered as such since it achieves the same purpose as reinsurance. This arrangement is used instead of facultative, in some instances, when the premium for the excess layer is less through use of a separate policy. It may also be used when the primary insurer does not wish to issue a policy for the full amount, even though a portion of it is reinsured, because of legal complications when policy limits must be revealed following certain types of claims.

When liability insurance is involved, both types of individual excess reinsurance are handled on a case basis. No treaties are used in most instances. The reinsurer evaluates each risk and makes a decision on acceptance. If accepted, the reinsurer specifies the rate or premium desired. Each case stands on its own with no treaties and no contingency commission arrangements, ordinarily. Informal agreements may be used, however, to specify the general types of risks to be submitted, and the procedures of handling applications and coverages. Some companies have even established automatic placement arrangements, but these are relatively uncommon and follow no set pattern.

2. Catastrophe excess reinsurance. Every line of insurance is subject to catastrophes. These are unusually large losses that ordinarily involve multiple risks. Examples are tornados, hurricanes, hail storms, floods, earthquakes, forest fires, and the like; these may involve damage to a large number or risks, each of which may be small. Automobiles and homes may average a loss of only $1,000 each in a catastrophe, but the aggregate may run in the millions of dollars.

Catastrophe excess reinsurance can also be used for an unexpected accumulation of losses from one risk. A contractor, for example, may be insured under a commercial liability policy and a workers' compensation policy, both in one company. The limits of exposure may fall within the insurer's retention. It is possible to conceive of a loss, however, when a large piece of equipment runs out of control, injuring many workers and members of the public. The aggregate loss for liability and workers' compensation could exceed the desired retention of the company; a catastrophe treaty could cover such an occurrence.

Still another use for a catastrophe excess treaty is as an alternative to pro rata reinsurance on large property risks. Instead of placing part of a large risk under a pro rata arrangement, the underwriter may use an excess reinsurance treaty. This almost always would be the same treaty as is used for multiple risks. Individual risks could be covered by the treaty on an automatic basis, with little or no information about each risk being given to the reinsurer. The same provisions apply as explained next. When the term "catastrophe reinsurance" is used, it is understood to include those single large property risks of companies using this arrangement instead of pro rata reinsurance.

Catastrophe reinsurance is *always* on a treaty basis. The rate or premium is specified in the treaty, and a contingency arrangement is rare but possible. Neither party has any choice in the placement of risks under the treaty, after the terms are settled. A major difference from other types of reinsurance is that no premium assignment of individual risks is made under catastrophe excess reinsurance. The reinsurer gets a flat amount of premium, or a rate that is applied to the aggregate premiums written by the company on the lines subject to the treaty. No identification is made of individual risks. Other than its knowledge of the general class of business written by the company, the reinsurer knows nothing about the characteristics or sizes of individual risks.

Catastrophe reinsurance often is placed in several layers, with each treaty covering only the excess above the company's retention any other treaties below it. Each treaty has an "attachment point" at which it becomes involved in the loss — this point occurring when the retention of the company is reached, plus any other treaties below it. Each treaty has a limit. The treaty, therefore, pays the loss above a certain amount (the attachment point) and up to its limit.

Catastrophe excess treaties seldom pay all of the loss within their layers. Rather, each treaty usually pays only 90 or 95% of the loss within its limit. The balance is paid by the company and is not reinsured. This arrangement keeps the company interested in avoiding catastrophic losses, since five or 10% of a loss involving several millions of dollars cannot be overlooked. In addition, this arrangement reduces the cost of reinsurance.

REINSURANCE PRACTICES — INDIVIDUAL RISKS

An underwriter usually may approach the reinsurance market in many ways, depending upon the circumstances of the risks involved. However, some insurers specify the details of the sequence in which reinsurance is to be applied and the limits of each. Even when the underwriter is free to use individual judgment, he or she will often follow the pattern that is subsequently described, because it is the most logical for most risks.

The first step is to determine the retention of the primary insurer. This is handled in the same fashion as was described earlier in this chapter. The next steps are different for the two major types of reinsurance.

Pro Rata Reinsurance

The second step for many property insurers is to use a surplus treaty. Some reinsurance arrangements have a first and a second surplus treaty; these are applied in layers, with the second treaty being used only if the amount of reinsurance exceeds the capacity of the first treaty, and then only for the excess amount.

The last step is to submit any excess above the surplus treaties to a facultative reinsurer.

Examples

As an illustration of a possible reinsurance arrangement for a large fire risk, assume that an application is offered with a total exposure at one location of $1,000,000. The underwriter has a retention of $50,000 and has two surplus treaties. The first treaty carries a maximum of $200,000 and the second treaty carries a maximum of $250,000. If a facultative reinsurer accepts $500,000 on this risk, the distribution is as follows.

	Amount of Exposure	Percentage of Exposure
Retention	$50,000	5%
First Surplus Treaty	200,000	20%
Second Surplus Treaty	250,000	25%
Facultative	500,000	50%
	$1,000,000	100%

Any loss, up to the full amount of $1,000,000, is shared in the proportions shown. Similarly, the premium is shared in the same percentages. However, the amount received by the primary insurer from the reinsurers may differ, because of differences in the ceding commission, which is that amount paid by the reinsurer to cover expenses and perhaps to furnish a profit to the insurer. Surplus treaties often have contingent commission arrangements under which a book of business (cessions) which is profitable to the reinsurer will result in payment of additional commissions to the ceding insurer. These arrangements are most common with first surplus treaties but may be used on any treaty. Facultative reinsurance does not have such a contingent provision oridinarily, since each cession is expected to stand on its own merits. Some type of contingent arrangement is possible, however. Terms of contingent provisions are usually more liberal on first surplus treaties because the volume of cessions is larger than on other treaties. For this reason, underwriters try to use these treaties as much as possible.

Pro rata reinsurance is placed in layers. The first surplus treaty ordinarily must be used to its maximum before the second is used, and facultative is seldom used until the treaties have been filled to capacity. In the previous example, a $100,000 risk would have a 50% retention and 50% in the first surplus treaty; a $300,000 risk would have a retention of $50,000, $200,000 in the first surplus treaty, and $50,000 in the second surplus treaty. However, once the cessions are made, each insurer shares in the entire risk on the basis of the percentage determined by the cessions on that risk; even small losses are shared among all of the insurers.

Excess Reinsurance

Excess reinsurance is the other type of placement used by an underwriter to spread large exposures among other insurers. It is an arrangement under which the primary insurer pays all losses up to its retention limit, and the reinsurer then pays the remaining portion of the losses up to its limit. This type of reinsurance is used almost exclusively by casualty underwriters. However, it is sometimes used by property underwriters and is becoming more popular, although pro rata reinsurance is still used for most property lines.

The procedure under facultative excess reinsurance is similar to that used under pro rata reinsurance. The underwriter issues one policy for the full limits desired, and then places the limits above the retention with the reinsurer. On the other hand, specific excess reinsurance requires the reinsurer to issue a separate policy for its share of the coverage.

The major difference under excess reinsurance lies in the fact that the reinsurer does not become involved in a loss, unless and until the loss exceeds the retention of the primary insurer. There is no sharing of small losses; the primary insurer pays all losses up to its limit and the reinsurer then becomes involved.

It is less common to use several layers of reinsurance for excess reinsurance than for pro rata reinsurance. While a liability reinsurer usually writes the entire excess amount above the retention of the insurer, risks with high liability limits may be reinsured in layers, with a portion of the premium being assigned to each layer.

For an example of excess reinsurance on a specific risk, assume that the policy is written with a liability limit of $5,000,000. The underwriter retains the first $100,000 and the first layer of reinsurance may not exceed $1,000,000. If a second layer of excess reinsurance were used to cover the exposure, the reinsurance would be as follows.

	Limit of Liability
Retention	$100,000
First excess layer	1,000,000
Second excess layer	3,900,000

Any loss up to $100,000 would be paid entirely by the insurer writing the policy, and every amount above $100,000 up to $1,100,000 would be paid by the reinsurer. A loss of $1,000,000 would be shared by the insurer ($100,000) and the first reinsurer ($900,000). Only if the loss exceeds $1,100,000 would the second reinsurer become involved and then only for the excess. The second reinsurer pays a maximum of $3,900,000 in this example (the total insurance protection is $5,000,000.)

Since recoveries under excess reinsurance are on an excess basis, the higher limits carry greatly reduced rates. The layer retained will be used for many more losses for two reasons: (1) most losses are relatively small, and (2) every large loss must exhaust the retention limit before involving reinsurance. In the previous example, the premium for the $100,000 retained limit might well exceed that for the top layer of $3,900,000. The amount of premium paid to each reinsurer will be determined by negotiation. Some of these placements are handled under treaties, but more of them are arranged by agreement between the insurer and reinsurer. A greater area of judgment is used in placing excess reinsurance than in pro rata reinsurance; in the latter type, the reinsurer simply gets the same proportion of the premium as it shares in losses. In excess reinsurance, it is a matter of judgment how often and how severe a loss will be large enough to involve the reinsurer. Obviously, the excess reinsurance seldom will become involved, but when it is, the loss can be large. Accordingly, the excess reinsurer must establish minimum premium to be sure that it receives enough premium for the rate, but costly, large loss.

Excess reinsurance is arranged by the insurer. The usual practice followed is for the producer to submit an application for the entire limit of liability desired. If the insurer wishes to retain only a portion of the liability, the underwriter ordinarily handles the contact with a reinsurer in obtaining either a facultative excess arrangement or a specific excess policy. Then the underwriter can quote a combined premium for the entire limit.

Methods of Placement

Several different methods of placing pro rata and excess reinsurance are now apparent. These are illustrated in Table 5.

1. If the underwriter writes only the retention and lets the policyholder (or the producer) secure a separate policy, the coverage is almost always on a pro rata basis. The insured, therefore, gets more than one policy.

2. If the underwriter places the reinsurance on a facultative (or surplus treaty) basis, the insured gets only one policy and may be unaware of the existence of the reinsurance.

TABLE 5
Comparison of Handling
Large Amounts of Insurance

Type	Arranged By	Basis	Name	Policies To Insured
1. Write retention only	Applicant or producer	Pro rata	Separate policies	Two or more
2. Facultative	Underwriter	Pro rata or Excess	Facultative Surplus, or Facultative Excess	One
3. Specific Excess	Underwriter	Excess	Specific Excess	Two or more

3. If the underwriter secures a specific excess policy, the underwriter handles the entire transaction, but the insured gets more than one policy.

There may be situations when an insured prefers only one policy. On the other hand, the use of facultative reinsurance on an excess basis may be more expensive than writing separate policies. When a cession is made under a facultative arrangement, the ceding company will want to recover its costs, and these may be higher than for a specific excess policy. Commissions to producers may be higher under insurance written by primary insurers than under a specific excess policy, too.

The offsetting advantages and disadvantages of these methods of handling large risks demonstrate that neither plan is preferred for all risks. Some applicants are covered more efficiently and economically under two or more policies. Others are more economically insured under one policy for the entire amount—letting the insurer secure reinsurance above its retention. Both methods are important to the underwriter, because they permit some flexibility while guaranteeing the ability to limit the exposure to an amount which can be retained safely.

The underwriter for a primary insurer handles the placements with a reinsurer. When these placements are on an individual, non-treaty basis, the underwriter is usually instructed by the insurer about the reinsurers which may be used. Within broad outlines, the underwriter usually has the authority to negotiate terms with the reinsurer.

A reinsurance underwriter follows the same general principles and practices as a primary underwriter. In other words, the reinsurance underwriter selects risks from those offered and accepts or rejects any risk. The underwriter classifies the risks, applies rates determines the forms. The reinsurer generally follows the primary insurance on forms and coverages, but not on rates. The reinsurer will charge the primary underwriter a rate, in one fashion or another, and the reinsurance underwriter tries to negotiate a rate that is acceptable.

The purpose of reinsuring part of a risk is to secure needed capacity and not a device for "dumping" undesirable business on a reinsurer. The primary underwriter must protect the reinsurance market by giving the reinsurer some good risks, as well as some poor ones. An insurer may insure all of a person's business, and then be asked to insure the "hot-rod" that the teen-age son has purchased. Or a businessman may open a new location in an undesirable area, or acquire a new subsidiary in a non-preferred type of business. Since the underwriter who accepts such business should be able to retain all of the undesirable exposures, an attempt should be made to restrict the policy to the retention. If forced to write a larger exposure, the underwriter may have to secure reinsurance; this should be done very rarely and only with full explanation to the reinsurer. A good reinsurance market is too valuable for an underwriter to jeopardize with a few poor risks.

Most reinsurance treaties are written with professional reinsurance companies, as are many facultative placements. However, some insurers place risks with other primary insurance companies, thus spreading the risk and achieving a degree of reciprocity. Most reinsurance with professional reinsurers was placed in Lloyds of London for many years. However, within the past several decades, United States companies have aggressively sought reinsurance, and now write a sizeable share of the premium volume.

REINSURANCE PRACTICES – CATASTROPHE PROTECTION

No matter how carefully an underwriter limits the retention or individual risks, there is always the possibility of loss involving two or more risks. These are called "multiple risk" losses, to distinguish them from single-risk losses. If they are large enough, they are called "catastrophes."

A catastrophe is a multiple risk loss of such magnitude that it causes the insurer concern. Naturally, the size of loss that qualifies as a catastrophe will vary by insurer. A $200,000 loss may be a catastrophe to one company, while another may not apply that term to any loss below $500,000. On an industry-wide basis, any loss over $1,000,000 is usually considered to be catastrophe.

Catastrophes may be the sum of a number of retentions, but entirely different considerations are used for retentions and catastrophes. Even when an underwriter knows that there is a good possibility of a catastrophe loss, the maximum retention can be retained on each individual risk. In extreme catastrophe areas, however, the specified retention per risk may be lower, but this is seldom the approach used by insurers. Rather the underwriter applies the normal retention, regardless of location. To do otherwise would limit the retention so severely that it would be difficult to realize a profit on any book of business.

An underwriter will retain the maximum amount of loss that he or she is willing to assume on that risk. It is obvious then, that if several risks are involved in a loss, the total loss may be greater than the underwriter wishes to bear.

Catastrophe Reinsurance

The solution is to purchase catastrophe reinsurance. This type of reinsurance is always written on an *excess* basis. The primary insurer pays the entire loss until the attachment point of reinsurance is reached. The reinsurer then pays the loss above that amount until its own limits are exhausted; sometimes the reinsurer pays the whole loss, but more commonly it pays only a percentage of the loss. The percentage, ordinarily 90 or 95%, is applied to the amount of loss above the attachment point; the loss above that point is determined and the reinsurer pays its percentage of that loss, with the insurer keeping the remainder without reinsurance.

Catastrophe reinsurance is commonly written in layers. Each one becomes effective when the previous layer is exhausted. The catastrophe reinsurance program for a fire insurance company might look like the following:

Retention:	$200,000
First Treaty:	90% of the next $500,000 over $200,000
Second Treaty:	95% of the next $1,000,000 over $700,000
Third Treaty:	95% of the next $3,300,000 over $1,700,000

This insurer would thus have reinsurance protection up to a loss of $5,000,000. The insurer would pay its retention plus its percentage share of each layer and the reinsurer would pay the balance.

Property underwriters are aware constantly of the catastrophe loss possibility. Buildings and personal property are susceptible to severe multiple risk losses from a multitude of perils: fire, riot, windstorm, tornado, hurricane, and many more. Since no area is immune from one or more of these perils, there are few, if any, property insurers that do not carry catastrophe reinsurance.

Liability insurers are not as susceptible to catastrophe losses. It is quite rare for such losses to occur, but the possibility is always present. The building owner and the tenant might each be insured in one company and both could be held liable for a large loss. A similar situation could occur when both the lessor and lessee of a truck or other equipment become involved in a loss. A situation could arise even in personal lines when both the owner of an automobile and the driver are held liable, and both may be insured in one company. There is no means of predicting such occurrences and no method to prevent a severe loss other than by purchasing excess reinsurance. For these reasons liability insurers carry such reinsurance to protect against these losses.

The cost of catastrophe reinsurance could be prohibitive for a liability insurer, if it were purchased alone. The losses are few in number but large in size, so the reinsurer needs to accumulate substantial premium in order to pay the rare losses which do occur. However, all liability insurers carry excess treaties to protect against large single-risk losses, as was explained previously. Hence it is logical and economical to combine catastrophe protection with a single-risk exposure in one excess treaty. This is common practice for liability insurers.

Those property insurers that protect against large single-risk losses by an excess treaty may also extend that treaty to cover catastrophe losses. There need be no dividing line between these types of losses; the reinsurer (or reinsurers) pays losses in excess of the specified retention, whether it is caused by one or many risks.

Property insurers using pro rata reinsurance on individual risks are *forced* to purchase excess reinsurance to protect against catastrophes. This results in a more complicated reinsurance program, but that is all. Catastrophe reinsurance is expensive enough and the exposure is common enough that treaties may be purchased without loss of efficiency, unlike liability insurance. When both pro rata and catastrophe excess reinsurance are used on property lines, only the retained amounts are covered by the excess treaties; the amounts ceded to pro rata reinsurers are disregarded in computing the retention and payments under the catastrophe reinsurance.

Catastrophe reinsurance is purchased by the staff of the insurer. The line underwriter is not involved directly in its negotiations. However, the general provisions of treaties should be known by underwriters. Many times, they are able to take steps that will minimize the exposure under the treaties, which in turn will result in lower reinsurance costs. For example, a personal lines fire underwriter may limit acceptance to a certain number or percentage of risks in a tract of homes located in a known catastrophe area, such as a tornado area or a forest fire exposure.

"Block limits" is a device used by commercial fire underwriters to limit their catastrophe exposure. Under this system, the underwriters accept the usual retention under the "line limit." Each acceptance is then recorded on a map or other document. A limit is set on the maximum exposure written within each block or other area; perhaps a subdivision is used, or a valley in a grass fire area. When the total insurance written in a block or other specified area reaches the limit, the underwriters will accept no further insurance in that area. This device is used quite commonly in fire insurance. It limits the maximum probable loss during any one catastrophe. However, there is always the possibility of a major catastrophe which could involve many blocks, so the use of block limits does not remove the need for catastrophe reinsurance. An effective block limit program will reduce the exposure to catastrophe losses, thus reducing the cost of excess reinsurance.

Line underwriters do not need to know the details of catastrophe reinsurance treaties either. The rates and treaty dates are quite unimportant to them. However, they must know the attachment point, the limits of the reinsurance and any exclusions in the treaty. Underwriters must operate within the framework of their approved retentions and the reinsurance their companies use, and must be careful not to overexpose the treaties by indiscriminate acceptance of risks on the theory that reinsurance will take care of any possible problems.

Underwriters also have the responsibility of suggesting changes in reinsurance. If they become aware that a sizeable exposure to the company is building up in a specific area, they should call this situation to the attention of their supervisors. Insurers may wish to secure special catastrophe protection, or to increase their limit under existing treaties. On the other hand, it may wish to instruct underwriters to restrict further writings in that area.

QUESTIONS FOR DISCUSSION

1. Given the fact that an underwriter accepts an above average risk, why is it still necessary for the underwriter to be knowledgeable about a company's liability or line limits?
2. Explain with an example, the significant differences between probable maximum loss and possible maximum loss.
3. In fire insurance parlance, the term "amount subject" is an important consideration to the underwriter. What is it?
4. Define the term "reinsurer," and its purpose, in general.
5. (a) What is the purpose of pro rata reinsurance?

   (b) In what circumstances are facultative and specific excess treaties involved?

   (c) Explain the procedures for handling an individual risk subject to facultative and treaty reinsurance.

   (d) Compare the similarities and differences between facultative and treaty reinsurance.
6. (a) For what line of insurance is excess reinsurance primarily used on individual risks?

   (b) Why is excess reinsurance unlikely to be used for property risks?

   (c) What is the purpose of catastrophe excess reinsurance?

   (d) Why can treaty, more so than facultative, reinsurance serve to the detriment of the reinsurer?

INTRODUCTION TO PART IV

BASIC FACTORS IN SELECTION

Underwriters perform their work, not on classes or groups of policies but on individual policies — that is, they underwrite one policy at a time. Part III is devoted to explaining the basic functions performed by underwriters and Parts V and VI describe how these functions are applied to individual policies. But before those basic functions can be applied to each line or type of policy, it is important to know what the underwriter is seeking. Little benefit is derived in selecting risks, classifying and rating them, applying policies and forms, and carefully handling retentions and reinsurance, unless the basic factors to be considered are understood. These other functions are necessary, of course, and must be learned thoroughly in order to qualify an apprentice as an underwriter.

The real question, however, is this: What is the underwriter seeking? Or, to put it another way, what factors are weighed by the underwriter when evaluating a risk? The answer is: there are a number of hazards which must be considered in every risk, regardless of the line of insurance being handled. These hazards are increased chances of loss, and to overlook them is to ignore a basic purpose of underwriting: to secure a profitable book of business.

It seems essential to pause before analyzing the separate lines of insurance and applying the basic functions, to studying these hazards. The separate lines of insurance could not have been analyzed at any time prior to the discussion of the basic functions in Part III because the actual practices followed by underwriters in identifying and controlling these hazards had not been previously discussed. At the same time, each of these hazards should be studied along with the discussion of each separate line of insurance, if not presented first, because these are the most important factors which underwriters must consider in the selection process. For these reasons the basic hazards are discussed in this part.

After this detailed analysis of the basic hazards, the hazards will be mentioned in later parts only as matters of reference, or where a particular problem exists. It is important to note, however, that they underlie every consideration of an underwriter.

Hazards are factors which contribute to uncertainty. There are many types of hazards, but they may be grouped into these four general categories.

1. *Moral hazard — caused by the personal acts of individuals.*
2. *Morale hazard — caused by the indifference of individuals.*
3. *Physical hazard — caused by objective material factors.*
4. *Legal hazard — caused by the operation of laws.*

These categories are discussed in the chapters which form this part.[1]

Underwriting deals in uncertainties. If an underwriter dealt only in statistics, such as might be the case if all available risks were written and the law of large numbers was relied upon to keep the book of business profitable, underwriting would be a dull, routine job. In reality, underwriting is an interesting, challenging task because many factors may contribute to uncertainty. The real contest involves discovery, evaluation, and control of hazards.

These hazards apply to all types of policies and may be viewed as permeating all kinds of risks and overriding other considerations. If severe enough, hazards must be controlled before the underwriter can consider other factors.

1. Some writers would add a fifth type: the environmental hazard. This is defined by the Urban Property Protection and Reinsurance Act of 1968 as "any hazardous condition that might give rise to loss under an insurance contract, but which is beyond the control of the property owner." The reference is to a greater possibility of loss from such perils as burglary and arson because of the characteristics of the neighborhood in which the property is located. This hazard is not yet defined well enough to be of much help to the underwriter, and the attempt to apply it can conflict with the current prohibitions against "redlining." In recent years, bombings which are politically or socially inspired have occurred, but more often in the best and most prestigious buildings, not in the slums. Perhaps social forces will generate a new type of hazard classification in the future, if it can be sufficiently identified to be of assistance to the underwriter.

15

Moral Hazard

Moral hazard is the increase in uncertainty caused by personal acts of indivduals. These acts may contribute to the probability or severity of loss, or both, and the individual creating the problem may be the policyholder or another person; the chance of loss is increased in any case.

Of all types of hazards, moral hazards are the most difficult to detect and, yet, may be the most dangerous. It is almost impossible to discover the thoughts of another person, certainly within the limited scope of investigation available to most underwriters. At the same time, it is obvious that any premium which equals less than the full value of the property will be insufficent if the insured plans to deliberately destroy the property.

Moral hazard may be present in every line of insurance. No underwriter can ignore it without incurring an increased chance of substantial loss. In spite of this universal and potential severity, its true nature is seldom understood. For this reason, its characteristics must be reviewed before an underwriter can consider the means available to guard against this hazard.

TYPES OF MORAL HAZARD

At its worst, moral hazard is synonymous with "moral turpitude." Such a term brings to mind such words as baseness, vileness, depravity and wickedness. This type of moral hazard is applied to policyholders who deliberately cause losses; for example, setting fire to buildings or automobiles; conspiring with thieves to steal cargo-laden trucks; making false entries in accounts in order to justify claims for nonexistent property.

Some underwriters think only of this type when they use the term "moral hazard." Based on such thinking, it is obvious that the resulting principle would be this: "It is impossible to underwrite against the moral hazard." It is indeed impossible to secure enough premium or to apply enough safeguards to protect the insurer against a policyholder who intends to attempt to defraud the insurer by deliberately destroying the property or misrepresenting the facts. Most types of moral hazard are not of this type. There are many cases when the mental attitude of the policyholder has increased the hazard, without any thought of a deliberate act. The underwriter must be alert to the possibility of these factors being present before comtemplating the taking of corrective action. The following are some of the common types of moral hazard.

Lack of Insurable Interest

A situation when the policyholder would profit from destruction of the property is when that person lacks an insurable interest in the property. There are cases when the ownership of property is less desirable than the proceeds from insurance. One example is an out-dated building situated in a business area with a high concentration of business and a shortage of parking space. The owner might receive rent from tenants, but could receive more if the building were razed and the land used as a parking lot. Under such circumstances, there is a great temptation to actually start a fire, or at least to avoid taking steps to prevent one.

Another example is the person who is unable to meet the payments on a loan and is faced with foreclosure and the resulting loss of the property. This situation occurs more frequently with vehicles, but situations may arise under many other conditions. The policyholder may be threatened by actual physical harm if payments cannot be met. The property may not be saleable at a price high enough to repay the loan; this is frequently the case with new vehicles that depreciate faster in the first few months than the loan payments reduce the principal. Even if the property has a high enough value to cover the loan, the policyholder may fear a deterioration in credit rating if the property is foreclosed or repossessed. When any of these conditions exist, there may be a temptation to "sell the property to the insurance company" by means of a total loss. In fact, many vehicle fires which occur along lonely stretches of roads are believed to be caused by just such circumstances.

Record of Questionable Acts

A basic tenet of underwriting is that the future can be foretold by the past. Many underwriting decisions are based upon the assumption that the record of the past will continue into the future. When an underwriter looks at the character of an applicant, the assumption is made that the character will not change in the future. Thus, if an applicant has resorted to questionable acts, perhaps subterfuge, in order to achieve goals in the past, it is likely that it will happen again in the future.

The most obvious example is an applicant who has had one or more questionable insurance claims. Arson is difficult to prove and allowances must be made for coincidences in order to avoid pre-judging a person. However, a record of several questionable losses should alert an underwriter to carefully check into the character of the applicant.

The record of questionable noninsurance transactions in the past should also provide a clue to the character of the applicant. An underwriter should be on the alert when learning of such past occurrences as conviction of receiving stolen goods, tax actions involving attempts at defrauding the government, and bankruptcies which hint at attempts to profit at the expense of others. Since a person who would be involved in any such activity might attempt to defraud the insurance company, the underwriter must watch for evidence of this moral hazard.

Poor Business Reputation

There is a fine line, perhaps an indistinguishable line, between actions that are illegal and those that are "sharp business practices." A person may avoid illegal transactions, but still have an unsavory business reputation. Perhaps that person constantly searches for technical loopholes to avoid an unprofitable business arrangement, rather than honor the intent of an agreement. Such a person might even repudiate contracts, secure in the belief that other parties do not wish to pursue legal remedies, possibly because the value of the contract does not justify the expense.

An unethical person can avoid violating any laws, but remains a poor person with whom to transact business because suppliers, employees, and customers often lose at his hands. The insurance underwriter must be extra careful because providing insurance is based on mutual trust and an applicant who is unethical in business dealings will often be a poor insurance prospect.

Evasion of Responsibilities

There are some who take steps to avoid responsibilities. The most common example is a person who puts the title to property in a spouse's name. There may be legitimate reasons for this type of arrangement but there are other cases when this practice is highly questionable. The inference is that this action will remove the property from a position where it could be used to satisfy business creditors. A businessperson who will go to such lengths to evade responsibilities is either unethical or is in a shaky financial condition, or both; either should be sufficient cause for an underwriter to exercise extreme caution.

Revenge

Property is sometimes damaged or destroyed as a means of securing revenge for a real or fancied wrong. An employee who is discharged may decide to "get even" by setting fire to the employer's property. A person who has been held in a prison or mental institution may also set a fire as a means of revenge for alleged unjust deprivation of freedom. In labor disputes, striking employees sometimes burn the homes and cars of strikebreakers. Acts of these types are difficult to predict in advance. Any hint at threats of this type should be investigated carefully; the threat may be real and would obviously increase the chance of loss.

Rebellion Against Social or Economic Conditions

Some types of property, under certain conditions are susceptible to deliberate acts of destruction. One example is the threat of damage during a strike; the striking employees may riot and set fire to property of their employer. Another example is the threat of damage to schools and other public property by rebellious students and political activists. Schools and public property were considered to be preferred property business for many years, but rioting, bombing and vandalism became so severe at the end of the 1960s that this class had difficulty in getting coverage at any price. The situation illustrated vividly the increase in losses that can be caused by a relatively small number of people who engage in deliberate acts of destruction. Underwriters must be constantly alert for conditions under which this type of moral hazard may develop. Changes can occur rapidly, requiring underwriters to adapt to new situations.

Cover For Crimes

Some fires are deliberately set in hopes that the evidence of a crime will be destroyed. Sometimes these acts involve outsiders, where the crime is burglary or even murder. Others involve employees or even the owner, with the crimes being embezzlement or tax evasion. Where conditions exist breeding such acts, it is obvious that the moral hazard is greatly increased.

Mental Instability

Persons with mental problems sometimes deliberately start fires. Pyromaniacs have a mental quirk which leads them to start fires for the pleasure that they derive from the flames and excitement: there is seldom any pattern to their acts, making discovery and prediction exceedingly difficult.

Mental instability can also lead to other types of losses. Individuals have been identified who deliberately throw themselves in front of moving vehicles, and fake serious injuries.

UNDERWRITING AGAINST MORAL HAZARDS

Underwriters must be alert constantly for the presence of moral hazards, and must take some action to offset the increased losses which would otherwise result when moral hazards are present. There is no line of insurance which is immune, so every underwriter must be always watchful for evidences of moral hazards. A successful underwriter is one who is alert at all stages of the underwriting process for evidences of this important problem.

Underwriting against moral hazards starts with obtaining information and interpreting it; this process is ordinarily performed concurrently with the same operations conducted for other underwriting processes. If a moral hazard is found which is too severe, the underwriter must decline or cancel the insurance. Otherwise, limitations are placed in the policy in order to control the hazard; usually these are limitations on recovery or exclusions of specified property. Related to these policy provisions but in a slightly different category are deductibles; these are often used to help control moral hazards. In practice, some policy conditions, as well as some deductibles, are used on policies *before* a moral hazard is discovered, perhaps to avoid an undiscovered hazard which can be disastrous, or as a means upon which to add specific restrictions. Finally, rate adjustments are sometimes used by underwriters as a means of offsetting the adverse effects of moral hazards. Each of these underwriting processes is discussed separately in the following pages.

Securing Information

The first step in any underwriting process is to secure facts. As they are secured, the information is used for various purposes. One of these purposes is to discover moral hazards. Thus, the underwriter seldom starts out by securing information which will reveal the existence or extent of a moral hazard. Rather, as the information gathered for such other purposes as eligibility, acceptability, rate classification, and reinsurance is looked at, the underwriter is alert for possible moral hazards.

When an underwriter discovers evidence of a moral hazard, it must be acted upon immediately. Sometimes the information contained in the original source document may give sufficient facts upon which to base a decision for action. At other times, more information may be requested in order to get further details to substantiate or negate suspicions, or to be certain that there is no mistake. Thus, every source of information available to an underwriter may be helpful in discovering moral hazards. These sources are discussed in detail elsewhere in this book[1] but some of them are mentioned here, with emphasis on the ability to reveal moral hazards.

1. *Application.* Many clues to moral hazards may be contained in the application. Previous losses, previous business experience, the person in whose name title is held, and many other clues may be revealed by use of the proper questions. If an inspection by the producer is required at the time the application is submitted, further clues may be found, such as evidence of poor housekeeping or poor business practices.

2. *Inspection reports.* The underwriter usually can use several types of inspection reports. Some may relate solely to classifications for rating purposes while others may relate to the physical conditions of premises. Another type is usually available for individuals and small businesses — one that includes comments about possible moral hazards.

3. *Special services.* Publications are available indicating business stability, ability of management, and the business reputation of most concerns. The most widely used service is *Dun and Bradstreet.*

4. *Local sources.* Important information may be obtained from books and other local sources, as well as from competitors and customers. The persons with whom a firm or an individual does business often can supply helpful information. Contracts can be made by special requests to inspection agencies or producers, or such company personnel as engineers may be utilized.

5. *Trade bureaus.* Some insurers maintain bureaus which accumulate the names of persons who have been involved in questionable claims. One bureau lists convicted arsonists plus those who have made claims under suspicious circumstances or have presented exorbitant or inflated claims. Another bureau maintains records on all automobile thefts, permitting identification of those repeaters who present many claims under similar circumstances.

6. *Motor vehicle records.* Most states maintain records of driving performances of licensed drivers in the state. These records are usually available to insurers, as to others, and can reveal the past accident and citation record of drivers.

7. *Claims reports.* As a claim is being investigated, the adjuster may encounter suspected moral hazards. Suspicions may be aroused by many factors of the claim

---

1.See Chapter 6 and each chapter in Part V.

and the actions of the policyholder. This report can be very helpful to the underwriter and should be considered as a valuable source of information.

8. *Engineering reports.* For some lines of insurance, engineering reports are needed. These reports are designed primarily for information about physical conditions, but an engineer (more often now called a loss prevention specialist) might find indications of a moral hazard which should be reported to the underwriter. The underwriter is then in a position to investigate further, although the engineer can discover and mention the apparent existence of problems.

9. *Producers recommendations.* The recommendations of the producer are always important to an underwriter. Sometimes the recommendation is furnished with the application while at times, the underwriter may point out to the producer the indications of a moral hazard, asking for a specific recommendation. The recommendations of a producer will be weighed differently, depending upon the profitability of the producer and the degree to which reliable opinions have been demonstrated. While final decision must lie in the hands of the underwriter, a strong recommendation from a profitable and dependable producer will have considerable influence.

Interpreting Information

From those sources just discussed, an underwriter can develop a great deal of information about the moral hazard of an applicant. Obviously, not every source is used on every applicant, but indications of possible trouble are watched for as the facts received for other purposes are reviewed. Then other sources may be used to get enough information to make an intelligent decision on the moral hazard.

As this information is reviewed, the underwriter will study the character of the applicant, keeping in mind the basic premise that a person will ordinarily act in the same manner in the future as in the past. Some of the important facets of the applicant's character are these.

1. *Personal habits.* A police record, a history of gambling, questionable associates, and similar factors must be viewed with caution by an underwriter. A preferred applicant is one who lives in a well-maintained home in an area where there is pride of ownership and a low rate of crime.

2. *Stability.* An important factor is the stability of the applicant. The underwriter looks at the employment record, how often the applicant moves from one residence to another, and the record of bill paying.

3. *Claims consciousness.* Some policyholders believe that insurance should pay for every loss they suffer, no matter how small. In some cases, the claims are questionable; the facts appear to be twisted in bringing loss within the scope of coverage. In other cases, claims may be legitimate but of such minor nature that they are really maintenance losses, not those for which insurance was designed. And, in still other cases, the frequency of claims is so great that it raises serious questions about moral hazard.

4. *Business risks.* All of these factors apply to a business because a business is run by individuals. There are other factors that must be watched in a business,

however. Housekeeping is one, and it concerns the cleanliness of the building and surrounding area, the maintenance of equipment and the safeguards used on machinery. Other factors are the way the books are kept, the regularity in which bills are paid, the relationship with employees, the business reputation of the applicant, and other such items.

As the underwriter studies the character of the applicant, he makes his decision about acceptability. If the moral hazard is too great, the insurance must be declined. If the moral hazard appears to be slight, the risk may be accepted without qualification. On the other risks, the underwriter must attempt to make adjustments that qualify the risk, as is explained in the next sections.

Employing Policy Provisions

The most common method of controlling moral hazard is through the use of policy provisions. Some of these protective provisions are printed in the basic policies and, thus, are a defense against the undiscovered moral hazards, as well as those which have been discovered. Other provisions are added by the underwriter to meet the circumstances of specific cases.

Provisions printed in the basic policies must be familiar to the underwriter. There is a tendency among some underwriters to ignore these policy provisions under the assumption that they are of importance only to the claims adjuster. Actually, each underwriter should be fully aware of these provisions in the type of policy being underwritten, since only in this way can it be known that certain minor moral hazards are controlled effectively. Without this knowledge, the underwriter may feel that the risk must be declined, or that some means of revising the policy to add needed safeguards must be found. Even worse, the uninformed underwriter may be under the impression that a certain hazard is controlled by a policy provision, whereas a careful reading may reveal that the provision is so worded that is does not exclude the particular situation intended.

The existence of these policy provisions that protect against some moral hazards should remove a considerable degree of worry or concern from an underwriter's shoulders. Obviously, it is less important to discover problem areas if the contract furnishes automatic protection to the underwriter. However, this actually presents more of a danger than a safeguard, for the underwriter might not worry about moral hazards. Then, a hazard which is beyond the scope of the policy provisions can be disregarded. In addition, even if the policy appears to exclude certain areas, a loss can cause serious claim difficulties and can result in an unexpected loss. For all of these reasons, it is essential that the underwriter be familiar with the policy provisions, and that every moral hazard discovered be weighed against these provisions. Only in this way can it be certain that intelligent underwriting has been applied to every moral hazard encountered.

Kinds of Common Provisions

These built-in policy provisions are generally quite similar among the policies used for the various lines of insurance. There are differences, and each underwriter should be familiar with those used. In the following discussion, the most common of these provisions are discussed, without any attempt to specify the differences among policies.

1. Fraud and misrepresentation — The entire policy is void if the applicant commits *fraud* in securing insurance or *wilfully misrepresents* or *conceals* any material fact or circumstance concerning insurance. An applicant can find the policy void at inception if a driving record is wilfully misrepresented, or a past history of burglaries on the premises has been concealed, or the ownership of the property has fraudulently been mistated. In each case, the fraudulent act must be material to the insurance purchased, before the coverage can be rescinded.

2. Title — The exact *title* to property must be revealed to the insurer, including any encumbrances. Furthermore, the policy may not be assigned to a new purchaser of the property without the written consent of the insurer. An applicant may not conceal a mortgage on the property; this is an important item in underwriting the moral hazard, and can be considered a material concealment, thus voiding the policy. Furthermore a policyholder may not secretly transfer title and insurance to another party; the underwriter must have an opportunity to secure information about each insured.

3. Cancellation — The insurer retains the right to *cancel* the insurance, with specified advance notice to the policyholder, without giving any reason for its action. Some moral hazards develop after the insurance is written, or are not discovered until late, and it is extremely helpful to an underwriter to be able to retire from the risk on short notice. If there is evidence that the policyholder intended to defraud the insurance company, but there is no absolute proof available, the underwriter could be sued for libel or defamation of character if this was stated as the reason for cancellation. It is valuable, therefore, not to be required to reveal the reason for the action.

This particular provision on cancellation is being superseded by laws that are enacted in many states. The laws restrict the right of the insurer to cancel the policy except for reasons specified in the laws, and they often require the insurer to give the reason to the policyholder. To the extent that these laws restrict the right of the insurer to cancel policies when moral hazards are present, they will interfere with the performance of the underwriter's duties. The underwriter who is faced with such laws must adopt other defences against moral hazards.

4. Reporting loss — The policyholder must give prompt written notice to the insurer of every loss and must provide a signed proof of loss upon request. A dishonest applicant may apply for insurance after a loss has occurred, and may delay the report until it is difficult to ascertain all of the facts. This policy provision prevents delayed reporting, and warns the policyholder that any false claim can lead to prosecution.

5. Settlement of loss — The insurer retains the right to repair the damaged property, to take it at an appraised price, or to replace it with other property of like kind and quality. A policyholder may find that a car is a "lemon," or that the land is worth more without a building on it, or that equipment is obsolete; the "solution" to this problem might be to arrange a loss and hope to receive cash from the insurance company, thus making a profit in both directions. A person will be less inclined to take such a step, however, upon learning that the insurer may elect to repair

or replace the damaged property, leaving the insured nothing better than before the loss.

6. Exclusion of certain property — The existence of some types of property is very difficult to prove after a loss. For example, after a fire a policyholder could allege that a large sum of money was on the premises and was destroyed in the flames, and an insurer would find it difficult to prove or disprove both the existence and amount of such property. A dishonest policyholder, therefore, could claim a loss for a large sum of money or of similar property, and could be successful in some cases. To prevent such problems, it is common for property policies to exclude such items as money, currency, securities, accounts, bills, deeds, evidences of debt, bullion, and manuscripts. Even when such property is not excluded, it is usually limited; an example is a limitation of $100 on money or $500 in securities.

7. Increase in hazard — A problem of constant concern to an underwriter is the possibility that the hazard will be substantially increased after the investigation is concluded. For example, an underwriter may accept a certain building if it is occupied by an office, but may reject it if the occupancy were a restaurant or a dynamite manufacturer. Of equal importance, but somewhat less obvious, is a change within an occupancy class; an example is a dry cleaning establishment which replaces its approved cleaning solvent with a dangerous solvent having a low flash point. To guard against such changes, property policies often provide that coverage will be suspended while the hazard is increased without approval of the insurer. Provision is usually made that such changes will affect coverage only when they are within the control or knowledge of the policyholder and are made deliberately.

8. Right of subrogation — Many claims are presented to insurers when a third party is responsible for the loss. A policyholder has a right to demand payment from the company insuring the policy. If collection from the third party is possible, the insured will, in effect, recover twice. While there is little possibility of this happening with most losses, the chance of unjust enrichment through collusion is quite possible. An example of a case involving collusion is when two people fake an accident, submit high claims for damages, collect from their respective insurers and divide the gain. In order to prevent this from happening, insurance policies contain a provision stipulating that the insured must assign — to the insurer — any right of action against a third party who is responsible for the loss. This is called subrogation.

9. Limitations on recovery — The last line of defense by those who prepare policy provisions intended to control moral hazard, is to limit the amount of recovery. A claim limitation which prevents undue enrichment will often reduce moral hazards. Some dishonest persons may try to improve their economic status by recovering an amount in excess of the property value from insurance policies, but several types of policy provisions are used to limit such recovery in an attempt to thwart such persons.

a) Limiting recovery to the actual cash value of property. Actual cash value is usually defined as being the replacement cost less depreciation and obsolescense, if any. Replacement cost means the cost to replace the property with materials of like kind and quality within a reasonable time after the loss. A person who owns a building that has an old roof cannot get the cost of a new roof from the insurance company. Rather, the insurer will deduct the depreciation and pay the balance. In effect, the property owner is paying a share for the use received from the roof. A property policy, unless endorsed otherwise, does not replace old property for new; it provides payment instead for the value of the old property, and the owner must pay the difference if a new piece of property is desired.

b) Providing that all policies share in a loss, if more than one policy covers the loss, rather than permitting full recovery under each policy, with the total exceeding the extent of loss or damage. An example, is the person who owns a building with value of $10,000 and purchases two policies, each for $10,000, with the expectation of collecting $20,000 in case of total loss. There are two types of policy provisions that can prevent double recovery. One provides that each policy will share in the loss in the same proportion that its coverage bears to all insurance covering the property. This is called a *pro rata clause.* The other type is an *excess clause,* specifying that the policy will pay only after all other policies have first paid up to their limits, and then only the remaining value, up to its limit. Both of these clauses are very effective in preventing double recovery.

c) Limiting recovery to the insurable interest of the policyholder. This means that the policy will pay no more than the actual loss the policyholder has sustained, whether it is a loss to physical property owned, or an adverse effect on the insured's position regarding potential future profits. Thus, if a policy is issued in the name of a partnership, one partner cannot collect the entire proceeds. If there is an encumbrance on property, such as a mortgage, the property owner can collect no more than the value of the property less the amount of the encumbrance. This is another provision that limits recovery to the actual loss sustained.

d) Excluding increased costs because of ordinances. Building codes are continually being ing tightened, so older buildings cannot be rebuilt in many cases without substantial increases in costs. For example, codes may require additional fire escapes, or enclosed stairwells with self-closing fire doors. Some ordinances provide that a building constructed prior to a specified date cannot be repaired if damage exceeds a certain percentage of the building value; it must be razed before it can be rebuilt, so obviously the cost to replace the building will be greatly increased because of such a law. To avoid the payment of such costs, which could substantially enrich a property owner, policies ordinarily exclude any increased cost of repair or reconstruction by reason of any law or ordinance regulating construction or repair.

Applying controls

In addition to these provisions which are printed in the basic policies, an underwriter may apply specific controls to individual cases. This will be done when the moral hazard is beyond the control of other provisions, but when an application is acceptable under certain conditions. The most common of these controls is an exclusion of specified property; a single item of jewelry might be excluded from a theft policy covering personal property. Another common control is to exclude a class of property under specified conditions. An example is the property taken on a business trip by a traveling salesperson who frequently reports theft losses of property taken from a motel room. Another control is to exclude the acts of a specified person; this person may be an infrequent but irresponsible driver of a vehicle. Still another tool is to exclude existing damage when it is discovered, such as a broken window in a store, or a damaged hood on an automobile. The list is endless, limited only by situations which appear to cover moral hazards, and the ability of the underwriter to offer insurance by restricting the offending item.

Using Deductibles

The use of deductibles is increasingly common and their amounts are increasing. These trends stem largely from the need to control costs of settling claims; it costs virtually as much to handle a $10 claim as one for $100. Another reason is the desire to reduce costs of insurance in the face of an increase in the number of losses and in their average costs. Premiums also can be held down if policyholders assume the small, frequent losses themselves. Thus, most increases in the use and amount of deductibles can be attributable to economic factors.

Deductibles, however, can be helpful in controlling some types of moral hazard, and part of the increase can be traced to this factor. An underwriter who wants to use a deductible on a policy or even on a group of policies, in order to help control moral hazards, will find a willing ally in the actuary who is attempting to reduce costs. Deductibles can be applied to a particular class of risk or to a type of policy, and whether the initiative comes from the standpoint of underwriting control or loss reduction, the net effect will help control moral hazards. On the other hand, a deductible can be used on an individual policy, specifically to control a moral hazard that has been discovered.

It is generally believed that most moral hazards are directly reduced as deductibles are increased. The smaller the share of loss the insurer pays, the less temptation there is to be repaired or replaced, as it usually is, the policyholder will have to assume the deductible, and this could be a financial burden. Another reason is the possibility that a fraudulent claim will be discovered and the perpetrator will be punished; the smaller the potential recovery, the less attractive is this risk.

However, some moral hazards are not reduced by deductibles. For example, if striking employees or disgruntled customers threaten to burn down a building, no amount of deductible will deter them. The weakness is that the deductible is charged to the policyholder, not to the party responsible for the loss. However, there may be a deterrent even to such losses in some cases, by encouraging the policyholder to take steps to reduce the chances of a loss. A more reasonable employer may be able to avoid acts of destruction by strikers, and a concerned distributor may be able to reduce the degree of dissatisfaction on the part of its customers. Thus, deductibles may have some effect on most types of moral hazard, even though the effect is slight or nonexistent when the hazard comes from other parties.

Employing Rate Adjustments

Insurance rates are established on the premise that little or no moral hazard exists in risks which are insured; obviously, they are inadequate if the probability or severity of loss is increased by the existence of a sizable moral hazard. An underwriter who cannot control the moral hazard by policy provisions or deductibles should attempt to balance the hazard with increased rates.

No rate adjustment will compensate for a serious hazard and if no other control can be found, the risk should be declined or cancelled. For lesser hazards, uncontrolled by other means, rate adjustments may be a solution. It is claimed by some underwriters that if the chance of loss is materially increased, no rate increase, within an applicant's ability to pay, will be sufficient to offset expected losses. The qualification of "within his ability to pay" is needed, and sometimes is referred to as an "affordable rate." It is apparent that a rate which is double the value of property (such as a premium of $20,000 for a $10,000 building) will solve any moral hazard, but is so unrealistic that it is beyond the scope of discussion. A reasonable limit might be 200, or 400% at most, of the usual rate. At these rates, only minor increases in hazard can be permitted, although an underwriter, perhaps, cannot measure moral hazard that closely.

Other underwriters, however, feel that minor moral hazards can be controlled by rate adjustments. This is particularly true when the apprarent hazard is vague, while the pressure is heavy to write the business. It is obviously better from an underwriting standpoint to get 50 or 100% more premium in such cases; if this does not result in a profit on these risks, it at least reduces the loss.

Another area where rate adjustments can help is in the application of surcharges for previous losses. If such losses are considered to be caused by moral hazards, a position which is often correct but sometimes debatable, then rate increases appear to help the situation. It is common in many lines to surcharge on the basis of previous losses, or to give credits for a clean loss record. Such action is obviously justified on the premise that past experience will probably continue in the future. However, a case could be made for the position that some losses, at least, are caused by moral hazards, and surcharges or credits are measures of controlling such hazard.

Rates for most lines in most states can be adjusted only with difficulty. Filings must be prepared showing the factors upon which the rate classes are based. It would be difficult, if not impossible, to prepare and secure approval for a schedule that increases rates a fixed percentage for "poor business reputation" or "a record of questionable claims." This situation probably restrains underwriters from using rate adjustments to control moral hazards more than a feeling that such control is unrealistic. For this reason, most rate adjustments aimed at such control are based solely on records of past losses, even though some losses may contain no suggestion of moral hazards. It might be possible, however, to increase rates because of past bankruptcies, if the property is in the spouse's name, and so forth, but this is rarely done.

Rate adjustments are too limited to be of much help to the underwriter who is confronted with a moral hazard. The real control remains in solid underwriting practices: get as much information about the situation as is reasonably possible; decide if the risk can be written and if so, on what terms; and then take the indicated action. Since moral hazards can be disastrous to underwriters, they must be underwritten with extreme caution.

QUESTIONS FOR DISCUSSION

1. Define "moral hazard," in general, and explain why it is often difficult to detect.
2. Give one example of the following types of moral hazard:
   (a) lack of insurable interest;
   (b) poor business reputation;

(c) revenge; and
(d) rebellion against social or economic climate.

3. What are some of the characteristics of individuals that should warn underwriters of a possible moral hazard?
4. Why is knowledge of policy provisions so important to an underwriter who is confronted with the possibility of moral hazard?
5. Explain some of the controls which underwriters can use to at least reduce the effects of moral hazard.

16

Morale Hazard

Morale hazard is the increase in uncertainty which is brought about by indifference or carelessness. Because of indifference, a policyholder may neglect ordinary precautions to protect against loss. Because of carelessness, a policyholder or other person may take actions which lead to losses. The result will be an increase in the probability or the severity of loss, or both.

Under many circumstances, the difference between moral hazard and morale hazard may be only one of degree. If the property owner actually takes steps to destroy owned property, that is a *moral hazard.* If that person fails to take steps which would help to protect against a loss, that is a *morale hazard.* The loss can be just as bad in one situation as the other. However, the morale hazard is usually considered as being not quite as dangerous as the moral hazard; the difference is slight and neither is easy to detect.

A morale hazard usually exists when the policyholder suffers little or no monetary loss when damage occurs. It is really a matter of attitude and it might even be subconscious — arising quite suddenly if conditions are changed or developing because of the existence of full insurance. Indifference is the key word in a morale hazard, characterized by such phrases as "I should worry" and "I don't give a damn."

Since morale hazard, like moral hazard, may be present in every line of insurance, lack of attention to it may increase the chance of loss. Morale hazard is even less understood than moral hazard, perhaps because it is more subtle, less obvious. In any event, every underwriter should be aware of the problems, but first needs to study its characteristics.

CAUSES OF MORALE HAZARD

Most people never present a morale hazard. They take steps to maintain and protect their property against loss. They exhibit a pride of ownership, an inherent respect for property, and an abhorrence of causing inconvenience or expense to someone else because of their carelessness. Where these characteristics exist, there is no morale hazard.

Other people do present morale hazards. They are the ones who are indifferent to causes of loss. There are a number of reasons for this situation, and they must be analyzed before the types of morale hazard can be understood.

Decline in Profits of Income. A morale hazard may develop when a person's income or profits are reduced. In such a case, the property owner has a reduced interest in maintaining the property or business that might be lost. Even if that feeling does not exist, there may not be enough money to take the necessary steps to prevent loss. Thus, there may be a morale hazard in cases when the policyholder actually prefers it to be otherwise, but is prevented by a shortage of money from taking proper care of the property.

Depreciated Value. Property eventually depreciates in value to the point when there is little incentive to maintain it, although most property is replaced before it reaches that point. If it is not replaced, its owner presents a morale hazard. Money cannot be spent to maintain the property in good condition because such expenditure would be uneconomical. Accordingly, the property will depreciate even further. The incentive for good housekeeping will decrease, and the opportunities for a fire or other loss will increase. Whether dealing with real property or personal property, an underwriter should be cautious about the morale hazard if value has depreciated greatly. An owner may not even think of actually destroying the property, so no moral hazard exists; but may simply let it deteriorate even more, until a loss is almost certain. This is a common example of the morale hazard

White Elephant. Property may become a "white elephant" even if it is in good condition and has not depreciated in value. There are a number of reasons why this condition may develop. A building is built in the wrong area, a resort fails to develop, a neighborhood does not materialize as expected, or a corner location is a poor choice for a particular type of business for inexplicable reasons. In other circumstances, a building may have been "right" for its location and may have been profitable business, but conditions have changed; a resort lake has become polluted or depleted; a neighborhood or community has changed its style; or an expressway has revised a traffic pattern. In fact, a moral hazard will often exist when property becomes a "white elephant," but not necessarily. Some property owners would not think of destroying the property. However, few owners take as good care of such property as they do for profitable property, and lack of proper maintenance soon results in increased chance of loss. Thus, a morale hazard is usually present or imminent when property becomes a "white elephant."

Small Financial Interest. A person who has only a small financial interest in property is less inclined to take care of it than one whose interest is substantial. Real property faces this problem when the mortgage is almost 100% of the property value. A person who pays only a few hundred dollars down on a home will take care of it if the neighborhood develops well; if the tract does not sell, or if other buyers do not maintain their property, the temptation is great to let the property deteriorate since the loss to the buyer would be slight if something happened to the property.

Hence the net effect is creation of hazard.

Personal property faces similar problems. A person who buys an article for "nothing down and no payment for 60 days" has less interest in taking care of the property than one who has made a sizeable down payment. This is particularly true of property that is both mobile and common, like an automobile; a driver with little financial interest may drive less carefully than a counterpart who has a substantial financial interest in his car. Thus, the morale hazard is present when the owner has little interest in taking care of the property.

Lack of Concern for Others. Some people exhibit a lack of concern for the safety of others. People are legally responsible for their acts, but liability insurance may transfer that responsibility to an insurer. If a person reacts to this transfer by assuming an attitude of indifference, a morale hazard is created. This is exhibited in the manner a person drives a car, takes care of property of others, and maintains owned property as regards the safety of others. These people would not deliberately injure another person nor damage property, so there is no moral hazard. On the other hand, there is a morale hazard because these people are not exercising the degree of care necessary in avoiding harm to others.

Improper Training or Knowledge. Many people perform tasks for which they are not properly trained, or about which they have little knowledge. A homeowner may permit trash to accumulate near a water heater or furnace, or may use gasoline to clean tools in a garage where a heater is located. An automobile driver who parks on a hill may not know how to set the brakes and crimp the wheels. These acts are not intended to cause losses, but the result could be serious injury or damage.

TYPES OF MORALE HAZARD

There are many reasons why morale hazards exist, as was explained in the previous section. Four separate types of morale hazards result from these conditions. People who are indifferent to factors which cause losses will exhibit one or more of them which increases the probability or severity of loss, or both.

Poor Housekeeping. A potential morale hazard is most often exemplified by poor housekeeping and it is also the easiest to observe. It is demonstrated in many ways, depending upon the occupancy of the building. A machine shop may fail to provide regular sweepings to keep floors free of chips and cutting oil. A retail store may fail to hire enough employees to keep stock in proper order, which may result in damaged goods and injured workers. Any business to which the public has access can increase the hazards by neglecting to keep debris picked up, floors repaired and aisles cleared. Any homeowner or business owner may allow trash to accumulate under a water heater and close to the pilot light, greatly increasing the possibility of a fire.

Whenever there is poor housekeeping, the chance of loss is increased. However, there may be reasons for this condition other than those described in this chapter, i.e., poor supervision and inefficient arrangement of the premises. Underwriting will be different for each reason, so the underwriter must attempt to discover the true underlying reason. Some of these conditions may be cured by proper loss control recommendations, but morale hazards are difficult to control. The methods of underwriting against morale hazards are discussed in the next section; it is vital at this point to realize that some types of morale hazards are similar to other conditions.

Poor Maintenance. Closely related to poor housekeeping, but different from it, is poor maintenance. It may be present in buildings, where it can be as unimportant as a need for new paint, or as serious as a worn roof or frayed wiring. In personal property, poor maintenance is evident in such items as worn bearings, chipped paint, torn upholstery, and the like. Some poor maintenance is merely unattractive, but much is positively dangerous. Any evidence of poor maintenance must be investigated carefully, because this situation could lead to more serious conditions. Furthermore, while poor maintenance, like poor housekeeping, may be caused by other reasons than indifference, the ultimate effects could be disastrous if the reason is a result of a morale hazard.

Poor Safekeeping. Still another example of morale hazard is poor safekeeping of property. When a person does not care what happens, there is less inclination to be careful in handling valuables. Money causes many of these problems, because it is so easily taken if it is not handled properly. It is fairly simple to protect money against most losses, but this does take some effort. A person who does not really care what happens will be careless in safeguarding money, and the chance of loss increases substantially. Some other property is almost as susceptible as money to losses that are increased by carelessness; articles on sale in many retail stores are highly subject to loss by pilferage and shoplifting. A careful proprietor will take steps in preventing such losses, but a careless one will suffer many losses.

Irresponsible Conduct. The fourth type of morale hazard concerns conduct which must be described as irresponsible. If a person does not feel a concern for the welfare and safety of other people and their property, that person has a tendency to act irresponsibly. Poor driving habits, the practice of leaving borrowed tools out in the rain, a neglect of the premises—these are examples of irresponsibility which is often related to other morale hazards.

UNDERWRITING AGAINST MORALE HAZARDS

Underwriters cannot perform an effective job of underwriting, unless they understand morale hazards and take the necessary action to prevent increased losses. Since morale hazards are present in every line of insurance, vigilance must be used at all stages of the underwriting process.

If a morale hazard is discovered during the course of securing and analyzing information, the underwriter must consider the steps to take. There may be cases when insurance must be declined or cancelled because of the seriousness of the hazard, although this is somewhat less frequent than when a moral hazard is revealed. More often, policies are written with provisions which help to control the increased morale hazard, enabling the underwiter to write the insurance and still avoid exorbitant losses.

Securing Information

The information received by an underwriter is used in many ways. In addition to such obvious uses as determining policy forms and rates, information should be analyzed to determine if any morale hazard exists. This type of problem becomes evident from various sources as they are searched for other reasons. An underwriter will seldom, if ever, gather information just on this problem, at least not until its potential existence has come to light.

Every source of information can be helpful in discovering a morale hazard. The original application often gives a clue, and somtimes gives sufficient information upon which action should be taken. Whenever any indication of a morale hazard is revealed, the undewriter should pursue it until satisfied that it is or is not a real problem, because a morale hazard can be serious.

Sources For Discovering Morale Hazards

The following are some of the sources an underwriter can use in his attempt to discover a morale hazard, or to secure more information about one.

1. *Application.* Answers to various questions on the application may give clues to morale hazards. Some examples are: indications that the property has depreciated heavily in value or is a white elephant; a loan on the property approximates the value of the property; or the accident record indicates a disregard for the rights of others. Also any indications by the producer of careless housekeeping or poor maintenance should alert the underwriter to possible morale hazards.

2. *Inspection reports.* The type of report which comments on financial and personal matters may give some clues to morale hazards. When an underwriter suspects that a morale hazard exists, special attention to the apparent problem areas should be requested.

3. *Special services.* Reports or publications that indicate business stability and profitability can give further information about potential morale hazards. Underwriters should use these services whenever a suspicion exists about a morale hazard.

4. *Motor vehicle records.* The driving records of all licensed drivers are available in most states. An underwriter may use such records in determining past attitudes of an applicant as reflected by the driving record.

5. *Claims reports.* A claims adjuster contacts policyholders under conditions that may reveal morale hazards. As a matter of fact, most insurers encourage adjusters to report their findings to the underwriters. These reports on present policyholders can be very valuable to underwriters and should be evaluated carefully.

Interpreting Information

As an underwriter analyzes the available information, it can be determined if the conditions present indicate a possible morale hazard. If so, more information may be requested in order to verify whether a problem actually exists. Not all sources of information will be used in each case; only those appearing to offer the best opportunity to develop necessary information will be used. Some of the factors to look for as information is analyzed are as follows:

1. *Financial Interest.* The extent of the applicant's interest in property is very important. The size of a mortgage or loan in relation to the value of the property is a valuable clue to the interest the applicant might take in preserving the property.

2. *Property Value.* An indication that the actual value is considerably below either

the amount of insurance or the value of similar property should be a warning that a morale hazard may exist. Any references to outmoded or excessively depreciated property should be investigated carefully.

3. *Profitability.* A decline in profits, particularly over a recent period, may indicate that a morale hazard is present. Even a sharp decline in income of an individual should be suspect and should call for further investigation.

4. *Poor Housekeeping and Maintenance.* When a report shows the presence of poor housekeeping or poor maintenance, the underwriter should suspect that morale hazards are present. There may be other reasons, of course, but these conditions could indicate morale hazards and further investigation is vital.

5. *Poor Safekeeping.* Applicants who appear to be careless in the handling of money or other valuables may present morale hazards. A competent underwriter will secure more information to see if this is the situation, or if other reasons cause this condition.

6. *Irresponsibility.* Many clues appear in various sources of information as to the degree of responsibility of the applicant. If there are indications that the person has acted in an irresponsible manner, the underwriter should take careful note, because this could well results in problems.

Employing Policy Provisions

Morale hazards, like moral hazards, also can be partially controlled by the use of policy provisions. Some of these provisions are printed in the basic policy, while others are added by the underwriter as a means of tailoring the contract to the specific circumstances.

The most important reason for using policy provisions is, however, different for an underwriter faced with a morale hazard than one faced with a moral hazard. The latter uses provisions that are designed to guarantee that the policyholder does not profit from a loss or that this will deter the policyholder from causing one. An underwriter with a morale hazard, on the other hand, does not need to be concerned about a deliberate act that causes a loss, but rather an indifference that permits loss causing conditions to develop. The intent of any actions an underwriter takes in combating a morale hazard, therefore, is to employ some provisions that will shock the policyholder into an awareness of the true situation. The underwriter will have a greatly increased chance of making a profit if the indifferent policyholder can be convinced to be more careful. A second reason for using policy provisions is the same for moral and morale hazards, i.e., the use of provisions will reduce losses if conditions worsen and loss does occur.

Provisions which are printed in the policy can help the underwriter control morale hazard, too. These are some of the same ones used to control moral hazards, but fewer are used for morale hazards and the reasons are different in some cases. The underwriter should be aware of these provisions and the protection they give, to understand the control available over morale hazards.

Common Policy Provisions

The most common of these provisions generally included in property and liability policies are as follows:

1. *Title.* The type of encumbrance on the property, and the name of the mortgagee or loss payee, appear in the policy. The amount of the encumbrance is not shown on the policy, but the policyholder is aware of the situation if the unpaid balance is large, because this information is requested on the application. An underwriter hopes that the applicant thus becomes aware that only the mortgagee will receive the proceeds of the policy and the applicant will not benefit at all if loss should occur.

2. *Cancellation.* Possibly the strongest weapon an underwriter can use against a potential morale hazard is the threat of cancellation. The property owner who does not take care of his property because it is insured, may change habits if the insurer threatens to cancel the insurance. Morale hazard is caused by adequate insurance which leads the policyholder to an indifferent attitude; the removal of insurance by cancellation destroys the base for this indifference. When an underwriter learns of poor housekeeping or poor maintenance and suspects a morale hazard, notification may be sent to the policyholder that the policy will be cancelled unless the condition is corrected. Such warning often shocks an indifferent person into a feeling of concern, thereby eliminating the morale hazard.

The laws enacted in many states have a tendency to destroy this protection to the underwriter because they limit the right to cancel policies. When an underwriter finds a condition such as poor maintenance or poor housekeeping during the discovery period (meaning the initial days of a policy during which a cancellation is permitted for any reason), the decision may be to proceed with cancellation instead of offering an opportunity for improvement. This situation tends to reduce the availability of insurance, but an underwriter must take the steps available in order to avoid undue losses. Naturally, these restrictive laws increase losses for morale hazards because policies may not be cancelled for reasons of carelessness after the discovery period.

3. *Exclusions of certain property.* Property policies commonly exclude such property as money, currency, and securities; when covered, a rather low dollar limit is used in most cases. These provisions help the underwriter in both of the basic ways. The policyholder might be shocked into exercising more care when it is realized that the insurance does not cover the entire loss. And if a loss occurs, the amount of the payment will be reduced on the property, the value or existence of which is difficult to determine.

4. *Limitations on recovery.* Several policy provisions are designed to limit amount of the recovery. These help the underwriter by reducing the amount of loss, if other measures have not avoided damage. While the existence of these provisions in policies may cause an indifferent policyholder to be more careful, their principal purpose is to reduce costs if losses do occur.

— One way to limit recovery is to place a limitation on the policy's share of loss, or to limit recovery to the excess over other policies. Almost all policies contain either pro rata or excess clauses, specifying that the total amount paid under all policies will not exceed the value of the property damaged or destroyed, regardless of the number of policies purchased. Since the morale hazard is caused by a feeling of indifference caused largely by the existence of insurance, this indifference could increase if the policyholder thinks collection is possible from each of several policies, and it could reduce when it is realized that this is not the case. Then if a loss does occur, the insurer may have its share reduced by the contributors from other policies.

— Another method of limiting payment is to apply a percentage participation on every loss. Some fire policies provide that on unprotected property, the insurer will pay only three-fourths of any loss. This three-fourths loss clause is designed to shock the property owner into realizing the importance of taking care of the property. A person who is required to pay one-fourth of every loss is more inclined to be careful about loss possibilities than one who will be reimbursed in full for losses. If a loss should occur, substantial reduction in payments are realized through the operation of this clause.

— The device of excluding certain acts of negligence is another device used to limit loss payment. Insurance policies ordinarily pay for acts of carelessness by policyholders. Indeed, most losses under property policies are traced to negligence on the part of the property owner can be avoided by the excercise of proper care. The problem is how to continue this traditional and basic concept without incurring overwhelming losses caused by extreme carelessness. The solution used in many policies is to exclude certain acts. A good example is found in policies issed to laundries and dry cleaners protecting against damage to customers' goods. These bailees customers policies usually exclude such acts of everyday carelessness as scorching, tearing, or discoloring articles of clothing on which work is being performed. In this manner, any morale hazard that is present because the insurer will pay for carelessness is removed entirely by the simple expendience of excluding certain careless acts.

— The final method is to specify the requirement of certain steps in order to minimize loss. The morale hazard can even exist after a loss occurs. Some people might be careful of their property while it is intact, but might feel after a loss has occurred that they have no further responsibility. They are inclined to walk away from the damaged property, letting the insurance company take over the entire responsibility. Such an attitude obviously can increase the amouint of the loss, because substantial reductions in ultimate damages can be realized if the proper steps are taken. Several clauses are included in some policies to help minimize the loss because of this hazard. A common one is to provide that there shall be no abandonment to the insurer off any property. The policyholder must retain title and primary responsibility for the care of the property. Another clause excludes loss caused directly or indirectly by negleect of the insured to use all reasonable means to preserve the property at and after a loss, or when the property is endangered by an insured peril such as fire in neighboring premises. Finally, most policies require the policyholder to assist in recovering the amount of the loss from the person responsible for the loss; this includes attending hearings and trials, assisting in securing evidence, and helping to obtain the attendance of witnesses.

All of these causes are designed to reduce the morale hazard after loss occurs. They try to change an attitude of unconcern into one of interest in reducing loss. These clauses are of primary interest to a claims person, but the underwriter is assisted by any step that reduces the amount of claims dollar paid. Morale hazards must be controlled wherever possible.

Those clauses, as just discussed, are printed in the policies issued to all insureds. Sometimes underwriters wish to add special clauses in order to cope with specific morale problems. These special clauses usually take the form of exclusions and are the result of a realization that proper degree of care is impossible under the circumstances. One type is an exclusion of a property class, such as property carried by a person on a business trip; some people may exercise due care of their property at home but be so careless of it while on a trip that insurance cannot be written at any reasonable rate. Another type is an exclusion of acts of one individual, such as an infrequent driver of an automobile; that person may be so careless that the underwriter is unwilling to write the insurance, unless this person's acts are excluded. The same problem may exist in many other situations, such as a child in the family who continually breaks windows in other buildings, or the person who is careless when hunting or playing golf. While all of these acts can be excluded, seldom does an underwriter do so. It is more common to refuse writing the insurance when the morale hazard of a family member, or a frequent user of the property, is such that some action is necessary.

Using Deductibles

The increasing popularity of deductibles is partly brought about by their help in controlling morale hazards, as well as their help in controlling the cost of claims and moral hazards. A morale hazard exists because the policyholder is indifferent to loss, and this is usually caused by a feeling that nothing will be suffered if there is a loss. Applying a deductible immediately changes the picture since the insured will have to pay a part of every loss. Thus a deductible is a powerful weapon against a morale hazard.

A problem with deductibles is that is it difficult to find one large enough to deter carelessness, without imposing too large a burden on the policyholder. A $500 deductible may be staggering to an elderly couple living on social security, but that amount would be unnoticed by a large corporation. Various deductible amounts are available on most policies, so an adaptation is possible. Applicants may select the deductible desired but this amount may not coincide with those of the underwriter. When a morale hazard is discovered and the underwriter wants to control it with a deductible, that underwriter must be free to require a deductible that is large enough to do the job, as an alternative to declination or cancellation of the policy. The current trend is toward larger deductibles in personal lines, away from the $25 and $50 amounts and into areas of $100, $250, $500, and even $1,000.

A special type of deductible became popular in the early years of the homeowners policy. This is the diminishing deductible — the most common being a $50 deductible that diminishes as the loss increases until it disappears with a $500 loss. This type of deductible is not as effective in controlling morale hazards as a flat deductible — that is, one in which the deductible is the same for every loss. It has been said that diminishing deductible may even increase the morale hazard because it tends to reward the policyholder who has the large loss. In fact, the diminishing deductible is no longer available through most companies in many states. Optional flat deductibles are more commonly used by underwriters when confronted with a morale hazard.

Employing Rate Adjustments

Insurance rates anticipate reasonable maintenance, housekeeping and care. If poor maintenance, poor housekeeping or carelessness is present, the rates will be inadequate and the underwriter either must secure an adequate increase in the rate or decline the coverage.

As with moral hazard, a serious morale hazard cannot be overcome by a rate adjustment. Even though the insured will not deliberately destroy the property, a loss is almost as certain if proper care is not taken. The only question is how soon a fire will occur if grease is allowed to accumulate over the grill in a restaurant, if trash if piled against a hot water heater, or if oily rags are kept in a cardboard box. No reasonable rate can compensate for the increased chance of loss under such circumstances.

Minor morale hazards can be overcome with rate adjustments. Sloppy housekeeping and poor maintenance can be rated, and some rate schedules charge for them. If a condition cannot be improved but is not so bad as to require cancellation, it is a help to secure additional premium. Perhaps the major advantage, however, is the warning to the insured that a rate adjustment gives. It may be the first time the seriousness of careless behavior is realized. More often, it will be recognized that a little care can save money in insurance premiums, and this is a powerful persuader to many people.

Rate structures which increase the cost because of previous losses can also help with minor morale hazards. Again, the additional premium is helpful, but the principal benefit is from the psychological impact on the applicant.

Increases in rates because of morale hazards are difficult to administer. Except for increases because of past losses, they are somewhat subjective: When is "poor housekeeping" so bad that it requires a surcharge? Furthermore, such rating factors are costly to apply; a report revealing the presence of a condition often is not precise enough for rating purposes, so a second report is required. Thus, additional rates for morale hazards are used rather sparsely, except for surcharges for past losses.

The principal help from rate increases, as well as other provisions, is the effect they have on the policyholder. Morale hazards stem from a feeling of indifference. If the policyholder can be shocked into being careful, the morale hazard is eliminated. Underwriters often use these tools in an effort to derive a favorable result because the goal of underwriting is to write insurance, not cancel it. However, if the morale hazard continues, the underwriter must reevaluate the situation because a continuing pattern of negligence and neglect can lead to serious losses, regardless of all other steps an underwriter may take.

QUESTIONS FOR DISCUSSION

1. Define "morale hazard."
2. Explain, with an example, why the difference between "moral" and "morale" hazard may be only one of degree.
3. Describe briefly, four examples of morale hazard.
4. Of the various types of morale hazard, which are more physical in nature than mental?

5. What are some of the clues for detecting morale hazard for which underwriters should be especially watchful?
6. Explain the ways in which policy provisions dealing with limitations on recovery can help to reduce loss costs.
7. Explain some of the controls which underwriters can use to reduce the effects of morale hazard.

17

Physical Hazard

Physical hazard denotes an increase in uncertainty caused by objective material factors. These factors may be the physical condition of an individual, the construction elements of property or the forces of nature. Whatever the type of physical hazard, it increases the probability or severity of loss, or both, beyond that which is contemplated in the rate.

It is easier to detect physical hazards than those which might be termed as psychological factors (moral and morale factors). Physical characteristics are specific and objective; many are capable of quite precise measurement, as well.

Physical factors are important in all lines of insurance, although their principal use is with property insurance. Indeed, differences in them are recognized by rate differences in most lines, such as youthful drivers of automobiles, unprotected risks for fire insurance, and Gulf Coast property for hurricane coverage. In contrast, a physical hazard exists when the characteristics of the individual risk are greater than those contemplated by the rate. The underwriter must differentiate between those factors which are contemplated in the rate and those which are not; the latter must be underwritten with extreme care.

TYPES OF PHYSICAL HAZARD

All physical hazards are objective, i.e., specific factors may be observed and measured. There is nothing mysterious nor secretive about them. However, they are not understood thoroughly by all underwriters, and such understanding is a prerequisite to proper handling. The first step, therefore, is to study the three major types of these hazards.

But before analyzing these three types of hazards, it is important to realize that a distinction should be made between those physical hazards about which something can be done and those about which nothing can be done. The line of demarcation is not always clear, and it may have a price tag on it — that is, some improvement in most physical factors is possible if someone is willing to spend enough money. From the standpoint of insurance, the maximum which ordinarily would be spent is the difference in insurance premiums which would result from its improvement. If the change is not economical from that standpoint, the underwriter must consider that nothing can be done about the condition, in most cases.

This distinction does not imply that the underwriter should be less concerned about one class than another. A physical hazard can be disastrous from an underwriting standpoint, whether it could have been corrected or not. On the other hand, the underwriting approach will be different between these two classes. Thus, the underwriter must constantly keep in mind the possibility of improving the physical risk, while attempting to understand and control the physical hazards. The three types of physical factors are as follows.

Physical Condition Of An Individual

Some insurance policies depend heavily on the physical conditions of individuals. A prime example is automobile insurance, where the physical condition of the driver can make all the difference between an accident and a safe trip. If rates are the same for all adults, and a typical policyholder is 40 and in good physical condition, consider the increased hazard of an applicant who is 90, blind in one eye, and subject to frequent heart attacks. The latter risk is a physical hazard. Not that there is anything wrong with an elderly person, but simply that the physical condition increases the chance of loss. Some insurers charge more for elderly drivers and some for physically impaired drivers. Lacking such a rate schedule, the underwriter is faced with a physical hazard.

Little can be done about physical hazards caused by the bodily condition of individuals. In fact, no amount of money can restore youth and vitality to an aging person. However, some improvements are possible, such as specially-equipped automobiles and prosthetic devices.

Construction Elements of a Building

Property insurance rating usually varies by the construction elements of the building, taking into account the materials used, the number of stories or fire divisions and such factors. Related to these are other elements which may also account for rating differences, such as occupancy, degree of police or fire protection, exposures from adjacent buildings, climatic and weather conditions, location, and facilities for controlling or minimizing losses. All of these elements may constitute hazards but most are contemplated in the rates.

A physical hazard may be caused by these elements if the exposure to loss is greater than is contemplated by the rate. This can occur because there are limits to the classifications used in all lines of insurance, leaving some risks with characteristics beyond the boundaries of the rate classifications. In addition, a physical hazard is said to exist when the construction elements present such a severe loss potential that the underwriter is unwilling to write the insurance at almost any rate. In the latter cases, the underwriter feels that no reasonable rate could compensate for the increased exposure.

Physical hazards are relatively easy to identify. They usually are subject to correction, and the techniques or methods of accomplishing the corrections are well known. On the other hand, the cost of correcting the condition may be entirely unrealistic. If there is no water available for fighting a fire it is possible to drill a well, but the expense probably is prohibitive. A frame building may present a substantial hazard when fire protection is weak and the occupancy presents a sizeable chance of a flash fire, but the underwriter scarcely can ask the owner to demolish the building and rebuild it with fire-resistive materials. Thus, many physical hazards are recognized but they cannot be corrected at a reasonable expense.

Other physical hazards can be corrected. Sometimes a minor change will reduce or eliminate the additional hazards. Other situations require careful engineering and some expense. The underwriter must recognize those that can be corrected before taking the required steps to secure improvements.

Forces of Nature

A third, but very important, type of physical hazard consists of the forces of nature which people have not been able to control. A small degree of control has been found for some of these forces, and people have learned to adjust to many of them, but others still rage beyond the influence of mere mortals.

Both direct and indirect insurance losses may result from the forces of nature. Direct damage to property is the most common and obvious. Tornadoes have been observed in almost all states, with the greatest frequency being in the "tornado belt" which consists of Texas, Oklahoma, Kansas, Nebraska, Missouri, Iowa, Illinois and Indiana. Lightning and windstorms cause damage in every state. Hurricanes create havoc along the Gulf Coast and the Atlantic seaboard, extending into New England on occasions. Earthquakes have been recorded in most states, but are most common on the Pacific Coast. Floods are common in many areas, sometimes accompanied by mudslides. Landslides are not unusual in hilly areas, particularly in the Western states.

In addition to the direct damage these forces of nature can cause, indirect damage also may result. Airplanes and other forms of transportation are prevented from moving, resulting in lost revenue and perhaps loss of business to their clients. Manufacturing and assembly operations are suspended during severe weather conditions, causing a loss of production. Additional expenses for living and maintaining vital functions which cannot be interrupted without serious consequences, such as hospitals and food preparation, are incurred during and after these catastrophes. Furthermore, indirect damage may be caused by forces of nature which are more common and less severe than the catastrophic events previously described; examples are snowstorms, blizzards, heavy rains and rising water.

Property insurance rates contemplate normal exposures to these forces of nature. Varying degrees of exposure are measured by rate differentials based upon past experience of the risks in an area. Thus, windstorm rates are higher in Kansas than in California, but earthquake rates are the reverse. An underwriter can determine fairly well, the general exposure to climatic conditions.

Physical hazard is found in those risks subject to increases in loss expectancy above those expected. One cause of this condition lies in the precise location of the risk; some areas are more susceptible to loss by the forces of nature than others. A hurricane may cause much more damage to a building close to the Gulf and located barely above sea level than to one situated on a bluff above the water or several miles inland. Earthquakes, on the other hand, cause more damage to structures located on filled ground than on rock.

Another cause of increased uncertainty of loss by the forces of nature is the construction and maintenance of buildings. Earthquakes cause more damage to brick structures than to frame buildings. Windstorms and rain may cause little damage to a building which is well maintained, but may damage seriously, a building with an old roof in need of repair. An owner of an automobile with good brakes and new tires is less likely to cause an accident on wet or icy roads than one with poor brakes and slick tires.

Still another cause of physical hazards is the degree of protection available. Good fire protection can do much more to minimize loss following the occurrence of a contingency insured against than can poor protection. An efficient warning system can permit the taking of steps which may reduce the extent of damage in a hurricane or windstorm. A good fire department may be able to recommend preventative steps that can be taken in advance, such as the repair of roofs. A strict enforcement of building codes helps in reducing losses from floods and earthquakes.

The underwriter must be aware of these situations where the exposure to loss by natural forces is greater than is anticipated by the rate. Those which can be corrected, such as a roof in poor condition, must be determined. Those which cannot be corrected by any reasonable means, e.g., a building constructed in a flood-prone area; one too close to the Gulf; or one situated on filled land astride an earthquake fault, must be identified.

The underwriter must separate those than can be corrected and those that cannot, before corrective measures can be applied to reduce these hazards.

UNDERWRITING AGAINST PHYSICAL HAZARDS

Physical hazards are easier to identify than to control. The first step, however, is to understand the nature and types of these hazards, and then to identify specific problem risks. Only then can the underwriter start to take steps to correct these hazards.

Identification of physical hazards is made by an underwriter while facts about a risk are being analyzed. Having discovered a hazard, the underwriter must determine if improvements are possible and practicable, and must decide upon the steps to take. Some cases will be so poor that the underwriter will have to decline or cancel the coverage, which is not an unusual situation. Often, however, physical hazards may be corrected, or controlled by policy provisions. These routes are preferable, because they enable the underwriter to retain risks that are potentially profitable.

Securing Information

An underwriter gathers information about physical conditions from many sources and it is from this information that it can be determined if physical hazards exist. Sometimes an underwriter will request information for the specific purpose of identifying physical characteristics, but more often items of concern will be encountered during the analysis of the general information available. There are four common sources from which an underwriter can gather details about physical hazards.

1. *Application.* Specific questions about physical conditions are asked on every application for property insurance, as well as applications for liability insurance where the physical condition of an individual is a factor. In the latter category, information is requested about the age, physical impairments, and chronic ailments of all regular drivers of vehicles. On property applications, questions are asked about the construction of the building, the type and condition of the roof, the condition of the premises, the housekeeping and the age of the building.

Applications for some types of property insurance ask for other information that is germane to the type of coverage requested. Some of these questions concern the size of the building, the type and condition of the heating system, the type of occupancy for which the building was originally constructed, the number of stories, the date when the building was last painted and rewired, and the condition of chimneys and flues.

All types of property insurance applications contain reference to the location of the risk and the type of protection available. The latter may involve such things as fire departments, police departments, private security forces, sprinkler systems or other applicable types. Questions may be asked about the distance to fire hydrants, the conditions of all access roads, the proximity to forest areas, and similar items of importance to certain types of insurance in various areas.

From all of this information, an underwriter can determine if physical hazards exist. Many of the answers give rating data, while other are necessary in determining eligibility. However, certain items of information or combinations of items may indicate that an increase in uncertainty is present. These evidences of problems may be in any of the three types of physical hazard. When they are encountered, they must be identified carefully; further information is desirable in many cases, too.

2. *Inspection reports.* The same inspection report used for identifying other hazards and for supplying rating information will also furnish physical data. The reports obtained from the many reporting companies will contain answers to the obvious questions about physical hazards. If additional specific information is desired, it should be requested by special notation. All types of physical hazards may be investigated, including information about the physical condition of a driver, the construction of a building and the climatic conditions of the area.

3. *Engineering reports.* Commercial property often requires specialized knowledge in order to identify its physical characteristics adequately. Engineers (Loss Prevention Specialists) are used in reporting upon physical conditions and commenting upon physical conditions and physical hazards. Although they may recommend improvements, only the underwriter can determine if the physical hazards, when weighed with other factors, make a risk unacceptable or not. These engineers may

be employees of the insurer or of a reporting company; in either case, they report on special conditions to which their attention is directed, as well as on general physical conditions.

4. *Special sources.* Various auxiliary sources are available under some conditions. If the suspected problem is the physical condition of a driver, a motor vehicle record may reveal any disabilities or physical impairments. For more data on building construction, occupancy and exposures, an underwriter may refer to the specific rate publication of the fire rating bureau, where this information is available on most commercial risks. If more detail is needed on the construction characteristics, it may be possible to secure a copy of the inspection form used by a rating engineer during the examination of the premises, or even a copy of the blueprints used for construction of the building. When the problem deals with a possible exposure to unusual forces of nature, descriptions of past weather patterns and major disturbances are available from the United States Weather Bureau and some fire rating bureaus.

5. *Claims reports.* The physical aspects of the risk, as evaluated by the adjuster, are requested by most insurers. These reports are usually factual and may reveal conditions that were not discovered in the initial search for information or were developed later. This type of information requires careful consideration by the underwriter.

Interpreting Information

All these sources can give an underwriter a wealth of detail about physical characteristics. Many different elements of construction and condition also may be analyzed. These elements are quite easy to identify and describe, certainly much easier than the psychological factors described in the previous two chapters. The gathering of information is thus no problem to an underwriter; photographs, blueprints, medical histories, engineering reports, and almost any other specific information is available.

The real problem in underwriting is in determining how to use the information. Some of it may reveal that a risk is unacceptable, such as a building that is smaller or older than the insurer ordinarily writes. Other information is also necessary for rating. All of it, on acceptable risks, must be analyzed to see if physical hazards exist. Few risks will be perfect in all respects, but most will be average enough to offer no problems. Others may present extraordinary physical hazards which must be controlled if the risk is to be considered as acceptable.

Typical conditions that create each type of physical hazard are described next.

1. *Physical condition.* The physical hazard is increased when the insured's physical condition is poorer than that contemplated by the rate. Age is a good example; an elderly person, meaning any one over 80 years, often is handicapped by age and thus is a poorer risk as an automobile driver. Not all persons over 80 are nonpreferred drivers, but many are. Therefore, when the available information indicates that a driver has approached or passed that age, the underwriter must check several sources to determine the person's exact condition.

The same type of procedure applies to other physical conditions that can increase the hazard. The defect may be adequately compensated, but the underwriter will not know this until enough information has been obtained. A person who has lost an arm or a leg will usually present an increased hazard, unless the car is specially equipped. An applicant who suffers from fainting spells, diabetes, or epilepsy may be a severe hazard, but the conditions may be controlled by medicine to the point where the chance of loss is normal.

Certain types of information should be sought from the standpoint of physical hazards from physical conditions. First, an underwriter should look for indications of problems. Then, if any are found, a further search is needed in order to determine, as accurately as possible, if the condition can be tolerated at the rate charged. A suspected problem may not really be a matter of concern, but the underwriter must be suspicious until sufficient information has been secured to enable a decision to be made.

2. *Construction elements.* The physical hazard is increased when any deficiencies exist in the elements of construction property. The facts usually are quite definitive: either a chimney is substandard or is it not; a roof is approved or unapproved. The types of conditions presenting problems are not likely to be obvious without qualifying factors being mentioned at the same time. In this respect, the construction element is usually reported in a different manner than the bodily condition of an individual.

There are many construction elements, as was explained earlier in this chapter, that can cause physical hazards but are balanced by other factors or handled by rating. The indication of a problem in this area is enough to cause more investigation and sometimes mitigating conditions will also be found. A building that is unprotected from a fire standpoint might have a private well which would reduce the hazards, but it is unlikely, however, that this aspect would have escaped special mention by the producer.

Still, an underwriter who is confronted with a suspected physical hazard must continue the investigation until all of the pertinent facts are determined. If the risk is a restaurant, the underwriter will want to know the frequency that grease is cleaned from the flue; if a jewelry store, the burglary preventative measures that have been taken; if an older automobile, whether there is any unrepaired damage. Only by asking enough questions and securing enough information can the underwriter exercise proper judgement in evaluating risks.

3. *Forces of nature.* Physical hazards exist when the forces of nature threaten an above-average frequency or severity of loss. All property is subject to loss from natural forces, and the rating structure usually takes this into account. What the underwriter is looking for, as information is received and analyzed, is an unusual situation not included in the rate. This will sometimes involve a trend which appears to be developing, under which a new weather pattern may be emerging. There may be similar cases where the expected frequency of loss is judged to be greater than is indicated by the bare statistical information being used in rating.

A more common use for information the underwriter receives is to identify circumstances of unusual severity. These situations require the weighing of several different factors which affect the severity of loss. For example, a well-constructed building might resist a windstorm, while one built of inferior materials or in a short-cut manner might suffer extensive damage. The same problem could result from property in need of repair, in need of proper maintenance, or even in need of proper housekeeping. Whatever the natural forces threatening damage to property, the underwriter must not only investigate the expected frequency of the disturbance, but must also analyze all other factors that could increase the severity of damage when a loss does occur.

Recommending Improvements

Physical hazards often may be reduced by improvements in the risk. After the underwriter has received and has analyzed the information, and has weighed the severity of the conditions, some action must be taken. Many times the proper action is to recommend that improvements be made, although occasionally the underwriter must conditionally decline the application; that is, refuse to write the insurance, unless specified improvements are made.

Most recommendations for improvement are in the area of construction elements. The wiring may be in need of replacement, the roof may need repair, a flue may need cleaning, or many other items may require improvement before the underwriter will accept the risk. These are the deficiencies revealed to the underwriter through sources of information. These are not, however, taken into account in the rating. The usual practice is for the underwriter to send a list of needed improvements, with a request that the producer notify the underwriter when the changes are made.

Some improvements are merely desirable, while others are mandatory. The underwriter may request certain changes as a means of improving the risk and helping the insured by preventing a possible disastrous loss. When the underwriter, in these cases, accepts the risk without these improvements, the physical hazard cannot really be considered great. Other hazards may be much more serious, so much so that the underwriter will refuse to write the risk unless the improvements are made. This is actually a conditional declination — actually a declination but with the condition that if the improvements are made, the risk will be accepted. Obviously, a conditional declination is not used, unless the risk is entirely acceptable with the exception of those physical conditions that can be improved.

Recommendations may also be used for other types of physical hazards, although this is uncommon. An underwriter may decline an application for automobile insurance for a paraplegic, unless his vehicle is equipped with special devices. Even some control over natural forces may be required by an underwriter. An application for landslide insurance could be refused until a hill or bank on the property is supplemented with certain types of vegetation, while other types of vegetation may also be required as protection against brush or forest fires.

Employing Policy Provisions

Physical hazards can be controlled to some extent by the proper use of policy provisions. As with the other hazards previously described, these policy provisions may be printed in the basic policy or added by the underwriter.

Three provisions are used in many types of policies for purposes of controlling the physical hazard, among other reasons.

1. **Cancellation.** The insurer almost always provides in the policy that it can cancel at any time, upon proper notice. This provision is helpful to the underwriter who encounters a risk whose physical hazard develops after the policy is written. An underwriter also can decline insurance on a new application showing a physical hazard, but it is not uncommon for such a hazard to develop later.

Even the laws which restrict the right of the insurer to cancel a policy, often will permit cancellation if the physical risk has changed materially since the inception of the coverage. When the laws do not provide for this, naturally the underwriter who encounters physical hazards on policies already written must continue to provide protection until permitted to retire form the risk, as a nonrenewal.

2. **Inspection.** Most policies permit the insurer to inspect the property or the records of the insured at reasonable times. This provision puts teeth into the cancellation provision, for it gives an underwriter who suspects that a physical hazard exists the right of inspection and verification. There may be cases when a source of information indicates the probable existence of a physical hazard. The underwriter, always reluctant to act without all available facts, will use the right of inspection to verify the actual conditions. Only if a serious problem is discovered will the underwriter cancel the policy or take other action.

3. **Suspension.** A common provision in property policies is one providing that coverage will be suspended while the hazard is increased. The severity of this provision is reduced by the requirement that such changes must be deliberate changes within the control or knowledge of the policyholder. A change in the occupancy is the principal cause of such suspension, along with prolonged vacancy.

This provision, like the cancellation clause, is designed primarily to avoid an unexpected loss caused by a physical hazard. However, a secondary purpose is to alert the policyholder to the threat of a loss because of the physical condition. An underwriter always prefers to see the problem corrected and the coverage continued rather than declining insurance.

While these three clauses are printed in the policies, others are available to underwriters since special problems need special handling. Many of these problems are not so severe as to warrant cancellation or suspension, but they do increase uncertainty. The most common of these provisions applied by underwriters to specific policies deal with exclusions of property. The underwriter may exclude such things as a roof which needs repair, an entire tool shed in poor condition, or damage caused by a named driver who is using other than a specially-equipped automobile. In addition to these very specific exclusions, a class of property sometimes may be excluded, such as any stock of merchandise stored in a flood-prone area or in other than a fire-resistive warehouse. Other endorsements may be prepared by underwriters, but these are used less frequently for physical than for psychological hazards. When a physical hazard exists, an underwriter is more likely to attempt to get the condition improved, and to cancel if it is not, than to try to tailor the contract to the condition as it exists.

Using Deductibles

Deductibles have been used extensively in recent years on property policies. These help control physical hazards and encourage the improvement of deficient conditions by requiring the policyholder to share in every loss. Deductibles are of little help to an underwriter who is faced with a physical hazard over which the policyholder has no control. When the hazard is increased by an insured's poor physical condition or a force of nature, the insured cannot reduce losses merely because he or she participates in every loss under the deductible amount. This is not to say that deductibles are not used under such conditions, they are, but not for the purpose of controlling the physical hazard. Rather, the deductible reduces the amount which the insurer must pay after a loss occurs and is used for this purpose. If an applicant presents a physical hazard over which he has no control, the underwriter might insist upon a deductible in order to reduce the cost if a loss does occur. To this extent. the deductible is helpful to an underwriter, but it does not really control the hazard.

On the other hand, a deductible may be helpful in circumstances when the policyholder has the power to reduce the physical hazard. A worn-out roof may be repaired, a fire-wall may be installed, or fire extinguishers may be installed; the incentive for improvements of these types might come from the imposition of a deductible, or a threat of one. For example, a building owner may let the roof deteriorate, thus increasing the physical hazard. However, if the insured must pay the first share of every loss, say $500, there may be motivation to repair or replace the roof. Just the threat by an underwriter to impose a deductible may be enough to cause the owner to repair or replace the roof, thus avoiding the deductible.

The distinction must always be made on the practicality of securing improvements, as mentioned earlier. If the hazard can be removed only by a prohibitive expense, such as drilling a well or rebuilding a structure, neither the threat nor the imposition of a deductible will motivate the property owner to correct the deficiency. Again, the deductible will help in reducing the amount of the loss the insurer must pay, but will not help in removing the physical hazard. The underwriter must be careful to make this distinction and not be led into believing that a deductible will help to control a physical hazard by encouraging corrective action of applicant, if the action is too expensive to be practical.

Employing Rate Adjustments

Basic insurance rates are promulgated on the basis of normal physical conditions. This means that when an underwriter encounters a physical hazard, a profit is possible only by limiting coverage through the use of policy provisions or deductibles, or by increasing the rate.

Serious physical hazards are beyond the reach of rate adjustments. No rate which is within the realm of being reasonable can compensate for such hazards as those created by an automobile driver who suffers frequent epileptic seizures, or a building so deteriorated that it could collapse at the slightest provocation, or a home built on pilings within a few feet of high tide on a section of a beach noted for its turbulence. Loss becomes a virtual certainty under such conditions and insurance is impossible at any premium.

However, many physical conditions are handled by specified rate charges. Most rate schedules provide for different classifications allowing for different physical characteristics, as well as other measurable factors. Conditions below average in specific items may carry increased rates. Construction elements within the normal range are classified into many possible rate combinations, with some rates being several times greater than others. Locations subject to the forces of nature are often rated by the degree of exposure to destructive elements. As risks are classified, the underwriter can apply these rate differentials. This can control physical conditions of these types by securing adequate premium and, since these are part of the rate structure, they are not considered to be physical hazards.

Other physical conditions may be of a size which can be controlled by rates, but the underwriter may find that no rate is available in the schedule used. The underwriter may feel that an extra charge should be made for a driver who has one leg, but no surcharge is in the company's rate table. Substandard wiring may increase the hazard, but not more than a higher rate would justify if it were available. A group of buildings built in a valley or canyon through which the wind blows frequently, are susceptible to windstorm severity greater than that of the surrounding area However, windstorm rates are usually established for large areas and increased rates for small areas are not available, even though the underwriter would be willing to write the risks at a reasonable surcharge. In all of these cases, the underwriter should use a higher rate if one is permitted by the rate structure used by the company. If a higher rate is not available, the exposure then becomes greater than is contemplated by the rate and it must be considered as a physical hazard.

Underwriters are not always permitted to use higher rates, regardless of their desirability. Rating laws in some states prohibit the use of rates which are other than those placed on file. Fortunately, many states are adopting "consent to rate" laws which permit the use of higher rates when these are justified by existing conditions. Underwriters should use these rate adjustments to counteract increased physical hazards whenever possible; otherwise, the only alternative, other than to lose money, is to refuse to write the insurance.

Rate adjustments for physical hazards can have another beneficial effect. They may cause the applicant to take the necessary steps to reduce the hazard. Naturally, this will not be the result where there is no cure, such as in some cases of poor physical conditions, or in situations where improvement would be prohibitively expensive. However, many physical hazards can be corrected with a moderate amount of expense. A policyholder may feel that it is better to spend money in improving the property than in paying it in the form of increased insurance premiums; the latter course leaves the risk with the same poor condition and nothing to show for the increased expenditure. The underwriter welcomes this response to the imposition of a higher rate because the improvement will reduce the exposure to loss.

Physical hazards must be underwritten carefully and the condition must be improved if possible. If the underwriter cannot obtain an improvement, a rate must be charged which is adequate for the increased exposure. If prevented from securing an adequate rate, the underwriter must then decline the insurance, unless instructed that the company intends to lose money on the risk or the class because of other factors than underwriting (such as political pressures, agency demands, or related business). From an underwriting standpoint, physical hazards are probably the most common ones encountered and they must be handled in one manner or another — if the risk is to be accepted by the insurer.

QUESTIONS FOR DISCUSSION

1. Define the term "physical hazard,' and explain why it may be easier to detect than moral and morale hazards.
2. Briefly describe each of the three physical hazard types.
3. Describe the four sources of information available to underwriters that can be useful in detecting physical hazards.
4. Explain some of the policy provisions which can be useful in controlling physical hazards.
5. What are some of the conditions which create physical hazards with individuals and with property?

18

Legal Hazard

Legal hazard involves the increase in uncertainty caused by the operations of laws and court decisions. Liability insurance is written to protect the policyholder against loss arising out of a situation for which he or she may be held responsible. Legal hazards exist when conditions are changed to increase the probability or severity of loss, or both. These changes may be caused by actions of the policyholder or by others. Whether the hazards are within the control of the insured or not, they do increase the chance of loss, or by the rulings of authorities whose duty it is to administer or interpret the law.

It is not difficult to identify legal hazards, although it may be difficult to locate them. In this respect, legal hazards have somewhat the same relationship to liability insurance as physical hazards bear to property insurance. Both are relatively easy to detect, when compared with psychological (moral and morale) hazards. Both physical and legal hazards are largely confined to their respective classes of insurance, although each can apply to the other classes of insurance under certain conditions.

TYPES OF LEGAL HAZARDS

Legal hazards are specific, objective hazards. They exist because of situations which are created and which can lead to penalties under the law. There is nothing mysterious or subjective about them, in the manner in which moral and morale hazards are difficult to identify and evaluate.

Common law has developed over the centuries and forms the basis for our legal system today. Any person who owns property, conducts a business, or just moves around other people, may perform some act that makes that person liable to another person under common law. Some of these acts include those committed by the person who is held liable, such as one who injures the other person or damages his property. Other acts may be those of omission, such as failing to protect the other person from harm. These exposures to loss are present for everyone, and are commonly protected by liability policies of insurance. The losses are uncertain but they are founded in our heritage, and are thus considered to be basic uncertainties connected with living and with conducting a business.

There are six types of legal hazards that can be identified as increasing the uncertainty of losses and they have been added to the common law. An underwriter must be alert to conditions under which these hazards exist.

Doctrine of Absolute Liability. Under certain circumstances, a person can be held liable even if not negligent; this is called absolute liability. Common law requires negligence before a person can be held liable, and even then may plead such defenses as contributory negligence (the other party was also negligent) and assumption of risk (the other party knew of the danger and assumed the chance of loss). Absolute liability denies these defenses and holds the person liable if someone is injured under almost any condition.

Examples of absolute liability may be found in many types of situations. In the personal field, a person is absolutely liable if he or she maintains a wild, undomesticated animal as a pet. A person who owns a dog which is domesticated is not absolutely liable, but a person who owns a Bengal tiger and keeps it in his home may be absolutely liable. If the tiger harms someone, the injured party can collect from the owner of the tiger, regardless of the circumstances. In the commercial field, a person who performs blasting operations may be absolutely liable. The extra-hazardous nature of this work removes the common law defenses.

Workers' Compensation Laws. A common legal hazard is the statutory requirement that an employer provide medical treatment to an employee who is injured in the course of employment, or who contracts a disease of some type because of employment. Common law defenses are denied the employer, who must pay even if blameless and the employee is so carelessd as to almost constitute deliberate self-injury. Employers must pay medical expenses, disability benefits, weekly indemnity, and death benefits to injured employees and their dependents. Every state has passed workers' compensation laws which are similar in intent but are very different in detail.

Compulsory Automobile Insurance. In some states, motorists are required to carry automobile insurance with specified minimum limits of protection. This coverage is designed to protect third parties who are injured by the automobile. The intent, therefore, is not dissimilar from the intent of workers' compensation laws. These laws change occasionally, adding another dimension to the uncertainty created by this legal hazard.

Contracts. People sign many contracts in the course of their business and personal activities, many of which can create legal hazards. Contracts which transfer liability from one party to another are sometimes signed with full knowledge and concurrence of the parties. Other times, they are signed because the party is at a disadvantage, and must sign in order to secure desired benefits. Many times the provisions of the contract which create legal hazards are not clear or are even unknown to the person asssuming the liabilties. Common situations are those under which one party agrees to hold the other harmless for liabilities incurred while the assuming party is engaged in commercial activities on the property of the other party. Examples of the latter are railroad sidetrack agreements and lease agreements. Slightly different conditions exist under contracts signed between contractors and subcontractors, under which the subcontractor holds the contractor harmless for accidents occurring in conjunction with a work project.

Legislative Actions. State and federal governments pass laws that cause legal hazards, too. Conditions arise which appear, to those making the laws, to require modifications of the common law. These statutes may affect specified persons or businesses and can increase the uncertainty of loss.

Judicial Decisions. The various courts interpret the laws, and sometimes create legal hazards where none appeared before. This type of legal hazard is the most elusive and uncertain, because it can create liabilities for situations which have already occurred.

UNDERWRITING AGAINST LEGAL HAZARDS

Underwriters handling most lines of insurance must be aware of legal hazards in order to perform this function properly. All types of liability coverages obviously are greatly concerned with legal situations, not only those which are contemplated by the policies but also those extra conditions which create legal hazards. Even property insurance must be concerned with the various liability situations which may arise. Leasing agreements may affect coverage under a fire policy. Contracts may determine when the title passes, a matter of concern to a property underwriter.

Underwriters need to be aware of the possibility of legal hazards as they analyze available information. They must know situations under which absolute liability is imposed, and be alert for such situations in individual risks. They should be familiar with the workers' compensation laws and compulsory automobile laws, if they work with those lines. They also need to know the climate and trend of recent changes in laws from both legislative and judicial sources. Finally, they must analyze all contracts which might cause legal hazards.

The action an underwriter will take in order to handle legal hazards depends upon the specific situation. Some cases will require rate adjustments, others must be handled by policy provisions, some may be absorbed with no changes, while others will require declination of the application. The first step in every case, therefore, is to determine as much as possible about the risk.

Securing Information

As information is secured and interpreted, instances of legal hazard will become apparent. Sometimes these instances are obvious, but other times they may be merely suggested by other facts. The underwriter must be inquisitive wherever there is a hint that these conditions exist.

A number of sources are available to the underwriter from which to determine if legal hazards exist. Some of these sources are described starting with the application.

1. *Application.* An application which is properly prepared and properly completed can indicate the existence of most legal hazards. Absolute liability may be

indicated by the business operations performed by the applicant or by other factors. Contracts should be described in sufficient detail to permit preliminary judgment whether a legal hazard may be present. The type of coverage and the state in which the applicant resides or operates will give further clues to the underwriter who is well-versed in the problems which can arise.

2. *Inspection Reports.* Some types of inspection reports can be helpful, although special reports or special attention items must be used. The type of report used for most other purposes will seldom give the necessary information on legal hazards. Inspectors can look for problems, such as the existence of sidetrack agreements, if they are so requested. Inspections by employees of the insurer, such as engineers, may also be helpful; again, their special attention ordinarily should be directed to suspected conditions.

3. *Copies of Agreements.* Often the underwriter will need to request a copy of the actual agreement or contract, in order to be aware of the existence or extent of legal hazards. In order to do this, the underwriter must request the producer to obtain copies, in most cases. When the copies are received, the underwriter must analyze them. If they are particularly complex, the assistance of an attorney may be required. There are so many situations that can arise under the multiplicity of contracts and agreements in use today, and particularly when the various laws and judical interpretations are considered, that a careful and informed analysis is required in order to understand where legal liability lies. An underwriter must have this understanding before he can identify and handle the legal hazards.

4. *Advisory Bulletins.* Continual changes are taking place in the laws and interpretations affecting liability. An underwriter, in order to be considered fully informed, must be aware of the laws being passed and the judicial interpretations being rendered in jurisdictions where he or she underwrites and in the lines being handled. Changes are made in workers' compensation and compulsory automobile coverages, as well as in other fields of liability. An underwriter may subscribe to services for information on pertinent changes. More practical for many companies is the practice of assigning specific persons at the staff level to secure these changes, screen them, refine them, and forward them to the underwriter who will use them. These persons may be in the legal department, and confine their distribution of information to the facts about changes which are made. In other companies, these persons may be in the staff underwriting department; they would be more likely to interpret changes and to suggest (or demand) changes in underwriting practices which will be in accord with the new conditions.

5. *Claims Reports.* During the adjustment of any type of claim, the adjuster may discover new or previously undisclosed legal hazards. The underwriter should encourage the inclusion of comments about these hazards in the claims report. Even if the adjuster is not aware of the full impact of the hazard, or is unable to investigate it completely, it should be mentioned in the report. The underwriter then may use another source to secure necessary details, and to take whatever action is needed.

Interpreting Information

The facts gathered by the underwriter will enable a determination to be made about the extent of the applicant's liability. If the exposure is no more than is contemplated by the rate, there is no problem, but if unusual hazards are discovered, further action is required.

Specific information will be available in most cases involving contracts and absolute liability. If a legal hazard is present, the underwriter may attempt to secure its removal, recommending that certain changes be made in contracts in order to remove the hazardous conditions. The underwriter may even suggest that operations which are considered to result in absolute liability should be abandoned or revised.

More generalized information will be available in most cases, upon which to analyze legal hazards. The underwriter must be alert for situations which have been, or may foreseeably be, affected by new laws or judicial decisions. Whether in fields of workers' compensation and compulsory automobile, or in fields of general liability, the underwriter must try to identify problems. Having discovered these problems, the next step is to try to either remove them or correct them, if possible. Perhaps operations or situations can be revised to reduce or eliminate these conditions.

Employing Policy Provisions

Legal hazards may be partly controlled by policy provisions. These can be provisions printed in the basic policy, or they can be added by the underwriter, as is the case in underwriting other types of hazards. There are three provisions found in most policies that can help control legal hazards.

1. *Cancellation.* The insurer retains the right to cancel the policy with advance notice to the policyholder. With this provision, an underwriter may cancel a policy if the circumstances have changed enough to create a legal hazard. The uncertainty may have increased because of such internal changes as the signing of new contracts, the embarking upon new endeavors which are subject to absolute liability, or the entry into new states. On the other hand, the problem may be external and beyond the control of the insured, such as new laws or adverse judicial decisions. In any case, the underwriter will first try to handle the increased exposure by various available means. If the exposure cannot be controlled, the coverage must be cancelled. This is the ultimate underwriting control, but it is essential only as a last resort.

Within the past few years, noncancellation laws have been enacted in many states. Most of them are aimed at automobile insurance primarily, but they may involve other lines. These laws supersede cancellation provisions in the policies, and may prevent mid-term cancellation by insurers. When this condition exists, the underwriter must carry the risk to expiration date, and then may refuse to renew. In the future, even the right to nonrenew may be impaired, but it is likely that renewal may be refused for specific reasons, and underwriters may hope that increased legal exposure will be among those reasons.

2. *Inspection.* An inspection of the pertinent activities of the policyholder is permitted under most policies. This provision lets the underwriter discover the legal hazards leading to underwriting action— even to cancellation. The underwriter, or a person designated by the underwriter, is granted permission to inspect lease

agreements, contracts, records of operations in various states, and other information that may cause legal hazards.

Nonstandard clauses may be applied by the underwriter in certain cases. When legal hazards are discovered which cannot be controlled by other means, the only alternative to cancellation is to exclude the problem area. The underwriter may prepare an endorsement to exclude a certain person or operation, or to provide that no coverage exists under specified contracts. These specific exclusions are quite severe and are used sparingly. However, they may be acceptable alternatives to cancellation.

3. *Endorsements.* Amendments to all policies of a specified type may be required by underwriters when some legal hazards arise. An example is a court decision that extends a policy beyond the scope intended by those who drafted it. The underwriter may endorse all policies to bring the coverage back into its intended limits by revising definitions or adding exclusions. These changes will, of course, be incorporated into the policies upon reprint. In the meantime, endorsements may be used by underwriters to control the hazard.

Using Underwriting Controls

Deductibles are not commonly used in liability insurance, although they are not impossible. Most insurers do not like them because they tend to cause the late reporting of accidents, especially when the amount of claim is below the amount of the deductible. The reasoning is this: the policyholder may demand a voice in the claim settlement since some of the money is directly the policyholder's; and also, it is sometimes difficult to recover the amount of the deductible from the policyholder after a settlement has been made. The latter reason is inherent in any liability situation because the company claims adjuster must be able to settle the entire loss at the proper moment, without delaying settlement while the deductible is forwarded by the policyholder.

Large commercial risks may be sophisticated enough in insurance matters to permit the use of deductibles. In these cases, a substantial deductible may help to control legal hazards. However, the potential size of liability claims renders deductibles almost meaningless in terms of prevention of losses; the policyholder is not likely to be more careful about signing contracts or expanding into new operations merely because of a requirement to absorb a relatively small amount in the form of a deductible. On the other hand, when there is a frequency of losses, a deductible may reduce the total amount of claims payment to a considerable degree. Thus, deductibles may be used by commercial underwriters in some situations, but not as commonly as in the property lines.

Another underwriting control deals with limiting the amount of insurance written. In liability insurance, this means placing a ceiling on the limit of liability under the policy. When an underwriter encounters a risk where a legal hazard is present, a limitation on the total insurance available may serve to reduce the hazard to one with which the company can live. This action may force the applicant to secure additional coverage elsewhere, or may force the applicant to take necessary steps to remove or reduce the exposure. Either alternative will solve the problem, from the standpoint of the underwriter.

Employing Rate Adjustments

Rates are available to the underwriter to use in attempting to control legal hazards, and surcharges may be applied to cover various situations. Some of these added costs are fixed, such as those for workers' compensation and compulsory automobile coverages. Others may be included in rate guides which are used by underwriters in determining rates which appear to be adequate for various contractual and absolute liability situations; if the exposure is greater than the contemplated rates. The underwriter must either secure the necessary approval to use special rates or must decline the risk.

Legal hazards caused by legislative actions and judicial decisions will ultimately be reflected in the basic rates. Until then, underwriters should attempt to use adequate rates for those hazards that are known and measurable. No rate allowance can be made for those which are not yet known, such as laws which have not yet been passed, or decisions which have not yet been rendered by the highest courts to which the cases are appealed. It is impractical to consider rate increases based upon such conjecture. The underwriter who anticipates a new law or an adverse decision may want to identify those files which could be affected, but should not attempt to take action based upon the contingency. When this adverse legislation or legal interpretation becomes evident, the underwriter may want to increase the rates to compensate for the increased exposure. The exposure to these legal hazards is one of the problems of the insurance business, and is the reason that underwriters like to have a little cushion in the basic rates.

QUESTIONS FOR DISCUSSION

1. Why are legal hazards more readily identifiable than either moral or morale hazards, but more difficult to locate than physical hazards?
2. Briefly describe the various types of legal hazards.
3. How can absolute liability be of concern to both insurers and insureds?
4. Explain, in general, the extent to which legal hazards can be controlled by policy provisions.
5. What are the advantages and disadvantages for using deductibles on liability exposure which commonly are prompted by legal hazards?

INTRODUCTION TO PART V

UNDERWRITING PRACTICES BY LINE OF INSURANCE

Although property and casualty insurance is divided into many lines and some of these lines are combined in package policies, their separate identities are fairly well maintained. The practices of underwriting, as applied to each of the major lines of insurance, are discussed in this part. Each chapter discusses a separate line, except that several minor lines are combined in Chapter 30. For ease of handling and for ready reference, the same basic outline is followed for each line. Briefly, this outline is as follows.

First, the scope of the line and its coverages are explained, along with some of the basic information about the line and its significance in the insurance picture. The description of coverages is relatively brief, being included only to provide an idea of the types of protection which are offered. An underwriter needs to know additional details about the lines being handled, but generally needs no more than this on other lines.

Discussed next are the underwriting factors. In these sections, each of the basic functions of underwriting is discussed separately in the same order as in Part III, with the general outlines of these functions explained in detail as they apply to all lines. The specific sections in the chapters on each line are as follows:

1. Selection of risks. Under each line, this function is explained in two sections. One concerns eligible risks, and contains a description of the types of risks generally eligible for the coverages. The other section looks at ineligible risks, approaching the selection function from the standpoint of an underwriter who attempts to define those risks he or she does not want to insure. This section deals with the actual underwriting considerations which are used to select risks for that particular line of insurance.

2. Securing information. As was explained in a previous chapter, the underwriter must "get the facts." Since many sources of information are available to underwriters, this section explains the sources generally used for each line and the types of information that can be secured from each source.

3. Classification and rating. An integral function of underwriting is the classification and rating of each risk. Specific details are not given; rate manuals are available for that purpose. These details vary between areas and companies and are frequently changed. In the following chapters, the general types of approaches are explained in enough detail to guide an underwriter in applying the information found in the rate manuals.

4. Policy forms. Another integral function of underwriting is in the application of policy forms. General indications are given for each line as to when policies are written and how much latitude the underwriter is given to make modifications. There are variations among lines, so general practices for each line are explained.

5. Retention and reinsurance. The final step in underwriting an application involves determining the amount of insurance to be retained, and securing necessary reinsurance to protect the company. Since many different practices are used, with variations by companies and by lines, the general approaches are explained in each chapter.

Some lines of insurance present special problems of a contemporary nature, such as social or legislative conditions. When these are significant, they are discussed at the end of the chapters. The chapters in this part, then, present a general picture of underwriting practices actually followed by underwriters for each line of insurance.

19

Personal Automobile

The largest single line of insurance in the property-casualty field is automobile insurance. It is written by about 900 individual companies, whose more than $73 billion of automobile insurance premiums estimated for 1985 accounted for 41% of the total writings of property and casualty insurance.[1]

While private passenger automobiles used for personal purposes constitute the bulk of this line, other vehicles are also included, such as private passenger automobiles used in business, motorcycles, motorbikes, golf carts, snow mobiles, dune buggies, and most other types of conveyances used for transporting people on public or private roads. Total private passenger automobile premiums were almost $58 billion in 1986.[2]

Commercial vehicles are considered to be a separate line of insurance by most insurers. This line includes trucks of every description, as well as other types of equipment and conveyances used in businesses. The next chapter explains the underwriting of commercial vehicles.

DESCRIPTION OF COVERAGES

Some knowledge of the coverages offered on an automobile insurance policy is necessary for an understanding of the underwriting process. While there are some differences between the policies used by various insurers, the following brief explanation generally applies.

The automobile insurance policy is a divisible contract; that is, each of the coverages is separate and distinct. The applicant may select any or all of the coverages,

---

1. "Review and Preview: Up from the Ashes," *Best's Review, Property/Casualty Insurance Edition*, Vol. 87, No. 9 (January, 1987), p. 16.
2. Ibid., p.83

in any combination, subject to only a few exceptions which will be noted, and subject to the approval of the underwriter. The contract itself may bracket several coverages for purposes of definitions and other provisions, but this is for ease of reading and economy of printing only.

Automobile Liability Insurance

The insurer agrees to pay all damages the insured becomes legally obligated to pay because of specified occurrences arising out of ownership, maintenance or use of the automobile. These accidents are of two types: bodily injury to other persons, and damage to property of others. In addition to paying for legal obligations, the insurer also agrees to defend the insured.

Bodily injury (BI) and property damage liability (PD) coverages are called "third party coverages" because they are concerned with damages to people other than the insured. The policyholder does not collect anything under these coverages, but benefits by having legal obligations paid by the insurer, as well as having legal defense furnished.

Bodily injury and property damage limits of liability are selected by the applicant from those offered by the insurer. Theoretically, a person should purchase limits that are adequate to protect that person's possessions and estate against an adverse lawsuit. In practice, many persons purchase the minimum coverage which is usually the amount needed to satisfy such state requirements as financial responsibility laws. (These laws have been enacted by almost all states to assure that an owner or operator of an automobile will be able to satisfy judgments in the event of bodily injury accidents, or property damage accidents over a specified amount. The penalties are such that most car registrants purchase liability insurance, this being the only practiced means of complying with the law.)

Maximum amounts of liability are limited only by what the insurer is willing to offer and the applicant is willing to buy. Liability limits are more often available on a single-limit basis, although split limits can be obtained, if the insured desires. When coverage on a single-limit applies, the limit is expressed as $20,000 or $50,000, for example. The amount so designated represents the limit of liability for bodily injury to one or more persons, as well as all property damage sustained in any one accident. When coverage is purchased with split limits, the amounts are commonly expressed in an abbreviated form, such as 15/30/10. The first number ("15" in this illustration) represents the limit of liability for bodily injury to one person, while the second represents the limit for bodily injury to all persons injured in a single accident; both are in thousands of dollars. The third number is the limit of liability for property damage arising out of an accident, also in thousands of dollars. Using the illustration of 15/30/10, the most that the insurer would pay because of the legal obligations of the insured for a single accident is $15,000 for bodily injury to any one person and an aggregate of $30,000 for bodily injury to all persons, plus $10,000 for property damage.

As a matter of comparison, an insured with 15/30/10 split limits has a maximum of $40,000 protection in the event of one accident involving both bodily injury and property damage, whereas the same insured with a single-limit of $30,000 would require a limit of $40,000 to be fully protected. However, if the injury to one person amounted to $20,000, the split limits of 15/30/10 would be insufficient to protect the insured, whereas the single-limit of $30,000 would be more than sufficent to protect the insured.

The cost of defense is in addition to these liability limits. However, there is a trend toward specifying that when the insurer pays the limit of its liability, it is no longer required to defend the insured against further claims arising out of that accident. For example, continuing the illustration previously used, if the insurer had paid $15,000 for bodily injury to each of two claimants ($30,000 in total), and then a third claimant presented a demand, the insurer is not required by the policy to defend the third claim.

The automobile underwriter will be concerned about the exposure to legal liability of an applicant and concerned about the size of the claim if one occurs. The underwriter will attempt to accept an applicant who is less liable to become involved in an accident in which that person is legally liable, subject to the other underwriting considerations. Since protection is provided not only for the named insured and spouse, but also for any resident of the household plus any other person who uses the automobile with permission, information is also desired about other drivers. The underwriter will attempt to relate the possibility of a loss and the maximum exposure, as represented by the liability limit requested, again subject to rates and other considerations.

Liability coverages are included in most automobile insurance policies, but not all. Some policies cover only the liability section of the policy, while others may only include physical damage coverages.

Uninsured Motorists Coverage

A person who suffers damages for which another person is legally liable may not be able to collect them if the other person does not have liability insurance. To protect against this contingency, an applicant may purchase uninsured motorists coverage (UM) which pays the damages as though the other party did carry liability coverage. In effect, the policyholder's own insurer steps into the shoes of the "absent" insurer for the other party and pays the policyholder.

This coverage was first introduced in the 1950s, and became so popular that by the end of the 1960s, most states required every insurer to offer it in conjunction with liability coverages. Many states require that it be included with every automobile liability insurance policy, unless the applicant signs a separate statement that this coverage is not wanted. While most states require that such coverage be written only for bodily injury, some states have applied it to property damage also; this seems to be the current trend. Uninsured motorists coverage is seldom, if ever, written alone. It is closely related to liability coverage and ordinarily written only on policies covering automobile liabilty insurance.

Underwriting of individual applicants for uninsured motorists coverage is virtually nonexistent. If liability coverage is written, the states usually require that this coverage be offered also. Even if this were not true, there is little selection possible for this coverage alone. On the other hand, the underwriter should be alert for trends on large groups of policies. It is apparent that if almost everyone carries liability insurance, there will be few claims under uninsured motorists coverage. Conversely, a territory in which a relatively small number of drivers carry bodily injury and property damage coverages will have an unusually large volume of uninsured motorists claims. Under the latter conditions, if a state requires that uninsured motorists insurance be offered, the underwriter must either seek additional premium for the coverage or restrict its writings in that territory to avoid poor loss experience.

The limit of liability is ordinarily the financial responsibility limit required by the state. The theory is that the policyholder is protected as though the negligent other party carried the minimum state requirement. Higher limits are offered in many states, and are required to be offered in an increasingly large number of states. Policyholders and regulators have become aware that minimum amounts of uninsured motorists coverage are inadequate for many people. An injured person may need higher medical limits if other insurance is not available, or higher loss-of-income limits if self-employed or if an employer does not furnish a salary continuation plan. Some policyholders may want to be able to recover more than the minimum amount for inconvenience, pain and suffering. Such people will want higher limits for uninsured motorists coverage. Companies ordinarily will not write these limits for more than the amount of bodily injury liability coverage, on the theory that a person should not be able to recover more than the amount of protection carried to protect others.

Underinsured Motorists Coverage

A person who carries higher limits of uninsured motorists coverage will do so to make available more than the minimum amount of coverage, if the other motorist is liable. The same need exists if the other motorist is uninsured or is carrying only minimum limits of liability. However, in the latter case, uninsured motorists coverage will not pay, because the other party is not actually uninsured.

This gap is filled by *under*insured motorists coverage (UIM). It pays up to its limit if the third party is liable but is carrying liability insurance in a lower amount than the UIM limit of the policyholder. In effect, it is the same as if the other party carried liability insurance in an amount equal to the limits desired by the policyholder. Since the other party does carry some liability insurance, that amount is deducted from the UIM limit carried (in most states). Figure 7 gives examples of insured motorists and underinsured motorists loss situations, using different limits carried.

Medical Payments Coverage

The insurer agrees to pay all reasonable expenses incurred within one year from the date of accident for necessary medical expenses. The insured and relatives are covered while in the described automobile or a non-owned vehicle, as well as though being struck by an automobile or in another automobile being operated by the insured.

FIGURE 7
Examples of UM and UIM Recovery
(Per Person) Assume $50,000 Loss

1. "B" Party is uninsured

Coverage	A	B	C
UM	15,000	100,000	100,000
UIM	—	—	100,000
Collect			
UM	15,000	50,000	50,000
UIM	—	—	—

2. "B" Party has 15,000 Liability Policy

Coverage	D	E	F
UM	15,000	100,000	100,000
UIM	—	—	100,000
Collect			
UM	Nil	Nil	Nil
UIM	—	—	35,000*

* 50,000 loss less 15,000 Liability Coverage

Medical payments coverage applies to "bodily injury, caused by accident." It pays for necessary medical, surgical, dental, hospital, nursing, and similar services, as well as ambulance and nursing care and even pays funeral expenses!

This is a first-party coverage. Since the policyholder and the policyholder's family receive direct benefits through having their medical bills covered, it could be considered as automobile accident insurance. Other persons may also receive benefits, but only those who are in the automobile owned or operated by the insured. Many people want to carry the coverage because they feel a moral obligation to pay the medical costs of guests injured in their cars. Furthermore, the payment of medical expenses probably prevents many law suits, and some of these law suits could be "friendly" suits which act to the detriment of the insurer. In any event, insurers generally encourage the writing of this coverage.

Limits for medical payments coverage are usually offered in the following amounts: $500, $750, $1,000, $2,000 or $5,000. As the cost of medical services increases, the natural tendency is for higher limits to be sold. In the 1950s, limits of $250 or $500 were common; now, insurers offer limits of $5,000 and even $10,000. Premiums are quite modest which is probably the reason that this coverage is ordinarily available only in conjunction with liability insurance.

Underwriting medical payments coverage is almost nonexistent, other than underwriting for loss frequency on the automobile policy in general. An excessive usage of this coverage should be investigated; perhaps the automobile has jagged parts that cause repeated injuries to occupants, or perhaps the driver is involved in many accidents. The cause of the losses will indicate the action that is needed, if any, such as cancellation of that coverage.

No-Fault Coverage

A number of states have enacted laws which require the offering of expanded first party coverage against bodily injury, disability or death. Medical payments coverage is the foundation, often in limits of $2,000 to $5,000, or for "reasonable and necessary" expenses without a dollar limit.

Other out-of-pocket expenses are also covered. Wage loss is included, up to a limit, such as $200 per week, and usually limited to about 85% of the actual loss, since these payments are not subject to federal income taxes. Replacement or substitute services are covered, to the extent of actual loss up to about $20 per day; these services include, for example, mowing the lawn, cooking the meals, or doing the laundry, which the injured party is unable to perform because of the accident. Funeral benefits of about $1,000 are included in some plans.

Some states require no-fault coverages as a type of expanded medical payments coverage. Others provide that these coverages are an exclusive remedy, and the injured person cannot sue a third party unless the out-of-pocket expenses exceed a specified threshold. The threshold, below which suit cannot be brought, sometimes is a dollar amount, such as $500, $750, or $1,000. Other times, it is a "verbal threshold." One law, for example, permits recovery in tort in the event injury or disease consists in whole or in part of:

(a) Significant and permanent loss of an important bodily function.
(b) Permanent injury within a reasonable degree of medical probability, other than scarring or disfigurement.
(c) Significant and permanent scarring or disfigurement.
(d) Death.

Physical Damage Coverages

There are several coverages available against damage to the described automobile. These are grouped under the common titles of physical damage or material damage. Together they account for about 40% of the total automobile insurance premiums.[3]

Comprehensive or (other than collision loss coverage). This is a broad coverage which pays for loss to the described automobile caused by accidental means, except as otherwise excluded. Thus, it is an all risks coverage, applying to all losses except those excluded, as compared to a named peril coverage which lists the perils or losses that are covered. The principal exclusion is collision (which is covered in

3. "Review & Preview," *Best's Review, Property/Casualty Insurance Edition*, Vol. 87, No. 9 (January, 1987), p. 16.

the next item). In fact, the easiest means of defining these coverages is to describe collision coverage first, and then state that all other losses are covered under comprehensive coverage. However, comprehensive coverage is traditionally placed before collision coverage in the policies.

Comprehensive car damage coverage has a few other exclusions. Most of them are obvious, such as war, radioactivity, wear and tear, freezing and mechanical breakdown. Glass breakage and loss caused by such perils as falling objects, earthquake, or colliding with a bird or animal are usually specified as not being caused by collision. This latter provision is important because many losses could be covered under comprehensive or collision, and it is best to clarify the intent before the loss occurs.

Collision. Damage to the automobile caused by collision with another object or with a vehicle to which it is attached is insured by collision coverage. Also, covered is "upset of the automobile," and the coverage is sometimes referred to as "collision and upset."

Towing and Road Service. This coverage pays for reasonable and necessary towing and labor costs resulting from disablement of the described automobile. It is used when a car will not start because the battery is dead, when a tire goes flat, when the motor overheats and stalls the car, and similar occurrences. A common limit of coverage is $25 per disablement. Towing and labor costs are covered up to that amount, but only for such labor as is performed at the place of disablement. Thus, if a tire develops a puncture, the cost of changing to a spare tire would be covered up to the limit of coverage, but the repair of the puncture made at the tire shop or service station would not be covered. The cost for this coverage is very low and is seldom, if ever, written without the physical damage coverages.

These material damage coverages may be written separately or in combination with other coverages, depending upon one's needs or desires. However, there are a few insurers that combine comprehensive and collision into one indivisible coverage, but this is not common. Deductibles are used to prevent small claims, to encourage carefulness on the part of the policyholder and to reduce premiums. Collision coverage is almost always written with a deductible, with $100 and $250 being the most common. Rarely is a collision deductible lower than $100; the trend is toward larger deductibles, $500 or higher. Comprehensive and fire-theft coverages were written without deductibles until the middle 1960s, generally, but then $25 or $50 deductibles became common. Inflation later caused increases in the minimum amounts offered. No deductible is used on towing coverage, however.

Underwriting the material damage coverages differs somewhat between the coverages. All of them, of course, are subject to the general evaluation concerning potential loss frequency as measured by the factors discussed in this chapter. In addition, towing and collision coverages are not ordinarily written on older cars, usually defined as those over 10 years old. Moreover, comprehensive and collision coverages are not written by some insurers to cover some of the less common foreign cars, because of the possible difficulty and delay in getting parts and in locating adequate repair facilities.

When a policyholder presents more losses under material damage coverage than the underwriter feels can be tolerated, there are several alternatives to cancellation. A deductible can be applied to comprehensive coverage; a higher deductible can be used on collision or comprehensive; or a specific exclusion can be used in some cases, such as to hub caps if the theft frequency has increased. Some underwriters may even require a comprehensive coverage deductible on all cars not kept in a garage at night, particularly in high crime areas.

UNDERWRITING FACTORS

Most automobile insurers define the general market area in which they expect to operate. Even if an insurer does not specifically or consciously adopt such a definition, its rate structure will limit its policyholders to one broad class. As will be seen, there are several distinct groups into which automobile insurance rates fall. An applicant who qualifies for a low rate will not accept an applicant who qualifies only for a high rate.

Each insurer will thus consider a section of the market as the risks acceptable for its protection. Beyond this, there are no acceptability lists, as such, for most automobile insurers. The broad and universal acceptability rule that a risk is acceptable if the auto is used for private passenger purposes, rather than commercial purposes, is in the very definition of the line.

Types of Risks

There are three broad groups of insureds, based on the type of risks generally acceptable: *preferred, substandard and standard.*

Preferred risks are those who are acceptable for the lowest rates. They have good driving records and have no convictions. They are stable in their employment and living habits, and they are mature in emotions, as well as in age. An insurer writing only risks of this type can use relatively low rates, enabling it to attract still more risks in this category.

Substandard risks are at the other extreme. They have one or more of the factors which lead to an abnormal number of claims: poor driving records, instability, and immaturity and are risks that have difficulty in getting insurance in the other markets. Companies which insure such risks necessarily have high rates and use rating schedules which can develop almost astronomical premiums. Those insurers that uses such rating systems are able to offer coverage to virtually all drivers, the only exceptions being drivers with very serious records, such as several hit-and-run citations or several accidents involving injuries, all within a few years. Theoretically their acceptability lists would be "all applicants." However, most applicants who can obtain insurance at lower rates would not consider themselves as likely candidates for substandard insurers, and this restricts the true acceptability list to the least desirable risks.

Standard risks are those who fall between the other two extremes. They have a few problems with their driving records or their stability or their maturity, but they are not substandard. Insurers of this group will use rates that are between the two extremes and will accept all applicants except those considered to be substandard.

The acceptability lists for standard risks will be larger than those used by either of the other groups.

Types of Insurers

Noticeable distinctions are present among insurers that write these three classes of risks. The differences are not in corporate structure (each type has stock, mutual and reciprocals) but in methods of operation. The same general differences apply to other lines of insurance, but they are much sharper in automobile insurance because of the intense competition, the tremendous size of the market and the relative homogeneity of the risk. Recognizing that there are notable exceptions in each class, the general characteristics are as follows.

Preferred risk companies tend to be independent. Some are huge national companies, while others are small, operating in special local markets. Many write through employees or exclusive agents or by direct mail. In total, they write well over half of the automobile insurance in many states.

Substandard risk companies are generally small, local insurers. The most obvious exceptions are those operated as running-mates for some of the preferred-risk insurers and a few of the standard insurers. Altogether, these companies insure only about five or 10% of the automobiles.

Standard risk companies are generally the bureau companies, making rates through a bureau, although some deviate. Most are companies that also write other lines; indeed, many are stronger in lines other than automobile insurance. This group contains the largest number of companies, but probably writes less than one-third of the automobile insurance premium.

Distinction Between Risks

The line of demarcation between acceptable classes of policyholders are indistinct. Specific applicants will often be insured in a different class than would otherwise be expected for a multitude of reasons. An average, nonpreferred risk may be written in a preferred risk company because of related business, or because of influence exerted by the applicant. A preferred risk may insure in a standard-risk company because the applicant likes the producer, or has related business with the insurer. Still another applicant may appear to be a preferred risk, but is declined because the driving record cannot be verified. These situations often arise because of underwriting considerations. An important fuction of the underwriter is to select those applicants fitting within the acceptability group considered by the company to be its segment of the market.

A few insurers have acceptability lists based on more precise factors. Some insure only nondrinkers on the assumption that they have fewer accidents. Other offer policies only to members of certain professions or types of employment, such as teachers, preachers or military personnel. Still others solicit certain age groups, perhaps senior citizens. In each case, the management of the insurance company has decided that it can best serve a specified market, and the acceptability list reflects that decision. These lists are usually defined so severely that the authority of the underwriter is circumscribed within the boundaries of these lists.

UNACCEPTABLE RISKS

Almost every insurer uses a list of risks considered to be unacceptable. The only exceptions are some of the substandard risk companies that attempt to offer coverages to each applicant at the same price, as was explained previously. Many factors determine the content of the unacceptable lists used. Companies vary in the degree of experience and knowledge of underwriting management and some companies are more alert than others to changes in exposure and sociological factors. Each insurer, therefore, must tailor its lists to the segment of the market it wants to write.

The following categories are used, in varying degrees, by most automobile insurers. Details of unacceptable lists are probably different for each insurer. In general, however, preferred risk insurers use more strict application of the following categories, while those writing at "standard" rates use many of these items but in a more liberal way.

Driving Habits

Studies have indicated that the driving record of an applicant is the best indicator of expected future accidents. For example, one report showed that, compared with a driver who had received no conviction over a three-year period, a driver with one conviction was 1.95 times as likely to have an accident within the next three years. Drivers with two convictions are 2.70 times as likely, and three convictions, the "times-as-many" factor is 3.54. The table continues to progress, indicating that a driver with nine or more convictions is 9.03 times as likely to have an accident as the driver with no convictions.[4]

The same report reveals that most drivers do not have many accidents or convictions. Over a two-year period, only 1.3% of the drivers had two or more accidents while another 10.5% had one accident. This leaves 88.2% of the drivers who had no accidents in two years. Extending the period to three years, 83% of the driving population was accident-free. Looking at these figures from another viewpoint, the average driver was involved in an accident only once every 12 years.[5]

Because of the evidence presented by these studies, many insurers consider as unacceptable, any applicant who has a poor driving record based upon a specified maximum number of accidents and convictions over a given period of time. For example, an applicant may be unacceptable if he or she has had more than two accidents and two convictions during the previous three years.

Definitions cause problems in establishing and administering these rules. An "accident" could be any accident in which the driver was involved, or it could be only those in which the driver was judged to be at fault. Some companies do not count accidents occurring while the driver was legally parked, or legally stopped for a traffic control device. Convictions can be equally difficult. It is common to excuse convictions for illegal parking, for failure to have a driver's license in one's

---

4. States of California Department of Motor Vehicles, *The California Driver Fact Book,* Report No. 29. Sacramento, California, Second Ed., July, 1976.

5. *Ibid.*

possession or similar offenses considered as having no reflection upon poor driving habits.

The underwriter often faces a dilemma in evaluating some of these accidents and convictions. The applicant feels, with much justification, that there should not be a penalty for a not-at-fault accident when the other party paid all damages. Similarly, some applicants feel that many citations are given in "speed traps" or in unusual circumstances or just because they are being "persecuted." On the other hand, the underwriter knows that an unusual frequency of such occurrences tends to indicate that the driver is careless or accident prone or does not practice defensive driving. The underwriter realizes, furthermore, that these studies include all accidents and convictions appearing on record in state motor vehicle departments, and any dilution of the rule will probably increase the chances of future losses. Finally, the underwriter knows that only a small minority of drivers receives any conviction or is involved in any accident over a short period of time. (The average driver receives one moving violation about every three years and one accident every 12 years.)[6] It is difficult, therefore, for an automobile underwriter to be persuaded that an applicant with three or four citations and a couple of accidents is a "typical" risk.

Still another problem with accident and conviction rules is when an applicant's driving record cannot be verified. The applicant may tell the producer, who in turn tells the underwriter, that he or she has had no accidents or convictions, but this cannot be verified. Perhaps the applicant has recently moved in from another country, or even from another state that does not exchange motor vehicle records. The underwriter must decide, within the limits of authority, if such a statement should be accepted. Many times the decision will hinge upon other underwriting factors, and an applicant whose driving record cannot be verified will be considered unacceptable, unless all other factors are flawless.

Accident and conviction rules are often some of the most difficult for an automobile underwriter to handle, for previous reasons mentioned. Judgment is required in many cases, if the underwriter wants to be fair, and this often brings nothing but criticism. The easy way is to use a rule as an absolute, with all applicants either qualifying or not, depending solely upon the record of accidents and convictions. This is not true underwriting, however. The unacceptable list may show a "poor driving record," and may define it, but the underwriter must administer it.

Another item often appearing on unacceptability lists of automobile insurers is related to the driving record. It concerns the driver's license of the applicant or the driver of the car. If a regular driver has no valid driver's license, the risk is ordinarily unacceptable. If a driver has had a driver's license suspended or revoked within a specified period of time, this risk also would be unacceptable for most insurers; some insurers may even consider as unacceptable, any driver who has ever had a license suspended or revoked.

---

6. *The California Driver Fact Book.*

Stability

Experience has taught automobile underwriters that the stability of the applicant is an important factor in measuring desirability, since instability in living factors apparently tends to indicate emotional instability, and that adversely affects driving habits.

People who change jobs frequently or who move frequently, or who live in transient types of quarters like motels or hotels, may give evidence of instability. A related problem is that the underwriter often has difficulty in securing more information through an inspection, in cases where the applicant is moving around frequently. For these reasons, automobile insurers often put on the unacceptable list, applicants who have had several residence addresses in a recent period, or have held more than a specified number of jobs, or who live at temporary addresses. This factor has increased in importance in recent years because people tend to be considerably more mobile, and more inclined to move often, than in previous decades. The underwriter, therefore, finds the job more difficult as this factor becomes more prevalent.

Age of Drivers

The underwriting criteria of most automobile insurers contains one or more references to age of the principal driver or of any driver. These rules are based upon solid foundations of experience and research. Youthful male drivers are a problem to automobile underwriters. Variously defined as being drivers under age 21, 25, or even 30, and sometimes differing by marital status, the class has many differences between companies. As an example, some insurers consider all single males who are principal drivers under age 25 as unacceptable. Many times the rule has exceptions, such as in situations when the parents have been insured in the company for a stated minimum period of time.

Starting in the 1950s, the problem of the youthful male driver began to get recognition. The problem did not abate during the following years. Studies have shown that teenage male drivers have twice as many accidents and more than twice as many citations as drivers over 20 years of age.

According to another study, there were 142.2 million drivers in the nation during 1978 who were involved in 31.5 million accidents of which 67,200 were fatalities. Of the total number of drivers, 10% or 14.2 million represented youths under the age of 20. This group was involved in 17.8% of all automobile-related accidents and 17.2% of all fatalities. On the other hand, those between the ages of 20 and 24 (16.9 million drivers) were involved in 20% of all vehicle accidents and 21% of the fatalities.[7]

Female youthful drivers escaped much of the criticism directed at the driving habits of their male counterparts. Through the 1950s and well into the 1960s, many underwriters theorized that females used their cars less at night hours, and were less inclined to show off or to alter their cars to make them more powerful. Still, a separate classification was created, and the experience soon worsened. Only when it became

7. National Safety Council, *Accident Facts,* 1978 Edition, Chicago, IL.

obvious that the losses were heavy on policies of females did underwriters change their opinions. They then realized that many females also liked to drive fast and to take chances. Even when this was not true, some young women let their boy friends drive their cars, particularly on dates, and the youthful male drivers exposure added to the adverse loss experience. By the end of the 1960s, underwriters recognized that youthful female drivers were also a problem and unacceptable lists were revised to include them, along with rate adjustments and other modifications.

Research has indicated that the major reasons for poor experience of youthful drivers are immaturity, lack of experience, absence of parental control and show-off tendencies. Because of these problems, and faced with unassailable statistics, many insurers use more restrictive accident and conviction acceptability rules for youthful drivers and require more evidence of stability. Other underwriters have tried other measures. Psychological testing of youthful applicants has been attempted by several insurers, in detecting, in advance, those with unstable characteristics. It has long been felt that youths who are hostile, who are emotionally immature, and whose entire attitude is one of aggression, are the problem drivers and can be discovered by testing. The basic assumptions of causes are probably correct. Unfortunately, no testing which is economically feasible has been found to be reliable. Several insurers have continued to experiment in this field, and they may find that it works for their clientele and their manner of operation. However, present indications are that underwriters find that their best hope for improved selection lies in more detailed studies of statistics concerning the population, its distribution and its trends.

At the other end of the age scale are the senior citizens. Controversy developed near the end of the 1960s on whether they are, as a class, better or worse drivers than the middle-aged group. (The arguments are presented in the rating discussion later in this chapter.) It is suffice to say here that some companies have an item on the unacceptable list referring to drivers over a certain age, usually 65 or 68. Even if the underwriters were convinced that senior drivers, as a class, are not a problem, many of the preferred risk insurers might keep them on unacceptable lists. As a general rule, they remain policyholders for a relatively short time; they may soon develop driving problems; and they seldom can offer much related business. In short, they may be average prospects, but seldom preferred. These comments refer, of course, to new applicants. Most insurers, perhaps all, will retain an older driver far beyond the age specified on the unacceptable list, so long as no adverse driving experience develops.

Occupation

Since the occupation of the applicant has long been considered an important underwriting factor, the unacceptable list of virtually every automobile insurer contains some occupational groups. Some of these unacceptable occupations are not difficult to explain or justify. Persons engaged in transient occupations, such as circus performers, race track attendants and migratory agricultural workers, are often difficult to locate for purposes of collecting premiums, serving processes of suit and mailing notices of cancellation or restrictions, as well as securing underwriting information. Even more obvious are persons engaged in illegal activities; it would be against public policy, as well as abhorrent to any responsible enterprise, to insure persons engaged in dope smuggling, for example.

Other occupations fall more within the realm of subjective factors, such as persons who "float" from job to job and from place to place. In general, and speaking in a relative sense in comparison with the general population, they tend to be less stable, less property-oriented and less respected as citizens.

However, these generalities are not true of all persons in these classes. Undoubtedly, there are exceptions in every occupational group. There are those who are as stable, family conscious and responsible as persons in any other occupation. The reason that these occupations have been listed as unacceptable is that a majority of the people in these occupations are not acceptable. Since it is expensive and often difficult to determine if a particular applicant is the exception, that person should be accepted. It has been easier, and more economical in such a large operation as automobile insurance, to consider all of the people in these occupations as unacceptable. However, an underwriter can always make an exception and consider such an applicant, even though starting out by assuming unacceptability.

This approach started to fade quickly near the end of the 1960s. Sociological trends in the country gave the major impetus to change, as "civil liberties" and "discrimination" became central issues. Automobile insurance is closer to being "social insurance" than most other types of property and casualty insurance and its underwriters are more conscious of social and political pressures. For these reasons, the trend is toward removing most occupations from unacceptable lists. Instead, underwriters consider each applicant on his or her own merits, regardless of occupation, although a few occupations may remain on unacceptable lists of companies who use them.

Other Personal Factors

A long list of miscellaneous personal factors are used by various automobile insurers. (The number varies among companies, but virtually all used some of these factors.) The most common of these unacceptable personal factors are those relating to the responsibility shown by the applicants toward others. A criminal record is a prime example. Excessive use of alcohol or drugs is another. However, other factors relate to circumstances beyond the control of the applicant, to some degree. Examples of these are physical impairment, noncitizens, persons in the country less than one year and applicants who cannot read or write English.

As was previously seen to be the case with occupations, there are reasons why these factors are on unacceptable lists. Some physically-impaired drivers may drive cars not properly equipped to offset their impairment or they may be subject to sudden and unpreventable seizures or attacks. Persons who cannot speak English tend to make poor witnesses in court, and they raise the suspicion that they drive cars without knowledge of our laws or ability to read our traffic signs. On the other hand, many of these people are good drivers. For this reason, the same trend is present here as is present in connection with occupations, i.e., the removal of these groups from unacceptable lists and the underwriting of individual applicants.

Within a few years, it is quite possible that all of these personal, subjective factors will be removed from the unacceptable lists used by automobile insurers. Underwriting caution guides may contain these factors, for they are legitimate subjects of underwriting concern. But future underwriters will tend to use objective factors, like accident and conviction records of drivers, as the only personal items on unacceptable lists.

Use of the Automobile

Most insurers writing private passenger automobile insurance do not wish to insure commercial uses of such vehicles. They are not prepared to handle such exposures, because they lack underwriting knowledge, rates or policy issuance requirements.

Because of this situation, automobile insurers often consider emergency vehicles equipped with red lights and sirens, messenger or delivery services, and rental car agencies as unacceptable uses. Also unacceptable in many companies are loan cars used by service stations and repair garages, demonstrator cars used by automobile dealers or salespersons and vehicles used by repair garages for delivering cars to customers. Still another category usually unacceptable is that in which the vehicle is used to carry others for hire or for instruction; and taxicabs, buses, trucks or trailers that carry workers to the job site or for hire.

There are other uses of an automobile, in addition to commercial uses, which are often unacceptable. The most common is a vehicle driven over a specified distance over a period of time, such as 30,000 miles per year. Underwriters realize that rates are based on averages and that excessive use increases the exposure to loss.

Physical Damage Factors

Unacceptable lists often contain references applicable only to the physical damage coverages: comprehensive and collision. Most factors in the unacceptable lists of automobile insurers are applicable to all coverages, but some may apply only to specified coverages.

The most common rule is that physical damage coverage will not be written on vehicles not garaged at night, if the neighborhood is one with a high crime record. The experience with thefts, or with hit-and-run collisions at night in some areas led to the insertion of this rule in many unacceptable lists. The use of more and higher deductibles on these coverages, particularly on comprehensive coverage, may make unacceptable risks acceptable.

Some automobile insurers will not write physical damage coverage on specialty cars, because of the difficulty sometimes encountered in securing parts and repairs. Other insurers will not write physical damage on any car unless liability coverages are also written, because the premium from a full coverage policy is needed in order to be able to investigate the risk thoroughly.

Vehicle Type and Performance

Unacceptable lists of many automobile insurers contain various references to the vehicle itself. Some of these factors relate to the type of the vehicle, while others are concerned with the performance characteristics of the car.

A number of basic vehicle types are unacceptable in many automobile insurers. Trucks, motorcycles, motorbikes, minibikes and midget cars are all traditional types not written by some companies. The newer class of multi-purpose recreational vehicles is also unacceptable in many companies. These are the recreational type of vehicles such as snowmobiles, sand buggies, dune buggies and amphibious crafts with a variety of trade names. Many automobile insurers prefer to write only the more standard types of private passenger cars, and prefer to leave the others to specialty writers.

Altered cars and sport cars became a problem to automobile underwriters in the 1950s and 1960s. These cars were either built or altered to develop more speed than ordinary stock passenger cars. Experience soon taught underwriters that losses were both more frequent and more severe than the average. A person who spends money and time to increase the speed and performance of a car is almost always a person who wants to see how a car will perform. A buyer who selects a fast, sporty car may have some show-off tendencies. Neither group has many members who can resist the temptation to drive a little faster than the rest of traffic, under certain conditions, nor to see just what the car can do under other conditions. These characteristics led underwriters to include both groups on unacceptable lists. "Altered cars" are usually defined by the degree of alteration performed; this often includes cars which are lowered, those which are decorated in a show-off fashion and those in which the power train has been changed. "Sports cars" are usually specified by make and model.

During the 1960s, automobile manufacturers embarked upon a program to stress power in private passenger cars. Engines and gear ratios were offered which could make almost any make of car into a "bomb on wheels." When underwriters recognized the problems presented by such cars (other names for these vehicles are "muscle cars" and "hot cars"), the classification of "sports cars" was eventually replaced by "high performance cars" in these unacceptable lists.

The energy crisis of 1974, and again starting in 1979, changed this picture. The gasoline shortage suddenly made "miles per gallon" a more desirable factor than power. Manufacturers raced to produce energy-efficient cars, not powerhouses. The problems of high performance cars virtually disappeared as a class, except for a few people who "souped up" their cars and were recognized as problem individuals, and some older-model cars with low weight-to-horsepower ratios. During future periods of lower gas prices, power may again be emphasized, requiring the attention of underwriters.

SECURING INFORMATION

The first step in underwriting automobile insurance is to determine if the applicant is acceptable or unacceptable under the lists used by the company, as has been discussed in the preceding sections. This is not to say that an underwriter applies these lists inflexibly because, to do so, would be to reduce underwriting to a mechanical, clerical function. However, applicants who are apparently eligible may not be always acceptable to the underwriter, while applicants on the unacceptable list may be sometimes acceptable.

The second step in underwriting is to get more facts upon which to base judgment. The usual method of gathering this information is to require that an application be submitted with answers to all specific questions. The same information would be needed even when the underwriter is considering an application over the telephone by a producer, or when requesting elaboration or verification from another source.

Application

Most insurers require that the producer submit an application for automobile insurance and that it be signed by the applicant. One purpose of the application is to obtain underwriting and rating information. It is generally believed that the signature requirement tends to supply answers which are more nearly honest and correct than if the applicant did not sign the application. In automobile insurance, the part of the application containing the declarations may be made a part of the policy, too.

The questions on the application are usually classified into three major categories.

1. Personal
2. Description and use of the automobile
3. Insurance information

The following is a list of the information requested under each of these categories. Naturally, different insurers use slightly different lists, either in the details requested or in the arrangement. However, most automobile insurance applications cover this information.

1. *Personal*

A. Full names, not only of the named insured but also of all drivers, and the relationship of other drivers to the named insured.
B. Mailing address of named insured, as well as the residence address of all drivers.
C. The age (or birth date), sex, marital status and license number of each driver, as well as the number of years the driver has been licensed to drive an automobile. If divorced, the date the decree was granted.
D. Approximate percentage that each car is driven by each driver.
E. Occupation and employers of all drivers.
F. Special information concerning youthful drivers. If they are in school, the name and distance to the school. If they qualify for discount, the academic standing and driver training certificate.
G. Information concerning stability factors, such as home ownership, years of residence at that address, length of employment with present employer, and the number of jobs held in the previous period, perhaps 5 years.
H. The accident record of all drivers, including details of all accidents while operating any vehicle during the previous period (such as five years), along with a statement of fault and the amounts paid.
I. The citation record of all drivers, including the date and type of citation, and covering traffic citations for which the driver was convicted, fined or arrested during the previous period (such as five years).

J. The name of any driver whose license has been suspended or revoked. (Some insurers want this information only for the previous period, perhaps five years, while others want the information regardless of when the suspension or revocation occurred.)

2. *Description and Use of the Automobile*
   A. Year, make, model, body style and serial number of the automobile.
   B. Estimated annual mileage. (Some insurers request the odometer reading to verify that the estimate is reasonable.)
   C. Name and address of the legal owner, if other than the applicant, together with the reason for a different owner if such is not obvious. On leased cars, the address of the lessor is requested.
   D. Name and address of the loss payee, plus the amount owned. (A loss payee is one who has loaned money to the applicant and has an interest in the automobile as security.
   E. Place of principal garaging if different from the residence address of the applicant. (Some insurers ask if the automobile is kept inside a garage at night.)
   F. Use of the automobile in business (driven in the course of employment) or on a farm.
   G. Use of the automobile in driving to and from work, including car pools and, if so used, the distance covered each day and each week.
   H. Any unrepaired damage to the automobile, defective equipment, alterations and special equipment.
3. *Insurance Information*
   A. Coverage desired, specifying limits and deductibles for which application is made, and the requested effective date.
   B. Identification of other vehicles owned by any driver and not covered under the application, along with the name of the insurers of such vehicles.
   C. The name of any driver who has ever been required to file proof of financial responsibility.
   D. The name of any driver who has ever had an automobile insurance policy cancelled, refused, or denied renewal, plus an explanation of the circumstances involved.
   E. Description of any physical impairment or mental disability of any driver.
   F. Information about the previous insurer: name of the insurer, policy number, whether is was an assigned risk policy (that is, whether is was written voluntarily or under compulsion) and whether the insurer cancelled the policy or denied renewal.

Most of this information is closely related to underwriting factors, as they were discussed on previous pages of this chapter. The questions are designed to develop information used by the underwriter in evaluating the risk. They can be related back to previous explanations of how the underwriter considers each factor, under such headings as: Driving Habits, Stability, Age, Occupation, Other Personal Factors, Use of the Car, Material Damage Factors, and Vehicle Type and Performance.

Some of the information requested on the application is not of interest to the underwriter. Examples are the serial number of the automobile and the address of the loss payee. This information is necessary for the issuance of the policy.

Motor Vehicle Records

Most states maintain records of accident involvement and citation of drivers licensed in the state. These records are available to automobile insurers, as they are to others, for a fee. Underwriters often check these motor vehicle records to verify the information furnished on the application. The factors of accidents and citations have become so important in underwriting automobile insurance that an accurate record is almost essential to proper underwriting. This is particularly important if other factors indicate that the applicant is borderline in acceptability.

Experience has taught underwriters that many applicants do not remember, with much accuracy, the accidents and citations with which they have been involved over a several year period. Some dishonesty is present, no doubt, but many drivers simply do not remember all of their driving records, nor incidents that have occurred. It is up to the underwriter, therefore, to request a motor vehicle record when there is a suspicion that the facts are different from the record shown on the application.

Some insurers consider accidents and convictions in determining the premium for automobile insurance. They secure a motor vehicle record on every applicant for rating purposes, and this record is then available for underwriting purposes also.

Inspection Reports

There are national and local companies that furnish inspection reports to insurers and others. This is the sole business of some companies and an important part of the business for others. An automobile underwriter requests an inspection report for one or more of several reasons. Probably the most frequent reason is to verify information concerning the driver and the use of the car. Since underwriting is usually different when youthful drivers are present, the underwriter asks that particular attention be paid to the existence of such drivers and their frequency of using the car.

Another important reason for requesting an inspection report is to develop or verify information concerning the appearance of the automobile itself. Still another reason for requesting an inspection report is to verify the accident and citation record. If this is the only information needed, it is usually an inexpensive method of securing a motor vehicle record. However, when insurers do not have access to state records in some territories, underwriters sometimes ask for the driving record from an inspection company.

In the jargon of underwriting, inspection reports are commonly called "credit reports." Apparently this is an outgrowth of the fact that one of the earliest companies furnishing inspection reports also furnished credit reports to other businesses. Whatever the reason for the name, the report furnished to an automobile insurer rarely, if ever, mentions the credit standing of the applicant. Perhaps this will change in the future; because studies have indicated that persons with poor credit ratings also have poor driving records. The studies are still inconclusive, and "credit reports" secured by automobile underwriters continue to be "inspection reports" or "investigation reports" at the time of this writing.

Experience of Other Insurers

Another source of information which is sometimes used by automobile underwriters is the experience of the applicant as recorded by the previous insurer. The purpose of these inquiries is to verify the accident record of the applicant because some accidents do not always appear on the motor vehicle record or the information is sometimes incomplete. Automobile underwriters, of course, do not decline insurance solely for the reason that the previous insurer may have cancelled the policy, but underwriters are interested in determining whether the same accident information they have received corresponds to that of the previous insurer.

Quite obviously, the completion of a request for this kind of information requires some additional handling expense. And, considering the fact that the automobile insurance business is highly competitive, this probably explains the reason this method of verifying information is used infrequently. However, when used, it is done a reciprocal arrangement — that is, an underwriter will provide assistance only when given the same assistance, when requested, from an underwriter of another company.

CLASSIFICATION AND RATING

When all underwriting information on an applicant is collected and compiled through the various methods discussed in the preceding pages, and this information indicates that the applicant meets, or at least tentatively meets, the company's underwriting standards, the next step for the underwriter is to classify and rate the applicant.

Classification

The classification is based upon the same information as is secured when determining the basic acceptability of a risk. An underwriter will automatically classify each applicant as the facts are reviewed. Thus, while classifying an applicant could be considered as an underwriting function connected with acceptability, it is really a function of rating. This is not to infer that the underwrting function disregards the classification process; it does not. For example, an important classification is youthful drivers, and the requirements for acceptability are different among age groups. These differences are taken into account while evaluating information, and it is immaterial whether the underwriting precedes or follows the actual classification. Thus, with these qualifications, it is correct to say that classification of automobile applicants is made as an adjunct to the rating structure.

There are many different classification and rating systems in use by automobile insurers, and probably no two independent companies have the same system. The insurers that belong to the rating bureau use a common system, with, perhaps, a few variations. (These insurers constitute a majority of the companies but a minority of the business, as was explained previously.) Because of this variance, no attempt is made here to explain, in detail, the plan used by any one company.

All automobile insurance rating plans use approximately the same classifications, and a brief explanation of the them is sufficient for an understanding of the detailed plans used by any one insurer. The first system explained applies to the liability, uninsured motorists, and medical payment coverages.

Basic Premium Classifications

Territory — This can take in a small portion of a city or a whole state. In addition, the territory varies with the coverages. For example, there may be several rating territories for liability insurance in a large city, while the rate for uninsured motorists coverage is often the same for an entire state.

Limits of liability — The premium is higher for applicants requesting higher limits of liability, within each classification for other factors, than for those buying lower limits. Thus, risks are classified by the limits requested.

Primary Classifications

Age, sex and marital status — These are very important classifications to an underwriter and are interrelated. The term "youthful driver" usually applies to drivers under age 25 or 30. However, youthful unmarried males are in one classification, youthful married males in another, youthful unmarried females in another, and youthful married females in still another. The distinctions by sex and marital status are seldom made for middle-aged drivers, but they could be. Many insurers use a separate classification for drivers over 65 or 68 years of age, but sex and marital status are seldom a part of such classification systems for "senior citizens."

Sex (gender) has been challenged as a rating factor, because of the Equal Rights movement. In Pennsylvania, the Supreme Court ruled that gender-based rates are prohibited, and the article describing this decision stated that this is "the latest in a growing number of judicial decisions nationwide prohibiting sex discrimination in insurance," and lists 15 states which have adopted equal rights provisions.[8] Even the age of the driver has come under attack, and both insurers and regulators are studying the possibility of using driving records as the sole rating criteria.

Use of the automobile — Separate classifications are used for automobiles driven in the course of employment and those driven only for pleasure. In the latter category, one classification might be used for cars not driven to and from work, another for those driven a short distance or a low number of miles to and from work (such as five miles each way, or 50 miles each week), and still another for those driven many miles in going to and from work. Another classification is used by some insurers, applicable to any of the other "use" classes, that applies a different rate to automobiles driven less than a specified number of miles, such as 7,500 miles per year.

Youthful driver discount — There are two discounts for which youthful drivers are acceptable under some classification systems. They are not uniformly used by all insurers, by any means. One is the good student discount, allowing a percentage credit on the premium for students in high school or college who maintain a specified minimum grade level. The rules are carefully drawn to identify those students who are acceptable and the grades permitted, along with certification by school officials. The justification for this discount lies in studies which have been conducted, indicating that a student who gets better grades has a better driving record. The rationale, as yet unproved, is that the good student is at home studying while a counterpart with lower grades is driving around, showing off and having accidents. Some insurers apply the discount only to youthful male drivers, while others permit any

8. "Pennsylvania Supreme Court Upholds Unisex Auto Ruling," *The National Underwriter* (October 26, 1984), p. 1.

young driver to qualify.

The other discount is for successful completion of a driver-training course. A percentage credit on the premium is given to those youths who can furnish evidence of such completion from approved courses. The rules on approved courses vary among insurers giving this discount and among the states to some degree. The reason for giving this discount, of course, is the hope and belief that a trained driver will have fewer accidents than one who is untrained. But even this basic premise has been challenged on some occasions. Some states are adopting universal driver training in high schools, which tends to reduce the value of the discount; since almost everyone will qualify, the so-called discounted rate is really the base rate.

Senior citizens — Some insurers apply lower rates to drivers over age 60 or 65. While these persons are probably not better drivers than those of middle age, they usually drive less and thus have fewer accidents. Discounts are offered to drivers in this group, sometimes as low as age 55, who have taken specially-designated driver training or refresher courses.[9]

Secondary Classifications

Driving records — Many insurers use separate classifications for those drivers who have had no accidents over the past period, such as five years. A smaller number of insurers also use separate classifications based on the number of convictions received by drivers, also over a specified recent period. The reason for these discounts was explained in the previous section of this chapter under the heading: Unacceptable Risks.

Years of driving experience — Some insurers use separate classifications for drivers who have driven only a short time, such as one, two or three years. The reason given for this distinction is related to the reason for considering a driving record that cannot be verified, as was also previously discussed under Unacceptable Risks.

Multiple cars — Most insurers allow a discount when more than one automobile owned by a family is insured in the company. Separate classifications are used for one car, two or more cars and a fleet (five or more cars).

Since these classification factors relate to "a driver," and there may be several drivers in a household, each with a different classification, the rating plans are refined to take these situations into account, as is described later in these pages.

Automobile performance — Some insurers also take into consideration whether the auto is of standard, intermediate or high performance, or a sports car.

Classifying Physical Damage Coverages

A slightly different system of classification is used for comprehensive and collision coverages. Most of the same factors apply, but no choice of coverage limits is given the applicant. In other words, the insured cannot choose the amount of insurance carried. The insurer merely offers only one limit of coverage, determined

---

9. Several companies offer 10% discounts to seniors who complete the "55 Alive/Mature Driving" program sponsored by the American Association of Retired Persons (AARP), according to "Older Drivers are Reconditioning their Skills," *Los Angeles Times* (September 22, 1986), Part V, p. 1.

in the fashion explained in the next paragraph. In effect, the applicant either insures the automobile 100% to its value, or does not insure it at all.[10]

Insurable Value

The "insurable value" of the automobile is determined by its cost when new, less depreciation for age and obsolesence. The automobile underwriter is not too concerned with value, because automobiles have such a ready market regardless of age or condition and the market value is virtually identical with the insurable value. All that is needed is to list the make, model and year of the automobile, along with its symbol, giving the classification for material damage coverages.

While this approach has been used for years by automobile insurers, there were some indications by the late 1960s that the results were often unfair to many applicants. It was at that time, too, that automobile manufacturers started offering so many options that the actual cost new of one automobile differed considerably from another automobile of the same make, model and year. Such options as a large engine, air-conditioning, full power equipment, and stereo tape players increase the cost of a car to almost double the price of a stripped-down car. Underwriters soon recognized the inequity of using a single rate for all cars that have the same base rate, but which have substantially different selling prices. However, they concluded that it is too expensive to secure the additional information and attempt to rate it, and they cannot decide when to start rating the "extras" and when to stop. Accordingly, the old system continues, but efforts continue to improve the system.

Coverage for full replacement cost with a new similar vehicle is being offered by some insurance companies. Policyholders are thus able to replace an insured auto which is totally destroyed with a new one, not a used car. Concerns about the moral hazard are similar to those expressed when replacement cost coverage was first offered on real property, but that insurance is now available and purchased on most eligible property. Experience has not yet demonstrated if the same result will be found on automobile risks.

Use of Deductibles

Deductibles are still another classification system used for material damage coverages. (Deductibles are seldom used in liability coverages.) A deductible on collision is virtually mandatory; no automobile insurer has written full collision coverage for many years. The usual deductible amounts are $100 and $250, although larger amounts of $500 and $1,000 are offered by many insurers. Higher deductibles have been adopted for a number of reasons: increased costs of repairs, inflation, more affluence and higher insurance premiums.

Comprehensive coverage has traditionally been written without any deductible, except by substandard insurers and by a few other insurers of youthful drivers. However, deductibles of $50, $100, and higher have been introduced along with the higher collision deductibles for the same reasons mentioned previously.

---

10. For a comparison with fire insurance on a home, where the applicant selects the amount of insurance desired (within limits), see Chapter 21.

Purpose of Classifications

All of these classifications are used by automobile insurance underwriters as a means of identifying the characteristics of applicants. As an underwriter encounters a specific factor, it is classified for reference. This not only enables him to apply different rules to different risks, but also helps in evaluating the entire risk, since most of the pertinent factors are reduced to classifications that can be used easily. Thus, one purpose for classifications is to facilitate underwriting.

Another reason for classifications is to achieve a homogeneity among risks. Competition is so prevalent among automobile insurers that each must set the boundaries of the classifications with precision; to do otherwise would result in mispricing some risks with potential loss to competitors. The applicant who is placed in a class which is rated too high will purchase insurance elsewhere. On the other hand, the applicant who is classed too low will tend to adversely affect the experience of the class, requiring its rates to increase. This situation, in turn, will cause other policyholders to seek insurance elsewhere. Since losses and expenses of all drivers within a class must be spread among all of them, each should be classified with other drivers having similar exposures.

Classifications must be defensible to producers, applicants, legislators and others. Thus, they should be logical, verifiable and fair. In addition, since they are the basis for rating by producers, they should be easy to explain and to understand.

The boundaries of the classes must be established by the use of judgment. Not only must past experience be used, but future trends must be considered, too. Underwriting judgment must be applied in a different form than when evaluating an individual application, but the same principles apply. Ordinarily classifications are established by the staff underwriters. The desk underwriter applies the classifications, but also observes changes which are desirable and recommends them to the staff.

Rating

Classifications are also used in rating. In fact, automobile insurance cannot be rated until classifications are established.

Private passenger automobile insurance is table rated, because the units of exposure are too small for any type of self-rating, and rates are too low to permit inspections in determining special rating factors that could be applied. Accordingly, rate tables are prepared by the insurer, usually by an actuary with the cooperation of the underwriters, or by a rating bureau. The rate tables are made available to producers, underwriters and rate clerks, and are applied quite rigidly. There is very little latitude in automobile insurance rating and very little judgment is allowed, too.

Some large independent automobile insurers are able to make their own rates. They have a sufficiently large volume of risks to produce credible statistics, even when analyzing a single state or territory. While there are not many such insurers, they write, collectively, more than half of the automobile premiums in most states. These insurers establish classifications, compute rates, file them with insurance departments as needed, print rate tables and distribute the tables.

Other insurers combine their experience through a rating bureau. A majority of the automobile insurers are in this category, although they write less than half of the premium. The bureau establishes the categories and rates and handles the other necessary details.

Automobile insurance has a high frequency of loss. Accidents occur with a frightening frequency, as can be easily verified by a few minutes driving on city streets and expressways. Although most accidents do not involve bodily injury, they do damage automobiles, which are becoming more expensive to buy and to repair.

Repair costs (labor and parts) also are escalating. In another study, it was determined that it would cost $37,014 to replace all of the parts of a totalled 1985 sport coupe which had a purchase price new of $10,682. It would be impractical, of course, to repair such an automobile after a total loss. The point is that costs of repairs are an important factor of automobile insurance, even when the damage is minor.[11]

Liability insurance rates are provided in tables for basic amounts of coverage, such as 15/30/5. Different rates are given for each class and each territory. An upcharge table (containing increased limit factors) is applied to the base rate in order to arrive at higher limits of liability. The increase for higher limits is relatively small, because few liability claims are large.

Medical payments coverage is rated with a flat amount for each limit. Within any one class and territory, one rate is given for $500 limits, another for $1,000 and so forth. Again, the increase for higher amounts is not large.

Physical damage coverages require classification by car symbols; these are based on the new price of the cars, but are given in tables. Most rating plans employ three age groups, such as current model, previous two years and older cars. With these factors, plus the desired deductible, the rate can be found in a table for each rate class, territory and deductible.

The preceeding brief explanation indicates that a great many different rates are used. Some rating systems used result in thousands of rates for any one state. However, as rates increase, pressure grows for even more classes. Each segment of the driving population that feels that it is better than others in its class, tries to obtain a separate classification. Often an insurer is found that offers such a distinction, and then other insurers follow in order to protect their business.

A prime example of this pressure for preferential rate treatment comes from drivers who have had no accidents. They feel they should be given lower rates, because they have not cost the insurer anything. The results of this pressure are evidenced by the various merit rating plans used by automobile insurers. Some base acceptability on accidents and convictions, while others use only accidents. Those with clean records are given lower rates, while those without them are surcharged; the net result is the same, but different approaches are used for various reasons. (The time period is usually two or three years.)

---

11. "What's a Nice Car Like You Doing with a Repair Tag like This?", *Journal of American Insurance*, Fourth Quarter, 1985, p. 16.

These merit rating plans sound logical and are appealing to many drivers. However, they are of questionable validity, since frequency of loss is low and most drivers qualify for reduced rates. This means that only a few are surcharged; hence, the rate for the majority is really reduced very little. Furthermore, there is serious question that a two or three year driving record is a sound measure of a person's driving ability. Finally, a driver who has been free of accidents for several years and then is involved in a collision in which he or she is slightly at fault, if at all, may resent a substantial increase in his premium, and may, at that time, seek out an insurer that will not apply a penalty for that one accident.

In spite of these obvious problems, pressures continue for more refined rating systems. Some appear to have merit; one of these include drivers whose annual mileage is low, such as below 7,500 miles. However, it is doubtful that statistics justify very many further refinements. The premium in each class and territory can be divided only a limited number of times before the figures become too small to be meaningful.

Automobile insurers spend a great deal of money in securing infomation upon which to classify risks properly and in maintaining classes and rates. However, the expense is a limiting factor on further expansion of classifications. Indeed, substantial economies could be achieved by employing only one or two rate classes, but this destroys homogeneity and is not acceptable to many of the insuring public. Regardless of the merit of a single class system, the competitive situation would not permit its adoption without a legislative directive that all insurers adopt the same system.

Thus, every automobile insurer uses a somewhat complex rating structure based on various factors concerning the driver and the car. A complicating situation occurs when there are two or more drivers for a car. Most rating systems require an estimate to the percentage of use for each driver and apply the classifications of the drivers on the basis of use. For example, a car driven by a middle-aged couple would have one rating classification if a 60 year old father-in-law operated the car 15% of the time, another if an 18 year old son operated it 20%, and still another classification would apply if that son drove it 40% of the time.

Rates for Senior Drivers

Rating elderly drivers has been a subject of controversy for years and various approaches have been taken. Few insurers rated drivers over 65 years of age in any different fashion from middle-age drivers until the mid-1960s. Studies then indicated that older drivers were more costly to insurers, leading many companies to apply a senior driver's surcharge of 10%, 25% or even higher. Some insurers used a higher percentage for the older drivers in this group, such as over age 70.

Further studies were made in 1969, some indicating that senior drivers were actually better risks than those in the 30 to 65 age group. By 1970, some insurers had removed the surcharge, others continued it, while still others (including the ISO) give a discount to drivers over 65. The inconsistency is apparently caused by relying upon different data, plus various interpretations of the available data. This probably will continue.

The arguments in favor of a surcharge for elderly drivers tend to focus upon the fact that as a person becomes older, there is an undenied loss of coordination and agility. Furthermore, older drivers are much more likely to have restricted licenses — that is, they must wear glasses while operating a vehicle, their driving may be confined to certain geographic areas or they may only be allowed to drive during daylight hours.

On the other hand, the arguments in favor of discounts for elderly drivers focus upon accident statistics reported by the states. In 1977, using reports from 24 state traffic authorities, it was shown that 9.2% of all drivers were 65 years of age or older and they accounted for only 6.9 of the fatal accidents and 6.3 of all accidents.[12]

What is the correct answer? Are elderly drivers entitled to a discount or should they be surcharged? This dilemma is not unlike that faced every day by an automobile underwriter: conflicting evidence must be evaluated. Most decisions of an underwriter, however do not affect such a large number of people as this one does. In addition, this problem is fraught with social and political implications of considerable magnitude.

Is it possible that elderly drivers are involved in fewer accidents and yet cost the insurance companies more in losses? At first glance, this appears to be impossible; someone must be in error. But a closer study reveals that perhaps the term "accidents" does not mean literally what it implies. Most states receive reports of accidents only when they involve bodily injury or substantial (over $200) property damage; most "accidents" which are "fender benders" are not reported. Is it possible that elderly drivers have more minor accidents, such as dented fenders in parking lots? This seems to be a reasonable conclusion. Generally speaking, older drivers will do most of their driving at relatively low speeds in their neighborhoods and they have difficulties in backing their automobiles because of physical limitations. Perhaps it is not illogical to assume that a large share of their losses are minor scrapes and dents — the types that are not reported to state motor vehicle departments, but those costing insurance companies a number of dollars under liability and collision coverages.

Further study is needed in order to determine the answer to this enigma and to substantiate or refute the theory previously discussed. Until this is done, this will remain one of the subjects on which underwriters must advise management, but the decision will be made at the staff level, often upon grounds other than pure underwriting. If the insurer's rating structure requires different treatment for elderly drivers, the underwriter is relieved of specific responsibility for that decision beyond verification of age.

POLICY FORMS

The automobile insurance policy language is not specified by statute in most states. While each insurer devises its own policy either alone or through a bureau,

12. National Safety Council *Accident Facts.* 1978 Edition, Chicago, Illinois, p. 54.

there is great similarity among the policies used, and almost every policy follows the general outline of coverages given at the beginning of this chapter.

The differences in policy provisions used by insurers are generally minor. There can be extra benefits under medical payments coverage, for example, or a unique exclusion under comprehensive coverage to handle a specific problem that an insurer has encountered. As a change is adopted by one insurer or bureau, it tends to be copied by others, because of the extremely competitive climate under which all insurers operate.

Underwriters have very little opportunity to modify the automobile insurance policy in their daily underwriting operations. The line is so huge and so standardized that almost every policy is virtually identical with all others. Even the insurers writing so-called specialty lines may use unique rating systems or acceptability rules, but their policies are quite standard.

However, there are situations when an underwriter may endorse the policy to amend the coverage. One such situation is when an applicant is acceptable except for one driver of the car. If the unacceptable driver is a regular or frequent user, the risk cannot be written. But if that operator is a son or daughter of the named insured and is in the military service or away at college, the policy can be endorsed to exclude any coverage while that person is driving the car. A wise underwriter obtains a signed acceptance of such restriction from both the named insured and the excluded driver, in avoiding future arguments. In a slightly different situation, the underwriter may wish to exclude all other permissive drivers or all of a class. Among the examples are a service station attendant whose fellow employees often drive each others cars; or a student in college whose roommates borrow the car. In some states, either or both of these types of restrictive endorsements are unenforceable and this appears to be the trend, since it tends to create situations under which innocent third parties may be unable to recover damages because there is no insurance. On the other hand, at least one state requires insurers to offer to exclude a problem driver, thus guaranteeing acceptability and a lower rate to the good drivers in the family.

Another situation when the policy can be modified is when an applicant has equipment in or on the automobile that the underwriter does not wish to insure. The equipment can be a car telephone, a special stereo player or custom wheels. Instead of declining insurance, the underwriter may accept the applicant subject to an exclusion of the offensive property. (An exclusion endorsement would be used for this.)

Some underwriters are concerned about customized cars and antique cars. Feeling that it may be difficult and costly to secure repair parts and to make repairs on such vehicles, underwriters will endorse the policy to exclude such extra expenses. This is an example of a situation when the underwriter may modify the automobile insurance policy.

Pre-existing damage is sometimes a problem to automobile underwriters, too. When a policy is issued covering physical damage, it is obvious that the underwriter does not intend to cover damage that existed before the policy was written. The policy does not cover such damages, of course, but considerable argument can arise. The claims adjuster may not even have known that some of the damage was pre-existing.

To avoid such eventualities, the underwriter might endorse the policy to specifically exclude the described pre-existing damage. Later on, the endorsement may be removed when satisfactory notification is given that repairs have been made.

RETENTION AND REINSURANCE

The problems of retention and reinsurance are of little concern to most automobile underwriters. Seldom are these problems encountered in day-to-day underwriting. However, situations can arise when an automobile underwriter needs to consider these problems.

Liability

A large share of all automobile insurance policies cover less than $25/50/5 liability limits. Most insurers retain the full exposure at these limits. On the other hand, each insurer has a limit beyond which it does not wish to be exposed. For one insurer, this may be $50/100/10, while for another it may be $250/500/100. When an underwriter encounters an acceptable applicant requesting limits in excess of the company's desired retention, the underwriter must reinsure the excess amount. The same situation arises when the underwriter does not wish to retain the limits requested for underwriting reasons. For example, some underwriters want low limits for youthful drivers; if the applicant insists upon higher limits, the only alternative to losing the risk is to reinsure the excess.

In automobile insurance, it is almost universal that the underwriter issues a policy for the entire limits requested and approved. Then the additional exposure is reinsured by means of an excess reinsurance treaty. These treaties are automatic. However, there are instances when desired liability limits are beyond the capacity of the treaty; in such cases, the underwriter or producer secures a specific excess policy covering only the excess of that policy. In this situation, the basic policy is written only for the lower limits.

There is a slight catastrophe liability hazard in automobile insurance. Two or more policyholders could simultaneously collide with a passenger train, causing a great deal of bodily injury and property damage. If each such policyholder carried the maximum retained limits of the insurer, the single occurrence could greatly exceed the desired retention. As excess reinsurance treaty is ordinarily carried to protect an insurer against such events, usually combined with the excess coverages on separate policies with high limits. The desk underwriter is not concerned with this catastrophe exposure, because the coverage is automatic and there is really no way to underwrite these catastrophes.

Physical Damage

The maximum value of most insured automobiles is low enough that underwriters do not concern themselves with the hazard of total loss. Almost any insurer can retain, safely, the value of most cars. However, some luxury or specialty cars can be worth $50,000 or more, which could strain the capacity of a small insurer. Furthermore, catastrophes can occur under physical damage coverages. Common examples are flood, windstorm, fire and earthquake. There is even the possibility of an accident involving several insured automobiles, such as the multiple-car accident that sometimes involves dozens or even hundreds of vehicles on a fog-bound expressway. Catastrophe reinsurance treaties are carried by most insurers to protect against these possibilities; they pay when the aggregate losses from a single occurrence exceed a stated amount. The automobile insurance underwriter is not involved with these treaties in normal activities, either.

SPECIAL PROBLEMS

Private passenger automobile insurance has more problems than any other line. In fact, it seems at times that it has more problems than all other lines combined. The reasons for the multitude of problems are not hard to find. Almost every family in the United States is affected by automobile insurance. The automobile has become virtually a necessity, and the laws in most states all but compel every driver to have insurance at the risk of losing a license. Every time that automobile insurance rates increase, almost everyone feels it and no one likes increased prices.

Added to these factors is the basic problem that insurers have very little control over the items determining insurance rates. Inflation can cause large increases in hospital and medical costs, in automobile repair costs, and in the costs of operating businesses. At the same time, highways are more crowded, more teenagers are driving, and automobile manufacturers are building more powerful and speedy cars which are also more fragile.

On top of all of these difficulties, and related to them, the very system under which insurers operate has been threatened. Politicans put limits on the right of insurers to cancel or nonrenew undesirable risks, they limit the right of insurers to use selection processes which are felt to be justified and they limit their right to charge adequate rates. Juries award damages in amounts unheard of just a few years ago. Even the fault system, under which a negligent driver is required to pay the resulting damages and purchases an insurance policy to protect against this contingency, is under severe challenge from many sides.

The automobile insurance underwriter is forced to operate under these difficulties. Most of the problems have already been discussed in this chapter: the demands for higher limits of protection, an increase in accidents, increased mobility of the population, more youthful drivers and the limitations placed on driver restrictions. A very serious problem, one that warrants attention, is the trend toward noncancellation laws. Most states prohibit cancellation of an automobile insurance policy, after a "discovery period" of about 60 days, except for a few specified reasons, such as nonpayment of premium. In addition, every year more states which have enacted such laws adopt more stringent controls. The next stop is to prohibit nonrenewal of policies; such legislation has been enacted in several states and this trend continues.

These restrictions require more careful underwriting when an application is first received. Gone are the days when an automobile underwriter could accept a risk with little or no investigation and, then, cancel it if experience turned bad. Today, the underwriter must select very carefully, gathering all available information within the first few days of receiving the application. Since these restrictive laws will undoubtedly result in tighter risk selection, an applicant who is borderline may have to be declined if the alternative is to keep the insurance forever, no matter how poor a risk the person is or becomes.

Automobile insurance has become a form of social insurance. The automobile still is almost a necessity and so is the insurance on it. Politicians have found that the automobile insurance is a good consumer issue. Under these conditions, the great field of automobile underwriting will become ever more of a problem and a challenge.

Still another problem has been the pressure for no-fault automobile insurance. The principal behind this approach is that bodily injuries should be paid by the insurer of the victim, regardless of fault. The purpose of this idea is to assure that all out-of-pocket expenses are paid promptly, with no need to determine fault. Savings are supposed to be realized because less investigation is needed, court costs and attorney's fees are reduced or eliminated, and little or no recovery is made for subjective complaints, commonly called "pain and suffering."

Many states, as well as the federal government began studies of no-fault plans about 1970 and, within the first couple of years, several states enacted modified versions. Minnesota enacted its plan on January 1, 1970 and Massachusetts passed a law in 1970 which became effective one year later. By 1985, 15 states had adopted laws which restricted the right to sue, and six states required the offer of payments regardless of fault but without disturbing the tort concept. In 1979, Nevada became the first state to repeal a no-fault law.

Underwriting is unaffected by most no-fault plans.

QUESTIONS FOR DISCUSSION

1. Of what direct benefit to an insured is automobile liability insurance?
2. Explain the amount of liability coverage provided under a single limit of $50,000 and split limits of 25/50/5.
3. (a) What prompted the need for uninsured motorists coverage?
   (b) Of what benefit to an insured is uninsured motorists coverage?
4. Why might an insured want to purchase underinsured motorists coverage when he or she already has uninsured motorists coverage?
5. Give three reasons why medical payments coverage should be purchased.
6. What purpose does the so-called "threshold" serve under some no-fault auto plans?
7. Explain the coverages available to insureds against loss to their autos.
8. What purposes do deductibles serve under physical damage coverage, and under what conditions might an underwriter impose them or require higher amounts?
9. Compare the characteristics of a preferred, substandard, and standard auto risk.
10. Why are underwriters often confronted with dilemmas when evaluating accidents and citations of insureds?

11. Briefly explain the significance of the following factors from the standpoint of underwriting:
    (a) driving habits
    (b) stability of the driver
    (c) age of the driver
    (d) occupation
    (e) use of the auto
12. What are some of the important factors underwriters must consider with respect to auto physical damage insurance?
13. Explain the sources from which underwriters can obtain information on auto insurance applicants.
14. What are the traditional considerations which comprise the primary classifications for auto insurance? For secondary classifications?
15. How is the amount of coverage established for the physical damage insurance of autos?
16. What is the purpose of classifications and why are they essential to the underwriter?
17. How may it be possible for some youthful operators to receive a reduction in their auto insurance costs?
18. (a) What is the purpose of auto merit rating plans?
    (b) What is it about merit rating that sometimes makes it of questionable value?
19. Explain some of the special problems created by autos and their impact on underwriting.

20

Commercial Automobile

A commercial automobile is a motor vehicle which is customarily used in the business, profession or occupation of its owner. It can have two, three, four, or more wheels operated on land. Within this class are many types of vehicles, such as private passenger automobiles, panel and pickup trucks, commercial tractors, trailers and semitrailers whether or not engaged in interstate commerce.

There are circumstances, however, when some vehicles can be considered as private passenger automobiles rather than commercial automobiles. The criterion lies with the use of such a vehicle. For example, a pickup truck owned by an individual (office worker) and used for transportation to and from work and for pleasure purposes is considered a private passenger automobile, while an identical pickup truck used by a gardener or carpenter in the business is considered as a commercial vehicle.

Public automobiles, on the other hand, can be of any type motor vehicle, such as private passenger, bus, or delivery sedan, so long as they are used as public or livery conveyances.

All of these vehicles, except personal automobiles of individuals, can be insured under various standard and nonstandard policies, depending upon their use. Most of the commercial automobile insurance is written under three *standard* policies of the Insurance Services Office: (1) the business auto policy, (2) the truckers policy, and (3) the garage policy. These three policies are called "coverage forms" under the 1986 commercial lines program of the Insurance Services Office, using the modular concept explained in Chapter 13 of this book. Since few changes in coverages were made, these programs will be discussed together, with significant changes noted where applicable.

BUSINESS AUTO POLICY

The business auto policy is used for all commercial vehicles except those written under the truckers and garage policies. Examples of insureds using the business auto policy are building contractors, service firms, bus and other public transportation companies and vehicles owned by municipalities and other public and private institutions.

Description of Coverages

The business auto policy (BAP) is a divisible contract. The applicant can select the coverages desired, subject to the approval of the underwriter. The coverages can include insurance on all autos, whether owned, non-owned, or hired. Alternatively, insurance can apply only to those owned autos described in the policy.

Coverages include liability, personal injury protection (no-fault), uninsured motorists coverage, and medical payments coverage. Physical damage coverages are comprehensive, specified perils, collision, and towing and labor. The policy is written on a single-limit basis, but split limits are available by endorsement.

Following is a brief description of the coverages:

- Liability Insurance
  The liability coverage is virtually identical to that covered under other auto policies. Recovery is based upon tort law. The insured is given protection against bodily injury and property damage caused by accident for which the insured is legally responsible, including defense protection. Minimum financial responsibility limits for trucks subject to the federal Motor Carrier Act were increased by the Department of Transportation effective January 1, 1985; the new limits are as high as $5 million, and this may cause problems to underwriters.
- Personal Injury Protection
  Personal injury protection is a statutory coverage required by the no-fault laws of some states. If the state has no such law, this coverage does not apply. When written, the benefits vary by state and are statutory. Nonetheless, the policy lists the benefits, which usually include medical expenses, rehabilitation costs, funeral expenses, loss of income, and the cost of replacement services. These coverages are paid regardless of fault, and are offset in many states by limitations on the right to sue. This protection applies to all vehicles, but is likely to have limited application for a business exposure because most operators of vehicles are already covered under workers' compensation insurance.
- Uninsured Motorists Coverage
  Uninsured motorists coverage is similar to that offered by the personal auto policy. It pays an insured for bodily injury caused by a motorist who is at fault but who is financially irresponsible. This coverage, like personal injury protection, will have limited application to business exposures.
- Medical Payments Coverage
  Medical payments coverage will pay a covered person for reasonable and necessary expenses incurred for injuries sustained by accident while occupying the insured auto. Medical payments, like personal injury protection and uninsured motorists coverage, will have limited use for business exposures.

Vehicle Exposures Covered

The vehicles which are insured for the above coverages are referred to as *co-*

vered autos. This term can apply to any auto, whether owned, nonowned or hired, or it may include only certain specified autos.

The selection of covered autos is handled in a somewhat unique way, through the use of numerical symbols which represent different types of covered autos. There are nine such numerical symbols available. When the insured selects a numerical symbol; as shown below, coverage applies as described:

(1) all owned, nonowned and hired autos.

(2) only owned autos of the commercial and private passenger type which are owned, including those acquired during the policy period. This also includes nonowned trailers which are attached to these covered autos.

(3) only private passenger autos, including those acquired during the policy period.

(4) all owned autos, other than private passenger autos, such as commercial trucks, including those owned autos which are acquired during the policy period.

(5) only those owned autos subject to no-fault insurance, including owned autos acquired during the policy period if they are required to have no-fault benefits.

(6) all owned autos which are subject to mandatory uninsured motorists insurance without right of rejection, in the state where such autos are principally garaged. This includes autos acquired during the policy period subject to this mandatory insurance.

(7) only those autos specifically described in the policy declarations for which a premium charge is shown.

(8) only hired autos, that is, autos leased, hired, rented or borrowed, other than autos of employees.

(9) nonowned autos, other than those leased, hired, rented or borrowed in category (8) above. Included in this group would be autos owned by employees.

Mechanics of Coverage

Given the numerical symbols from (1) through (9), the appropriate symbol is placed opposite the coverages as listed in the policy declarations. For example, if the symbol (1) were to be placed opposite liability coverage, the named insured would have liability insurance on all owned, nonowned and hired autos. If medical payments coverage were desired on private passenger autos only, the symbol (3) would be designated opposite the medical payments coverage as listed in the declarations.

There may be times when the underwriter is unwilling to give an insured comprehensive liability coverage, which is symbol (1). Examples could be when a business changes autos too much and does not keep adequate records so that it is difficult to determine the annual exposure when the policy is audited. Another example is when a business has had too many claims involving owned autos, some of a questionable nature. Whatever the reason, the underwriter may only want to provide coverage on specifically described autos, in order to have better control over the exposure. In such cases, the symbol (7) must be designated opposite the liability coverage. However, it might be an undue burden upon the insured if the symbols (8) and (9) also were not designated. The reason is that an insured might not have a hired and nonowned auto exposure at policy inception, but either or both could arise during the policy period. If those symbols were not to be designated and the insured were to sustain a loss involving a nonowned auto, there would be no protection. (This would be excess, because primary coverage for an employer is available under an employee's personal auto policy, if a policy is in force and the limits are adequate to protect both the employee and employer. If the policy of the employee is inadequate, the employer can look to its nonowned auto coverage for excess protection. If an employee does not have insurance, the nonowned auto coverage of the employer becomes primary.)

Another important point about the mechanics of coverage is that when the symbols (1) through (6) are used on any coverages, the insured receives automatic coverage on any owned covered autos which are acquired during the policy period. But when symbol (7) is used, a newly acquired auto is covered only when two conditions are met. The first is that the insurance company already covers all autos which the insured owns for the coverage provided, such as all autos, private passenger autos only, or all owned autos other than private passenger vehicles. The second condition is if the insured informs the insurance company within 30 days after the acquisition that the auto is to be added to the policy.

Automatic liability coverage for temporary substitute autos is given under the 1986 program. Coverage applies for a temporary substitute auto if a covered owned auto is out of service because of its breakdown, repair, servicing, loss, or destruction. Under older policies, the insured needed to purchase hired auto coverage to get this protection.

Physical Damage Coverages

There are four physical damage coverages an insured may choose for its autos: comprehensive, specified perils, collision, and towing and labor. The following is a brief description of those coverages.

- Comprehensive Coverage

  Comprehensive coverage reimburses the insured for direct and accidental loss or damage to the covered auto from any cause, except as otherwise noted. The exceptions when coverage does not apply are (1) loss or damage stemming from an auto's collision with another object, and (2) when the perils which cause a loss are specifically excluded. The collision exposure, of course, can be insured under collision coverage. Losses by certain perils are excluded because they are not accidental in nature, such as wear and tear; they are catastrophic in nature, such as loss by war and nuclear weapons; or they are insurable for an extra charge. An example of the latter is loss to any sound receiving equipment, such as CB or two-way radios. Comprehensive coverage seldom is purchased by a business on its commercial vehicles. The loss potential from such perils as dents and scratches do not have much impact on the use of these vehicles. Considering the limited exposure for loss or damage, the cost of coverage would be excessive.

- Specified Perils Coverage

  Under specified perils coverage, the insured's auto is covered against damage or loss by six perils: (1) fire or explosion, (2) theft, (3) windstorm, hail or earthquake, (4) flood, (5) vandalism or mischief, and (6) the sinking, burning, collision or derailment of any conveyance which is transporting the covered auto. These six perils are provided as a package. Thus, if a business garages its commercial vehicles and the concentration of values is exposed to fire and/or vandalism, the insured has coverage on both of these. In addition, protection is given for the other perils as well, at a cost which usually is less than if the insured had purchased comprehensive coverage. Sometimes an underwriter may require a deductible, especially when an insured has had several of the same type of losses. The deductible, if it is high enough, may force the insured to exercise more loss control.

  The 1986 commercial program of the Insurance Services Office uses the term "cause of loss" instead of "perils," and adds lightning as one which is covered.

- Collision Coverage

  Collision coverage applies to damage or loss when an insured auto collides with another object, or when it overturns. Mandatory deductibles of $500 or $1,000, or even higher, are usually used. Vehicles are highly susceptible to damage by collision. A deductible is seldom a burden to a business, particularly in relation to the values of most commercial vehicles.

- Towing and Labor Coverage

  Towing and labor coverage only applies to private passenger autos. Payment is limited to $25 for towing and labor costs on a disabled covered auto. It is a requirement of this coverage, however, that the labor be performed at the site of disablement. If repairs can only be made at a garage, the only expense that will be covered is the towing service.

  The $25 limit does not appear in the form under the 1986 commercial program of the Insurance Services Office. Various limits may be purchased, with the applicable limit being shown in the declarations.

Vehicle Exposures Covered

The selection of covered autos for physical damage coverages is handled in the same way as it is for liability coverages. However, there are only five such symbols available. When the insured selects one of these numerical symbols, coverage applies as shown:

(2) all owned autos (commercial and private passenger).

(3) all owned private passenger autos

(4) all owned autos, other than private passenger autos.

(7) only specifically described autos for which a premium charge is shown in the declarations.

(8) all hired autos, including those autos which the insured leases, hires, rents borrows from others, except autos of an employee.

Mechanics of Coverage

Given the numeral symbols (2), (3), (4), (7) and (8), the appropriate symbol likewise is placed opposite the coverage as listed in the policy declarations. For example, if the insured desires comprehensive coverage and tow and labor coverage on its owned private passenger autos, specified perils on its commercial autos, and collision on its hired autos, symbol (3) would be placed opposite comprehensive and towing and labor coverages; symbol (4) would be placed opposite the specified perils coverage; and symbol (8) would be placed opposite collision coverage. If the insured had 10 private passenger autos and only wanted four of them covered for comprehensive coverage, symbol (7) would be appropriate.

When symbols (2), (3) and (4) are used, there is automatic coverage on any covered autos acquired during the policy period. But when symbols (7) and/or (8) are used, a newly acquired auto for the foregoing exposures is covered only when two conditions are met. The first is that the insurance company already covers all autos for that coverage or it replaces an auto the insured previously owned which had that coverage. The second condition requires the insured to notify the insurer within 30 days after acquisition that the vehicle is to be covered for the physical damage protection in question.

Other Commercial Auto Policies

Other policies and coverages are available in connection with commercial auto exposures.

GARAGE POLICY

The standard garage policy is a package program designed for auto dealers (franchise and nonfranchise). It may also be written for nondealers in such related businesses as service stations, repair garages, storage garages and parking garages. The coverages available are garage liability, automobile liability and physical damage, garagekeepers coverage, and auto dealers physical damage.

The following is a brief description of each such coverage option:

- Garage Liability Coverage

  The garage liability coverage is somewhat similar to the coverage provided by a commercial general liability policy. It covers the exposures of premises and operations concerning a garage or dealership. It also covers products liability, completed operations, limited contractual liability, and work performed by independent contractors.
- Automobile Liability Coverage

  The automobile liability coverages can apply to use of owned, nonowned or hired vehicles. Where applicable, personal injury protection (no-fault) can be purchased for eligible autos, along with auto medical payments and uninsured motorists coverages.
- Automobile Physical Damage Coverage

  The physical damage coverages available to covered autos are the same as that which is available under the business auto policy: comprehensive, specified perils, and/or collision coverage, subject to any deductibles.

- Garagekeepers Coverage
The garage liability coverage excludes damage to property, including autos in a dealers or nondealers care, custody or control. However, protection sometimes is desired against damage to property of others, for purposes of goodwill. To meet those needs, two forms of garagekeepers insurance are available against damage by the perils of comprehensive coverage, specified perils, or collision. The first one is garagekeepers legal liability coverage. This is a bailee type of coverage which pays for damage to property of others in the garage's care, custody or control, but only when the garage is legally responsible for the resulting damage.

  The second form is garagekeepers coverage which pays without regard to liability. Naturally, it is more expensive than the legal liability form. This coverage pays for damage to the property of others on an excess basis if other insurance applies, or on a primary basis when no other insurance is applicable. For example, if a customer has comprehensive and collision, the latter subject to a $100 deductible, on the auto and it is damaged by a garage, the coverage of the garage would pay the excess of any damage or, in other words, the $100. However, if the customer did not have any kind of physical damage on the auto, the garagekeepers coverage would pay for the actual cash value of the damage to such auto.

- Dealers Physical Damage Coverage
Dealers physical damage coverage is designed to cover the exposures of damage to a dealer's autos which are used in the business, as well as those on consignment or held for sale. Coverage can be obtained for comprehensive or specified perils and collision, and can be written on a reporting or nonreporting basis. Nondealers physical damage coverage applies to owned autos and to any incidental exposure involving autos held for sale by nondealers. The same perils available to dealers applies here as does the reporting or nonreporting form.

Vehicle Exposures Covered

The vehicles to be insured under the above garage coverages must be identified on the policy. Numerical symbols are used, as for other commercial autos. However, these 11 symbols designate different classes of vehicles, as follows:

(21) can only be used by dealers. It provides liability and medical payments coverages on *any* auto, whether owned, nonowned or hired, except damage to autos of cusomters.

(22) can be used to provide liability coverage for a nondealers *owned* autos. It can also be used for dealers and nondealers to provide physical damage and uninsured motorists coverage on owned autos.

(23) can be used to designate liability and medical payments coverages for a nondealer's owned private passenger autos. Also it can be used to designate physical damage and uninsured motorists coverage on a dealer's and a nondealer's owned private passenger autos.

(25) used to designate no-fault auto insurance on owned autos for dealers and nondealers.

(26) to be used only when certain owned autos are subject to compulsory uninsured motorists insurance, without right of rejection. However, if a dealer or nondealer wants uninsured motorists coverage to apply to all owned autos, symbol (22) can be used, and symbol (23) can be used to provide uninsured motorists coverage on all owned private passenger autos.

(27) can be used to provide liability and medical payments coverages on specified autos of a nondealer. It also can be used to designate other coverages for dealers and nondealers but only with respect to specified autos.

(28) used to handle hired auto exposures only. (A dealer which uses symbol (21), covering any auto, would not need to use this symbol.) However, symbol (28) cannot be used for autos of the nondealer's employees, nor for the no-fault, uninsured motorists and medical payments coverages. This symbol can be used alone or in conjunction with symbols (22), (23), (24) or (29) to provide liability or physical damage coverage on hired autos.

(29) used to obtain liability or medical payments coverages for autos not owned by the nondealer but used in the garage business, such as autos of employees. An auto dealer who selects symbol (21) would not need to also select symbol (29) because the former covers any auto.

(30) when used, signifies that garagekeepers coverage is to apply to a dealer or nondealer.

(31) provides physical damage coverage on autos consigned to a dealer for sale.

(32) a blank symbol which can be used for any exposure that develops and is not handled by any of the other symbols.

When symbols (21), (22), (23), (24), (25), (26), and (28) are used, there is automatic coverage on any auto which is acquired during the policy period, depending upon the class of autos and the coverage to which the symbol is meant to apply. Symbol (27), on the other hand, requires that any autos newly acquired during the policy period are covered only when the same two conditions are met as before. The first is that the insurance company already covers all autos for that coverage. The second is that the insured notifies the insurer within 30 days after acquisition that the auto is to be insured for the coverage desired.

Examples

Given the symbols and the coverages they represent, coverages for the autos and other exposures are triggered by inserting the appropriate symbol or symbols after the coverage is listed in the schedule.

Consider, for example, a nondealer such as an auto repair shop which owns one tow truck and three private passenger autos. The named insured wants liability coverage on the owned and any nonowned autos, comprehensive and collision on the three private passenger autos, specified perils coverage on the tow truck, mandatory uninsured motorists coverage on all of the vehicles, and garagekeepers comprehensive coverage. The following would be how the coverages and symbols would appear:

Coverages	Covered Autos
Liability insurance	22,29
Uninsured motorists insurance	26
Garagekeepers insurance Comprehensive coverage	30
Physical damage insurance Comprehensive coverage	23
Physical damage insurance Collision coverage	23
Physical damage insurance Specified perils coverage	24 or 27

Assume in this next example that an auto dealer owns five pickup and panel trucks, and nine private passenger autos. The dealer desires liability insurance on all autos, medical payments on the owned private passenger autos, comprehensive and collision coverage on the private passenger autos, specified perils coverage on the trucks, garagekeepers comprehensive and collision coverage, and specified perils coverage for autos on consignment. The following would be the symbols and coverages.

Coverages	Covered Autos
Liability insurance	21
Medical payments coverage	23
Garagekeepers insurance Comprehensive coverage	30
Garagekeepers insurance Collision coverage	30
Physical damage insurance Comprehensive coverage	23
Physical damage insurance Specified perils coverage	31
Physical damage insurance Collision coverage	23

The procedure in selecting the coverages against the exposures is not difficult, once one gets familiar with the scope of each such symbol and its application.

TRUCKERS POLICY

The truckers policy is designed for any person, firm or corporation which is in the business of transporting property for another. Thus, moving firms would be considered to be truckers, as would common carriers and even contractors who use their vehicles to haul materials of others. But not included as a trucker is a person, firm or corporation which transports its own cargo or cargo of another exclusively, such as a contract carrier.

Description of Coverages

The truckers policy is almost identical to the business auto policy, except that the former policy has a modified definition of the persons insured provision. The truckers policy also has a trailer interchange coverage which handles a common exposure of truckers.

Thus, the truckers policy provides liability insurance and can be written to provide personal injury protection (where applicable), uninsured motorists, medical payments, and the same physical damage insurance coverages as provided under the business auto policy.

- Trailer Interchange Insurance
  Trailer interchange insurance is designed to cover the exposure created by a trailer interchange agreement among truckers. Under this agreement, several truckers may agree to haul one another's trailers as a matter of scheduling convenience. The problem is that the truckers policy, like other automobile policies, excludes liability for damage to property of others in an insured's care, custody or control. The trailer interchange insurance solves this problem by providing the same physical damage coverage, and applicable deductibles, on nonowned trailers within this arrangement as are applicable to the insured's own units.
- Truckers Insurance for Nontrucking Use
  When a trucker hauls cargo of another, using the latter's trailer on a one-way trip, the trucker will have protection under the automobile policy of the firm for whom the cargo is being conveyed. But when the trailer is unhooked from the trucker's vehicle, the trucker is without insurance. For protection in this instance, the trucker needs "truckers insurance for nontrucking use," which is available by endorsement, because it will provide the trucker with protection while the truck-tractor is not used for trucking use. This insurance is also commonly referred to as "bobtail" liability insurance.

  Instead of detaching the trailer at the point of destination, the cargo may be unloaded and the empty trailer hauled back to the point of origination. If, under a lease agreement, coverage for the trucker ceases after the cargo is unloaded, the trucker has no protection while returning the nonowned trailer. To overcome this coverage gap, the "truckers insurance for nontrucking use" endorsement can also be used. This protection is sometimes referred to as "deadhead" liability insurance.

Truck Exposures Covered

The vehicles considered to be insured, referred to as *covered autos*, depend upon the coverages desired. The selection of covered autos is handled in the same way as with the business auto and garage policies, except that different numerical symbols are used for truck risks. There are nine such numerical symbols available:

(41) any auto, whether owned, nonowned or hired, is covered for liability. This

is the equivalent of symbol (1) of the business auto policy.

(42) owned autos only. This can be used to effect coverage for liability, medical payments, uninsured motorists and physical damage coverages. It is the equivalent of symbol (2) of the business auto policy.

(43) owned commercial autos only. This serves the same purpose as symbol (42), except that it is used to insure owned commercial vehicles of the truck, tractor or trailer type. This is the equivalent of symbol (4) of the business auto policy.

(44) owned autos subject to no-fault insurance. This is the equivalent of symbol (5) of the business auto policy.

(45) owned autos subject to compulsory uninsured motorists law. This is the equivalent of symbol (6) of the business auto policy.

(46) specifically described autos. This provides nonfleet coverage to the same extent as symbol (7) of the business auto policy.

(47) hired autos only, that is, those hired or rented, such as commercial autos owned by employees, but not private passenger autos owned by employees. This is similar to symbol (8) of the business auto policy.

(48) trailers in the insured's possession under a written trailer interchange agreement.

(49) trailers of an insured which are in the possession of another trucker under an interchange agreement, for physical damage insurance.

(50) nonowned autos only. Covers exposure of an insured created by use of nonowned autos in the insured's business. This is equivalent to symbol (9) of the business auto policy.

Mechanics of Coverage

Given the numerical symbols from (41) through (50), the appropriate symbols are placed opposite the coverages as listed in the policy declarations. This handling is the same as that which is used with the business auto and garage policies.

CLASSIFICATION AND RATING

The next step for the underwriter is to classify the risk (different classifications are used for liability and physical damage coverages) and then, the risk can be rated and the final underwriting decision reached.

Classifying the commercial vehicle is basic to underwriting and to rating. This requires the underwriter to determine first what rules are to apply, that is, private passenger autos, trucks, tractors and trailers, public autos or garage autos. Then the underwriter refers to the classification section for that particular rate class.

Liability Classification — Trucks

Since use of the vehicle is extremely important in risk selection, the underwriter must determine the use classification or rate class as one of the first steps in analyzing the information which is presented. Reference is then made to that classification during the balance of the underwriting, as well as in rating the risk.

Rate classes for trucks, including truckers who transport goods of others, are found in tables prepared by insurers or bureaus. The ISO tables are used by many insurers, while others use independent tables that differ in some ways. According to the ISO approach, trucks, truck-tractors and trailers are subject to two major methods of classifying and rating.

The first concerns *other than zone rated risks*. Included here are trucks, truck-tractors, and trailers, including lightweight trucks, regularly operated within a 200 mile radius of the principal place of garaging.

The second involves *zone rated risks.* These include trucks, truck-tractors, and trailers, other than lightweight trucks, regularly operated beyond a 200 mile radius from the principal place of garaging. This latter class usually involves vehicles subject to the truckers policy.

To classify commercial vehicles for both zone and nonzone risks, the underwriter must consider the vehicle's size, which depends upon weight, its use (intensity), and radius of operation.

Vehicle Size. There are four size classes of trucks depending upon their gross vehicle weight (GVW) or the maximum loaded weight as designed. These are as follows:

(1) Light trucks — GVW of 10,000 pounds or less.
(2) Medium trucks — GVW of 10,001 to 20,000 pounds; including crawler type trucks.
(3) Heavy trucks — GVW of 20,001 to 45,000 pounds.
(4) Extra-heavy trucks — GVW over 45,000 pounds.

There also are two size classes of truck-tractors which are motorized vehicles with or without a body for transporting cargo, and equipped with a fifth wheel coupling for semitrailers. They are categorized by their gross combination weight (GCW) or, in other words, their maximum loaded weight in combination with a semitrailer.

(1) Heavy truck-tractors — GCW of 45,000 pounds or less.
(2) Extra heavy truck — GCW over 45,000.

Business use. Vehicles can be classified into one of three use classes. If a truck, truck-tractor or trailer is subject to more than one of the following uses, the highest classification applies, unless 80% of the use is in a lower-rated class.

(1) Service use encompasses vehicles used for transporting the insured's personnel, as well as tools, equipment, and on an incidental basis, supplies from one work location to another. This classification is intended for vehicles which are parked the majority of the time at work locations, or, in other words, have a low intensity of usage. A building contractor's truck would be an example.
(2) Retail use encompasses vehicles which are used to pick up and deliver property to households. Trucks of grocers, dry cleaners, or appliance deal-

ers are examples.

(3) Commercial use encompasses vehicles used to transport property that do not otherwise come within the service or retail uses. A truck of a wholesale distributor or a manufacturer is an example.

Radius of use. There are three radius of use classes.

(1) Local use means that the vehicle is not regularly operated beyond a radius of 50 miles from the place of principal garaging.

(2) Intermediate use means that the vehicle is operated beyond a radius of 50 miles but not regularly beyond a radius of 200 miles from the place of principal garaging.

(3) Long distance use means that the vehicle is regularly operated beyond a radius of 200 miles from the principal place of garaging.

Classification of Trailers

Trailers and semitrailers are classified according to use or by weight in the following manner:

Semitrailers are those equipped with a fifth wheel coupling device for use with truck-tractors, with a load capacity over 2,000 pounds.

Trailers are those units, other than semitrailers, with a load capacity over 2,000 pounds.

Service or utility trailers are trailers or semitrailers with a load capacity of 2,000 pounds or less.

Secondary Classification

For certain special classes, an additional or secondary rate factor must be established. These classifications, which do not apply to zone rated risks, include manufacturers of various kinds, truckers (common and contract carriers), food delivery, special delivery such as armored cars and parcel post, waste disposal, farm vehicles, dump and transit mix vehicles, and contractors.

Liability Classification and Rating — Summary

The primary classification of a vehicle must first be established, considering the size, use, and radius of operations. Next, any applicable secondary factors must be applied to trucks, truck-tractors, and trailers used in special industry classes and not zone rated. The resulting factors are applied to the base rates for the liability exposures to be covered. To this product is applied any fleet rate discount. A fleet consists of any risk that owns five or more motorized vehicles of any type, other than mobile equipment.

Zone rated risks, which are commonly written under the truckers policy, are developed in the same manner as above except that special zone factors are applied depending upon the vehicles' geographical scope of operation.

Physical Damage Rate Factors

Physical damage insurance costs depend upon the vehicle's *age group, original cost new* and *size class*. For trailers, size class is not a factor. There are six age groups. The current model year takes age group 1, the first preceding year takes group 2, and so on. Original cost new is the retail cost which the original purchaser paid for the vehicle and its equipment, plus all federal, state and local taxes.

Deductibles are used extensively with physical damage insurance. It is not uncommon to find deductibles of $500, $1,000 or even higher on all types of physical damage coverages.

ACCEPTABLE RISKS

Insurers of commercial vehicles generally aim toward a particular segment of the market or, in other words, on certain classifications of risks. One insurer may specialize in long-haul trucks, another in log trucks, and still another in motor carriers that carry goods of others for hire. Some insurers, of course, attempt to cover virtually all of the market spectrum.

There are some commercial vehicle risks which are not very different from some personal automobile risks. A prime example is an automobile used in business. There is a degree of overlap between these lines. An automobile may be used by a salesperson and classified as a "business use" under personal automobile insurance, while an identical vehicle used to deliver drug store orders or fried chicken to customers who telephone their orders to the store, are considered commercial risks. Since there is no difference in the vehicles, the *use* of the vehicle is the determining factor.

There is such a slight difference in rates that some automobile insurers that do not write large trucks offer coverage to smaller truck risks. As a group, these smaller truck risks are quite different from large ones. The former include vehicles used for deliveries, short hauls, and for carrying tools or small equipment. These risks do not need the loss control and engineering programs which are important to large truck risks, while the values at stake, plus the potential of huge losses, are much smaller than are found in the larger truck risks. Accordingly, smaller trucks do not need a great deal of specialized underwriting, other than basic automobile underwriting, and much of the underwriting is very similar to that done by personal automobile underwriters. Thus, these risks form a large group of acceptable risks for many insurers.

Large truck risks, on the other hand, comprise a heterogeneous group, many of which require quite specialized underwriting. They often need road patrol service, loss control and engineering programs and sophisticated rating. Many trucks and many truck lines specialize; that is, they handle only one product and, perhaps, operate in only one market. Seldom do insurers specialize to that great an extent, although some have tendencies in that direction and consider as eligible, only certain types of applicants.

Since the trucking industry is big and complicated, truck insurance is too. There are many aspects that can be considered in establishing acceptability: each insurer must first decide the market segment in which it intends to operate. From there, it must establish its acceptability rules to fit that market. A large insurer may even include several subdivisions, each aiming at a segment of the market and each having its own acceptability rules.

UNACCEPTABLE RISKS

There are no substandard commercial auto insurers in the same sense as there are substandard insurers of personal automobile insurance. But, even so, all insurers of commercial autos use unacceptability lists in order to reach a particular segment of the market. However, there is such a diversity of market that the number of insurers in the commercial vehicle field makes it possible for almost any risk which may be unacceptable with one company to be acceptable with another.

Those commercial auto insurers that write a fairly broad spectrum of the market without attempting to specialize and use rates which are approximately the same as bureau rates might possibly use unacceptability lists containing the following factors.

Age of drivers — older drivers are unacceptable because of their comparative inability to respond quickly to emergency situations. Youthful drivers are also unacceptable under some conditions. Long haul trucks are particularly suspect if the drivers are under 21, and especially if they have poor driving records.

Use of commercial vehicles — many uses considered as extra-hazardous are unacceptable. Some common exclusions, by general class of the factors which would be considered by an underwriter, are the following.

1. Trucks with an unusual catastrophe exposure, such as emergency vehicles, trucks hauling explosives or bulk liquid petroleum gas, tank trucks carrying gasoline or other flammable liquids and trucks servicing oil fields.

2. Commercial vehicles with a greater than average mileage or exposure to accidents, such as taxicabs, door-to-door ice cream vendors, coffee or lunch wagons, rubbish and garbage haulers, junk and salvage operations, rental car agents and vehicles used to deliver newspapers.

3. Unusual types of vehicles or exposures, such as house movers, road construction equipment, auto-home cars, trucks on which special equipment is mounted and trucks used to haul workers as passengers.

Radius of operations — trucks hauling certain types of products beyond a certain radius are considered too hazardous for many insurers. Higher rates are available for longer hauls, but these particular risks usually are considered more hazardous than rates contemplate. Special handling or special rates are, therefore, needed. Some of the products in this category are fruits, vegetables, grain, product, livestock, fish, meat, poultry, and Christmas trees. A common denominator of these products is a degree of perishability or need to reach a market within a short time, and truckers hauling such products more than a relatively short distance are often inclined to drive as rapidly as possible in order to reach the market early. (A radius of operations exceeding 50 miles is generally considered to be the limit for these products.)

SECURING INFORMATION

A commercial auto underwriter follows the same steps in the underwriting process as a personal automobile underwriter. Both of them must first determine if a risk is acceptable or uncceptable under the insurer's rules. The commercial auto underwriter ordinarily exercises considerably more judgment in the area of acceptability, and is given greater latitude and is more inclined to take into account such factors as related business and amount of premium.

All automobile underwriters use the same sources of additional information upon which to base acceptability, too. There are some different sources available, but the application is the primary source for both.

Application

The commercial auto application is not inherently different from the personal automobile application. Both furnish information for rating, as well as underwriting; both are usually signed; and neither is made a part of the policy.

The usual classification of the questions in the application show these major categories.

1. Personal
2. Description and use of the vehicles.
3. Insurance information.

Since private passenger automobiles often are combined on policies with commercial vehicles, many of the questions parallel those used for insuring automobile insurance, but there are questions or parts of questions, which pertain only to trucks. The following information is obtained on these applications, although details differ by insurer.

1. *Personal*

A. Full name of the applicant including the firm name, if any. (The usual practice is to secure the name of the person or persons who are applying, followed by the "d.b.a." which stands for "doing business as.") If a partnership, the names of all partners are needed.

B. The structure of the firm, whether an individual partnership, or corporation.

C. The business address and mailing address of the applicant.

D. Names of all drivers and the relationship to the applicant.

E. The age (or birth date), marital status, and driver's license number of each driver, and the number of years of driving experience for each driver.

F. The approximate percentage that each vehicle is driven by each driver.

G. The occupation or job assignment of each driver.

H. The accident record of all drivers, including details of all accidents while operating any vehicle during the previous period (such as five years) and with a statement of fault and the amount paid.

I. The citation record of all drivers, including the date, type of citation, and type of vehicle being driven, and covering traffic citations for which the driver was convicted, fined, or arrested during the previous period (such as five years).

J. The name of any driver whose driver's license has been suspended or revoked. (This is even more important for a truck driver than an automobile driver because of the greater exposure to large losses. Many insurers ask for this information for a longer period of time, often without any limitation of time.)

2. *Description and Use of the Vehicles*

A. The year, make, model, serial number and description; body type, truck tonnage, trailer length.

B. Information regarding value, such as the original cost new, including accessories and equipment, the actual cost of any equipment, the date purchased, and whether the vehicle was new or used when purchased. (Some insurers require a "brake and light certificate" on trucks over a specified age, such as ten years, to ascertain that those vital parts are in satisfactory operating condition.)

C. Name and address of the legal owner, if other than the applicant.
D. Name and address of the loss payee, plus the amount owed.
E. The place of principal garaging of all vehicles, if other than the mailing address of the applicant.
F. For private passenger automobiles, the usage in business or in driving to and from work, and the estimated annual mileage.
G. For trucks, the type of commodities hauled, whether used for retail or wholesale delivery; whether the truck is for hire or rented to others, and if it is used in any other business. Also, if it has more than one rear axle, and if it is ever used to haul a trailer.
H. Any unrepaired damage to the vehicles, defective equipment alterations, and special equipment.

3. *Insurance Information*
   A. The coverages desired, specifying limits and deductibles for which application is made, and the requested effective date.
   B. The name of any driver who has ever been required to file proof of financial responsibility.
   C. Description of any physical impairment or mental disability of any driver.
   D. Whether any insurer has ever cancelled, refused, or declined renewal of this type of insurance for the applicant, plus an explanation of the circumstances involved.
   E. Information about the previous insurer; name of the insurer and policy number.
   F. For trucks, whether each is equipped with a camper.
   G. Any filings, which must be made with a motor carrier regulatory body. (For example, the Interstate Commerce Commission requires proof that liability insurance is carried by all motor carriers under its jurisdiction, and the insurer must file a certificate showing that insurance is in force. An underwriter is interested in knowing about such filings because most of them, like the I.C.C., cover all equipment of the policyholder. For that reason, the underwriter wants to get premiums for all equipment. Furthermore, the liability of the insurer is absolute as respects claimants, so the underwriter cannot rely on policy conditions or exclusions to deny coverage.)

Other Questions

A special fleet application is used for applicants having multiple vehicles, usually five or more. In addition to the preceding information, additional questions are asked, along the following lines.

Equipment: A complete description of each piece of equipment and the coverage desired on each; type of fuel used and any seasonal use; location where stored when not in use; and whether leased to or from others.

Repair facilities: Information concerning the repair facilities mentioned by the applicant; and details of the schedule and location of service and maintenance.

Operations: Commodities transported and the routes traveled; details about average and longest trips made; information about the drivers, whether sleeper cabs are used or schedules are broken to permit rest periods; the terminal use and number of non-driving employees; and a description of any unusual features of the business.

When writing garage liability insurance, a supplemental application is used to develop information peculiar to the operation. Questions are asked about any loan cars available to customers, about equipment rented to others and if a dealer, the type (e.g., franchised, non-franchised, farm implement, etc.).

Since there are coverage options for specific exposures, the application indicates the ones that are desired. For those to be insured, additional information is required. Non-ownership liability is one of the options, and the underwriter will be interested in learning about the number and type of employees who are to be covered. Since all employees are covered under the usual garage liability policy, this generally refers to the employees of other business operations conducted by the applicant. Garagekeepers liability insurance is another option and for this coverage, the underwriter wants to know the maximum number of cars stored or parked, and whether they are kept in a locked enclosure while the premises are unattended.

A different supplemental application is used when writing cargo coverage. It calls for a description of vehicles, type of cargo, ownership of the rig and whether fire extinguishers are available on trucks. (Some insurers use detailed applications in order to determine if the cargo may at any time consist of merchandise which is unusually subject to theft, such as alcoholic beverages, tobacco, drugs and furs.)

Most of the information secured from the application is related to underwriting, because it helps the underwriter in evaluating a risk. However, some of the information only is necessary for rating or issuing the policy.

Motor Vehicle Record

State records of the accident involvement and citation convictions of drivers are available to a commercial automobile underwriter and other persons. Some underwriters check motor vehicle records of all drivers in order to ascertain their ability to drive a motor vehicle properly. But in truck insurance, unlike other automobile insurance, rates are seldom affected by the past accident or citation record of drivers.

Inspection Reports

Reports of inspection companies are available to commercial underwriters for the same purposes as they are to personal automobile underwriters. Both will order "credit reports" to secure more information about drivers or to substantiate (or correct) answers given them on the application.

Commercial underwriters often order expanded reports containing additional information about the condition and use of the vehicle. These reports will develop such information as additional equipment not revealed to the underwriter, about the business record and reputation of the applicant and about any questionable driving history of any of the operators.

An important item often developed only through an inspection report is information concerning drivers who may take their trucks home at night. Sometimes this aspect is not mentioned to the producer at the time the application is completed. If a firm permits its employees to do this, it may be increasing the insurance risk. One added hazard is the driver who uses the truck to take groups of friends to parties or picnics. Still another is when the driver rents the truck to others, perhaps for group parties or picnics. The underwriter is interested in information of this type because the employer can be held liable for any injury or damage caused by the operation of the truck and, as the owner, would at least have to defend against suits. Such defense and any damages awarded would be provided by the insurance policy, unless the underwriter made specific provision to exclude that exposure.

Engineering Reports

Underwriters of trucks often use special loss prevention and control engineers to supply important information. Some insurers employ their own engineers, while others subscribe to the services of one or more of such companies furnishing this service.

One type of engineering concerns a report on physical factors. A specialist inspects all vehicles and completes a report for the underwriter. This is a portion of the function of an inspection company report; indeed, an inspection report may satisfy this need for some risks. However, a loss control report can go into greater detail concerning the maintenance of the equipment, the repair facilities, the cargo carried, the attitude of the drivers and similar factors.

Another type of loss control is safety promotion — a continuing service. A person performing this function ordinarily reports on physical factors, but will go farther. Possible activities are to conduct safety meetings for drivers, operate safety programs or contests, teach drivers how to report accidents and work with the scheduling of drivers. The latter factor is particularly important because drivers should not be scheduled for long trips beyond their safe physical limits; or not expected to complete trips within such a short period of time that they must violate the speed laws in order to meet schedules.

Still another type of loss control concerns road patrol. Those involved cruise the highways observing the policyholder's vehicles. They watch for speeding, poor driving, faulty equipment and other observable factors. A record is kept of each truck observed, so that the policyholder can check the location and time that a driver is seen in order to verify that the records are correct and that the driver is not deviating from the approved routes. Also, many of the road patrol cars are equipped with radar to enable the loss control specialist to measure the speed of the vehicle accurately. Since it is necessary to park the car on the shoulder of the road in order to operate the radar, and parking on most expressways is permitted only in emergency cases, this practice is becoming more difficult.

Any one loss control specialist may perform any or all of these functions. Many are ex-truck drivers and are able to report the pertinent facts about the vehicles and drivers to the underwriter. With this information, the underwriter can do a better job of evaluating risks. In particular, the underwriter can learn whether the drivers accept the safety programs or may be expected to comply. Even more important, the underwriter can find out the attitude of management; one of the true keys to success in writing truck insurance is to have the wholehearted support of the truck line management in these safety programs.

The loss control specialist can do more than try to improve the risk and to report the facts to the underwriter. That person can be of great value to the underwriter by expressing an opinion about the desirability of the risk. The specialist's responsibility in this regard differs among insurers; some insist that a decision be made and reported on the acceptability of the risk, while others feel that it is not the job of the specialist to evaluate a risk, but only to report facts. The former seems to utilize best the knowledge of the loss control specialist. If trained properly, the specialist should know the type of risk the insurer wants. Often that person is in the best position to make a qualified decision because the producer is not trained in these details; the credit reporting company does not know the insurer's philosophy; and the underwriter cannot actually see the risk. It seems most effective for the loss control specialist, therefore, to report the facts and to give an evaluation of the risk. The final decision, of course, must remain with the underwriter who has access to other information not available to the loss control specialist, such as related business influence of the applicant and desire to accommodate the producer.

Experience of Other Insurers

Commercial auto underwriters sometimes exchange information just as personal automobile underwriters do. Letters to prior insurers are used to request this information. As with automobile insurance, the purpose of these letters is to verify the accident record of the applicant. No underwriter will cancel a policy simply because another insurer has cancelled it, but the reasons for the action are of interest. Perhaps the problem can be avoided or the rate may be adjusted for the exposure, but to do so facts upon which to base the decisions are needed. Commercial auto underwriters do not use this device of checking with former insurers as much as automobile underwriters. This is partly the result of better record keeping by commercial risks, as compared to individual — that is, the commercial applicant is much more likely to be able to furnish details of past accidents than is the average individual. It is also the result of the complexity of many truck risks, which would cause an unreasonable burden to furnish the experience information.

POLICY FORMS

Commercial auto insurance policies, like personal automobile insurance policies, are written under either bureau policies or independently. Even so, most such policies used by insurers are similar. However underwriters have more authority modifying commercial policies than personal automobile policies and, because commercial insurance develops more premium, underwriters are permitted more opportunities to investigate risks and adapt coverages to conditions which are found to exist.

Commercial insurance covers a wide range of operations, too. A farm truck or a light truck may have a premium which is comparable to an automobile policy, with the underwriting being not very different. But, on the other hand, fleets and extra-heavy trucks often develop large premiums, requiring careful underwriting and specialized handling. About the only similarity between these extremes is that all must cover the financial responsiblity requirements. For that reason, there is a limit beyond which the underwriter cannot go in reducing coverage or excluding some areas of protection.

It also should be emphasized that high premiums mean different things to different people. When an automobile insurance policy has a high premium, the underwriter knows that the risk is less desirable; the driver may be young and inexperienced or has a poor driving record, or both. However, when a commercial policy develops a high premium, the underwriter knows that a large-scale operation is involved, along with an opportunity for more profit. Large premiums may be generated by risks having large trucks, a fleet, a long-haul operation, etc.

Commercial auto underwriters may endorse policies to exclude certain undesirable drivers or to permit only certain classes of employees to drive. They can permit only certain coverages, such as fire and theft instead of comprehensive, if the operations or vehicles warrant the reduced coverage. They may exclude some equipment, too, if they do not wish to insure it, along with pre-existing damage — with the exclusion being removed upon satisfactory evidence that repairs have been made.

A fairly common limitation placed on some types of truck applicants is one limiting the commodities carried or the operating radius, or both. Rates are based on representations, and it is not unusual to guarantee the accuracy of the information by providing no coverage if the limitations are exceeded. Then, if infrequent extensions are needed for special trips, the underwriter may again endorse the policy, this time extending protection to other goods or territories, for an additional premium. Coverage is usually not granted if trucks are rented to others under a lease or contract, and there is no coverage for permissive users of the trucks either, other than employees in the course of their employment.

RETENTION AND REINSURANCE

Underwriters of commercial auto insurance often face problems of retention because of the high liability limits usually needed for entire exposures. It is to their advantage, therefore, that they know how to handle reinsurance. Faced with an application for high liability limits, the commercial auto underwriter has two choices. Both of these approaches are common and each has its advantages.

The first approach is to write the policy for the entire amount requested and then to secure reinsurance to protect above the desired retention. Reinsurance is usually obtained on a facultative basis, with the underwriter applying to the reinsurer for coverage on the specific risk. However, automatic treaties are sometimes arranged, under which the underwriter can bind the reinsurance. The cost of the reinsurance is usually negotiated and then included in the total premium charged to the policyholder who is usually unaware of the reinsurance. The advantage of this arrangement is that the applicant gets one policy, the underwriter controls the entire account and loss adjustments are handled by one claims adjuster.

The second approach is for the commercial auto underwriter to write a policy for the amount which he or she desires to retain, and then to leave the problem of buying a specific excess policy for the balance of the coverage desired in the hands of the producer. This approach, which is more accurately described as an excess insurance, is always placed on a specific basis for each applicant. The cost of the excess placement is, of course, paid by the policyholder to the excess insurer. The main advantage of this method is that in case of a suit whereby the policy must be revealed to the claimant attorney, the primary policy alone can be disclosed, leaving the excess policy and its high limits unrevealed. Another advantage to the commercial auto underwriter is that the retention can be limited to the desired amount and the primary underwriter need not be concerned with any higher limits desired. A disadvantage of this arrangement, on the other hand, is that the excess policy may have a high minimum premium which increases the total cost of the insurance protection. The rates for the excess policy are often quite low because the policy does not apply to any loss not exceeding the limits of the primary policy.

Since catastrophe liability reinsurance is carried by all commercial auto insurers, underwriters must be aware of the coverage and exclusions of the treaty. With such a treaty, the underwriter can retain higher limits than without this protection. Such treaties exclude certain types of risks and may have higher points of attachment for some risks than others. The treaty, or a combination of treaties, cover those rare, but possible situations, when the limits of several policies are involved in a single loss. For example, an owner of one truck could be driving another firm's truck while on an errand for a third firm and all could conceivably be held liable for an accident.

Catastrophies are also possible under material damage coverage. It is not unusual for a truck line to have a dozen or more trucks in one lot or at one terminal at any one time. A fire or flood could destroy all of the vehicles, and if the trucks and trailers were loaded and more cargo was stored in the terminal awaiting shipment, the entire loss could total millions of dollars. The commercial auto underwriter, therefore, should be aware of the coverage provided by reinsurance treaties secured to protect against these contingencies, as well as the exclusions or limitations of such treaties.

A commercial auto underwriter also must be familiar with all facets of the risks being insured. Not only must all of the pertinent facts about the vehicles themselves and their operations be known, but also the effect of any contingency on the insurer. Thus, an underwriter must know the reinsurance arrangements applicable to each of the policies issued.

Truck Cargo

Insurance which protects against loss of cargo is classified as inland marine insurance under every definition used. However, it is so closely allied with truck insurance that it sometimes appears near the commercial vehicle section of the automobile manual. Cargo coverage is ordinarily written as an endorsement on a truck policy, although it can be written as a separate policy. There are two forms, one of which can be used in any one situation. The first is an owner's form, covering property belonging to the policyholder and carried on owned vehicles. The second is for truckers who transport goods of others; a cargo policy covers their legal liability as common carriers, bailees or warehousemen for loss or damage to goods carried by them, or held by them.[1] Both of these forms cover cargo under approximately the same provisions, in spite of the legal differences between insuring one's own property or one's liability for loss to property of others. There is no standard

1. This same division between those transporting their own goods and those hauling the goods of others is used in classifying trucks, as was mentioned earlier in this chapter.

form for either type, but the forms used by most insurers are similar.

Most cargo policies cover on a specified perils basis — that is, on such perils as fire, windstorm, flood, explosion, collapse of bridges, perils of the sea while on a ferry, and collision or overturning of the vehicle carrying the cargo. Theft is available but is underwritten very carefully, with the type of cargo being a prime factor of consideration. Even when theft is covered, it is common to exclude petty theft and pilferage for many types of cargo. The usual exclusions are delay, inherent vice, loss of use or of market, war and nuclear contamination. Other exclusions sometimes used, depending upon insurer and type of cargo, are riot and civil commotion, strikers, leakage, breakage, and loss from rough handling, poor packing or faulty loading.

"All risks" coverage is sometimes written for owners. Under this form, the usual exclusions are shrinkage, breakage, leakage, marring, scratching, dampness, extremes of temperature and changes in flavor or color.

All forms require that the truck which will transport the cargo be described in the policy. A limit of coverage per truck is used, as well as an aggregate limit per occurrence and coverage is excess over other insurance.

Rates are largely a matter of judgment. Usually the rate is specified per $100 of cargo coverage for each truck, although some insurers write truckers on the basis of gross receipts, with a rate applied to the receipts as reported monthly by the policyholder. Sometimes a rate table is used as a guide; such tables commonly contain several groups of rates, by type of goods, such as produce, dry freight, lumber, livestock and gasoline. When a table is used, it shows the rate for an average policyholder, with modifications expected for those who are different from the norm. The judgment used in establishing the rate, whether setting a rate or modifying a table rate, is based on such factors as the distance and route to be traveled, the locality, the type of truck and goods and the financial standing of the policyholder.

QUESTIONS FOR DISCUSSION

1. For insurance purposes, what is the criterion that distinguishes a private passenger auto from a commercial auto? Give an example.
2. a. For whom is the business auto policy intended?
   b. For whom is the garage policy intended?
   c. For whom is the truckers policy intended?
3. Why might personal injury protection, medical payments and uninsured motorists coverages of the business auto, truckers, and garage policies have limited application to businesses?
4. Compare symbol (1) and (7) of the business auto policy from the standpoint of (a) auto exposures covered, and (b) coverage on newly acquired vehicles.
5. What is the difference in coverage between a business auto policy written with symbol (1) and a business auto policy written with symbols (7), (8) and (9)? Why might an underwriter be reluctant to provide coverage under symbol (1)?

6. Assume a business has four private passenger autos and six trucks. The business wants comprehensive and collision on the private passenger autos and specified perils and collision on the trucks. What are the appropriate symbols?
7. Explain the two types of garagekeepers coverages that are available. What is the purpose of garagekeepers insurance?
8. For what reasons might a business need dealers physical damage insurance?
9. In what ways is the coverage of the truckers policy similar to the business auto policy?
10. Explain the difference between "bobtail" and "deadhead" liability.
11. Briefly discuss the criteria in classifying a trucker subject to zone or other than zone rating.
12. Why may truck cargo insurance be necessary?
13. What two truck cargo insurance coverages are available?

21

Personal Liability

Almost every individual faces some type of exposure to liability caused by his or her negligence. This personal liability can stem from any number of ways, but popular sources are an individual's or family's residence premises and personal acts. Many suits arise because hazardous conditions at a person's residence lead to bodily injury. A sidewalk in need of repair or an unattended swimming pool are just two examples of the type of hazards which can lead to claim for injuries because the owner does not take the necessary steps to avoid the inevitable. Too, a person's careless use of rented watercraft or premises leading to property damages are other examples of situations that can place a person's assets — home and savings — into jeopardy.

One of the more common methods of securing coverage against many such personal liabilities is to purchase a comprehensive personal liability insurance policy or CPL. Actually this form of coverage is commonly procurred with a purchase of a homeowners policy because it forms an integral part of that contract. However, those who do not have a homeowners policy or the need for one can still purchase this coverage as a separate contract. (A farmers comprehensive personal liability insurance policy or FCPL policy is also available to those engaged in certain farming operations. It is somewhat similar to the comprehensive personal liability insurance policy, but is has some additional coverages dealing with liability stemming from certain farm operations. This policy is discussed in Chapter 37.) A business owner who has a commercial liability policy on the business, and is a sole proprietor, may add the CPL coverage for personal exposures to the commercial policy.

While most comprehensive personal liability insurance is written under standard language of the Insurance Services Office, there are many independently filed versions, too. These usually differ from the standard approach in relatively minor ways.

For those who feel that comprehensive personal liability insurance is insufficient in certain areas, some form of personal umbrella liability insurance also can be purchased. Since personal umbrella insurance complements comprehensive personal liability insurance and, as a matter of fact, since the latter is required as a prerequisite to purchasing the former coverage, particulars of personal umbrella liability insurance also are discussed in this chapter.

DESCRIPTION OF COVERAGES

In spite of the fact that there are many versions of comprehensive personal liability insurance, there are many features of this package policy.

—Personal liability coverage provides protection for insureds, the named insured listed in the policy declarations and his or her spouse, resident relatives of either and any person under age 21 in care of the insured, whose negligence causes bodily injury or property damage or both, subject, of course, to the exclusions. Combined into one insuring agreement are coverages for bodily injury, property damage and employers liability. The policy is written with a single limit of liability — the limit of which is the maximum the insurer will pay for bodily injury (to one or more persons) or property damage arising out of one occurrence. The usual minimum limit is $25,000, but higher limits are available up to $500,000.

Employers liability coverage applies to residence employees whose duties deal with the maintenance or use of the insured premises or even away from such premises so long as the same type of duties are performed. This coverage does not apply, however, if the insured has a worker's compensation policy which covers such employees or if the insured should have purchased such insurance and failed to do so.

—Fire legal liability coverage makes an exception to the care, custody or control exclusion and provides liability insurance for damage to premises or house furnishings used by, rented to or in the care, custody or control of the insured. Such coverage, however, is limited to damage arising out of fire, explosion, smoke or smudge caused by the sudden, unusual and faulty operation of any heating or cooking unit.

—Medical payments insurance is automatically included without additional premium on basic coverages — that is, on such coverages that are contemplated by the basic premium charge for coverage. This means that when certain additional classifications of exposures are added to the policy which require extra charges for personal liability coverage, extra charges are also required even for basic medical payments coverage. An example could be any additional residence premises maintained by insureds other than the named insured and spouse. Medical payments insurance is usually written for a minimum per person, per accident limit of $500, but higher limits are available. In fact, underwriters often seek to write higher limits because the underlying reason for this insurance is to pay promptly certain bodily injury claims in order to avoid costly lawsuits. Medical payments insurance does not apply to the insured or family members. It is designed to cover injuries to others, not to be a health insurance policy.

—Physical damage to property of others coverage is automatically included without premium charge, too. This coverage is similar to medical payments insurance in that it has nothing to do with the legal liability of the insured; coverage applies without regard to fault. It is frequently described as coverage for the "moral obligations" of the insured. Thus, for example, if an insured borrows a neighbor's power tool and accidently burns out the motor, the insured may feel morally obligated to pay for the damaged property, in spite of the fact that the policy may not cover such loss because of the care, custody or control exclusion.

There are, however, several important safeguards which protect insurers against any possible abuses of this nonliability coverage. For one, coverage usually carries a maximum $500 limit for any one occurrence, thus limiting the protection to relatively minor losses. For another, the insuring agreement stipulates that the insurer will pay for the actual cash value of property damaged or destroyed by an insured or the insurer may elect to repair or replace the property up to the $500 limit. Finally, some forms contain a specific provision stating to the effect that any payment made under this coverage does not constitute an admission of liability on the insured's behalf.

With these safeguards, it is difficult to imagine that a policyholder, no matter how dishonest, could defraud an insurer for an amount which makes the effort worthwhile.

Personal Umbrella Liability Cover

For some people, comprehensive personal insurance is not enough. For one thing, they may need higher limits — $1 million, $5 million or more — than those usually offered as maximum amounts by insurers. For another, some people may want to complement bodily injury liability coverage with personal injury liability coverage. The latter includes such offenses as libel, slander, defamation, false arrest, invasion of privacy and wrongful eviction. Any one of these offenses can be just as damaging and possibly more expensive than bodily injury claims which are limited to physical harm claims of others. Those persons in this category, therefore, who feel that they need broader protection should explore the idea of purchasing a personal umbrella liability policy.

A variety of personal umbrella liability policies are offered by insurers to provide protection excess of underlying liability insurance. These are nonstandard and each insurer has its own rules on the limits required with underlying policies. Common limits required as prerequisites to personal umbrella insurance are: $50,000 comprehensive personal insurance; $100/300/10,000 automobile liability; and $50,000 for other exposures such as watercraft and aircraft. However, if insureds carry limits on underlying policies in excess of minimums, their premium for the broader coverage is somewhat less costly than otherwise. This stands to reason because the higher the limits on underlying policies, the less chance of an umbrella policy coming into use.

In addition, personal umbrella liability insurance is intended for catastrophe-type claims; insurers are not interested in covering small claims. To uphold this intent, umbrella policies that cover certain exposures that are not covered by underlying policies also are subject to deductibles in varying amounts. These deductibles are commonly referred to as self-retentions and vary in amount by insurer and applicant. While some insurers offer umbrella insurance without deductibles, most insurers usually require a minimum but offer higher ones for additional reductions in premium. On occasion, however, underwriters may exercise their right and demand higher self-retentions than the minimums when they feel that a particular risk is not otherwise insurable because of some unusual exposure to loss.

Finally, while personal umbrella liability policies are designed to provide broader protection than is available on other personal liability insurance policies, they should not be interpreted as being all-inclusive, as some people have been led to believe. Each such policy must be studied to determine whether it will fulfill the needs of a particular risk.

UNDERWRITING FACTORS

Acceptable and Unacceptable Risks

Since most comprehensive personal insurance is written as an integral part of homeowners forms, acceptability of the former coverage rests primarily with the acceptability of the latter coverage. However, even when CPL policies are written under separate contract or by endorsement to fire or casualty policies, acceptability tracks rather closely with the acceptability of homeowners forms.

From a homeowners manual rule standpoint, almost every individual is eligible for coverage, including comprehensive personal insurance, except those who are engaged in the occupation of farming. Thus, whether an individual (or two individuals as partners) is an owner-occupant of a dwelling, a tenant of a multiple occupancy building or the eventual owner-occupant of a dwelling under construction, coverage may be written.

However, this should not be taken to mean that the mere fact that a risk qualifies according to manual rules for a homeowners policy or a CPL policy that the risk will be written. There may be instances when an applicant for a homeowners policy meets the eligibility rules of the manual but is still rejected by the underwriter for some reason. If this were to happen, an applicant still could probably purchase personal liability coverage, if the reason for rejecting the applicant rests solely upon some physical aspect of the dwelling conducive to loss from such perils as fire, windstorm or water.

For the most part, few applicants for personal liability insurance are rejected by underwriters. Those persons who are engaged in illegal activities, such as notorious gamblers or those who conduct business pursuits on premises which are capable of causing a good deal of argument as to coverage after loss may be examples of those who may find it difficult to obtain coverage. Too, applicants with abnormal exposures to loss will usually find it difficult to purchase coverage, especially for high limits. Among those in this category are individuals who have swimming pools or have attractive nuisances which are not properly safeguarded; those who own vicious animals or those who have mischievous children; or those who own speedboats or large watercraft and permit their children to operate them. It is not unusual to find some insurers even rejecting applicants who are wealthy. The underlying thought here is that such persons offer an unusually large exposure to suit. The milkman, for example, who trips over a loose brick in the sidewalk and cuts his hand or leg may quickly overlook that event if it occurs at some residence in a middle-income area. But if this were to occur at the premises of some wealthy person, he might threaten to sue for a large sum.

Personal umbrella liability insurance (which affords high limits of coverage, such as $1 million or more, above an underlying policy) is underwritten in a variety of ways depending upon insurer philosophy. Some insurers have acceptable lists which preclude some probable troublemakers, such as any person who has had unfavorable publicity; any person presenting a moral hazard; those who have unusual exposures to libel and slander suits, such as broadcasters and newspaper reporters; or those whose activities subject them to considerable publicity, such as actors, actresses, professional entertainers, professional athletes, public lecturers, labor negotiators and politicians.

Aside from these factors, some insurers will readily write the umbrella coverage when it also provides all underlying coverages which are normally required as prerequisites for coverage. Other insurers do not require that they have the underlying coverages but only that such underlying coverages with other insurers remain in force. In some cases, underwriters of personal umbrella insurance will not go to any great length in securing underwriting information other than an application — their thoughts being that if an insurer willingly provides underlying coverages at lower limits, the risk is usually considered as acceptable for the broader coverage. But if an underwriter discovers certain adverse qualitites of an insured, he may still reject coverage in spite of any underlying insurance because umbrella liability insurance is intended to cover catastrophic-type claims.

SECURING INFORMATION

Since comprehensive personal insurance is ordinarily written in connection with a homeowners policy, much of the information about the risk will have been secured from the other coverage. Whether this is the case, or whether the CPL policy is written alone, there is certain information which is important to the underwriter.

Application

Most insurers require that an application be submitted by the producer, as with other lines. The application for comprehensive personal insurance, either alone or with other coverage, gives information that is necessary for underwriting, rating, and policy issuance. It is ordinarily signed by the applicant, and the statements made in the declarations section are repeated on the declarations page which is a part of the policy.

Specific questions differ by insurer. However, most applications include these major categories.

1. Personal
2. Description of the premises
3. Insurance information

The following information is developed from most applications for comprehensive personal insurance.

1. *Personal*

A. Name of the applicant.

B. Mailing address and residence address of the applicant.

C. Age (or birth date) of the applicant and spouse, and the marital status.

D. Occupation and employer of applicant and spouse.

E. Information concerning stability factors, such as ownership of home and how long a resident at the present address.

F. A description of losses of the type which would be covered by this insurance during the previous period, such as three years.

2. *Description of the Premises*

A. The number of units or apartments in the building.

B. Whether the applicant is owner or tenant.

2 C. Other premises owned by the applicant.

D. Any business or farming which is conducted on the premises.

E. The number of rooms held for rent by renters or boarders.

F. Number of full time residence employees.

G. If an apartment, whether maid service is furnished.

H. A description of other buildings on the premises, in addition to the residence.

I. Whether there is a swimming pool on the premises.

J. Any unusual hazards, such as dangerous animals on the premises, water skiing by any member of the family, or child care duties (such as baby sitting) of any member of the family.

3. *Insurance Information*
   A. The limits desired, and the requested effective date.
   B. Explanation of the circumstances if any insurer has ever cancelled, refused, or denied renewal of this type of insurance.
   C. Information about the previous insurer, name of the insurer, policy number, and reason for changing insurers.

When comprehensive personal liability coverage is written with another policy, as it usually is, the application is consolidated for all coverages. All of this information, therefore, overlaps that required for most other types of personal insurance.

However, most of this information is needed for proper underwriting the coverage. While it is true, as explained previously, that not a great deal of underwriting is generally performed on comprehensive personal insurance, there are cases when the underwriter's suspicions are aroused. In those cases, all of the factors which often appear to be superfluous are weighed carefully before a decision is made.

Personal umbrella applications tend to ask more information about an applicant's liability exposures than any other factor. While there is no uniformity in the information requested or in the arrangement of the applications, the questions generally fall within the same categories as on the comprehensive personal insurance application. Most personal umbrella applications develop the following information.

1. *Personal*
   A. Name and age of applicant and all family members.
   B. Mailing address of the applicant.
   C. The occupation of the applicant.
   D. A description of losses of the types which would be covered by this policy during the previous period, such as five years. Some applications specify "all losses," while others ask for those over $1,000 or $10,000.

2. *Premises and Exposures*
   A. All residence locations, type of interest (own or lease), number of swimming pools at each and acreage, if farms.
   B. All automobiles owned, type and principal driver of each, where garaged and rate classes.
   C. All boats, owned or leased, with descriptions of type, speed, horsepower and length of each, operators of such watercraft, location of operation and whether any underlying policy has restrictions on water skiing.
   D. All aircraft owned or used with descriptions of each.
   E. Employers liability or workers' compensation exposures with number of domestic servants and farm employees.
   F. All business pursuits or business properties of the applicant.
   G. Plans of any family member to enter an automobile or boat race, contest or exhibition.

3. *Insurance Information*
   A. The limits and effective date reported, plus the amount of the retention for self-insured exposures.
   B. Schedule of all applicable underlying policies: automobile, comprehensive personal liability, boat, aircraft and employers liability or workers' compensation insurance.

The description should include the name of the insurer, the policy number, the policy period, the limits on the policy and the premium.

C. Specific information about other policies such as if comprehensive personal liability provides coverage for business pursuits or business properties, or if any policy has endorsements which eliminate coverage or reduce the limits of liability with respect to any of the insureds or any exposure.

Inspection Reports

The same inspection companies used for other lines are also used to furnish more information on personal liability coverages.

Inspections for comprehensive personal liability insurance are usually combined with inspections for the other coverages ordinarily written on the same policy. If the underwriter wants more information about the automobile or fire coverages, he or she will ask for information about the corollary CPL exposures. Particularly on the inspection forms for the homeowners fire policy, where CPL is an indivisible part of the contract, one section furnishes information solely about the CPL factors.

On the other hand, inspections are rarely made on policies written for comprehensive personal liability coverage alone. The premium is too small to permit much investigation; there are many cases when the cost of a "credit report" amounts to one-half the annual premium for the CPL policy. For the same reason, when the CPL policy is part of another policy, the underwriter would not request any inspection, unless there were also reservations about the automobile or fire portions of the policy.

Personal umbrella applications are often investigated by means of an inspection report. The underwriter is concerned about unknown or unusual exposures. More information is desired about the character of the applicant, since large amounts of liability coverage are involved.

Experience of Other Insurers

The underwriter may choose to ask the previous insurer about its experience with the applicant. However, this is seldom done for comprehensive personal liability alone, for the same reasons that inspection reports are seldom ordered under this situation. Presumably the other insurer would report CPL coverage experience along with other losses under a combination policy. The loss frequency on CPL policy is very low, so it would be rare that much information about these exposures would be gained through this means.

Sharing the experience of personal umbrella coverage is the exception rather than the rule, too. There are any number of reasons for this. For one thing, there is very little in the way of previous claim experience under this type of coverage. For another, the applicant is not apt to forget nor ignore mention of claims on the application considering the fact that umbrella coverage is meant to cover catastrophic-type claims.

CLASSIFICATION AND RATING

Classifying and rating comprehensive personal liability insurance is a relatively simple matter however written — that is, when included along with a homeowners policy or written separately.

Acutally, when this coverage is written with a homeowners policy, the premium for basic coverages is automatically included. However, when an insured has such additional exposures as other residence premises, watercraft, recreational vehicles or when part of the premises is occupied as an office, professional, private school or studio, they must be classified according to the classes and codes of the homeowners manual and additional charges made for them.

When this coverage is written separately — that is, by separate policy or by endorsement to a property or automobile policy, the classifications and rates are usually in the Commercial Lines manual. When coverage is written in this manner, the producer or underwriter need merely determine the exposure of the insured — as stated in the application — and classify it according to the classification and codes of that manual. The state rate pages indicate the rates for these various classifications at basic limits and by territory.

Rates are quoted for basic limits: a single limit of $25,000 applies for any personal liability of the insured and the basic medical payments limit is $500. Upcharge or increased limit tables provide percentage increases for higher limits which are then applied against basic premiums to determine the total charge for the exposure. There are cases, however, when increased limit tables are on a dollar basis rather than on a percentage basis; this is common when coverage is written with a homeowners policy.

Personal Umbrella Insurance

Being a nonstandard coverage, personal umbrella liability insurance is rated in a variety of ways. Some insurers, for example, apply a flat amount against underlying coverages and limits, while other insurers apply factors to basic limits of underlying coverages.

Certain underlying coverages are required before an insurer will write the umbrella coverage, but whether the insurer requires the underlying coverages, too, is a matter of choice. Generally, the more underlying coverages in force and the higher the limits on such coverages, the lower the charge for umbrella insurance. Available, too, are self-insured deductibles. These play an important role on premiums, since the higher the deductibles chosen, the lower the charge for umbrella insurance — subject, of course, to minimum premiums that usually apply.

POLICY FORMS

Comprehensive personal liability insurance is avaliable in a variety of forms but differences among them are fairly few. The bureau forms — those written in conjunction with homeowners forms and those available under separate contracts —

have the advantage of standardization, although those used by independent insurers provide an offsetting advantage of being flexible when changing conditions or adverse court decisions require prompt modifications.

Personal umbrella liability policies, on the other hand, are not standardized. Each insurer writes its own policy which is modified by the underwriter to meet the requirements of the applicant; to adapt to the unique situations presented by different underlying forms of coverage; and to satisfy the demands of the underwriter.

There are many similarities in these policies, of course. The basic policies, before modification, provide coverage that does not differ a great deal between insurers. But it takes careful study to discover this fact because most such policies are completely dissimilar in appearance and format.

RETENTION AND REINSURANCE

One of the least of the problems facing the underwriter of comprehensive personal insurance is retention. However, a need for reinsurance can exist and the underwriter should be aware of the problem.

There are two situations in which reinsurance is needed. The first arises when a policy is written with high liability limits. Most insurers can retain the entire exposure of \$25,000 or \$50,000 limits. When the limits are \$100,000 or higher, most insurers secure a reinsurance treaty to cover any single loss occurrence in excess of the desired retention of the insurer. The second situation arises when two or more policyholders are involved in a single loss. This is unlikely but is slightly more possible than under automobile insurance. It is conceivable that two partners, each with their personal liability coverage insured by the same company, could be involved in a boat or aircraft loss because one owned the craft and the other was operating it. This catastrophe exposure is always covered by the same treaty or treaties as for high limits of coverage on one policy. It is not unusual to find several layers of reinsurance treaties, each layer excess over the underlying layers because the potential exposure can be half a million dollars or more. It is conceivable that a specific excess policy could be bought on a certain risk, but this is rarely done.

The personal umbrella policy is really a type of excess policy, and any insurer writing the limits of liability required under the policy must have reinsurance arrangements carefully made in advance. The underwriter in this situation is almost a reinsurance underwriter and must know precisely how each application is to be ceded or reinsured before it can be accepted.

QUESTIONS FOR DISCUSSION

1. Why is comprehensive personal liability coverage considered to be a package within itself?
2. How does medical payments coverage under CPL insurance differ from medical payments coverage under personal automobile policies with regard to the persons covered?

3. To what extent does the CPL make exception to the general exclusion of damage to property in the care, custody or control of the insured?
4. (a) For what reasons might a person desire or need a personal umbrella liability policy?

   (b) What do underwriters usually require from the standpoint of underlying coverage before a personal umbrella liability policy will be written?

22

Commercial Liability

Everyone — from an individual who owns an apartment house or operates a store to the largest corporation or institution which provides products or services — faces a multitude of exposures which may require the paying of damages stemming from negligence. Everyone, therefore, needs protection against crippling lawsuits. Claims may arise out of conditions on premises, during operations away from premises, from any assumed liability, from any products sold or work completed by such individuals, commercial enterprises or institutions, to name a few. Insurance offered to protect any such risk as the result of possible liability is commonly referred to as commercial liability insurance.

All commercial liability insurance protects against the contingency that the policyholder will be sued for alleged negligence resulting in bodily injury or property damage to others. Thus, it operates under precisely the same principles as automobile liability policies or personal liability policies of individuals. There are no legal reasons that all of the liability exposures are not covered under one policy, but the divisions are traditional and not likely to be abolished soon and, hence, each liability policy is careful to exclude other types of liability exposures.

Like personal liability insurance, commercial liability protection is widely sold because most businesses do not attempt to operate without this insurance. On the other hand, the commercial area is much more complicated than the personal area, offering a number of coverage types and requiring a substantial degree of training for underwriters who wish to be proficient in all of its aspects. As for knowledge possessed by policyholders of this insurance coverage, undoubtedly more commercial insureds are cognizant of their policy details than are insureds of their personal policies, but there are many business owners who buy coverage they are told is correct without ever understanding the terms of the contract.

In spite of the fact that many commercial liability policyholders are not familiar with the details of their coverage, they consider it to be very valuable to them. A business could become bankrupt overnight by a liability claim resulting from a substantial adverse judgment. The benefit from a liability insurance policy, therefore, is very real because it protects the assets of the business by providing legal defense and payment of judgments in the event of serious loss.

Some of the unfamiliarity by policyholders with commercial liability coverages results from its many complexities. The terms are couched in legalistic language which insurers feel is necessary in a contract that may appear before a court of law for adjudication. Furthermore, the myriad of business situations requires a large number of contracts and adaptations to contracts in order to accomplish the intended results and still keep the premium within reason. This complexity of exposures to be covered must be kept in mind in order to understand the reason for the many types of commercial liability coverages available.

DESCRIPTION OF COVERAGES

The coverages of commercial liability insurance can be categorized in numerous ways. For purposes here, they are grouped into seven general classifications.

1. Owners, Landlords and Tenants Liability (OL&T)
2. Manufacturers and Contractors Liability (M&C)
3. Products Liability and Completed Operations
4. Contractual Liability
5. Contingent Liability (Owners and Contractors Protective)
6. Miscellaneous Liability
7. Professional Liability (Physicians, Surgeons, Dentists, Hospital, Miscellaneous Medical and Lawyers)

These classifications have been used for a number of years. However, they are completely changed under the simplified-language commercial forms program of ISO. That program is described later in this section. First, though, the traditional classifications will be explained for several reasons: (1) they are still used by a number of insurers who write on independent forms; (2) they furnish a bridge to the new approach for underwriters who have used the older classes; and (3) they may help to clarify classifications for new underwriters.

All of these traditional classes, except for professional liability, ordinarily have been combined into one contract referred to as "comprehensive general liability" — discussed later in this section. Some insurers issue policies covering only one or more of these individual classes, so they will first be explained separately.

Owners, Landlords and Tenants Liability

Owners, landlords and tenants liability insurance is intended for every person or enterprise which is subject to claims for damages stemming from any negligence when such exposure rests *primarily* on premises. Thus, those who own, rent, use or lease premises, whether for residential or commercial purposes, come within the category of OL&T coverage. Owners of property may be held liable because of a condition in the property whether they operate the premises or not. Even if an accident arises solely out of operations, an owner will usually be named in a suit, and therefore, needs defense coverage. Landlords of property are also susceptible to suit because they exercise some control over premises. If a visitor to an apartment trips over a loose tile or is injured in an elevator, that person will probably name the landlord in a suit, along with the tenant. Tenants, on the other hand, are almost always involved whenever an accident occurs because they are the ones most obviously present. Too, they are most likely to have control of conditions and will need defense against virtually any claim for damages on the premises. However, this is not to say that OL&T coverage is restricted to premises. Quite to the contrary, there is also coverage off-premises — provided it is necessary or incidental to the on-premises exposure. What is an operation *necessary* or *incidental* to the premises, however, is a question that is sometimes difficult to answer. It depends upon the type of risk covered and the negligent act giving rise to claim.

Among those classes of risks which come within the category of OL&T coverage are apartments, hotels, motels, clubs, banks, restaurants, theaters, office buildings, retail stores and wholesale distributors. (Risks involved in manufacturing or contracting operations come within the category of M&C coverage as is explained later.) Thus, almost any type of commercial enterprise is eligible for OL&T coverage.[1]

While coverage is primarily concerned with on-premises legal liability — the insured must be proved negligent before the insurer is obligated to pay — there are times when the insured will want medical bills of the injured to be paid, even when there is no liability. The insured may feel morally obligated to pay for such medical bills or may feel that it is a necessary part of its goodwill to do so. An insured, therefore, can also purchase medical payments insurance in various amounts, although some insurers are reluctant to write this coverage on target risks like hotels, bowling alleys, rooming houses and schools.

When it becomes necessary to do so, the OL&T policy may be expanded in scope to include coverage against any bodily injury or property damage arising out of structural alterations which involve changing the size of or moving buildings or other structures, new construction or demolition whether performed by or on behalf of the insured. Since these exposures are excluded in the basic contract, an additional coverage part must be attached and an additional premium charged. The premium is calculated on either one of two factors: (1) Cost; the premium is based upon the cost of the project with the rates quoted on each $100 of such cost, or (2) Remuneration; the premium is based upon remuneration with rates quoted on each $100 of such remuneration.

Aside from this additional coverage, the premises-operations exposure of the OL&T policy is rated either on an area or frontage basis. For area, the rates are usually quoted on each 100 square feet of such area, while frontage is usually quoted on each

1. Technically, a risk does not have to be of a commercial nature to be eligible for OL&T coverage. Coverage for private residences and multiple family dwellings — two, three or four families — may also be written. In most cases, it is a matter of choice whether an insured wants to insure the premises under the OL&T form or some other form, such as homeowners or comprehensive personal liability. On the other hand, there are insureds who are ineligible for one reason or another under other forms of coverage and must seek this alternative of insuring their liability exposures under an OL&T form.

linear foot. (Vacant land is an example of property rated on the basis of frontage.)

Manufacturers and Contractors Liability

Manufacturers and contractors liability insurance is intended for every person or enterprise which is subject to claims for damages stemming from any negligence when such exposure rests primarily *away* from premises. Thus, those who own, rent, use or lease premises for purposes of manufacturing goods or contracting various services come within this category of M&C coverage.

As previously mentioned, risks which come within the category of OL&T coverage are those whose exposure to liability rests primarily on premises and incidentally away from premises. Risks categorized under M&C coverage, on the other hand, are those whose exposure to liability rests primarily away from premises and incidentally on premises. A building contractor, for example, has more exposure to third party liability at the construction site than at the business office. So, too, with a manufacturing concern. It may have some public traffic on premises but its employees — salesmen, truck drivers, etc. — can create enormous exposures to liability which relate directly, of course, back to the employer. Thus, emphasis between on premises and away from premises coverage is one of the points of distinction between M&C and OL&T coverages.

There is yet another perhaps more important distinction between the two and that deals with the rating basis. Since most exposures relating to M&C risks are away from premises of the insured, it obviously would be insufficient from a premium standpoint to base charges on area as is done for most OL&T risks. Since the primary exposure of M&C risks (other than products liability or completed operations which are discussed later) is away from premises of the insured and primarily the cause of employees, a more equitable system of rating exposures is with payroll. Generally speaking, the more the payroll, the greater the exposure to loss. While most M&C risks are rated on payroll, this rating basis should not be taken to mean that it is the best way to measure exposure. There are probably many other better measures but not to be overlooked is the problem of promulgating them. Even the system of payroll creates problems because of the various records that must be kept; but this system is more equitable a measure than area.

With the possible exceptions of the rating basis and the fact that all operations in progress by the named insured are covered without the restriction of being necessary or incidental to the insured's premises, coverage of the M&C policy corresponds to the OL&T policy and is, therefore, limited in scope. Thus, when it becomes necessary to do so, the M&C policy may be expanded in scope to include coverage against any bodily injury or property damage arising out of operations performed for the insured by independent contractors. For example, this exposure may arise when a manufacturer decides to expand a section of this building and hire an independent contractor to perform the work. Since this exposure is excluded in the basic contract, an additional coverage part (owners or contractors protective liability) is required along with an additional premium. The premium is calculated on the basis of cost with rates applied to each $100 of cost.

The M&C policy, unlike the OL&T policy, is not usually written with medical payments insurance because there is seldom any need for it — the primary exposure of the insured away from insured premises.

Products Liability

Any firm that manufactures, distributes, or sells a product has a potential liability if a user of the product suffers bodily injury or property damage. Claims could be presented by a person cut by a piece of glass in a bottle of milk, by one whose skin is blemished by a cosmetic, by another who loses control of an automobile because of a faulty pin in the steering apparatus, and so on ad infinitum.

Products liability is a relatively recent liability line, but it is growing fast. Claims are increasing every year, while settlements and judgments are reaching astronomical proportions. This tremendous growth is probably caused by a combination of inflation, increasing claims consciousness on the part of many members of the public, more liberal warranties and emphasis on warranties in advertising, expansion of the law of warranty, increasing complexity of products resulting in more allergies and other unexpected results, the concept of strict liability, and the trend toward more liberal awards by juries.[2] Whatever the cause, there in no doubt that products liability is a problem line. Sales are increasing rapidly, making this the fastest growing liability line. At the same time, the line is unprofitable and threatens to become worse, in spite of substantial rate increases.

There is some evidence that this line cannot be written for some classes of risks at any price which is even remotely reasonable. At the same time, of course, these risks are anxious to buy this protection. Some of the problem businesses are bakers, restaurants, cosmetic manufacturers, soft drink bottlers, and patent medicine manufacturers. Products liability may well become the largest liability line, perhaps second only to automobile, and it may be giving the greatest problems to underwriters and insurers, again possibly second to automobile.[3]

Products liability is written for many risks. The coverage is amended frequently and is not standard among all insurers. Basically, however, it applies to claims arising out of the products, or reliance upon a representation or warranty made with respect to a product. Coverage applies to possession, consumption, handling or use of the product and any resulting bodily injury or property damage that occurs *away* from premises owned by or rented to the policyholder and after the insured has relinquished physical possession of the product to others. On premises coverage is given only to restaurants, hotels and clubs.

Completed Operations Coverage

A closely related protection of products liability coverage that is optionally writ-

---

2. "One of the most disturbing things about products liability cases is that the manufacturer or the retailer is never present when the mouse is found in the bottom of the soft-drink bottle or when the worm is discovered in the breakfast roll. Thus, the defense is in a very difficult position in trying to prevent a judgment against him." —Mehr, Robert I. and Cammack, Emerson. *Principles of Insurance,* p. 326. 6th ed. Homewood, Illinois: Richard D. Irwin, Inc., 1976.

3. For a detailed description of the problems of Products Liability, including a description of the Consumer Product Safety Act of 1972, see *CPCU Annals,* Vol. 27, No. 1, March, 1974.

ten is completed operations coverage. A basic OL&T or M&C policy will cover damages while installation or service is being performed away from the policyholder's premises, but not after the operation is completed. There are many cases when work is finished but the buyer has not yet accepted the job, or when a defect or improper installation causes injury or damage.

Completed operations coverage starts when the job is completed, but does not cover pickup or delivery, or the existence of tools or uninstalled equipment. This is a valuable coverage for those who install or repair equipment or machinery for others, such as air conditioning, heating, and similar contractors, as well as those who construct dwellings or buildings or any portions of them.

Contractual Liability

There are essentially three ways in which persons can become legally obligated for damages: (1) through their own negligence, i.e., failure to exercise the proper degree of care required by the circumstances; (2) through a breach of contract; or (3) through assuming the liability of others, i.e., the policyholder agrees to hold harmless another person for any subsequent liability to the extent specified in the contract. (These contracts are often referred to as "hold harmless" agreements and are insurable under contractual liability insurance — if they otherwise are not in violation of any statute or against public policy.)

Why would one party voluntarily assume the liability of another? There are a number of good business reasons. If a shipper wants a railroad spur track constructed or operated on the property, in order to facilitate shipping, the railroad will require assumption of any liability which might arise out of the spur. The terminology used is that the shipper agrees to indemnify, or to hold harmless, the railroad. A tenant or lessee might be required, as one of the terms of the lease, to hold the owner harmless. A utility company wanting to share the use of the poles of another utility company will be required to assume the entire liability arising out of the poles. Sellers of equipment may, as an inducement to sales, agree to assume the liability of the buyers arising out of the equipment. Large buyers, such as government agencies, may require hold harmless agreements in all contracts for goods and equipment they purchase, using their tremendous buying power to coerce eager sellers. Each of these organizations or individuals whose liability is assumed would probably be covered under their own liability policies if the agreements were not in effect.

At one time, contractual liability insurance was difficult to purchase without first undergoing some rigid underwriting.[4] Thus, if an insured had signed a hold harm-

4. Not a subject of this type of contractual liability are "incidental contracts." These are automatically covered under OL&T and M&C forms without additional premium charges but only to the extent defined. These incidental contracts are usually defined as meaning "any written (1) lease of premises, (2) easement agreement, except in connection with construction or demolition operations on or adjacent to a railroad, (3) an undertaking to indemnify a municipality required by municipal ordinance, except in connection with work for the municipality, (4) sidetrack agreement, or (5) elevator maintenance agreement." If an agreement does not fall within this definition, it must then be added to the policy for an additional premium.

less agreement and desired insurance, one of the first things that person was required to do was to submit a copy of the contract so that the insurer could determine the scope and insurability of the agreement. Such agreements were sent to home office underwriters or legal departments for review and, in the meantime, coverage could not be bound. Many insurers have since liberalized their underwriting policies — probably because of competitive pressure — so that it is relatively easy for most insureds to purchase contractual liability insurance.

Contractual liability insurance — for other than incidental contracts — can be provided in one of two ways: (1) on a designated contract basis, or (2) on a blanket basis. In either case, an additional form is usually required in order to provide such coverage.

Under the first approach, insurers that use the policy forms of the ISO, for example, must attach a coverage part entitled "Contractual Liability Insurance (Designated Contracts Only)." On this form must be indicated the contract to which insurance applies, e.g., limited, intermediate or broad form, the desired limits and the additional premium for the coverage.

Several factors affect the premium charge, e.g., cost per unit of exposure and desired limits but the most important factor depends upon whether the contract is considered to be a limited, intermediate or broad form agreement. When an agreement is categorized as a limited form, it usually means that contractual liability insurance will protect the indemnitee (the person who requires the signing of the contract) for any liability which is the result of the person who is performing the work or the person who is assuming the liability as specified in the contract by the indemnitee. Under an intermediate contract, coverage is provided to the indemnitee when resulting liability is the cause of both the indemnitee and the person who signed the hold harmless agreement. The broad form follows the intermediate in covering the negligence of both the indemnitee and the person who assumed such liability, but goes one additional step and even covers liability due solely to the negligence of the indemnitee. It is this form, in particular, which must be underwritten very carefully.

Under the second approach, blanket contractual, an insured is provided with automatic coverage sometimes on a nonreporting basis and other times on a reporting basis ranging from 30 to 90 days. However, when written this way, automatic coverage is usually restricted to intermediate form contracts and even then subject to some limitations. It is rather obvious, too, that insurers are selective on the type of risks that will be given blanket coverage. Large construction contractors who are involved in agreements involving architects and engineers probably will not be among those risks acceptable for blanket contractual. In other words, these types of risks will be on prohibited lists of insurers. If a large contractor, therefore, has blanket contractual and is involved with broad form hold harmless agreements, that contractor more than likely will have to insure those contracts on a designated contract basis.

Contingent Liability

As previously explained, liability of one person can sometimes be transferred to another through hold harmless agreements which are sometimes insurable under contractual liability insurance. However, there are occasions when liability cannot be transferred to another. One such example is when one party contracts to perform certain work for another party and each has responsibilities which cannot be transferred. Excavating work beside a sidewalk may require both the contractor and owner of premises to maintain adequate warnings to protect pedestrians from bodily injury. While there may be an attempt to transfer such liability onto one of the persons involved in this work, it is sometimes uncertain whether the transfer is legally effective. Besides, any injured person will probably name both the owner and contractor in a suit, so the owner needs defense coverage even if that owner is able to shift the ultimate liability to the other person. Owners or contractors protective liability insurance is the coverage that is needed for this kind of contingent liability. (There are a variety of coverages available to cover contingent liability and owners or contractors protection liability coverage is one of them.)

Both the OL&T and M&C policies can be written to include owners or contractors protective liability insurance merely by adding that coverage part to the policies. An insured who has an OL&T policy would need this coverage if that insured were to hire a contractor to build an addition to a present building. The reason for this is, the OL&T policy specifically excludes bodily injury or property damage arising out of structural alterations which involve changing the size of a building whether such work is performed by the insured or someone else. The contractor would normally have primary protection in case negligence leads to suit, and the owner of premises — with this additional coverage — would at least have defense coverage if brought in on the suit, too.

Since an M&C policy generally excludes bodily injury or property damage arising out of operations performed for the insured by independent contractors, there is also a need for owners or contractors protective liability insurance under this policy, too.

There are several related types of contingent liability insurance that are rated separately by some insurers. The type of exposure is the same as owners or contractors protective liability. A landlord may lease all of a property to one tenant, the owner retaining no control over elevators, boilers or any other part of the operation of the premises. The owner in this situation needs a landlords protective policy. A tenant may share a building with other tenants, the tenant sharing the operation of elevators but having no control over the maintenance of the elevators; the tenant needs a tenants protective policy. A newspaper or a dairy may contract delivery to persons it regards as independent contractors; a principals protective policy is needed. There are other similar types of exposures and policies to cover them.

Miscellaneous

Fire legal liability can be described as miscellaneous coverage. It can be written in connection with almost any other type of liability insurance, and is seldom if ever written alone when written under a liability policy. However, it may be written under a fire policy. It covers the legal obligation of the policyholder for injury to, or destruction of, premises rented or leased to the policyholder.

Since most liability policies exclude property in the care, custody or control of the policyholder, fire legal liability coverage is needed to protect against one's liability for fire damage to non-owned buildings or portion thereof that may be controlled by another. It is not fire insurance on the building; rather, it covers only liability arising out of the policyholder's negligence; liability assumed under contract is not covered, however.

Personal injury liability is a liability coverage that does not apply to bodily injury or property damage. Instead, it covers such acts as libel, slander, defamation, false arrest, invasion of privacy, malicious prosecution and wrongful eviction. Almost every type of business has a potential exposure to alleged damage under one or more of these acts, but the coverage was not widely sold until relatively recently. (It is now more popular, and is sold with virtually every commercial liability policy.)

Advertising liability is another liability coverage that does not apply to bodily injury or property damage. It coversd offenses committed by an insured in advertising, broadcasting, publishing or telecasting. Included is injury caused by wrong descriptions of prices, as well as the failure of products or services to conform with the advertised performance or quality. (This coverage, along with personal injury liability, is automatically included in every policy issued under the simplified-language commercial program of ISO described below.)

Elevator collision is a separate optional coverage. A person who is accustomed to handling vehicle coverages is startled to think of "elevator collisions." Where can an elevator go to collide with something? However, with a little thought one can visualize such accidents occurring, such as the elevator doors closing on a package or part of an object which is put in an elevator.

Since such accidents seldom happen, the annual premium for this coverage is generally about two or three dollars a year. The coverage insures against damage to the elevator and to any other property which is owned, used by, or rented to the policyholder, or in the insured's care, custody or control.

The simplified-language commercial forms program of ISO does not consider this to be a liability exposure. Coverage is available only on a special property form.

Professional Liability

Professional persons and organizations for whom they work are subject to liability suits because of real or alleged errors committed in the practice of the profession. They can also be held liable for the acts of others for whom they are legally responsible. There are two general classifications of professional liability. The coverages are almost the same, but are tailored for the needs of the policyholders. The subclasses use different titles: malpractice liability for the medical profession, and errors and omissions insurance for other professions.

Malpractice liability is the term used for physicians, surgeons and dentists. It covers claims for malpractice, error, or mistake, and includes both acts of commission and omission. Coverage can include any person engaged in the medical profession: general practitioners, medical specialists, anesthesiologists, all types of dental surgeons, optometrists, chiropractors, physiotherapists, X-ray laboratories, and veterinarians.

While nurses and others who assist doctors may be covered under the policies of doctors, they may also have their own malpractice policies. Hospitals are policyholders of malpractice liability insurance, too.

The complexities of a claim for, say, leaving a sponge in a patient during surgery can be imagined easily: the surgeon, the nurses, the hospital, and probably the assistant surgeon and anesthesiologist will all be named in the suit. If each is covered by a different insurer, the defense can be complicated. It does not even help if all parties are insured by one company — which is ordinarily a desirable situation with two or more defendants. If it is admitted that someone erred and the sponge were actually forgotten, the only question becomes one of determining which person was responsible. Thus, each party can offer an effective defense only by showing that another party was careless.

An important feature of medical malpractice insurance, which is the opposite of other forms of liability insurance, is that the insurer may not pay any claim without the approval of the policyholder. This provision, which is unique in the liability field, is based on the fact that payment of a claim is tantamount to admission of liability and, thus, to admission of malpractice. A medical practitioner depends heavily on reputation and cannot permit the insurer to proclaim, by paying a claim, that there has been an error in the practice of the profession. Because of this provision in the policy, a large percentage of medical malpractice claims go to trial rather than being settled without recourse to the courts. And, because the evidence requires expert testimony to evaluate medical malpractice, defense is very expensive.

The tremendous underwriting losses on medical malpractice liability in the mid-1970's led to the development of "claims-made" forms. The traditional approach has been to write "occurrence" forms, under which every loss which occurred during the policy period was covered. The problem is that some medical losses may not be presented as claims until many years later, usually because the patient is unaware of the alleged malpractice. The insurer may be forced to pay large claims, long after it had closed the books on that policy period. Inflation, plus the escalation in the size of judgments, caused serious losses not contemplated when the premium was established.

The "claims-made" coverage corrected this problem, as is explained below.

Errors and Omissions Liability (generally called (E&O) is the term more commonly used for all other professions. It can cover some occupations which might not be termed "professional" under most definitions. Perhaps it is more accurate to say that it is used for those who advise others or manage the affairs of others. Examples are insurance agents and brokers, accountants, corporation officers and directors, druggists and architects.

The coverage under an errors and omissions liability policy applies to acts committed or allegedly committed by the policyholder or others at the policyholder's direction. It can include advice to take a certain step which turns out to be detrimental to the client, or failure to tell of steps which should be taken. Whenever a client suffers loss because of the real or imagined act or advice or the policyholder, a claim may be presented.

These claims are sometimes complicated and expensive to defend, but are generally not quite as technically complex as medical malpractice claims. The responsibility for the error is usually easier to establish than under malpractice and so E&O policies ordinarily permit insurers to settle claims without permission of policyholders.

One class of professionals not covered under an errors and omission policy is teachers. They have a potential liability for their acts in connection with laboratories, manual training, physical training and maintaining discipline. Their protection can be written under a CPL policy.

Comprehensive General Liability

The comprehensive general liability policy, traditionally referred to as the CGL policy, is a combination of general (as opposed to automobile, professional and personal) liability coverages of the types previously discussed, but by no means limited to those. Thus, under this basic policy, there is coverage for premises and operations, owners or contractors protective, products liability and completed operations. However, contractual liability for other than those defined under "incidental contracts," must be specifically added when coverage is desired. Even so, the advantages of the CGL policy over an M&C or OL&T policy are obvious; coverages are automatically included in the CGL policy and, unless they are needed or desired, they can simply be designated in the policy schedule as "not covered" or excluded by endorsement.

To those basic coverages which are automatically included can be added a multitude of other coverages, e.g., broad form property damage, personal injury liability, elevator collision, fire legal liability, personal liability, druggists liability, garage liability and liquor liability to name a few.

In addition to these advantages of the CGL policy is another perhaps important one of providing coverage not only on those existing hazards at policy inception but also those which are newly created during the policy term.

Professional liability could be included on a Comprehensive General Liability policy, but is more commonly written as a separate contract.

Commercial General Liability

The simplified-language commercial forms program of the Insurance Services Office (ISO) uses a new approach to the structure and rating of commercial liability insurance. Coverages are modernized and standardized between monoline and package policies.

Note that the term "CGL" means "Commercial General Liability" under this program, and not "Comprehensive General Liability" as before.

The coverages, as described in the previous pages of this chapter, are combined and rated in a new manner. Also, alternative "triggers" for coverage are made available. These approaches may replace the former methods of writing and rating this line.

Classification: The separate coverages described earlier in this chapter are combined under two sublines: (1) premises/operations and (2) products/completed operations. New classification codes are used to identify five groups: (1) mercantile, (2) manufacturing or processing, (3) buildings or premises, (4) contracting or servicing, and (5) miscellaneous.

Rating: The types of exposure are more closely related to the rating structure by the adoption of some new rating factors. Offices use the number of square feet of area, as do lessor's risks. Apartment rates are based on the number of units. Mercantile, manufacturing and processing risks are rated by gross sales. Contracting and servicing businesses use payroll to determine the rate. Contracting risks use the total cost of the work as the basis for the rate.

Coverage "triggers": Historically, commercial liability claims were "caused by accident." Later, this was changed to "causedd by an occurrence." This "occurrence trigger" remains as one of the types of coverages written, and probably will remain for some time as the one most commonly used for most policies. However, some risks present a "long tail" exposure, which means that the claims which have occurred are not known or presented until many years later, thus making it very difficult for insurers to establish adequate rates or claims reserves.

A "claims-made" coverage trigger corrects this problem. It has been used for a number of years on professional liability, particularly medical malpractice (as described above). Claims are covered only if they are "made" during the policy period, which usually means that a third party claimant has notified the insurer that redress is being sought for an injury. Claims-made policies provide that they will not cover any injury which occurs before the "retroactive date," which ordinarily is established as the effective date of the first claims-made policy issued to a specific business. Also, claims-made policies may permit the reporting of claims after the end of the term of the policy; the ISO program provides for both limited automatic Extended Reporting Periods and optional unlimited extensions at additional premium.

(The underwriting of claims-made forms is discussed in the Special Problem section at the end of this chapter.)

UNDERWRITING FACTORS

Acceptable Risks

Most casualty insurers write a broad spectrum of risks with little concentration on lines, unless they are specialty companies. Too, many insurers write at rates which are lower than bureau in order to select the preferred risks, which more often means declaring unacceptable those risks that it does not want. There is such a wide variety of rating plans available that most insurers find that they can write most classes and still operate within the framework of the risks which are considered to be their markets.

Every commercial enterprise, no matter how large or small, can use commercial liability insurance, and almost all of them are able to find an insurer willing to offer the coverage, even if the premium is not to the liking of the applicant. Without actually creating a substandard class of applicant, nor a class of insurers primarily writing substandard risks, insurers generally have a market for all risks. Those risks presenting unusual exposures may have to search for an insurer but there are a variety of rating plans designed to accommodate most risks, so that even those insurers that write "standard" risks can usually accommodate substandard ones.

Unacceptable Risks

Commercial liability insurers, individually, use lists of risks considered unacceptable. These lists vary by the market the insurers are trying to reach, as well as by the rate flexibility insurers want to employ. For those insurers writing in a somewhat inflexible manner, meaning that the underwriters have a limited degree of authority to establish or modify rates, an unacceptable list is required.

The following list gives the major factors that a commercial liability underwriter would probably consider. The risks indicated as unacceptable are not taken from any one insurer's list, but are illustrative of the risks that an insurer might use if it operated in a rather inflexible manner with rates which are no more than bureau, and perhaps slightly less.

Personal Stability. One of the most important elements in commercial liability insurance is the stability of the owner of the business. A risk would be unacceptable if there were serious questions about this factor.

Either of the following items might make a risk unacceptable, too, and both of them would certainly put a risk in an unacceptable category.

1. Does not have a record of meeting obligations. Such a record demonstrates that premium may not be paid, and the insured may not be in business very long.
2. Has a policy record, or is considered uncooperative. These factors could make defense of a suit difficult. The insurer also needs cooperation in reducing hazards which might cause losses or in settling claims.

Business Reputation. A business often has a reputation which is separate and distinct from that of the owner. Since it is the business that can cause loss, the same questions could arise if one or more of the following items are present. Just one of the following can make the risk unacceptable.

1. In business only a short time. A new business does not yet have a reputation, and statistics show that a large percentage of new businesses fail within a short time.
2. Questionable legality or respectability of the business. The insurer might need to bare all facts about the business in court, in case of a loss.
3. Not in a respectable neighborhood. This fact is a clue to the respectability of the business itself.
4. An indication that the insurance is being purchased only for a short term convenience. The expenses of writing a commercial liability policy are so great that an insurer can make even a small profit only if the policy remains in force for a number of months.
5. Has been cancelled by another insurer, or has a record of many past losses. These factors tend to indicate that further experience may not be good.

Physical Aspects of the Premises. Liability losses are caused by physical defects in the premises. An underwriter might consider an applicant with such defects as unacceptable because of possible injury resulting from the defects. In addition, these factors indicate the attitude of management toward safety and cooperation.

1. Housekeeping poor, or premises not orderly. The inherent hazards from slipping and other injuries give a clue about the attitude of the owner.
2. Maintenance is poor. The above factors provide the possibility that the business is in poor financial condition.

3. Premises located in run-down or unstable areas. Such conditions tend to breed a lack of responsibility and a degree of claims consciousness.

Operations of the Business. Certain business operations present a greater exposure to loss than others. If the underwriter is not permitted adequate latitude in establishing premium rates, any risk with these characteristics may need to be considered as unacceptable.

1. Products which are liable to result in an abnormal number of claims.
2. Subsidiaries engaged in operations which could cause claims difficulties, such as foreign operations.
3. Contractual obligations which increase or render ambiguous the potential liability of the applicant.
4. A necessity for coverage for hazardous operations, such as a requirement of collapse coverage for a contractor engaged in excavating for underground utilities.
5. An excessive exposure, such as an unusual advertising program.

In addition to all of these, many insurers consider as unacceptable, certain risks or coverages under the various policies or coverages. These prohibitions are usually based on the background knowledge or predjudices of the underwriting staff, or on actual experiences. Examples of possible unacceptable risks of this type are these.

1. Premises medical payment coverage for hotels, rooming houses and schools.
2. Contractors who perform demolition work.
3. Products which are unusually hazardous, such as chemicals, drugs, ammunition, food and plastics, or which are new products which may become hazardous or which may be used in hazardous circumstances.
4. Contractual liability assumed when applicant has assumed an excessive liability of another party.
5. Under professional liability, brain surgeons and transplant specialists.

SECURING INFORMATION

A commercial liability underwriter must first determine that an applicant is eligible under the rules established by the company. The next step is to secure more information in order to determine if the applicant is acceptable.

The primary source of information is the application, although other sources are sometimes used for supplemental information. In all cases, the underwriter will be looking for facts upon which to establish classifications, rating and coverages, as well as to determine acceptability.

Application

Some type of application is necessary for every commercial liability applicant. It is an absolute necessity in order to determine the exposures and to write and to rate the policy properly. Underwriting information will also be developed by this information, as well as by other questions which are usually included. The application is usually signed by the applicant but is not made a part of the policy. The questions on the application are usually classified into three categories.

1. Personal
2. Description of operations and exposures
3. Insurance information

While there are many differences in the details of the applications used by insurers, the following information in indicative of most of them.

1. *Personal*
   - A. Full name of the applicant, including the firm name, if any. The latter is designated "d.b.a.," meaning "doing business as." The names of all partners in a partnership are needed.
   - B. Structure of the firm, whether an individual, partnership or corporation.
   - C. Business address and mailing address of the applicant.
   - D. Stability factor, such as citizenship, home ownership, age, marital status and policy record of the applicant.
2. *Description of Operations and Exposures*
   - A. Locations of all premises used by the applicant, with information concerning ownership or tenancy and the portion occupied by the applicant.
   - B. Description of all classifications of hazard, as described and coded in the rate manual, which exist at the time of application or are expected during the term of the policy. Include territory and premium basis, the latter also taken from the manual.
   - C. If applicant uses a subcontractor, the expected cost of the subcontract during the policy period, with codes and rates for owners and contractors protective liability coverage.
   - D. Contractual obligations and descriptions of sidetrack or other hold harmless agreement for contractual liability coverage.
   - E. Particular information about raw materials and markets in which selling is conducted, if products liability coverage is desired.
   - F. Detailed information, sometimes on a supplemental application, for professional liability insurance: type of practice, professional associations to which the applicant belongs, professional licenses held, questions about X-ray equipment for medical practitioners, and complete details about any suit for professional liability which has ever been filed against the applicant.
   - G. Information about the advertising program of the application.
   - H. Details about subsidiaries owned, the type, number and operations.
   - I. Details about any foreign operations of the applicant.
   - J. Any employer's liability exposure such as under the federal longshoremen's act.
   - K. If vehicles are to be covered, all of the information about the vehicles and drivers, as is explained in Chapters 19 and 20.
   - L. Stability factors for the business, such as how long it has been in operation, the type of neighborhood, and the housekeeping of the premises.
   - M. Physical factors, such as the construction of the building, the type of heating used, and the physical condition of the premises.
3. *Insurance Information*
   - A. The limits of liability and the types of coverage requested, along with the proposed effective date.
   - B. Details concerning any previous declination or cancellation of insurance by another company.
   - C. Information about the previous insurer and the coverage carried, including past losses.
   - D. Existing insurance for some of the coverages with other insurers, since it is not unusual to have more than one insurer for a large business.
   - E. If vehicles are to be covered, information about the drivers, filing requirements, and other items as explained in the chapters on vehicles in this Part.

Inspection Reports

The commercial liability underwriter often uses inspection reports by outside companies. The same inspection companies furnishing reports for commercial vehicles are available for reporting on commercial liability exposures.

Reports are sometimes used to verify information given in the application. Since most commercial general liability policies cover many exposures, it is particularly important to the underwriter to ascertain all types of liability hazards which exist.

Reports are also used to secure more information about the type of applicant and operations. The questions on the application are fairly detailed, but sometimes the answers merely whet the appetite of the underwriter for more detail. He or she may request that the inspector specifically report upon certain items which are not fully explained, or may order a general report which will answer some of the suspicions or the desire for more information about the entire risk.

Engineering Reports

Two types of reports are used for commercial liability. They are the same as two of the types used for commercial vehicles; indeed the same people often report for both lines.

One type is a report of physical factors. This may include the premises, the operations, the product manufactured, and any other aspect of the risk to be covered. A report of this type could be completed by an inspector of a reporting company, and an inspection report will usually contain information on some physical characteristics.

The other type of report concerns loss control. Even as an engineer conducts safety programs for drivers, so will a commercial liability loss control specialist work with the safety features of the risk. Sometimes this means only observing unsafe conditions and reporting, to the underwriter, the recommendations for operational changes which will reduce the possibility of loss, such as the installation of quality checks, realignment of equipment, or even a complete change in the operations performed.

Still other times, the specialist may arrange with the policyholder's safety committee for a continuing loss control program which is designed to eliminate conditions which might contribute to a liability loss.

Engineers are often company employees, but there are separate companies that sell this service. In either case, the engineering of many types of risks may be combined for truck and liability policies, because many commercial businesses use their own trucks. On both kinds of policies, the underwriter is interested in receiving information about the physical aspects of the risk, and also about the attitude of management toward reducing exposures to loss. As with truck insurance, a commercial liability risk needs the cooperation of the management in order to maintain a profitable operation from an insurance standpoint.

The engineer for a commercial liability risk is ordinarily expected to express an opinion on the desirability of the applicant for the guidance of the underwriter. As was explained in the discussion on truck underwriting, the engineer's report may be the best source of information available to the underwriter.

Experience of Other Insurers

Commercial liability underwriters seldom exchange information about the past loss history of a particular applicant. The coverages are so different and so complex that any meaningful report would require more time for completion than an insurer usually wants to devote for the benefit of a competitor.

CLASSIFICATION AND RATING

The classification of a commercial liability applicant is quite involved, as compared with many other lines of insurance. The cause of the complication is the broad scope of coverages included under this general heading of commercial liability. The underwriter must gather a great deal of information about the applicant before classifying and rating a risk — and considering its acceptability at each of these stages.

Manuals are provided by each insurer, or by the bureau to which an insurer belongs. The manuals are indispensable because they contain codes for each type or classification of occupancy. Definitions are often quite detailed in order to establish the correct codes between similar types of risks. For example, a "club" might be used for a fraternal organization, for a golf course, for swimming, for luncheon groups, for rental to various groups, for horseback riding, and so forth. A number of different classifications might be used, each with its own code. The rating may be different, also, such as being based on the number of members, the size of the building or payroll.

Although rating differs among insurers, the following general rules are ordinarily used. Each type of coverage has an applicable minimum premium, but it varies so greatly that it is mentioned in the following discussion only when this may be a significant factor. (The 1986 ISO program, described above, changes some of these classification and rating factors. Only the major changes are identified below.)

Owners, Landlords and Tenants

The principal hazard in risks of this type is on the premises themselves, rather than any business away from premises. Because of this, most OL&T risks are based on the area of the building. This particularly applies to such occupancies as stores, hotels, apartment houses and motels.

Rates are given in the manual. They apply to each 100 square feet of floor space of the building. Reduced rates may be used for areas used only for storage or heating. For some risks, frontage rates are used; they are applied to the linear feet of the property abutting on the street, and are applied only to the ground floor.

Many refinements may be made in the classifications. An applicant often occupies only a portion of a building but owns the entire building, so the portion occupied may be rated on that classification and the balance under applicable or combined classifications. Parking areas may be covered at no additional premium if customers are not charged for parking, except that extra premium may be applied to such occupancies as bars, restaurants and stores. If customers are charged for parking, a separate classification is used and a separate rate is applied.

Premises medical payments coverage is rated separately. An insurer may use flat rates, or may use a percentage of the applicable liability premium for the risk.

Manufacturers and Contractors

The operations performed by the applicant and employees are the principal hazards in M&C risks. For this reason, they are usually rated on a payroll basis. (Manufacturers are rated on gross sales under the simplified-language commercial lines program of ISO.)

The manual rates apply to each $100 of estimated annual payroll. A fixed, arbitrary amount is usually specified for each proprietor, partner and executive officer. Employees are often divided into different categories with different rates applying to each; examples are clerical office employees, outside salespersons, truck drivers, and managers. A contractor who constructs buildings may perform a number of types of work, such as painting, masonry, electrical, roofing, and carpentry. Payroll must be kept separate for each classification, since different rates apply to each.

Many other bases for rating are used for special operations, as previously mentioned. Some have a rate per $100 of sales, for certain types of manufacturing. Others are based on each $100 of gross receipts, such as some type of beverage concessionaires and the rental of contractors' equipment. Still others are on the basis of each article, such as each boat in a boat-rental business or each ski lift in a resort.

Escalators — Passenger Type

Classifications by use are applied to passenger escalators. Further classification might be made by type of occupancy with which the escalator is used: office or bank, steamship piers and lessor's risk only. Each classification has a code, and each code has a flat rate per landing within each territory.

Elevator collision coverage is likewise based on the classification codes of elevators and hoists as is given in a table.

Products Liability

Many OL&T and M&C manual classifications have separate codes for product liability and completed operations coverages. The manual also shows these codes. The basis for rating is shown with each code. Some of the bases are the same as for M&C liability: sales, gross receipts, or each article. Bottlers and breweries have a rate applying to each 10,000 bottles or cans filled. Service stations may be rated on the basis of each 10,000 gallons of gasoline sold. (The simplified-language commercial forms program of ISO uses the same exposure base for Products/Completed Operations as for Premises/Operations.)

Contractual Liability

Some types of contractual agreements are covered without additional charge by most insurers. These usually include sidetrack agreements, easements, and lease of premises agreements.

Other types are judgment rated. The exposure varies so greatly by the details of the contract that no published rates are available. The underwriter must analyze each agreement and arrive at a rate which is mutually agreeable to all parties.

Professional Liability

Many different types of rating are used for the professional liability coverages, because of the varied nature of the professions included within this general category.

The medical profession is first classified by specialty: surgeon, general practitioner, veterinarian, and so forth. Different classifications may then be used, depending upon the type of practice or organization: self, partner, member of a clinic, on the staff of a hospital, etc. Each of these classes has a code and a rate. These are ordinarily quoted at a flat rate for a year's coverage.

Other professions, those for whom errors and omissions coverage is the common term, are handled differently. It is more common for these people to be employed by a firm, and the coverage is purchased by the firm. Each type of profession has its own code. Within each code, the rates are usually given to apply to each person engaged in that work, whether an accountant, insurance agent, architect, or whatever. Different rates might apply to those persons who perform certain tasks than for others.

Some professions are handled in a different manner. Druggists, for example, usually find that their liability coverage is rated on a gross receipts basis, or perhaps on the basis of a flat rate per store. Teacher's liability, on the other hand, is rated on the basis of each teacher.

All of these rates are subject to constant review. The field of professional liability is changing so rapidly that an underwriter must keep abreast of current legal decisions and other trend factors in order to maintain adequate rates, as well as to evaluate applicants correctly. For the same reason, underwriters are usually given authority to modify the rate for a specific professional liability applicant, if unusual factors are present.

Contingent Liability

Different codes are used for different types of owners or contractors protective liability. For example, one code and rate may apply for general construction work, another for specific types of construction, and still another for all other types of contingent liability. Rates are ordinarily applied to each $100 of total contract cost (or remuneration) and may be reduced for higher amounts, such as over a $1,000,000 contract cost.

Fire Legal Liability

Fire legal liability coverage is not direct insurance on property, but rather coverage for liability stemming from the policyholder's negligence. Still, the exposure is based largely on the same factors as are used for rating fire insurance: construction, operations, fire protection, and exposures from other occupancies or buildings.[5]

Thus, the rate for fire legal liability insurance is a percentage of the applicable fire rate. Different insurers use different rates, but common approaches are to use something like 25% of the published flat rate or the published coinsurance rate, or perhaps the 80% coinsurance rate. Minimum premiums are particularly important for this coverage, because the rates per $100 of insurable value may be quite low.

Personal Injury Liability

The rates for personal injury coverage are usually related to the rate for basic OL&T or M&C liability because the same underlying factors are present. Typical rates might be 10 or 15% of the basic rate; variations might be made for such factors as a private police force or plant guards employed by the applicant.

---

5. For more details, see Chapter 24.

Comprehensive General Liability

The CGL policy is a package of all other applicable liability coverages.[6] Its rating is simply the sum of the applicable premiums of all coverages included. The policy must be handled carefully in one respect, as concerns classification and rating. It is a broad policy that covers almost all exposures. Thus, if the applicant does not want a particular coverage, it must be specifically excluded. Otherwise, it must be included in the rating, if there is any exposure. Vehicle coverages may be added to the CGL policy. Again, the applicable rates are used. When vehicles are added it is referred to as a comprehensive-automobile general liability policy.

Credit may be allowed for certain liability coverages already in force. Company rules may vary, but usually a complete description of the other policies is required so that the comprehensive general liability policy may be endorsed to provide that it does not cover those liabilities until the other policies expire.

Audit Policies

Many commercial liability policies are written on an audit basis. This means that an estimated (or deposit) premium is collected at the inception of the policy, with an adjustment to be made at a later date. At the conclusion of each term, usually one year, the policyholder must report the required information: gross receipts, sales, numbers of units, or whatever is used as the basis for rating.

Obviously, this system is used only on larger policies when premiums are substantial. The insurer will want to be sure that the applicant keeps records in such a manner that reports can be made properly and promptly. Obviously, it is used most often on comprehensive general liability and comprehensive-automobile general liability policies, since they usually include more coverages.

The advantage of this type of rating is that the policyholder pays only for the actual exposure to loss. If audit is not used, the underwriter will always tend to estimate too high, to protect against any unforseen growth. The policyholder who can handle an audit policy can reduce the insurance costs. The underwriter likes it, too, because the insurer is getting a rate for the actual exposure, thereby eliminating the guesswork.

Limits of Liability

Commercial liability policies, like other types of liability insurance, are written with specified limits applying to each accident or to each occurrence. Where split limits are used, the base is usually $250,000/50,000. Single limits are sometimes used, and the base is usually $25,000; an annual aggregate is occasionally employed, such as $25,000. Each type of liability insurance has its own upcharge or increase limits table. This is a table showing the percentage increase applied to the base for each limit desired. (The simplified-language commercial forms program

6. It is not a true "package" as the term is used in the insurance industry. The CGL policy covers only the various types of liability insurance, while a true package policy includes more than one type or line of insurance. See Part V for a more complete explanation of package policies.

of ISO uses single limits only, and also contains rather complex aggregate limits which are applicable to all coverages under the policy.)

Each manual description, code section, or rate section contains a reference to the increase table applicable. Some tables are used for a number of coverages, but on the other hand, different types of rating for a single coverage might use different tables.

POLICY FORMS

Commercial liability policies are not specified by statute. Hence, there are many variations in policies used by the various insurers, but there is a general similarity within the policies used for each type of coverage. Each type of commercial liability has its own policy, tailored to the requirements of the coverage. The insuring agreements are quite similar, but beyond that there are many differences. The comprehensive general liability policy is fairly standard among insurers and is becoming increasingly popular; in fact, recent years saw a trend with some insurers writing almost all risks under the CGL policy because it can be tailored to fit most needs.

The simplified- language commercial forms program of ISO uses modular policy forms which are the same for monoline and package policies. The liability portions are standardized for all risks, although endorsements are needed to handle specific situations, of course.

The large variety of coverages and risks presents a wide range of underwriting problems. The underwriting and handling are quite simple and routine on some risks, such as service stations, small stores, and neighborhood repair shops. On the other hand, the liability coverages for a hospital or a drug manufacturing concern require expert handling by a well-trained underwriter.

A common trait to all commercial liability coverages is individual risk underwriting. Even the simpler types of applicants need careful attention in order to identify the potential loss exposures. The underwriter often applies limitations or exclusions to those applicants who present extraordinary exposures and where it is not deemed advisable to rate for the hazards, either because the applicant is unwilling to pay the extra premium or the underwriter is unwilling to assume the exposure. Almost any type of commercial liability policy may be endorsed by the underwriter to exclude or limit specific hazards, operations, premises, or persons.

Manuscript policies are not uncommon for large risks. However, the comprehensive general liability policy is so broad that it usually can be modified to fit most applicants. The printed policy, before modifications, excludes aircraft, boats off premises, war, liquor liability, workers' compensation, and the usual "property in the care, custody or control of the policyholder."

Contractors

Special exclusions apply to certain contractors, unless the policy is amended otherwise. These are known as the "XCU" exclusions.

Contractors whose policies specifically cover or exclude these items are those engaged in excavating types of jobs. A major hazard in such construction is the damage that may be done to other property because of the construction. The clauses exclude damage to the property of others caused by explosion or blasting (X), by collapse of or damage to buildings caused by excavation work (C), or by damage to underground wires or pipes caused by mechanical excavating equipment (U). Other clauses, less often encountered, are for property damage for loss of property rights to oil or other mineral substance below ground (D), or by damage to property above the surface caused by a blowout of a gas or oil well. (E).

The classification section of the manual indicates those codes to which the XCU exclusions are to apply. The underwriter accepting an applicant who is classified under one of those codes will place the XCU exclusion on the policy. The underwriter may remove the exclusion for additional premium, if convinced that the contractor will conduct the operations in such a manner as to eliminate or reduce the liability exposure from these hazards. The simplified-language commercial forms program of ISO automatically includes a rate loading for the classes which previously carried the XCU designation.

The (D) and (E) exclusions may also be removed under certain conditions, depending upon the decision of the underwriter after reviewing all of the pertinent facts. In all cases, a judgment rate is used to remove the exclusion.

RETENTION AND REINSURANCE

An underwriter of commercial liability coverages faces many reinsurance problems. While a large share of policies carry limits of liability that most insurers can retain, there are many that demand very high limits. The underwriter must know the retention limits available to him, and when to apply the various limits.

Above the retention, the underwriter must secure or arrange reinsurance. This can be done in one of two ways, using the same alternatives as a commercial auto underwriter.[7] The primary underwriter can issue a policy for the entire amount requested, and secure reinsurance to protect above the retention limit. Or the underwriter can issue a policy for the desired retention amount, and let the producer obtain a specific excess policy for the balance needed.

No matter how reinsurance is arranged for a single risk, the underwriter still faces a catastrophe exposure. It is not unusual for a judgment to be secured against several parties jointly; for example, an award could be made against a surgeon, the anesthesiologist and the hospital; or against a bottler, the wholesaler and the retailer. An underwriter who has retained the full limit on each of these risks, assuming that the company insured more than one involved in a joint suit, could be faced with a catastrophic loss. A reinsurance treaty is carried by all commercial liability insurers to protect against this possibility. Coverage is automatic and the premium is established by the insurer, not the underwriter. However, the latter must be aware of the existence of the treaty to know the degree to which the insurer is protected.

---

7. See Chapter 20.

The underwriter also must know the exclusions and provisions of the treaty so as not to inadvertently rely on coverage for a particular risk that is not covered by the reinsurance.

SPECIAL PROBLEM

Underwriting Claims-made Policies

Claims-made policies present new and difficult challenges to commercial liability underwriters. The basic coverages are the same as under an occurrence policy, but the operations are very different. In order to understand these differences, one must be familiar with the concept of a "coverage trigger."

An insurance policy covers many different kinds of events. The insuring agreement and the exclusions go into great detail in defining the kinds of events that are covered. In order to qualify for coverage, an event must meet the condition of the insuring agreement which causes the policy to come into play: the coverage trigger. For liability insurance policies, the most common triggers for coverage have been accidents, occurrences, and claims-made.

Another way of looking at the concept of coverage trigger is to think of it as the type of event which is the condition precedent of the policy agreement. If the company agrees to pay, on behalf of the insured, liability on account of *accidents* during the policy period, the condition precedent is that the insured must be liable for an accident, which is normally thought to be a fortuitous and sudden event.

Contrast this to a policy that is triggered by an *occurrence* during the policy period. This is a very different trigger because the event may not necessarily be accidental. It may even be intentional, although normally there is no coverage for intentional acts unless the consequence of the act is not intended. The event clearly need not be sudden, since the term "occurrence" includes continuous or repeated exposure to conditions. In these respects, the coverage provided by an occurrence basis policy may be much greater than the coverage provided by a policy that has identical terms except that it is triggered by accidents.

The "occurrence" trigger has proved to be much more costly to the insurance industry than was originally contemplated. Very large claims were brought under novel theories of law, and both the defense and the payment of claims drained the assets of the insurers. In addition, the stacking of policy limits compounded the problem. Since occurrence type losses cover a period of several years, in some cases courts have ruled that policy limits for each year apply separately. As a result, companies have found themselves exposed to their policy limit multiplied by the number of years of coverage they provided. In other words, the limits have stacked on top of each other.

In response to this problem, companies that specialized in the kinds of business especially prone to this type of loss (frequently called "long tail" lines of business) started to introduce policies with a new coverage trigger, the *claims-made* form.

Purpose

The purpose of claims-made policies is to control the tail on long tail lines of business. The word "tail" in the insurance business refers to claims that are classified as incurred but not reported (normally abbreviated as IBNR). Claims are not reported either because they are not recognized yet as claims, because the harm has not yet developed, or because the responsible party has not yet been identified. An example of the first type of claim is in an asbestosis case. A person exposed to asbestos over time is injured at each exposure. However, it is not until many years after the first exposure that a diagnosable case of asbestosis will develop. The party or parties responsible for the exposure to asbestos may be responsible for the injury of asbestosis, but they have no way of knowing who the injured person may be until many years after the exposure.

The tail is controlled by a claims-made form but not by an occurrence form. The reason is that under an occurrence form, a claim such as the asbestosis loss will be covered even though the policy may have expired 10, 20, 30 or even more years ago. The only condition is that the occurrence be during the policy period. In contrast, under a claims-made form, once the policy expires, if no claim has been made, there is no further exposure to the company under that policy. Under a claims-made form the claim would be covered, but only one limit would apply, in contrast to the stacking of occurrence forms.

It is important to distinguish tail from reserve development. Reserve development is the tendency of liability claims to grow during the period after they have been presented and before they are settled. The tail is completely cut off by a claims-made form, but reserve development is not affected at all. The reason is that reserve development takes place on known losses, as further information on them is developed. Tail refers only to claims that are not yet known to the company.

Conversion to a Claims-made Form

A claims-made form may be a reduction in coverage when compared to an occurrence form. As a result, the insured may purchase a claims-made form only when there is no other alternative. However, there are some advantages to the insured in a claims-made form. First, there is an initial rate reduction compared to occurrence rates. Next, there is a coverage advantage in that the coverage trigger is much more certain than an occurrence trigger. It is easier to determine if a claim has been made than it is to determine if injury has occurred. This certainty of coverage should lead to a reduction in disputes between insureds and their carriers. Finally, the policy that covers the loss is the one that the insured most recently purchased. It will be much more likely to reflect current coverage needs than would a policy purchased decades ago.

From the point of view of the insurer, it is certainly desirable to cut off the exposure to tail losses, because it brings much more certainty to current results. Instead of the two unknowns of (1) tail (or IBNR) and (2) reserve development, only reserve development remains for business written on a claims-made form. However, just as the form is not all bad from the point of view of the insured, it is not all good from the point of view of the insurer. First, the rate reduction associated with claims-made will reduce current income. Since the discount is larger for recent conversions to claims-made, the reduction is especially severe in the first years. In addition to the reduction in premium, the cutting off of tail losses will also mean that the investment income from those loss reserves will be lost.

On balance, conversion to claims-made coverage remains a distinct advantage for the insurer. The only IBNR that would remain would be composed of the remainder of the IBNR from prior occurrence from coverages, plus losses from these sources:

1. The actual in-force book of business (as with direct property coverages); or
2. Any extended reporting period coverage that is sold.

The result would be to bring the break-even level for third-party business much closer to that of first-party business, where almost all losses are reported promptly and so little loading for IBNR claims needs to be made.

Initial Selection

Before making a decision on any risk, the underwriter requires complete information regarding the operations and history of the prospective insured. In underwriting a claims-made form, more is needed. First, a history of liability insurance coverages is needed; and second, a more complete loss history is needed. In addition to prior losses, the underwriter will need to know about prior events which could become claims under the policy which is being requested.

The history of insurance coverages is needed both to evaluate exposure and for proper rating of the coverages that are being offered. If the prior coverage was written on an occurrence basis, the new claims-made policy will cover events that occur and are reported during its policy period. It will also cover, on an excess basis, events which occurred during prior policy periods and which are covered by an occurrence basis policy. Thus, the coverages provided and the limit of liability of prior policies should be examined to see if they will be sufficient should an occurrence basis claim surface.

If the underwriter does not wish to provide excess coverage, there are alternatives: a retroactive date may be applied, or claims arising out of specified events may be excluded. These choices will be examined more fully below.

If the prior coverages were written on a claims-made basis, the underwriter must be careful to avoid causing a gap in coverage. In this situation, the possibility of a coverage gap is caused because of the presence in claims-made forms of retroactive dates. A retroactive date is a cutoff date for coverage of occurrences which took place before the claims-made policy was in force. Occurrences which took place before the retroactive date are not covered; occurrences which took place after the retroactive date are covered.

A common error made by underwriters is to automatically advance the retroactive date to the new inception date at the renewal of a claims-made policy. This will create a coverage gap for the insured. The only way the insured can obtain coverage for this period of time is to exercise the extended reporting period option (ERPO) in the expiring policy. No gap is created if the retroactive date of the new policy is the same as that of the expiring policy, and no gap is created if neither policy has a retroactive date.

Source of Information

If the policy is a renewal to the underwriter, the underwriting file of the expiring policy will be the source of most information. This is the most credible of all information available to the underwriter. On the other hand, if the account is new to the underwriter, an application must be substituted.

The application is needed for two primary reasons. The first is that the information contained in the application is needed to determine the conditions for the policy. The conditions are the presence or absence of a retroactive date, what the date is if one is needed, or the events which should be excluded from coverage. The second reason is that the application contains the information needed for rating a claims-made policy.

The rating information that is needed is in two parts. The first is the standard rating information that is needed for occurrence basis policies, such as receipts, payroll and so on. In addition, in claims-made forms, a discount is allowed in the early years after conversion from occurrence basis forms. The reason for the discount is that IBNR or tail claims will be covered by the prior occurrence basis policy; the claims-made policy that replaces it will only respond to occurrences after the retroactive date.

As time goes by, the number of claims that are made against the claims-made policy based on occurrences prior to the retroactive date are reduced, so the discount decreases with each renewal. Therefore, in order to determine the amount of discount to allow, the underwriter must know when the insured first was covered on a claims-made form. This date will normally coincide with the retroactive date.

Prior Loss History

In underwriting practice, it is generally believed that past claims are a predictor of future experience. This is as true for the claims-made underwriter as it is for the occurrence basis or accident basis underwriter. In addition, the claims-made underwriter has an additional interest in the prior loss history of the insured. Without a retroactive date, or with a retroactive date that goes back to occurrence policies, a claims-made policy can provide coverage for losses that have already occurred. (This aspect of a claims-made policy is sometimes called the "nose" of the policy, as a parallel to the tail feature of coverage after expiration of occurrence basis policies.)

This excess coverage nose can mean that the claims-made policy provides broader coverage than an occurrence basis policy would. As an example, consider the Drunken Sailor Tavern. In December, the crew of the Good Ship Lollipop rented a car and drove to the Drunken Sailor for an evening of fun and relaxation. Unfortunately, the evening stretched on a bit too long, with the result of considerable rowdiness on the part of the crew. While they drove home, the driver lost control of the rented car and bounced into several other vehicles, with resulting damage to both cars and people. Three of the injured have sued the Drunken Sailor under the state's dram shop law, but it is known that at least two other people suffered injuries.

The Drunken Sailor's liquor liability policy renews in January. If it is renewed on an occurrence basis, the renewal policy will not be affected by the claims that will be brought by the two other injured people because the occurrence was during the prior policy period and will be covered by that policy. If the renewal is on a claims-made basis with no retroactive date, it will apply in excess of the policy that was in effect at the time of the occurrence. It is this effect of the nose that makes the claims-made policy broader in coverage than an occurrence policy under some circumstances.

Because of the nose, the underwriter will normally use a retroactive date. The date selected will normally be the effective date of the insured's first claims-made policy. In the case of the Drunken Sailor Tavern, all of the claims for the accident would be covered by prior occurrence basis policy. The retroactive date would cut off coverage under the claims-made renewal policy for the other two injured people because the occurrence was prior to the retroactive date.

Selection Criteria

Insureds who face the possibility of occurrence or long tail claims are obvious candidates for claims-made policies. Examples are most forms of professional liability, environmental impairment liability coverage, and some specialty products and completed operations liability policies involving things such as medical equipment, industrial machinery or aircraft products.

The introduction by ISO of the simplified-language Commercial General Liability policy, with its claims-made option, has expanded the number of insureds for whom a claims-made form may be considered. Should the underwriter accept "main street" business on a claims-made form?

One consideration is expenses. In handling a claims-made policy, the company will incur much higher than normal underwriter expenses because of the additional information that is required to properly rate and underwrite the coverage. In addition, claims expenses will be increased because of the need for more policy information (especially information relating to retroactive dates) than is needed for occurrence basis forms. Because of this higher expense load, underwriting management may establish minimum premiums below which insured will not be considered for claims-made coverage. For example, if a company determines that the additional expense of handling claims-made forms is $200 per policy, and this should represent not more than 2% of the policy premium, a policy minimum of $10,000 is needed to develop the $200 in extra expense dollars. Once the minimum premium threshold is passed, the more the premium exceeds that number, the lower the percentage of the premium which is represented by the fixed additional expenses. Therefore, to a small extent, the larger the general liability premium is, the better the risk is for claims-made coverage.

Another consideration is the discount allowed off the occurrence basis rates for the claims-made form. The rating technique that ISO has selected is a flat discount for each major line of business (that is, one discount for premises/operations and another one for products/completed operations). Within the broad classes, no distinction is made with respect to the possibility of tail losses. An astute underwriter may find a premium redundancy in risks that have a higher degree of tail losses (and that will thus have more tail losses cut off by the claims-made form than will the average risk).

In the premises/operations exposures, no one class of business stands out as having a greater degree of tail than any other class. It is possible that there is an advantage in urban exposures as compared to rural exposures. If urban locations are more susceptible to suits because of a greater claims-consciousness on the part of city dwellers, then a risk with an urban location will have more tail losses cut off by the claims-made form than the same risk with a rural location would have. The discount for the claims made form may leave a rate redundancy for the urban location and a rate redundancy for the rural location. This distinction is only speculation at present.

For products and completed operations exposures, no distinction is made in the rating procedure to distinguish useful lives of the product or work. There thus appears to be some rate inadequacy for products or work with short useful lives, since a shorter period of existence means that there is less time for the product or work to cause harm. On the other hand, there appears to be some rate redundancy for risks whose products or work have long useful lives. For example, bakers would be poor claims-made insureds. Bakery products will be consumed rather soon after they are distributed, and there is a fairly short period of time in which they can cause injury. Relatively few claims will be cut off by the claims-made policy form, and so the discount allowed will be a larger credit than is justified.

In contrast, a general contractor constructs buildings that are expected to last for many years. If the contractor's work is defective, losses from the defect may not surface for many years after the work is complete. As a result, more claims will be cut off by the claims-made form for a general contractor than for the "average" completed operations insured. The discount for claims-made still leaves a rate redundancy for this type of insured.

Finally, there are some technical considerations the underwriter must weigh in considering claims-made applicants. These apply to the resources the company has for handling claims-made accounts. For example, the claims department must have a method to keep track of retroactive dates regardless of the location where the claim is handled. Also, the underwriting department must have the capability of keeping track of both the retroactive date and of the conversion from an occurrence form in order to be able to properly rate future renewals of the policy.

Terms

Once the information is gathered, and the underwriter has decided to offer a claims-made form, the next decision is what terms should be offered. The choices that must be made are as follows:

1. Should there be a retroactive date?
2. If so, what date should it be?
3. Should there be an exclusion for any particular event or product?

Whatever is decided in regard to these issues should be communicated in writing to the producer in the form of a proposal letter. Even though the producer has the primary responsibility to explain the ramifications of the coverage to the insured, that job cannot be performed unless the producer gets that information from the underwriter. Moreover, most errors or omissions will be eliminated if the underwriter makes it a practice to prepare a proposal letter for each claims-made account, regardless of whether it is new or a renewal. Each succeeding policy term will be different from the last, so a new proposal letter each year will be very important.

Retroactive Date

If a retroactive date is not used, or if the date that is used goes back to occurrence basis policies, the claims-made policy will provide nose coverage. Nose coverage involves considerable adverse selection. That is, the insured may know of a potential (but not yet reported) claim. In order to increase the limits of liability available to cover this claim, the insured may convert from occurrence to claims-made basis coverage with nose coverage. This situation will be very difficult for the underwriter to recognize and avoid. As a result, it will normally be best to include a retroactive date that coincides with the date of conversion from occurrence basis to claims-made basis coverage.

If nose coverage is offered, careful analysis is very important. The major consideration is the quality of the prior coverage. If there have been losses, the prior policy may be nearing exhaustion of its limit, either because the occurrence may result in further claims or because the aggregate limit is exhausted. Another possibility is that the prior coverage was covered by an insurer that is not financially strong. It does little good for the prior policy to be primary if the company is unable to pay the claim. In either case, a retroactive date should be used.

Another issue that must be examined is if the prior policies were written for limits of liability and with coverages broad enough so that the claims-made underwriter can be confident that the occurrences that are within the policy periods of the prior policies will be adequately covered by those policies.

This kind of analysis will be familiar to underwriters who deal with umbrella liability, where the quality of the underlying insurance program is an important underwriting factor. The major difference is that the claims-made underwriter must expand this analysis to include the coverages the insured carried for the past several years, not just for one prior year.

Even if the underwriter is satisfied with the prior coverage, a retroactive date may still be needed because of past occurrences that may result in future claims. Further, the pattern of past losses may point to a problem that may be repeated in the future, such as claims arising out of a known defect in a product. In both cases, a retroactive date may be useful in aiding the underwriter to provide coverage to an otherwise unacceptable risk. It is not the only, or even necessarily the best solution, and other alternatives will be discussed below.

Prior Claims-made Coverage

If the expiring policy is a claims-made form, the choice of whether or not to use a retroactive date will already have been made on the prior policy. Frequently, the underwriter will wish to follow the earlier choice. That is, use the same date if there is one, and not use a date at all if there is none.

As mentioned earlier, attempting to add a retroactive date to a policy that does not have one, or to advance the retroactive date if there is one, will create a coverage gap for the insured. To obtain coverage, the insured must exercise the extended reporting period option of the expiring policy, and pay the extra premium for doing so. In order to fairly compare costs, the extra premium for the ERPO (or tail) must be added to the cost for the renewal coverage with the advanced retroactive date.

This potential coverage gap caused by an advanced retroactive date is one of the major criticisms of claims-made policy forms. The underwriter has the power to deprive the insured of coverage, merely by advancing the retroactive date at renewal. True, the insured usually has the right to purchase an extended reporting period under the expiring policy, but this may be for a limited time, and may be at a cost which is prohibitive for that client. In order to avoid this criticism, underwriters renewing a policy in the same company ordinarily should not advance the retroactive date. Similarly, if the insured is changing insurance companies, the new underwriter should use the same retroactive date as the expiring policy, if it is at all possible. Ethical considerations require that protection at a reasonable price be afforded to all clients.

If underwriters insist upon advancing the retroactive date when the insurance company is changed, this will tend to 'freeze" the client in one company. This, also, is one of the potentially-adverse effects of claims-made forms. Competition may prevent this change in the retroactive date, because the increased cost to purchase the extended reporting period option may raise the total premium to a non-competitive amount. However, if competition does not do this effectively, clients will suffer, and underwriters will be seen to be violating their duty to consider the interests of their clients, as well as to protect their insurance companies against too many claims.

Choice of Date

If a retroactive date is selected, what date should it be? The basic idea of a claims-made form is that it covers claims that are made during its policy period. If the prior form was an occurrence basis form, the retroactive date can coincide with the inception date of the new claims-made policy. The insured will be covered for old occurrences under the expired policy which was in effect at the time of the occurrence, and for new occurrences under the claims-made policy. There will be no coverage gap in this circumstance.

If the prior policy was a claims-made form, whether a renewal or a new account to the underwriter, a coverage gap will be created unless the retroactive date remains the same on the new policy. This gap occurs because occurrences within the prior policy period will not be covered by the expired policy, since the claim will have been brought too late, and they will not be covered by the new policy because they occurred before the retroactive date.

This information must be communicated to the producer so that the customer can be alerted to the need to purchase the tail or extended reporting period option on the expiring policy. This is another example of the importance of a proposal letter for each claims-made policy.

As a matter of practice, once a retroactive date has been selected, it is normally continued unchanged on all subsequent claims-made policies. Extraordinary circumstances, such as a known occurrence that is likely to mean claims in future policy terms, may cause a change in this pattern. Absent this, it is best to follow the customary pattern.

Other Options

In most cases, the retroactive date by itself is sufficient protection for the underwriter. There are occasional exceptions.

Consider, for example, the Jolly Roger Printing Company. Jolly Roger undertook a job to print labels for the Lucretia Borgia Chemical Company. One of the batches of labels was for bottles of a dangerous poison. Through an error, Jolly Roger neglected to include any warning on these labels. Subsequently, several people were poisoned because of this lack of warning. They sued and won a substantial award from Jolly Roger.

In considering this account for liability coverage, the underwriter may suspect that more claims may arise out of the defective batch of labels, but may consider Jolly Roger to be an acceptable risk except for these claims. A retroactive date would not be helpful here, since the date of the occurrence or occurrences is not known; the event will not occur until another person is poisoned, which may have already happened, or may not happen until well into the next policy term. The retroactive date will not affect bodily injury that has not yet occurred. This is in contrast to the earlier example of the Drunken Sailor Tavern, where the injury occurred prior to the retroactive date.

Instead, the underwriter may offer coverage with a retroactive date (to avoid providing excess coverage for the people who have already been injured) and with an exclusion for all claims arising out of the defective batch of labels (to avoid covering the liability for injuries caused by the labels to people who have not yet been injured). This exclusion for a specific outstanding product of the insured is an option under the simplified-language commercial forms program of ISO[8]

Another option is the specific occurrence exclusion.[9] This endorsement may be used in cases where the underwriter is willing to provide coverage for everything except the claims arising out of a specific event, such as a major accident, and where a retroactive date will not be used.

For example, consider the Deadly Poison Manufacturing Company. After careful review, the underwriter determines that Deadly Poison is an acceptable risk except

8. The ISO form designed for this purpose is CG 27 02 (02 86).

9. The same form—CG 27 02 (02 86)—is used for this purpose. Its title is "Exclusion of Specific Accident(s), Product(s), Work or Location(s)."

for one problem. There was a leak of some poison into the air around Deadly Poison's plant about a month earlier. Liability arising from the leak will be covered by the occurrence basis policy currently in force.

In converting to claims-made coverage, the retroactive date will not protect the underwriter from claims arising out of the spill. In this case, the underwriter will want to specifically exclude claims arising out of the leak. To avoid coverage for other IBNR claims not related to the leak, the underwriter will also want a retroactive date that coincides with the effective date of the claims-made policy.

Reinsurance

A final issue that will arise before the policy is issued is the effect the claims-made form will have on the reinsurance available to the underwriter. There are two different kinds of reinsurance, treaty and facultative, and the effect on each will be different.

Treaty reinsurance is designed to cover a book of business for a company. For example, a company may have a treaty for its workers' compensation business to protect it in the event of losses which exceed a certain predetermined limit. In contrast, facultative reinsurance is purchased to cover a specific risk.

For the underwriter, the impact from treaty reinsurance will likely be relatively minor. It will be confined to general restrictions in the insurer's underwriting requirements. For example, an insurer may require that products liability for manufacturers of machine tools be written only on a claims-made form. Such a restriction may be the result of a requirement in the insurer's general liability reinsurance treaty.

In dealing with facultative reinsurance, claims-made issues will be more critical for the underwriter. If facultative reinsurance is to be used for a claims-made policy, care must be taken in the following areas:

1. The retroactive date on the policy must coincide with that on the reinsurance certificate.
2. If an exclusion of prior accidents or products is required, the primary carrier and the reinsurer must specifically agree on it.
3. The primary policy may create an obligation for the carrier to offer an ERPO (tail) at a specific price. The reinsurer must also agree to be bound by this obligation.

Events During the Policy Term

Once the claims-made policy is written, most transactions will not be different from an occurrence policy. There are some exceptions.

Reinstatement of Aggregate Limits

The first issue is the question of reinstating aggregate limits of liability. Although this is not exclusively a claims-made issue since aggregate limits of liability also appear in occurrence and accident basis policies, most claims-made policies are likely to have aggregate limits of liability. In the event of a large loss, the insured may lose all protection because the policy limit is exhausted. Reinstatement of limits may be requested.

Another reason for such a request may be to create concurrency of aggregate limits with umbrella coverage. In this case, if there have been no claims made against the policy, notification of this fact to the umbrella carrier will be sufficient. If there have been claims, the limit over which the umbrella is to attach will be reduced, and the umbrella carrier may request that the primary policy's aggregate limit be reinstated.

The underwriter's initial reaction may be an automatic rejection. After all, why should the company desire to reinstate coverage? Since the aggregate limit is likely to be a multiple of the occurrence limit, the request to reinstate coverage will be after several large losses. The answer is that it is a business decision. If the events that caused the losses are unlikely to reoccur, or if the premium is large, or both, it may be a good business decision to reinstate the limit.

Certificates of Insurance

The second issue in which a claims-made form differs from an occurrence form during the course of the policy term is in dealing with certificates of insurance. Certificates are extremely complex documents involving four different kinds of interests:

1. The insured;
2. The certificate holder;
3. The producer; and
4. The company providing the insurance.

The purpose of certificates is to provide evidence of the existence of insurance coverage. For example, before hiring a contractor to construct a building, the owner may require a certificate of insurance to show that the contractor carries liability, automobile and workers' compensation insurance.

Claims-made coverages can cause complications for the certificate holder because of the tail problem that the claims-made form is designed to handle. That is, if the occurrence takes place after the expiration of the policy term, the information on the certificate will likely be obsolete. Certainly, no coverage will be available after the expiration of the policies that are certified. Because of this, certificate holders may try to impose restrictions by means of the certificate. The underwriter must be alert to this and be careful not to certify anything that is not within control. For example, consider a real estate developer who may require certificates of insurance from all contractors and subcontractors. In the case of claims-made coverages, the developer may require that coverage for completed operations be carried for a period of time after the project is finished, even if it is well beyond the policy term of the current policy. If a certificate of insurance is drawn to reflect such an agreement, it must be rejected, since continuation of the coverage is not within the underwriter's control. It is primarily within the control of the insured, so any assurance regarding the kind of insurance the insured plans to carry in the future must come directly from the insured, not through the insurance company via the certificate of insurance.

Increased Limits

The final issue that may arise mid-term is "new limits." This issue arises when an insured under a claims-made policy requests an increase in the policy limit. This new limit—the difference between the higher limit requested and the limit previously provided—will have a retroactive effect. Because of this retroactive effect, there is the possibility of adverse selection in providing new limits.

For example, the Careless Electric Contracting Company purchased a claims-made liability policy effective January 1 with a retroactive date of January 1 and a limit of $300,000 each claim. In April, Careless completes a job wiring a new building. In May, Careless learns from newspaper reports that the building has burned down and the damages are $500,000. Although no claim has yet been made, Careless suspects the fire may have been caused by faulty wiring and therefore requests that the policy limit be increased to $500,000 each claim.

On the other hand, insureds will want to increase their limits of liability for many reasons unrelated to adverse selection. Possible reasons include inflation, social inflation (increase in losses because of new laws or interpretations of laws), and increase in the insured's net worth.

In granting a request for new limits, the underwriter may simply agree to it despite the possibility of adverse selection, or the underwriter may choose to add a second retroactive date that applies only to the new limits.

Normal practice is to agree to provide new limits without changing the retroactive date. The possibility of adverse selection is recognized, but it is accounted for with an increase in the rates. Insurance policies in general, and claims-made policies in particular, are extremely complex documents. Multiple retroactive dates would add to this complexity immensely. (On umbrella and excess policies, underwriters might use a later retroactive date because of the large amounts of coverage which are exposed; presumably those insureds who require these high limits are more sophisticated and can handle the increased complexity.)

Issues at Expiration

Having completed the policy term, the final area of consideration is the renewal process. The issues to be considered can be broken into two sections, one in which renewal is offered and the other in which renewal is not offered.

If Renewal is Offered

Just as in the first term of a claims-made policy, on renewal a new proposal letter should be prepared. On renewal, the same issues will surface. The underwriter should inform the producer of the retroactive date (it should not be advanced, unless the insured is advised to also exercise the extended reporting period option). The proposal letter should also cover the extended reporting period option in the proposed renewal policy, and finally, it should cover any special endorsements excluding particular products or events.

On the renewal, the claims-made discount will be lower than it was in the prior year if the retroactive date is not advanced. The reason is that the next year's policy covers claims for occurrences that happen both during its policy period and during the prior year. For each additional year in a claims-made program, the discount continues to be reduced because another year's worth of tail is added to the coverage.

If Renewal Coverage is Not Offered

If, for whatever reason, the policy is not renewed, the insured will have the option of purchasing the extended reporting period option.[10] By exercising this option, the insured in effect converts the expiring claims-made policy into an occurrence basis coverage. Actually, the effect is even greater than this; the expiring policy is endorsed to respond to claims that are made at any time within the option period, as long as the occurrence upon which the claims are based happened before the expiration date of the option policy. In other words, the retroactive effect of the ERP goes all the way to the retroactive date (if there is one) or indefinitely if there is not a retroactive date.

It will be up to the underwriter to calculate the premium for the ERP. In the ISO's version of the claims-made policy, there is a premium cap of 200% of the policy premium for the exercise of the ERP option. However, the actual premium will be subject to the underwriter's judgment.

In some cases, 200% will not be an adequate premium for the value of the tail (or ERP). For example, an event may have occurred during the term of the claims-made policy which would be likely to result in large claims (perhaps an explosion at the insured's place of business that results in injuries) even though no claims have yet been bought. It is very likely that 200% is not an adequate premium in this case.

Normally, no such event will have occurred. In that case, the proper premium for the ERP is the difference between the claims-made premium and the occurrence premium. This difference should reflect the number of years the insured has carried claims-made coverage. That is, the difference should be charged for each year of claims-made coverage, and those differences should be totalled. This total should be adjusted upward to reflect the lost investment income because the premium will be collected after the policy period, not before it. (A rough measure of expected investment income is the interest rate the company charges on its premium finance plan.) Finally, the total should be adjusted downward to reflect any reduction in limits of liability available because payment of claims has reduced the aggregate limit of the policy.

Summary

Claims-made coverage is new to most underwriters, but it is necessary to understand since the simplified-language ISO CGL policy has a claims-made version. There is a great deal to learn about the workings of this form of coverage. The underwriter must be particularly cautious to avoid creating an unintended coverage gap. The purpose of the claims-made form of coverage is not to avoid paying legitimate claims, but is instead to more precisely identify which policy and which limit of liability applies to any particular claim.

---

10. The ISO version contains an optional unlimited extended reporting period. Limits, such as 3 years or 5 years, may be used in individual company programs, particularly for professional liability.

QUESTIONS FOR DISCUSSION

1. Why is commercial liability insurance important to a businessman?
2. Explain the basic coverages under OL&T and M&C liability coverage, and differentiate between these two classifications.
3. Give 5 reasons why products liability claims are increasing every year.
4. What types of businessmen need completed operations coverage?
5. Why would one party voluntarily assume the liability of another?
6. What liability coverages are included under the basic comprehensive general liability policy?
7. Explain why rates are based on the following different factors:
   a. OL&T: floor space
   b. M&C: payroll
   c. Products: various
8. Explain why policy limits may be "stacked" under occurrence policies but not under claims-made policies.
9. Why is there an initial rate reduction under a claims-made form?
10. What happens if an underwriter advances the retroactive date at the renewal of a claims-made policy? Why does this happen?
11. Explain "tail" losses. Do they exist under claims-made forms?
12. Explain why "there is the possibility of adverse selection in providing new limits" under claims-made policies.

23

Personal Fire

Fire insurance on dwellings and contents is one of the oldest lines of insurance. It started in England soon after the great London Fire of 1666 and soon spread to the American colonies. Fire insurance grew with the United States, sharing in much of the romance and adventure of the early years of the Republic. As the country matured, fire insurance expanded to furnish protection against more property and more perils.

For many years, personal fire insurance was a leading source of income and profit to insurance companies. It was one of the largest lines and even when other lines became larger and thus more important, personal fire remained a steady, reliable source of business. Except for a few catastrophe years, it supplied consistent profits to insurers. Underwriting was specialized and underwriters were very knowledgeable concerning this one line, particularly so since changes in underwriting occurred slowly. Thus, personal fire insurance manifested the height of stable, consistent, profitable insurance.

This beautiful picture was shattered during the decade of the 1950s. Pressures were brought to expand the perils covered by the dwelling fire policy and in rapid succession the industry adopted the additional extended coverage endorsement, the broad form, and the all risks form. Before underwriters could adapt to these massive though evolutionary changes, a revolution came to the industry and changed the entire picture. The homeowners dwelling package policy was introduced in the mid-1950s and was an instant success. It covered everything that was in the personal fire policy, along with theft and personal liability coverages, all at discounted rates.

The preferred risks in the personal lines field rushed to the homeowners policy. Within a few years, most of the best personal fire policyholders were lost to the new package. Perhaps this development was beneficial to property owners, producers and insurers; that is another subject covered in a separate chapter. From the standpoint of dwelling fire business, the result was little short of disastrous. Almost overnight, a line which had enjoyed insuring the cream of the homeowners business in America was reduced to covering only risks which were not eligible for the package policy: rental units, old homes, and property owners who neglected their property or were otherwise considered as nonpreferred risks. The term "residual risks" was soon applied to these properties that were denied the benefits of the package and those that suffered a relatively large ratio of losses.

Personal fire underwriters realized that new techniques would be required in order to return the dwelling fire line to a profitable position. Enough volume remained to hurt the insurers if the line was unprofitable, so underwriters began serious efforts to find means of ending the losses. The underwriting program they developed is the subject of the discussion on underwriting in this chapter. However, the current picture on coverages, both property and perils, is explained first.

DESCRIPTION OF COVERAGES

Personal fire insurance is quite uniform among insurers and is quite strictly controlled. Some companies use independent forms, but even they are very similar to those used by other companies regarding the descriptions of property and perils. There are some differences among geographic areas of the country, but these differences are minor and the following explanation is generally correct.

Property Coverages

Dwelling. The first item covers the building, which must be occupied principally for dwelling purposes. Multiple-family dwellings are included, with a maximum number of family units ranging from four to 20, depending upon the rules used in the state. Also covered under this section are additions in contact with the dwelling, and materials or supplies located on the described location or adjacent thereto which are intended for construction, alteration or repair of the dwelling. If not insured elsewhere, coverage also extends to equipment and fixtures relating to the dwelling.

Private Structures. Coverage applies under this item to garages and other structures on the premises but not in contact with the dwelling. Most forms automatically extend 10% of the dwelling amount to apply to private structures appertaining to the described premises; if this is insufficient, additional coverage may be purchased.

Contents. Personal property in a dwelling or on the premises is covered under this item. All household and personal property usual or incidental to the occupancy of the premises as a dwelling is covered, except for such property as automobiles, animals and boats. Off-premises coverage is granted, usually with a 10% limitation on the amount of contents.

Rental Value. All forms extend coverage for the fair rental value of the dwelling or portions thereof; that is, basic forms cover the rental value whether the dwelling is rented to others or occupied by the insured. The most expensive forms cover only if property is rented to others. The insured-occupant is covered better under additional living expense insurance. In each case, the usual extension is 10% of the dwelling amount and additional coverage may be purchased when desired.

Additional Living Expense. Rather than paying only the fair rental value if the policyholder is forced out of the home by a covered loss, the more expensive forms pay the necessary increase in living expense. This is a more realistic approach to covering the additional out-of-pocket expenses incurred by the policyholder. The usual extension is 10% of the dwelling amount, with provision for buying extra coverage, if desired.

Improvements and Betterments. If the policyholder does not own the dwelling, up to 10% of the contents covered may be applied to the improvements, alterations and additions made to the dwelling and private structures.

Trees, Shrubs, Plants and Lawns. Under the more expensive forms, five percent of the dwelling amount may be applied to cover trees, shrubs, plants and lawns. The perils are restricted, with no coverage applying for such perils and windstorm, hail and falling objects.

*Debris Removal.*The basic policy covers the expenses incurred in the removal of debris of covered property if caused by an insured loss.

Replacement Cost. Basic fire insurance policies cover the actual cash value of the property. Actual cash value is usually defined as the replacement cost at the time of loss less depreciation; depreciation may be physical or it may be caused by obsolesence. The more expensive fire forms cover the dwelling and private structures, not contents, for the full replacement cost without deduction for depreciation. Usually excluded from this coverage is such property as carpeting, cloth awnings, domestic appliances and outdoor equipment. It is required that the property be insured to at least 80% of replacement costs in order to receive this extra coverage; otherwise, actual cash value is paid, or the proportion which the amount of insurance bears to 80% of the replace cost, whichever is greater.

Perils Covered

With the use of "readable policies," the term "peril" has been replaced by "cause of loss." The Insurance Services Offices adopted a Dwelling 77 Policy Program which uses "Basic Form DP-1," and similar identification of other forms, with some new terminology and format but with few substantive changes from prior forms.

Some current forms have dropped the term "Extended Coverage," automatically including all basic perils in the named-peril forms. However, the ISO Basic Form retains the old term, permitting these perils to be added or not, as the client wishes.

Because various forms are now available, the following discussion is general, and may not conform in detail with any one policy. The ISO Dwelling 77 titles are used.

1. Basic Form DP-1:

a. Fire, lightning and removal. The basic perils covered by every fire policy are fire, lightning, and damage caused by removal of the property from premises endangered by the perils insured in the policy. The word "fire" has been interpreted to refer only to a "hostile fire," not to a "friendly fire;" the latter means a fire which is confined to the place where it was intended to be, such as a fireplace or stove.

b. Extended coverage endoresement. Almost every fire policy covering habitational risks is endorsed to cover the extended coverage perils, unless a more complete form is used. There are eight perils included within this endorsement; in fact, it was customary in years past to refer to it as "eight-point coverage." Without listing all of the details of descriptions and exclusions, the perils are these.

A. Windstorm
B. Hail
C. Explosion, including the explosion of accumulated gases or unconsumed fuel within the firebox or combustion chamber of any fired vessel. Excluded under this peril is loss by explosion of steam boilers or steam pipes, water hammer and shock waves caused by aircraft. The latter are generally known as "sonic boom."
D. Riot and riot attending a strike. This includes direct loss by acts of striking employees while the building is occupied by the striking employees, but excludes resulting damage due to change in temperature or humidity. This peril had little application for many years, but the riots which occurred in many cities from the middle 1960s into the 1970s caused an interest in this peril; these events demonstrated the value of including many perils in a policy rather than permitting applicants to select the perils they feel they need.
E. Civil commotion. This is little distinction between riot and civil commotion. The latter is generally considered to be a riot of prolonged duration in which there is defiance of civil authority, although less defiance than would constitute insurrection (which is excluded).
F. Aircraft. This means only loss resulting from actual physical contact of an aircraft or object falling therefrom, with the property covered. Therefore, a "sonic boom" is not covered under this peril.
G. Vehicles. Damage resulting from physical contact of a vehicle to the property is covered, but excluding damage caused by a vehicle owned or operated by the insured or a tenant of the described premises. Damage to fences, driveways, walks, lawns, trees, shrubs and plants is excluded.
H. Smoke. This coverage is limited to sudden, unusual and faulty operation of a heating or cooking unit, and only when the unit is connected to a chimney by a smoke pipe or vent. Smoke from a fireplace is not covered.

c. Vandalism and malicious mischief. This coverage is an option for additional premium.

2. Broad form DP-2:

Dwelling buildings and contents may be covered under a broad form policy. This is a named-peril policy which covers all of the previously described perils, plus a number of others. The most important of these perils, either new or modifications of others, covers damage to the property by the following perils.

A. Vandalism and malicious mischief.
B. Damage done by burglars, but not property taken by burglars.
C. Aircraft and vehicles, including damage done by a vehicle owned or operated by an insured or tenant of the property. However, damage by such a vehicle to driveways, walks lawns, trees, shrubs, and plants is not covered.
D. Smoke, including all damage by smoke except from agricultural smudging or industrial operations.
E. Falling objects. Damage to the interior of the building, or property in the building, is covered only if the building first sustains damage to the exterior.
F. Weight of ice, snow, or sleet. Excluded are such items as television antenna, outdoor equipment, cloth awnings, fences, lawns, trees, shrubs and plants.

G. Collapse. This refers to collapse of a building or a part thereof, but not settling, cracking, bulging or expansion.
H. Accidental discharge, leakage, or overflow of water from within a plumbing or heating system.
I. Sudden and accidental cracking, burning, or bulging of hot water heaters.
J. Breakage of glass which constitutes a part of the building.
K. Freezing of plumbing and air conditioning systems and domestic appliances.
L. Sudden and accidental injury from artifically generated electrical currents to electrical appliances and fixtures.

3. Special Form DP-3:

Dwelling buildings, but not contents, may be covered under an "all risks" form which generally is called a *special form*. In general, this form covers all of the perils previously listed, plus unnamed perils. Actually, the exclusions are written carefully enough so that there are few perils which would be covered under this form and not under a broad form.

There are exclusions in the so-called *all risks* form, of course. Most of them are perils for which insurance cannot be purchased, such as wear and tear, deterioration, mold, contamination, mechanical breakdown, cracking or settling of foundations and loss caused by vermin or domestic animals. Some exclusions conceivable could be removed by an underwriter, although most companies do not have rates for this action; these exclusions are vandalism and malicious mischief while the building is vacant for more than 30 days; loss by freezing if the building is vacant for more than four days and due diligence has not been exercised to maintain heat; and loss by freezing or thawing to fences, patios, swimming pools and foundations.

Earthquake is excluded, but a separate coverage may be purchased from most companies for an additional premium. A substantial deductible applies to this coverage in order to keep the cost down by avoiding payment for the many small cracks caused by every earthquake, as well as the cracks present in most homes because of normal settling but not noticed until an earthquake occurs. The deductible ordinarily is 2%, 5%, or 10% of the value (actual cash value or replacement value, whichever applies) of the property, depending upon the state and policy form used. However the newer forms are using a more understandable approach of 5% of the total amount of insurance applying to the subject property. Specific coverage may be purchased for contents, as well as for buildings.

Flood is also excluded. This coverage is not written by any company alone, but the Federal Flood Insurance Program was instituted in 1970 to make this coverage available. Private companies sell and service flood insurance, ceding the premium (less expenses) to the federal government, which pays all losses. Only in designated communities may this coverage be purchased, those which have taken steps to control construction in flood-prone areas. Mudslide is also covered, along with flood. On the other hand, landslide is not covered, so the policy exclusions apply and few companies write this coverage.

UNDERWRITING FACTORS

Acceptable Risks

Insurers which write personal fire insurance follow somewhat the same pattern as insurers of personal automobile insurance. This is not surprising, since these are the two largest lines of coverage in the personal field, excluding package policies. In each case, companies may consider themselves as insurers of preferred, standard or substandard risks, and each type would delineate the specific risks that would be acceptable.

Fire insurance is less stratified than automobile insurers, as regards the preferred or nonpreferred classes. In automobile, the majority of the premium is in preferred-risk companies, a sizeable share is substandard, and relatively little is written at so-called standard rates. In fire insurance, the largest share of the coverage on dwellings and contents is written by the standard companies — those that write at bureau rates. A substantial amount of premium is written by preferred-risk companies — those that write at lower rates than bureau, and this share is increasing steadily. On the other hand, only a small portion of habitational risks are written at surcharged rates by companies which consider themselves to be substandard fire insurers.

Preferred-risk fire companies usually establish general acceptability rules. They desire the owner-occupied dwellings of average or better construction in steady or improving communities. Many of these companies write insurance through exclusive agents or employees and attempt to guide the solicitation to these types of risks. Because they write at rates which are lower than average, they feel that only risks above average are acceptable. However, it is not easy to determine the "average" in factors as indefinite as those inherent in dwelling risks. Perhaps it is more accurate to say that these companies, since they do not write the below-average risks, attempt to write those that are average or above.

Standard companies, on the other hand, consider most risks to be acceptable. They attempt to avoid the true substandard risks, but many of them are written by this class because of related business, or simply because the underwriter does not realize the nature of the risk. By far the largest number of companies are in this category and they consider as acceptable, all risks except those at the very bottom of the scale.

Substandard writers are much less important in the habitational fire line, but they do exist. As with automobile insurance, they might consider all risks as being acceptable and would be delighted to write some preferred business. Realistically, however, their acceptable risks are the older, smaller, run-down dwellings in declining neighborhoods. Isolated dwellings might also be within their acceptability group, as well as habitational risks exposed to fires from forest or brush areas and to windstorm from tornadoes and hurricanes. Those dwellings and contents which have problems from the standpoint of fire underwriting may be written only in the substandard market, at rates substantially above average.

Unacceptable Risks

Personal fire underwriters tend to use rather lengthy unacceptable lsits, somewhat as personal automobile underwriters do. These lists guide the producers in the risks they should submit and help the underwriters to select the better ones. Personal fire is a line that is underwritten by class rather than individually; thus it is similar to automobile underwriting on this point. The use of unacceptable lists, therefore helps in the class underwriting.

Judgment plays a large role in determining unacceptable risks for each company. The point at which to draw the line is imprecise, so different insurers use different rules. However, they tend to follow the same general approaches. A description of the unacceptable risks for a preferred risk company usually include these factors.

Age of Dwelling. A universally recognized factor is the age of the dwelling. Older residences, constructed under less stringent building codes, may have substandard wiring and heating, faulty electrical equipment and defective equipment for heating and cooking — all leading causes of fire in dwellings. Deterioration may be so great that the structure has little value, or comprises a physical hazard merely because it is in disrepair. Many older dwellings are in the poorer part of cities, often in mercantile or manufacturing areas, where good housekeeping is rare. Recognizing those factors, the problems still remains about what year to start considering risks as unacceptable. Some underwriters use 25 years, with older dwellings being unacceptable, while others may specify 30 or 35 years. Still others use the end of World War II as the dividing line, perhaps specifiying 1945 since few residences were built during the war years of 1941 to 1946.

Size of Dwelling. Small homes are unacceptable in most preferred-risk companies. The usual sizes below which applicants are unacceptable are 700, 750 or 800 square feet. While the exact dimensions are subject to variation, the reasons are the same. Small homes are usually older than average. They usually contain substandard, or at least minimal quality wiring and heating. A fire will involve a larger proportion of the structure than in a larger house; a kitchen fire may damage one-tenth of a medium-sized home, but one-half of a small home. Since the value of the home and its contents is relatively low, the premium naturally will be small, perhaps too small to cover the acquisition expenses plus the cost of claims.

However, every producer and every fire underwriter knows that some small homes are very desirable risks. A house may be small because it was built for a retired couple. Such a home may have been of the finest materials and under the most strict code requirements. Still, such a risk is unacceptable under the rules of many companies. This is so because there are too few desirable applicants of small homes; hence, it is easier to make all such homes of that size unacceptable. An exception could be made by the underwriter, of course. Under the concept of class underwriting such exceptions would seldom, if ever, be made. The cost of securing adequate information by which to determine whether an exception can be made is too great for the amount of premium involved. A small house will develop only a small premium, and the underwriter cannot afford to secure reports and other types of information needed before an exception can be made.

Class underwriting is exemplified very well in the matter of small dwellings.

A line is drawn and smaller homes are unacceptable. The few applicants with smaller homes who are desirable must remain unacceptable because it is uneconomical for the underwriter to attempt to determine if an exception is justified. Any one of these small homeowners could be accepted, but the underwriter would need to secure reports on so many that are not acceptable, and would receive so little premium on the ones acceptable that it is simply poor business practice to attempt to locate that one which is acceptable.

Inferior Construction. A dwelling built of interior materials or in an inferior manner is usually unacceptable for preferred rates and sometimes for standard rates, as well. Examples of inferior materials could include roll-type roofing on peaked or pitched roofs, plywood siding, substandard wiring or size of framing. Inferior types of construction may include nonstandard installation of electrical fixtures, wide space framing and inadequte insulation around heating ducts. Many of these conditions will exist in older homes. These conditions may also exist in homes situated outside of a city or town; in fact, some dwellings are deliberately built beyond the reach of building codes in order to reduce construction costs. Thus, many of these homes are unacceptable because of age or lack of fire protection, in addition to poor construction.

Low-valued Dwellings. Many companies consider, as unacceptable, all applicants with dwellings and personal property below a specified minimum. These amounts vary by insurer. One reason for this rule is simply that policies on low-valued property will develop very little premium. Even if a minimum premium is established in an attempt to obtain enough money to cover the cost of issuing the policy, this leaves nothing with which to pay losses. Another reason for making this class unacceptable is that low-valued homes generally are dilapidated, maintained in poor condition and apt to attract careless occupants. As a general rule, people who are careless in their living habits tend to live in low-valued, dilapidated dwellings so a dual problem is encountered. It is true that low-valued homes ordinarily are old and poorly constructed, but even if these factors are not present, low-values on buildings and contents may make applicants unacceptable.

Inferior Neighborhood. Pride of ownership is an important factor in personal fire underwriting. An owner who has pride in the home, in its appearance and surroundings is likely to be a desirable risk, than a person who does not have such pride in the property. Some homes are located in neighborhoods which are so deteriorated that no pride of ownership is evident in any of the houses. Most homes in these areas are rentals, poorly maintained and with poor housekeeping. Vandalism, arson and damage by burglars also may be greater in such areas, as in the chance of fire from neighboring structures. These are called *environmental hazards*, meaning those that increase the chance of loss but which are caused by conditions beyond the control of the property owner. Such habitations offer unusual exposures and are unacceptable in many companies.

Unusual Loss Exposures. Certain areas of the country are susceptible to catastrophe losses from forest fires, grass fires or brush fires, while other areas are exposed to hurricane or tornado losses. Since these exposures are greater than some companies wish to accept, insurers place such risks on unacceptable lists.

Unusual types of heaters have also caused problems; kerosene and wood-burning stoves have caused fires if not properly installed, and some underwriters have prohibited such risks (when they can be identified).

Isolated Risks. Some permanent homes, as well as many vacation homes, are located outside the limits of a city or a town and are quite isolated from other dwellings. However desirable these may be from an aesthetic viewpoint, they increase the chance of serious loss. One problem is that no competent fire department may be available to suppress a fire. Another problem is that if a fire should start, notification to a fire department might be delayed. If the property owner is home, there may be no means of calling for aid; if no one is at home, the fire may not be observed until it is beyond control. Finally, even if a fire department should be summoned promptly, the trucks may be prevented from rendering aid, especially when the roads are blocked by snow or mud.

Prohibited lists for some companies attempt to handle these situations by specifying certain risks as unacceptable. The usual approach is to prohibit dwellings located beyond the limits of a city or town, unless they meet specified requirements. Some of these conditions are: that there be a fire department that will respond, that there is a telephone on the premises, that the house is within a reasonable distance of other residences, and that the house is located on a year-round accessible road.

Hazardous Occupancies. Some dwelling-type buildings are occupied as boarding houses, rooming houses and nursing homes. Since these occupancies may increase the chances of loss, some companies make them unacceptable, while others limit the exposure by limiting roomers or boarders to no more than one or two.

Vacant Property. A dwelling is vacant when it contains no personal property. A new dwelling is vacant after it is completed and before an owner or tenant moves in. An old dwelling is vacant when one occupant has moved out and another has not yet moved in. A vacant building presents none of the hazards caused by people, such as smoking, heating and cooking. This advantage, however, is far outweighed by the increased hazard inherent in vacancy. Dirt and dust will settle, hobos or tramps may move in, rats may build nests, vandalism may be present and fire reporting will most certainly be delayed. The moral hazard may increase if the vacancy is caused by an inability to sell or rent the house, too. These increased hazards are recognized by limitations in policies regarding certain perils if a building is vacant beyond a specified time. An underwriter may consider any vacant buildings as unacceptable and will make exceptions only if concrete evidence is presented that the vacancy will terminate within a short period of time.

Responsibility Lacking. A person who demonstrates lack of responsibility is unacceptable in many cases. Most dwelling fire policies cover many perils, some of which are susceptible to an increased chance of loss when the property is not maintained properly. Applicants who use drugs or alcohol to excess, who are not financially sound, or who have criminal records are usually unacceptable because they do not demonstrate the type of responsibility that is necessary under a property insurance policy.

Previous Losses or Cancellation. Although losses under fire insurance policies are relatively infrequent, an applicant who has incurred any loss within a period, such as three years, is unacceptable under the rules of some companies. An exception might be made, but only after complete explanation of the circumstances is made. In the same fashion, cancellations or nonrenewals or fire policies are not common, so such action by insurers indicates that a problem does exist. Those risks who have been cancelled are also unacceptable for many companies, with acceptance possible only after satisfactory explanation.

History of Arson. Loss by arson is a particular problem to fire underwriters. If the applicant has suffered losses by arson, or is in a neighborhood where arson has occurred with frequency, careful investigation is needed. There are many motives for arson. Where fire setters are active in an area, the reasons are probably social unrest, juvenile mischief, carelessness or pathological disturbances. Individual instances of arson may be caused by revenge, spite, attempts to cover up other crimes or fraud for insurance purposes. Some people are mentally disturbed or dishonest, and insurance cannot be written profitably for them. An even more serious condition exists in some areas where the public attitude toward private property, particularly that of others, has become so casual or disrespectful that the insurance mechanism cannot function properly. Such risks, or risks in such areas, are unacceptable in most companies.

Inadequate Insurance to Value. Securing proper insurance to value is one of the prime requisites to the profitable writing of fire insurance. An applicant who will not insure to value must then be unacceptable. The minimum permitted by most companies is 50% insurance to value, meaning that the amount of insurance on each item is at least 50% of the value of that item. Some companies require more, such as 70 to 75%. Replacement cost coverage, on the other hand, is given only when the property value equals or exceeds 80% of the replacement cost; most underwriters require that figure as a minimum for acceptability. On policies without replacement cost coverage, the "value" used in the requirement is actual cash value (ACV), which traditionally is defined as meaning "replacement cost at the time of the loss, less depreciation." The depreciation can be physical, functional, or economic, and if applied correctly, usually results in the ACV approximating the market value. In fact, there is a feeling in some areas that ACV means market value, although this is not yet widely accepted.

SECURING INFORMATION

A personal fire underwriter must secure considerable amounts of information about risks that are submitted and, while some facts will determine eligibility, others are needed in order to determine acceptability. While several sources are available from which an underwriter can secure this information, the application is the most important one in most cases and is the first one available.

Application

Factual information about the risk is given on the application. Much of the information describes physical factors, but other questions furnish answers on the charcter of the applicant. Most companies do not require the signature of the applicant, since no part of the application is made a part of the policy, except the description and location of the property and coverage.

Applications are quite uniform in requesting the items which will be repeated on the policy, but there is no uniformity about other information. Most applications, however, develop the same general information which can be classified in these categories.

1. Personal
2. Description of property
3. Insurance information

The following information is generally requested in each category, on a typical application.

1. *Personal*

A. Applicant's full name, which should correspond to the name or names on the title.
B. The interest of the applicant in the property, such as joint tenancy.
C. Applicant's mailing address.
D. Property locations.
E. Applicant's marital status.
F. Age and occupation of applicant and spouse.
G. Stability of the applicant, as reflected in such factors as how long at this address and number of jobs in a recent period.
H. Previous losses of the type covered by the policy for which application is made, over a recent period.

2. *Description of Property*

A. Information about the building: construction, type of roof and number of units or apartments.
B. Information about fire protection: the fire district or area in which the building is located, the distance to the nearest responding fire station and the nearest fire hydrant.
C. Size of the dwelling, the number of stories and description of attached or detached garages.
D. Age of the dwelling and the roof.
E. Type of heating systems and fuel.
F. For risks outside of a city or town, information about exposures to forest or brush, whether there is a telephone and a year-round accessible road and the distance to other dwellings.
G. If contents are covered, the estimated value of all household goods and personal property and whether the applicant owns the dwelling.

3. *Insurance Information*

A. Perils for which coverage is requested.
B. Amount of insurance desired on each item of coverage and any deductibles requested.
C. Proposed effective date.
D. Name and address of a mortgagee or loss payee.
E. Description of any other insurance on the property.
F. Information about the previous insurer: name of the company, type of policy and amount of insurance, policy number and whether the policy was cancelled or non-renewed by a company.

Inspection Reports

While personal fire underwriters use inspection reports on some risks, their usage is considerably less than that of many other underwriters. One reason for this limited use is the fact that fewer moral hazards are present than in many other lines. Another reason is that the eligibility rules are drawn rather tightly, so that most eligible risks are automatically acceptable.

When inspection reports are desired, they are ordered from the same companies used for other policies. Several types of reports are available. One type is a comprehensive report which includes a considerable degree of information about the applicant and the property; this type would be requested when the underwriter is concerned about the moral and morale hazards. Another type includes little information about the applicant, and instead, concentrates on the physical aspects of the risk. Still another type is strictly a physical inspection, including only the exterior of the dwelling and the neighboring premises; these are sometimes designated as "drive-by" or "sidewalk" inspections.

Physical inspections are made by company employees, in some cases. Certain insurers with considerable volume of personal fire insurance employ inspectors in areas of the greatest concentration. In addition, many companies ask their employees who travel in the field, such as special agents or commercial engineers, to inspect an occasional risk for a particular purpose. The latter practice is quite expensive in most cases, although costs are hidden, so underwriters use it only in special cases, such as those in a particular hurry or for a prominent applicant where an inspection by an outside company might be undesirable from a political standpoint.

Photographs

Since the physical condition of the building is one of the most important factors in personal fire underwriting, a photograph of the exterior of the dwelling is very helpful. A picture can tell the underwriter more than a lengthy description about the construction and condtion of the building. Photographs are available with inspection reports and most of them are secured from this source, although an underwriter may request a photograph with any type of inspection report. However, some companies require the producer to submit a photograph with all applications or on specified risks.

A significant problem with photographs lies in the fact that the camera angle is all-important. A head-on view of the front of the house will reveal nothing about the sides or rear. A picture taken too close will not show the surrounding area. One taken from too great a distance will not disclose such physical problems as a worn roof, while trees or other buildings may interfere with a good picture. Because of these difficulties, some underwriters require two photographs, each taken from opposite corners at a medium distance.

Experience of Other Insurers

Underwriters of personal fire insurance exchange information on their experience with somewhat less frequency than on many other lines. Premiums are often small, perils are somewhat restricted and loss frequency is relatively low, all causing some reluctance to take the time to exchange information. However, some companies do reciprocate in this regard and occasionally develop enough information to justify the effort.

CLASSIFICATION AND RATING

Most fire insurance is written under rules and rates established by a rating bureau. A few companies promulgate independent rules or rates for personal fire, but almost all follow the bureau.

There are two reasons that fire bureaus are used so universally. One is that few companies write a sufficient volume to enable their own statistics to be credible. Unlike personal automobile insurance, where a few independent insurers write a large share of the risks, personal fire insurance is divided among many companies, with none writing much more than about five percent of the total. With a large number of risks spread among so many companies, it is more economical to combine statistics through a bureau and the results are more credible, too. The other reason is that personal fire insurance risks have a much lower frequency of loss than many other lines, notably personal automobile insurance. On the other hand, severity of loss is greater in fire insurance. The low frequency and high severity make it necessary to combine a great number of risks in order to secure reliable experience upon which to base rates. Only through rating bureaus can most companies secure this reliability.

Classification Factors

Personal fire risks are classified by a number of factors before the rate is developed. The underwriter is responsible for assigning these classifications from the information available. The most common classifications are the following.

Dwelling Construction

A basic classification factor is the construction of the dwelling which is insured, or in which the insured property is contained. Some of the types are frame, frame-stucco, brick, stone and brick veneer. Rates for the frame types are higher in most cases.

Type of Roof

The combustibility of the roof is a factor in personal fire insurance. Wood shingles and shakes may carry higher rates than composition shingles, metal or tile roofs; the former are called unapproved, while the latter are classified as approved.

Number of Dwelling Units

Most rating plans require classification by number of dwelling units in the building. As an example, one and two family units may carry the same rate, three and four units a different rate and dwellings containing more than four units may be rated as apartments under commercial fire.

Type of Occupancy

The rate for dwelling buildings is lower for owner-occupied residence than for those occupied by tenants. This differentiation recognizes the importance of pride of ownership in property insurance. In addition, tenants, as a class, take less care of the property, a fact which logically leads to higher rates for this group.

Degree of Fire Protection

A critical classification concerns the degree of fire protection available. Not only does this mean the quality of the fire fighters who respond, but many other factors as well. The supply and distribution of water, the type of fire alarm system, the quality of police protection and the building laws are factors to be considered. Others are the enforcement of laws which relate to hazardous materials and the structural conditions of the area which can affect the potential for catastrophes.

The classification system used for fire insurance is based upon the grading of cities and towns which is applied by the bureaus. Each area is assigned a national board class rating. The lower the number, the better the protection. No city has even been graded lower than two, and the highest number is 10. The latter denotes a complete lact of protection, and in most states, classes nine and ten are called "unprotected."

Rate tables are prepared using those classification factors. Personal fire risks are class rates, not individual rates. Each applicant is classified by the various factors and then the rate is determined from a table. (The rate is shown in cents per $100 of coverage.) While different rates apply for building and contents coverages, fire rates for residential risks are the same regardless of the amount of insurance carried, with the sole exception of earthquake coverage which may use a coinsurance clause.[1] The rate is the same for the first $100 of coverage as for the last $100 purchased, too. The principal deterrent to under-insurance is the application of insurance-to-value rules by underwriters. Without these rules, many applicants would recognize that almost all losses are relatively small, and that they could insure against all but the unusual loss by purchasing only a few thousands of dollars of coverage.

One modification has been made by some state bureaus in an attempt to overcome the tendency toward under-insurance. This was the adoption of a loss constant, which is a flat charge added to all policies to cover the small losses which will occur regardless of the amount of insurance carried. Under this rating system, the basic premium is first determined by multiplying the rate times the amount of insurance. Then a flat amount is added to the basic premium in order to arrive at the final premium — this loss constant being the same for all policies within each classification. An alternative method for using the loss constant is to show in a table, the final premium for each $100 of coverage, or for each $1,000 and provide for extrapolation; either method arrives at the same result.

Still another modification has been used. The traditional method of fire rating has been to use a flat rate per $100 of coverage, regardless of the amount of insurance carried. The first modification, as described above, was the loss constant, which resulted in a higher rate for smaller policies. The next step was to modify all levels of coverage by the experience of each level. Statistics showed that higher-valued homes produced a poorer loss ratio than those with medium values, but still not as poor as homes with low values. This was referred to as a "saucer effect" of rating with higher final rates per $100 being used for both low-valued and high-valued risks. Adjustments are made as values change. For example, rates for dwellings might be higher for those valued below $60,000 and above $10,000.

Fire rates are given on an annual basis. Some policies are written for a term

---

1. See Chapter 24 for an explanation of coinsurance clauses.

of three years in order to meet the requirements of mortgagees and the desires of insurers. In most cases, however, personal lines policies are paid annually, with the premium being computed each year.

Personal fire rates are adjusted at irregular intervals, but most bureaus appear to consider changes approximately once a year. The loss ratio method of computing rates is used, employing the combined premium and losses of all member and subscriber companies. The experience for a long period is used, perhaps five years for the peril of fire, in order to achieve stability; more weight usually is given to more recent years. A period of 10 or even 25 years may be used for some catastrophic perils, such as hurricanes.

As previously mentioned, most companies are members of the bureaus for personal fire insurance; they use the bureau rates without modification. Many other companies are subscribers to the bureaus, using the bureau rates and rules but with deviations in some or all classes. The deviations are based upon the loss and expense statistics of the deviating company, so a reasonable size is necessary before a deviation can be justified. The deviation may be based upon lower losses because of superior selection, or upon reduced operating or acquisition expenses. In any event, deviations are almost always expressed as a percentage below the bureau rate and are quite commonly applied only to specified classifications.

A few large independent companies promulgate their own rates, but most of them use approximately the same methods and classifications as the bureaus, although a few have adopted different systems. These independent rate structures are designed either to achieve economies in handling the rating or to accomplish a preferred selection of specified classes of risks, or both. While the number of companies using independent rating is small, this group does include some of the companies which are among the top writers in premium volume. For the most part, insurers are much more inclined to use independent rates on personal fire insurance than on commercial fire.

A few personal fire risks are charged rates which are above those promulgated by rating bureaus. Some of these may be written at a "negative deviation," that is, at rates which are at specified percentages *above* bureau rates. Most, however, are written either in the surplus lines market or under "consent-to-rate" laws; both of these systems are relatively rare in personal lines, and are explained in the chapter on commercial fire — where they are used more commonly.

POLICY FORMS

Fire insurance is written by virtually every company in every state on a standard policy to which are attached various forms and endorsements. Actually, fire insurance is the classic example of a prescribed, standardized policy which is incomplete until forms are added. The fire policy is prescribed by law in many states. In others, a standard policy is required by the insurance departments, while in the balance of the states, general practice and promulgations of the rating bureaus have resulted in one policy that every company uses. Only a few local farm mutuals are exempt from using the standard policy, in most states.

The 1943 New York standard fire policy is now used exactly, or with slight modifications, in almost every state. It contains two parts. The first is the face of the policy, containing the general agreement between the company and the insured. The second part is the numbered lines, containing the conditions applicable to the insurance. These conditions are fairly general because they are used in the basic policy insuring any type of property against loss by fire, from a small household contents policy to a large apartment, store or manufacturer. Many of the provisions of the standard fire policy are inapplicable to personal fire risks, or are modified by the forms attached. Otherwise, the provisions of the standard policy are applied.

A trend toward requiring "readable" policies started in the late 1970s. The standard fire policy cannot possibly conform to any reasonable standard for easy readability. This problem has been solved by new regulations of laws which permit fire policies to be written in other than the standard form, provided they furnish at least as much coverage. This trend, which is not yet complete, probably will eventually abolish the standard fire policy, as such.

The policy itself contains no space or format for typing the name and address of the policyholder, the term of the policy, or the amount of insurance and premium. Until the early 1950s, the typing of this type of information was placed on the forms which were attached. Since then, it is customary to type or print by computer the basic information on the face of the policy and to refer to the attached forms by number. In this manner, the standard fire policy and the forms attached to it are united into one contract. (Chapter 13 of this book describes this change, as it applies to all lines of insurance.)

The forms contain the definitions of the property, extensions, applicable exclusions and special permits or modifications of the standard policy. In personal fire insurance, the basic form is the dwelling and contents form. It includes all that is necessary to insure the property which may be covered under a personal fire insurance policy. However, no additional perils are covered by this forrm beyond fire, lightning and removal which are specified in the standard fire policy. Most personal fire policies also include the extended coverage endorsement or E.C.E. This may be added by a separate endorsement. However, since it is so common, it is generally printed on the same piece of paper as the dwelling and contents form. It is clearly specified that extended coverage is a separate endorsement in spite of this combination for convenience.

In a few states, still another form may be added to cover more perils. This is the additional extended coverage endorsement, adding a few of the perils described earlier in this chapter under the broad form. The A.E.C. endorsement, as it was called, was an evolutionary step between extended coverage and broad form coverage, but it did not survive in most states beyond the late 1950s.

The broad form and special form approaches are different. Rather than attach still more perils to the policy which already had the dwelling and contents form, E.C.E., and the A.E.C. endorsements added on it, a new method was used. All of the provisions of these other forms were included in the broad form and special form, as were applicable, so only one form needed to be added to the standard fire policy.

The result was a more simplified contract, one that can be understood with some degree of ease. These policies, which are now easily the most popular of the personal lines policies, still contain the general provisions of the standard policy and the specific provisions of the form, with some of the latter modifying portions of the former. A fire policy is generally more difficult to read than other policies written as a unit, but the broad form and special form have simplified the personal fire policy as much as possible, so long as the standard policy must be used.

Other forms and endorsements are used on some personal fire policies. Almost all of these are specified by the rating bureaus to meet certain conditions. Some of these clauses restrict coverage, others give special permission, while others are required by rating rules. Underwriters have little latitude in using most of these clauses because they are precisely specified in the bureau rules. However, underwriters may decline to give some of the extensions or they may apply certain exclusions. Thus, some degree of tailoring the policy is permissible, although the mass handling of personal fire insurance usually prohibits much specialized treatment of individual risks.

On occasion underwriters may write their own endorsements to fit special cases. With blank endorsements supplied among the bureau forms and endorsements for this purpose. An underwriter will sometimes exclude certain property or apply special requirements and these may be written by the underwriter and typed on the blank endorsement.

Deductibles are specified by the rating bureau and deductible clauses are placed in the forms or added by endorsement. Often these are mandatory, so the use of the clause is automatic. However, sometimes deductibles are optional, so the underwriter may require the use of a certain deductible for underwriting purposes. In fire insurance, it is more common to select an endorsement that provides for the desired deductible, unlike most other lines that merely specify the amount of the deductible on the face of the policy.

Deductibles on personal fire policies were slow in receiving approval. Premiums were so low that little credit could be allowed for deductibles. When broader coverages were offered, the added perils generally carried optional deductibles. Soon after, deductibles were offered on windstorm and hail because of the severe losses which were occurring under these perils. Gradually those deductibles spread to other perils and were made mandatory. Later, some states required deductibles on all personal fire policies, while most states offered them as options. When deductibles are optional, policyholders may choose not to use them. Underwriters, however, may require them on certain risks, or perhaps on all risks, as a means of controlling small, frequent losses.

Independent forms are quite uncommon in personal fire insurance. The policy itself, of course, is specified for all companies. Most companies find it more economical and practical to use bureau forms than to develop their own. A few companies that specialize in personal fire insurance actually print their own forms, but seldom do these vary substantially from the bureau forms.

One problem involved in the use of fire forms is concurrency of coverage. This is the provision in all fire policies specifying that each insurer will pay only its proportion of any loss when there is more than one policy on a risk whether the policy is payable or not. Thus, if one policy is different and should exclude a type of loss which another does cover, the one which covers will pay only its share of the loss and the balance of the loss would be uninsured and, therefore, assumed by the insured. It is not common for personal fire insurance to have two or more policies on one piece of property, as it is in commercial fire. However, underwriters sometimes limit their retention on some risks, such as very expensive homes or those unusually threatened by catastrophic losses. The producer must then place the risk with two or more policies. When this occurs, it is highly important that the coverages be concurrent. The underwriter should check carefully to be certain that the policy covers precisely the same perils and conditions as all other policies on the property. This requirement of concurrency, therefore, is one of the principal reasons that almost all companies use the bureau forms.

Another problem faced by a company that desires to prepare its own forms is the specificaiton of certain mortgagees. Lending institutions play an important role in fire insurance. They are permitted to establish reasonable requirements about the policies they will accept, although they are prohibited by law in many states from coercing borrowers to write the insurance in specified companies. It may not be unreasonable for mortgagees to refuse to accept nonstandard forms. Even if the coverages are substantially the same, or the independent form is more comprehensive, a mortgagee might feel that it does not have the time to check many different forms. Most mortgagees probably would accept independent forms, but the potential problems are enough to keep most companies from attempting to prepare their own fire forms.

RETENTION AND REINSURANCE

Since personal fire insurance generally covers relatively low amounts of coverage at any one location, underwriters of this line are not regularly involved in reinsurance. However, some risks are fairly large and have catastrophe exposures, so the subjects of retention and reinsurance must be familiar to personal fire underwriters.

From an individual risk standpoint, the underwriter must consider all of the exposure at one location. Not only would this include the dwelling and its contents, but also the extensions to private structures, rental value or additional living expense, and others, where these are additional amounts of insurance, as they often are. Most fire companies establish maximum retentions at any one location, such as $100,000 or $250,000. The underwriter then accepts any personal line risk up to that retention. If that is not enough to take care of the needs or desires of the applicant, the underwriter can suggest to the producer, that another policy be written in another company for the balance, or as an alternative, the underwriter may have a facility for placing part of the exposure with the reinsurer, either on an automatic basis such as a surplus treaty, or on a facultative basis. In those cases, the reinsurer acts as another company would in paying its pro rata share of each loss.

Some fire insurers use excess reinsurance for larger risks. When such a treaty is in effect, the underwriter's retention, before the application of reinsurance, is usually high enough to cover all personal line risks. The company writes all of the coverage and collects on each loss above its net retention from the excess reinsurer.

The catastrophe potential is a matter of constant concern to a fire underwriter. Almost every section of the country is subject to losses by windstorm, hail, hurricane, or catastrophe fire, and some of the losses can be very large. Some companies attempt to limit their exposures in specified areas where these catastrophe potentials appear to be the greatest. In these companies, underwriters indicate on maps or on lists, the location of each risk which is accepted. When the limit is reached, no further exposure in that area is accepted. This type of control is not common in personal fire insurance but it is practiced by some companies in some areas. Probably the most common areas are those subject to hurricanes, brush fires or earthquakes.

Virtually all fire insurers carry catastrophic excess reinsurance. This reinsurance protects against multiple-risk losses in excess of the stipulated amount. The attachment points varies considerably by the size and distribution of the risks of the reinsured company, and it may be different for various perils. If the company uses an excess policy for individual risks, that coverage may be expended to cover catastrophe exposures, as well. Although these treaties are arranged by home offices, underwriters should be aware of the provisions in order to determine the amounts of exposure they face.

QUESTIONS FOR DISCUSSION

1. Give 2 items of property covered under the dwelling item, in addition to the building itself.
2. List 5 examples of specific articles which are covered under the contents item, and 3 which are excluded.
3. Compare the perils covered by the extended coverage endorsement and the broad form policy in these respects:
   a. List 2 perils which are covered under both, and explain the differences.
   b. List 3 perils covered only under the broad form policy.
4. Explain the difference in approaches between a named-peril policy and an all-risk policy, and show why an all-risk form on a dwelling building has a higher premium than a broad form policy.
5. Describe the underwriting significance of the age, size, construction, and value of dwellings.
6. Why are photographs important to underwriters?

24

Commercial Fire

Fire insurance on commercial buildings and contents is an old, well-established line of insurance — much older than most other property and casualty insurance lines — but not quite as old as personal fire insurance. However, most commercial fire insurance is now usually written as a part of commercial package policies, and so the monoline coverage is not growing as much as would be expected. In 1985, fire and allied lines insurance equalled $5,658,000 of premiums written, and most of these apply to commercial lines. The fire coverage was profitable, but allied lines caused underwriting losses. The total share is 3.7% of all property/casualty premiums in 1985.[1]

Commercial fire insurance has avoided the extreme decline which personal fire insurance has encountered over the years, but the former has not enjoyed as steady or profitable an experience as the latter did during the decade when personal fire was a leading profit line. Commercial fire is more subject to large losses and is more sensitive to changes in the economic condition of the country; fire losses to commercial property tend to increase as the economic picture worsens.

Commercial fire insurance has not become a "residual market" as has personal fire insurance. Still, the same trends are apparent, with package policies being offered to most classes, accompanied by substantial discount for the better risks.

As more of these preferred enterprises become insured under packages, the experience on the remainder will no doubt worsen. In fact it appears to be quite predictable that commercial fire underwriters will face somewhat the same problems as those which have faced personal fire underwriters. This means that new techniques will have to be developed in order to avoid underwriting losses. However, commercial fire insurance generally has been written in a steady, conservative pattern. For

1. "Property Insurance Marketing — 1985," *Best's Review, Property/Casualty Insurance Edition*, Vol. 87, No. 7 (November, 1986), pp. 102-104.

this reason, the adjustment to a "residual" status may cause little disruption. (The present underwriting programs are explained in this chapter, after explanations of the policy coverages.)

DESCRIPTION OF COVERAGES

Commercial fire insurance is one of the most uniform of all lines, with almost all companies using the same forms. Coverages are controlled by rating bureaus and few companies attempt to prepare independent forms except for specified classes. The following description is indicative for virtually all companies in most states.

Property Coverages

Building. The first item of coverage on a policy is the building. This includes the entire building or structure, as well as fixtures and machinery used for the service of the building. Additions to the building are also covered; this encompasses such property as platforms, conveyors, bridges and canopies.

Business Personal Property. Business personal property of every description is covered under this item, including that which is classified as stock and described under the next item. Coverage applies while the property is contained within the described building and while in the open, subject to a specified distance from the building or premises. Coverage may also apply away from the premises when temporarily removed, but is limited to a dollar amount.

Stock. Stock of goods and merchandise of every description is covered under business personal property. The intention is to cover stock which is being held for sale or for manufacture, regardless of the stage of manufacture or preparation at the time of the loss. Also covered are the materials and supplies which enter into the manufacture, packing, or shipping of the goods. This property is protected while in the building or in the open — the same as other personal property.

Personal Property of Others. This item covers the personal property of others which is in the care, custody or control of the insured.

Improvements and Betterments. A tenant may alter a building or install improvements to make it more suitable for the occupancy. The tenant does not have a right to remove the additions when leaving, because those items which are attached to the realty become the property of the building owner. However, the tenant does have an insurable interest in the improvements, because he or she would be deprived of their use in case of damage. This "use interest" is covered under Business Personal Property.

Loss of Business Income. When a commercial risk is damaged by fire or other peril, there may be a loss of sales or income for many months. The loss of earnings is insured under Business Income Coverage (formerly called "business interruption insurance" or "use and occupancy (U & O.) insurance"), a type of consequential loss coverage. The direct damage to the property is paid by the basic policy, but consequential loss is paid only if this added coverage is purchased, to protect against loss of earnings. These earnings consist of two parts: the net profit, which would have been earned if the business had continued to operate and the fixed charges and expenses which necessarily continue during the period of partial or total suspension of business.

Extra Expense. Some businesses cannot afford to interrupt their operations; examples are newspapers and diaries. These enterprises must continue to operate at almost any cost. Their primary need is for more money to cover the extra expense which will be incurred in renting temporary quarters, hiring additional help, advertising and moving of equipment. These additional costs can be covered by purchasing extra expense insurance, which is now included in the Business Income Coverage Form. Ordinarily, every commercial risk can use either business interruption or extra expense insurance, and many risks can use both.

Leasehold Interest. A person who leases property from others may suffer a loss if a favorable lease is cancelled because of damage by fire or another peril. Most leases contain clauses providing that the lease will be terminated if the premises are damaged to a specified extent. The loss, which is caused by the necessity of the lessee to pay a higher amount for a new lease, is covered by leasehold interest insurance. The difference in the lease amounts is paid for the balance of the lease.

Replacement Cost. The standard fire coverage applies to the actual cash value of the property, which is usually defined as replacement cost at the time of loss, less depreciation and obsolesence. The depreciation and obsolesence may be removed by purchasing replacement cost coverage. Ordinarily only buildings are acceptable, but personal property may be written on a replacement cost basis if the underwriter is willing.

Perils Covered

With the use of "readable policies," the term "Peril" has been replaced by "causes of loss." Also, the limited coverage form is now called "Basic Form." It includes the fire perils (mandated by the Standard Fire Policy) and the former Extended Coverage perils.

So as not to confuse those insurance students who have studied the older forms, the following discussion uses the older terminology. Note, however, that the current forms which are generally used do not make this distinction nor use the name "Extended Coverage." Rather, all of these causes of loss are listed in the Basic Form — plus vandalism and malicious mischief.

1. Basic Form

a. Fire, lightning and removal. The basic perils covered by every fire policy are fire, lightning, and damage caused by removal of the property from the premises endangered by the perils insured in the policy. The word "fire" has been interpreted to refer only to a "hostile fire," not to a "friendly fire;" the latter means a fire which is confined to the place where it was intended to be, such as fireplace or stove.

b. Extended coverage endorsement. Almost every fire policy is endorsed to cover the extended coverage perils, unless a more complete form is used. There are eight perils included within this endorsement; in fact, it was customary in years past to refer to it as "eight-point coverage." Without listing all of the details of descriptions and exclusions, the perils are these.

A. Windstorm
B. Hail

C. Explosion, including the explosion of accumulated gases or unconsumed fuel within the firebox or combustion chamber of any fired vessel. Excluded under this peril is loss by explosion of steam boilers or steam pipes, and water hammer.
D. Riot and riot attending a strike. This includes direct loss by acts of striking employees while the building is occupied by the striking employees. This peril has had little application for many years, but the riots which occurred in many cities from the middle 1960s into the 1970s caused an interest in this peril; these events demonstrated the value of including many perils in a policy rather than permitting applicants to select the perils they feel they need.
E. Civil commotion. There is little distinction between riot and civil commotion. The latter is generally considered to be a riot of prolonged duration in which there is defiance of civil authority, although less defiance than would constitute insurrection (which is excluded).
F. Aircraft. This means only loss resulting from actual physical contact of an aircraft or object falling therefrom, with the property covered. Therefore, a "sonic boom" is not covered under this peril.
G. Vehicles. Damage resulting from physical contact of a vehicle to the property is covered, but excluding damage caused by a vehicle owned or operated by an insured or a tenant of the described premises.
H. Smoke. This coverage is limited to sudden and accidental loss or damage, but excluding smoke from industrial operations or agricultural smudging.

2. Broad Form. Buildings and contents may be covered under a broad form policy. This is a named-peril policy which covers all of the previously described perils, plus a number of others. The most important of these perils, either new or modifications of others, covers damage to the property by the following perils.

A. Falling objects. Damage to the interior of the building, or property in the building, is covered only if the building first sustains damage to the exterior.
B. Weight of ice, snow or sleet. Excluded are lawns, trees, shrubs and plants.
C. Collapse. This refers to collapse of a building or a part thereof, but not settling, cracking, bulging or expansion.
D. Accidental discharge, leakage, or overflow of water from within a plumbing or heating system.
E. Breakage of glass which constitutes a part of the building.
F. Sinkhole collapse.
G. Volcanic action.

3. "All-risks" form. Buildings and contents may be covered under an "all-risks" form which generally is called a *special form.* In general, this form covers all of the perils previously listed, plus unnamed perils. Actually, the exclusions are written carefully enough so that there are few perils which would be covered under this form and not under a broad form.

There are exclusions in the so-called *all-risks* form, of course. Most of them are perils for which insurance cannot be purchased, such as wear and tear, deterioration, mold, contamination, mechanical breakdown, cracking or settling of foundations and loss caused by vermin or domestic animals. Some exclusions conceivable could be removed by an underwriter, although most companies do not have rates for this action.

Earthquake is excluded but a separate coverage may be purchased from most companies for an additional premium. A substantial deductible applies to this coverage in order to keep the cost down by avoiding payment for the many small cracks caused by every earthquake. The deductible ordinarily is 2% or 5% of the value (actual cash value or replacement value, whichever applies) of the property, depending upon the state and policy form used. However, some forms use a more understandable approach of 5% of the total amount of insurance applying to the subject property. Specific coverage may be purchased for contents, as well as for buildings.

Flood is also excluded. The coverage is not written by any company alone, but the Federal Flood Insurance Program was instituted in 1970 to make this coverage available. Only in designated communities may this coverage be purchased, those which have taken steps to control construction in flood-prone areas. Mudslide is also covered, along with flood. On the other hand, landslide is not covered, so the policy exclusions apply and few companies write this coverage.

Special Programs

Some classes of risks are acceptable for special combinations of coverages in certain states. These special programs are multiple peril policies in the commercial line and the most popular are as follows.

Manufacturer's Output Policy. This policy covers all risks to personal property, including products, of manufacturing risks. Building coverage is not included. Property is covered at the described location and in transit, with separate limits specified for each. Flood and earthquake are covered in transit and may be covered on the premises and theft is covered but may be excluded. Risks are classified by industries, with many different ones being specified.

Industrial Property Policy. This policy is broader than the manufacturer's output policy, covering all risks on finished stocks wherever located, and also other personal property except in manufacturing or processing locations. Building coverage may not be included. Reporting and non-reporting forms are offered and mandatory deductibles apply.

Commercial Property Coverage. Mercantile risks may purchase this form including retail, wholesale and related occupancies on an all risks coverage basis on a reporting or non-reporting form. Rates are promulgated by bureaus on an account basis. Only personal property is acceptable. The coverage offered under this form to retail and wholesale stores is somewhat similar to the inland marine block policies.

Office Contents Form. The contents of offices are acceptable for this all risks form, except such risks as physicians and surgeons, as well as offices located in stores or factories. Coverage applies on premises and away, subject to deductibles and coinsurance clauses. Rates are based on the basic fire and extended coverage rates plus a loading.

Public and Institutional Property Program. The P.I.P., as it is generally known, is offered to schools, churches, hospitals and governmental units. Blanket coverage is written on all real and personal property against the perils of fire, extended coverage, vandalism and malicious mischief, and sprinkler leakage. An inspection program is included, with substantial rate credits being offered for risks which qualify.

A 90% coinsurance clause is used, as are deductibles. Minimum premiums are substantial in the early years of the program, but have been reduced considerably. The program offers lower cost, broader coverage and a loss prevention program.

These special programs are multiple-peril policies, and could be classified as multiple-line since both fire and theft coverages are included. However, they are not true package policies as the term is used today, because commercial package policies must include both property and liability coverages. These special multiple-peril policies include coverages written in fire, crime and inland marine lines, but all are in the property field. These policies are discussed here because fire and related perils are the principal exposures in most cases, and because most of these programs are not separate policies but are special forms attached to a fire policy.

These special programs are tending toward obsolesence, as commercial property and package policies become broader and more standardized. It is likely that the use of common policy provisions plus special endorsements will remove the need for these special combinations of coverage.

UNDERWRITING FACTORS

Acceptable Risks

Commercial fire companies are less inclined than most insurers to stratify themselves into preferred and nonpreferred writers. Most companies write most types of risks.

A major factor in determining acceptability is the size of the risk. Some companies try writing the larger commercial risks, specializing in the service and loss prevention requirements of such risks. Others try to avoid the large exposures, preferring to write small to medium-sized risks. There are no specific dividing lines, of course, but most companies tend to write more toward one size than the other.

Some companies use other than bureau rates. The largest group of these, although only a small minority of the companies, are those that deviate — that is, they write at lower rates than most companies. These deviating companies attempt to select those risks that appear to be average or better for their classes. This type of selection is more difficult in commercial fire than in many other lines because commercial fire rates are promulgated to measure the loss exposure quite closely. Nevertheless, some companies try to select the better risks within each category.

Other companies write at surcharged rates. Those companies, which are few in number, deliberately seek the hard-to-place risks, i.e., those which appear to have a greater-than-average loss expectancy. Such companies, like other substandard writers, would be glad to write preferred risks, but realistically consider the nonpreferred risks as being unacceptable for their insurance.

Unacceptable Risks

More often than not, commercial fire underwriters avoid the use of unacceptable lists. These underwriters instead select on the basis of individual risks rather than to rule out many of them by unacceptable lists. It is more common for commercial fire underwriters, therefore, to consider rates and other factors on each applicant and to make decisions on a case basis.

Companies which use lists may divide the risks into the following four categories:

1. *Acceptable:* Most risks fall into this group, unless they have problems in such areas as condition of the property, maintenance of the property, or financial conditions.

2. *Caution:* Most risks in this group are acceptable but some individual risks are not. This might include such classes as amusement parks, large department stores, and wearing apparel retailers.

3. *Submit for Approval:* Most risks in this group are not acceptable, but some are. The producer may submit these risks to the underwriter but may not bind the company without prior approval. Every company list will vary, but might contain such risks as aircraft parts manufacturers, restaurants, and appliance sales-and-repair stores. A company may decide to consider a risk in these categories only if the entity has been in business, with good experience, for a stated period of time, such as three years.

4. *Unacceptable:* Perhaps 10 to 20% of the risks will be completely unacceptable to a company. Fire insurers depend more upon reinsurance than most types of insurers, and reinsurance treaties often prohibit certain risks. A company cannot, of course, consider accepting a risk upon which no reinsurance exists. In fact, this is one of the few areas where underwriters do not have the authority to accept any risk, whether on a list or not. Most reinsurance treaties prohibit such unusual risks as bridges, exhibition halls, and national monuments. In addition, company rules may consider, as completely unacceptable, those risks which the company believes to have a high exposure to catastrophe or other losses. Examples may be bowling alleys, explosive manufacturers, and food processors.

Deviating companies, those desiring to write only preferred risks, use some unacceptable lists. Sometimes these are just guides, but sometimes they contain listings of prohibited risks. The lists vary considerably by company, but most of them probably consider the following factors.

Age of Buildings. Underwriters must consider the fact that, in general, older commercial structures tend to become dilapidated and hazardous, especially in urban areas where low values eventually lead to poor housekeeping and maintenance. They must also consider the fact that most building codes are somewhat lax in former years and, if heating and electrical systems have not been properly maintained or replaced since then, they most certainly will be considered unsafe by today's standards. While it is difficult to select an age of a building beyond which care should be exercised by underwriters, some feel that those that were built 25 years or more is a safe figure. In spite of the fact that many buildings which are older than that figure are in better shape than some of the newer ones because of proper maintenance and repair, they are on many unacceptable lists in order for underwriters to investigate such risks thoroughly before accepting them for coverage.

Isolated Risks. Some commercial buildings are located in so-called unprotected areas — those where the fire protection is minimal or nonexistent. While the rates are high, some companies consider such risks as unacceptable because total losses are common; a small fire in a protected risk will probably be a total loss in an unprotected risk, in many cases. In addition, many buildings are constructed beyond city limits in order to avoid stringent building codes. It may be difficult, therefore, to ascertain which structures are below standard. Hence, it is easier to consider all of them as unacceptable.

Vacant Property. A commercial building containing no personal property is considered to be more hazardous than an occupied building, by many commercial fire underwriters. Even a new building is subject to scrutiny until it is occupied. The first impression of a layman is that a vacant building is subject to none of the hazards of many occupancies: cooking, heating, smoking and the like. However, experience has proved that vacant property is more subject to vandalism and malicious mischief losses because it is empty; to windstorm damage since no one is present to secure loose fittings; to the problems caused by rats and other rodents; and to the hazards of uninvited guests, such as transients. As an example of the latter, after two transients died in a fire started in an abandoned building in an effort to keep warm, a Los Angeles Fire Department captain estimated that "in a city of the size of Los Angeles, perhaps a dozen or more transients are burned to death in abandoned buildings in a given year. Street people have to find a place to bed down."[2] Tragic as this from the standpoint of human lives lost, it is of concern to property underwriters primarily because each of these fires damages the buildings.

Moral hazard is even more of a problem in vacant property. If the vacancy is caused by a shift in population or business, or by construction elements which make it unsuited for most occupancies, or by poor economic conditions, it may become a burden to the owner. Faced with no income and a steadily deteriorating building, the owner may decide to "sell" it to the insurance company by means of a carefully arranged fire.

For these reasons, vacant property is unacceptable in many companies. A critical factor in acceptance is the length and cause of the vacancy and the expectations for the future. An underwriter is concerned about the type of occupancy which can be expected, for it is of no value to secure occupancy if the type of business conducted by the tenant makes the risk unacceptable under another rule.

Hazardous Occupancies. Certain occupancies are unacceptable in many companies. These are the occupancies which have demonstrated a loss experience that is worse than average. Some of them are traditionally considered high-risk occupancies. Others fluctuate, being considered acceptable or even preferred at some times and unacceptable at others. The following list is indicative of the approach used by some preferred risk companies.[3]

- Bowling alleys — have been considered hazardous for years, and are even

---

2. "Bodies of Two Transients Found after Fire Destroys Abandoned L.A. Building," *Los Angeles Times*, November 8, 1986, Part I, p. 31.

3. For more detail on occupancies and other aspects of this subject, see Robert B. Holtom, *Commercial Fire Underwriting*, Second Edition, (Cincinnati: The National Underwriting Company, 1984).

prohibited under some reinsurance treaties. Poor loss experience is charged to the large, undivided area, concealed ceiling spaces, smoking and cooking.

- Supermarkets — A series of huge total losses caused many underwriters to turn away from supermarkets and, sometimes, from all grocery stores. Principal problems are large, undivided areas, refrigeration equipment, overloaded circuits and poor housekeeping.
- Restaurants — A number of serious fires in restaurants has made it difficult for owners or operators to secure insurance in many markets. Fire and grease are inherent in restaurant operations and can lead to major fires if uncontrolled. Both frequent cleaning and proper installation of chemical automatic extinguishers are required by many underwriters before restaurant risks will be accepted.
- Woodworking risks — have unusual exposure to loss, whether lumber yards, sawmills, cabinet shops or refinishers. Upholstering is related occupancy which is also considered hazardous. Sawdust, lint, varnish, storage and handling are some of the hazards which may contribute to large losses. Some reinsurance treaties exclude woodworking risks, as do most deviating companies.
- Amusement and recreational property — such risks as theaters, auditoriums, lodge halls, dance halls, country clubs and resort or seasonal property are on some unacceptable lists because the hazards of each of these may be greater than in the average commercial risk.
- Specified retail and service risks — are on many prohibited lists, such as antique shops, surplus stores, auction houses, auto wrecking, bakeries, cleaners, garages and body shops with spray painting, ladies ready-to-wear, self-service laundromats, pawnshops and welding shops.
- Specified manufacturing risks — Some of the more common manufacturing establishments considered unacceptable by many companies are explosive manufacturers, cotton gins, distilleries, furriers, foundries, machine shops, metal workers, and manufacturers of awnings, tents, boxes and chemicals.
- Schools and public buildings — For many years, insurers considered schools and public buildings to be highly preferred risks. Special programs of broad coverage and low rates were developed, and competition was keen. The riots and acts of vandalism which started in the late 1960s changed the pattern completely. Suddenly these risks had difficulty in buying coverage. Rates were increased, coverage was reduced and high deductibles were required. These classes furnished an excellent example of the extent to which commercial fire underwriting can be affected by outside influences in the social and economic areas. They also demonstrate forcibly the necessity for underwriters to be fully aware of circumstances surrounding them, to be flexible enough to adapt to changing conditions, and to recognize when new underwriting factors arise in various types of risks.

- Storage facilities — Certain types of storage facilities are considered unacceptable by some underwriters. Examples are truck terminals, box storage, furniture storage, cold storage and warehouses.
- Miscellaneous classes - A number of other risks may appear on unacceptable lists of some companies. Some of the more common are nuclear facilities, bridges and tunnels, fruit and vegetable packing houses, granaries, feed mills, hay stacks, bars and taverns, boarding and rooming houses, dehydrators and evaporators and hotel or motel properties.

Inadequate Insurance to Value. It is crucial to the success of a commercial fire underwriter that adequate insurance to value be written. Therefore, an applicant is unacceptable if not insured to value. The minimum acceptable to most companies is 50% of the actual cash value, applicable to each item separately. A commercial fire underwriter has some devices available to help secure insurance to value. The most common is a coinsurance clause, which is explained in a later section of this chapter. Whether such a clause is used or not, an applicant who will not meet the insurance to value requirement usually is considered to be unacceptable. Some companies have employed various types of programs to maintain the insurance to value after a policy is issued. These programs attempt to offset the adverse effects of inflation on property values. One type is an "Inflation Guard Endorsement" which automatically increases the amount of coverage by a predetermined percentage, such as 1, 2, or 3% per quarter of the year.

History of Arson. Applicants who have a history of arson or who live in a neighborhood with a history of arson are generally considered unacceptable. The reasons for the arson are important, but fire rates are too low to permit much leeway for fires which are set deliberately. An applicant who has been convicted of arson, or who has had several suspicious fires, must be investigated carefully before an exception to the unacceptable rule can be considered. Too, a neighborhood where arson has been common may make an individual risk unacceptable, unless there are reasons to believe that the specific applicant is not affected. Arson fires are a major cause of loss, and studies have been conducted to develop indicators of possible arson. Underwriters may avoid losses by watching for these early warning signs.[4]

New Materials. A problem for commercial fire underwriters in recent years has been the introduction of new materials, particularly plastics, that have not been tested by fire engineers and whose susceptibility to loss has not been taken into account in rating. It is difficult to identify such risks in an unacceptable list, but an underwriter may consider manufacturers or processors of new materials as unacceptable.

Poor Financial Condition. The financial condition of a commercial fire applicant is very important. One reason is that a marginal company usually has the tendency of cutting costs in the areas of housekeeping and loss preventative practices. Another reason is the tendency toward moral, or at least morale, hazards when the

---

4. For a more complete discussion of the arson indicators, see Robert B. Holtom, *Commercial Fire Underwriting*, p. 122.

business is not profitable. Some underwriters attempt to specify the financial conditions that are not desired, but most try to weigh all factors and make a decision. In either case, a poor financial condition may make a risk unacceptable.

Time in Business. The failure rate during the first few years for new businesses is very high. Some underwriters require at least one year or three years of successful operation under the same management, to be more certain that management has adequate knowledge and capitalization.

SECURING INFORMATION

A commercial fire underwriter needs to secure a great deal of information about most applicants in order to be able to select risks properly. As previously mentioned, some of the information is intended to determine eligibility, but more is pointed toward acceptability. Many sources of information are available. The first one used is the application, and occasionally it provides all of the needed information.

Application

The application for commercial fire insurance is primarily designed to develop physical information, although some questions are aimed more at personal characteristics of the owner or manager. Most of these applications do not require the signature of the applicant and the application is not made a part of the policy, beyond a repetition of the identifying facts about the risk and the coverage.

There is no uniformity to the information requested by insurers. The factual data needed for the policy is the same, but other questions vary considerably. A general description of the important information requested by the average company can be divided into three categories.

1. Personal
2. Description of property
3. Insurance information

The following information is secured in each category.

1. *Personal*

A. Full name of the applicant, including the firm name, if any.
B. The structure of the firm, whether an individual partnership or corporation.
C. Business location and mailing address of the applicant.
D. Location and description of all premises owned or occupied by the applicant.
E. Number of years that the applicant has been in business.
F. The product handled by the applicant, along with a description of process used, materials involved and type of equipment employed.
G. Details of all losses of the types covered by the policies for which application is made, during a previous period of, perhaps, five years.

2. *Description of Property*

Commercial fire underwriters have established an unusual classification system for the physical factors of risks. They consolidate all information under four headings which are called the COPE factors: construction, occupancy, protection, and exposure.

A. Construction: This includes a description of the type of materials used in the building and roof of the structure owned or occupied by the applicant. Such a description may include the size of the building, the number of stories, a description of all structures on the premises, the age of building and the type of heating system and fuel.

B. Occupancy: A description of every occupancy on the premises is needed, including that of the applicant if that person conducts a business there. This includes the amount of floor space occupied by each tenant, hazards of the occupancy and any special arrangements to reduce those hazards.

C. Protection: Both public and private protection must be described. Information about public protection should include the city or fire protection district within which the risk is located, and the national board class by which the area is graded. Private protection includes sprinklers or other automatic extinguishers, hand extinguishers, watchmen, fire alarm systems and any other devices which are used.

D. Exposure: The chance that a loss will communicate from another risk is called the exposure. It may come from another occupancy within the building or from another building nearby. The degree of separation should also be described, whether in terms of distance, fire walls or whatever is relevant. Exposures may also come from non-building sources, such as from an adjacent field or forest.

3. *Insurance Information*

A. The perils for which coverage is requested.

B. The amount of insurance desired on each location and each item of coverage, any deductibles requested and any coinsurance or other clauses desired.

C. Proposed effective date.

D. Name and address of any mortgagee or loss payee.

E. Description of any other insurance on the property.

F. Information about the previous carrier: name of the company, amount of insurance, policy number, and if the policy was cancelled or nonrenewed by the company.

Inspection Reports

Commercial fire underwriters use inspection reports, but not to the degree that this source is used by those handling many other lines. Other sources often are able to offer better physical and financial information that can most inspection companies.

When inspection reports are used for commercial fire, they are requested from the same companies providing reports for other lines. These companies generally are most effective in reporting upon the reputation and moral hazards of the applicant. The report may indicate the type of neighborhood, the apparent business success or prospects of the applicant and similar subjective information. When an underwriter desires to check upon these factors, inspection reports are a good source.

Some inspection companies also may be able to report on the credit standing and financial condition of businesses. Others have inspectors who are trained as engineers and can report on physical conditions. Both of these types of information may be gathered from inspection companies, but specialty sources are used more commonly.

Financial Reporting Services

Commercial fire insurance is subject to losses from policyholders who are in financial difficulty, more than most lines. Arson is difficult to detect, and even harder to prove, leading to the belief of experts that many fires are set deliberately. Many of these dishonest losses are caused to furnish relief from financial difficulties, and are called "fires of convenience." It is important, therefore, that a commercial fire underwriter attempt to determine the financial condition of most applicants.

Companies supplying financial data are able to help underwriters, too. Books are published showing the financial rating and condition of most businesses, while more detailed reports are available upon request. Since these companies are thorough and reliable, underwriters should have access to their data whenever the need seems to exist; some underwriters, in fact, check all applicants for this type of rating.

Engineering Reports

The physical condition of a risk and recommendations for improvement are of great concern to commercial fire underwriters and loss prevention specialists are available to supply this information. Some are company employees while others work for companies that supply this service for a fee.

Many underwriters request engineering reports on all but the smallest risks. The complexity of the reports will vary by the size and nature of the risk. In all cases, the underwriter is primarily interested in the facts concerning the physical factors of the risk: construction, operations, storage, housekeeping, wiring and other aspects. Usually the underwriter also wants to know of the recommendations for improvements which are made by the specialist, because risks which are almost acceptable may be satisfactory if certain changes are made. Finally, the specialist may be asked to submit a recommendation on the desirability of the risk.

Bureau Reports

Fire rating bureaus are used by most commercial fire companies. Rates may be available in rate books, rate cards, microfiche, electronic format for interface with an insurer's automated system, and by telephone or written inquiry. The rate information which the bureaus supply, in most states, contains basic information concerning every commercial risk: construction, occupancy, public protection, and exposures may all be identified, to some degree, from these rate publications. More detailed reports are available from the bureaus, in many cases, where further information is needed.

Maps are published for many cities showing every building within designated areas. These maps may be coded or colored to indicate various charcteristics of construction and protection. From these maps, each risk, and those which expose it, can be identified and analyzed.

Experience Of Other Insurers

Commercial fire underwriters tend to exchange information about experience somewhat less than most other underwriters. Loss frequency is relatively low, so most experience is meaningless. The physical factors are more important than other factors in most cases. Even when moral and financial factors are significant, the experience of a previous insurer will seldom be helpful, because conditions may change, and current conditions on these lines are the most critical factors. Some commercial fire underwriters do reciprocate in exchanging experience, in spite of these drawbacks. If they occasionally develop information which may not have been revealed elsewhere, they will feel that the effort is justified.

CLASSIFICATION AND RATING

Almost all commercial fire insurance is written under the rules and rates promulgated by fire rating bureaus. Some companies, of course, deviate a fixed percentage from the rates, but all, except a few specialty companies, follow the bureau pattern.

The reason for uniformity in classifications and rates is the complexity of the risks. Many factors must be taken into account because of the heterogeneous nature of commercial fire risks. Most classifications cannaot use rate tables, but contain such varied elements that each risk is rated separately.

Factors Considered in Classifying and Rating

Four major factors are used in classifying and rating commercial fire risks. These four factors must be considered by bureau engineers who establish the rates. These are the same four items used by underwriters as logical means of organizing information received from various sources available. The only types of information not falling within these classifications are the personal information concerning the applicant; the psychological factors, measuring the moral and morale hazards, including financial, economic and personal elements which may affect the risk. All other factors are physical, and may be grouped into these four items.

These four major factors, as described previously, are construction, occupancy, protection, and exposure, the COPE factors. A brief description of each one follows, as they are used in rating.

1. Construction. A basic consideration in rating and underwriting is the construction of the building insured or containing the property insured. Various types of materials may be used, such as wood, stucco, steel, cement and so forth. These materials may be grouped into such classifications as fire-resistive, semi-fire-resistive and combustible. The type of roofing material is also important and the various materials are grouped into two classes: approved and unapproved.

Other less obvious factors may enter into the construction consideration, too. One of these is the number of fire divisions in the building — that is, the extent the building is divided into sections with proper partitions restricting the spread of fire. Another is the degree to which the building may have been remodeled or converted for an occupancy different than that for which it was built originally. Remodeling and conversion often result in false ceilings, open spaces, inadequate electrical circuits and other hazards. These factors are of vital interest in the selection of risks, as well as in rating.

2. Occupancy. The use of a building, and the type of business within it, constitute the occupancy. Multiple occupancies are common in commercial buildings, so the underwriter and rater must identify all occupancies. Many considerations enter into the occupancy factor. The type of operations performed are critical; inherent hazards exist in such operations as spray painting, cooking, furniture refinishing and the handling of flammable liquids and gases. The materials being used are important. Some materials are more flammable than others, meaning that they are more likely to burn. Others are more susceptible to damage by smoke or water which is used to extinguish a fire.

Smoking, cooking, air conditioning equipment, heating, woodworking, and many other potential hazards of occupancies also must be considered. Even a vacant building has its hazards; while those caused by people and operations in other occupancies are not present, the unique hazards of vacancy do exist.

3. Protection. Prevention, detection and extinguishment of fires is the concern of the protection factor. Public protection refers to the public fire department, plus such factors as water supply, code requirements and police departments. Private protextion involves automatic sprinkler alarms, watchman services, portable extinguishers, chemical systems and many other means of preventing, detecting and extinguishing fires.

4. Exposure. The chance of loss from an outside source is called the exposure. The outside source may be from another building, from grass or brush in fields, from railroads, or from many other exterior exposures. An exposure may also be presented from other occupancies in the building, so a great deal of information must be secured about such occupancies. In addition, the degree of exposure is important, involving the questions of distance between risks, fire divisions (with fire walls, fire doors and other protective features), openings through stair wells and air ducts, and all other factors which could prevent or contribute to the spread of fire. The degree to which the outside sources expose the risk to loss is important, therefore, in underwriting and rating.

These four COPE factors are used by the rating bureaus in establishing specific rates for each location. The rates are computed by the application of rating schedules — a function performed by the bureaus. So far as rates are concerned, a commercial fire underwriter need only know the factors which are taken into consideration for information and guidance; an underwriter does not have to know the mechanics of computing the rates.

Specific rates are published and arranged by street address. The rate pages contain notations identifying the COPE factors, so an underwriter can get a brief indication of the most important items. The detailed pages which identify the characteristics and show the rate computations are available upon request from the bureaus. Thus the rating information is helpful to underwriters, but these factors are not used by underwriters in classifying and rating risks. Rather, any rater or coder can locate the address of the risk and determine the applicable rate, whether for building or personal property.

However, some classes are rated by tables instead of by specific location. These are the classes which have a greater degree of homogeneity than most commercial risks. State rules vary, but in many states, as high as 50% of the commercial risks may be class rated. This often includes apartments, churches, service stations, and mercantile risks which contain not over 5,000 square feet and are not over three stories in height.

New buildings, and occupancies which have changed, are rated by tariffs. These are lists of charges which are made for certain rating factors. By tariff rating a risk, an underwriter can determine a reasonably accurate rate which may be used until the rating engineers have had an opportunity to determine the proper specific rate.

Commercial fire rates are customarily given as annual rates for each $100 of insurance written. Although underwriters do not compute rates, no commercial fire risk should be underwritten without a consideration of the rate. A relatively high rate indicates that there may be problems needing investigation. A relatively low rate may be a problem if it is too low, especially on risks require reinsurance, because there may not be enough premium to cover expenses and still have enough to pay inevitable infrequent losses. Underwriters must know the average rate for the protection, occupancy and other factors of the risk before they can determine whether a particular rate is high or low. Experience is invaluable in this regard.

Coinsurance

Coinsurance is an important factor in rating commercial fire insurance. A coinsurance clause, also called an average clause in some jurisdictions, is a device used to encourage more insurance to value. Most fire losses are small so an applicant could insure only a small percentage of the values and secure coverage in full for most losses. Underwriters usually have a rule that they will not accept a risk which is insured for less than 50% to value. But often, it is difficult to ascertain the actual value, particularly on equipment and stock.

With a coinsurance clause, an applicant who will agree to carry a fixed percentage to value will receive a substantial reduction in rate. A common percentage is 80, although others may be used. An 80% coinsurance clause means that if the property is covered by at least 80% to value at the time of the loss, the loss will be paid in full, up to the policy limits. If there is a deficiency, the policyholder will share in every loss in the percentage that the coverage was deficient.

A coinsurance clause is a valuable rating device which reduces the premium for an applicant who complies with its requirements. Whether such a clause is used or not is unimportant to the underwriter, unless there appears to be a deficiency. In this case, good public relations requires the underwriter to question the applicant and producer carefully before writing a policy with an apparent coinsurance penalty. Sometimes an error in valuation will be found, while a misunderstanding will be uncovered in other cases. Under some circumstances, deliberate underinsurance may be permitted, but these cases are rare.

After all of these computations, the bureau rate is determined. Ordinarily computations are different for building, personal property, and each of the other coverages. (Some companies then apply a deviation, which is a percentage reduction in the rate. It is not uncommon to use a deviation only on certain classes of types of risks.) The final rate for the company then is multiplied by the amount of insurance for that coverage in order to obtain the premium amount.

Bureau fire rates are prepared by means of applying a complicated rating formula. Adjustments are seldom made on the basis of loss experience in commercial fire insurance. Rather, corrections are made in some of the factors as the risks with those factors develop good or bad loss ratios. Past experience is a guide, but fire rates are not developed on a completely statistical basis. The rating structure is too complex, using specific rates developed under a schedule system, to be able to supply a statistical support for each rate. Thus, the approach used is to modify some of the rating items in the schedule on a judgment basis.

Few companies prepare their own rates for commercial fire insurance. Some do so for specific classes, particularly those subject to table rating. The engineering analysis required on each risk in order to determine the correct rate is so time-consuming and costly that the only practical appraoch is to consolidate this function through a rating bureau. The fire rating bureaus perform this function for most companies, while special rating organizations furnish rates for some companies on specified risks, such as large manufacturing plants which may have unusual factors present.

Some commercial fire risks have difficulty in securing fire insurance because the rates appear to underwriters to be inadequate. These situations usually arise because changes in certain classes appear to increase the hazard but have not yet entered into the rating. A few companies use "negative deviations" under which they use bureau rates with a percentage increase. More of these hard-to-place risks find coverage in the surplus line market, which is composed of companies and producers operating under rather strict state regulations. Most of these companies are not admitted carriers in the states, and are able to write at higher rates when conditions justify these actions. Most states, however, require certification that the normal market will not write the business and they impose a special tax on these premiums. Even so, the non-admitted market is more flexible than the rather rigid domestic market, both in rates and in contracts which may be tailored to the needs of some clients.

Consent To Rate

Another technique used in some states is "consent to rate" laws. These are specific provisions under which companies may write risks at rates that are higher than bureau rates, thus avoiding the necessity of placing the risk with a surplus line market and still furnish insurance. The requirements are rather strict, requiring a signed form by the applicant agreeing to the higher rate, a statement by the producer that a market cannot be found at regular rates, and approval by the state insurance department of each rate proposed to be used under this program. This technique was adopted in the 1960s in an effort to make insurance available to those risks which have had difficulty in securing coverage. It also is a valuable tool to the underwriter who wants to write an applicant but feels that the rate is inadequate for the exposure.

POLICY FORMS

Commercial fire insurance is written by almost every company on the same standardized forms. The standard fire policy itself is prescribed by law or regulation in most states and the forms and endorsements are promulgated by bureaus and are used almost universally.

The forms are uniform for most companies, too. There are two reasons this uniformity exists in commercial fire insurance. One is the fact that few companies write enough coverage, or at least enough different classes of coverage, to enable them to be able to prepare satisfactory forms. The other reason, even more important, is that many risks are so large that two or more companies often share in writing the insurance and concurrency requires that the policies be identical. If policy provisions are not the same, the apportionment provision in the policy provides that each company will pay only its pro rata share, leaving uninsured any amount not covered by one of the policies. A few specialty companies or pools might issue their own forms. Otherwise there is no competition on policy forms among commercial fire insurers.

The basic commercial fire form is the building and personal property form. It adds no perils, but defines the property, gives some extensions of coverage, inserts some exclusions and specifies limitations.

Under the simplified-language commercial forms program of ISO, separate forms are added to show the policy conditions, the covered Causes of Loss, Business Income Coverage, and other additional coverages. Previous programs used the approach of adding endorsements for more perils, such as the extended coverage endorsement and the vandalism and malicious mischief endorsement, plus other endorsements for added coverages. A declarations form contains information on the address, description and amount of insurance.

Endorsements containing warranties are used on commercial fire insurance policies. These are agreements under which the insured contracts to the truthfulness or existence of certain conditions and facts which are essential to the validityy of the policy. Automatic sprinkler warranties limit the right of the policyholder to turn off the sprinklers. Watchman warranties provide that the insured will maintain a watchman service. Cleaning fluid warranties specify the types of fluids that may be used by a dry cleaner. Warranties of these types are used on many risks. The underwriter accepts the application on the assumption that these conditions will be met, and uses warranties to be sure that circumstances will not change to the insurer's detriment. Each such warranty is printed or typed on a form which the underwriter uses.

Other forms contain clauses which may limit the amount of recovery following a loss, under certain conditions. The most common is the coinsurance clause, which was explained previously. Another is the stipulated value (agreed amount) clause, in which the underwriter agrees with the policyholder that the amount of insurance on the policy does indeed meet the requirements on the coinsurance clause. Obviously, this clause would be used only when the underwriter is certain, by means of an appraisal or otherwise, that the amount of coverage does equal or exceed the required amount. Still another is a distribution clause, spreading the insurance over all locations operated by the insured. This clause is used when coverage is written on a blanket basis to cover several locations, and its purpose is to assure the underwriter that adequate coverage is carried at each location.

Deductibles are used on most commercial fire policies. Their adoption was slower than in many other lines, but deductibles are now common on all perils. One reason for their popularity is the reduction in premium which they can offer. A more important reason is the desire of underwriters to avoid the expense of small claims.

Thus, the principal use of deductibles is as an underwriting tool, although it is common to apply deductibles to all risks of a given class, and then to provide that they can be removed only with the permission of the underwriter and the payment of additional premium.

RETENTION AND REINSURANCE

Commercial fire underwriters are the largest users of reinsurance among all underwriters, as a general rule. Values of commercial risks are so great, and the chance for huge losses is so ever-present, that a majority of the risks are reinsured in one manner or another.

The underwriter must determine how much of the exposure to retain, on an individual risk basis. This is done in order to assure a profitable operation and to avoid the shock of large losses. There are two concepts which must be understood: line limits and block limits.

Line Limits

Line limits are the maximum amounts which may be retained at any one location. Each company determines its line limits which may vary by construction, occupancy or protection. A basic rule is that the total exposure must be considered. This is the total amount of insurance that could be involved in a single loss, including buildings, personal property and such extras as business interruption. Each location is considered separately. At one location, all property which predictably would be involved within one loss is totalled. Where there is more than one building on a lot, the construction of each and the distance between them are considered by the underwriter in making the decision on whether both should be counted as one location or not. Each fire division is considered as a separate location; the term "fire division" has specific meaning, including only divisions of a buidling having unbroken walls of approved fire wall material, or if pierced, equipped and self-closing, approved fire doors.

Block Limits

Block limits are the maximum exposures an insurer is willing to assume within any one city block. The usual practice is to mark, on some reference material, the amount of retention at each location. When these aggregate the limit within a block, no more coverage may be written in that block. The amount of the block limit is usually set by the company and administered by the underwriter who may find it most efficient to enter the amount of each policy on the maps used to secure information about each risk. Another method is to indicate each policy on the rate pages, to use line cards, which are small index cards used to record such items as the policyholder's name and address, the type of occupancy and the amount of insurance; if these cards are filed by location, block totals may be gathered easily. Any method may be used, but the underwriter is charged with the responsibility of not exceeding these block limits.

When a risk is presented which exceeds the line limit, or which would push the exposure above the block limit, the underwriter must take steps to avoid coverage above the limit. The easiest step, in many cases, is simply to offer writing only the amount the underwriter can absorb, and let the producer place the balance with one or more other carriers. This approach is commonly used in commercial fire insurance.

However, when an applicant insists upon only one policy, or the producer cannot place a portion of the coverage elsewhere, the underwriter who wants to write a part of the line must write it all and then reinsure the rest. Some companies have established reciprocal provisions under which they will accept a portion, called a cession, from others; the result is the same as if each had directly insured a portion of the lines. More often, the underwriter reinsures the extra coverage with a professional reinsurer. Companies usually are given surplus treaties under which the primary underwriter is permitted to bind the reinsurer up to agreed limits, usually a multiple of the amount retained. Above that amount, or in its place if no treaty exists, the underwriter must apply to the reinsurer on a facultative basis, with the reinsurer having the opportunity to accept or decline the cession.

Under any of these types of reinsuring a portion of the risk, the reinsurers share with the primary carrier on a pro rata basis. The net effect is the same as though several carriers issued policies on a risk. Each company gets its pro rata share of the premium and pays the same share of expenses and losses. This is the common, traditional method of handling large lines of commercial fire insurance.

In recent years, some fire reinsurance has been placed on an excess basis. For various reasons, a reinsurer does not want to share on a pro rata basis; the principal reason being that a rate may be inadequate for the exposure. The excess reinsurer, in this case, will stipulate a rate or premium which it demands for its excess share, and the primary carrier must use the balance to pay its part of the losses. Under this arrangement, the reinsurer is not involved in any loss which does not exceed the retention and pays only in excess of the retention on larger losses.

There are two terms the underwriter must know in order to handle line limits, block limits and reinsurance: PML and Per Cent Subject. PML stands for "Probable Maximum Loss," which is an estimate of the largest loss which is expected to occur. It is always expressed as a percentage of the property. The underwriter applies judgment to determine the estimate of the largest expected loss, taking into account such factors as construction, distance between building, fire divisions and type of protection. "Per Cent Subject" is an abbreviation for "percentage of risk subject to one loss." All property at each location is considered, so a single location would be 100% subject. In using these terms, the underwriter uses PML unless his company's rules specify otherwise because PML is the greatest probable loss and represents the best judgment of the underwriter, while per cent subject is merely a mathematical determination of the greatest possible loss. (Most line and block limits and retentions for reinsurance, use PML.)

Catastrophe reinsurance is used to protect the company against conflagrations; windstorms or other catastrophes. The reinsurance is always written on an excess of loss basis. Most companies combine commercial fire catastrophe reinsurance with treaties used for other lines, such as personal fire. The underwriter ordinarily has little control over the treaties, because they are arranged by the staff. But the amount retained by the underwriter on each risk will have an effect on the recoveries and thus, ultimately, the cost of the reinsurance. In addition, the underwriter can affect reinsurance by the type of risks written, their dispersion and the coverages written.

QUESTIONS FOR DISCUSSION

1. Explain how personal property is insured under a commercial fire policy, and why different coverages may be used.
2. Why do commercial businesses insure against consequential losses? What types are available?
3. Are vacant commercial buildings considered to be more or less hazardous than those which are occupied? Why?
4. List 4 occupancies which are often considered to be more hazardous than the average, and explain the reasons.
5. Explain 3 sources of information which are available to the commercial fire underwriter but not to the personal fire underwriter.
6. List and explain the COPE factors used in classifying and rating commercial fire risks.
7. (a) Differentiate between line limits and block limits.
   (b) Define PML and Per Cent Subject.

25

Personal Crime

Every person has some personal property that can be taken away by a theft or other crime. Since there is less chance of this occurring for many people than having the property damaged by a fire, less personal crime insurance is written than person fire insurance. Still, the hazard is there, and insurance is needed to protect against loss. Personal crime insurance is strictly a property type of insurance which protects a person against loss of, or damage to, personal property by theft, burglary or robbery.

PERSONAL CRIME COVERAGE GROUPS

There are three different classifications of insurance used to protect personal property against crime losses. They developed through the evolution of insurance in the United States. The only reason for the different approaches is the historical background under which they grew. A very brief description of these three groups is as follows:

Personal crime policies, particularly the broad form personal theft policy are classified as casualty insurance, although they cover only property. The coverage is always on a named peril basis and includes only the crime perils and may be covered on a blanket basis or scheduled basis. (These coverages are described later in this chapter under the section entitled "Personal Crime.")

Inland marine policies, such as the personal property floater and the personal articles floater are classified as inland marine insurance, and they cover only property. The coverage is usually on an all risks basis but some policies use the named peril approach. All of these policies cover other perils in addition to crime; fire perils are usually included, and most policies include at least as much coverage as broad form fire policy on personal property. Some policies also cover on a blanket basis while still others require a scheduling of the property to be covered. (These policies are described in Chapter 27.)

Dwelling package policies are simply composed of one of the two previous policies, lifted intact and placed in the package, along with coverage on the dwelling building, contents, and comprehensive personal liability insurance. Most package policies, including the bureau homeowners policy, use the broad form personal theft policy as the contents portion. However, some independent package policies use inland marine policies as the base for the personal property, usually a named peril policy. (These policies are discussed in Chapter 35.)

The crime coverages which are the subject of this chapter are sold in a limited volume. Never one of the leading volume classes in the property-casualty field, they did enjoy a fair growth after World War II until the late 1950s. Then the homeowners policies swept the nation, and sales of the separate crime coverages decreased rapidly. There are still some policies sold, but the principal reason for analyzing the underwriting factors now is to be able to build a solid understanding of the line in order to handle dwelling package policies more intelligently. By far the bulk of these coverages are found in the package field.

CRIME COVERAGE DEFINITIONS

Essential to an understanding of crime coverages is knowledge of the meanings of certain terms. While the terms are often used interchangeably by laymen, they have different meanings and, since some policies cover only one or two of these terms, the underwriter should have a working knowledge of them. The following definitions apply to all policies insuring against crime perils.

Burglary—involves the felonious taking of property from within a building or room by actual force or violence, of which there are visible marks made upon the exterior of the premises.

Robbery—involves the felonious or forcible taking of property of another by violence or threat of violence. The popular term is "hold-up" but this is not used in insurance policies.

Theft—involves any act of stealing. It includes burglary and robbery, and is broad enough to mean any unlawful taking of property without the consent of the owner. The legal term meaning the same thing is "larceny."

Mysterious disappearance—concerns the vanishing of property by means which are unknown or puzzling. If the owner knows how the property disappeared, such as a watch dropping into a lake from a boat, the loss is not covered under this peril. Gradually, there are three requirements for coverage: (1) the place from which the property disappeared must be certain; (2) the time during which it disappeared must be certain and reasonably limited; and (3) the loss must be puzzling and inexplicable. Property which is simply lost or mislaid is not covered under this peril. Mysterious disappearance coverage is generally considered as an extension of the theft peril, although it has evolved into a separate peril.[1]

Blanket coverage—is concerned with all items of property covered under one amount. The full amount of the insurance applies to any property covered, with no requirement that any item of property be described in the policy.

Specific coverage or scheduled coverage—involves separately listing each item of property (or described in a schedule) with a separate amount of insurance applicable to each article.

DESCRIPTION OF COVERAGES

There are only two policies of the personal crime type in general use. One is the broad form personal theft policy, formerly called a residence and outside theft policy, and the other is known as a personal theft policy (limited form).

Brief knowledge of the coverages is necessary for an understanding of the selection and rating factors. The policies are quite standard, being prepared by a bureau and with few modifications made by independent insurers.

Broad Form Personal Theft

Personal property owned by the policyholder or members of the family is covered under the broad form personal theft policy. The premises must be of the residential-type, but incidental office occupancies are permitted, such as a doctor's office in the home. The term "premises" includes the dwelling, garage and any other private structure on the premises.

Coverage A: Deals with property at the described premises and also property in a bank or safe deposit company, and in an occupied dwelling not owned by or rented to the insured, where the property has been placed for safekeeping. This is the basic coverage of the policy; without at least $1,000 insurance under Coverage A, no coverage may be written under Coverage B.

Coverage B: Deals with property away from the described premises, anywhere in the world. All personal property is covered, except property pertaining to the business, profession or occupation of the insured. Property is covered anywhere except in any other residential premises owned by, occupied by, or rented to the insured with the exception that coverage does apply at premises where the insured is temporarily residing. This coverage is optional; when written, it is a separate section from Coverage A and requires an additional premium. It is not an extension of Coverage A; in fact, there is no overlapping, and coverage may apply only under one section or the other, never both.

Perils covered: Both coverages (A and B) protect against theft or attempted theft,

---

1. For a comprehensive discussion of Mysterious Disappearance, see *The fire, Casualty and Surety Bulletins,* Casualty and Surety Volume Burglary Tab, Pm-pages (Cincinnati: The National Underwriter Company).

including burglary, robbery and mysterious disappearance. Not covered is mysterious disappearance of a precious or semi-precious stone from a ring or other setting. Also included under Coverage A is damage to the interior of the residence building, and damge to the property in the residence, caused by theft, vandalism or malicious mischief.

Blanket coverage: Most insurance on these policies is written on a blanket basis, covering all personal property for one amount. Limitations of coverage are placed on money and securities (usually $100 and $500, respectively). Excluded is property specifically insured elsewhere and property not owned by the insured.

Specific coverage: It is possible to schedule property — having a separate amount of insurance apply to the scheduled items. All insured property can be scheduled, or some can be scheduled and the rest insured on a blanket basis. Most scheduled property must be fully described in the policy; an exception is a collection of coins, stamps, or silverware, which may be covered as a collection.

Divided coverage: It is also permissible to divide the property into two groups under Coverage A. One section includes unscheduled target items, such as jewelry, watches, furs, precious and semi-precious stones and articles of gold and platinum. The other section is for all other property. It is important to note that neither section contains scheduled items; this is blanket coverage which is divided into two broad classes.

Personal Theft (Limited Form)

The description of the insured personal property and the premises is the same as under personal theft as it is for broad form personal theft coverage. There is only one coverage, applying both on and off premises, world-wide. However, jewelry and furs are not covered under the item applying to other property on a blanket basis, so a separate item is used; the coverage may be blanket or specific.

The perils covered are theft, burglary and robbery, but not mysterious disappearance. Damage to the interior of the buildings is covered if caused by theft or attempted theft. Vandalism and malicious mischief damage to personal property is covered within the building or away from the premises.

Limitations of coverage are the same as under the broad form personal theft policy. In addition, boats are not covered. Theft of property from an unattended automobile away from the premises is excluded, unless there is visible evidence of forcible entry into the automobile and losses are not covered to property in a dormitory or in a fraternity or sorority house.

This policy is somewhat more limited than the broad form and is much less common. It is the broad form which is used in the homeowners policy, and that is where most personal theft coverage is written today.

UNDERWRITING FACTORS

Acceptable Risks

Although personal crime insurance is almost never written alone, there are very few circumstances under which an insurer would write such a policy without having other coverages for the applicant; the few exceptions would be to accommodate an influential producer or client.

The reason that this coverage is written only in connection with other coverages is that crime insurance has become a high loss line. The increase of all types of crimes has caused an astronomical increase in losses under theft insurance. Policies covering only theft perils became unprofitable.

In order to help offset this poor experience, insurers generally require other coverages to be written for the applicant. The usual requirement is for fire insurance on the dwelling and personal property, since this is closely related. However, it is also desirable to have other policies, such as automobile and comprehensive personal insurance in the personal lines and any available commercial coverages. The most common means of handling this requirement is to write a homeowners policy, which includes fire, theft, and CPL, all as integral parts of the policy.

For these reasons, insurers do not think of acceptable risks for personal crime coverages alone. Rather, the acceptability list is twofold: First, applicants who have other policies with the insurer; and second, applicants who are acceptable for other coverages. Thus, the acceptability risks for other policies tend to determine the acceptability for crime insurance.

There is little competition for personal crime coverages because of the adverse loss experience. Most insurers write at, or near, bureau rates. Some may even deviate, but not much, and then only because they generally write all insurance at deviated rates and because they hope to attract customers for other lines.

Unacceptable Risks

Underwriters of personal crime coverages must be extremely careful in the applicants they accept. The borderline between a profitable and an unprofitable risk is narrowly defined and hard to identify. To guide producers and the underwriters, rather lengthy unacceptable lists are used by most insurers.

Personal crime insurance has become unprofitable because of the increase in thefts and other criminal acts, as was mentioned in the previous section. That, alone, would cause cautious underwriting and carefully drawn unacceptable lists. However, there is a much deeper reason for careful underwriting. This is the inherent problem of writing a type of insurance which has the following adverse characteristics.

1. The moral hazard is greater than in any other type of insurance. A loss is difficult to prove, because there are no charred remains as there is from a fire, no damaged automobile as there is from a collision, no injured body as there is from a fall. The property is gone, often without any visible evidence that a crime has occurred.[2]

2.The problem has been well stated thus: "A basic principle of inland marine underwriting is that a risk of poor moral hazard cannot be insured at any price. In addition, corrective actions usually have little effect in such cases." (The theft exposure is identical between inland marine and personal crime coverages.) S.S. Huebner and Kenneth Black Jr., *Property Insurance,* p. 356. 4th Ed. New York: Appleton-Century-Crofts, 1957.

2. The applicants most likely to have a loss are the ones who apply for protection. This is true of all insurance, of course, but there are leveling factors in many lines. The state's financial responsibility laws almost force every responsible driver to carry automobile insurance; the mortgagee or lessee insists that the borrower maintain fire insurance; the state laws require employers to purchase workers' compensation insurance. No such compulsion exists for crime insurance, and the result is that this line has the smallest proportion of potential risks actually insured as compared to any other major line of insurance. This is adverse selection at its worst.

3. A large proportion of the insured property is highly mobile and easily concealed. In addition, many of the items are relatively quite valuable. Because of these facts, it is quite easy to present a questionable claim. An underwriter has enough troubles without trying to control a line which inevitably will have suspicious losses.

4. The definitions of losses covered under the policies are extremely broad. This is particularly true with policies covering mysterious disappearance as a named peril.

5. Underinsurance is an even greater problem than for fire insurance. After all, it is not impossible, though unlikely, that a building and its contents will be totally destroyed by fire. But theft of the entire contents of a home, including all personal property is extremely rare. For this reason, most applicants are interested in purchasing on a minimum amount of insurance. There is no coinsurance clause on most crime policies and none on personal crime, so the incentive for full coverage on many fire policies is absent here. Because most applicants tend to purchase low amounts of coverage, the premium for each $1,000 of insurance must be quite high. This, in turn, discourages future applicants from buying more than the minimum amounts, thus perpetuating a poor condition.

Faced with these problems the underwriter of personal crime insurance tends to be cautious. A list of applicants who are considered unacceptable is usually prepared. The list differs by insurers, but usually include the following characteristics.

Target Risks. Some applicants are in a class that are considered targets for thieves. Prominent in this class are wealthy persons and celebrities. A well-planned burglary or robbery often nets a sizable amount of plunder. Homes situated in isolated areas are also target risks, particularly if there is some evidence of affluence. Not only are these target risks considered unacceptable because the expected frequency of losses is high, but they are also a problem because they often have high values in property which are easily taken. Jewelry, furs and sterling silver are so much a characteristic of this class that they are called "target items" in the parlance of underwriters. When the potential for both frequency and severity of loss is high, the applicant must be considered unacceptable.

Hazardous Occupations. There are a number of unacceptable occupations which are less glamorous than the movie stars, politicians and millionaires who are considered as target risks. Some of these other occupations offer a great exposure to loss because of the travel connected with them. In some cases, this is simply the result of expensive clothing that a salesperson must carry in order to make a good impression, and is highly susceptible to theft. In other cases, display cases and samples are carried, and the concentration of values in portable goods makes a tempting target for a burglar in a hotel or a thief in a parking lot. In still other cases, a salesperson who lives alone, or who takes the family along on the business trips, increases the exposure to a burglary loss of the property left in the home.

On a completely different tack, other occupations are unacceptable because they offer increased exposures to loss for other reasons. Many of these are people who drift in their work. Examples are race track employees, agricultural workers and circus performers. Other occupations that are undesirable because of frequent shifting of jobs are waiters, bellhops, bartenders and professional entertainers.

Home and Neighborhood Undesirable. Many of the factors which are important in fire insurance underwriting are also important in crime underwriting. This is logical, since both lines insure property; the principal difference is in the perils covered. A home that is poorly maintained, has an unkept yard, or is used for illegal purposes give evidence that the occupant has little regard for property. An owner who will not take care of the real property, probably will not protect personal belongings. An important key to preventing crime losses is to make it difficult for the thief to commit a crime, so the underwriters must consider, as unacceptable, any applicant who gives evidence of not trying to protect the property.

In similar vein, a home in a deteriorating neighborhood makes a poor prospect for crime insurance. When people show little regard for keeping their area neat and clean, they usually have little respect for property rights. Deteriorating neighborhoods are often high-crime areas. When this is the case, the underwriter will consider unacceptable, those applicants living in such areas.

Responsibility Lacking. Persons demonstrating lack of responsibility toward others are unacceptable for crime insurance. Those with criminal records and those who use alcohol or drugs to excess can be considered to be persons in such a category.

Previous Losses. An applicant who has suffered previous crime losses is ordinarily considered unacceptable for crime insurance. This does not mean that an underwriter never accepts such applicants; it means that the producer should submit the application to the underwriter before writing the insurance, together with all facts about the losses. The underwriter will look carefully at the circumstances. If there was only one loss and it was uninsured, the underwriter may conclude that the victim was moved by that occurrence to seek insurance or to listen to the sales approach of the producer. In such cases, the underwriter might accept the risk if the circumstances surrounding the loss does not indicate a likelihood of a repetition. On the other hand, a series of losses generally indicates that the applicant is in a target position or does not take care of the property, or both. This person is unacceptable until the circumstanes are changed drastically. An example might be when losses were caused by a neighborhood band of thieves, and the applicant had moved to another city.

Risk Not Solicited. An applicant is generally unacceptable who has not been solicited for the insurance by the producer, but instead has come to the producer for coverage. As was explained earlier in this section, most people who could use crime insurance do not buy it. The ones who do apply are those who consider that they are likely to have a loss. There are exceptions, of course, but as a starting point, one who asks for crime insurance is unacceptable. This is particularly true if the applicant carries no other insurance with the company, and this is one of the reasons that "related business" is almost a prerequisite for many insurers.

SECURING INFORMATION

The first step in underwriting any line of insurance is to determine whether the applicant is acceptable. In crime insurance, this is a rather formidable step, because the unacceptable list is fairly long in the percentage of applicants it names; without other insurance in the company, many applicants simply are not acceptable.

The next step is to secure as much information as possible about the applicants who appear to be acceptable, and in some cases, those who do not. A good underwriter of crime insurance will be curious, even suspicious, of every applicant, but will also give careful consideration even to the most unlikely looking prospect. The basic tool with which to gather the information is the application. Other sources are used for more details.

Application

A signed application is required by almost all crime insurance underwriters. It contains statements which must be answered and the underwriter relies upon those statements. However, the application is not actually made a part of the policy. The application differs greatly among insurers. Generally the questions cover approximately the same subjects and can be classified into three major categories.

1. Personal
2. Description of property
3. Insurance information

The information requested under each of these categories normally includes the following for most insurers.

1. *Personal.*
   A. Full name of the applicant.
   B. Mailing address of the applicant.
   C. The location of the property, including specific information if the mailing address is a post office box or otherwise is not specific in describing the location.
   D. Marital status of the applicant.
   E. Age and occupation of applicant and spouse. Also, whether or not the applicant travels in the performance of the duties of the occupation, and if so, how often and by what means of transportation.
   F. Stability factors, such as home ownership, how long the applicant has lived at this address, how long with the present employer, and how many jobs in the previous period, perhaps five years.
   G. Previous crime losses suffered by the applicant during the previous period, such as five years.
2. *Description of Property*
   A. Building description: Number of buildings on the premises, number of family units if an apartment, construction, type of roof and siding, age and size of the building, and information whether the applicant owns or leases the premises.
   B. Personal property: Total value of all personal property, value at each location if more than one is described, and descriptions including values of all target items (jewelry,

watches, sterling silver, and furs) over a stated amount such as $500 per item.

C. Security information: Whether the premises is in a developed area or not; any protective devices on the premises; and if an apartment, whether maid service is furnished.

3. *Insurance Information*

A. Coverage desired, the limits for both blanket and scheduled items, deductibles and the requested effective date.
B. Complete descriptions of all scheduled property.
C. Information about the previous insurer: Name of the insurer, policy number, type of coverage, whether the insurer cancelled the policy or denied renewal.
D. Any business pursuits on the premises, and number of roomers or boarders.
E. Name and address of a loss payee or other holder of lien such as a chattel mortgage. (The underwriter of crime insurance may be interested in this information although it is of primary importance to the policy issuance clerk.)
F. Description of other insurance on the personal property.

Inspection Report

The underwriter of crime insurance depends heavily on inspection reports by outside companies. These inspection companies generally are the same ones who furnish reports on other personal lines, such as for automobile and fire insurance.

Easily, the most important reason for reports concerning applications for crime insurance is to check on the moral hazard. This is such an important part of crime underwriting, as was mentioned before, that an underwriter having the slightest suspicion of a moral hazard must do everything reasonable to determine the facts. A good report will describe previous losses, comment upon the income and living habits of the applicant, verify the existence and condition of the property, and give information about friends and associates of the applicant. Any suspicious or borderline aspects should be developed fully.

The financial condition of the applicant is an important part of an inspection report. Naturally, the information desired is not merely the apparent financial status, but also the actual condition. The credit rating of the applicant may be an important factor, and thus the term "credit reports" for these inspection reports is more applicable than under many other lines of insurance.

The physical condition of the premises is ordinarily of secondary interest to the crime underwriter. If any obvious defects are present, or if the preoprty is in a rundown condition, this is of interest, of course, These are the obvious factors, however, that any reasonably well-trained inspector can find and report. An engineer would seldom be used for personal crime reports because the physical hazards are usually much less important than the moral hazards. There would be exceptions, such as in a home with a high concentration of values and some protective services such as vaults and alarms. A loss prevention specialist may be able to recommend improvements, and can report to the underwriter on the effectiveness of the devices.

Experience of Other Insurers

Crime underwriters tend to exchange information more than most underwriters, with the exception of automobile insurance applicants. The frequency of crime losses is relatively low, so an underwriter is anxious to learn if an applicant has presented claims to the prior insurer. The usual procedure is for an underwriter to send a letter, usually a form letter, requesting information about prior losses. The underwriter for the prior carrier ordinarily can merely enter the information on the letter and return it.

Obviously, this practice is followed only with insurers that reciprocate. In spite of its value to underwriters, it really is not a common practice, and is done on a small minority of applications. It can be a valuable tool when it can be used.

CLASSIFICATION AND RATING

Personal crime policies employ several classifications factors. These are needed for allocating amounts of insurance and for rating. There are several steps needed to arrive at the rate, and they are similar between the two policies.

Broad Form Personal Theft

Allocation of insurance: The broad form personal theft policy has several possible alternatives under which the property can be covered, as was explained earlier in this chapter. The lowest rate applies to scheduled property. The next high rate applies to divided coverage, with a portion of the insurance applying to target items and the balance to all other property. The highest rate is for full blanket coverage.

The applicant, in conjunction with the producer, decides upon the allocation of insurance desired. The underwriter normally accepts the requested allocation if he or she accepts the risk. However, there may be cases which will require a different allocation as a prerequisite to acceptance. Insurance to value is a problem in crime insurance as it is in other types of property insurance. The underwriter may require a different distribution of the insurance if this will result in better insurance to value. As an example, consider an applicant who possesses $10,000 of jewelry and furs and $10,000 of other personal property; if this owner believes that any crime loss will involve only one of these groups, he or she can purchase blanket coverage of $10,000 and be protected against any loss. The underwriter may well feel that the increased rate for blanket coverage is not sufficient to offset the fact that there is only 50% insurance to value. In such a case, the underwriter could require that divided coverage be applied, thus being much more certain to get insurance closer to 100% of value.

Occupancy: Most rates use two classes of occupancy. One is for dwellings and small apartments having one through four family units. The other classification is for multiple-occupancy buildings of five units or more.

Territory: Large territorial classifications are used, many of them containing two or more complete states. Thus, the territorial variations in hazard are recognized roughly, but with much less refinement than is found in most other lines of personal insurance.

Amount of Insurance: Rates are provided in tables, for each $1,000 of insurance. The highest rate applies to the first $1,000. Rates for additional amounts are reduced in steps, with the lowest rate usually applying to each $1,000 over $5,000 of insurance. Three rate schedules are given for each territory: One for divided coverage (with the same rates applying to both sections), another for blanket coverage, and a third for specific coverage. Coverage B premiums are given separately from Coverage A, and are usually lower. Only two rate schedules are needed because divided coverage is not available for the off-premises coverage.

Personal Theft (Limited Form)

Allocation of insurance: The limited form has only two classifications under which insurance is allocated. The first is blanket coverage. As previously explained, one part of the blanket coverage may be used to cover jewelry and furs, and the other part used for all other property. The second classification of insurance concerns specific insurance.

Underwriting of the limited form is less concerned with the allocation of insurance than under the broad form. Target items (jewelry and furs) are not covered unless an amount of insurance is applied under either the blanket or scheduled sections.

Occupancy: The same classes of occupancy are used for the limited form as the broad form.

Territory: The same territories are used for both forms.

Amount of Insurance: Rates per $1,000 are given in tables. The amounts of insurance under the blanket coverage are added together in order to determine the amount of insurance to be applied to the rate table. For example, a policy with $3,000 blanket on jewelry and furs, and $5,000 on other property, would have $8,000 insurance. The rates are reduced for large amounts, as under the broad form. Specific insurance is rated at the next level on the table above the blanket amount; in the example just given, if $1,000 specific coverage were written, it would take the rate applicable between $8,000 and $9,000.

POLICY FORMS

Personal crime coverages are fairly uniform among insurers. There is no prescribed policy other than that promulgated by the rating bureau. And, while, some independent policies are used, there are few important variations in the basic printed policies.

Underwriters have some latitutde in endorsing policies to fit particular situations. One type of endorsement is designed to increase the coverage, with an additional premium. By this practice, policy limitations of $100 on money and $500 on securities may be increased.

Other endorsements limit coverage. Some of these are available as a means of reducing premium, as well as helping to correct a frequency of small losses. Deductibles are the best example of these. Another is to delete all perils except burglary, thus removing the coverage away from the premises, as well as other perils on the premises. Other restrictions are used by underwriters to avoid unwanted exposures. A limitation may be placed on target items, and a business trip exclusion may be used to avoid exposure while the policyholder is traveling away from home on business. The endorsements to accomplish these changes are fairly standard. However the underwriter occasionally drafts a special endorsement to fit a unique situation.

RETENTION AND REINSURANCE

A large percentage of personal crime policies are written for quite low amounts of insurance, such as $5,000 or $10,000. On these policies, underwriters are not concerned about the exposure to large losses, they retain the entire exposure without question.

However some personal crime policies protect high values of property. On these, underwriters want to limit their exposure. This is accomplished by securing reinsurance to protect the insurer above a stated amount. It is not customary in personal crime insurance for several insurers to cover the property of one applicant, although this is possible. It is much more common for an underwriter to accept the entire exposure and then to pass along to the reinsurer, a portion of the risk. The reinsurance may be on an excess basis or on a pro rata basis, such as with a surplus treaty. The reinsurance is usually combined with other lines, such as commercial crime, so the personal crime policies tend to follow the pattern used by the insurer.

Underwriters seldom worry about catastrophe losses on personal crime insurance. Still, a multiple policy loss is possible, such as by a burglary of a number of safe deposit boxes in a bank or vault. Catastrophe reinsurance is usually combined with other lines because the minimum premium would prohibit a treaty for personal crime alone. Thus, the retention and protection is ordinarily determined by lines and more premium and greater exposure.

QUESTIONS FOR DISCUSSIONS

1. State the perils covered by (a) personal crime policies, and (b) personal inland marine policies. Which approach is used in dwelling package policies?
2. (a) Differentiate between burglary and robbery.
   (b) How does mysterious disappearance coverage compare with theft coverage?
3. In what ways do blanket coverage and specific coverage differ?
4. Explain 3 characteristics which might make an applicant not acceptable for personal crime insurance.
5. Why might an underwriter not accept an applicant who had come to the producer for coverage?

26

Commercial Crime

Every business is exposed to loss by theft or other crime, in much the same fashion as individuals are exposed. Commercial crime insurance is more widely sold than personal crime coverages, but still there is less crime protection sold than fire protection. Most commercial crime policies protect an insured's property against loss or damage by such crime perils as theft, burglary and robbery.

COMMERCIAL CRIME COVERAGE GROUPS

The same general classifications of insurance protection against crime losses are found in commercial lines as in personal lines.

Commercial Crime Policies. There are many different types of policies included within this category which are classified as casualty insurance. (These policies are discussed in this chapter.)

Inland Marine Policies. There are also many types of policies covering commercial risks that are classified in this category of inland marine. Some are all risks while others are on a named peril basis. Most of them cover many perils other than theft and can be written on a blanket or scheduled basis. These policies are described in Chapter 28.

Commercial Package Policies. Crime coverages are not an integral part of most package policies; in that respect, commercial and personal packages differ. However, much crime insurance may be added using the same forms as are used for commercial crime or commercial inland marine coverages. (These policies are discussed in Chapter 36, entitled "Commercial Lines Package Policies.")

DESCRIPTION OF COVERAGES

Many different commercial crime policies are offered, actually numbering in the dozens. They cover the gamut of businesses to be protected and perils to be covered. Classification of this myriad collection of policies could be approached in several ways, but a logical grouping is to use the following three classes, the first being a class of property and the other two, types of occupancies.

1. Money and securities.
2. Mercantile risks.
3. Special occupancies.

A brief description of the most popular policies written in each class (prior to the simplified-language commercial crime program of ISO) will give an idea of the scope of coverages within commercial crime insurance. Traditional names for the coverages are used; the simplified-language crime program of ISO replaces many of these names with "Plans" and "Coverages," under the modular concept, but some of the former names are used, and it will probably be many years before the familiar terms are dropped. The terminology may change periodically, but the general types of coverages are these.[1]

Money, Securities and Records.

Money and Securities Broad Form — This offers protection against destruction, disappearance or wrongful abstraction of money and securities both on the premises and while being conveyed by a messenger off the premises. It also covers other property taken by a burglar from a safe, loss to cash registers and cash drawers by theft and damage to the premises by a burglary or attempted burglary. Each insured location may be scheduled or a blanket coverage may be written to cover all locations of the policyholder.

Money and Securities Destruction — This coverage differs from the money and securities broad form in one respect: the money and securities destruction policy covers only loss caused by destruction, not by theft or disappearance. Both cover destruction by the perils of fire, flood, windstorm, riot and others.

Paymaster Robbery — Protection is given to money and checks intended for payroll purposes taken by robbery from a custodian engaged in regular duties in connection with the payroll. Damage to furniture and other property is also included, as is kidnapping of the custodian. For an additional premium, the more comprehensive paymaster broad form policy may be written, covering all risks of destruction, disappearance or unlawful taking of money and checks.

Combination Crime — This policy, formerly called "Comprehensive Dishonesty, Disappearance and Destruction" ("Comprehensive 3D") is a broad policy that permits the combining of several separate coverages. These coverages are: (1) Employee dishonesty, much like a commercial blanket bond or blanket position bond; (2) Coverage inside premises, including the protection of the money and securities broad form and the safe burglary form; (3) Coverage outside of the premises, taken from the custody of a messenger; (4) Money orders and counterfeit paper currency coverage, applying to such property taken in good faith in exchange for mer-

1. A summary of the different ways the simplified language crime coverage forms can be used to approximate the coverage of particular crime policies in the previous crime program may be found on the B-pages of the Crime tab in the Casualty and Surety Volume of the *FC&S Bulletins,* (Cincinnati: The National Underwriter Company).

chandise; and (5) Depositors forgery coverage, corresponding to the coverage given under a depositor's forgery bond.[2] In addition, it is permissible to add other coverages, such as burglary of stocks of merchandise and office equipment, Policies can be written with separate limits applicable to each part, or a single limit per occurrence.

Mercantile Risks

Mercantile Open Stock Burglary — Coverage is provided against loss of merchandise, as well as furniture, fixtures and equipment from within the premises by burglary, attempted burglary, or robbery of a watchman. This is not a theft policy, since it covers only while the premises are not open for business; however, theft coverage may be added for additional premium, subject to a deductible and with no coverage for mysterious disappearance. A coinsurance clause is used which varies by territory and type of merchandise, and a schedule may be used, with separate amounts at each location, or blanket coverage may be applied to any location.

Mercantile Robbery — This policy covers money, securities and other property by robbery or attempted robbery. There are two coverages that can be written separately, one inside the premises and the other outside. The inside coverage also applies to damage to the premises by an actual or attempted robbery. The outside coverage applies while the property is in the custody of a messenger. A special provision is made for service stations because the employees may be robbed while they are outside of the building; the entire premises are covered under the inside coverage section for an additional premium that is less than insuring each employee under the outside coverage.

Mercantile Safe Burglary — Money and securities, as well as other property, are covered against loss by burglary from within a safe or vault. Only described safes or vaults are covered, they must be located within the premises, and they must have been closed and locked by all combination and time locks with which they are equipped. The property must be taken by force or violence leaving visible evidence on the exterior of the safe or vault. In addition to money and securities, other types of property are covered, but they must be locked in the safe or vault. This is not a stock burglary coverage, nor does it apply to valuable papers or accounts receivable.

Storekeepers Burglary and Robbery — Small and medium-sized stores seldom purchase the other types of commercial crime insurance because the minimum premiums for each coverage are too high. To offset the problem, this policy was devised, and has become the most popular of the burglary and robbery forms. It covers seven different items: (1) inside robbery of money, securities, merchandise and equipment; (2) outside robbery of money, securities and merchandise; (3) kidnapping after the premises are closed for business; (4) safe burglary; (5) burglary from a night depository or the home of a custodian; (6) open stock burglary with a $50 limit on jewelry and tobacco; and (7) property damage by burglary or robbery. The same amount

2. Bond coverages mentioned in this chapter are described in greater detail in Chapter 31.

of insurance applies to each item and may be as low as $250.

Broad Form Storekeepers Policy — Small and medium-sized stores may purchase this policy, instead, which covers considerably more than the storekeepers burglary and robbery policy. It is similar to the latter in offering relatively low amounts of insurance ($250 minimum) which is applicable to each item. However, the policy is more like the 3 D policy in scope of coverage. There are nine separate coverages with the principal coverages going beyond the storekeepers burglary and robbery policy. These are employee dishonesty, depositors' forgery, and counterfeit money coverage. Employee dishonesty coverage protects against any fraudulent or dishonest act committed by an employee who takes money, securities, merchandise or other property. Depositors forgery covers outgoing instruments such as checks and promissory notes against forgery or alteration. Counterfeit money coverage protects against loss resulting from the acceptance, in good faith, of money orders and counterfeit paper money.

Special Occupancies

Banks — There are two policies designed for banks and other financial institutions. One is a combination safe depository policy having two parts. The first part protects the liability of the financial institution for loss of a customer's property left in a safety deposit box. This coverage is really a liability insurance, but it is handled by a commercial underwriter because of its similarity to crime policies. The second part of the combination safe depository policy has two sections. One covers loss to a customer's property by burglary or robbery or damage by other perils. The other section covers damage to the premises by burglary, robbery, vandalism or malicious mischief. This second part is not a liability-type of coverage, since it pays regardless of fault. Few financial institutions purchase this second part.

The other policy designed for financial institutions is actually offered to the customers themselves. A person who deposits valuables in a safety deposit box can secure all risks coverage or just burglary and robbery protection.

Office Burglary and Robbery — This policy is very similar to the storekeeper burglary and robbery policy. The only important difference is that the office form covers theft or property used in an office rather than stocks of merchandise.

Churches and Fraternal Societies — Policies are available to cover money, securities, and other property against loss by burglary, robbery, theft and larceny. More limited forms cover only money and securities. Coverage applies to loss within the premises, within a night depository, in the custody of a messenger, and damage to the premises by a burglary or theft.

Innkeepers Liability — This policy covers the legal liability because of injury to, or loss of, property belonging to guests while the property is on the premises or in the possession of the innkeeper. While this is a liability coverage, the greatest hazard is from crime, so the policy is traditionally handled by a crime underwriter.

Warehouseman's Liability — Like the innkeepers liability policy, this covers the legal liability of the policyholder for property or others in his or her care. It is also handled by crime underwriters.

UNDERWRITING FACTORS

Acceptable Risks

Commercial crime insurance, like personal crime insurance, is seldom written alone. Most insurers require either an actual policy in another line or a promise that such a policy will be written upon expiration, before accepting a crime application.

Commercial crime losses have increased tremendously in recent years, which explains the reluctance of insurers to offer insurance against these losses for many types of businesses.

Other commercial insurance is often a prerequisite to writing crime insurance. Fire, liability, automobile, workers' compensation — any or all of these help to make the underwriter more inclined to accept the crime exposure. Thus, the acceptability lists of these other lines would tend to determine the acceptability of commercial crime. Many insurers consider crime coverages as accommodation business, and do not actively seek to write this insurance, or at least not without supporting business.

Since there is little competition, there is little rate cutting in commercial crime lines. Rates are fairly standard among all insurers. Virtually the only deviations are by companies that deviate on all business they write.

Unacceptable Risks

Commercial crime underwriters face most of the problems of their personal crime counterparts. Both use rather lengthy unacceptable lists in an attempt to improve selections.

Moral hazard is a major problem; it is not difficult for a dishonest policyholder to present all of the proper evidence of a crime to a business risk. The firms that consider that they are most likely to have a loss are generally the only ones most interested in buying the insurance. Much of the property has high concentration of values and is easy to conceal or to sell to others because the risks most likely to buy crime insurance are those dealing in jewelry, furs, tobacco and the like. Many of the policies are quite broad, and underinsurance is a constant problem. Any applicant is considered as being unacceptable if personal habits, character and moral standing are not above reproach.

The underwriter of crime coverages in commercial lines, as in personal lines, tends to use unacceptable lists that are quite long. Most of these lists include the following subjects.

Location and Neighborhood. Burglaries and robberies occur more frequently in some neighborhoods than others. Where these high-crime areas are too small to be rated for the exposure, an underwriter will avoid writing crime insurance there.

Police Protection. The quality of policy protection differs between areas. Since good police protection is a deterrent to crime, those areas with low quality protection are considered unacceptable for crime insurance by many insurers.

Business Reputation. Because of the extreme moral hazard in commercial crime insurance, any applicant with a poor or questionable business reputation must be considered unacceptable. Related items might also appear on the list, such as the associates of the applicant and the types of business conducted by neighbors and associates.

Previous Experience. An important factor is the past loss experience of the applicant and the past insurance experience. Some businesses appear to be targets for criminals, and no underwriter wants to write such a risk without careful consideration. A poor loss experience would make an applicant unacceptable. In the same fashion, a risk which had been cancelled by another insurer is probably susceptible to loss or is uncooperative, and either reason is sufficient cause for placing any applicant who was cancelled or rejected by another insurer on unacceptable lists.

Insurance Values. An applicant is usually unacceptable if the insurance values are out of line with the apparent needs. If values are too low, perhaps the business is operating on a shoestring, or perhaps is just trying to underinsure. If the values are too high, this raises suspicion that some unrevealed operations are being conducted on the premises. The chance of loss on commercial crime insurance is so great that an underwriter must take all steps to write average risks, not unusual risks.

Protective Devices. Many devices can be used to protect against crime. Not only are these helpful in preventing losses, but they are also indications of the attitude of the owner toward the handling of the property. Some people feel that the existence of an insurance policy removes any obligation on their part to take precautions against loss. An underwriter will usually consider as unacceptable, those applicants who do not have at least the minimum protective devices. In robbery insurance, this may include pushbutton alarms which a guard can trip to send a signal to a central station, a bandit-resistive enclosure, or an armored car for carrying cash. In stock burglary insurance, the requirements may be cylinder-type dead bolts for all doors, bars on all off-street doors and windows, burglar alarms, and guards on duty during all hours that the business is not open. In safe burglary insurance, the type and amount of property insured may call for various classifications of safes, both as to fire resistance and burglar resistance; on many unacceptable lists are safes that can be carried away by burglars. The underwriter will try to reduce, by means of the unacceptable list, those risks with a higher-than-average probability of loss attributable to easy access to the premises, flimsy structures, and a lack of available protective devices.

Susceptibility to Loss. There are a number of other factors that make property more susceptible to loss. Some of the items often appearing on acceptable lists are these: applicants, particularly those wishing to insure stocks of goods, who do not have adequate bookkeeping systems and thus may have difficulty in preparing complete reports following a loss. Applicants whose buildings are poorly constructed or maintained, or are not sprinklered (for some coverages). Applicants for warehouseman's liability whose buildings have entrances and exits which are not controlled entirely from inside the building, or whose warehouses are not fireproof or bonded. Applicants who do not exercise proper precautions in the handling of money, both while the premises are open for business and when they are closed.

Hazardous Occupancies. Most unacceptable lists for commercial crime insurance contain many specific occupancies. These can be grouped into the following categories.

- Occupancies where the public has relatively free access to the property, such as coin-operated laundries, arcades, parking lots and refreshment stands.
- Occupancies visited by a questionable or transient-type of client, such as pool halls, dance halls, bowling alleys, gambling places, taverns and saloons.
- Occupancies which present an extraordinary target for robbery of money, such as banks, finance companies, check cashing offices, liquor stores, motels and hotels, fairs, utility bill collection offices, restaurants, food markets and taxicab companies.
- Occupancies which present an unusual target for burglary of property, such as antique and art dealers, liquor stores, furriers, jewelers and gem dealers, drug stores, wig shops, radio and television shops, sport shops, tire stores and pawnbrokers.

SECURING INFORMATION

Commercial crime underwriters use lengthy unacceptable lists as the first step in determining acceptability. It is obvious from the comments concerning unacceptable risks that there are many factors about which the underwriter will be concerned.

The first step in gathering the information for analysis is securing a completed application. Other sources are used freely, too.

Application

As with personal crime insurance, a signed application is required by many commercial crime underwriters because the application contains vital information about the applicant. While the underwriter relies on the statements, the application is not attached as part of the policy.

In actual practice, most insurers use several applications for commercial crime coverages because different policies require different information. It is customary to group several related policies on one application; obviously some insurers would decide on different groups than others, so the format of the applications varies considerably among insurers. The information is fairly uniform, however, and can be classified into three major categories.

1. Personal
2. Description of premises and property
3. Insurance information

Under each of these categories, the following information would be requested by most insurers.

1. *Personal*

A. Full name of the applicant, including the firm name, if any.
B. The structure of the firm, whether an individual, partnership or corporation.
C. Business address and mailing address of the applicant.
D. Location of all premises owned or occupied by the applicant.
E. The number of years that the applicant has been in business.

F. Product handled by the applicant.
G. Details of all losses of the types covered by the policy applied for during the previous period, such as five years.

2. *Description of Premises and Property*

A. Description of the building occupied by the applicant, including construction, whether sprinklered or not, the fire protection available, and exposures by other occupancies in the building or in adjacent buildings. In addition, the amount of floor space occupied by the applicant in the building, and its location in the building.
B. Information about the potential ease of entrance, the floor upon which the applicant is located, whether all windows are barred, the types of locks on doors and windows and if the building is well-lighted at night.
C. Neighborhood information, such as its general characterisitics, types of business, and whether it is declining, steady, or improving. Sometimes the underwriter may want to know if the risk is on a main highway leading out of the city, since this could provide ready escape to a criminal.
D. The hours and days that the business is open.
E. Preventative and warning systems, such as the existence and types of burglar alarms, any guard system and the police protection available.
F. Number of employees, including the number in each job classification for some policies.
G. The type of account books kept, as well as other records which could facilitate the settlement of a loss.
H. If cash is covered by the policy, the number and types of cash registers.
I. If safe burglary is covered, complete descriptions, rating, date of purchase and original cost of each safe.
J. If custodian coverage is included the numbers and descriptions of the property ordinarily in their possession.
K. If comprehensive 3D coverage is desired, details about audits employee classifications, the countersignature system and the verification of bank accounts.
L. If valuable papers coverage is requested, complete descriptions of all valuable papers, including their values by groups. Information concerning the maintenance of duplicate copies of the papers. Also a complete description of the safe or vault in which the papers are kept when the premises are not open for business.
M. If accounts receivable coverage is to be written, a complete description of the safe or vault in which the records are kept when not in use: the manufacturer, the class of safe and the rating shown on the label, and information on whom issued the label. In addition, the underwriter will want to know the estimated percentage of uncollectible accounts to the total accounts receivable for each of the past three or five years, as well as financial data which will indicate the solvency of the applicant.

3. *Insurance Information*

A. The policy and coverages desired, specifying limits, deductibles, and other optional factors and the requested effective date.
B. Information about the previous insurer, and a complete explanation if any previous insurer ever cancelled, declined or refused renewal on commercial crime insurance.
C. Description of any other crime insurance on the property.
D. Details if any employee has ever committed a fraudulent or dishonest act in the service of the applicant or any other employer.

Inspection Reports

Commercial crime underwriters often use reports from inspection companies. There are many possibilities of loss, and also many protective devices available, so it is important to know as much as possible about each applicant.

Since moral hazard is a major consideration, one of the most popular reports is that which relates the apparent business standing of the applicant. Various companies used to inspect risks, give reports on credit ratings, and investigate current financial standings. Some of these companies can also give some information about the physical conditions at the applicant's business.

The importance of the physical factors cannot be overemphasized. It is essential to know about the layout of the store or business, the types of protective devices used, the rules which are used to protect property, the degree to which these devices are actually used and the rules followed. Company inspectors or loss prevention specialists are often used to develop this information; these may be the same people who handle other commercial lines also, such as trucks, liability and fire. These persons can report on conditions which could affect the desirability of the risk.

Almost as important, loss prevention specialists can recommend improvements and help to secure their adoption. These improvements can be in the area of physical factors, such as better locks, new alarms and other detecting devices, and other ideas which are seldom known to an average business owner. On the other hand, the recommendations may be in procedures, such as better ways to handle cash, tighter controls on inventories, and other programs that are also strange to the uninitiated, but which may help a great deal in preventing crime losses. The loss prevention specialist may merely recommend improvements and let the underwriter and producer attempt to secure compliance by the applicant, or may take an active part in getting adoption of the recommendations.

Experience of Other Insurers

Commercial crime underwriters, like those who handle personal crime, tend to exchange information about the past loss history of applicants more than in many other lines. Past losses given such important clues to exposures to future loss, and to the protection of property that this becomes an important item of information.

The problem of exchanging experience in commercial crime insurance is in the mechanics. It is often difficult to locate the needed records. Other than that, there is a fairly free exchange of information with no reluctance to share experience.

CLASSIFICATION AND RATING

Many types of commercial crime insurance require classification before the rate can be determined. In these cases, the classification is also important to the underwriter. As the latter gathers information about the applicant, the various classification factors are applied. These guide as the requirements for each risk are verified, such as safe warranties and coinsurance clauses.

Even in those types of policies when special classification is not needed, the underwriter performs a classification and takes the rate and premium into consideration. These rating factors and price determinations are very important to crime underwriters.

Steps in Rating

The first step in rating some types of commercial crime insurance is to determine the classification. This means the trade group in mercantile coverages: open stock, robbery, safe burglary, and the storekeepers burglary and robbery. Each policy uses its own trade group (such as discount houses, drug stores, dry cleaners, etc.); the lists are different for each policy. The classification for safe burglary coverages deals with construction classification of the safe, based upon the thickness and construction of the door and walls, the burglar-resistive factors used, and the type of occupancy.

The base rates for these policies are determined from tables, using the classifications established. Other policies used different methods of determining base rates: per messenger for paymaster robbery; number of employees in each category for comprehensive 3 D; a percentage of the 100% coinsurance fire contents rate for valuable papers and accounts receivable coverages (usually 150% and 40% respectively); per number of apartments or bedrooms for innkeepers liability; and simply per location for church insurance. All commercial crime rates are given per $1,000 of insurance, and the rate per $1,000 is lower as the amount of coverage is increased, for many coverages. The gross premium is determined by multiplying the rate by the amount of insurance.

Territorial multipliers are then used for most types of commercial crime insurance in order to measure the differences in various parts of the country. These multipliers are different for each type of policy.

Discounts and surcharges are applied next. These modifiers are used more in commercial crime insurance than in any other line. Some of the discounts are for push button alarms connected with a central station, automatic alarms with central station or outside bell, bandit resistant enclosures, approved messenger bags, armored cars or guards for conveying property, businesses open 24 hours per day, tear gas systems on safes, guard services with various provisions for types of reporting, barred windows, and special locks on doors and windows. Surcharges are used for such factors as robbery from a janitor, and the exclusion of forcible entry on the mercantile open stock burglary policy.

Some policies are other rules that affect rating. For example, the 3D policy has extra charges for additional locations under the employee dishonesty coverage, and different rates are used for blanket and specific coverage under the church policy.

The net result of all of these computations is the final premium. The underwriter considers the amount of the premium in determining if the application is acceptable; the insurer will want to receive sufficient premium to cover the estimate of loss potential. All lines are subject to experience and schedule rating, if further adjustments are desired.

POLICY FORMS

Most insurers use policy forms that are quite similar whether insurers use bureau forms or independent forms. Crime policies, unlike the majority of property and casualty policies, include definitions of the perils covered. Burglary, robbery, and theft are usually defined, and the courts have upheld the right of insurers to use definitions differing in some respects from statutory definitions.

Underwriters use endorsements in modifying some of the policy provisions to fit various situations and needs. Deductibles are often used, both to reduce exposure to losses and to decrease premiums; in fact, the prevalence of petty theft and shoplifting make deductibles almost a necessity on money and stock under many coverages. The amount of the deductibles can range from $50 to as high as $1,000 or more.

Other endorsements are used in modifying coverages to meet the desires of applicants. Mercantile robbery coverage can be endorsed to cover a custodian in the home. Vandalism and malicious mischief protection can be added to a mercantile open stock burglary policy. Fire coverages may be excluded if this action avoids an overlap of coverage. As a matter of practice, most policies automatically exclude the peril of fire, because it is almost always covered under a fire policy.

Perhaps the greatest use for endorsements is to assure that high standards of protection are maintained. Among the requirements are alarms, barred windows, better safes, and improved procedures for handling cash and merchandise. Indeed, crime losses have increased so greatly that some applicants are finding that they cannot buy crime insurance at any price, unless they take major steps to protect their property against loss.

RETENTION AND REINSURANCE

Commercial crime underwriters recognize the possibility of large losses. They protect against this exposure by securing reinsurance treaties.

It is not common in crime insurance for several insurers to share a line. Rather, an underwriter will write the entire amount and reinsure a portion of it. The reinsurance is usually on an excess basis, although pro rata treaties are sometimes used. Unless an insurer writes a large volume of crime insurance, it ordinarily combines the reinsurance with other lines, perhaps with personal crime and fire insurance.

Catastrophe losses are seldom a concern to the commercial crime underwriter. However, to protect against the slight possibility of a crime involving several policyholders in one event, it is customary to write the excess reinsurance policy to cover a single occurrence, whether one location or several.

QUESTIONS FOR DISCUSSION

1. List the 3 major types of protection given by the Money and Securities Broad Form Policy.
2. Describe the coverage under a Paymaster Robbery Policy.
3. Differentiate between Valuable Papers coverage and Accounts Receivable protection.
4. List the basic coverages under a Comprehensive 3D Policy.

5. What types of property are protected under (a) Mercantile Open Stock Burglary, and (b) Mercantile Robbery?
6. Why would liability policies, such as Innkeepers Liability and Warehouseman's Liability, be handled by crime underwriters?
7. Describe the types of protection devices used to protect against crime.
8. Why are deductibles considered almost a necessity under many types of Commercial Crime Coverages?

27

Personal Inland Marine

Inland marine insurance is a relatively recent line of coverage and one of the hardest to define. It developed from extensions of ocean marine insurance to cover inland transportation risks. As more coverages were needed, policies were extended to apply to personal property under many situations. Since fire and casualty companies were prohibited by law from expanding into other lines they could not offer the variety of coverages needed. The marine companies were not restricted in this fashion, so they developed many new types of policies. After a period of conflict and uncertainty, agreements were reached on the property and perils that could be classified as inland marine.

Most inland marine policies cover a multitude of perils, either on a named peril or all risks approach. Only personal property may be insured — any coverage to buildings is incidental, except such structures as bridges, tunnels, piers, wharves, pipelines, radio and television towers, antenna and cranes. Policies are written either on a scheduled or blanket basis. Some inland marine forms are uncontrolled, leaving a great deal of discretion in the hands of the underwriter.

Personal inland marine insurance, however, is quite firmly defined. Policies, rates and forms are fairly uniform for all insurers. Unlike personal crime policies, there are many different policies available which together amount to substantial volumes of premium.

The development of homeowners package policies has reduced the volume of blanket personal inland marine insurance sold, because most personal property coverage is now written in package forms. On the other hand, package policies have greatly increased the awareness on the part of the public for the need of personal property insurance, particularly against crime perils. Since package policies offer limited coverage for certain property, the popularity of scheduled policies has increased. Although these scheduled policies may be written separately, they may be added to package policies also, but they remain separate inland marine policies even when they are physically attached to package policies.

Virtually all personal inland marine policies cover the same as a fire and extended coverage policy, plus theft, burglary, robbery and transportation perils. Some cover on an "all risks" basis, with the usual exclusions being wear and tear, breakage of fragile articles, mechanical breakdown, marring and scratching, dampness of atmosphere, extremes of temperature, damage by insects or vermin, and refinishing or repairing processes.

DESCRIPTION OF COVERAGES

There are three broad classes of policies.

1. Blanket policies
2. Scheduled policies
3. Boat policies

The term "floater" is used with each of these classes, except boats. This is one of the confusing terms which is used by inland marine underwriters. To a layman, the only property described in this chapter which "floats" is a boat, but this is not the terminology used by the trade. Rather, the term "floater" refers to a policy covering property wherever it is located. In a manner of speaking, the insurance "floats" along with the property. A common misconception is that coverage needs to be worldwide in order for the policy to be called a "floater;" some cover only in the United States and Canada. It is required, however, that property be of a type which is transported with relative ease and is not limited to a fixed location in order for the term "floater" to be used. The latter distinction is necessary because certain fixed property can be insured under inland marine insurance. (In Chapter 28 such commercial property as neon signs and bridges are described as insurable under inland marine policies.)

The types of coverages classified as inland marine are specified in the Nationwide Marine Definition which was published by the National Association of Insurance Commissioners in 1953. This definition has been revised several times since then, including a new Definition in 1976, and has been adopted in most states. Interpretive bulletins are issued occasionally by a special organization called the "committee on interpretation," clarifying specific cases which are not clearly within or outside of the definition. Within the broad bounds of these rules, a large number of policies are issued, covering many types of property. The most common policies in each of these personal inland marine classes are described briefly as follows.

Blanket Policies

Personal Effects—The only property covered is personal effects such as are usually carried by tourists and travelers, including luggage, clothing, toilet articles and the other items usually taken by a person on a trip, all on a blanket basis. Excluded are tickets, money, passports, and merchandise. Coverage is all risks, with a limitation on property stolen from an unattended automobile, unless the automobile is fully enclosed and locked. A limitation of $100 per article and 10% of the coverage applies to target items.

This policy is quite limited in the property which is included. Coverage applies only while away from the domicile, although a separate extension is available to cover there also. Relatively few of these policies are sold. The common name for this policy is the personal effects floater. It was formerly known as the transit floater and is still sometimes referred to by that name.

Travel Baggage — This is a limited form of a personal effects coverage which is on a named peril basis — including loss by fire, lightning, transportation perils including the stranding or sinking of a boat, collision while in an automobile, and theft from a hotel room or a common carrier. This is a very limited policy and is sold in conjunction with travel accident insurance mostly by travel agencies.

Personal Property Floater (PPF) — Under this "all-risks" policy, all nonbusiness personal property is covered, "owned, used or worn by the insured and members of the insured's family of the same household." Coverage extends to the dwelling if the damage is caused by theft, and to the interior of the dwelling if caused by vandalism or malicious mischief. Limitations apply to unscheduled target items, stamps, coins, money, and securities. Scheduling is permitted under the same terms as the scheduled policies described later. Coverage applies world-wide, with a limitation on property ordinarily situated throughout the year at residences other than the principal residence of the insured.

This very broad policy was developed in the 1930s and eventually became the leading personal inland marine policy from the standpoint of premium volume. Until the advent of package policies, it was the favorite personal property policy other than fire insurance. The PPF was adopted as the personal property coverage of the best and most expensive of the package policies, thus continuing its role as the "top of the line" coverage. Today, then, PPF is written principally for condominium and apartment dwellers.

Householders Protective Policies — Bureaus and insurers have developed these policies bearing different names but are generally similar. They cover the same property as the PPF. Coverage, however, is on a named peril basis, insuring against loss by fire, lightning, extended coverage perils, vandalism and malicious mischief, water damage, burglary and robbery. Some policies also cover against theft, many of them with mysterious disappearance covered under a presumption of theft. Limitations are similar to those of the PPF, but scheduling is not generally permitted. Coverage applies world-wide with the same restriction on property in secondary dwellings as the PPF.

These policies enjoyed a brief period of popularity in the 1950s, but were generally replaced by homeowners dwelling package policies. Some independent package policies used the limited householder forms as the personal property coverage, rather than the broad form personal theft policy of the casualty field which was used in most packages.

Personal Articles Floaters (PAF) — This is a policy on which particular classes of valuable personal property may be scheduled. Each of the classes described below may be written on the PAF, either as a separate inland marine policy or as an addition to a homeowners policy. This combined form is a convenient alternative to the use of a number of separate policies, and has become the principal contract now used to insure personal property on a scheduled, "all-risks" basis.

Scheduled Policies

Jewelry — Property which may be covered under a scheduled policy includes personal jewelry, watches, rings and the like, but not silverware or plated ware; such items as pens, pencils, flasks, cigarette cases and trophies may be insured. Precious stones may be covered when used for personal adornment; loose stones are not considered to be "jewelry." Coverage is written on an "all risks" basis with the usual exclusions. Valuation is on an actual cash value basis unless specifically provided that the value for each item is agreed upon and valued coverage is issued. Many jewelry policies are on a valued basis. Each item is scheduled and no blanket coverage is extended. Coverage applies world-wide.

Furs — This policy covers furs and garments trimmed with fur or consisting principally of furs. Coverage is on an all risks basis, while valuation is usually on the basis of actual cash value. Each item must be scheduled except that ensembles (such as a matching coat and hat) may be blanketed. Coverage is world-wide.

Cameras and Projectors — All types of personal cameras and projection equipment may be covered, on an all risks basis. Valuation is ordinarily made on the basis of actual cash value; seldom will an underwriter agree to pay a stated amount under a valued policy, preferring to apply depreciation in order to control the moral and morale hazards. Each item must be described and insured separately, except that small items (such as carrying cases, holders and filters) may be covered on a blanket basis up to 10% of the total amount of insurance placed on scheduled items. World-wide coverage is provided.

Musical Instruments — Coverage may apply to any type of musical instruments except household instruments not ordinarily taken from the residence, such as radios, television sets, tape recorders and record players. All risks coverage applies and either actual cash value or agreed value applies. All items must be scheduled, except that miscellaneous equipment may be blanketed if it is not over 10% of the total amount of insurance on scheduled items. Also school owned instruments insured in the name of the school board or the municipality may be covered on a blanket basis if the 100% coinsurance clause is used. Coverage is world-wide.

Silverware — Property which may be insured is personal silverware, goldware, pewterware, or platedware, except such items as pens, pencils and flasks which must be covered under a jewelry policy, not a silverware policy. Actual cash value is ordinarily used. Coverage is on a blanket basis; seldom is a schedule employed. Coverage is world-wide.

Fine Arts — This policy covers such articles as paintings, etching, statuary, rare books, manuscript and antique furniture; recognition is given to the fact that such property may have a cash value in excess of its utility value. All risks coverage is provided with a specific exclusion of damage resulting from any repairing, restoration or retouching process; breakage of such fragile articles as porcelain and art glass windows is excluded, unless caused by fire and other specified perils. A valued basis is used because of the difficulty in establishing the value of many articles after they are damaged or destroyed. All items must be scheduled. However, it is permissible to blanket small items up to 10% of the scheduled amount of insurance, and such blanket coverage is on an actual cash value basis. Coverage applies only in the United States and Canada, and does not apply while the property is on exhibition at fair grounds or on the premises of any national or international exposition.

Stamp and Coin Collections — Coverage may apply to two types of property: philatelic, including all types of postage stamps, covers, proofs, etc., and numismatic, including rare and current coins, paper money, medals, coin albums, frames, cards and the like. All risks coverage applies, with special exclusions of damage caused by fading, creasing, scratching, tearing, thinning, dampness, and damage from being worked on or handled. Mysterious disappearance is not covered unless the property is an actual part of a stamp or coin collection. Theft of property from an unattended automobile is excluded, too. Unscheduled property is covered on an actual cash value basis with a maximum amount applicable to any one stamp or coin, and with a 100% coinsurance clause required. Valuable items, such as those with a valuation in excess of $100, should be scheduled with the insurer agreeing to pay the stated amount or to replace the property (but not for more than the amount insured). Coverage is world-wide.

Golfer's Equipment — This policy covers golfing equipment, including golf clothing, other clothing while in the club house lockers, golf clubs, golf bags and related property. All risks coverage is given except that golf balls are protected only against fire and burglary. Actual cash value is used, and only blanket covers is provided. Coverage is world-wide.

Sports Equipment — This policy is designed to cover guns and fishing tackle of individuals; it does not cover golf equipment, photographic equipment, boats, or motors. Coverage is on an all risks basis with various company forms using such exclusions as rust, fouling, mechanical derangement, explosion of guns, breakage of glass or fishing equipment, and damage while being worked on or repaired. All property must be scheduled, and actual cash value is used. World-wide coverage is provided.

Wedding Presents — A special policy is available to cover wedding presents of all types, so the types of property which may be included are broader than under any other policy. All risks coverage is given, and the usual exclusions. Actual cash value is used on blanket coverage, but articles may be scheduled on an agreed-value basis. An 80% coinsurance clause is used, but this can be reduced to 50%, the latter being a more reasonable figure in view of the difficulty in estimating the values of gifts with much accuracy. However, the rates are so low that the minimum premium usually provides an adequate amount of coverage, except for a very large wedding. The policy becomes effective a long time before the wedding. The amount of coverage may be increased as additional gifts are received, too. Protection may start at any time for which application is made, but the wedding date is shown in the policy and coverage ends 90 days afterwards. Coverage is world-wide.

Bicycles — This policy insures only bicycles which are scheduled. The all risks coverage excludes such perils as rust, gradual deterioration and damage while being worked on or reparied. It is not permissible to cover motorbikes or any type of motor-powered conveyance. Either actual cash value or agreed value may be used. A $5 franchise clause is used, under which no claim is paid if the damage is less than that amount and the damage is paid in full if it exceeds that figure. World-wide coverage is given.

Boat Policies

There is no accurate dividing line between the boats covered as inland marine insurance and those considered as ocean marine insurance. Traditionally, inland marine includes rowboats, canoes, outboard motors, and their appurtenances; ocean marine insures inboard motor boats, yachts, and similar boats in which the motor is installed as a part of the boat. This distinction is used by some experts. However, the dinstinction is unclear in actual practice, partly because of the development of such hybrids as inboard-outboard motor boats and partly because of such developments as relatively large boats with powerful outboard motors (sometimes in pairs) and small boats with inboard motors.

Each insurer, therefore, draws its own line. Some insurers use 26 feet in overall length as the dividing line; those under that size are considered inland marine, and those over are consider ocean marine. It is important to make this distinction because large boats travel long distances and encounter situations where the unique, stilted language of the ocean marine policy is necessary for proper protection. (See Chapter 29 for more details on ocean marine insurance.) On the other hand, inland marine forms are more readable and can be handled better in conjunction with travel trailers and other types of vacation property.

Inland marine boat policies can cover not only the boat itself, but also outboard motors, boat accessories and even boat trailers. Three types of coverages are offered by most insurers. Easily the most common is an all risks policy, with such exclusions as wear and tear, weathering, damage by marine life, and theft of equipment which is not permanently attached to the boat. A 100% coinsurance clause usually is mandatory.

The second contract, in order of popularity, is a broad named peril policy. It usually covers fire, lightning, windstorm (but only while the boat is on land), theft of the entire boat or motor, collision or overturning of a transporting land conveyance and perils of the sea.

The third policy, one which is seldom used, is a limited named peril policy. It covers all of the perils of the broad named peril policy except perils of the sea. Thus, it does not cover such losses as sinking, stranding and water collision.

Most inland marine boat policies offer other optional coverages in addition to damage to the boat and its equipment. One of these covers the legal liability of the policyholder for damage to other boats and contents, if the damage is caused by collision with the insured boat while it is afloat. A dollar limitation is used, ordinarily $1,000. This is a liability coverage and includes defense of any suit alleging damage which could be covered. Bodily injury is not covered by this section of the policy, but another section is similar to comprehensive personal insurance covering bodily injury and property damage arising out of the ownership and use of the boat and its covered equipment. However this latter section seldom is sold because most boat owners need the broader protection of a full comprehensive personal insurance policy.

Medical payments coverage may also be included. This pays reasonable medical expenses incurred by accidents arising out of the ownership or use of the boat and equipment, provided the use is with the permission of the policyholder. For an additional premium, guest medical payments coverage may be extended to apply tow water-skiers towed by the boat.

UNDERWRITING FACTORS

Acceptable Risks

Personal inland marine insurance is seldom written alone. There may be underwriters who will accept a boat policy alone, and perhaps a blanket type of policy, but rarely a scheduled policy. Underwriters usually want the broader base which is given by insuring more than one or two articles of property.

These policies, other than boats, have all of the crime hazards that were discussed in Chapter 25 concerning personal crime insurance. In addition, inland marine coverages have many more perils, usually on an all risks basis; while this increases the premium, it also increases the chance of losses.

Underwriters generally require that other policies be written for the applicant in order to spread the exposure. Scheduled articles are seldom written unless the residential fire insurance or homewoners package policy is written, too. Thus, the acceptability list is ordinarily based on that of other lines.

In general, there is not a great deal of competition for personal inland marine lines, by themselves. Some insurers deviate because that is their common practice, but most insurers write at bureau rates.

Unacceptable Risks

Personal inland marine insurance is underwritten very carefully. Because there are so many possibilities of fraudulent losses, lengthy unacceptable lists are used. The major problems are the same as those discussed in Chapter 25 concerning personal crime insurance: moral hazard, adverse selection, property which is both mobile and valuable, broad coverages and underinsurance. Some of these are more applicable than others to some classes. For example, much property covered by a personal property floater is bulky household furniture and appliances, so the underwriter of that policy is less concerned about mobility. Too, many scheduled policies are written only with an appraisal, so underinsurance is seldom a problem.

However, the all risks nature of most personal inland marine policies causes more concern to underwriters. The moral hazard becomes the real problem, and special steps are taken to avoid or control it. In general, underwriters will try to accept only applicants who have adequate financial resources and those of high integrity. Many times they will require either that the producer be personally acquainted with the applicant or that satisfactory references be furnished. Special attention will be given to the background of the applicant, as well as to occupation, source of income, personal habits and financial condition.

Since careful underwriting is needed, the underwriter will seek to avoid undue exposures by publishing rather extensive unacceptable lists. Such lists will contain the following items, for most insurers.

Target Risks. There are many persons who are targets for losses of the types insured by most personal inland marine policies. Burglaries are more common among wealthy persons and celebrities than among the general populace. Thus, such persons may be on unacceptable lists, along with professional entertainers and others who are in the public eye. Even single and divorced people present an increased target for crime losses. The writing of such "target items" as jewelry and furs is handled carefully for all of these classes.

Hazardous Occupations. Certain occupations present great exposures to theft and other perils. Most unacceptable lists, at least for all inland marine coverages except boats, including gambling operators, persons employed in illegal activities and traveling salespersons.

Home and Neighborhood Undesirable. Since most inland marine policies include perils ordinarily included in fire insurance policies, the same maintenance and housekeeping requirements are used. Scheduled property is even more susceptible to improper care of property, and a neighborhood which is above average in exposures; many unacceptable lists show residences in buildings where the primary occupancy is commercial, too.

Responsibility Lacking. Even more than in personal crime insurance, a person who demonstrates a lack of responsibility is unacceptable for personal inland marine insurance. Not only those with criminal records and excessive users of alcohol and drugs are unacceptable, even persons with poor financial ratings are on these lists. An underwriter cannot write an all risks policy for irresponsible persons and still hope to make a profit. Every applicant must be trustworthy, filled with integrity, careful with the property and have little or no moral hazard.

Previous Losses or Cancellations. A person who has suffered a previous loss of the type insured under the policy applied for will be unacceptable, and an underwriter needs a complete explanation of the circumstances before accepting the risk because circumstances which cause one loss may well cause another. The same is true of an applicant who has had this type of insurance cancelled or an application refused by another insurer. These actions indicate the existence of problems which the producer must explain to the underwriter before the risk can be accepted.

Rules for Jewelry. Special unacceptable risks are usually shown for scheduled jewelry. Students not living at home are unacceptable. Mens' rings and accessories are unacceptable, unless the applicant is a substantial individual with other policies placed with the insurer; one of the worst classes of jewelry is a single ring owned by a man because he is apt to remove it daily. Also unacceptable are jewels which are cracked, chipped or with flaws and jewelry needing repair.

Rules for Musical Instruments. Specific unacceptable lists for musical instruments for scheduled coverages are often used. Some of them used by some insurers are instruments owned or used by school children or in dance bands or orchestras, and such instruments as electric guitars, bass fiddles, drums, mikes and amplifiers.

Rules for Sports Equipment. The unacceptable lists for scheduled sports equipment may include gun clubs, unless separate policies are written for each member. Items which are often considered unacceptable are tobogaans, water skis, snow skis, decoys, camping equipment and underwater equipment. Applicants must have unusually good character and good personal habits and be in good financial condition, particularly for equipment with high values.

Rules for Bicycles. Most insurers prohibit bicycles used in professional racing or in delivery or messenger services. Rental bicycles are unacceptable, as are all bicycles with motors. Applicants who live in neighborhoods where the theft hazard is high are unacceptable for this broad coverage, too.

Rules for Boats. Some of the general qualifications, as discussed, also apply to boats. In addition, specific unacceptable lists are generally used. There is great variance among insurers, but many consider the following risks as unacceptable: homemade boats, boats constructed of canvas or of military surplus; hydroplanes, air boats, catamarans, or amphibious craft; racing or experimental boats; epoxy fleck construction (because of the expense in making repairs); boats used in commercial operations; boats not in good condition or not showing careful maintenance; and boats older than 10 years old.

Applicants may be unacceptable if they are under 21, over 70 years of age, or in the military service (unless other business is written in the company, such as their automobiles). Since a poor driver of an automobile will probably be a poor driver of a boat, many insurers consider any applicant who cannot qualify for an automobile insurance policy unacceptable, taking into account such factors as marginal or poor driving record and physical impairments. (The interest of underwriters in high performance automobiles has caused many insurers to be aware of the same problems in boats; some unacceptable lists refer to horsepower-to-length ratios.)

SECURING INFORMATION

In personal inland marine insurance, as in other lines, the first step in underwriting is to determine if the applicant is acceptable or not. This line has a fairly long unacceptable list and many applicants are not acceptable, particularly if they do not have other insurance in the company.

Even among those who appear to be acceptable, the underwriter will be cautious of many. A great deal of information will be needed to satisfy that the applicant is acceptable. Also, of course, additional information may be secured about applicants who appear to be unacceptable, if good reasons are given why such risks should be considered. There are several available sources of information with the application being first in time and in importance.

Application

Almost every personal inland marine underwriter requires a signed application on every risk, since the answers to the questions are very important guides to a final decision. However the application is not made a part of the policy, except for the schedule of approximate values by category under the prsonal property floater, as will be explained. Applications are not standard in any degree, among insurers. However, most of the questions are generally the same and can be classified in these categories.

1. Personal
2. Description of property
3. Insurance information

Typical information requested under each category is as follows.

1. *Personal*

A. Applicant's full name.
B. Applicant's mailing address.
C. Property location, if different from the mailing address.
D. Applicant's marital status.
E. Age and occupation of applicant and spouse, and whether travel is required in connection with his or her occupation.
F. Applicant's stability as reflected in such factors as home ownership, how long at this address and on present job, and number of jobs in a given recent period, such as the past five years.
G. Previous losses of the types covered by the policy applied for, over the past three or five years.

2. *Description of Property*

A. Information about the building: its type (private dwelling, apartment, semi-commercial, hotel, etc.), number of family units if a multiple-unit building, type of roof and siding, age and size of the building, and applicant's status regarding ownership or lease. (On policies where the location exposure is not a major factor, many of these details may be omitted.)
B. Information about security: protective measures such as burglar alarms and safes, status of the neighborhood regarding the degree in which it is built up and whether servants have access to the premises.
C. Blanket policies: the total value of all personal property and target items, and the value of all property ordinarily situated throughout the year at other residences. For the personal property floater, the applicant's estimate of the value of unscheduled property by categories such as clothing, books, rugs, cameras, etc. These are declarations of the applicant and tend to give more information to the underwriter. It also helps to prevent underinsurance. The list is copied and made a part of the policy.
D. *Scheduled policies:* Some special information is needed for these policies.
   (1) Furs and jewelry: If the property is owned or worn by other than the applicant, such details about that person as age, marital status, occupation and relationship to the applicant.
   (2) Cameras and projectors: If the applicant is other than an amateur, details about the use of the equipment.
   (3) Musical instruments: If the instruments are used for other than amateur purposes, or by a young person, details about the use of the instruments and the age of the musician.
   (4) Fine arts: If not specifically made a part of the insurance information, details about where the property is ordinarily situated and facts about any other display or exhibition of the items.
   (5) Guns: If the applicant is a member of a gun club, the name and address of the club.
E. *Boat policies:* Answers to a number of additional questions are required, such as these:
   (1) The general condition of the boat and any existing damage.

(2) Where the boat and equipment are stored when not in use.
(3) Deatils if the boat is used for racing or in commercial enterprises.
(4) The maximum speed of the boat, as well as its length and horsepower.
(5) Descriptions of fire extinguishers, bilge pumps, ship to shore radio, and similar equipment.
(6) Any physical impairment or mental disability of the applicant or any other operator of the boat, and the driving record (of both automobiles and boats) of all operators of the boat, along with date of birth and driver's license number (automobile) so that the record can be verified.

3. *Insurance Information*

A. Coverages and limits of insurance desired, deductibles and the requested effective date.
B. Descriptions of all scheduled property, in detail.
C. Appraisals of all scheduled property over a stated amount, such as $500, of these classes: jewelry, furs and fine arts. These must be current appraisals by reliable dealers or appraisers, and they must be in sufficient detail to permit accurate identification to help recover stolen property, as well as to aid in settling loss. If the property is fairly new, such as under five years, the bill of sale may be used, but this must show the actual price paid for the property. The underwriter must avoid accepting a statement of "insurable value" on property allegedly sold at a "sale price" because the moral hazard is greatly increased if the amount of insurance exceeds the price paid for the property. It makes no difference if the purchaser wants to feel that a bargain price was received or if the property is always sold at the "sale price" and the inflated "insurable value" is a myth; the problem remains any time insurance exceeds the price paid.

The amount of insurance on appraised property is ordinarily the full appraised price, but sometimes insurance is written for less than the appraised amount. Actually the appraisal merely establishes the value of the property, much as cost per square foot is used to establish the value of a dwelling for fire insurance purposes. The underwriter and the applicant (usually through the producer) can agree upon any amount of insurance to be written. Many underwriters insist upon 100% of the appraised value; those who do not, ordinarily want at least 80% to that value.

D. Information about the previous insurer: name of the company, type of policy and amount of insurance, policy number, and whether the previous insurer cancelled the policy or declined to renew.
E. Name and address of any holder of a chattel mortgagee or a loss payee.
F. Description of any other insurance on the property.

Inspection Reports

Personal inland marine underwriters use inspection reports quite freely. They request such reports on many applicants, using the same reporting companies as are used for other personal lines coverages.

The most important factor of concern is the moral hazard. Coverages are so broad, and properties are often so valuable, that all circumstances which could possibly cause an increased moral hazard must be checked carefully. (Personal contact by a trained inspector is the best source of this information.) In addition, the report should comment upon the neighborhood, living habits of the applicant, occupation and business associates and social activities. Another important item is simply verification that the insured property exists; the producer is supposed to see the property, but this is not always done. The worst possible moral hazard is created by an all risks policy on nonexistent but high-valued property.

Closely related to that factor is the financial condition of the applicant, and this should be another area of reporting. As was indicated in the discussion on acceptable risks, applicants with poor financial ratings are not to be written. The factor of responsibility, as indicated by a good financial or credit rating is highly important in writing personal inland marine coverages.

Scarcely less important is the physical condition of the premises. While dwelling buildings are never insured under inland marine policies, their condition gives an important clue to the care of property that the applicant demonstrates. All risks coverage could be highly unprofitable if many policyholders were careless in their handling and maintaining of property. An inspector can also report on physical protection of the insured property, such as safes and alarms. Some insurers use special inspectors or loss prevention specialists to help in the installation and maintenance of such protective devices, for policyholders insuring high values of property.

Experience of Other Insurers

Underwriters of personal information insurance exchange information more freely than in most other lines. It is so important to uncover applicants who fraudulently or otherwise present an abnormal number of claims that it is to the mutual benefit of all underwriters to exchange experience information. This is not to say that it is a common practice, for many insurers do not exchange information, but it is a helpful device when used.

The common practice, when experience is exchanged, is for the underwriter to send a form letter to the previous insurer, for completion since policies differ in their coverages, it is customary to specify the types of policies involved.

Marine Surveys

A boat underwriter has the advantage of the availability of marine surveys. These are detailed reports containing most factors of interest to an underwriter about the boat itself: condition of the boat, condition of the motor, protective devices, seaworthiness, etc. The surveyors are experts in the field and can give a much more detailed and accurate report than most producers.

Marine surveys are seldom used on small boats or outboards, but may be used on the larger boats insured under inland marine policies by some insurers. Their principal use, however, is in the field of yachts, which are ordinarily classified under ocean marine.

CLASSIFICATION AND RATING

Each of the three classes of personal inland marine insurance is classified differently. In each case, the classification is made during the underwriting process, as information is received. Thus classifications are important to underwriting, as well as to rating. Rating is based on class rates, because such coverage is quite homogeneous and a substantial volume of statistics is available. The rating method which is used is different for each of the three major classes.

Blanket Policies

The relatively simple personal effects and travel baggage policies are rated from tables and the only classification needed is to determine the amount of insurance and territory.

The personal property floater is more complicated. The first step in the classification process is to determine the fire insurance contents rate applicable to the location of the principal residence. If the rate is subject to an 80% coinsurance credit, as is the case of many apartments and commercial buildings, the net rate after that credit is used. The next step is to determine the territory because the theft exposure varies by territory. From the territorial table, the "loading" is determined; this loading is the additional premium required for all of the perils except fire. (However, in some territories, where windstorm is a particular hazard, a separate windstorm loading may be used.) The loading decreases as the amount of coverage increases. For example, one rate per $1,000 may apply for the first $5,000 of insurance, a lower rate for the next $10,000, and so forth. The amount of insurance is determined from the statement of values in the declarations; ordinarily, the insurance must be at least 80% of the estimated value.

Householders protective policies are rated much like the personal property floater. The contents fire rate is the base; some insurers use the fire and extended coverage rate or even the broad form rate, depending upon the breadth of the policy. A loading is used, varying by territory, and is reduced for larger amounts. (Scheduled coverages which may be attached to these blanket policies are rated exactly like the separate policies, as described next.)

Scheduled Policies

Most scheduled articles require only classification by territory. Rates are reduced for higher amounts of coverage for most articles. Fine arts is an exception. It is first necessary to get the basic fire rate for contents, so the first step is to classify just as for fire insurance. The flat contents fire rate is used for property located in dwelling buildings, usually with an arbitrary credit of 25% and the 100% contents fire rate for commercial structures. To this basic rate is added a loading from a table with variations by territory.

Boat Policies

The first step in classifying and rating boat insurance is to establish separate values for each class of property: boat, motor, accessories and trailer. Boats and motors, either or both, are usually divided into two classifications by those insurers that consider all boats under 26 feet in length as inland marine insurance. One classification is for boats having a maximum speed under 35 miles per hour, and the other over that figure. Separate rate tables are used for these two classifications.

The next step is to determine the deductible to be used on boats and motors. Then a rate table is used by class and deductible, giving rates per $100 of insurance. Separate tables are used for accessories and trailers, again containing rates per $100 of insurance.

Liability and medical payments coverages are rated differently. Most insurers first divide the boats into two classifications: powered and sailboats. Powered boats are divided by horsepower, and sailboats by length; each class has three or four groups. Thus, there may be six or eight classifications shown in the rate tables for any one territory. Rates are then based on the liability limits desired; many insurers include $500 medical payments coverages with the liability, while others have separate tables. Another table is used for rates that apply to guest medical payments coverage for water skiers, although the market for this coverage is quite restricted; few companies offer it in view of the substantial injuries that can result.

POLICY FORMS

Handling of policy forms is different for each of the three broad classes of personal inland marine insurance.

Blanket Policies

Most blanket policies are written on a scheduled property floater policy. The scheduled property floater is the basic inland marine policy whose provisions are included in most inland marine policies with the exception of boats. This is usually accomplished by adding forms to the skeleton form. Apparently it is one of the peculiarities of inland marine insurance that this policy is called a scheduled property floater although it is used with blanket, as well as scheduled coverages. This policy is somewhat like the standard fire insurance policy in that it contains only the general conditions and provisions; it is nothing until the applicable form is attached to it. Special forms are printed for each of the types of blanket policies, and they contain all of the details about the property covered. Thus the basic policy plus the applicable form constitute the contract. However, some insurers write so many personal property floaters (PPF) that they print the entire contract as one policy form.

The underwriter may amend the PPF or the householders protective policy in a number of ways to fit the needs of the applicant or the demands of the underwriter. The limitation on property in secondary residences may be increased by endorsement for one thing and the dollar limitations on stamps, coins, money and securities may be increased for another. Additional coverage may be written on target items by scheduling, as is explained subsequently. (All of these are standard endorsements.)

Deductibles are very common on blanket inland marine policies, particularly on the personal property floater. The coverage is so broad that the insurer would be "nickel and dimed to death" if no deductibles were used. Anytime a policyholder loses a pencil or spills ink on a tablecloth, a claim could be presented under a PPF policy. In order to keep a broad policy but still cover only the unanticipated losses, underwriters use deductibles on virtually all policies of this class. Deductibles of $100, $200, or even higher are common. In addition to helping the underwriter, they also serve to keep the premium lower, of course.

The underwriter may develop special endorsements to fit special needs, too. For example, if a policyholder frequently travels on business and has suffered several theft losses from a hotel room, the underwriter may decide to exclude property which is carried on a business trip.

Scheduled Policies

There are three separate methods for writing scheduled property. The first is similar to the method used for blanket coverage: a descriptive form is attached to the basic inland marine policy, the scheduled property floater. The second method is to add the description of the scheduled property to the personal property floater, householders protective policy, or homeowners dwelling package policy; in the latter case, the form for scheduled property is complete in itself, forming a policy within a policy.

The third method is the most common. This involves the use of the personal articles floater (PAF), which combines in one form, the most common provisions of scheduled articles. Each of the scheduled policies shown in this chapter, with the exception of the wedding presents and bicycle policies, is included in the PAF. This combination form is used for two reasons: the common provisions are placed together on the form, avoiding duplication; and more than one type of property may be scheduled without increasing the minimum premium. The latter reason is quite important because each class of property has its own minimum premium. This is often so high (because of the expenses of issuing the policy) that many prospects cannot afford to buy the insurance. With the PAF, several classes may be insured within the minimum premium for one class, under certain conditions. The coverage itself is identical with that given by separate scheduled policies.

Actually, the personal articles floater is simply a combination of several scheduled policies in one. The PAF form still must be attached to a basic policy; this can be the basic inland marine policy if no other coverage is written, or it can be a blanket floater policy or homeowners dwelling package policy.

Valuation of scheduled property is a particular problem to the underwriter. Appraisals are often demanded, as was explained in a previous section of this chapter. The underwriter must decide if an appraisal is acceptable or not. If it is, a copy is usually kept in the files for later reference; it is not attached to the policy. Naturally, if the appraisal is not accepted for one reason or another, the coverage is declined, unless an acceptable appraisal is submitted.

The valuation as shown on the policy is often a source of misunderstanding. There are two possible approaches. The most common one is to specify the amount of insurance applicable to the described property. This is the limit of liability; it indicates the maximum that the insurer will pay for loss of, or damage to, the described property. The loss is settled on the basis of the actual cash value at the time of loss. Furthermore, policy forms provide that the insurer's liability is limited to the amount that it would cost to repair or replace the property with materials of like, kind and quality. These provisions concerning actual cash value are the same in scheduled policies as in blanket policies; they are not changed by the fact that a specific amount of insurance is shown for a single described piece of property.

A *valued policy* may be written, however. The applicant may wish to insure for an agreed amount, guaranteeing to receive that amount in case of a total loss to the property. This is usually accomplished by showing on the form, instead of "limit of liability," the words "insured for and valued at," followed by the amount. The underwriter may be reluctant in issuing a valued policy because of the potential increase in moral hazard, particularly if the property is or may become less valuable than the stated amount. On the other hand, some property is insured more properly for a stated amount than for actual cash value. An example is an antique or a work of art; the value is extremely hard to establish if the property is totally destroyed or stolen. In such cases, the underwriter is wise to "settle the loss in advance" by agreeing with the applicant upon the proper value before the policy is written.

As previously indicated, fine arts are usually written on a stated value basis. Other property may be written that way under some conditions, such as a rare jewel, a handmade camera, a violin which is an heirloom, or a rare stamp.

Each of the classes of scheduled property under the personal articles floater may be endorsed to tailor the coverage to the requirements of the underwriter or the desires of the applicant. Some of the most common are these.

Jewelry: If the property is customarily kept in a safe deposit box at a designated bank, the policy can be endorsed to provide that no coverage applies while the jewelry is out of the safe deposit box without advance notice to the insurer that it will be taken out. The rate is greatly reduced for this endorsement, but a pro rata additional premium at regular rates is charged for the period of time that the jewelry is out of the safe deposit box.

Furs: Depreciation is a major problem with furs. The underwriter can endorse a specific percentage of depreciation which will apply each year. The effective date of the reduction is ordinarily the anniversary date of the policy when written for a three-year term. A better practice, however, is to require periodic re-appraisals in order to ascertain actual values.

Cameras: Sometimes the list of items covered on the policy is too long to type and attach to the policy with any degree of ease. In such cases, the underwriter can endorse the policy to specify that the property insured is that which is scheduled in the file kept in the insurer's office. This method saves considerable trouble and expense for policyholders who frequently change their camera equipment because they need only to notify the insurer and the policy does not need to be changed.

Musical instruments: A bulky list of articles can be referred to in the policy and kept by the insurer, as under the camera policy. Also, a limited form of coverage is available for bands and orchestras, covering such named perils as fire, lightning, windstorm, flood, theft (with an exclusion of theft from unattended automobiles), and transportation hazards; this form is a separate policy and is not used with the personal article floater.

Silverware: Although it is possible to schedule all silverware, the underwriter usually prefers blanket coverage with a separate limit of liability applying to each class of property for which coverage is desired: (1) silverware and silver-platedware, (2) goldware and gold-platedware, and (3) pewterware.

Fine Arts: When blanket coverage is used, as is permitted for an amount not to exceed 10% of the scheduled amount of insurance, the underwriter usually attaches a 100% coinsurance clause applicable to the blanket coverage, and specifies that actual cash value applies to those items. The coinsurance clause is not used on scheduled property, but most underwriters try to write at least 80% to the appraised value.

Wedding Presents: The regular policy form excludes breakage. For an additional premium, the underwriter usually will cover breakage of glass, china, marble, earthenware and other brittle articles by endorsement.

Boat Policies

Unlike other personal inland marine policies, which are quite uniform in coverage, boat polices are not at all standard. There is not even any uniform distinction betwen the boats that are covered under inland marine forms and those considered as ocean marine. The diffeence is more than academic because policies are quite dissimilar. The ocean marine policy, sometimes called a yacht policy, is written in the cumbersome, traditional language used by ocean marine underwriters for centuries. This form is used for most inboard and inboard-outboard boats, or at least for most of those over 26 feet in length. (This line of insurance is discussed in Chapter 29.)

The inland marine boat policy is used for most outboard motor boats, as well as for the smaller inboard and inboard-outboard motor boats by some insurers. The policy is written in the same type of language as other inland marine policies, and personal automobile policies. The arrangement is more like an automobile policy, with a printed policy designed to handle most risks and with the typed information about the policyholder, the boat, and the coverage either placed on the first page or placed on a separate form attached to the policy.

RETENTION AND REINSURANCE

Since many personal inland marine policies cover substantial amounts of insurance, underwriters protect against too great a concentration of insurance by purchasing reinsurance. This may be on an excess basis or a pro rata basis. In this respect, handling is similar to that of personal fire insurance. However, it is not customary for one underwriter to accept part of the line on an inland marine risk and let the producer place the balance with another insurer, although this is sometimes practiced.

In considering the total amount of risk at one location, the underwriter needs to consider other insurance written by the commpany. For example, an insurer might write a fire insurance policy and a personal property floater policy on a dwelling and its contents. Another problem is when a scheduled policy is added, or when an increase is made in an existing schedule. The underwriter must always know the total amount of risk at one location, and be prepared to reinsure the excess over the desired retention of the company.

Catastrophe losses are quite possible under inland marine insurance, too. The policies are so broad that they expose the insurer to such losses as flood, landslide and earthquake, as well as the more common perils of fire and windstorm. Excess policies of reinsurance are carried by inland marine insurers. Often these are combined with other lines, such as commercial inland marine and fire. Each insurer must consider all covered lines in setting the attachment point and the limit of reinsurance purchased.

SPECIAL PROBLEMS

The popularity of "collectibles" has caused problems in recent years for Inland Marine underwriters. This refers to the so-called "limited edition" of such items as medallions, coins, records, ingots, plates, spoons, dishes, bells, statuary, etc. Estimates have run as high as 1,000 of these editions being introduced each year. Studies have shown that roughly 80% of these are now worth less than when they were issued.

Guidebooks are available to help underwriters determine the current value of most of these issues. It is important to know the value in order to avoid over-insurance with its attendant moral hazard, on the one hand, and under-insurance with its lack of adequate premiums, on the other hand.

Values of these "collectibles," as well as of jewelry, furs, and many other items, should be verified periodically, certainly no less often than every three years.

QUESTIONS FOR DISCUSSION

1. Are personal inland marine policies written on a named-peril or all-risk basis? Explain.
2. Explain the difference between blanket policies and scheduled policies. Give an example of each.
3. (a) List and describe 4 types of property which may be scheduled under personal inland marine policies.
   (b) List factors which might make some applicants unacceptable for those types of coverage which you named.
4. Explain the coverages and purpose of the PAF.
5. Describe 2 approaches to valuation which are used.

28

Commercial Inland Marine

Commercial inland marine insurance, like personal inland marine, covers many different types of property against a multitude of perils. These coverages evolved to meet the needs of commercial enterprises — needs that could not be met adequately by monoline insurers which wrote only fire or casualty coverages. Marine underwriters alone had the authoriy to write broad floater-types of policies, so they developed policies to cover the hazard of transporting property.

Today these policies are written in fairly simple language — at least, it is simple in comparison with the old marine policies with their endorsements to cover "inland" exposures. Some of the policies are quite standardized while others are actually manuscript policies, written to fit the characteristics of the applicant's business. The simplified-language commercial property program of ISO includes commercial inland marine in the modular form, for use as a monoline policy or as part of a package.

Crime perils are an important part of many commercial inland marine policies. As was explained in the chapter on commercial crime insurance, these two classes of commercial crime and inland marine comprise the major methods of writing crime insurance for businesses; the third method, that of placing coverage in commercial package policies, is the newest and still the least used of the three. However, unlike commercial crime insurance written by casualty insurers, commercial inland marine policies cover a great many other perils. Indeed, many are written on an all risks basis, and the others usually contain a long list of perils which are covered.

Commercial inland marine insurance is basically property insurance. Some liability exposures are protected by certain of the policies, particularly bailee liability exposures. Personal property is the primary subject of commercial inland marine insurance, but some coverage extends to building; such structures as bridges and tunnels may also be covered.[1]

The Nation-wide Marine Definition specifies the lines which may be insured as inland marine, as was explained in the chapter on personal inland marine. Many acceptable classes are listed in rather general terms, and other classes are listed which are not permitted as inland marine risks. In spite of these delineations, it appears that almost any insurance protection on personal property, other than merchandise in course of manufacture, storage, or permanent location can be squeezed into the inland marine coverages. Even the latter limitations are not absolute, because some forms, such as the jewelers block and dealers forms, cover merchandise and fixtures at fixed locations.

With this broad scope of insurance, it is not surprising to find inland marine underwriters among the most imaginative and innovative in the industry. They are more likely to try to change a policy to meet a specific need than to decline it because it does not fit the norm. They use standard coverages where these are suitable, but they will not hesitate to write a policy if this is needed. They handle a classification of insurance which contains many different types of policies, so it is essential that they remain receptive to all offers from applicants and producers.

The term "floater" is used in commercial inland marine, as in personal lines, and it always refers to a coverage which moves along with the property to protect it wherever it is located, within its defined limits. Another term peculiar to inland marine insurance, this one to commercial only, is "block," as in the jewelers block policy. This term appears to be adapted from the French "en bloc," which means "all together." Block policies provide all risks coverages for certain classes of dealers.

DESCRIPTION OF COVERAGES

There are literally dozens of different commercial inland marine policies available, covering a wide range of coverages and risks. For convenience, they can be divided into the following five groups.

1. *Transportation Policies.* These cover property while in transit, through one means or another. Also included are the instrumentalities of transportation, such as bridges and tunnels.

2. *Dealers Block Policies.* As was mentioned in the chapter on commercial fire insurance, stocks of merchandise in the hands of dealers may be covered for fire and related perils under a fire policy. Many dealers want, and are willing to pay for, all risks coverage with protection applying wherever the property is located, not just on the described premises. A variety of dealers block policies are available to meet these needs.

3. *Equipment Floater Policies.* Many commercial enterprises have equipment that often moves from place to place, and is subject to a multitude of perils. Fire

---

1. Business Income coverage should also be written on many of these types of policies. For a complete discussion of the needs and problems, see "Time Element Exposures in Inland Marine," *Strategies for Insurance Coverages Manual* (The Merritt Company, Santa Monica, California), II-A-4.4.

insurance is not broad enough and crime insurance does not cover many of the perils, so these inland marine forms have been prepared. They cover many types of equipment, from livestock and signs to scientific instruments and radium.

4. *Stock Floaters.* Stocks of mechandise are subject to many situations under which broad floater coverages are needed. Goods may be sent away from the premises for processing purposes by someone else, such as heat treating, degreasing and annealing of metal; tanning of leather; and recapping of tires. Other goods are rented to others or consigned to them for resale. In still other cases, raw goods are purchased at one location and shipped long distances before reaching the processing plant. All of these situations may be insured under inland marine policies.

5. *Bailee Policies.* The liability of a bailee for property of others in custody may be insured as a liability policy, as was discussed in the chapter on commercial liability insurance. Such policies pay only if the policyholder is negligent; that is, does not exercise reasonable care in protecting the property as required by the circumstances. Many bailees realize that they can not plead their legal rights without losing so much good will that they may easily be forced out of business. The answer then is to purchase bailees customers goods insurance, covering the property against many perils, with no regard to legal liability for the loss.

The most common policies within each of these groups are described briefly as follows.

Transportation Policies

Truck cargo coverage may be written either as a separate policy or as an endorsement on a truck insurance policy. (This coverage was disussed in Chapter 20, along with other commercial automobile coverages.) One form covers the shipper of merchandise who uses owned trucks, while the other covers the legal liability of truckers (those who haul for hire) against claims for loss or damage to merchandise that they are carrying.

Shippers of merchandise may protect their interest in property while it is in transit by purchasing a *transit policy.* Coverage applies from the time the merchandise leaves the premises of the policyholder until it reaches its destination. The types of conveyances on which merchandise is carried are specified in the policy, and coverage applies while the merchandise is in such storage, or on such docks or wharves, as is incidental to the transportation. Coverage can be on a named peril basis, including such perils as fire, lightning, windstorm, flood, collision, perils of the sea and theft (usually of an entire package only, not pilferage). The policy can also be written to cover on an all risks basis except for such exclusions as delay, dampness, war, strikes, goods carried on deck, shipments refused by the receiver, and failure of the policyholder to use reasonable means to protect the property following a loss.

The regular transit policy just described is usually written on an open basis, under which all shipments of the kind of merchandise described in the policy are covered. When some shippers do not need this continuous type of protection, they may purchase a specific coverage — *trip transit policy* — whenever they have need of the protection; coverages are similar to those of the transit policy.

A shipper who uses parcel post may insure each package with the post office department of the federal government with a *parcel post policy.* This is a cumbersome method for those who ship frequently by parcel post, so an insurance form has been developed under which insurers may protect this exposure. It is an open form under which the shipper keeps a record of the shipments and reports them periodically to the insurer.

The policy covers the property while it is in the custody of the post office department until it arrives at its destination. All risks protection is provided, with certain exceptions, such as a limitation to name perils on property which is easily susceptible to deterioration, and an exclusion of loss to property which is improperly wrapped or addressed. A dollar limit is applied to each package, too.

A *registered mail policy* is ideal for shippers using registered mail to ship jewelry, precious stones, securities, money and similar property, and want broader coverage than is available from the post office department. This open policy is available, covering all risks except war. A dollar limit is placed on each package and a higher limit on the total shipments in any one day from the shipper to any one addressee. Banks and security dealers are the usual purchasers of this policy and carry very high limits.

Banks, trust companies, security dealers and others who act as transfer agents often ship such securities as bonds, stock certificates and coupons by first class mail. A *first class and certified mail policy* covers such shipments on an all risks basis, excluding only war. Other shippers may use certified mail; this coverage may be endorsed on the policy.

Some shippers use armored cars or messengers to deliver jewelry, money, etc., instead of using registered mail. An *armored car and messenger policy* covers the same property as the registered mail policy and on the same terms.

Instrumentalities of transportation and communication such as bridges, tunnels and viaducts are covered as inland marine insurance, although they are structures attached to the land. The reason for this is historical: fire insurers were unwilling to offer the broad protection needed by such structures, such as collapse, collision, flood, ice and earthquake. Only inland marine underwriters would write such policies, so when the Nation-wide Marine Definition was adopted, it recognized this situation and included this type of property under inland marine.

A fairly standard form is used for insuring bridges and tunnels. It is extremely broad, being an all risks policy with such exclusions as war, strikes, wear and tear, gradual deterioration, and neglect of the policyholder to use reasonable means to preserve the property after a loss.

Underwriters of inland marine insurance write policies to fit the needs of other properties of this type. Some of these properties are radio and television transmitting towers, power transmission lines, pipe lines carrying oil, gas, or water, and such water facilities as piers, slips, docks and wharves. Each has its own special hazards and needs, so special policies are written by the underwriter for each risk.

Builders risk coverage is available to cover during the construction of a bridge or similar structure. Even business interruption coverage is written for those structures which would suffer a loss of income because of damage, such as toll bridges.

Dealers Block Policies

The original "block" policy was the *jewelers block.* It was developed because of the need for broader coverage than was available under fire and crime policies, such as theft and transit coverage. Coverage applies to all stock of merchandise usual to a jewelry store, both on and off premises; the policy is called a floater, and coverage does apply wherever located, but most of the coverage actually applies at the described business premises of the policyholder. All risks coverage is provided, with exclusions applying to infidelity of an employee, and such perils as loss of market, delay, gradual deterioration, defective packing, mysterious disappearance, inventory shortages, and damage resulting from work upon the covered property. Without special endorsement, the policy does not cover property at exhibitions, loss by earthquake or flood, and property in show windows against loss by theft.

Dealers in construction and mobile agricultural equipment may insure their stocks of merchandise under an *equipment dealers policy.* It covers such property as binders, reapers, harvesters, tractors, plows and similar farming equipment, as well as such construction equipment as pneumatic tools, road scrapers, compressors and their accessories. Coverage is all risks with such exclusions as corrosion, rust, freezing and extremes of temperature, flood and inventory shortages. Tires and tubes are covered only for fire, theft and windstorm, unless damage is coincidental with other loss.

Many types of dealers may insure their stock under a *dealers policy.* Examples of these dealers are those who handle cameras, musical instruments, stamps, coins, fine arts, furs, and marine supplies. Retailers, wholesalers, and distributors may be insured under this policy. All risks coverage is given, with the exclusions being similar to the jewelers' block policy, but changed as needed to fit the type of property covered.

Another exception to the general rule that inland marine coverages should be floaters, or at least should have some degree of mobility, is found in the policy insuring *neon and electric signs.* The reason again is the desire of the owners for broad, all risks coverage. Only certain signs are acceptable: neon and electrically-operated mechanical signs; nonmechanical signs and billboards are not acceptable, even if illuminated. Each sign insured must be scheduled on a policy, with a complete description of the sign, its location, and lettering on it and the amount of insurance. All risks coverage applies even while the sign is in transit, but breakage is not covered during transit or during installation, unless caused by fire, lightning or collision or overturn of a conveyance carrying the sign. Deductibles are almost always used.

Commercial Floater Policies

A *contractors' equipment floater* is used to insure the movable equipment of contractors engaged in road building, mining, dam building and other jobs using heavy and expensive machinery. Steam shovels, concrete mixers, earthmovers and draglines are examples of the type of equipment which may be included. However, autos, trucks, automotive equipment designed for highway use, and stationary apparatus may not be insured under this policy. Each piece of equipment covered must be scheduled, except that blanket coverage may be used for incidental items like shovels and wheelbarrows, with a coinsurance clause. Named peril coverage is more commonly used, however. It is similar to a fire and extended coverage policy plus flood, collapse of bridges, collision of a transporting conveyance and earthquake. Theft may be included if the underwriter feels that the risk is not too great. All risks coverage is sometimes written, too, accompanied by such exclusions as gradual deterioration, wear and tear, overloading of lifting machines and infidelity of employees.

Mobile agricultural equipment owned by a farmer and used on a farm may be insured under an *agricultural equipment floater.* Cotton pickers, threshers, harvesters and combines are examples of the types of equipment which may be covered. The usual method is to schedule all equipment, with a provision for blanket coverage of incidental items up to 10% of the value of scheduled items and with limits on each unscheduled item and on the aggregate of all such items. Some insurers also offer a blanket policy, but they usually exclude large equipment such as harvester-thresher combines. Both forms commonly use an 80% coinsurance clause on the aggregate of unscheduled items and on each scheduled item. All risks coverage is afforded by both forms, and the same general exclusions as the contractors' equipment floater. Deductibles are usually used, too.

Blanket coverage may be written on all animals of a particular class of livestock, such as horses, mules, cattle, sheep and swine under a *livestock floater.* One common form covers all animals of the described class with an 80% coinsurance clause and a stated limit of liability for each animal. Another popular form requires 100% insurance to value because the limit for each animal is determined by dividing the amount of insurance by the number of animals in that class, although a limit per animal is usually specified. Scheduling of specific animals having unusual value is permitted by most insurers, too. Coverage is on a named peril basis, usually covering death or destruction only resulting from or made necessary by fire and extended coverage, flood, earthquake, collapse of bridges, being hit or run over by vehicles other than those owned or operated by the insured, and theft (excluding mysterious disappearance and escape). For an additional premium, most underwriters will extend the protection to include such perils as drowning, accidental shooting, electricity and attacks by dogs or wild animals. Freezing and smothering in snowstorms or blizzards are usually excluded.

Surgical and scientific instruments, as well as equipment owned or used by a policyholder in the medical or dental professions may be insured on a *physicians and surgeons equipment floater.* Even furniture and fixtures may be added by endorsement. Property is covered wherever located, and it is ordinarily permissible to limit coverage to the types of property usually carried by the policy holder. All risks coverage is given, with the customary exclusions.

Scenery, costumes, and equipment associated with the theater and of the type that can be carried around the country may be insured under a *theatrical floater.* Named peril coverage is given, being basically fire and extended coverage plus flood, theft and transportation perils. A 100% coinsurance clause also is used.

Many other types of equipment may be covered under various inland marine floater policies. Some of these are morticians equipment; patterns and dies; equipment and paraphernalia of lodges and fraternal organizations; radium used for medical or scientific pusposes; and vending machines. Some of these policies are fairly standard, being prepared by the rating bureaus, while others are written by the underwriter to fit the needs of the applicant.

Stock Floaters

Garment contractors — a clothing manufacturer who sends goods to contractors or subcontractors away from the premises has a chance of loss if the goods are destroyed in transit or while goods are at the shop of the processor.

Named peril coverage is given, including fire, extended coverage, water damage, burglary and sprinkler leakage. For an additional premium, the underwriter may extend the coverage to loss by strikes, vandalism, malicious mischief and theft. Consequential damage may also be included and can be important to the manufacturer who sends parts of garments to different processors because additional loss can be suffered if some of the parts are destroyed.

Owners of motion picture film rented to others can purchase a *motion picture film floater* to protect against loss to the film. The same policy may be used to protect the original negatives of a motion picture during its filming and processing, before copies can be made. The entire cost of production can be wrapped up in these negatives, most of it requiring reproduction if the film were damaged or destroyed.

A *wool growers floater* is usually needed by an owner of wool while the wool travels through the various processes from shearing to the purchaser. The storage time is indefinite, the warehouse locations may not be known, and values may change, all requiring a special floater policy for adequate coverage.

The owner of cotton needs the same general type of protection as the owner of wool and can get such protection under a *cotton floater.* However, the value of the cotton stock tends to vary more than wool because of additions during the harvesting season; a reporting form is, therefore, used. The policyholder reports purchases to the insurer from the gin near the growing area, and reports sales to purchasers who may be across the country or even across the ocean.

Many types of property are shipped under conditions which require special *transit floaters.* Expensive advertising displays, component parts of airplanes, large transformers built for a specific job are all examples of the types of risks offered to inland marine underwriters. There are no prescribed forms or rates, so underwriters of these policies must be able to weigh such various factors as distance and type of transit, damageability of the property, value of the property, the ability to repair or replace the property and the possibility of recovery from the carrier as determined from the bill of lading and the financial condition of the carrier.

Sales floaters — Many manufacturers and jobbers place property in the hands of dealers for sale to the ultimate consumer, with title being held by the manufacturer or jobber. Consignment is one of the methods, and may include consignment for trial or exhibit.

Floor plan is another method; this is used for automobiles and household appliances. Under each of these arrangements, the stock may be covered as inland marine insurance, because there is a degree of transit involved even though the property is ordinarily at a fixed location. However, consignment floaters may not cover property for more than 120 days after it arrives at the premises of the consignee. Most of these floaters are on a named peril basis, but all risks coverage may usually be secured, particularly on floor plan policies.

Dealers who sometimes sell merchandise on a deferred payment basis need *installment sales floaters.* Their security is the right to repossess the property if the payments are not made. Since damage to the property could destroy that security, they need insurance against loss or damage while the property is in the hands of the purchaser. A company that finances such sales may also need this coverage. Policies offered by inland marine companies may be either on a single interest basis, covering only the interest of the seller, or a double interest basis, covering both the buyer and the seller. A reporting form policy or a specific amount of coverage may be used. In any case, named peril policies are issued, generally covering fire, extended coverage, earthquake, flood and transportation hazards. Common exclusions are damage caused by improper packing, rough handling, or mechanical breakdown, and such perils as theft, robbery, and misappropriation by an employee or the insured or anyone else to whom the property is entrusted.

Property which is being installed on the premises of another remains the property of the seller until it is accepted by the buyer. *Installation floaters* may be written to cover such property, particularly for large equipment such as elevators, air conditioning equipment and electrical generators. The property is covered while in transit, during installation, and sometimes during testing, but coverage stops when the buyer accepts the property or the interest of the policyholder ends.

Accounts receivable — The accounts receivable policy insures the policyholder's inability to collect outstanding balances because records are destroyed in an insured loss. Coverage is on an all risks basis, so it protects against fire, theft, malicious destruction and many other perils. Excluded are accounting errors, fraudulent or dishonest acts of a policyholder or officer, and alteration of records to conceal the wrongful taking of money, securities or other property. The policy requires that records be kept in a described safe or vault when not in use and when the premises are not open for business; temporary coverage off premises may be purchased for an additional premium. The limit of recovery is stated in the policy and is usually determined by monthly reports of values.

Valuable Papers and Records — This is an all risks policy covering documents, records, books, deeds, abstracts, and similar papers and records. It does not cover money or securities. The safe or vault in which papers are kept is described in the policy, and the insured property must be kept in that safe or vault at all times when the premises are not open for business, except while the papers are in actual use. Blanket coverage can be written, in which case the papers are covered on a replacement cost basis. A better coverage for most papers is available by scheduling, with losses settled on an agreed amount basis. Since the policy covers all risks, it protects against theft and burglary, as well as many other perils; excluded are such perils as wear and tear, gradual deterioration, and dishonesty of the policyholder or officer (employee dishonesty is covered but only to the extent of any losses resulting from an attempt to conceal an embezzlement).

Bailee Policies

Laundries, dry cleaners and dyers, rug and carpet cleaners, tailor shops, and similar establishments have property of their customers in their temporary custody. The bailee may obtain a *bailees* customers goods policy to protect the customers goods against specified losses, regardless of the negligence or lack of negligence on the part of the bailee. The policies are not standardized but are tailored to fit the needs of the applicant by the underwriter, and of course under terms which are acceptable to the underwriter. Named peril policies are generally used, ordinarily covering against fire and extended coverage perils plus theft, earthquake, flood and transportation perils. The actual cash value of customers' property is the limit of liability; some policies specify an aggregate limit for each location of the policyholder, but some do not specify any limit. In either case, the policyholder is required to keep accurate records of receipts so that the premium may be determined. Deductible clauses are usually used, but sometimes all losses are covered with the policyholder given authority to settle losses under a stated amount, such as $100; both methods avoid the expense of handling small claims.

Owners of fur coats often leave coats with a furrier for cleaning, alteration, repair, or storage. A *furriers customers policy* covers such property while in the custody of the furrier policyholder, during transportation and while on the premises. All risks coverage is given, with the usual exclusions; an important exclusion is damaged due to any process. The amount of liability is usually established monthly by means of reports by the furrier to the insurer, stating the total valuation in storage and in each of the premises of the furrier.

People who do not own freezers often rent cold storage lockers, and the operator of the locker has the same type of liability as any other bailee. A *cold storage locker bailee floater* pays for damage to the property of customers. Policy provisions are generally similar to those of policies used for laundries and dry cleaners.

Many manufacturers depend upon subcontractors to do part of the processing work. The subcontractor becomes a bailee for the property not owned, but is in his custody for processing. The subcontractor, therefore, can secure a *processors' liability* policy which is generally similar to those available to laundries and dry cleaners.

An innkeeper (the operator of a hotel or motel) often has property of others entrusted for safekeeping. For example, a customer who rents a room may place valuables in the hotel safe. A checkroom for coats and hats in the dining room is another example of a sizable exposure. If the operator merely wants to insure the legal liability, he or she may purchase an *innkeepers liability policy* which was previously described under commercial crime in Chapter 26 (with the explanation that this liability coverage is traditionally handled by a crime underwriter rather than a commercial liability underwriter, because the greatest hazard is from crime). However, if the operator wishes to be able to reimburse customers for damage to their property in custody even if the damage is not caused by negligence, the oepra-tor may purchase a type of bailees customers goods policy, from an inland marine insurer. The policy is similar to others of that type, but is almost always on a named peril basis. Many policies exclude mysterious disappearance, as well as delivery to a wrong person. Care must be taken, in writing the policy, to be specific whether the policy covers or excludes carelessness by employees of the operator in handing out property.

UNDERWRITING FACTORS

Acceptable Risks

Commercial inland marine coverages are more likely to be written alone than either commercial crime or personal inland marine policies. Many commercial inland marine risks are somewhat unique and can stand alone when handled by an experienced underwriter.

More than many other lines, this class requires that an underwriter who is expected to handle the entire range of policies must have considerable training and experience because some of the coverages are quite complicated. Each coverage must be exactly the right one for the applicant. It is common to tailor the policies to the individual needs of the risks, and the rating often contains an element of judgment. All of these characteristics, therefore, require special underwriting.

Insurers of commercial inland marine may be divided very roughly into two categories. The first consists of the relatively few insurers that try to offer all, or most, of the coverages written in this line. Their rates are generally similar but many variations are possible, depending upon the knowledge and background of the underwriter and the philosophy of the insurer. Each insurer wants to write as much business as possible but is seldom interested in cutting the rate too far in order to accomplish this. These insurers always like to get related policies, of course, but they require them only in certain classes or on certain risks where the maximum rate that can safely be charged appears to be inadequate for the potential exposure; sometimes it can help to write other coverages and look at the entire account as a unit. On the other hand, these insurers give considerable weight to the producer, usually writing the more complicated or unusual policies only for those producers who write a fair volume of business with the insurer.

The other category of insurer consists of those companies that write only the more common, standardized inland marine coverages. This group contains many more insurers than the first group, but it probably makes up less premium. The list of coverages written by these companies varies considerably, depending upon the related lines each insurer is attempting to support. A typical list might contain some of the equipment dealers, such as mobile agricultural equipment; some contractors equipment floaters and agricultural equipment floaters, livestock floaters; and limited bailee policies, perhaps only for laundries, dry cleaners, cold storage lockers, and innkeepers. These insurers write commercial liability and fire on these risks and feel that they must offer the related inland marine coverages in order to protect the entire account. Their acceptable risks will, therefore, tend to follow the acceptable risks for these other lines. Most of the policies written by these insurers are quite standard in coverage and rating, so the underwriters do not need to be so highly trained as those specializing in inland marine. Rates for these insurers tend to follow bureau rates, often with a small deviation if the insurer tries to deviate on all lines.

Unacceptable Risks

Commercial inland marine coverages are quite broad, many being of the all risks type. It is natural, therefore, that the underwriters are cautious of the risks that they write. They tend to use unacceptable lists to guide producers, more than some other lines. On the other hand, it is probably true that more exceptions are made in this line than in most others, after the underwriters have received enough information to satisfy themselves that such exceptions are justified.

Moral hazard is the most serious problem because of the broad coverages. Crime perils are covered under most policies, so the problems described in Chapter 26 as applying to these perils are all present. In addition, there can be moral hazards under other perils.

The unacceptable lists are different for each insurer and for each coverage. Generally speaking, however, unacceptable lists for commercial inland marine include most of the following subjects.

Business Reputation. The reputation of the business, including its owners and their associates, is of extreme importance. A poor or even questionable reputation makes a risk unacceptable.

Adequate Records. Many policies are on a reporting basis, or otherwise were dependent upon the maintenance of adequate records. These records can determine premium and also fix the limit of liability if a loss should occur. An applicant who does not maintain adequate records is unacceptable.

Physical Features. Most inland marine policies cover basic fire and extended coverage perils, as well as additional perils. The underwriter, therefore, will usually start by qualifying the applicant for commercial fire insurance, as described in Chapter 24. An applicant who does not qualify for fire insurance is unacceptable for inland marine insurance.

Insurance Values. An applicant whose insurance values are not in accord with the apparent needs is unacceptable. Underinsurance may indicate a poor financial position, while apparent overinsurance raises the suspicion that there are some unrevealed operations, or that the applicant hopes to profit by the insurance. A fairly accurate statement of values is required with 100% insurance to value on many policies.

Each class of risk, or type of policy has its own unacceptable list. These vary greatly among insurers. Some of the more common rules that make some of these risks unacceptable are the following.

Bridges Under Construction. Applicants are unacceptable unless the application is accompanied by detailed plans of the bridge, plus an engineering report that has been completed and signed by an engineer associated with the project.

Jewelers Block. Among those unacceptable are risks without experienced and trained personnel, without adequate safes and proper security, and without good ratings for credit and finances.

Equipment Dealers. Applicants with construction and agricultural equipment of the types which are stored in yards are unacceptable, unless the yards have adequate fencing. Guards or alarm systems are sometimes required, too.

Dealers. Most dealers in heating and air conditioning equipment, office machines, household applicances and the like are unacceptable, unless they have an approved protective system against burglars.

Contractors Equipment Floater. Many insurers place on the unacceptable list such risks as loggers, lumbering operations and mountain road builders.

Agricultural Equipment Floater. Unacceptable lists often include equipment in areas subject to flooding, or equipment rented to others, such self-propelled machinery as mechanical cotton pickers or harvester-thresher combines when used for custom farming, and any custom farming beyond a limited distance such as 75 miles. Farms not operating profitably usually are prohibited, too.

Livestock Floater. An applicant is not acceptable for most insurers, unless experienced in raising animals and in caring for them, and with proper facilities presenting good apperaance. Specifically unacceptable are animals in open range, horses used exclusively for show or racing, livestock owned by carnivals and circuses, and livestock being transported to stockyards or already there. Coverage is ordinarily not written for autioneers, nor for veterinarians if the coverage is intended to cover the animals owned by others while in the care of the applicant for treatment.

Physicians and Surgeons Equipment Floater. There is little moral hazard in this class because the equipment is needed to conduct professional work, particularly the "little black bag." Carelessness is the greatest problem, so the previous loss history might make a risk unacceptable. Theft and burglary, particularly of money and narcotics, may be a problem, however,

Bailees Customers Goods. Unacceptable are applicants located in undesirable locations, those situated in frame or unprotected buildings with poor fire protection and no burglar alarm, those with poor loss record, and those whose premises are not clean and orderly. Cleaning methods and type of cleaning solvents are important; many underwriters will not accept an applicant using solvents with a stated flash point or lower. Self-service or coin-operated laundries and dry cleaners are often unacceptable.

Furriers Customers Goods. The quality of storage facilities is the most important underwriting qualification. Unacceptable are those who are not both good fire and good burglary risks; thus, they should have sprinkler systems, fireproof vaults and control station alarms. A risk is unacceptable if it employs any persons who cannot be bonded. Previous losses are critical; a risk with a record of previous losses would be unacceptable whether those losses indicated susceptibility to a particular peril or just carelessness on the part of the applicant or employees.

Cold Storage Locker Bailee Floater. The type of equipment used with these risks makes them paticularly vulnerable to certain types of losses. Equipment failure from an insured peril can result in considerable loss, so an automatic auxiliary unit is usually required. Since equipment needs proper care, a risk should not be written if the financial status is so poor that maintenance might be neglected. Fire suppression may be difficult in these risks, so adequate fire protection is required and an unprotected risk would be unacceptable. Some types of refrigerant gases are poisonous and applicants using them would be unacceptable, too.

SECURING INFORMATION

Commercial inland marine underwriters must first determine if an applicant fits within the acceptability rules, and then whether it is or is not on an unacceptable list. Having determined that an applicant is indeed eligible, there is much more information needed to determine acceptability.

The application is the primary source of information. Often it is backed up by a supplemental application, which usually is submitted as another part of the original application but it is one that may be requested later. Other sources of information are also used.

Application

A signed application is required by most commercial inland marine underwriters. The information about the business and its owner are very important to the underwriter, but the application itself is not made a part of the policy. It is common to use a basic application, or perhaps several basic applications grouped by general type. Every applicant must complete (or have the producer complete it) a basic application containing general information. The applicant then also submits a supplemental application giving answers to specific questions about this type of business. Some insurers combine related occupancies on one supplemental application to reduce the number of application forms required.

In general most applications contain questions that may be grouped into three categories.

1. Personal
2. Description of operations, premises and property
3. Insurance information.

Under each of these groups, the following questions are asked by most insurers.

1. *Personal*

A. Full name of the applicant, along with the firm name, if any.
B. The structure of the firm: individual, partnership or corporation.
C. The business address of the applicant, and the mailing address if different.
D. Type of business conducted by the applicant.
E. Number of years that the applicant has been in business.
F. Details of all losses of the types which would be covered by the policy applied for, during a previous period, such as five years.

2. *Description of Operations, Premises and Property.* Each coverage requires different information on these subjects. Examples of some more common policies and their questions are these.

A. Equipment dealers: description of the buildings and yards, type of fencing used, devices used to protect the property against theft and vandalism, description of the types of equipment sold, the approximate value of equipment on hand at the minimum and maximum periods, description of any repair or maintenance facilities and operations, and information concerning the rental of equipment to others. The limit of insurance for each location must be specified, both within buildings and outside.

B. Dealers: the application for dealers in heating and air conditioning, household applicances, office machines and the like must contain detailed information concerning the stock for the past year (some insurers require two years). This includes such items as gross sales, maximum inventory, and the average values of property of others in the custody of the applicant — all separated by each class of property

C. Agricultural equipment floaters: description of all equipment to be covered, including manufacturer, serial number, year built, date purchased, and cost; information about the farm, covering type of farming, number of acres, and if the applicant owns it or not; complete information if the equipment is ever loaned to others, where the equipment is stored when not in use; and details if any custom farming is conducted, including a description of where work is performed and the percentage of the applicant's total operations that are represented by custom farming. (The latter term refers to performing farming operations on the land of another, for hire.)

D. Contractors equipment floaters: a complete description of all equipment to be covered (as explained in the previous paragraph); the nature of the work in which the contractor specializes (such as excavation, paving, or construction); where the equipment is stored when not in use; complete information if the equipment is ever loaned to others; and the geographic limits within which the equipment will be used, plus special mention of use in mountainous areas.

E. Livestock floaters: description of all livestock to be covered, with details on specified animals to be covered under a schedule and number of head of each type of animal under blanket coverage, along with breed or type and value of animals; where the animals are kept, and whether or not they are grazed on open range; and information about special animals, such as where and when they are exhibited or to whatever use they are placed.

F. Bailee policies: complete description of the buildings in which the operations are conducted; types of operations performed; approximate values of customers' goods on hand at any one time; and special hazards of the occupancy, such as coolants, solvents, heat used, etc.

G. Cargo and transit policies: details of the product; the conveyances upon which it is to be shipped; potential liabilities of the carrier and the shipper; trade restrictions that might affect the shipment; and such information about the shipment itself as the type of packing cases used, description of any containerization employed, the type of packing used and the shipping department markings.

3. *Insurance Information*

A. The policy and particular coverages desired, with details of limits, deductibles, and other pertinent features of the policy, along with the requested effective date.

B. Information about the previous insurer of similar coverage, including the rate for the previous policy, and a complete explanation if that insurer or any other that has ever cancelled or declined similar coverage.

C. Details if any employee has ever committed a fraudulent or dishonest act in the employment of the applicant or any other employer.

D. Name and address of any loss payee or mortgagee.

Inspection Reports

Commercial inland marine underwriters often use inspection companies to obtain additional information. There are so many differences in the operations and exposures to loss that the underwriter must seek considerable information.

Physical factors are often determined by an inspection report. The applications for commercial inland marine policies tend to contain less questions than many other lines about such important factors as the neighborhood, the types of records kept, the number of employees and protective devices used. One reason for this lack of information is that a number of policies almost need to be combined on one application in order to avoid the necessity of printing an overwhelming number of applications, and little room is left for these additional questions. Another reason is that the producer must furnish considerable basic information about the applicant, and there is a limit to the amount of information that can be expected. Still another reason is that since the rate and often the coverage depend on the individual risk, the underwriter needs specialized information anyway, and gets only basic qualifying information from the producer.

Physical inspections are often conducted by the same independent inspection companies used for other lines. Since they are able to answer questions sent to them, they are fairly effective on most coverages.

Large inland marine insurers use their own inspectors. In some cases, these are the same persons who handle other commercial lines of insurance. In other cases, they are specialists. The coverages are so broad that specialized information is often invaluable to the underwriter. A trained loss prevention specialist can help install protective devices or procedures, and can furnish information of such an unusual nature that an underwriter may not even think to put it on an inspection form. When moral hazard is a major problem under some types of inland marine insurance, inspections by outside companies are used to develop information indicating the presence of an undue moral hazard.

Experience of Other Insurers

Commercial inland marine underwriters are less inclined to exchange loss history than most other commercial underwriters. One reason is the multiplicity and variety of coverages; it is of little help to secure information about a previous policy, unless the precise coverages are known. Another reason is that many policies are judgment rated, and underwriters are more reluctant to share any information which might tend to reveal their "secrets" to a competitor.

Some experience is exchanged, particularly on the more common, standardized coverages, and with companies writing a broad book of insurance rather than specialized coverages. Where an underwriter can find another who will reciprocate, the past loss history can be very helpful.

CLASSIFICATION AND RATING

There are fewer classifications within commercial inland marine coverages than in most other lines. The reason is that there are a great number of policies, so just the selection of a type of policy amounts to classification. Furthermore, there are a relatively small number of risks that buy each policy, and any further classification reduces the size of each class to the point that the experience would not be credible.

Many times, the equivalent of classifying is conducted during the underwriting process when the applicant is fitted to the right policy. Some commercial inland marine policies tend to overlap, and the underwriter must decide upon the proper policy as the information received is evaluated.

Rates are published by rating bureaus for all of the standardized coverage. Most insurers use these rates, some with a deviation, because each class is so small that few, if any insurers have sufficient volume to be able to calculate their own rates. Modifications in these rates are sometimes made to allow for certain characteristics of risks.

However, rating bureaus do not inspect any individual risks, but they do promulgate specific rates for each policy of some types, particularly the jewelers block policy. The insurer secures from the applicant, a complete and signed proposal, forwarding it to the bureau for purposes of determining the rate. The rate is based on the size of the city, protective devices, the nature of the business and the applicable fire insurance rate.

Many inland marine policies start the rating process with the applicable contents fire rate. A loading is added for additional perils, and debits or credits are applied to compensate for special features of the risk. Some forms, as for dealers, also take into account gross annual sales, protective devices used, and the limit of coverage applying at each location and in transit.

The more common, standardized policies are rated by tables which are contained in manuals. Equipment floaters and livestock floaters, for example, are rated by finding the applicable rate for the coverage, according to the territory in which the property is located, and applying that rate to each $100 of insurance.

At the other extreme are policies on bridges and tunnels. No two of these structures are alike, so each rate must be calculated separately. When an insurer that is a member of, or subscriber to a rating bureau, submits all pertinent information about the property, including details of construction and its present condition, the bureau will prepare a rate. Other insurers secure rates by having the underwriter apply knowledge and experience to arrive at a judgment rate.

POLICY FORMS

Commercial inland marine policies are written on a variety of policy forms and there is little uniformity among them. However, standard forms are available for the more common policies. These are used by most insurers, although underwriters often write their own endorsements to tailor coverages to fit the needs of each case. Many of these policies are printed in forms which are attached to the scheduled property floater policy, which is the basic inland marine form — as was previously explained in the chapter on personal inland marine. Those which are not so attached, but are printed as complete policies within themselves, include the general provisions of the scheduled property floater.

Manuscript policies are used for some classes, particularly for instrumentalities of transportation and some of the more complex block policies. As the name indicates, these policies are written by hand and then typed as the policy itself. There are so many differences in these coverages that standardized policies simply cannot handle them. This is not to imply that the underwriter starts out with a blank piece of paper and creates an entire contract. Rather the underwriter picks up portions of other policies, such as the basic provisions of the scheduled property floater and modifies them as the situation requires. Engineering reports and specifications, mortgagee agreements and other documents are checked and incorporated in the policy as needed. The writing of such contracts obviously requires many years of experience and thorough knowledge of the subject.

RETENTION AND REINSURANCE

Commercial inland marine risks often consist of high values, and the underwriter knows that protection must be secured against a shock loss. However, it is not common for two or more insurers to share the writing of a risk — such as is done in commercial fire insurance — because of the nonstandard coverages and rates used for many inland marine policies. Thus, the underwriter must write a policy for the entire amount of insurance, and then reinsure above the amount retained.

Pro rata reinsurance is seldom used for inland marine insurance, although it is not impossible. When used, the underwriter cedes the exposure that exceeds the amount of the retention to the reinsurer. For standardized coverages, the cession may be under an automatic treaty, but for unusual or judgment rates risks, facultative reinsurance is used.

The use of excess reinsurance is more common. The underwriter retains an amount of exposure, which may be only $10,000 or may be $100,000 or more, depending upon the insurer and the type of coverage. Specific excess reinsurance then is secured, but usually not on an automatic basis. However, many insurers have treaties which cover, on an excess basis above a stipulated amount, all risks the underwriter has accepted. Such treaties commonly exclude bridges, tunnels, and other instrumentalities of transportation because each of these risks requires special handling and represents large exposures. A reinsurer which has written a treaty to cover such exposures as a television dealer policy can scarcely be expected to cover a potential loss to a bridge worth many millions of dollars.

Reinsurance treaties commonly exclude target risks by name, such as the Mellon Collection of Fine Arts, the Frick Collection of Fine Arts, and the New York World's Fair Fine Art Syndicate. Treaties are revised occasionally to add other risks considered to be of an unusual target nature and with large accumulation of values.

Insurers that write modest amounts of inland marine insurance often combine the reinsurance with other lines, such as fire insurance. It is not common to combine these property lines with casualty insurance in one reinsurance treaty.

Catastrophes are of little concern to inland marine underwriters, other than on specific risks. However, the broad coverages expose an insurer to catastrophe losses by flood, earthquake, fire and similar perils, so reinsurance must be carried. The catastrophe cover may be combined with excess reinsurance on single large risks or it may be combined with fire insurance on other lines.

QUESTIONS FOR DISCUSSION

1. Are commercial inland marine policies more concerned with property or liability exposures? Explain any important overlaps.
2. List the 5 groups of commercial inland marine policies, and briefly describe each group.
3. Whose interest is protected under a transit policy?
4. Explain why neon and electric signs are insured under inland marine policies which generally require a degree of mobility in the property which is covered.
5. Explain the concept of bailee policies, including who buys them and what property is protected.
6. Why is the moral hazard a serious problem when underwriting commercial inland marine policies?

29

Ocean Marine

Ocean marine insurance, which has evolved over a period of hundreds of years, is the oldest known form of insurance. Today it is a highly specialized line, using terms in its contracts that are unique and almost incomprehensible to laypersons. These unusual provisions and terminology, more than the basic outline of this insurance, make it difficult for property and casualty underwriters to understand.

Ocean marine insurance is written by only a few United States companies; most of it is written by foreign insurers. It comprises about 1% of the total property and casualty premium in the United States, and this premium — over $1.1 billion — is concentrated in the hands of only a few companies. The coverages are so specialized, and most insurers lack so many qualified underwriters to handle them, that over half of the total ocean marine business is written by only about 15 companies.[1]

DESCRIPTION OF COVERAGES

There are four major types of coverages under ocean marine insurance: hull, cargo, freight and liability. Although policy variations exist among these four major coverages, a general discussion of these four coverages encompasses most policies.

Hull. Coverage on the vessel is called "hull insurance." There are four types of vessels into which subdivision is made: sail, auxiliary sail, steamer and motor. A different type of classification may be made for purposes of assigning forms: commercial ships, yachts and motorboats. Coverage may be written to cover one vessel or a fleet, as well as for a specific trip or for a stated period of time.

Cargo. Insurance on the cargo carried by a vessel is the largest type of marine insurance in terms of premium volume. It can be the most diverse, too. A single vessel

1. "Insurance Premium Distribution — 1983," *Best's Review Property/Casualty Insurance Edition*, (July, 1984), p. 15

may contain many different types of cargo, each representing a different interest. There are two broad classes of cargo: general (consisting of a variety of goods being shipped by one or more interests), and full (a single commodity which is being shipped by one interest). Another type of classification for cargo is under-deck or above-deck; the latter refers to all cargo above the main deck of the vessel, whether covered or not.

Freight. Insurance on freight refers to coverage on the money paid for transporting goods. Thus, it protects the interest of the owner of the carrier in the income the owner can derive from the operation of the vessel. If the vessel is damaged to the extent that it cannot carry goods, the owner of the vessel will suffer a loss of freight.

This use of the term "freight" is somewhat confusing to persons not familiar with ocean marine insurance. A common meaning of the term "freight" is "a load or goods transported by a carrier;" thus, it is synonymous with "cargo." The other meaning of the term "freight" is the one used in ocean marine insurance: "the charge made for transporting goods."

Liability. When liability insurance is provided in connection with ocean marine insurance, it is called protection and indemnity (P and I) insurance. It covers the liability of the owner or operator arising out of the operations of the vessel. The liability may be concerned with persons, cargo, other property or penalties imposed by laws or regulations. This coverage is almost invariably issued on a separate policy from other ocean marine coverages for commercial vessels, although it may be combined for yachts. Most discussions of ocean marine insurance do not include P and I insurance, but it is an essential coverage for vessels and cannot be ignored.

The perils covered under an ocean marine policy are described in the "policy forms" section of this chapter. The quaint wording is interesting to read but requires explanation for clear understanding.

UNDERWRITING FACTORS

Acceptable Risks

Ocean marine insurers are specialty writers, handling a line of business considerably different from other property and casualty lines. Marine underwriters use their own terminology and they have their own ideas about underwriting. They deal with special class of risks — those who travel in international waters.

In spite of the differences, ocean marine underwriters use the same general approaches to acceptable risks as do most other underwriters. Some want only the best classes, some write less preferred risks at higher rates, while others try to accommodate most applicants. As a general rule, it is safe to say that all of the larger insurers consider almost any risk as acceptable. Those companies writing a smaller volume tend to limit themselves more severely, such as requiring substantial other policies in the company before the marine exposure is acceptable. Some insurers in the latter group are inclined to consider only those applicants who receive the highest rating on surveys; these companies lack either the knowledge or the desire to attempt to rate risks that have some problems.

Specific classes may have special acceptability rules. For example, yachts may be acceptable only if they are over a stated length, such as 25 feet. (Shorter crafts are considered to be inland marine risks.) Other insurers may use a minimum valuation of pleasure boats for ocean marine insurance, such as $10,000; again, those with a lower valuation are considered inland marine.

Unacceptable Risks

Ocean marine underwriters try to avoid writing those risks possessing undesirable characteristics of substantial importance or those in too great a quantity. An ocean-going vessel is unable to receive help in a short time, unlike most land-based risks. The underwriter must be certain, therefore, that the quality of the risk is high enough to assure a reasonable degree of certainty that the voyage will be completed safely.

Unacceptable lists, as such are not used by ocean marine underwriters, other than those writing only limited types of risks. However, each underwriter has a number of factors considered as making risks unacceptable. There are six different categories which may be analyzed in determining if a specific risk is acceptable or not. Underwriters may prepare unacceptable lists based on these same six factors.

1. *Nationality.* Long experience has taught underwriters that people of some nationalities are more suited by temperament to a life on the seas than others. This adaptation of the captain and crew can be invaluable in time of crisis. An insurer, therefore, may, from its own experience, place on the unacceptable list, all vessels of certain nationalities.

2. *Ownership and Management.* In the ocean transport business, as in all other businesses, some owners and managers are less desirable than others. Some are careless about maintaining their vessels in good condition, and some do not spend the money to secure proper equipment. There are some who also are unable to secure competent officers and crewmen. Still others have a poor reputation for fair dealing with insurers after disaster strikes. Underwriters prefer not to insure these less desirable people and may identify these problems on unacceptable lists. They will not publish lists of unacceptable owners as such, but may put, on unacceptable lists, such wording as "vessels whose owners do not hire competent officers" or "vessels which are not maintained in good condition."

3. *Physical Condition.* The seaworthiness of a vessel, its interior condition with respect to cargo, its age, and its structural characteristics are all vital factors to underwriters. The power of the vessel, the material of which it is built, and the equipment also are important. Cargo carried in a vessel unsuited for it, or improperly equipped to handle it, can be seriously jeopardized. Underwriters, therefore, may develop combinations of specific factors they consider as making the risk unacceptable.

4. *Types of Cargo and Packaging.* Some types of cargo are extremely subject to damage by dampness or shifting. Type of packaging is very important in preventing damage caused by these perils, as well as by theft and pilferage. Underwriters usually require specified types of packaging for certain cargo and may publish these

requirements in an unacceptable list. The age of the vessel is important for cargo coverage; surcharges are usually applied if the vessel is over 20 years old.

5. *Season of the Year.* The season during which the voyage is to be made can be important. Ice can cause damage to vessels and cargo during certain seasons in colder climates. Storage of perishable goods in some ports may be a problem during certain seasons, too. Underwriters may consider those applicants who appear to present unusual hazards from the standpoint of the seasons as unacceptable.

6. *Evidence of Poor Faith.* Ocean marine insurance is based upon good faith and fair dealing between the policyholder and the underwriter. While this is true of all insurance, it is particularly true of this line. The underwriter cannot see the vessel or arrange for its inspection during much of the voyage and must depend upon the policyholder's integrity to reveal unusual conditions which might affect the insurance. When an owner of a vessel or a ship is found to evidence poor faith or unfair dealing, that risk must be considered unacceptable. An ocean marine underwriter, more than most underwriters, cannot tolerate moral hazard.

Yachts may involve special unacceptable rules. A yacht is defined as a vessel used for private pleasure purposes. Thus, a vessel used in a commercial enterprise is not considered to be a yacht, although it may have been built as a yacht. Different ocean marine companies use different rules on unacceptability. Miliary surplus vessels and all vessels powered with automobile conversion engines may be unacceptable in some companies. Any yacht with a speed capability of 40 knots or more may be unacceptable in others. Even the operator may be a subject of unacceptability — such as an operator of a yacht who is under age 21 or who has a poor automobile driving record.

SECURING INFORMATION

Ocean marine underwriters have some unusual facilities at their command for securing information about specific risks. These sources are important because the nature of the line requires that the underwriter secure considerable amounts of information. An underwriter, particularly for larger companies, will seldom rely on an unacceptable list. Rather, an ocean marine underwriter will search for as much information as possible before deciding upon the acceptability of an applicant.

Application

The starting point for ocean marine insurance, as with other lines, is the application which is submitted by the producer. Although the application may involve a huge ship or one of many cargo items, it contains substantially the same information as others. Applications contain information which is typed on the policy, but the application is not made a part of the policy. Standard provisions are printed on the back of the application and special conditions may be specified on the face of the application, all of which are restated in the policy when issued.

Applications are different for every insurer. However, there is a similarity with most of the questions covering the same categories. These can be classified into three groups:

1. Personal

2. Description of vessel, cargo, and voyage
3. Insurance information

The following information is generally requested, for each category.

1. *Personal*

A. Applicant's full name and firm name, if any.
B. Applicant's business address, and mailing address if different.
C. Type of business conducted by the applicant.
D. Length of time the applicant has been in this business.
E. Details of losses of the types which might be covered by the insurance, during the previous period, such as five years.

2. *Description of Vessel, Cargo and Voyage*

A. Vessel: Whether the vessel is being insured, or the carrier of the cargo, information is needed. The questions concern the material with which the vessel is built, its engine and horsepower, its structural plan, its equipment, its provisions for handling and storage of cargo and its condition, both interior and exterior.
B. Cargo: If cargo coverage is requested, the underwriter must know the type of cargo, its degree of preparation or completion of assembly, its materials, its perishability, the type of packaging being used, and other questions which vary by the type of cargo. If coverage is requested only on the vessel, most of this information will still be needed, although it may be in more general terms; the safety of the ship may be jeopardized by cargo which is poorly packaged or improperly stowed. Every type of application must indicate all of the kinds of cargo to be carried, since one type could have an effect on others.
C. Voyage: Applications made for coverage on a specific voyage must contain answers concerning destination, the ports of call before reaching the destination, the route to be followed, and any unusual circumstances anticipated. Applications for future shipments of a number of cargoes will give the same general information on each proposed shipment, though in less detail.

3. *Insurance Information*

A. The policy and coverages desired, the approximate date of the sailing, the name of the vessel, and the ports of shipment and destination
B. For cargo coverage, the kinds of goods and number of packages.
C. Name and address of any loss payee.
D. Any special conditions desired, in addition to those standard clauses printed on the back of the application.

Classification Societies

There are several classification societies that set forth details of vessels for whom a classification is requested. Two of the most popular are The American Record, and Lloyd's Register. These societies publish books giving information about the builder, type of machinery, construction, type of ballast, name of owner and former owner, country of registry and so forth. Underwriters check with the societies on every risk, realizing that some may be more reliable or impartial than others.

Classification in an inferior society infers that a lesser classification would be given in a more reliable society. If there is no classification in any society, it means either that the construction is so poor that no society will classify it, or that it is so superior that the owner does not wish to spend the money to secure a classification.

Surveyors

Marine surveyors are persons who are specially trained to furnish reports on the condition of vessels. Underwriters request reports from these surveyors on any risk they feel needs more detailed information. Even on risks shown in the books of the classification societies, the underwriter may wish assurance that the vessel has not deteriorated or suffered damage. Some of these surveyors are employed by the companies, somewhat like engineers in other lines, while others are independent and make surveys for many insurers, being similar in this respect to inspection companies. A marine survey contains many details about the vessel and may include recommendations for improvements or repairs.

Maps, Charts and Port Books

Underwriters maintain maps, charts and port books in their offices or have access to them. By referring to these sources, they can gather much information about the geographical conditions that may affect the voyage. Various vessels and cargoes may be affected by winds, currents, the depth of water in certain ports and similar factors, and the underwriter should refer to current records in order to secure detailed information that will help in the evaluation of the risk.

Producers

The producer is an important source of information for all lines, but is more valuable for ocean marine insurance than for most others. This is particularly true of the brokers who arrange the placement of a large share of the ocean marine risks, especially on the vessels. These brokers represent the applicants in dealing with the underwriters and are able to supply the answers to most questions. Many other risks are handled by agents who may be located anywhere because the shippers of cargo are situated in every state. These agents can furnish information about the cargo too, but may not be well informed on details of the vessel or the voyage.

Yachts are submitted by agents of the company, and these agents often are the same ones who produce other lines. Yachts may be written in conjunction with other coverages needed by the owner. These producers can furnish the same type of general information as for other lines, too.

CLASSIFICATION AND RATING

Ocean marine risks are not classified for rating purposes, as such. It is true that most vessels appear in the books of the claasification societies, but the purpose of these societies is to see that vessels are seaworthy from a construction standpoint for the trade in which they will operate. Vessels are built according to the requirements of a society, but not under the jurisdiction of the society. The list which is published by a classification society is helpful in establishing rates and helpful in underwriting, but the classification does not directly determine the rate. In this respect, ocean marine insurance is different from most property and casualty lines, with classifications being established for the latter lines and rates being determined quite precisely from the classifications.

Ocean marine rating is based on judgment — on an individual risk basis. The underwriter weighs many factors and then arrives at a rate under which the underwriter is willing to accept the risk.

Vessel: Some of the more important factors considered are those relating to the physical characteristics of the vessel. These include the material of which the vessel is built, the structural plan, the engines and power supply and the condition of the vessel. Also taken into account are such factors as the route planned for the voyage, the time of year and the type of cargo to be carried. Other items of consideration are the reputation of the captain and crew, the nationality of registry and the renown of the owner.

Cargo: Perhaps the most critical factor is the susceptibility of the cargo to damage. There are so many perils that can damage goods at sea and in various ports that the underwriter must consider the degree of susceptibility to various types of damage. In recent years, one of the most important factors concerns the ports through which cargo will pass because of the pilferage that frequently occurs. In addition to the reputation of ports based on the supervision used, critical factors conducive to pilferage are the types of cargo and the manner of packaging. Another factor in rating is the kind of cargo that will be stowed with the cargo under consideration; some materials are subject to considerable damage from certain other materials in case of leakage or spillage. Even the type of cleaning of the hold between voyages can be important to certain cargoes. Finally, of course, all of the characteristics thus far described as applicable to the vessel must be considered by the underwriter of cargo.

After considering all of these factors, the underwriter arrives at a rate considered to be reasonable. Each risk is somewhat unique and no fixed rate can be used. After arriving at the rate which appears to be correct, the underwriter may find that it needs to be revised. For one thing conditions may have changed. For another, competition in the international market is keen, and adjustments may need to be made in order to secure the business.

These comments about judgment rating are not meant to imply that the ocean marine underwriter simply fabricates a rate out of thin air. Actually, an underwriter draws upon extensive experience, and is able to apply informed judgment concerning the conditions which the risk will face. A large body of statistics has been developed over the centuries, so a judgment rate is well grounded in solid experience.

Ocean marine rating, unlike most other lines of property and casualty insurance, is free from regulation of state rating laws. One reason for this is the necessity of considering many complex factors in determining rates. More important, however, is the necessity of revising rates to meet competition. Without this freedom, there would be little ocean marine insurance written in the United States.

Yachts are often rated from tables, with a rate per $100 of value applied to the amount of insurance. Since yachts are more closely akin to outboard motor boats than ocean-going steamers, in many cases, they are handled more like inland marine insurance. Companies that do not consider themselves as ocean marine insurers may write yacht coverages. Often this protection is handled in conjunction with a substantial account of a policyholder. Because of this unusual handling, yachts may be rated from a table, with little or no judgment applied. Not all yachts are in this category — larger ocean-going yachts are handled more like commercial vessels. In almost every case, however, a yacht is written on the unique policy used for ocean marine risks.

Protection and indemnity insurance is rated by an unusual method. The limit of liability is stated in the policy, but the rate is applied to the gross weight of the vessel. Another feature which is not common in liability coverages written in other lines is the use of deductible. Ocean marine underwriters deal with commercial enterprises, and claims can be presented at any place in the world, so it is logical to provide that the shipowner pay small losses.

POLICY FORMS

The ocean marine policy is a quaint relic of days long past. The words are amusing but unintelligible to a person not versed in their meanings. The same general wording is used throughout the English-speaking world, and has evolved from the policies used more than 300 years ago. Changes are made by adding new words, such as additional perils. However, the language itself has been tested so thoroughly in the courts of the world that no underwriter would dare to make any changes. Marine underwriters, brokers and marine lawyers can understand the policy, but undoubtedly few other persons can make similar claim.

There is no standard form of policy which is required by law. Each insurer uses its own policy form, but these are very similar in wording. In this respect, ocean marine insurance is different from fire insurance because the latter uses a policy which is prescribed by the state law.

However, the ocean marine policy is similar to the fire insurance policy in construction. Both use a printed, basic policy as the foundation for all risks. To this basic policy, the underwriter may add forms which specify the particular clauses and agreements applicable to the specific risk. Some of these forms are printed for certain classes of risks, while others are typed for individual tailoring by endorsement.

In ocean marine, problems usually arise from the added forms. The basic policy has been thoroughly interpreted, but some of the added forms contain wording which has not been tested in the courts. The forms are held to overrule the basic policy, since they supposedly represent the specific wishes of the parties. If the wording is not prepared with extreme care, the result might be different from that which is intended. In addition, the customs established in world trade play a part in interpreting the intentions of the policy.

TERMINOLOGY — DEFINITIONS

Terminology used in ocean marine policies is unique. The more important terms which are peculiar to this line are described briefly.

Perils Clause

Probably the most important part of an ocean marine policy is the list of perils contained in the "perils clause." This is the list "touching the adventures and perils" which the insurance company "is contented to bear, and takes upon itself in this voyage." The perils are described as being "of the seas, men-of-war, fires, enemies, pirates, rovers, thieves, jettisons, letters of mart and countermart, reprisals, takings at sea, arrests, restraints and detainments of all kings, princes, or people, of what nation, condition or quality soever, barratry of the master and mariners, and all other perils, losses and misfortunes that have or shall come to the hurt, detriment or damage of the said goods and merchandise or any part thereof."

Two groups of these perils are particularly important today.

1. Perils *of* the Sea: These are the losses which occur in the course of navigation. The most important ones are stranding, sinking, collision and heavy weather.
2. Perils *on* the Sea: Fire is the listed peril which can be classified as a peril *on* the sea (in contrast to the perils *of* the sea). Such consequential damage as smoke, heat and odor are included also.

The other named perils are of minor importance today. Few vessels are lost in the latter part of the 20th century from pirates, rovers, thieves or by barratry (the willful misconduct by the captain or crew to use the vessel without the consent of the owner but to the detriment of the owner). Most of the other common clauses are qualifying clauses of the "perils clause."

General Average

Sometimes a portion of the vessel or cargo must be jettisoned to save the entire venture. If this act is done because of a peril of the sea, the general average clause applies. (The word "average" is derived from a French word meaning "loss from a peril of the sea.") The general average clause provides that a loss which is voluntarily incurred by a portion of the vessel or cargo in order to save the entire voyage from impending disaster is shared by all interests involved.

This provision is applied when the vessel is endangered and a sacrifice is made to prevent loss to the vessel or cargo. The interests who suffer loss under these conditions are reimbursed by the other parties, providing the venture is successful and the party seeking reimbursement is free of fault in the danger. The loss settlements are complicated, but the principle must be understood by marine underwriters.

Particular Average

Every *partial* loss which is not a general average loss is called a "particular average loss." None of the other interests contributes to the payment for the lost property; it is borne by its owner, or paid under the particular average clause. Most marine losses are of the particular average type. Perils of the sea, as well as perils on the sea, may be involved.

A special provision of the particular average clause is that which limits the recovery to the proportion that the amount of insurance bears to the valuation stated in the policy. When insuring a vessel, therefore, it is essential that a fair valuation be used. Cargo is valued at its market value, using complex calculations. This average clause provision tends to guarantee that proper insurance to value is carried.[2]

Free of Particular Average Clause

Policies may be written with a "free of particular average" clause (F.P.A.). Under these policies, specified types of particular average losses are not covered; ordinarily only such perils as stranding, sinking, fire and collision with another vessel are covered. Thus, this is a qualifying clause which is quite restrictive in its coverage. Slightly different wording is used on American and English policies, but the general intent is similar. Obviously, the word "free" translates into "relieved of," except that it really means "relieved of a portion of the particular average clause."

Average Payable Inrrespective of Percentage

A common clause now used provides for "average payable irrespective of percentage." In effect, this clause waives the average clause provision of the particular average clause, and does not impose a penalty for underinsurance.

Franchise Average Clause

Ocean marine policies customarily use a franchise clause rather than a deductible clause. A deductible provides that an amount will be deducted from the total amount of the claim. A franchise provides that if the amount of the claim is below the franchise amount, nothing will be paid; if over that amount, the claim is paid in full. The reasons for using these clauses are the same as for other lines: to reduce the cost of the insurance and to avoid the necessity of handling small claims. The amount of the franchise clause is determined by the underwriter on a judgment basis, depending upon the damageability of the property. (A franchise clause is considered to be a type of average clause.)

Subrogation Clause

Cargo policies cover on an all risks basis. When a loss such as pilferage occurs, the company pays and then subrogates against the vessel owner. However, if the loss is by a peril *of* the sea, no subrogation is made.

Collisin Clause

Liability for collision with another vessel is covered under the hull portion of the policy. The coverage is described in the "running down clause" (R.D.C.). On commercial vessels, it is not uncommon for the hull to be covered under a separate policy from the P and I insurance. The hull policy provides that it will pay for collision liability. On a yacht policy, where one policy covers both the hull and P and I (as well as guest medical payments plus coverage under the longshoremen's and harbor workers act), collision coverage is paid under P and I on an excess basis.

Bottomry Bonds

When a shipowner or cargo owner borrows money and pledges the vessel or

2. This average clause provision of ocean marine insurance is similar to the coinsurance clause used in the fire insurance policy. In fact, the coinsurance-type clause is called an "average clause" in some fire jurisdictions.

cargo, the evidence of the transaction is called a bottomry bond. The loan is to be repaid at the conclusion of the voyage; but if the vessel is lost, the debt is cancelled. (These loans are seldom used today.)

Inchmaree Clause

The inchmaree clause is added to marine policies to extend coverage to another peril such as damage to cargo from the bursting of boilers and other defects in the machinery of the vessel. The inchmaree clause holds that such losses are not covered under the basic perils of the policy. This clause is now added to all policies covering property in vessels propelled by mechanical power.

Doctrine of No Deviation

It is implied in the ocean marine contract that the vessel will not deviate from the planned voyage. If an unexplained and unnnecessary deviation is made, the insurance may be void. The policy does permit deviations without prejudice to the insurance, however, when caused by weather conditions or unavoidable accidents.

RETENTION AND REINSURANCE

After the ocean marine underwriter has accepted the risk, prepared the policy and detemined the rate, the underwriter still needs to face the problem of a possible catastrophic loss. Ships can sink with total losses to vessels and cargo and no one insurer can survive such loss alone. It is customary for many insurers to share in the writing of insurance on the vessel itself. Each insurer participates in the share of the risk it desires. No one insurer, therefore, suffers too much and reinsurance is not needed.

Cargo insurance, on the other hand, ordinarily is written by one insurer for each merchant, often on an open policy which permits a tremendous concentration of values on a single vessel. Reinsurance is used to distribute the exposure among many insurers. The following discussion relates only to reinsurance of cargo policies.

The retention of an underwriter is a specific decision. There are no rules other than those set by the company. The usual practice is to retain a rather conservative amount, partly to avoid all shock losses and partly to avoid too much accumulation of exposure that stems from more than one insured cargo being carried in the same vessel.

Most of the major types of reinsurance are used by ocean marine underwriters. Quota-share treaties are used when the underwriter needs to share all of the risks with the reinsurer, perhaps because of a shortage of capital. A modification of this is to share, on a participation basis, all risks moving over specified trade routes.

Excess treaties may be written in two forms under ocean marine practices. Excess of line reinsurance protects the company when its combined line of insurance on one vessel exceeds its retention. All exposures must be considered, whether hull, cargo, or freight. This type of reinsurance is adequate if the underwriter knows exactly the exposures faced on each vessel. Often, however, open policies are insured on cargoes, and the underwriter may not know when several cargo policyholders may use the same vessel, such as with coastal traffic in the United States.

In these cases, excess of loss reinsurance may be purchased, attaching when the retention is exceeded in any one loss. (This is a type of catastrophe reinsurance.)

Ocean marine reinsurance may be covered by treaties providing automatic coverage or by facultative placements. The latter are placements of individual risks on a judgment basis.

Ocean marine insurers often become reinsurers, also. Many reinsurance syndicates are composed of a number of insurers, as well as some professional reinsurers. In this manner, an ocean marine underwriter can achieve a much greater spread of risk than is possible on a direct basis. This practice is much more common here than on most property and casualty lines, thus demonstrating still another of the unique features of ocean marine underwriting.

SPECIAL PROBLEMS

Ocean marine underwriting is inextricably linked with the problems and developments of the shipping industry. The latter has encountered several new and unique situations in the years since World War II.

One of these problems is the tremendous increase in the cost to build and repair ships. This increase has made it more difficult to place the entire insurance on some ships. The value of the hull, combined with the value of cargoes at inflated prices and with the concentration in larger ships, causes need for a large amount of insurance on one voyage.

A type of vessel which has increased in importance and also in size in recent years is the tanker. Some of these are huge vessels transporting large amounts of petroleum. The tankers are expensive and values are high on each voyage. Compounding the problem, are large tankers that have suffered a disturbing number of casualties at sea. The losses to vessel and cargo are serious enough, but a new problem is caused by the pollution from large amounts of crude oil spilled on the oceans. Beaches, harbors, and other craft have been polluted in this fashion. The liability is not always certain, but the prospects of future losses of this type, perhaps with even more damage, are sufficient to trouble ocean marine underwriters.

Because of a federal anti-pollution law which became effective in 1970, most ocean marine insurers in the United States formed a pollution liability pool in order to provide coverage to owners, operators and charterers of vessel or boats in case they become liable for oil pollution cleanup costs. To the existing prohibition of oil pollution under the law of 1970 is yet another law which became effective in 1972 imposing statutory liability on the spillage of hazardous substances. These acts impose a statutory limit of liability which is the lesser of the following two amounts: $100 per gross ton of the veseel or $14,000,000. Coverage provided through the Water Quality Insurance Syndicate policy parallels the liability agreements stipulated in those laws.

Another problem lies in the use of containers for cargo. The time-honored methods of packing and loading cargo were inadequate in the post-war period. Pilferage caused tremendous losses, damage was high, and handling costs became almost prohibitive.

The ideal solution appeared to be found with the development of containers. These are large boxes roughly the size of the semi-trailers used with trucks. The containers are packed and sealed at the factory of the shippers, carried by flat trailers behind trucks or on railroad flat cars, and loaded quite efficiently into ships which are designed to handled the containers.

This rosy prospect has failed to materialize fully, however. The packing is sometimes improper, and damage is not discovered until arrival at the destination point. Also, many shippers are unable to fill a container resulting in considerable lost space. Most ironic of all, use of containers fail in the area where their principal benefit is expected; pilferage continues but is much harder to detect because the containers are resealed and forwarded. Even worse, pilferage is replaced in too many instances by the theft of an entire container. In spite of these problems, the use of containers continues to grow. Some ships are built to handle an entire cargo of containers.

New techniques in containerization are being developed, but each one appears to increase the problems for underwriters, rather than reduce them.

Ocean shipping is involved in international law, political maneuvers, national prestige, and other factors which are beyond the scope of insurance. Still, the ocean marine underwriter must deal with all of these problems, and attempt to make a profit in the meantime. This is a unique, fascinating task.

QUESTIONS FOR DISCUSSION

1. List the 4 major types of coverages under ocean marine policies.
2. Explain the meaning of "freight" as an item of insurance under an ocean marine policy.
3. Explain 4 of the characteristics of risks which could lead underwriters to reject an applicant for ocean marine insurance.
4. Differentiate between:
   (a) perils of the sea and on the sea.
   (b) a "particular average" and a "free of particular average" clause.
   (c) a franchise clause and a deductible clause.
5. Describe the use of containers in the handling of ocean marine cargo, and explain its significance to underwriters.

30

Miscellaneous Casualty Coverages: Glass, Power Plant, and Aviation

Three additional coverages in the casualty insurance line are glass, power plant, and aviation, and each one is important to underwriters. However, none of them is of sufficient importance to most underwriters to warrant a complete discussion of the underwriting practices.

Each coverage has a different reason for not requiring a full discussion. Glass insurance is fairly simple and is almost always written as an adjunct to property insurance. Power plant coverage, often called boiler and machinery insurance, is written by a very few companies and requires technical training in order to handle the engineering and underwriting of it. Aviation insurance is written almost exclusively by pools, requiring special knowledge and techniques; the smaller plans written by a few companies are handled very much like other types of insurance.

For the sake of simplicity, each coverage is discussed separately in this chapter.

GLASS INSURANCE

Insurance against the breakage of glass is an unusual type of coverage in several ways. It is an old type of insurance, and it is one of the simplest. There are very few exclusions and the average premiums are low, yet no more than 25% of all glass is insured. Although this is a property-type of coverage, glass insurance is traditionally considered to be casualty insurance. Finally, unlike other property coverages, the insurer replaces the broken glass in almost every case, rather than paying for the loss in money.

The coverage is on an all risks basis with the only exclusions being losses caused by fire or war; fire losses are covered under a fire insurance policy, and virtually every insurance policy excludes loss by war. Coverage applies to the described glass, frames, temporary repairs, and removal of any obstruction that prevents replacement of the glass.

Breakage of glass constituting a part of a dwelling structure is covered under broad form and special form fire policies and the comparable home-owners policies. Losses are subject to the deductible applicable to all perils, which usually is $100 or more. Thus, if any one window in a home is broken, except for a large picture window, there would be no recovery, but several windows broken in one loss may result in recovery.

Glass coverage may be written on both dwellings and commercial buildings on a scheduled basis. A glass schedule consists of the measurements and type of glass, as well as any lettering. In addition to panes and plates, a glass policy may cover glass bricks, stained glass, leaded glass and many other types of glass.

Residence glass coverage may be written on a blanket basis, with a limit of $50 for all damage arising out of one occurrence. Dollar limits apply to such categories as stained glass and radiant heating panels.

UNDERWRITING FACTORS

Acceptable Risks

Most insurance companies write glass insurance, but all of them write it as an accommodation line. This is not to say that a company will not write a glass policy alone on a specific applicant, but such circumstances are rare. The premium is so low, and the coverage fits so well with other coverages, that glass insurance is seldom written as the sole policy in a company.

Commercial insurers usually offer glass coverage as a companion to commercial property lines. However, it could be written in conjunction with commercial liability insurance, too. The acceptability factors for the other lines ordinarily control the acceptability for glass insurance.

Personal lines companies formerly offered blanket residence glass coverage in conjunction with dwelling fire and homeowners policies. This covered all glass in the dwelling, regardless of its value, and with no schedule required. As deductibles on the basic policy increased, the concept of no-deductible coverage on this one type of loss became less logical. Loss frequency sometimes became a problem, noncancellation laws started to appear, and personal fire lines became less profitable. As a result, most companies stopped writing this blanket coverage. It is now available in only a few companies, where its acceptability is determined by the related fire coverages.

Most companies write scheduled glass coverage on dwelling and homeowners policies. The acceptability is seldom a separate consideration. Rather, the acceptability of the basic policy will apply, and the glass coverage is added with little additional underwriting.

Unacceptable Risks

Insurers seldom use unacceptable lists for glass insurance. As a general rule, if a risk is written for other coverages, the glass is acceptable for coverage.

There is one type of applicant who is considered unacceptable by most underwriters, however. This is the one who has an abnormal frequency of loss. Since the premium is low and most losses are total, an insurer cannot tolerate very many losses even though they are small in the amount of money paid for each loss. Sometimes the frequency is caused by the location of glass. An underwriter would consider, as unacceptable, an applicant with a loss frequency pattern if the glass were in an area subject to riot or rock throwing, or in a location where autos and trucks often threw stones through the glass, or where abnormal windstorm or hail conditions cause an unusually large number of losses. In other cases, a loss frequency might be caused by structural problems or careless employees or children playing ball. Whatever the cause, the high frequency of loss can make a risk unacceptable.

Account underwriting is one key to unacceptability. An unusually high glass loss frequency may not make a risk unacceptable if the balance of coverages are sizable and profitable. On the other hand, an underwriter may decline to write glass coverage if there is little related insurance or if the other policies are borderline or unprofitable.

Certain types of risks are less desirable for glass insurance, and they are often considered unacceptable (subject to account underwriting). One type is the risk that is most likely to have glass losses, such as liquor stores, bowling alleys, greenhouses, poolrooms, taverns, amusement arcades and theaters. Another type is the risk having an unusually high value in glass, such as bent glass or plates with complicated lettering and designs. Another type consists of glass that is difficult to replace; memorial windows is a good example. Still another type includes glass that has a high probability of loss; an example is glass painted on 25% or more of its surface with uneven expansion often resulting in cracking. One more type is one which has an above average probability of loss just in the course of replacement, such as signs with neon tubes and lettering.

SECURING INFORMATION

An underwriter must secure complete information before issuing a glass policy. The physical factors of the risk and the neighborhood are most important. While much of the background information will usually be available on related policies, a complete description of the glass itself is essential.

Moral hazard is of great importance to most underwriters, but not to the glass underwriter. The policyholder has nothing to gain from a glass loss, because the value is low and the insurer almost always replaces the glass rather than paying for the loss in money. On the other hand, the policyholder always suffers some inconvenience and may lose some business because of broken glass.

The application for glass insurance generally includes most of the information required for a fire policy: information about the applicant, the premises, the type of business and previous losses. In addition, a complete description of the glass is required, including size, type and location. For residence glass coverage on a blanket basis, the insurer requires nothing more than the fire information with an indication that the glass coverage is requested.

The glass underwriter almost always requires inspection of the glass. The inspection may be made by the producer, but if the values are other than nominal, an inspection or a survey by an independent company or by an inspector or loss prevention specialist of the insurer is almost mandatory. In addition to supplying underwriting information, an inspection will verify the size and other factors upon which the rates are based, often resulting in an increased premium. A good inspector may also be able to suggest means of minimizing the possibilites of losses.

CLASSIFICATION AND RATING

It is imperative to the underwriter that glass be properly classified and rated. Only in this way is the underwriter certain of receiving an adequate rate in the face of many difficulties. One of these difficulties is the frequent inaccurate description of the glass; most producers do their best to classify glass properly, but it is a complicated process and errors do occur. Another difficulty is the low premium for most glass insurance. However, the major difficulty is the extreme selection against the insurer; adverse selection is probably worse than in any other line. Only a low percentage of glass is insured, and the majority of the insured glass is in large metropolitan areas with their attendant high incidence of crime and vandalism. Perhaps even worse, many policyholders do not insure all of their glass, only that which has the greatest exposure to loss. There is a degree of selection against the insurer in most lines of insurance, but in no other type of property insurance is there selection against the insurer within a risk. When other insurance is purchased, it applies to all of the property, but a glass applicant may insure only certain items.

An underwriter attempts to offset these disadvantages by keeping rates as low as possible, thereby hoping to attract more customers. Lower rates are offered for glass having a lower exposure to loss in an effort to achieve full insurance on all glass in a risk and to avoid adverse selection.

Rating Factors

There are six rating factors for glass insurance to which the underwriter must apply the applicable classifications and then the rates. These factors are as follows.

1. *Size of the glass* — The exact measurements must be specified, giving allowance to the setting.

2. *Kind of glass and type of setting* — From a table called a "directory of glass," a classification is determined for each kind of glass. For example, plain plate may be class A; colored mirrors, class C; and bent glass, class D. Glass which is clamped or screwed in place, rather than completely enclosed in a frame, usually requires an increase of one class.

3. *Basic cost* — A rate table is used to secure the basic cost for the size and class of glass. The rates are in dollars and cents.

4. *Position in the building* — The rates are modified by the position of the glass in the building. Percentage modifiers are used for each class. For example, "one" may be used for class A glass on the ground floor, "one-third" for certain locations inside the building, such as in lobbies, and "two" for refrigerator cases.

5. *Occupancy* — Discounts are applied for specified occupancies. Thus, a 50% discount may apply to hospitals, museums, libraries and churches, while a 75% discount applies to mausoleums.

6. *Territory* — The final rate is partially dependent upon the territory in which the glass is located. Territorial modifiers are based upon the freight costs from the manufacturer, as well as on the hazard of breakage in each area. A number of terri-

tories are used, each with a factor to increase or decrease the rate.

Glass is generally rated strictly from the manual. The hazards and costs are taken into account by the rather complicated rate structure used. Rating by individual risks is not common in glass insurance. Even superior risks, such as wired glass or mesh glass, are classified separately and rated by the rate tables.

Experience rating of glass insurance is permitted in some states. It applies only to large risks, such as those developing more than $300 of annual premium by the rate tables.

Glass rates are established by national bureaus. Most insurers either use these rates or deviate from them by a fixed percentage. Few insurers attempt to develop independent rate tables for glass.

Some overlapping of coverages occurs whenever glass insurance is sold. Many glass losses could be covered under other coverages. Losses by explosion, riot, windstorm, and non-owned vehicles would be covered by extended coverage; losses by earthquake, by the earthquake damage assumption endorsement and so forth. To the extent that these coverages and the glass policy both cover the same losses, there is a degree of redundancy in the rates. Any of these losses would be covered first under the glass policy. Since glass is scheduled on the glass policy and not on the other policies, the glass policy is primary under the Agreement of Guiding Principles.[1] The other policies, therefore, have some rate redundancy because they cover the losses in the absence of a glass policy, and are relieved of that exposure when a glass policy is written. The degree of overlap is not large, for most glass losses in commercial risk are caused by vandalism, and the vandalism coverage in fire insurance usually excludes glass breakage. Only a small portion of the premium for extended coverages and the other overlapping coverages is allocated for glass breakage. For that reason, the rate redundancy is not large. Still, the existence of some redundancy makes it desirable — from the standpoint of a property underwriter — for both coverages to be written in one company, in addition to the obvious savings in claims handling by having all coverages in the same company.

POLICY FORMS

The glass policy is one of the simplest insurance forms in use to cover an important line. It provides for a description of the glass, briefly states the coverage and exclusions and makes provisions for settling losses. It can cover a single page if the typed material (name, address, description, premium, etc.) is placed on a separate face sheet.

---

1. The Agreement of Guiding Principles is a set of stipulations concerning which of two or more policies will pay for specified losses. Some cases provide for one policy to be primary and the others excess, while others require proration among policies. The principle that applies to glass insurance provides that a scheduled policy will be primary when compared with blanket policies; all commercial glass is scheduled on the policy. Not all insurers have agreed to use these principles, but most insurers follow them in the settlement of losses.

The comprehensive glass policy is a standardized contract. Its provisions are not required by statute or regulation, but virtually all insurers use it without change. It may be used to provide specific or blanket coverage, too.

Deductibles are sometimes used in glass insurance on scheduled glass. A common approach is to make the deductible a percentage of loss, rather than a fixed amount. A rate credit is allowed for the deductible, perhaps 10% for a deductible of 25% of each loss.

RETENTION AND REINSURANCE

Glass exposure at any one location is seldom large enough to be of concern to an underwriter. All of the coverage is retained in the writing company, subject only to regular excess reinsurance.

An excess reinsurance treaty would come into play only under two conditions. The first is a loss at one location exceeding the retained amount; this could be a large glass exposure, or it could be, and much more commonly will be, a glass loss in conjunction with another loss. For example, an explosion in a building could damage the structure, as well as its equipment and glass. An insurer with an excess reinsurance treaty applied to all lines can collect for glass losses, as well as other losses.

The catastrophe loss is a second condition under which an excess reinsurance treaty could be involved with glass losses. An explosion or sonic boom could break glass over a wide area, causing a reinsurance claim. An earthquake, a hurricane, or a windstorm can break a large amount of glass, resulting in losses above the attachment point of an excess treaty, too.

POWER PLANT INSURANCE

Insurance against loss caused by accidents to boilers and machinery is a highly specialized type of coverage. It covers both direct and indirect loss to many types of pressure vessels, electrical machinery, and other types of equipment, as well as damage resulting from their accidental bursting or breaking.

Formerly written only as a separate policy, this coverage has been recognized as a part of a businessowner's commercial exposure. The coverage has been available as an addition to a commercial package policy and is included as a modular part of the simplified-language commercial forms program of ISO, so it can be written with other commercial policies and packages.

DESCRIPTION OF COVERAGES

A large variety of industrial equipment can be covered under the boiler and machinery policy. This equipment may be grouped into three categories.

1. Boilers and similar equipment using pressure to generate energy. Examples are steam cookers, refrigeration apparatus, laundry equipment, and low-pressure steam or hot water used to heat buildings.
2. Electrical equipment, such as motors, converters and generators.
3. Machinery and engines of the types using steam turbines, flywheels, governors, blowers and gears.

Many people tend to think only of boilers when boiler and machinery insurance is mentioned. Actually, much of the common need for this protection is involved with modern equipment found in offices and apartments; elevators, escalators, air conditioning, central heating units, pumps for swimming pools and the like.

Any of this equipment can cause loss by bursting, breakdown, disintegration, cracking and so forth. The causes of the losses may be improper maintenance or operation of defective parts or assembly, failure of control devices, etc. Whatever the cause and type of loss, the resulting direct and indirect damage can be considerable.

The power plant policy covers direct loss or damage in the following cases.

1. Damage to property of the policyholder, both to the insured object and to other property.
2. Extra costs incurred in repairing or replacing the damaged property in the fastest possible way, including expenses for temporary repairs, overtime, air shipments, etc.
3. Property damage liability, paying for liability to the property of others caused by an insured accident.
4. Bodily injury liability, covering the policyholder's liability for injury to persons by an insured accident. This coverage is optional. It excludes liability under workers' compensation laws, but otherwise covers employees.
5. Legal expense and investigation in connection with claims under property damage and bodily injury liability.

Indirect loss is covered under four situations by power plant insurance.

1. Use and occupancy, paying for loss casued by business interruption as a result of an insured accident.
2. Outage, paying a stipulated amount for the period that an insured object is out of use. A proportionate amount is paid for partial failure of equipment to operate.
3. Consequential loss, protecting the policyholder against loss by spoilage to perishable goods caused by interruption of power, failure of refrigeration, burn-out of motors, or other accidents which cause damage by interrupting power, heat, refrigeration or light.
4. Power interruption, paying a stipulated amount for the period that a public utility is unable to supply power. This policy is purchased by the user of power and indemnifies against loss resulting from the partial or total deprivation of power.

UNDERWRITING FACTORS

Acceptable Risks

Only a few companies write power plant insurance. In fact, more than 45% of the business was written in 1984 by the three largest companies.[2] Obviously, a high degree of specialization in underwriting has developed.

These few companies consider almost all applicants to be acceptable. Related business cannot be a factor, nor can the acceptability for other lines of insurance. Boiler and machinery insurance stands alone with little consideration being given to other lines.

Unacceptable Risks

Power plant insurers consider few applicants as being unacceptable. The largest class which would not be written consists of those risks who will not maintain their equipment properly.

2. "Insurance Premium Distribution — 1984," *Best's Review Property/Casualty Insurance Edition, Vol. 86, No. 3 (July 1985), p. 15.*

Producers generally are permitted to bind this type of insurance, but acceptability is dependent upon the risk meeting the requirements of company inspections which are rigid. Unacceptable are risks with poor maintenance, poor experience and those having mechanical defects. For producers without binding authority, no unacceptable list is used. The insurer inspects every risk, so it can decide which ones to accept.

Some insurers indicate, in agent manuals, the type of risks they consider to be problems, even though they are not unacceptable. Among these risks may be chemical manufacturing plants, motors in steel mills, extrusion machines, balers, turbogenerators and Yankee dryers in paper mills.

SECURING INFORMATION

For producers with binding authority, a complete application is required. In addition to the usual information about the applicant, the business, and the loss experience, a complete description of the objects to be insured is required. Most applications also require a detailed explanation of the present policy protecting the objects.

For producers who do not have binding authority, the power plant underwriter does not require an application, unlike underwriters for other lines. All that is needed is a memorandum containing the name and address of the applicant, the type of business, and the name of the person to contact, The insurer will always inspect the objects, so it can supply its own description. Under this arrangement, the producer must submit the application a week or more in advance of the date of expiration of the present policy, but is relieved of a considerable amount of detailed work.

CLASSIFICATION AND RATING

Most insurers use the classification and rating system promulgated by the bureau. This system includes no territorial differences in rates. Objects are first classified by type; examples are boilers, water heaters, steam turbines and vacuum tanks. The next factor is the number of each type to be insured. An additional division is made by the number of locations at which objects are located.

The standard limit of coverage is $5,000, but higher limits may be purchased. Each object has its own "object rate." To this is added a one-time "location charge," which is basically a charge for making inspections. Rates are quoted in dollars for each object and location, and for optional coverages and limits. The underwriter ordinarily will compute and quote the premium if he or she is willing to accept the risk.

An important factor when considering the rate for power plant insurance is the inspection service which accompanies the policy. The inspection is conducted by experts and may help to prevent a serious loss. In fact, a primary purpose of this insurance is to prevent loss, and more than half of the premium dollar is allocated to inspections. Naturally, this increases the expense factors used in determining the rates. This also helps to explain why underinsurance is so prevalent in this line. Many times, the inspection service can prevent a loss, so little protection is needed against losses. This inspection service is one of the most important parts of the coverage and unique in its scope.

POLICY FORMS

While most insurers use the form prepared by the rating bureau, a copyrighted policy was used for many years.

The basic policy contains the general provisions applicable to all risks. Schedules are attached, each containing a definition of an insured object and including special provisions for that type of equipment.

RETENTION AND REINSURANCE

Catastrophe losses are always possible when insuring power plants. The direct and indirect losses can amount to substantial sums. Excess reinsurance is purchased by every insurer writing this line.

Pro rata sharing or surplus treaties are not used, however. A large portion of the premium is spent on engineering, making it impractical to share or cede a portion of the total risk. Thus, the only type of reinsurance which fits this line is excess reinsurance.

AVIATION INSURANCE

Underwriters for most companies seldom encounter aviation risks. All of the large aircraft and most of the smaller ones are written by pools, with producers submitting applications directly to the pool for underwriting and issuance; insurance companies share in these pools in predetermined shares. However, a few large companies write insurance for private planes, and a true multiple line underwriter should have a nodding acquaintance with avaiation insurance.

DESCRIPTION OF COVERAGES

The coverages of the aviation policy are similar to those of other lines, particularly automobile insurance, but the hazards are somewhat different. There are two basic parts of the policy.

1. Protection against damage to the aircraft. Aviation insurance parallels ocean marine in referring to this as "hull insurance." It is generally written on an all risks basis, too.

2. Protection against liability suits arising out of the ownership or operation of the airplane. There are five sections of liability coverage.

a. Injury to persons other than passengers.
b. Injury to passengers.
c. Property damage.
d. Medical payments.
e. Voluntary settlements. This is an unique coverage which commonly is called "admitted liability insurance." It offers to pay a prearranged sum to passengers who are killed or injured in the aircraft, regardless of legal liability. It may even be extended to include crew members, for additional premium. A condition of receiving the stipulated amount is the execution of a release of liability; if the claimant refuses to sign the release, this offer is withdrawn and the passenger then has the protection of the section affording liability coverage for passengers.

A number of other miscellaneous aviation policies or coverages are also available. Among these are the following.

1. Hangarkeeper's liability, protecting the bailee's liability for aircraft in the bailee's custody for repair or storage. Generally, this is available only as a part of an airport liability coverage.

2. Airmeet liability, covering the general liability of the sponsors of an airmeet or airshow. This is usually written as a seprate coverage.

3. Airport liability, protecting all liabilities much like a commercial liability policy.

4. Workers' compensation for employees of airports, airlines, and others.

5. Products liability, covering manufacture, repair or sale against liability arising out of alleged defects.

All of these basic and supplemental coverages are similar to their counterparts in other lines of insurance. The underwriter must consider the unique characteristics of aircraft when compared with the subject of other insurance. For example, large sums are involved in one craft, with modern commercial jets costing many millions of dollars. The pilot must be well-trained and in good physical condition for the safety of the passengers and the aircraft. Finally, in many states the laws of negligence have been modified to hold the owner or operator of an airplane absolutely liable under many conditions.

UNDERWRITING FACTORS

Acceptable Risks

Any owner or operator of an aircraft is acceptable for aviation insurance, except those who have demonstrated such a disregard for safety and maintenance that they are uninsurable. Pilots without adequate experience at flying the aircraft or the proposed operations may encounter difficulty in securing insurance at average costs. Owners of older aircraft or aircraft which had limited production also may find it difficult to secure coverage.

Aviation pools generally write every classification of aircraft. Not being companies, they are not concerned with related business. However, they do try to select risks which will have good experience, in order to make a profit for their member companies.

The individual companies writing aviation insurance generally consider only the smaller private aircraft to be acceptable. Many of these are written as accommodation lines for substantial policyholders of other lines in the company or for influential producers.

Unacceptable Risks

Aviation underwriters, particularly for pools, do not find it practical to publish unacceptable lists because of the wide variety of exposures and risks and combinations of them which are encountered. Since a great degree of rate flexibility is available to the aviation underwriter, consideration is given to almost every risk.

An airplane is not insured if it is not in good condition and does not receive proper service. The owner must be a responsible person and the pilot must be experienced in relation to the performance characteristics of the aircraft and the intended uses. Poor loss experience could be grounds for declining to write a risk, if the experience were caused by factors indicating that unacceptable underwriting conditions are present.

SECURING INFORMATION

Verbal presentation to the underwriter is the primary source of information to the aviation underwriter; ultimately supported by a completed application. Information that is required includes make and model of the aircraft, horsepower of the engine, date purchased, purchase price, use which is planned for it, names and experience of the pilots, arrangements for its maintenance and a description of any added equipment.

Every airplane that is insurable has an airworthiness certificate, and the classification must be shown on the application, whether normal, utility, transport, acrobatics, etc. A supplemental application is sometimes used to secure information about the pilot: the rating, the number of hours that the pilot has flown solo by type of airplane, total flying time during the preceding quarter or half year before the date of the application, night flying time, and the record of violations of civil aeronautics regulations.

Inspection is an occasional source of underwriting information, and some underwriters employ experts to inspect risks and furnish reports. There are also a few companies that inspect aircraft and their owners and operators on a fee basis. These inspections are concerned with the physical facts about the airplane and its operators.

The underwriter is also interested in personal factors. An applicant in weak financial condition may not be able to afford proper maintenance and, therefore, try to cut corners. A pilot with a reputation for taking chances or for speeding in an automobile may not be a safe pilot either. Factors of these types can be investigated through the same credit reporting companies that other underwriters use.

CLASSIFICATION AND RATING

The aviation underwriter classifies acceptable risks in several different ways. The first, and most basic classification is by type of use: commercial, private business and pleasure. The commercial class includes those who carry passengers or cargo for a fee, and also includes instruction. The private business class is quite large, and includes business firms and individuals who use planes to transport executives, salespersons, records, emergency orders of small parts, and the like. The classification of "pleasure" applies to individuals and groups who operate planes for personal use, whether for the enjoyment of flying or for getting to vacation spots more quickly.

Liability rates require further classification. The number of seats in the aircraft is a factor when insuring bodily injury to passengers, since the charges are on a per seat basis. The type of liability is another factor, because passenger liability costs more than liability for bodily injury to the public. Naturally, the premiums are higher for higher limits of liability, although the rates for each layer are lower than the previous layer, as in other types of liability insurance.

Rates for protection against damage to the hull are also based on other classification factors. The size of the airplane is important. The type of aircraft is also a factor, such as seaplanes or land planes. Finally, the age of the plane is considered, with a loading used for older planes because the amount of insurance is less, but repairs must be made with new parts. Hull coverage for aircraft is rated on the basis that the airplane is new and that it is insured to full value; rates are quoted per $100 of insurance.

Aviation rates are not determined from fixed tables, as are most other rates in the property and casualty insurance field. The aviation underwriter usually has a schedule showing minimum and maximum rates, but is given considerable latitude in determining the exact rate. The underwriter applies judgment to the facts and quotes a rate. Some of the factors considered are the business and standing of the applicant, financial condition of the business, intended use of the aircraft, age and condition of the equipment and experience of the pilots. All of these are taken into account, along with the competitive picture. Thus, it can be seen that the aviation underwriter actually determines the rates to be charged, in addition to deciding acceptability of risks.

POLICY FORMS

There is no standard aviation policy. Competition is a factor in offering more liberal coverages.

Deductibles are often used, both to avoid small losses and to encourage careful handling by making the policyholder pay the first portion of each loss. Also available is a similar provision called a participation clause, under which the policyholder pays a stated percentage of each loss, regardless of size. The percentage may be 10 or 25%, and avoids the necessity of the policyholder paying all of a loss up to a deductible amount of, say, $1,000; the participation clause involves the insurer in every loss. Rates are adjusted for deductible and participation clauses.

RETENTION AND REINSURANCE

The catastrophe potential is one of the major concerns of aviation underwriters. This is the principal reason that most aviation insurance is written by pools; most insurers want only a moderate exposure to shock losses, and the pool device is more efficient and less costly than reinsurance for most insurers, when the catastrophe potential is so great. This is also the reason that the few carriers that do write this coverage will limit their acceptance to small aircraft.

The liability exposure is tremendous. Even a small airplane can crash into a school or a packed stadium, killing many people, injuring others and damaging property. Add to this exposure, the problem of passenger liability for commercial aircraft carrying hundreds of passengers, and the ultimate liability loss can amount to many millions of dollars.

The hull exposure is fantastic for some of the modern jets. An airplane which costs many millions of dollars can crash and be totally destroyed, without any warning. Added together, the potential losses from one occurrence are staggering. The prospect of two fully-loaded passenger jets colliding over a large city is enough to make any underwriter seek protection under heavy reinsurance treaties or to spread the exposure among many insurers by means of the pool device.

QUESTIONS FOR DISCUSSION

1. State the exclusions under a Glass Insurance Policy.
2. Explain the problems, under glass insurance, of:
   (a) loss frequency
   (b) moral hazards
3. List 4 types of equipment which may be covered under power plant insurance.
4. Give examples of both direct and indirect loss covered by the boiler and machinery policy.
5. Explain the unique role of inspections in power plant insurance.
6. Describe briefly these coverages under the aviation policy:
   (a) 2 basic parts
   (b) 3 supplemental coverages.
7. What are the personal factors considered by aviation underwriters, and why are they important?

31

Fidelity and Surety Bonds

Fidelity and surety bonds are not considered insurance, technically, but they are handled by casualty insurance companies, as well as by bonding companies, so they can be considered as comprising a line of insurance for all practical purposes.

The major differences between insurance and bonds should be understood (after which no further allusion is made in this chapter to the technical fact that bonds are not insurance). An insurance policy is a contract between two parties, the insurer and the insured. A bond is a contract among three parties; the bonding company is called the surety or obligor, the insured party or the one for whom something is being done is the obligee, and the party who has an obligation to the obligee is the principal. In insurance, the insurer pays the insured if there is an occurrence of the insured event and the insured is faced with a financial loss. In bonding, if there is an occurrence of an insured event, the insurer pays the insured only if, in addition to the necessity of a financial loss facing the insured, the principal fails to perform as promised. In insurance, there is no obligation as a part of a contract, for the person causing the loss to repay the insurer; there may be subrogation, but this is not a contractual obligation. On the other hand, in bonding, there is a contractual promise that the principal will reimburse the surety for any losses paid by the surety because of the failure of the principal. And finally, insurance policies can be cancelled by either party, whereas bonds are not normally cancellable.

Thus, a bond is a guarantee by the surety to an obligee that if the principal does not perform as promised, the surety will pay on behalf of the principal. The surety does not expect to pay, and a share of the premiums are generally considered to be service fees for the use of the surety's name.

DESCRIPTION OF COVERAGES

There are two major classes of bonds: fidelity and surety.

Fidelity bonds reimburse an employee for loss of money or other property caused by the dishonest acts of its bonded employees. Fidelity bonds are often described as "honesty insurance." Among large groups of employees, some losses are to be expected, based on the averages, and many of them will be of the same general types. In addition to guaranteeing to reimburse the employer, the surety may investigate employees, help prevent losses by surveying the methods of the employer's operation, help establish programs to prevent losses and uncover dishonest acts, and furnish the implied threat of punishment for dishonesty which only a large outside firm can supply. (Few of these, however, are carried out in actual practice.)

The term "fidelity bonds" has been used for many years, but has been replaced under a program adopted by the Surety Association of America. The modern term is "dishonesty insurance." Since it will take some time for complete adoption of the new title and revised coverages to become popular, this section will first discuss the traditional approach and then the more recent policies.

Surety bonds guarantee to one party of a contract (obligee) that the other (principal) will perform according to the contract; if not, the surety is responsible. Each case is handled individually and is somewhat different. In additon to being responsible for the performance of the principal, the surety gives assurance to the obligee that the principal has the necessary financial strength, ability and honesty to perform according to the contract. Thus, surety is basically a credit function.

Many types of classifications of bonds can be made. The following method of classifying bonds appears to be the most logical.

Fidelity Bonds

Individual bonds — An employer is protected against the dishonest acts of the person who is named in the bond. For example, a small company may decide to bond only the treasurer, by name.

Name schedule bonds — This is, in effect, a combination of two or more individual bonds. Each person must be listed by name, with a specific amount of coverage applicable to each person. Changes may be made, either additions of new persons or deletions, but each person must be named in order to be covered. As an example, a company might bond, by name, the treasurer and two accountants.

Position schedule bonds — The difference here is that only the positions are listed, not the names of the individuals. Changes in employees can be made without notification to the bonding company. However, if the number of employees in a covered position should change, the bonding company must be notified or the employer will be penalized. Any position or positions may be covered, but all employees of each covered type must be included.

Blanket bonds — All employees of the insured are covered on a blanket basis. No listing of positions or individual names is required. The coverage is broad, and this is the most popular kind of fidelity bond. There are two types of blanket bonds. One is the *blanket position bond* under which each employee is covered up to the amount of the bond; the maximum liability of the bonding company, is therefore, the number of employees who are involved in the crime times the penalty of the bond.

The other is the *commercial blanket bond* under which all employees in the aggregate are covered up to the amount of the bond; the entire penalty of the bond is available to pay any one loss, regardless of the number of employees involved in the crime.

Blanket bonds for financial institutions — Many special forms of blanket bonds have been developed to meet the needs of banks, savings and loan associations, credit unions and other financial institutions. The most popular is the *bankers blanket bond.* It covers not only fidelity risks of a bank but also burglary, robbery, hold-up and other theft hazards to such property as money, stamps, securities, jewelry and gems. This is a broad coverage, protecting against almost all risks except carelessness, incompetence and clerical errors.

Forgery insurance — Businessowners and families have a risk of financial loss caused by forgery of a signature to a check, or alterations in negotiable instruments. The *depositors forgery bond* is the most common coverage for a business, covering outgoing instruments only. The *family forgery bond* is designed for individuals and covers both outgoing and incoming instruments, as well as losses because of acceptance in good faith of counterfeit money.

Blanket crime — This policy, formerly called "Comprehensive 3 D," is a combination policy which includes commercial crime coverage in addition to employee dishonesty coverage under a blanket bond or a position bond, and forgery coverage of the type offered under a depositors forgery bond. It is described in Chapter 26 in greater detail because most of the coverages protect against losses by crime. As explained in that chapter, terminology is changing with the advent of the simplified-language commercial forms program of ISO.

Broad form storekeepers policy — This is another combination policy, somewhat similar to a blanket crime policy. Like the latter, its principal coverages are against crime perils, so it is described in Chapter 26, too. This policy also covers employee dishonesty and depositors' forgery, and adds protection against counterfeit money losses.

Credit card forgery insurance — Individuals and businesses that use credit cards to purchase goods and services are exposed to losses arising out of the use of the cards. A lost or stolen credit card may be used by a forger, a signed receipt may be altered to show increased charges, for a person entrusted with a card may misappropriate it for that person's own use. For a commercial risk, a separate policy may be written, or the coverage may be endorsed on a bond, or on a blanket crime policy. For an individual, coverage may be endorsed on a family forgery bond or on some personal lines property and liability policies. In recent years, the most popular coverage of this class by far is the *credit card and depositors forgery coverage endorsement* which is automatically included in most homeowners policies and may be added to personal automobiles policies. In addition to the two coverages expressed in its title, credit card and depositors forgery also covers loss sustained through acceptance in good faith of counterfeit money.

Since January, 1971, when an amendment to the federal Truth in Lending law went into effect removing most of the risk associated with lost or stolen credit cards from the holder and onto the card issuer, there has been speculation about the need for credit card coverage. In spite of the fact that the maximum liability of a card user is $50, credit card coverage is likely to be retained, especially in conjunction with homeowners forms because of the relatively low cost and the fact that coverage also includes depositors forgery and counterfeit money coverages, as well as coverage for legal expenses in connection with either a credit card or depositors forgery loss.

Dishonesty Insurance

The program offered under the jurisdiction of the Surety Association of America to replace "fidelity bonds" contains new coverage approaches. These coverages may be written as separate policies or in conjunction with the simplified-language commercial forms program of ISO.

Schedule A — Small employers without a high turnover of employees have the option of specifying the names of covered employees or the titles of their covered positions. Since one or more employees or positions may be named, this replaces individual bonds, name schedule bonds, and position schedule bonds.

Blanket A - Larger companies, where there may be a high rate of employee turnover, are better served with blanket coverage. As before, no listing of positions or individual names is required. However, only the employee blanket coverage is available. The blanket position coverage is no longer offered; this coverage was popular because the maximum recoverable was the bond limit times the number of employees involved in the loss. Somewhat similar coverage can be obtained by writing a position schedule coverage (described in the above paragraph) with a listing of each employee who occupies each position, the number of employees in such positions, and a limit for each such position. After a loss, then, the limit may be multiplied by the number of employees involved in the loss, provided those employees are identified and there are not more employees in a position than were declared.

Surety Bonds

Fiduciary bonds — Persons who are appointed by a court to carry out the provisions of a will or trust deed are required to deposit a bond to guarantee that they will perform their duties properly. One type is called a *probate bond,* which is required of the person appointed as executor of a will or administrator if there is no will, assuring proper performance in administering the estate of a decedent. Another type is called a *conservation bond,* which is issued for persons having a responsibility for the administration of the property of others, separate from decedents; examples are guardians, those charged with a duty to manage the affairs of a person who has been judged incompetent because of insanity, and trustees under a deed of trust to manage property under the terms of the trust instrument. Still a third type is an *insolvency bond,* required of persons appointed to conserve the assets after insolvency and to protect the interests of creditors.

Court bonds — A special class of bond is the court bond. It is filed by a party who is engaged in litigation as a requirement for obtaining a legal remedy. One type is a bond furnished by a plaintiff to reimburse a defendant for losses caused by an injunction on the use or disposition of property. Another type guarantees payments of judgments which will be required of the unsuccessful party in an appeal to a higher court. Still another type guarantees that an accused person will appear for trial on charges that he or she has committed a crime.

Public official bonds — Persons elected to public office are often required by law to deposit bonds which guarantee that they will perform the tasks assigned to them in their positions. One type applies to those who handle public funds, such as treasurers and tax collectors, guaranteeing honesty in the handling of, and accounting for, the funds, as well as in the faithful performance of their duties. Another type applies to those having responsible positions, protecting the public against unsupervised acts which cause losses, and the individual citizen against illegal acts which adversely affect a person or property. These bonds may be on an individual, schedule or blanket basis.

License and permit bonds — Many businesses are subject to licensing on federal or local levels. Bonds may be required to assure the proper performance of duties specified for the license. One general type guarantees that the licensee will act in conformity to the regulations applicable to the occupation. Another guarantees that the licensee will account for the taxes, fees, and other monies collected or held by for the government, or for a private party under some commission or consignment arrangements. Still another general type is that of permit bonds — requiring proper performance under a permit to hang a sign over a sidewalk, to cut down trees, to engage in certain types of contracting or repairing occupations, etc.

Contract bonds — A principal who contracts to perform a specified task for an assured is often required to furnish a bond under which the surety guarantees the performance. One type of bond guarantees specific performance and terminates when the principal has satisfactorily completed the task. The other type promises to pay damages to the obligee and terminates when the principal has indemnified the obligee for any damages resulting from failure to perform the contract. There are several categories of contract bonds. One guarantees that a bidder will, if accepted, enter into a contract and perform the task (bid bond). Another guarantees construction, to an acceptable conclusion, of buildings and other structures, or performance under other contracts such as supplying coal to a project (performance bond). Still another assures the completion of a contract to supply materials or articles under specified conditions (materal and supplies bond). Finally, another category guarantees the quality or durability of a specified material or article, such as a pump which is guaranteed to perform satisfactorily for five years (maintenance bond).

Miscellaneous bonds — There are many other types of bonds available, each designed to meet a particular need. Some guarantee that lost promissory notes and similar certificates will not appear at a later date and cause loss. Some guarantee the payments of installments on time purchases, of savings placed on deposit, or mortgage installments due, and of rents. Even insurance may be involved; agents may be required to furnish bonds for the payment of taxes; insurers may be required to furnish bonds for obligations incurred in different states, and employers wishing to self-insure, to guarantee the payment of workers' compensation benefits may be required to furnish bonds as guarantees.

UNDERWRITING FACTORS

Acceptable Risks

As previously mentioned, bonds are written by two types of companies. One type is the specialty company which concentrates on the writing of bonds, and the other type is the casualty company which writes bonds as well as other lines.

Specialty companies writing bonds are relatively few in number, but they write a large share of the bonds. Their underwriters are very knowledgeable in bonds, often being thoroughly familiar with many of the common sources such as contractors and courts. Most of these companies write every type of bond. This does not mean that they write all applicants; indeed, they may be quite strict in declining applicants who do not measure up to all of the qualifications of secure, dependable principals. A specialty company makes its entire profit from bonds, so it maintains a broad line of eligible risks and a tight pattern of acceptable risks.

While there are a large number of casualty companies, many of them write few of the really large and complex bonds — those with substantial premiums. These companies write much of their volume in license and permit bonds, credit card forgery, and employee dishonesty policies. Underwriters in these companies may be thoroughly familiar with the types of bonds written by their companies, but seldom are they skilled in handling all types of bonds.

A bond underwriter may be just as skilled regardless of the type of insurer because knowledge of the details and ramifications of the various bonds is needed. Therefore, an underwriter in either type of company may be just as capable of selecting risks as in the other type. However, there is no escaping the fact that acceptability differs by company. An underwriter for a specialty company will consider all risks as acceptable, subject to a strict unacceptable list, while an underwriter for a casualty company writing accommodation bonds may consider as acceptable, only those applicants already insured by the company, and then only for certain types of bonds.

From the standpoint of the applicant or the producer, the matter of acceptability is similarly circumscribed. An applicant needing any of the more complex bonds must approach an underwriter in a specialty company, as must an applicant with little or no related business. A publc official may be an excellent example of the latter. On the other hand, an applicant with a substantial commercial liability of commer cial crime account will most likely request a simple bond from that company, and particularly so if the firm's financial condition is so weak that it might be considered to be borderline on acceptability for the bond alone. Thus, the account concept of underwriting makes it possible for an applicant to secure a bond in a multiple line company when the applicant might be refused a bond by a specialty company.

Unacceptable Risks

Each of the two major classes of bonds has its own unacceptable list. The underwriting is quite different for each class.

Fidelity Bonds

The fidelity bond reimburses an obligee (employer) against loss of money or property arising out of a dishonest act of the principal (employee). Since there can be no loss unless the employee has been guilty of a dishonest act, it is obvious that selection must be based on the background of the employee and the opportunity furnished to accomplish a dishonest act.

The importance of checking the background of employees was emphasized by federal statistics which indicated that bank employees stole $382 million in 1984, "nine times more than bank robbers." In retail stores, "employee theft is far more serious a business liability than shoplifting and burglary," with insurance claims exceeding $344 million in 1984. The study estimated that worker thefts or embezzlement in all types of industries "may cost more than $1 billion yearly."[1]

The employee is the prime selection target. The bonding company occasionally spends a sizable share of the premium in checking the background of the employee. Each worker, for whom a bond is requested, is required to complete a form giving details of past work experience, and sometimes the police record. The underwriter considers unacceptable, any employee whose past record included instances of embezzlement, forgery, stealing, fraud, wrongful abstraction, misappropriation, or any form of dishonesty which might affect the handling of the employer's property. An exception might be made by an underwriter if the employee was hired for a job in which there was no opportunity to harm the employer by a dishonest act; such an exception would follow careful consideration of all factors, so any employee with a record of dishonesty must be considered as unacceptable.

Another factor is the protection against dishonesty which is built into the system used by the employer. A prudent employer will use checks, audits, and accounting procedures which are designed to remove opportunity for dishonest acts, and to uncover aberrations almost immediately. While it is true that some of the most elaborate systems have been breached, it is also certain that many potential thefts and embezzlements have been thwarted by tight systems which control the handling of money, securities and other property. An employer would be unacceptable if the firm had not adopted a system which is reasonably secure.

Surety Bonds

The surety bond guarantees the obligee that the principal will perform as agreed under contract. There is no loss if the principal does perform, so selection is based on the principal's ability to carry out the obligations. There are three basic criteria to consider: integrity (character), ability (capacity), and financial strength (capital). These are important in varying degrees for each type of bond.

Court bonds primarily require financial strength. Most of these bonds require the principal to make payment under specified conditions and, since these conditions are often beyond the control of the principal, the ability to pay is most important. Applicants for these bonds are unacceptable if their financial strength is

1. "Bank Workers Steal More than Robbers," *Whittier Daily News* (January 15, 1986), p. A 10.

uncertain. There are some types of court bonds where integrity is very important, such as bail bonds which guarantee that a person will appear for trial. Applicants without unimpeachable honesty are unacceptable, unless collateral is deposited, as is explained below.

Public official bonds are more concerned with integrity and ability than financial strength. It is more important to prevent a loss of this type than to try to reimburse injured parties after a loss, and only the integrity and background of the principal can control this factor. An applicant is unacceptable if there are serious questions about honesty or the ability to perform all of the duties.

Contract bonds require all three factors. Failure on the part of the contractor appears almost inevitable if the contractor is dishonest, does not have the ability to carry out the terms of the contract, or financial condition is so weak that the contractor may not be able to purchase supplies or meet payrolls. An applicant who is deficient in any category is unacceptable, with the possible exception of a weak financial position where collateral is deposited.

Special training of underwriters is needed just to enable them to determine whether the financial condition is sufficiently strong. Each case is different, but a rough rule of thumb sometimes used is that the net worth of the applicant must be at least 10 times the amount of the bond. If the underwriter feels that there is not sufficient financial strength, the applicant will be considered unacceptable, unless one of two possible corrective steps are taken: One is to secure an indemnity agreement from the principal or another party with sufficient financial resources to be reliable. Under such an agreement, the surety is reimbursed if it is required to fulfill the agreement of the bond. The second solution is to require collateral, i.e., cash, bonds, certified checks, Treasury notes, bank certificates of deposit, or other property acceptable to the underwriter. The collateral is returned to the principal, if the contract is performed; otherwise, it is transferred to the surety if the principal fails to perform. An applicant of questionable financial strength is unacceptable, unless a satisfactory indemnity agreement is submitted or an acceptable collateral is placed on deposit.

Contract bond applicants are underwritten very closely by some underwriters, particularly those writing bonds on contractors who are borderline but who have related business in the company. These underwriters might list as unacceptable, any applicant who does not meet the net worth requirement previously mentioned (at least 10 times the bond amount) plus a ratio of current assets to current liabilities which is at least two to one. In addition, they may require a working capital of at least a stated amount, such as $5,000 or $10,000; a record which shows no incidence of defaults; and sufficient experience in the line of work, perhaps of 10 years duration. These factors are weighed against the volume of other insurance written in the company in order to determine acceptability.

Many small contractors are unable to meet these bonding requirements and are, therefore, denied access to many potential contracts. In an attempt to correct this situation and to stimulate the development of small contractors, the Small Business Administration of the federal government has a program that provides that the SBA will reimburse a surety up to 90%. The intention of the program is to encourage more bonding since the surety has only a 10% exposure.

SECURING INFORMATION

A bond underwriter follows the same basic steps as other underwriters in obtaining information in which to underwrite risks. The first determination is whether the risk is acceptable under the company's rules, and is not on the unacceptable list. Then all of the available information is weighed carefully in order to determine if the applicant is acceptable.

More latitude in applying judgment is given to bond underwriters than to many other underwriters. Many complex, interrelated factors must be considered. In order to make sound decisions, a considerable volume of detailed information is required. There are several sources of information, with the application being the first and most complete source.

Application

A bond application is not, basically, any different from applications for other types of insurance. Information for rating, as well as for underwriting is furnished. The application must not only be signed; it must also be witnessed or even notarized for many types of bonds. It is not, however, made a part of the bond, because the bond cannot be denied in case of a misrepresentation, as is possible with most other policies handled by insurance underwriters. The applicant is bound under the terms of the bond, as well as by the signature on the application.

Applications differ by company, but the questions usually fall within these major categories.

1. Personal
2. Description of bond
3. Insurance information

Typical questions which are usually included under each category are as follows.

1. *Personal*

A. Full name of the applicant, including the firm name, if any. If a partnership or corporation, the names of all partners or principal officers are required.
B. Business address and mailing address of the firm or employer.
C. Type of business conducted.
D. How long in business at this location, how much experience in this type of business, and if the applicant has ever failed in business.
E. How long the applicant has lived in the city, and if a citizen of the United States or not.
F. Description of any lawsuit, lien or judgment pending against the applicant.
G. If the applicant is a business, a financial statement is required; this may be submitted with the application or may consist of inserting figures on a blank balance sheet printed on the application.
H. For employee's fidelity, additional information about the employee is required, such as date of birth; ownership of home or other real estate; amount of debts and personal liabilities; other sources of income; details of any arrest or imprisonment at any time in the past; and employee's present title and position; and details about every employment over a past period of time, such as ten years.
I. Names, addresses, and occupations of references (usually at least five) who are unrelated to the applicant but with whom the applicant is personally acquainted.

2. *Description of Bond*
   - A. Type of bond needed.
   - B. Name and address of obligee or the position to be covered, or similar pertinent information.
   - C. Details of the contract, bid specifications, or other information needed to identify the type and nature of the undertaking.
   - D. For employee's fidelity, the amount of the applicant's authority to sign checks and such other documents as warehouse receipts.
3. *Insurance Information*
   - A. The limit of the bond and the requested effective date.
   - B. Names of the bonding companies that have furnished bonds in the past, including the types and amounts of the bonds.
   - C. Details, if the applicant has ever been refused a bond, or has applied to any other source for this bond.
   - D. Description of any other bonds now in force.

Reference Letters

Applicants for most types of bonds are required to furnish names and addresses of several references. Ordinarily the application specifies that the applicant must be unrelated to these persons but must know them personally. Since the integrity of the applicant and a past record of any trouble are very important to the underwriter, a letter is often sent to these references. The answers to these letters receive careful scrutiny by the underwriter. Most of these letters contain no criticism because any applicant of normal intelligence will list only those persons who are friendly and who will be inclined to help. For this reason any hint of criticism will immediately cause the underwriter to become suspicious.

Employees for whom a fidelity bond is sought are ordinarily required to furnish information about their previous employment, including the names of their supervisors. Letters are usually sent to these persons, particularly for the most recent periods of employment. The answers are more likely to contain criticism than those received from character references because the employee has no opportunity to screen them. The underwriter weighs these facts, of course, but will be cautious if there are any indications of suspected or proven embezzlement or other types of dishonesty.

Inspection Reports

Inspection companies are available for securing further information about applicants. These are the same companies used by other underwriters on other lines, but the reports are directed toward the factors of importance to a bond underwriter. An inspector may be able to discover evidence that an applicant moves with shady acquaintances, lives beyond the apparent income, or appears to be in financial difficulties. Sometimes an inspector can secure financial data which indicates that the applicant is less financially sound than appeared from the figures furnished to the underwriter. Inspections might even reveal facts about previous behavior or activities indicating a lack of ability to perform the task for which the bond is issued.

Specialized inspection companies are used by the underwriters of some bonds. These inspectors might be able to recommend technques or physical arrangements which can prevent dishonest acts by employees. Other inspectors may prevent other types of losses by uncovering factors which could lead to failure to perform. For example, an expert in contractual work may be able to determine that a contractor has underbid a job and might be expected to have difficulty in completing it. Much of the premium for many bonds is supposed to be used to prevent a loss rather than to pay a loss after it occurs, so investigation is an important tool for a bond underwriter.

CLASSIFICATION AND RATING

A bond underwriter uses acceptable and unacceptable lists to determine basic eligibility of an application and, then secures information from several sources in order to determine acceptability. If a risk is accepted, the next step is classification and rating.

The classification of bond applicants and the rating are not clerical functions but, instead, component parts of the underwriting process. The underwriter must determine the classification to be used which is often subject to some judgment. Rates are generally determined by the classification, but the underwriter must take them into account as one of the important factors to consider.

Classification

Fidelity bonds, covering individuals or groups of people, are classified into two classes. One is the "average" risk to which basic rates apply. The other class includes "classified lines" — those whose exposure is either above or below that of the basic risks. Most businesses fall within the category of "classified lines." The specific classifications, and thus the rates, are determined by types of business. The position of the individual is also a factor in individual bonds but not for schedule bonds.

Fidelity bonds of the blanket type are classified and rated by the number and type of employees. Two classifications are used. Class (1) includes officials and executives, as well as bookkeepers, managers, clerks, and all others whose regular duties include the handling of money or merchandise, plus a percentage of all other employees not in Class (2) (five percent of the first 100, and one percent of the balance). Class (2) includes specified types of employees, such as demonstrators and outside salespersons.

Surety bonds are classified in many ways, depending upon the type of bond. Contract bonds, for example, are classified by the type of construction and the percentage of the contract price which will be covered by the bond. The bond underwriter must know and assign the proper classification, and then determine the correct rate.

Rating

Most bonding companies are members of, or subscribers to, the Surety Association of America and use the uniform rates promulgated by that association. Some companies are independent and prepare their own rates, but even some of these purchase the association rates and use them exactly or as guides. Generally, the specialty bonding companies — those concentrating on writing this class of business and writing, in the aggregate, most bond business, use the association rates, too. The companies writing bonds more as an accommodation to their property-casualty policyholders are more likely to use rates which are slightly different from those of the association. Apparently the reason for the latter situation is that these companies feel that the small volume of accommodation bonds which they write cannot really hurt them, and they need attractive rates to keep their policyholders from using other markets for bonds, and perhaps then for other coverages.

Fidelity bonds are rated from a manual, except for the very large bonds which are experience rated. Manual rates are shown for each $1,000 of the amount of the bond, and reduce in steps as larger amounts are written. Many bonds are written in multiples of $2,500, and one rate may apply for the first $10,000, for example, and then a reduced rate applies for the next $25,000. Bonds with a face amount of more than $100,000 on individual and schedule bonds are specifically rated by the association, with allowance being made for the loss experience of the specific firm.

Surety bonds are usually rated by applying a manual rate to the amount of the bond or, in the case of contract bonds, to the contract value.

The Surety Association gathers statistics from all member companies in order to make rates. Bond rates include allowances for losses and for other expenses like commissions, taxes, and overhead — the same as for other lines of insurance. In addition, a specific allowance is made for service, and in some types of bonds, the service charge is a large share of the premium. Court bonds, for example, may require considerable investigation. Many types of bonds require investigation, and furnish excellent examples of cases where money spent for investigation may more than pay for itself in reduced losses. Of course, the underwriter must apply good judgment to the facts revealed by the investigation, if satisfactory results are to be maintained.

Collateral is required on certain bonds, particularly if the applicant has a poor financial standing. With aequate collateral, losses under the bond should be minimal. This is another example of a situation where the principal component of the rate is the service charge; it covers the cost of investigation and supervision of the applicant, and also includes the fee for lending the credit and the name of the bonding company.

Bond underwriters, for most companies, have only a limited opportunity to adjust rates. Some rates, in fact, are fixed by law and may not be changed by the underwriter. This line, more than most others, uses standard rates for most companies. However, the underwriter does have some latitude in classifying applicants. The major involvement of the underwriter, with the rates and premiums, is to weigh the exposures against the premium. Underwriting selectivity must be more accurate in cases where there is no latitude to adjust rates. A bond underwriter, working against fixed rates and small allowances for losses therefore must exercise extremely good judgment in order to be successful.

BOND FORMS

Bond forms are not specified by law, except for some bonds involving public officials or the public interest. However, the Surety Association publishes standard bonds and forms and these are used by most companies. Thus, a bond underwriter has no more oportunity to adopt bonds than to adjust rates, as a general rule.

An interesting situation is found in the bonds for financial institutions. There are six different bond forms, designated by number, each applying to certain types of insititutions and offering different protection. These forms — developed by the Surety Association in cooperation with the pertinent trade associations — are broad, comprehensive forms, giving good protection, but furnishing no opportunity to an underwriter to make modifications to fit specific risks.

Deductibles are usually employed under fidelity bonds in order to encourage employers to adopt preventative measures. These deductibles are strictly underwriting deductibles, applied by an underwriter in an attempt to reduce losses rather than by a producer in an effort to reduce premiums; as a matter of fact, credits for deductibles are quite small. Since bond contracts are generally quite simple and quite inflexible, the underwriter must understand the contract, but seldom tries to change it.

RETENTION AND REINSURANCE

A bond underwriter must be thoroughly conversant with the retention limits of the company and with the various means available to reinsure exposures above the retention.

The maximum retention under bonds is fixed by law in most jurisdictions; a federal requirement, for example, is that no single bond may exceed 10% of the company's capital and surplus. Many companies use lower retentions as a means of reducing the exposure on single losses. In addition, bond underwriters often limit their retention in order to avoid too great a concentration on one class of risks or on one specific principal, such as one contrator.

Reinsurance is used to reduce the exposure. Most of it is placed under reinsurance treaties, with the reinsurer automatically accepting the exposure ceded to it. Some facultative placements are made, but they represent only a small percentage of the total. Virtually all surety reinsurance is on a pro rata basis, although there is some trend toward an excess basis on fidelity coverages.

Co-suretyship is sometimes used. It is the practice of having two or more companies sign the bond. The intention is that each company will share in the premium and losses. However, the nature of bonding is such that the principal may sue only one of the companies. The co-sureties exchange indemnification agreements to assure equitable allocation in cases where they are sued severally instead of jointly. Co-suretyship is also used sometimes to assure more protection under a large contract, and may be used to spread patronage over many companies.

The bond underwriter must know where and how to reinsure the bond that is written. The underwriting of applicants must be based on a careful evaluation of many items of information. The work is only partly completed when the underwriter has determined acceptability, classified and rated the risk and applied the bond forms. The underwriter must still protect the company from losses which are too large for it to bear easily. Reinsurance, therefore, is the tool used by the underwriter to limit the retention and still be able to write bonds for all types and sizes of applicants.

QUESTIONS FOR DISCUSSION

1. Explain the major differences between insurance and bonds.
2. Differentiate between fidelity and surety bonds.
3. List 6 types of fidelity bonds, and 4 types of surety bonds, and explain each one.
4. Discuss the statement that "bonds are written by two types of companies."
5. Explain the use of references as a source of information for bond underwriting.

32

Workers' Compensation

A special set of provisions for meeting one's obligations for injury to another person is established for employers. These provisions comprise workers' compensation or, under some conditions, employer's liability insurance. This line is second only to personal automobile insurance in size. In 1985, it accounted for more than 9 billion dollars of premiums. This is 13% of the total property and liability premiums.[1]

Employers have had a liability for workers injured on the job, for a long time. Formerly, however, there were many loopholes under which the liability could be avoided; contributory negligence, assumption of risk and the fellow servant rule are three examples.

During the early part of the twentieth century, workers' compensation laws were enacted in all states to remove these defenses. Similar laws were passed to provide compensation for longshoremen and harbor workers, who are subject to federal laws. The basic intent of all of these laws is the same: to guarantee that employees receive medical care and other compensation for injuries sustained in the course of and arising out of their employment, regardless of their own carelessness or that of a fellow worker.

Beyond the basic principle, which is the same for all states, the provisions are different for each state. Every state excludes some employees, while the definition of covered employees varies widely. The laws differ in the coverage provided for employees travelling in other states. In fact, one of the major problems is that of extraterritoriality. This concerns the question of which law applies when an employee

---

1. "Workers' Compensation, Inland Marine, Fidelity and Surety — 1985," *Best's Review Property/Casualty Insurance Edition*, Vol. 7, No. 8 (December, 1986), p.8.

is hired in one state and is then injured in another. Some states require all employers to secure workers' compensation insurance, some exclude certain employers, and some permit excluded employers to elect whether they want to be included under the law. One writer refers to the various methods of providing workers' compensation as "a crazy-quilt design,"[2] while another says that "their most striking feature is their dissimilarity."[3]

The source of the workers' compensation insurance also differs. Some states have monopolistic state plans, under which no private insurer may operate, while others have state funds which compete with private insurers. An employer operating in several states may find that some of the insurance must be written in state funds, although the balance of the coverage is in an insurer of the employer's own choice. Too, many states permit self-insurance, as an alternative to either a monopolistic state fund or private insurance.

Since a workers' compensation insurance underwriter obviously must know the law or laws which apply to applicants, discussion such as that given in this chapter necessarily must be very general in scope. The following sections describe the broad characteristics of workers' compensation insurance.

DESCRIPTION OF COVERAGES

Every workers' compensation insurance policy covers the employer's statutory requirements as the first coverage. Nearly all states also include employer's liability as a second coverage, so this is discussed, too. However, an employer should purchase both coverages, because there are circumstances under which each of the coverages is applicable.

Workers' Compensation Insurance

This coverage — workers' compensation — specifies that the insurer will pay all benefits prescribed by the applicable state, meeting the obligations imposed on the employer by law. The policy seldom specifies the type of employees covered. No uniformity exists among the various jurisdictions, particularly in relation to casual, irregular work. Some states specify the number of days per month, or hours per day which are required to bring the employee under the law. Since the laws differ, are subject to change, and over-ride a policy anyway, it is not customary to specify these details in the policy.

Other provisions are likewise specified in the law and not in the policy. Some of these are the amount of benefits to be paid injured employees, the system used to administer the law, and the methods under which benefits are secured. There are no limits of coverage specified in the policy, the insurance must cover all prescribed

---

2. Earl F. Cheit, *Injury and Recovery in the Course of Employment*, p. 25 (New York: John Wiley & Sons, Inc., 1961).

3. C.A. Kulp, *Casualty Insurance*, p. 95, 3d Ed. (New York: The Ronald Press Company, 1956).

benefits.[4] Automatic coverage applies at all locations and for all operations of the policyholder to which the workers' compensation laws apply. This is required by the laws of most states, but is now provided in the policy. On the other hand, these are state laws and the coverage applies only in those states listed in the policy.

Workers' compensation insurance is a pure case of liability coverage without fault. The employer, who is the policyholder and who pays the premium, may be completely free of any fault in an accident. The employee may be careless to the point of total ignorance and is injured only because of his or her own carelessness; still, the employee can collect. In exchange for what appears to be an unjust burden, the employer is freed from any potential suit for damages because of the accident. Workers' compensation benefits are an exclusive remedy; the employee has no other right to see the employer because of the injuries.

Employer's Liability Insurance

This coverage — employer's liability — is roughly the same as other types of liability insurance. It provides that the insurer will pay all sums the insured employer is obligated to pay because of bodily injury or death to employees, but does apply to any liability under any workers' compensation law; thus, excluded under this coverage are benefits payable under any workers' compensation law. If the injured employee is entitled to protection of the workers' compensation law, the employer must carry that coverage; the employer's liability coverage will not apply. Also excluded is liability under any contract or agreement.

In some states, an employer may elect to bring excluded employees under the act. If this election is not made, the employer purchases voluntary workers' compensation insurance to cover them. By doing this, the employer also has employer's liability protection. If this election is made, the employer should purchase employer's liability insurance. In most states, employer's liability coverage with a limit of $100,000 per accident usually is provided along with workers' compensation insurance at no additional charge.

---

4. The incongruity in acceptability and the insufficiency in benefits, in coverages and in safety standards are among many reasons the whole system of workers' compensation insurance is presently under attack by the federal government. And, unless states take the initiative to improve and upgrade their workers' compensation laws, the threat of federal takeover will become a reality. Federal laws are already in existence to improve the system. One of these is the Williams-Steiger Occupational Safety and Health Act of 1970. Under this act, which became effective in August 1971, the Department of Labor has the responsibility of formulating safety and health standards for all businesses engaged in interstate commerce. Safety inspections are then conducted and fines levied when employers are found to be in violations of work standards. As for benefits, the National Commission on State Workmen's Compensation Laws has recommended that by July 1973, weekly benefits for death and disability be equal to 66-2/3% of the state's average weekly wage and that by July 1975, the maximum be increased to 100% of the state's average weekly wage.

UNDERWRITING FACTORS

Acceptable Risks

Workers' compensation insurers offer coverage more to type of businesses than to what might be called "preferred" or "substandard" risks. They generally write a broad segment of the market. Many insurers write workers' compensation only in conjunction with other lines of insurance, usually commercial liability or commercial vehicles. In these cases, the acceptable risks obviously would be those which the insurer considers acceptable for the other lines.

However, some insurers specialize in writing workers' compensation, while others write the line without any requirement concerning related business. Such insurers generally consider all applicants, feeling that the rating structure is a fairly accurate measure of the exposure. But there are some insurers that concentrate on specific classes of business.

In most states, it is incorrect to refer to insurers which "write at lower rates," because all insurers must charge the same rates. Competition is furnished either by dividends or service, or both. In any event, insurers must decide the basis upon which they wish to compete. This, in turn, tends to delineate the risks which are really acceptable for each insurer.

Unacceptable risks

Workers' compensation insurers usually use lists of risks considered unacceptable, the same as for other lines. These lists differ by insurers, and relate generally to the segment of the market the insurer is trying to reach. The following is a list of the characteristics which might be considered as making an applicant unacceptable, especially for an insurer desiring to pay high dividends. (As is explained in a later section, workers' compensation rates are the same for all insurers, but dividends may be used as a competitive measure.) These are illustrative of the types of things an underwriter practicing selectivity would consider.

Hazardous Occupations

Probably the greatest concern of an underwriter for workers' compensation or employer's liability insurance is the hazardous nature of some occupations. The peril insured against is that of injury to an employee, so the underwriter will try to avoid those occupations which are more hazardous than the average. From experience and studies, the underwriter may construct an unacceptable list somewhat along these lines.

- Hazardous manufacturing, such as chemicals, batteries, acid, rubber, magnesium, glassware, foundries and asbestos.
- Hazardous construction, such as dams, excavation, sewers, bridges, tunnels, oil pipe lines and dredging.
- Hazardous operations, such as amusement parks, mining, movie production, saw mills, electric power, circuses, athletic teams, horse shows and boys camps.

Physical Aspects of the Business

Injuries to workers can be caused by defects in the premises or equipment. The underwriter might put, on the unacceptable list, any applicant whose property has such defects. Furthermore, an underwriter may analyze the following factors as being indicators of management's attitude toward maintaining safe working conditions.

- Housekeeping which is poor, or premises which are not neat and orderly, indicate careless attitude. Such conditions also furnish more chances for employees to fall and injure themselves.
- Maintenance which is poor is often an indication of poor financial condition, as well as being a direct hazard to workers.
- Premises which are located in deteriorating neighborhoods usually are less maintained and often employ a class of workers who are more claim conscious than average.
- Buildings of such an age or construction that they might collapse in a windstorm or earthquake, injuring workers in the buildings.

Business Reputation

An important element in writing insurance for any commercial enterprise is the stability and reliability of the business. An underwriter would probably consider unacceptable, an applicant who does not meet the following qualifications.

- In business one year or more, in order to demonstrate stability and to be able to establish a favorable reputation for safe operations.
- A legal and respectable business, in order to have a better chance of attracting respectable, honest employees.
- An owner who is a stable, reliable, and a law-abiding citizen, in order to have another measure of the good handling of employees which must be expected.

History of Past Losses

Important factors in underwriting are the frequency and types of past losses. In some ways, this can encompass all of the other factors. Faced with a poor history of past losses, the underwriter needs to ask: "Why should I expect next year to be any better?"

SECURING INFORMATION

An underwriter of workers' compensation and employer's liability insurance follows the same steps as underwriters for other lines: first determine eligibility and then acceptability. The primary source of information is an application, but other sources are also available.

Application

A completed application is customarily used to secure underwriting and rating information. Some companies require that the applicant sign the application. The application, by showing the statements on the declarations page, is considered to be a part of the policy in some states. While applications differ among insurers, the questions can generally be classified in these three categories.

1. Personal

2. Description of operations and exposures
3. Insurance information

An idea of typical questions used on applications can be secured from the following list, which is based on a number of applications in use.

1. *Personal*
   A. Full name of the applicant, including all partners and the trade name.
   B. The structure of the firm: individual, partnership or corporation.
   C. Business address and mailing address.
2. *Description of Operations and Exposures*
   A. Description and classification of all business operations conducted by the applicant and its addresses.
   B. Detailed information about employees: number of full-time, part-time and seasonal employees, average age, as well as specification of the age of the oldest and the youngest and if any donated or volunteer help is used.
   C. Transportation of employees: how, if at all, they are transported while on the job, and if automobiles or other conveyances are used by employees in performing their work.
   D. A complete description of the type of operations performed by the business and precisely what each employee does.
   E. Whether the applicant is a licensed contractor or subcontracts work to others.
   F. Any contemplated change in operations or in the duties of employees.
   G. Payroll information: approximate current monthly payroll, variations expected monthly and details about the making of payroll records.
   H. Information concerning any athletic teams sponsored by the applicants in states where they are covered under the policy.
   I. If a farm, details about acreage at each location, type of farming operations performed and if the applicant's employees perform work on the farms of others.
   J. Stability factors for the business: how long in operation, type of neighborhood and housekeeping.
   K. Physical factors: construction of the building and physical condition of the premises.
3. *Insurance Information*
   A. Limit of liability if employer's liability is written.
   B. Requested effective date of the policy.
   C. Report of payroll: specification of the times at which the applicant will report to the insurer the total payroll for each classification used.
   D. Details concerning coverage, if any, to be provided relatives, partners, officers and others not necessarily covered automatically.
   E. Details concerning any previous declination or cancellation of coverage by a previous insurer.
   F. Information about the previous insurer and past losses.

Inspection Reports

The workers' compensation underwriter uses inspection reports by outside companies to give more information about some applicants. Many times these reports will parallel those ordered by the commercial liability underwriter, since these coverages are often written together; much the same information is desired for both lines.

One purpose of a report is to verify the information about the applicant. The workers' compensation underwriter may want to verify that the operations are exactly as told, and that there are no hazardous operations which were not described. The underwriter may also want to check on the duties of the employees, and the amount of payroll (to help determine the proper rate).

Another purpose of a report is to secure more information about the stability and reputation of the applicant. The answers on the application about previous businesses or about the housekeeping may lead the underwriter to request more details. An inspection company can often furnish details which the applicant and the producer fail to provide, either carelessly or deliberately.

Engineering Reports

An underwriter of workers' compensation may call on a loss prevention specialist for information. As with inspection reports, these are quite similar to the reports requested by an underwriter for commercial liability, and the same person may report on both lines. A report by a loss prevention specialist on physical factors may be of more help to the underwriter than one by an inspector because of the technical background of most loss prevention specialists. The underwriter may be concerned about the danger to employees inherent in certain operations and will want to know if proper precautions are being taken.

Loss control is a very important contribution by the engineer. Probably more losses have been prevented by safety programs under workers' compensation than under any other line of insurance. Some insurers pride themselves in the high quality of safety promotion they furnish their policyholders. A well-trained loss prevention specialist can cooperate with a safety committee or other group to promote safety very effectively. Signs posted in strategic places, requirements of safety shoes and goggles, guards on certain pieces of equipment — these are just a few simple illustrations of the type of loss control which has done a great deal to reduce injuries to workers in many industries. A true loss control program can be very extensive, requiring the services of a well-trained person. Fortunate indeed is the underwriter who has capable experts ready to help reduce losses in the risks which the underwriter accepts.

Loss control is so important to workers' compensation insurance that it gives a quick picture of the type of management in the applicant's company. If management cooperates wholeheartedly in a safety program, the underwriter will be reassured considerably about the character of the applicant. On the other hand, a management who resists safety efforts should be evaluated very carefully; the company may be operating on a shoestring, it may be a fly-by-night operation, or it may be just uncooperative in everything. Regardless of reason, an applicant who resists a safety program for workers' compensation should be evaluated carefully by all underwriters, whatever coverages are requested. Thus, a good loss prevention specialist is not only of help to the underwriter in preventing losses, but is also helpful in reporting on the attitude and cooperation of the management.

Loss prevention specialists are usually employed by the insurer, but may be connected with outside companies. In either case, the same people often inspect risks for trucks, commercial liability and workers' compensation. On all lines, the same general information is needed by underwriters — physical conditions and attitude of management. In all cases, the specialist usually is expected to furnish recommendations to the underwriter on desirability of the risk, and sometimes on changes which could be made to improve the risk.

Experience of Other Insurers

Underwriters of workers' compensation seldom exchange information about the loss history of applicants. Losses are a matter of public record, and are so complicated that insurers would not usually want to spend the time needed to give adequate information to help a competitor.

CLASSIFICATION AND RATING

The classification and rating of workers' compensation risks are more standardized than for any other line, in most states. Every insurer must use the same classifications and the same rates, as specified by the applicable state rating board. Competition, other than on the basis of service, is possible only by payment of dividends; these are paid after the policy period ends and cannot be guaranteed in most states.

There are many variations of classification and rating among state plans. The following general discussion is intended as a guide to the principles involved. Applicable manuals must be consulted for the rules in each state.

The state rate manual contains a detailed listing of most types of business. A classification code is published for each business; in many cases, separate codes are used for different occupations which might be present. The classifications are established by the state board and occasionally are the subject of much dispute; a new process might be placed under one classification by the board, while the employer protests that the operation should be under a different (and lower rated) classification.

Another section of the manual gives the rates for each classification code number. The rate is applied to each $100 of payroll, unless a different basis is specified, such as "per employee." "Payroll" means not only money paid in wages, but also in substitutes for money. The amount applied may be established by the employer; otherwise, an arbitrary table is used to specify the amount to be used for board, lodging and tips. Also included are bonuses, commissions, overtime, holiday pay, and so forth. However, in some states, a maximum remuneration per employee is specified, such as $300 per week, for purposes of applying rates.

Loss and expense constants are used in many states. The loss constant applies for each state, and is basically a means of establishing a minimum premium for loss payment purposes; it is shown in the classification pages of the manual when it is used. The expense constant is simply a minimum amount, such as $10, which is added to each policy to cover the expenses of insurance; it is usually not applied to larger policies, such as $500 or more premium.

Various rules are used to cover audits, deposit premiums and premium adjustments. These are carefully specified in the manuals and differ by state. In the same category are such rules as how to classify clerical office employees, salespersons, messengers and drivers, as well as multiple-operations enterprises, aircraft and commissaries. Partnerships or joint ventures are covered, but the partners or members are covered only while acting within the scope of their duties for the insured company.

Special classification and rating rules apply to private residences and farms. Distinctions are made between inservants, outservants and occasional servants. Special minimum rules are used, but the rating otherwise is quite standard.

Higher limits of liability for employer's liability coverage are rated by a special table. Generally speaking, a relatively small percentage increase in premium is applied for higher limits.

Athletic teams sponsored by the applicant are covered and a separate premium charge is made. Separate classifications are used for each type of team, and the premium varies by the classifications.

Large risks are acceptable for special rating. Experience rating is available when the premium exceeds a certain amount, such as $3,000 in three years; the table rate is modified by the actual experience of the risk. Some states require a minimum of one year in business before experience rating can be applied. In one state schedule rating is used on certain large industrial risks; the table rate is modified by the degree that equipment in the plant is guarded. Retrospective rating is offered to risks of specified size. Under one plan, the figures for workers' compensation and commercial liability are combined, as well as for automobiles, burglary, and glass, at the applicant's option, in order to arrive at a premium that reflects, quite accurately, the actual experience of the policyholder. Interstate rating is permitted by most states, too.

POLICY FORMS

The insurance policy used to cover workers' compensation is the most strictly regulated policy in the casualty field. State laws generally specify what must be included and what may not be in the policy. In view of this situation, coupled with the fact that workers' compensation laws differ so greatly, it is quite surprising to find that a standard policy is used in most states. The secret is in the endorsements that are used to fit the standard workers' compensation and employer's liability policy to the requirements of each state. Some states provide for such substantial differences that separate policies are used in each of those states. The National Council on Compensation Insurance (NCCI) introduced a revised standard policy in 1983, for use in most states, using readable language and a modern format.

An underwriter is seldom able to adjust coverage as can be done in many other lines. While there are a number of endorsements available, most are designed to meet requirements of the law. So far as compulsory workers' compensation is concerned, the underwriter has very little coverage flexibility, although a few states permit endorsements excluding named persons, specified operations, or specific locations. Voluntary coverages under the policy, however, permit some degree of judgment.

One of these flexible areas is voluntary workers' compensation. It is possible for an employer to agree to offer workers' compensation benefits to those employees who are not subject to the workers' compensation law. The employee cannot be forced to accept these benefits as an exclusive remedy; if the employee does not wish to give the employer a release in exchange for the benefits, no coverage will apply and the sole remedy is then employer's liability. The applicant must specify the states in which the coverage is to apply, and must name the classes of employees to be covered, such as domestic servants or agricultural workers.

Why would an employer choose to provide benefits against which there are no defenses? Obviously, such a course does not appeal to everyone. Some employers feel morally obligated to pay for the expenses of some workers if the injury occurs on the job, regardless of fault. These situations arise most frequently with employees who have served for many years or who are close to the family of the employer. An accident policy could be purchased to cover medical expenses, but better coverage is given by workers' compensation because of the additional benefits of disability payments. Also, a lump sum is paid to the surviving family in case of death.

In a state with a monopolistic state fund, voluntary workers' compensation can be written only through the state fund. Additionally, an employer can purchase only employer's liability coverage from private companies in those states, if available. Therefore, the best course to follow is to bring exempted employees under the state fund, if this is the desire of the employer.

Another area in which a small degree of choice is offered is the field of occupational disease — such disease is entirely separate from occupational accidents. The best known of these diseases is silicosis which is caused by exposure to silica dust, but there are many others. Workers' compensation, coverage A of the policy, covers occupational disease and may not be amended; that is, the policy is broad enough to cover this exposure but state laws differ greatly in what is actually covered within each state.[5]

The basic workers' compensation policy covers only in those states listed in the policy declarations. (Those states which will be mentioned are those where the employer conducts business or contemplates conducting business during the policy period, except monopolistic state funds: *Nevada, North Dakota, Ohio, Washington, West Virginia* and *Wyoming*. This means that if a company has employees traveling in states outside of its usual operating territory or the company hires new employees in a state that is not within its normal jurisdiction, the company would be without protection if any of these employees were subsequently injured, unless those states are listed in the policy declarations. After the policy is written or renewed, one of two endorsements may be attached to provide the needed protection in states not contemplated when the insurance was written.

The first of these is the all states endorsement. Its purpose is to reimburse the employer for benefits he must pay under the laws of states listed in that endorsement; and it also provides employer's liability for claims stemming from operations of the business. However, coverage does not apply in states having monopolistic state funds, nor to any penalties or fines imposed upon the employer for noncompliance with state workers' compensation laws. While there is no charge for this endorsement, premium charges are made for any exposure which arises in those states listed in

---

5. About two-thirds of the states cover all occupational diseases, most of the other specify those to be covered, while two states do not compensate them at all. Earl F. Cheit, *Injury and Recovery in the Course of Employment*, p. 17.

that endorsement. In any event, an underwriter should never use this endorsement when a known exposure exists, but only when an unexpected and unforeseen exposure requires protection.

The second of these endorsements is the broad form all states endorsement which was introduced for use in most jurisdictions (except monopolistic state funds) in January 1973. Instead of being a reimbursement form like the all states endorsement, it provides insurance in all states listed in the endorsement — if the issuance of a policy is sufficient to bring an insured under the compensation law of the state in question. If a policy is not sufficient to bring an insured under the law of the state where an injury has been incurred by one of its employees, the insured is reimbursed in essentially the same way as if the all states endorsement were in effect. This broad form also provides employer's liability coverage. While this endorsement can be attached to the policy in lieu of the all states endorsement, there is an additional charge for its use. The cost is a flat $25 for each annual period or less. If an insured does not wish to purchase this coverage, the all states endorsement can be requested instead. In no event can both endorsements be attached to the policy.

An important factor to keep in mind when evaluating the policy used for workers' compensation insurance is that the provisions of the law supersede any inconsistencies in the policy. Furthermore, any subsequent change in the law applies automatically to all outstanding policies. These facts tend to emphasize the point that an underwriter of workers' compensation insurance does not attempt to underwrite through the contract.

RETENTION AND REINSURANCE

A workers' compensation underwriter is in a unique position from the standpoint of exposure retention. The insurer is not permitted by law to limit the amount of its liability. A number of employees could be injured in one accident on the employer's premises and the workers' compensation insurer would be required to pay benefits to each employee. The underwriter can protect the insurer only by purchasing excess reinsurance.

Employer's liability, on the other hand, can be handled in the same fashion as other types of liability. Specific excess reinsurance may be purchased to cover each large risk. However, it is much more common to purchase treaty reinsurance which applies when any occurrence exceeds a stipulated amount.

Because of the similarity of workers' compensation and employer's liability, it is common to secure one excess reinsurance treaty protecting against each loss occurrence above a specified amount. The retention might be $25,000, $50,000, or any other amount which fits the needs of the insurer and is agreeable to the reinsurer.

The frequency of large losses on these types of coverages is quite low. In order to avoid a high minimum premium, many insurers combine this reinsurance protection with that carried on commercial liability. There is a catastrophe potential on the latter coverage, so an excess reinsurance treaty is purchased. (Refer to Chapter 22 for further explanation of this point.) That treaty is often extended to cover against infrequent, but potentially catastrophic, large losses under workers' compensation and employer's liability insurance.

Another possible approach is to use an aggregate excess reinsurance policy. Since many losses are small, a regular excess per loss coverage would be very expensive if the retention level was set low enough to be really helpful. An aggregate excess coverage will give protection if the accumulation of these small losses should exceed a specified percentage of the earned premium. By this means, the underwriter protects against the possibility of a substantial impact because of a large number of small losses.

SPECIAL PROBLEMS

In addition to state laws, a federal compensation coverage extends protection to employees engaged in maritime occupations. The Longshoremen's and Harbor Workers' Compensation Act is intended to be an exclusive remedy for disability and death occurring upon federal navigable waters and adjoining areas.

Underwriting problems arise because of the confusion as to which employees are covered under the USL&HW act. A 1972 revision was intended to clarify the status of workers on small boats on piers and terminals. In some respects, the status became more confused.

Specially-trained underwriters are used by most companies to deal with the complex problems of applicants whose activities may involve maritime occupations.

QUESTIONS FOR DISCUSSION

1. Explain the concept of workers' compensation as "a pure case of liability coverages without fault."
2. List several types of hazardous occupations from the standpoint of a workers' compensation underwriter.
3. What types of physical conditions might be of interest to a workers' compensation underwriter?
4. Discuss these aspects of workers' compensation from an underwriting standpoint:
   (a) monopolistic state funds
   (b) all states endorsement
   (c) broad form all states endorsement

INTRODUCTION TO PART VI

UNDERWRITING PACKAGE POLICIES

Package policies, which had their start in the mid-1950s and have attained tremendous growth over the years, present unique problems to property and casualty underwriters. Much of the problems stem from the fact that packages, in general, involve so many facets of insurance that every underwriter must understand them if he or she is to comprehend the total underwriting picture.

To better understand the concept of packaging, Chapter 33 discusses the specific principles that are involved in packaging, such as the reasons for the concept, its advantages and disadvantages and its aspects on pricing and competition.

Then Chapter 34 is devoted to discussing underwriting problems peculiar to package policies. One of these is the practical problem concerning the background and knowledge of underwriters. Should several line underwriters each handle their specialties and then agree on the action to be taken, or should one multiple-line underwriter handle the entire policy? Another problem deals with the relative profitability or desirability of component coverage included in the package. Must each component coverage be profitable, or can some of them be unprofitable? If the latter, how can an underwriter determine the extent of unprofitability permitted under some coverages? These aspects are some of the subjects of discussion in this chapter.

Chapters 35, 36 and 37 discuss underwriting practices involving the three major types of package policies: personal lines, commercial lines and farms. Each chapter follows the same general format as that used in the discussions of specific insurance lines in Part V. First, the background and development of packages are discussed, along with explanations of the packaging situation in the current insurance picture. Following next are explanations of coverages with references to component insurance lines. Basic functions of underwriting are explained in the same order as under the discussion of specific lines previously mentioned; selection of risks, aspects of acceptable and unacceptable, methods of securing information, classifying and rating risks, policy forms and retention and reinsurance. Each chapter also contains the approaches actually used in the underwriting, and the extent to which multiple line underwriting or separate line underwriting is used in actual practice.

Finally, Chapter 38 deals with the concept of all lines packaging. Since these policies are not actually being used, at least in the United States, this chapter is devoted to discussing some of the problems of this approach, along with the possibilities for future development.

33

Principles Of Packaging Insurance

The first insurance companies in the United States were formed to meet specific needs, and as other needs developed, companies were started to write insurance which would meet those additional needs. In this manner a number of companies came into existence, each formed to write a particular type of insurance. First fire, then windstorm, and soon boiler, plate glass, workers' compensation, burglary, liability — each type of insurance protection having companies to write it.

Regulation of insurance followed the same lines. However, companies were grouped so that they could write more than one line within the group. The two groups were property and casualty.[1] The property coverages are traditionally fire, extended coverage and allied lines, inland marine, and marine. Casualty coverages include liability, crime, plate glass, boiler, machinery, aviation, and accident and health.

Under this system, property coverages could not be written in a single policy with casualty coverages. This however, did not prevent the development of two types of combination policies: one combining similar lines within one of the major groups, and the other combining coverages within a line itself. Some of these have been referred to as packages, but each one is confined to only one of the major groups and thus does not fit the commonly accepted requirement that a package policy must include at least one coverage from each of the two major groups of property and casualty. An example of the first type of combination policy, that which combines coverages within similar lines, is fire and windstorm, or personal liability coverage combined with an automobile liability policy. Examples of the second type — coverages combined within a line — are the extended coverages that include a number of perils previously sold seperately, and the comprehensive liability policy which

1. A third group was life insurance, which is still completely separate and not handled by property-casualty underwriters. Accident and health also is available with life insurance.

combines various personal liability coverages for the protection of a policyholder's liability.

Actually, several policies did develop during this monoline period which included more than one line of insurance. Marine insurance had developed in England on the basis of including liability and hull coverages in one policy and competition forced the same pattern upon United States underwriters. The jewelers block policies combined fire coverages with the casualty coverages of burglary and theft, and developed out of a true need for broad coverage. Boiler and machinery insurance, on the other hand, has been permitted from the beginning, as a combination of property and liability coverages.

The most popular of these combination policies was the full coverage automobile policy. For many years, an automobile owner could only be protected by two policies, one for liability and the other for physical damage. The clumsiness of this arrangement was offset to a large degree by the practice of two insurers combining their coverages on one piece of paper. Technically, two contracts were written, but the appearance was of one policy and the public accepted this arrangement eagerly.

All of these combinations were steps toward true package policies, although, theoretically, some of them are actually packages. In the common use of the term in insurance circles, however, they are not package policies.

EXPLANATION OF PACKAGE POLICIES

A package policy, as the term is used today, is a multiple-line policy since it includes within a single policy, two or more coverages formerly written only as separate policies, and has at least one property coverage and one casualty coverage.

An insurer may be a multiple-line company and may not even write package policies. But a multiple-line insurance company may write both property and casualty policies; this is permitted in all states. A multiple-line insurance policy includes within one contract, two or more coverages traditionally written as separate lines of insurance. (Some states were much slower in permitting package policies, but now all states permit them.)

Divisible and Indivisible Aspects

Package policies may be either divisible or indivisible in nature. A divisible policy is rated by combining the rates for each component coverage, either with or without discounts; thus, the total premium is the sum of the premiums for each of the coverages. An indivisible policy has a single rate and premium for all coverage included within the policy. Both divisible and indivisible policies require minimum coverage which always include at least one property line and one casualty line, and both types permit other coverages to be added for additional premiums at the option of the applicant.

Divisible policies commonly have much more flexibility; thus, a divisible policy for a class might require only fire, extended coverage, and basic liability, while permitting the addition of broad form fire coverages, theft, and such liability coverages as medical payments. An indivisible policy on the same class might require broad from fire, theft and medical payments coverages. An indivisible policy is much more likely to have mandatory relationships among the component parts, while the divisible policy has less restrictions.

Reasons for Packaging Concept — Advantages

There are several reasons package policies were developed. One is that the policyholder can secure one policy instead of two or three to cover the insurance needs. Another reason is that separate policies tend to leave coverage gaps, and a package policy can avoid these gaps if it is properly written. Still another reason is the relative ease of writing broad coverages, because all of the property exposures can be combined in one policy and thus may be covered on an all risks basis without a long list of perils. Finally, but perhaps most important, packaging can result in lower premiums.

There are several reasons that underwriters like package policies. One is the ability to observe all of an applicant's exposures at one time, presenting a complete picture of the risk. When separate policies are written, the underwriting and loss information is separated. The information an underwriter develops about an applicant can be used, at least to some extent, in evaluating other policies. With a package policy, the entire picture is in one place.

Another reason underwriters like package policies is that a much greater spread of risk is achieved. When theft coverage is only written alone, it is purchased almost exclusively by people who feel that they have a definite exposure to theft loss. Other people have some theft loss exposure, of couse, but it does not seem large enough to justify purchasing an insurance policy. The result is adverse selection, a condition which underwriters abhor. The package policy changes all of this; now every applicant purchases theft insurance (assuming that it is part of the package, as it is for most homeowners policies) even if the exposure is slight. The same can be said of comprehensive personal liability insurance. The CPL policy combines into one contract, the protection for the person with a vicious dog, for a neighbor with unruly children, for another who shoots guns, and for still others with swimming pools and a penchant for entertaining; each receives the protection needed, plus much more rarely needed, all at a price that is very little more than a policy written on each peril alone. This principle applies equally well when the CPL policy is made a component part of a package policy — requiring every applicant to purchase the coverage whether a need for it is felt or not.

Still another reason that underwriters like package policies is the better insurance which may be written because of premium savings. The alert producer who sells the first package to an applicant does not merely save some money; the producer usually secures better coverage for the client in addition to, or perhaps in place of, a premium reduction. This means better insurance to value, and this is of extreme importance to a property underwriter. Even the broader coverages the producer sells, in lieu of premium reductions, are beneficial to the underwriter because this gives the insurer another dimension in which to spread risks; everyone buys vandalism coverage, for example, rather than just the person who feels that there is a particular vandalism exposure.

A rather surprising reason why underwriters like package policies is the manner in which they can write coverages that may not be profitable otherwise. One small portion of an applicant's insurance needs may have so many problems that it is almost impossible to write it. The underwriter may not have a facility for getting a surcharged rate, and knows that the insurer will lose money on that line without such a rate. Under the line system of organization, each line must be profitable; at least it must come close to breaking even in those cases when an entire account is involved. Under a package policy, one unprofitable section may be lost wihtin others which are profitable, so the underwriter is able to furnish a market to all of the applicant's insurance needs and still make a total profit.

Finally, an underwriter likes package policies because they give a larger amount of total premium with which to operate. When the homeowners package policy was only a few years old, it had caused substantial increases in the average premiums of personal fire insurers. With more total income and more premium per policy, the underwriter can do many things. More inspections can be ordered, thus improving the selection of risk. The producer can be paid more dollars of commission (even though the percentage is lower), a fact which encourages producers to give an underwriter better risks. The underwriter also has more money with which to pay inevitable losses under any type of insurance.

Disadvantages of Packaging Concept

With all of the advantages of packaging, it is not difficult to see why package policies have become almost an instant success. But there are some disadvantages, of course. One is the higher premium that must be charged if the policies are too broad and losses are too many. Another disadvantage, from the standpoint of the consumer, is the very size of a package policy; covering many properties and exposures, it often tends to become confusing and hard to read; and a single large premium is due all at one time. From the standpoint of the underwriter, the package policy is difficult to rate for exposures that are largely unknown. An underwriter also occasionally encounters conflicts which naturally arise under policies traditionally written by different underwriters. The rating problem can be mastered in time, but insurers suffer underwriting losses during the transition. There is also conflict between property and casualty underwriters. This is discussed in more detail in the next chapter.

These disadvantages are not of sufficient size to curb the growth of package policies. Packages have become one of the major types of insurance and all indications point to their continued growth and development.

PRICING AND COMPETITION

Underwriters have marketed package policies successfully because of one primary characteristic: package discounts. There are other advantages, as previously mentioned, but there is little doubt that the outstanding success of packaging in insurance is due largely to reductions in premiums. The only other factor in this growth that can be compared with discounts is the increased dollar commissions producers can realize by selling package policies instead of separate policies.

Reasons for Package Discounts

There is no rule that says packages must have discounts. Underwriters are fully capable of writing packages which are simply the sum total of the premiums of the components coverages; additional charges can even be made. There are a number of inherent factors, however, which have led to discounts on every package that thus far has been introduced.

One of the three basic reasons given for package credits is the economics of issuing policies. With separate policies, an above-average homeowner might buy four insurance policies: fire insurance on the dwelling and contents, theft insurance on contents, comprehensive personal liability coverage, and automobile insurance. The producer must complete four applications; the underwriter must handle four files; the policy issuance section must prepare and mail four policies; and the accounts section must collect premiums for four policies. This process is repeated at each renewal, compounded by the fact that different policy terms may be used on these four policies: one or three years for fire, theft, and the CPL policy, and six months for automobile insurance.

How much more economical to issue only one policy! One application, one file, one policy to type, one collection to make — it seems obvious that this is the perfect solution. However, there are a few flaws. Automobile insurance probably cannot be included because this line requires so many rating factors that a combination would strain the capabilities of the computers. It would actually cost more to include automobile coverage in the package. Besides mortgagees on dwellings often insist upon three-year fire policies, and what automobile underwriter wishes to freeze the rate for three years? Thus, automobile insurance is usually omitted from the package — losing any chance of achieving savings on the largest of the four policies, representing well over half of the homeowner's premium on the home and possessions.

The other three policies — fire, theft and comprehensive personal liability — can be combined. There are some savings by issuing fire and theft coverages together, and perhaps CPL coverage (although many insurers previously endorsed the latter on automobile policies, which is quite economical itself). These savings must be offset, at least to some degree, by one expense of writing and printing new policies, preparing educational and training programs, adopting revised accounting procedures, and so on.

The conclusion reached by most underwriters is that no demonstrable economies can be achieved in policy handling. Package discounts, if any, must come from other sources.

Another basic reason for package credits is the superior selection that can be achieved. This selection results from two characteristics of package policies: one automatic and one controllable. The automatic improvement in selection results from the cessation of adverse selection. Under a policy which includes theft, as a basic peril, every purchaser buys theft insurance, not just those who feel so greatly exposed to theft losses that they are willing to buy insurance, and at no small premium, to protect that exposure. This characteristic, therefore, is valid and justifies a discount.

The other characteristic is controllable, and involves acceptability of risks. Underwriters offer package policies only to above-average risks. For example, if all of the homes in a city range in value from $15,000 to $30,000, the underwriter might set the minimum amount of insurance at $25,000. If it is a fact that lower valued homes represent the less desirable risks, this rule would tend to place the better risks in the package. In addition, more strict rules were adopted. Among these are that only newer homes (perhaps under 15 years of age) are acceptable. With these tools, underwriters have lured the better risks to packages, a practice which justifies package discounts.

The third basic reason that was advanced as a reason for giving package credits is the rate redundancy that is present in separate policies when they were combined. As one example, consider damage done by burglars to a home; the damage is covered under a broad form or special form fire policy, and it is covered under a theft policy. If these two poicies are combined, the premium charged under one of them for coverage by burglars is redundant. The same principle is true for other perils and property, such as property scheduled on a personal articles floater attached to a homeowners package policy, because both the PAF and the content fire policy cover the property aganst loss by fire, windstorm and some other perils. Rate redundancy, therefore is justifiable reason for allowing a package credit.

In Summary, there may be no economies in handling policies, but there are savings resulting from superior selection of risks and rate redundancy. These savings justify rates which are lower than the total of the component parts. As a matter of fact, rating laws of most states prohibit rates which are excessive; and perhaps insurers would have been required to give package credits if they had not been otherwise offered.

The problem, of course, came in deciding upon the amount of package credit. In the early years, about 15% was considered as a correct amount, but this was soon modified for different lines. There was no historical guide by which to measure the savings from selection and redundancy, so judgment was freely applied. Competition, too, played a role in setting the credits for package policies. Early loss ratio results on package policies were good, so a competitive race began. Policies were broadened and rates were reduced. Before long, the foreseeable adverse trend developed and package policies became a losing line.

Effects of Competition

Under pressure of competition, all of the rules leading to profits were violated. Minimum coverages were reduced almost to the vanishing point. Seasonal property was written. So much selling and advertising were conducted that many people expected to collect for every loss, and insurers were denied the benefit of no adverse selection. Insurance-to-value requirements were lowered, in the face of increasing costs to rebuild and repair property. Broad coverages were written, with low or no deductibles, almost begging for claims to be presented. Finally, rates were lowered to ridiculous levels; these were areas where a careful shopper could buy a homeowners package policy for no more than a fire and extended coverage policy on the same property. As underwriting losses continued, underwriters began tightening rules and rates. The package business started to settle down to a less glamourous line and more of a regular type of insurance, requiring careful underwriting and adequate rates. The class now is generally profitable, but subject to the same cyclical fluctuations as other classes.

In the meantime, the property which was not acceptable for a package had its own problems. The class consisted of the smaller, older dwellings often occupied by tenants. Some of the owner-occupants of these homes could not afford the more expensive package policies. As more and more package policies were written, the percentage of preferred risks which carried only fire and extended coverage was reduced.

These dwellings and contents which were not acceptable for package policies became known as "residual risks." The line soon became unprofitable and rates were raised substantially. The problems of this class are not those of the package underwriter, but this development should cause concern to every underwriter. It is not often that a large line like personal fire insurance can change from a highly profitable, highly desirable line to a problem "residual" class, within one decade. One of the results of this development was increased pressure from governmental agencies on insurance companies and these pressures are felt by all types of underwriters.

In sumamry, competitive pressures lead to broader policies and lower rates. Sales are good and average premiums rise. Losses increase even faster and some package policies become unprofitable. In addition, the residual business not acceptable for packaging becomes unprofitable and expensive, leading to pressures for relief. The development of package policies is actually a mixed blessing for underwriters.

SELECTION OF PACKAGE RISKS

The underwriter of any type of package policy must follow certain basic rules in selecting risks. The details involved in this process under specific policy forms are discussed in later chapters, but the following basic rules generally apply.

The definition of the available market and the preparation of a policy to fit that market is always important. This is of particular concern to package underwriters because the stability which has reached most other lines of insurance has not yet been reached in the package field. In other lines, a few new coverages or adaptations are developed each year by insurers, but few major changes are made. In the package field, on the other hand, it appears that the potential for new coverages and new markets is still great. Alert underwriters are constantly developing new policies to fit markets which had not even been recognized earlier.

There are limits to the development of new policies, even if they have not been reached yet. One limit is statutory in nature; coverage cannot be combined in a policy if such packaging is prohibited by law. There are laws in most states on this subject, the most common being those prohibiting the packaging of workers' compensation with other property-casualty coverages.

While it is possible to package any lines not prohibited by law, it is not always practical to do so. One restraint is the demands of mortgagees, some of whom specify the coverage they will not accept in a policy covering property in which they have an interest. Another restraint is in the rate redundancy present in the lines; if there is little or none, the underwriter may be able to offer very little package credit, and sales thus will be discouraged.

Whatever else is considered, a package policy will succeed only if it appeals to acceptable risks. There is no point in writing a policy which is so highly specialized that no customers are available. It may be possible to develop a policy which will cover all known hazards involved in traveling to the planet Mars, but there will be so few buyers, at least in this decade, that the underwriter will starve while waiting for business.

Even though some risks are acceptable from a technical standpoint, there may be other reasons certain coverages should not be packaged. An outstanding example is automobile insurance; no major package includes it. There have been efforts by independent companies to write packages which included auto, both in personal and commercial lines, but most have been withdrawn and the rest are not well known. No one seems to want automobile coverage included in their packages. There is little or no chance of a package discount, because automobile coverages are so automated that no savings would result from packaging. And, because loss experience has been so poor in recent years, there is no room for reduced premiums under any circumstances. Furthermore, underwriters do not want a term of longer than one year on automobile, and many insurers prefer six months, while some packages are written for three-year terms. Applicants find that the inclusion of automobile coverage tends to raise the total premium to such a large amount that they cannot pay it in one sum. For that reason, most spread the payment, a situation which is automatically present if automobile is written separately with a different renewal date. Even producers feel that the more careful underwriting, after a frequency of claims on automobile insurance can cause the entire package to be cancelled, so they prefer to keep automobile insurance separate from other lines.

Competition also restricts the type of package policy which may be written, from a practical basis. If competitors are offering a package that includes theft at little more premium than a fire policy with CPL coverage, an underwriter would be ill-advised to develop a Fire-CPL package. When competition has popularized a certain package, there is little to be gained by offering a policy with slightly less coverage. An underwriter may tap a new and profitable market by developing a policy with some added coverages, particularly if the additional cost is low, but it is unproductive to offer less coverage, unless substantial economies can be offered also.

Having selected a market, the underwriter must develop a package policy to fit its needs and then determine a premium structure for it. If the premium includes a credit for economies in handling of policies, no special underwriting is needed. However, if allowances are made in the premium for other reasons, careful selection must be practiced; otherwise, the credits will not be justified and the premium will be inadequate.

The major package credit is given because of the acceptability of risks. The "cream" of the class may be the target for writing the policy, and this is defined by such charcteristics as home ownership, no commercial occupancy in a home, no manufacturing on the premises of a commercial risk, and not more than one location covered. If any of these characteristics are the basis for a package credit, the underwriter must select risks carefully to be sure that they fit the established rules. Nothing can destroy the experience quicker than the acceptance of risks with a greater exposure to loss than the rate structure contemplates.

This factor of selecting risks is a special problem to package underwriters. Of course, all underwriters must select risks which fit within assigned categories, but package underwriters will take a class for which a rate is established, and package a portion of that class with a rate credit because of the definitions of acceptability; any laxity in enforcing the parameters of acceptability will lead to an erosion in loss experience.

There is still another problem facing package underwriters, as a class. They must be more careful in selecting risks which are homogeneous than those underwriters of separate lines. The latter must achieve homogeneity in order to realize profits, but this is not too difficult in many lines. A commercial underwriter may be able to place all frame retail stores in one category and achieve homogeneity. Similarly, a commercial liability underwriter may combine all retail establishments in one class.

The package underwriter must consider many different lines. Consideration must be given to the construction of the building, occupancy, theft hazard, liability exposures, and so on. A package policy for a shoe store must be underwritten on many more factors than "retail stores." If some liquor stores are accepted under the shoe store package, the homogeneity from a fire standpoint may not be violated, but from a crime standpoint it is seriously eroded. There are more perils and exposures under a package policy than under any of the separate lines comprising the package, and the addition of these perils and exposures requires more careful selection in order to achieve homogeneity.

The underwriter of package policies must follow different rules than the underwriter of a single line. It is not enough to combine the rules for the separate lines; it is ridiculous to pile up the unacceptability lists for each component line and consider this as the list for the package. A multiple-line package policy may be simply a combination of separate policies or it may be a completely new contract which includes the major provisions of other lines. Regardless of the format, there are special package rules that must be followed and these rules, as explained, must guide every package underwriter if an underwriting profit is to be achieved.

QUESTIONS FOR DISCUSSION

1. Define the term "package policy," and relate it to "multiple-line companies."
2. Explain the difference between divisible and indivisible package policies.
3. List the major advantages and disadvantages of the package concept.

4. What are the 3 basic reasons given for using package credits?
5. Explain the meaning of the term "residual risks" and show why these risks may be a matter of concern to underwriters.

34

Underwriting Package Policies

Until the advent of multi-line package policies, insurance was underwritten on a line basis. Each line of insurance was separate and an underwriter seldom handled more than one line.

Some cross-handling of underwriting was sometimes attempted, but it was always in related lines. Thus, a fire underwriter would handle some inland marine lines, but seldom would handle casualty insurance. The size of the insurance company and the underwriting department sometimes determined the lines handled by an underwriter. Some insurers wrote so little inland marine, for example, that they could not have a specialist; so a fire underwriter handled it. This situation was possible even in some fairly large companies because some of them specialized in certain lines and wrote others only as an accommmodation. Of course, small insurance companies wrote so little insurance in some lines that their underwriters handled several lines just to keep busy. Other than those situations the only time an underwriter handled more than one line was during cross-training.

There were advantages to this system. Underwriters became very proficient in their specialty lines. Many spent an entire working career in one line of insurance, such as fire, inland marine or commercial liability. The result was a corps of thoroughly trained, highly proficient expert underwriters. Many of these underwriters knew policies in detail, could quote rates almost automatically, and could recommend proper coverage for every situation. A producer, therefore, could count on receiving expert help and advice when presenting a specific problem to an underwriter.

On the other hand, there were disadvantages to this system, even under the monoline laws then in effect. Producers found that an underwriter in one line was completely ignorant of other lines. Clients do not have fire insurance problems and inland marine insurance problems, they have insurance problems. A producer trying to handle those problems was forced to deal with two or more underwriters, and their recommendations did not always agree. The fire underwriter might demand one type of protective device while the inland marine underwriter insisted upon another. It was not surprising that producers and their clients eagerly adopted the multiple-line concept when it was introduced.

The line concept of underwriting had serious disadvantages from the standpoint of underwriters, too. An ambitious young underwriter found promotional possibilities blocked by an older underwriter. The possibilities of moving to another line were not great, and even then the underwriter must start over again as a novice and try to learn a new craft.

Older underwriters operated as journeymen under an old guild system. There were few opportunities of learning to underwrite except by training under an experienced underwriter, almost as an apprentice. Newer underwriters then found their training rather severe and limited, their chances for promotion light, and their opportunities for moving to other lines quite restricted. These disadvantages undoubtedly reduced the number of bright, ambitious, eager young people who sought lifetime careers in underwriting. Those who were in the underwriting jobs, but had not yet reached a level of "senior underwriter," were anxious to adopt any change which would permit them to grow and to advance without working as apprentices for 30 years. It was against this background that multi-line policies were introduced in the 1950s. All of the circumstances seemed to be right and these package policies prospered.

MULTIPLE-LINE UNDERWRITING

Multiple-line policies require multiple-line underwriting; this appeared to be an obvious fact to many insurance people. The first package policies were scarcely off the contract writers' drawing board before underwriting departments were being realigned on a multiple-line basis.

The first true package policies were in the personal lines field — personal lines underwriters, therefore, were the first to go multiple-line. Before anyone could determine if the concepts were sound, commercial packages were introduced and commercial lines underwriters were also changed to the multiple-line approach. Within a period of a very few years, probably not more than five, most multiple-line insurers had changed the structure of their underwriting department from line to multiple-line.

Under the multiple-line concept, every underwriter handled multiple-line policies and also several lines of separate policies. Not all types of policies were immediately placed under package policies and some probably never will. However, if the underwriter can handle a package policy containing fire, inland marine and liability insurance, why should that underwriter not handle separate policies within each of these lines?

The logic of the multiple-line approach to underwriting appeared to be unassailable. The overnight success of package policies guaranteed that they would be a permanent part of the insurance business. Insurance companies introduced package policies and realigned their underwriting departments in a flurry of activity that must have been rivaled only by the great Gold Rush of the previous century.

However, one degree of specialization remained. Personal lines package policies developed along different lines than commercial packages, and the basic differences between those groups were recognized. The pattern soon developed of having two sets of underwriters: personal multiple-line underwriters and commmercial multiple-line underwriters. The only exceptions to those reclassifications were in those few lines that were not included in package policies for one reason or another; principally, ocean marine, workers' compensation, fidelity and surety, boiler and machinery and aviation.

A multiple-line underwriter handles entire package policies and also handles separate policies that come within underwriting jurisdiction. Thus, a personal lines multiple-line underwriter not only underwrites a homeowners package policy; but also underwrites those lines of personal insurance dealing with automobile, fire, liability, inland marine and crime.

The advantages of this new approach became obvious. One underwriter, not several, handled all of the insurance needs of a client; the producer received answers to all of the questions from one underwriter; a single decision was made concerning acceptability, protective devices, deductibles, and all of the other types of decisions an underwriter must make.

Perhaps most important of all was the fact that all insurance needs of a client were underwritten by one person. One of the advantages of a package policy is that it combines the entire insurance needs into one contract. The underwriting department carried this concept one step farther by having one underwriter handle risks, whether they were combined in one policy or not. Under the old system of line underwriting, a policyholder who presented several cigarette burn losses within a few months might find the contents fire policy cancelled. Under the multiple-line concept, the underwriter first looked at the entire account; if the automobile, crime, and personal liability coverages were profitable, the underwriter probably would not have taken action on the contents fire policy, or on the package policy which covered contents against loss by fire.

The disadvantages of the multiple-line concept in underwriting soon became apparent. Many package policies become unprofitable, and this was a factor in reevaluating the organization. However, many disadvantages became quite obvious long before the loss experience worsened.

The principal problem was that there were few underwriters trained to handle multiple-lines. Some had been cross-trained, of course, and some had been transferred from one line to another; so, they were reasonably proficient in more than one line. Few of these were experienced in more than two lines, however, and several lines were included in the duties of many multiple-line underwriters. Since most underwriters were proficient in only one line, massive training program was started. Considering the extent of the training that was needed, the newness and growth of the multiple-line policies, and the lack of knowledge on the part of producers because of the newness of the policies, it is somewhat of a wonder that the insurance industry survived this period.

Most underwriters simply did not have sufficient experience in all lines to become good multiple-line underwriters. Each one could handle one or two lines proficiently, but each was untrained in others. Since the background training was different, some underwriters were better in certain aspects of the multiple-lines, while others did their best in different lines.

Producers found that they still could not always get expert answers to their questions. An underwriter could give all of the answers on a multiple-line policy, but this was not much help in a problem case if half of the answers were guesses. It became apparent that, since producers are seldom experts in any one line, they should be able to take their problems to underwriters who were experts. The only way to achieve that expertise, it appeared, was for the underwriter to specialize, not to try to handle all lines.

It is obvious, therefore, that the multiple-line approach to underwriting has many problems, with the disadvantages often outnumbering the advantages. As insurers realized this, many of them went back to some type of a line underwriting concept. Some insurers, of course, had never adopted the multiple-line approach. They were joined by others who reversed their organization charts, returning to the concept of having underwriters specialize by line, at least for some policies.

UNDERWRITING BY LINE

The return to underwriting by line for some or all policies offered few problems under single line coverages. One of the main problems was in the admission that a mistake had been made; organizations, like people dislike to reverse themselves and to admit that a new concept is not as good as a former one. Another problem was in meeting the psychological needs of the underwriters: Having enjoyed the thrill of being master of all lines, it was hard for underwriters to return to the more narrow confines of single-lines. Some insurers had created higher positions for multiple-line underwriters, and these better jobs were not available for everyone returning to monoline underwriting.

Package policies were quite a different matter. There are inherent problems in having multiple-line policies underwritten by single-line underwriters. Is only one line underwritten and the rest ignored? If several underwriters handle on policy, what happens when only one wants to decline writing the coverage? Who makes the final decision? Several different arrangements have been tried in an effort to solve these problems.

One solution is to have one underwriter responsible for the policy with an arrangement to refer all policies with problems involving other than that person's specialty to other underwriters. For example, if fire is the dominant line in a particular package, the fire underwriter is the responsible underwriter. This person handles the fire line; if it is acceptable and there are no problems in the other line, no other underwriter is involved. If there are prob lems in crime or liability, for example, the fire underwriter then refers the file to the applicable underwriter or underwriters handling crime or liability insurance.

This first appraoch has two serious disadvantages. One is that responsibility for an underwriting decision must be fixed with absolute certainty. Under the last example, assume that all circumstances are satisfactory and the exception of crime coverage, and the crime underwriter feels that the application should be declined. Assuming that crime is an integral part of the package, who makes the final decision that all coverages be written or the entire policy declined? The crime underwriter reviews only on specialty, so that person cannot be gien final authority. The fire underwriter attempts to weigh all factors, but cannot determine whether the poor crime situation outweighs the desirable factors or not.

The second disadvantage is even more serious. This arrangement presupposes that the lead underwriter can recognize problems in other lines. How is one person to know if a problem exists, unless there has been extensive training in other lines? In the previous example, what would have happened if the fire underwriter had not seen any crime problem and had not referred the file to the crime underwriter? It is extremely dangerous to underwrite by ignorance — to assume that everything is all right simply because an untrained person does not see a problem.

This first approach, which has been tried by some insurers, is doomed to failure. If the lead underwriter is not trained to recognize problems in all lines, it is inevitable that some losses will occur which could have been prevented by a trained underwriter. If the lead underwriter is well-trained in all lines, he or she might as well be called a multiple-line underwriter and avoid the referrals to others. True, there is a slight difference between recognizing the existence of a problem and knowing what to do about it, but the difference is too minor to make much difference; an underwriter who recognizes a problem has already completed most of the underwriting, and it takes very little more training to learn how to finish the job.

Another approach which has been tried is the committee system. Each line is underwritten by an underwriter who specializes in that line. Then the comments of each one are brought together, generally in a meeting and a final decision is made. For example, the fire underwriter may approve the risk if a deductible is applied, the inland marine underwriter may require the installation of a protective device, and the liability underwriter may feel that the risk is acceptable as submitted. These separate decisions are combined into one package underwriting decision.

One of the disadvantages of the committee system of underwriting package policies is its clumsiness. The application must be routed to several underwriters which causes delays. Each underwriter must attach comments, or make notes on them to take to the meeting. This is a slow, cumbersome method of underwriting and insurance application.

Another disadvantage is the problem of making the decision in some cases. An application may be acceptable to all of the underwriters, except the liability underwriter who feels that the liability exposures are so great that the application should be declined. Since a decision on the entire package must be made, some type of arrangement must be made to reconcile the differences. The usual practice is to assign the decision-making to the underwriter with the greatest amount of premium. On one type of package, the fire premium may be the largest of those included in the polciy; on another, the liability premium may dominate. This method of making the decision tends to disregard problems in the lines which are smaller but which could cause many losses. It also presupposes that each underwriter is capable of making decisions involving several lines, which is not always true. Other insurers may provide that the most experienced of the separate underwriters, or perhaps the one who seems to show the greatest degree of underwriting proficiency, will make the final decision. The difficulties under these arrangements may be even greater because the underwriting problems of the major lines may be disregarded, and the result could easily be disastrous.

A third approach to package underwriting which has developed as a modification of the committee system places the ultimate underwriting decision in the hands of an underwriting supervisor or manager. This person must have general knowledge of all lines, but does not need specialized knowledge. The system seems to work best when the supervisor has specialized knowledge in one or more of the major lines included in the package, but it is more important that that person have a general understanding of underwriting principles. A package application is referred to each of the line underwriters under this approach, as under the committee approach, and each supplies an evaluation and recommendation. The difference is that under this system, the supervisor makes the final decision after securing ideas and comments from many specialists and discussing the application with them.

The supervisor approach depends heavily upon the ability of that person, of course. If this person is a good, all around underwriter, capable of making sound decisions on many aspects of insurance, the system can work. However, such people are scarce, and the industry has done little to develop them. There are not many people who can handle such an assignment, but when one is found, this can be an effective system of underwriting package policies.

Both the committee and the supervisor approaches bring the knowledge of many specialists to bear on each risk. When the underwriting factors are complex or the exposures are varied, such specialization can be very helpful. The producer can write package policies and still get the expert help of specialists. The applicant also receives a policy put together by experts for the exposures.

At the same time, both of these systems have disadvantages. They are slow, clumsy and time consuming. Like many other programs put together by a committee or by compromise, the policies may represent only the best compromise that could be reached, whether it is the best arrangment for the applicant or not. Producers find that these systems are unsatisfactory if an early decision is necessary, as it often is when selling insurance. The committee cannot decide anything until every line has been analyzed thoroughly, and even when the supervisor has the authority to make a decision, is not likely to do so until each of the specialists has given an opinion.

TRENDS IN PACKAGE UNDERWRITING

None of the approaches to package underwriting has proved to be ideal for all types of packages. A multiple-line underwriter can make decisions based on his or her own knowledge, but many times that knowledge is inadequate. One specialized line underwriter can handle packages and refer problems to others, but there is serious danger that some major problems will be overlooked. A committee of underwriters can bring together the expert handling of many specialists, but the final decision may have to be based more on the ability to secure a compromise agreement than on sound underwriting principles. A supervisor who leads the committee and has authority for its decisions can bring together both specialized knowledge and centralized authority, but will be swayed by line underwriters, unless the supervisor has the rare qualities of leadership and multiple-line knowledge.

Insurers have not yet found the one best method of underwriting package policies. Probably there is no single system best suited for all policies. Although the present trend is to use different approaches for different types of packages, the major divisions of personal and commercial generally have determined the type of underwriting to be followed.

Personal Lines

The homeowners dwelling package policy is a fairly uniform contract for all personal risks, as weritten by all insurers. While there are some differences among the policies, almost all of them are rather uniform combinations of broad coverage on dwellings, fire perils, plus theft on personal property, and comprehensive personal liability. The optional additional coverages are along the same lines, except for the personal articles floater which is a personal inland marine line.

Almost all of the premiums and exposures on personal packages are related to property, with most of it being fire. An underwriter trained personal lines fire insurance thus can handle most of these policies. The theft portions of the packages are either taken from the personal crime policies written as casualty insurance or from the personal inland marine field. In either case, the underwriting problems are closely related to those of fire insurance. The theft exposure is great and can be a major source of loss under personal package policies, but an experienced fire underwriter can learn how to underwrite personal crime coverage without too much trouble.

The only remaining part of the basic personal package is comprehensive personal liability insurance. Only a small portion of the total premium is reprsented by this line. Of more consequence is the fact that the CPL policy seldom receives very much underwriting attention whenever it is written. This is almost always a secondary coverage, and there seems to be little that an underwriter can do in underwriting this coverage. At any rate, the underwriting factors which are considered for the CPL policy, such as moral hazard, claims consciousness and undue hazards, are all related to the property coverages. An underwriter who handles the fire and theft coverages of the package has already secured the information needed to underwrite the CPL coverage, and the decision on the property coverages applies to CPL coverage, too. For these reasons, it takes very little additional training to enable a property underwriter to handle the CPL portion of the package.

An experienced fire underwriter can handle the underwriting of a personal package policy after some additional training in crime and comprehensive liability coverages. This additional training is not difficult, so most insurers handle it in this manner.

The underwriter is now a true multiple-line underwriter, handling three separate lines of insurance. This can be done effectively because one line (fire) comprises the bulk of the package, while the other lines (crime or inland marine and liability) are closely related to fire and are underwritten on roughly the same factors.

The one remaining problem is with the personal articles floater, on which are scheduled such target items as jewelry, furs and silver. An inland marine underwriter handles these as separate lines of insurance, applying considerable skill to avoid the problems inherent in all risks coverages on target property. When a PAF is added to the personal package as an optional endorsement, the question naturally arises whether specialized underwriting is needed. One important consideration is the type of property being scheduled; much of it is relatively low-valued furs or jewelry which is scheduled just to secure adequate coverage, because of restricted coverage to such property given in the package. Some of the scheduled property, however, may be quite valuable and needs careful underwriting. Another consideration is the extent to which the information gathered in order to underwrite the package will apply to the scheduled items. In most cases, every essential item of information will be available excepting only the appraisal and description of the scheduled property. In a few cases, however, there will be quite a bit of information still needed, such as where the property is kept when not in use and the social habits of the applicant.

The package underwriter can be taught rather easily to handle most personal articles floaters. After underwriting an $80,000 home with $40,000 on unscheduled personal property, there is seldom much concern with scheduling a $4,000 fur coat or a $3,000 ring for the applicant's wife, provided an appraisal is furnished. However, a different problem is presented by a $200,000 home with $100,000 on unscheduled personal property, plus a schedule of $125,000 in jewelry; careful underwriting is needed, and this may require the help of an inland marine underwriter.

Most insurers use multiple-line underwriters for personal package policies. Most of these underwriters have been trained in personal lines fire insurance, and have received additional training in crime, inland marine and personal liability coverages. In most companies, these underwriters also handle personal articles floaters, but provision is generally made that the package underwriter may refer any scheduled items to an inland marine underwriter. While the expert on scheduled property is expected to give an evaluation of the risk on the PAF, the final decision rests in the hands of the package underwriter.

In multiple-line policies for personal risks, multiple-line underwriters are used. The policies are relatively simple. They are primarily geared to one line, and an underwriter can learn to handle the entire policy without undue difficulty. In the one line of scheduled property where there has not been adequate training, the underwriter can secure the evaluation of an expert and relate it to the entire policy.

Commercial Lines

Commercial package policies are somewhat uniform as written by insurers, but there is considerable difference among the policies offered to different risks. The basic policies cover fire perils for buildings and contents, plus commercial liability coverages. Additional coverages are available for many classes of applicants and some of these can be quite complex.

Some commercial package policies are not too different from personal lines packages insofar as the relationship of the various lines are concerned. An apartment house package is largely constructed of fire coverages, with the liability exposures being relatively small. A trained commercial fire underwriter would need only to learn a rather simple line of liability insurance in order to be able to handle most risks. Many of the optional coverages, on the other hand, are property related, such as rental income insurance. However, a few optional coverages for some risks can present problems to a fire underwriter, such as elevator or boiler coverages.

Other commercial package policies are not so easily classified. The liability exposure may be greater than the fire exposure on a restaurant package, a manufacturer's package or an accountant's package. Some of these risks may be so heavily oriented toward liability coverages that the commercial liability underwriter can handle the entire package after a brief training session in fire insurance. Many others are rather evenly balanced between property and liability lines, so an underwriter would need to know each component line of insurance thoroughly.

Most commercial package policies are rather complex and have relatively large values exposed to loss. With the exception of those related heavily to fire, such as apartment house packages, the exposures are sizable in both of the major lines of fire and liability. Many of these policies also contain coverages for some of the more complex and expensive lines like commercial crime, commercial inland marine, glass, and even automobile or truck insurance. Each of these lines is a career in itself, if an underwriter is to have thorough knowledge of the subject, but there are few underwriters who are knowledgeable in all of these lines.

Some insurers may write only the more simple types of commercial packages; those with a primary exposure of fire coverages. Such insurers may use multiple-line underwriters, as are used on personal packages; these underwriters would handle all policies by referring problem areas to specialists for evaluation.

Most insurers write a fairly broad spectrum of commercial package policies and are expanding regularly into more classes of risks. But few of these insurers are blessed with multiple-line underwriters who can handle all of the many exposures which arise on a large share of the policies. These insurers, therefore, must use several underwriters on each package application in order to secure adequate underwriting on all lines.

The usual practice is to have a supervisor or lead underwriter bear the responsibility for the package policy. Specialists in the various lines contribute their evaluations of the risk, but the final decision rests on one person. Some insurers use the supervisor of the section for this lead position, while others use an experienced underwriter — one who has had considerable background in commercial underwriting, hopefully in two or more lines. Such an underwriter could be called a multiple-line underwriter, but has less authority than the title implies because this person is expected to secure evaluations from several specialists, rather than handling all lines alone.

Commercial package policies are too complex to be handled by one underwriter, except for the simpler classifications of risks. Most insurers use several underwriters, one for each specialty, and assign the ultimate authority for the policy to a supervisor or lead underwriter.

Profitability of Packages

Regardless of the type of organization used for the underwriting department on package policies, the same principle of profitability applies. This principle was not recognized by most underwriters in the early days of packages and is still violated by some underwriters today. However, it was the primary cause of realignment of package underwriters.

One approach to package profitability is to insist upon profitability for each component coverage. The advocates of this position argue that any one line includes potential losses which can more than offset the premium on the entire package. This is a conservative, safe approach which is designed to stifle sales. Many applicants have one problem line, but their entire account is profitable. One reason for packaging coverages is to bury the problem areas in the overall policy. To deny this possibility is to deny one of the values of packaging and to limit the market. The committee approach to underwriting heads toward this result, because each specialist wants to be sure that this one line will not suffer undue losses. This is a weakness of committee underwriting, and it is also a restriction on the development and growth of packages.

Another approach to the profitability of packages is to consider only the profit potential of the major line and to disregard the others. The underwriters using this approach usually do so from ignorance, not realizing the potential losses from what appear to be minor lines. This is an optimistic, unrealistic approach. There are some applicants who are highly preferred risks on all lines except one, and that one can be very poor. Such applicants attempt to hide the poor line in a package, realizing that they probably could not get coverage for the problem line otherwise — certainly not at discount prices. The underwriter who follows this approach may make a profit for a short time, but is doomed to failure over the long haul. The multiple-line underwriting system has this weakness under all policies having any substantial portion of the package in lines with which the underwriter is not reasonably familiar. In fact, even a minor line in a relatively simple package has the potential of losses which can make the entire package unprofitable. The multiple-line underwriter, therefore, must receive thorough training in all component coverages; without such training, the package policy will not be profitable.

The only practical, realistic approach to package underwriting, therefore, is to recognize that some of the component coverages may lose money, but that these losses must not offset the profitability of the other lines to the point that the entire package is unprofitable. There is no reason not to include in the package, certain lines which may be unprofitable in themselves. The essential requirement is that this unprofitability must be more than offset by the profitability of the other lines. The size or importance of each line is irrelevant. The important factor is to keep the potential losses on the entire package within the limits of profitability, and the essential underwriting requirement is to make a profit on the package, even though losses are greater than the premium on the fire line or the liability line.

The duty of the underwriter is to write insurance at a profit. This is true of separate insurance lines and of package policies, when those package policies are viewed as a unit. The package underwriter should strive, therefore, to make a profit on the package, regardless of the experience on each of the component coverages.

QUESTIONS FOR DISCUSSION

1. (a) What is meant by underwriting "on a line basis?"
   (b) What are its advantages and disadvantages?
2. Explain the multiple-line concept of underwriting, including the advantages and disadvantages.
3. Underwriting package policies by line can be approached in 3 different ways. Explain each, with its advantages and disadvantages.

35

Personal Lines Package Policies

The concept of package policies started in personal lines and has achieved its greatest growth there. The first true package policies in personal lines were written in the mid-1950s with rapid growth. The total premiums earned was approximately $16 billion by 1986.[1]

The name most commonly used for the personal lines package policy is "homeowners policy." This is the name used by the rating bureau for its policy, one which is written by most companies in the field. Those companies issuing independent policies generally use the name "homeowners" and follow almost exactly the same coverages. For all practical purposes, the names "personal lines package policy," "homeowners policy," "dwelling package policy," and "homeowners package policy" are synonymous and may be used interchangeably.

In the early days of personal lines package policies, both divisible and indivisible policies were offered. Within a few years, the indivisible policies won the contest, and now there are very few divisible policies available. The indivisible homeowners policy is now used almost universally, with a few modifications in some independent forms. (The basic coverages are rated from a table, with no separate premiums being shown for component parts.)

The homeowners policy is a combination of a personal lines fire policy on the dwelling and its contents, a residence theft policy and a comprehensive personal liability policy. A tenants policy is identical except that no coverage applies to the dwelling, other than the usual tenants improvements and betterments coverage included

---

1. "Review and Preview: Up from the Ashes," *Best's Review, Property/Casualty Insurance Edition*, Vol. 87, No. 9 (January, 1987), p. 86.

in a fire policy on contents.[2] Various combinations of coverage are offered, using the options under the fire policy generally, resulting in several types of policies being available. In every case, all of the basic coverages are included with no option to remove any of them. If an applicant does not desire theft protection or personal liability coverage, this person should not purchase a homeowners policy because the premium is an indivisible one.

The dwelling is the key to most of the homeowners policy. Coverage on it is written in even thousands of insurance. A minimum amount is specified in the rules, ordinarily about $8,000. Other private structures are covered by an amount of insurance which equals 10% of the dwelling amount. Personal property is automatically insured in an amount equal to 50% or 60% of the dwelling coverage. Additional living expense coverage is 10% or 20% of the dwelling amount, depending upon the policy. These automatic relationships help to assure proper insurance to value, especially on personal property. (Additional amounts may be purchased on each coverage.)

Comprehensive personal liability coverage is written with a minimum of $100,000 on liability, $1,000 on medical payments, and $500 on physical damage coverage for the property of others. Additional amounts may be purchased on only the first two coverages just as those personal liability policies written separately.

DESCRIPTION OF COVERAGES

Homeowners policies are fairly uniform. There are some differences in forms used by independent companies, but most of them are quite similar to the bureau forms which are followed by most companies. Some variations are used in certain states, but the use of a national forms bureau for this class has helped to achieve substantial uniformity. The following discussion applies generally, but details may differ in bureau or independent policies.

Types of Policies

Several types of policies are available, the names and combinations of which have changed over the years. Originally, policy A was a limited coverage, B was the broad form, and C covered on an all risks basis. These forms were numbered, being constructed somewhat as follows.[3]

1. Basic Form. The building and contents are covered only for fire, extended

2. It takes a little time for the uninitiated to become accustomed to the contradiction in terms. A "homeowner" is one who owns a home, so a "homeowners policy" should be available only to such persons. One of the paradoxical terms in insurance is a "tenants homeowners policy," meaning a homeowner who does not own a home. There is no logical explanation other than to state that the same "homeowners policy" was a good term for the original package, and it carried forward when the same coverage, except for the dwelling, was made available to tenants.

3. The only differences are in the property coverages. The personal liability section is the same for all types.

coverage, vandalism and malicious mischief, and glass breakage, plus theft for personal property. These perils are explained in detail in Chapter 26.

2. Broad Form. The property coverages are the same as those under the broad form fire policy. This means the perils under the first policy, plus the added perils of falling objects, collapse, freezing, and the other broad form perils. Personal property is also covered by theft.

3. All Risks and Broad Form Combination. The building items are covered under the provisions of the special form; this is an all risks coverage with specified exclusions. Personal property is covered the same as under the second policy; broad form plus theft.

4. Broad Form on Content Only. The tenants form covers only personal property in the property section. The perils are the same as under the two preceding policies; broad form plus theft.

5. Deluxe Form. All property is covered on an all risks basis. Building coverages are the same as the special form fire policy, on the third homeowners policy type. Personal property is the same as the personal property floater, the "best" of the unscheduled policies written in the personal inland marine line. The PPF is described in Chapter 27.

Coverages

Homeowners policies are divided into two sections: Section I contains the property coverages which are found in coverages A through D. Section II is for the personal liability portion, coverages E through G. The liability coverages are described in more detail in Chapter 21. The provisions of the homeowners policy are identical with those of the CPL policy.

A. Dwelling — The dwelling building is covered precisely the same as under a personal lines fire policy.

B. Separate Structures — A separate amount of insurance applies to garages and other appurtenant private structures located on the premises, except those used for commercial or farming purposes. The amount of insurance is 10% of the amount of the dwelling.

C. Unscheduled Personal Property — Personal property is covered if it is owned or used by the insured. Excluded are animals, birds, automobiles, property of roomers or renters, and articles held for sales or as samples. In most policies, the entire amount of the coverage may apply anywhere in the world. The automatic amount of coverage is 50% or 60% of the dwelling amount. The minimum under the tenants policy is $4,000.

D. Loss of Use — Additional living expense is covered, and is usually the full extent of the coverage, since the owner is required to live on the premises. However, a portion of the premises may be rented to others, and rental value coverage is included for this exposure. The automatic amount for both of these combined is 10% of the dwelling amount on the Basic Form, 20% on the other building forms, and 20% of the personal property amount under the tenants form.

E. Personal Liability — The liability of the insured for bodily injury or property damage arising out of personal acts or conditions on the premises is insured under this coverage. Also included is fire legal liability, affording a degree of protection to property which is in the custody and control of the insured. It covers property damage to the dwelling or house furnishings used by or rented to (but not owned by) the insured, if the damage arises out of fire, explosion, or smoke or smudge caused by the sudden, unusual and faulty operation of any heating or cooking unit. Thus, if a tenant causes such a fire to the dwelling, protection will be given under this coverage.

F. Medical Payments — This coverage pays for all reasonable medical expenses incurred because of accidents on the premises or elsewhere if caused by the insured, but excluding injuries to a member of the insured household.

G. Physical Damage to Property — Loss to property of others is covered here, if the loss is caused by the insured. This is a nonliability coverage intended to cover accidental damage caused by a person, either while visiting another person or while using that person's property.

Extensions

The property coverages are extended to cover debris removal. Trees, shrubs, plants, and lawns are covered by a five percent extension of coverage A, under the same conditions as a fire policy. Replacement cost coverage is supplied to buildings, with the same provisions as are found under a personal lines fire policy. Improvements and alterations to the building are covered under the tenants form, as under a fire policy. In some states, a limited amount, such as $250, may be applied to cover fire department service charges.

Optional Coverages

Some optional coverages are the same as under a fire policy, such as earthquake coverage. Others are additional amounts on property limited by the policy, such as the $200 limit on money and $1,000 on securities. Still others are on new coverages, such as a coverage which removes the exclusion of property stolen from unattended automobiles.

An important optional coverage is that which supplies all risks coverage to scheduled articles. The policy has a $1,000 limitation on all jewelry and fur items, in the aggregate, stolen in any one loss, as well as a $2,000 limitation on theft of guns and silverware. Complete protection for these items can be obtained by purchasing a personal articles floater, using the same coverages as under a personal inland marine policy. Although there is no dollar limitation on other types of property, such as cameras and musical instruments, the protection is broader under the all risks PAF, so it is not uncommon to schedule many of the classes offered by the PAF, under a homeowners policy.

UNDERWRITING FACTORS

Acceptable Risks

Personal lines package policies have specific rules on eligibility. A complete policy can be issued only on owner-occupied homes, or a secondary dwelling owned by the insured and not rented to others. The home can be occupied by not more than four families. Business occupancies are not permitted on the premises, except for incidental office occupancies such as a real estate office or an insurance sales office.

The tenants form may not be written for owners of dwellings. But non-owners are eligible whether they live in a dwelling or an apartment.

Companies have their own ideas about acceptability among those risks that are eligible by the rules. In the early days of package policies, most companies tried to limit acceptability to the newer and better homes. The theory was that only the preferred risks should be offered these coverages. One of the reasons given for the rate discount used for the package policy was the superior selection of risks which could be written. Premiums were considerably higher than for simple dwelling fire policies, so many prospects could not afford the package, it was reasoned. Few people had purchased theft coverages, so it was felt that only those who were rather well off, financially, would be interested in purchasing a package policy which automatically included theft coverages.

The limited eligibility did not last long. The package policies were almost instant sales successes and soon almost everyone wanted to purchase the new coverage. Producers appreciated the higher commissions resulting from larger premiums, so they sold the policies aggressively. As many people recovered losses from thefts or were reimubursed for other rather unusual claims, almost everyone wanted the new "broad" policies. Actually, all of the coverages contained in the package had been available in separate policies before, but few people realized this. Homeowners policies became synonymous with "broad form" or "all risk" coverages in the minds of many people, including many in the insurance community. As more applicants requested package policies, the eligibility guides were relaxed. Now almost any homeowner or tenant can purchase a homeowners policy.

Acceptability guides for companies are now constructed along lines similar to those used for other lines. Companies writing personal fire and inland marine insurance at deviations, continue the deviations under homeowners policies, and practice the same type of selection patterns. Most companies use the bureau forms at bureau rates and accept all but the substandard risks. However, a few companies use surcharged rates and write the poorer risks.

The types of policies have somewhat different acceptability patterns. At least, they are considered differently from the standpoint of preferred or nonpreferred risks. The basic form appeals more to the owners of low-valued homes because of the limited coverages. However, some companies are very selective on this form and do not encourage its sales; they may write it at bureau rates even if they use deviations on other forms. At the other end of the spectrum, the deluxe form appeals only to the wealthier prospects because of its broad coverage and relatively high premium. Most companies offer it very cautiously, or not at all. Few of these forms are written; the other forms cover most perils and at substantial savings.

Tenants are written by most or all of the companies writing homeowners policies, in spite of the fact that experience has worsened. Some companies reduced deviations on this class or insisted upon higher deductibles in efforts to achieve profitability. Some risks, of course, were more preferred than others, and companies generally used the same acceptability patterns, but with a little more caution on tenants.

The Broad Form and Special Form are easily the most popular of the homeowners policies, and a very large share of the policies are written on these forms, particularly if the tenants form is not counted. Most references regarding this class of insurance refer to these two forms which are quite similar in their coverages; their acceptability pattern generally follows the personal lines fire picture, too.

Unacceptable Risks

Personal lines package policies are subject to rather long unacceptable risks. This is not unexpected, because these policies are closely allied to other lines of personal insurance; in fact, the package includes several of those lines. Class underwriting is practiced, therefore, and unacceptable lists are of aid in carrying them out.

The starting point in many preferred risk companies is that any risk which is on the unacceptable list of one of the component coverages, is unacceptable for the package. This is a fairly common practice. Thus, the fire list would apply and would include older homes, small homes, inferior construction, low-valued dwellings, inferior neighborhood, unusual exposures, isolated risks, hazardous occupancies and vacant property. Minimum insurance to value rules would appear on the unacceptable list too. An example might be any risk which would not carry at least 80% to the replacement cost of the dwelling.

Package underwriters would probably include these unacceptable risks because of crime problems: target risks, hazardous occupations, undesirable home and neighborhood, and risks which are seeking insurance. Even the relatively few unacceptable rules of the personal liability line might be used, such as wealthy persons, unfenced premises with a swimming pool or other dangerous attractions to children, and families with vicious dogs or unruly children.

Most package underwriters, even those not writing at preferred rates, attempt to avoid those applicants who are problems on any line. When lack of responsibility or lack of interest in maintaining property is discovered, the risk is unacceptable for the broad coverages of the package policy. An applicant with a record of previous losses, particularly suspicious losses, will usually be unacceptable until the underwriter can ascertain the facts. Similarly, when another company has cancelled or nonrenewed a risk, most underwriters consider it unacceptable until the reasons for the action are learned.

A fairly-recent problem to underwriters of homeowners policies is the large number of unrelated persons living together.[4] This group has been identified by many

4. "The number of unmarried couples living together in America has jumped sharply to top the 2 million mark for the first time," with the estimated number about 2.22 million unmarried-couple households, according to the Census Bureau. "Cohabitation by Unmarrieds Up Sharply, Bureau Reports," Whittier *Daily News,* December 17, 1986, p. A8.

different terms. "Mingles" was used to identify those persons of opposite sexes who are single but live together as though they are married. Some institutions have used "significant other" to identify substitutes for "spouse." The Census Bureau, seeking a neutral term, tried "co-habitee," and then settled on POSSLQ (pronounced "poss'l-cue") to identify Persons of the Opposite Sex Sharing Living Quarters. The situation, if not the term, is of concern to underwriters because of the uncertainty of ownership of many items of personal property, as well as the instability which might result. These arrangements are not necessarily unacceptable, but are on the caution lists of many insurers.

Another problem facing underwriters of homeowners policies is the tremendous increase in working mothers. By the mid-1980's, nearly two-thirds of American mothers with children at home were in the work force.[5] Only 5.7% of the 83.5 million households in the United States consist of a working father, a homemaker mother, and two or more children.[6] The difficulty presented to underwriters is that most homes are now unattended during most of the day, and thus are more susceptible to burglaries. Some insurers attempted to place these residences on the unacceptable list, or at least on a caution list, but soon recognized that this action was too restrictive. Today, this is seen to be a problem, but it is not handled by unacceptable lists.

The broad range of perils under the homeowners policy causes some use of unacceptable rules by perils. The use of the unacceptable lists of the separate lines tends in this direction. Underwriters sometimes are inclined to decline an application because there seems to be an increased hazard in one of the component lines. However, it is at this precise point that package underwriting differs from line underwriting. Perhaps a fire underwriter is justified in declining an applicant who has an above-average chance of fire loss. The same is true for a crime underwriter and a crime hazard. A package underwriter, however, must attempt to consider the entire policy, with its many coverages and perils. The chance of a small, infrequent fire loss or crime loss may not be automatic grounds of declination. A package underwriter must consider that, with a substantial increase in premium, more losses can be paid and a profit can still be realized. Perhaps the underwriter cannot tolerate a loss frequency which is the sum of each of the coverage parts because there is a package discount, but the underwriter should think in that direction; that is, the underwriter should expect more losses under the package policy than under a fire policy, a crime policy or a liability policy.

From this underwriting standpoint, it is not realistic to use all of the unacceptable lists of the component lines. Some companies do try to shorten the package unacceptable lists to account for this factor. Most underwriters, however, prefer to retain fairly long unacceptable lists, usually including virtually all of those applicants that may have problems. Of course the underwriter can make exceptions to the lists and

---

5. "The News Brief — The Nation," *Los Angeles Times* (May 11, 1986), Part I, p. 2.
6. "New Housing Needed," *Whittier Daily News* (June 23, 1985), p. 6.

accept any applicant, so it is not critical that unacceptable lists are long.

Homeowners policies developed poor experience in the early 1980's, with the loss ratio rising to 71% in 1985.[7] Some of the factors causing this deterioration were inflation, the increase in crimes, and a greater awareness of the broad coverages under these policies on the part of policyholders. At the same time, there was strong suspicion that part of the problem was in underwriting. Too many allowances were made for unusual frequencies of loss, on the theory that more losses were expected. Competition prevented needed rate increases and the adoption of overdue deductibles and limitations, and many risks were accepted which did not really qualify for a package, certainly not at preferred rates.

Crime losses have become a major problem for homeowners insurers. One study showed that home burglaries and other crimes against residences accounted for nearly one-third of insurance costs for homes and apartments. Furthermore, these crime losses increased more rapidly from 1979 to 1981 than they did for any other insurance line.[8]

Experience was good in the early years of homeowners policies, and again in the late 1970's. This line followed most other lines into unprofitability in the 1980's, and will not return to underwriting gains until premiums are increased and underwriting again focuses on making a profit on the entire package.

SECURING INFORMATION

All of the sources available to the underwriters of the component lines are available to package underwriters. Some of this information is for rating, some for determining eligibility and some for ascertaining acceptability.

The application is the basic source of information as with other lines.

Application

A personal lines package policy application is completed by the producer, along the same pattern as for other lines. Most of the information requested on applications for the component lines appears on the package application. This does not necessarily mean that the package application is three or four times as long as other applications because there is a considerable amount of the information which is repeated on each personal lines application. However, a typical package application is longer than the application for any single line which is included in the package.

Applications for package policies contain questions on both physical and psychological factors, with a closer balance on these groups than most applications. A package policy is basically a fire policy, so considerable physical information is needed. At the same time, a sizeable share of the premium and exposure is on crime

---

7. "Property Insurance Marketing — 1985," *Best's Review, Property/Liability Insurance Edition*, Vol. 87, No. 7 (November, 1986), p. 22.

8. "Crime Losses in Property-Casualty Insurance," *All-Industry Research Advisory Council*, July, 1984.

and liability coverages, thus requiring that attention be paid to more subjective factors.

Most package applications require the signature of the applicant. Although the application is not made a part of the policy, the basic coverage information is repeated on the front of the policy. Therefore, uniformity in the coverage section is common, but there is no pattern to the other questions among insurers. The questions will generally fall within these three categories.

1. Personal
2. Description of property
3. Insurance information

A typical application will request the following information in each category.

1. *Personal*

A. Applicant's full name, which should correspond to the name or names on the title to the property.
B. The interest or type of ownership of the applicant in the property.
C. Applicant's mailing address.
D. Property location.
E. Applicant's marital status.
F. Age and occupation of applicant and spouse. If travel is involved in conjunction with the occupation, details about frequency and length of trips and means of transportation.
G. Stability factors, such as length of time at this address and with present employer, and number of jobs in a recent period.
H. Previous losses of the types which would be covered by the policy, over the past three or five years.

2. *Description of Property*

A. Information about the building: construction, type of roof and number of units or apartments.
B. Information about fire protection: the rating of the fire district, and the distance to the nearest fire hydrant and the nearest responding fire department.
C. Size and age of the dwelling: age of the roof, number of stories and description of all other structures on the premises.
D. Type of heating system and fuel.
E. For risks outside of a city or town, information about police protection, exposures to forest or brush, whether there is a telephone and a year-round accessible road, and the distance to other dwellings.
F. Estimated total value of all personal property, and descriptions including values of all target items (jewelry, watches, sterling silver, and furs) over a stated amount, such as $500 per item.
G. Security information, such as protective measures (burglar alarms and safes), type of neighborhood and whether maids or other servants have access to the premises.
H. If articles are to be scheduled, pertinent information concerning use, condition, age and other factors. This information may be requested on a supplemental application because of the details required on a variety of coverages.
I. Unusual hazards from a liability standpoint, such as swimming pools, dangerous animals, water skiing by any member of the family, and child care or baby sitting duties of any member of the family.

3. *Insurance Information*

A. Type of policy requested.
B. Amount of insurance desired on each coverage, and any deductibles requested.
C. The proposed effective date.
D. Name and address of any mortgagee or loss payee.

E. Description of any other insurance on the property.
F. Any business pursuits on the premises, and number of boarders or roomers.
G. Appraisals by reliable dealers on all articles which are to be scheduled.
H. Information about the previous insurer: name of the company, type of policy and amount of insurance and policy number.
I. Complete explanations if any policies which would apply to the coverages for which application is made have ever been cancelled, declined or nonrenewed.
J. Information about any previous losses in the past three or five years of the types which would be covered under the policy.

Inspection Reports

Underwriters of personal lines package policies use inspection reports more freely than most other underwriters. There are so many coverages in the policy which offer exposures to loss that careful investigation is needed.

Inspection reports are ordered from the same companies used for other personal lines. There are several types of reports available, depending upon the area of concern. If the only apparent problem is the physical condition of the premises, an exterior report of the "drive-by" type may suffice. If more physical information is desired, such as to verify the existence of certain articles or the presence of liability hazards, a more complete physical report may be ordered. Both types of physical reports are similar to those used for personal fire insurance, and may be supplied by company employees in some cases.

Most inspections on package policies are requested on special reports covering the varied exposures found under the policies. Inspection companies have prepared forms which may be tailored by type of policy to give the pertinent information. These reports will include interviews with applicants and neighbors, covering both physical and moral factors. Comments will be made concerning fire and allied perils to the dwelling and contents, crime exposures, and possible liability problems. A report of this magnitude is requested on every application when there is suspicion of a moral hazard or when values are a cause for concern. Many underwriters, however, tend to use these comprehensive reports on every inspection of a package applicant; if there are physical problems, these could lead to other problems which might cause loss under these broad policies. (The additional cost is justified in many cases.)

Photographs

Since a considerable portion of the exposure is of a physical nature under a personal lines package policy, a photograph of the exterior of the building can be quite helpful. These photographs can reveal many problems which are not disclosed in written reports.

Companies using photographs on personal lines applicants will request them on packages, also, since the same advantages are present. In both cases, photographs may be ordered in conjunction with an inspection report, or insurers may require that they be furnished by the producer.

Experience of Other Carriers

Personal package policy underwriters tend to exchange information more freely than most underwriters. There are many opportunities for losses, so an indication of experience by other insurers can be very helpful. Homeowners policies are fairly uniform, making a meaningful exchange of information rather simple. Many package underwriters, therefore, try to secure loss information from previous insurers that will share its experience.

CLASSIFICATION AND RATING

Most personal lines package policies are written under the rules and rates promulgated by fire or multiple-line rating bureaus. A few companies prepare independent rate structures for packages, but most insurers follow the bureau pattern.

A principal reason for this uniformity is the fact that the homeowners policy follows, very closely, the structure established for personal fire. Many of the coverages are similar to those offered in fire lines, and the rates are based on the same factors. It is natural, therefore, that companies follow, in the package policies, the concept of bureau rates which are so firmly established for fire policies.

The fact that more companies use independent rating structures on packages than fire insurance demonstrates that when larger risks are involved, more opportunity exists for independent action. Premiums are considerably higher on packages, reflecting greater loss frequency because of the broad coverages included. This situation permits more companies to develop credible experience upon which to base their own rates. Some large companies, and some smaller ones, use independent rates for packages, although the vast majority use the bureau program.

Early personal lines packages were rated by simply computing the aggregate premium for the coverages included. The total of these premiums, with about a 15% package discount, gave the total package premium, when rounded to the nearest even dollar. As more experience developed, the package policies were rated more on their own losses. One difficulty was caused by the frequent changes which were made in the coverages. Some of these changes broadened the protection in an attempt to meet the needs of policyholders, as well as to meet competition. Other changes reduced coverage because it developed that the premiums were inadequate to cover all of the perils, and there was no desire to increase the premium too much. In any event, both types of changes occurred often enough to make it difficult to rate on experience because the data was not homogeneous.

Problems sometimes arise under the current practice of rating homeowners and under the separate lines on the actual experience of each. In theory, the better risks are written on the homeowners program, so the package rates should be lower than the component coverages. This theory, however, does not always operate perfectly.

On the one hand, the homeowners experience can be so good that the package rates are unrealistically low in relation to the separate lines. Actual cases have arisen when the package costs very little more than the costs for a broad form fire policy on the dwelling and personal property; the crime and the CPL coverages are almost free. This situation puts heavy burdens on underwriters because almost everyone wants the package, even those who are not normally considered to be eligible. Careful selection must be practiced, therefore, to avoid accepting unacceptable risks.

However, the broad coverages of the package can sometimes raise loses of this class. Perhaps those people who purchase package policies pursue borderline claims more vigorously than those with fire policies. Perhaps the fault lies in the ratemaking process. Whatever the cause, situations have arisen when a package policy costs more than the separate coverages. Even more of a problem arises in those cases when a complete homeowners policy costs more than a broad form fire policy on the dwelling plus a tenants package policy. The rules ordinarily prohibit the writing of a tenants form on the owner of the dwelling, but loopholes sometimes are found. This situation also causes trouble for the underwriter, who is expected to write profitably on the basis of the rates established for each policy. In fact this became a problem during the 1970s when the tenants policy was unprofitable in many areas, but the rates had not been adjusted accordingly.

The actuaries and bureaus that promulgate rates must attempt to maintain a balance between the package and the component lines. Each coverage must generally stand on its own experience, but a proper relationship must be maintained. Otherwise, the underwriters are placed under severe strains in their attempts to offer insurance to every acceptable risk and, at the same time, make a profit.

Homeowners premiums are analyzed every year and are generally adjusted every two or three years. The loss experience under the entire policy is considered, since the policy is indivisible. The same long-term consideration is given to catastrophes as under fire insurance.

Rating Factors

Since most of the exposure under the homeowners policy concerns property, many of the same rating factors are used as on personal lines fire, plus one from crime insurance. The following are the most common.

Construction of Dwelling — The same definitions as in fire insurance apply to packages. However, in most states these factors are grouped into only two classes: *brick* and *frame.* All others are placed within one of these two classes.

Degree of Fire Protection — The same national board classifications are used for personal packages and personal fire. However, more classifications are grouped for rating purposes under package policies, resulting in a more simplified rate structure.

Geographic Area — The different exposures to crime losses are taken into account in establishing rating territories. In any one state, one or more territories may include the major urban centers, another one or more might include the smaller cities, and a final territory may apply to the small towns and rural areas. Some of the larger cities may be divided into two or more territories. It is essential to know the location of the risk in order to determine the geographical area.

Number of Dwelling Units — The eligibility rules of the package policy limit the number of units in the building, for a complete package. Only one through four and two unit dwellings are eligible but three and four unit buildings carry a different rate. All states permit tenants policies in apartments, and the number of dwelling units is necessary in order to determine the rate.

Rate tables for the homeowners policy are relatively simple to use. For a complete package (one which includes coverage on the dwelling building), a letter symbol is determined from the construction, roof, and fire protection class. For each letter symbol, the rate tables for each territory contain the annual premium for each $1,000 of coverage on the dwelling. (These premiums are given in even dollar amounts.) For amounts of coverage above those in the tables, a stated amount per $1,000 is added. The premiums are based on coverage on the dwelling building and start with the minimum amount, usually $8,000. There is no maximum.

Tenant policies are rated by the amount of coverage on personal property. Renters in dwelling buildings, usually up through four units, are rated by the same factors as are used for rating complete package policies. Those in apartments and commercial buildings are rated by first determining the applicable fire and extended coverage rates, then grouping these rates into about 10 rating groups and establishing premium tables by those groups, with the actual premium shown for each $1,000 of coverage on personal property. Different premium tables may be used for various deductibles, or premium credits or debits may be shown to modify the deductibles which are automatically applied.

Various options are available: For extra premiums, increased amounts can be purchased on personal property, private structures, additional living expense and on money and securities. Higher limits of liability and premises medical coverage may be obtained for more premium; the handling of limits under division II — liability of the policy is similar to that used under a comprehensive personal liability policy. Thus, additional premium is charged for liability protection on other residences, on vacant land and on watercraft.

Other coverages and perils may be added, each at appropriate premiums. Coverage for personal property susceptible to theft from unattended vehicles may be purchased, removing the exclusion in the policy. Scheduled items may be added, using the rates and rules of the inland marine personal articles floater. The earthquake peril may be added to buildings and contents by endorsement, at the fire rates and rules.

Most personal line packages are issued on a one-year term basis. When a three-year term is used, only the policy contract is fixed for three years; premiums are handled as on an annual policy.

Most insurers are members of, or subscribers to, the rating bureaus and use the rules and rates without change, although some deviate, usually by a fixed percentage. A few companies operate independently for package policies, but most of them follow the bureau pattern quite closely. The same considerations are present as on personal fire, although many companies that deviate, do so only on fire or on packages, and use different percentages for each line. A long and complicated list results from compiling the fire and package deviations for just a single state because of the many variations used.

It is rare for a company to write package policies at rates above those charged by the bureau. Package rates contain a discount based, at least in part, on the preferred quality of the risks. Applicants who are not in the preferred or standard categories, seldom are offered packages. Separate policies are more commonly issued to them. (Seldom does a company use a negative deviation on homeowners policies, although this practice is sometimes followed.)

POLICY FORMS

As previously stated, personal lines package policies are prepared by bureaus and used without change by most companies. The few insurers that write independent policies use the same general format in almost every case.

State laws formerly prescribed that every fire insurance policy be issued on the standard fire policy adopted in that state. The homeowners policy is basically a fire contract, and most states required the standard fire policy to be included. However, this approach has been changed in all states in order to accomodate the readable policies. Today, all states include the same material as the standard fire policy in homeowners policies, but written in a less technical form.

Personal packages follow the same general format as fire policies: a standardized policy back containing provisions common to all policies, and forms attached specifying details of the specific coverages purchased.

The policy back contains the provisions of the standard fire policy and other conditions common to the homeowners policy, including the complete section II — liability of the policy, since the comprehensive personal liability section is the same for all policies. The front portion of the policy also contains typed information such as the policyholder's name and address, the policy dates and the amounts of insurance and identification of the attached forms.

The policy forms are attached without any further need for typing. These are standard provisions, one for each of the five types of forms. The forms contain additional perils beyond those covered by the standard fire policy and specify the extensions, limitations, and exclusions applicable. Each form is complete in itself, along with the policy back, for the coverages they provide.

Endorsements (most are specified by the bureau) may also be attached to cover special circumstances. They provide additional coverages, such as theft from unattended automobiles or the earthquake peril. The personal articles floater is attached with its specification of coverage on each scheduled item or class. Other special permits or provisions may also be added.

Underwriters may write their own endorsements, too. This is relatively uncommon under homeowners forms, but occasionally an underwriter will want to exclude an article of property, an exposure such as theft while the insured is travelling on business, or exclude a vicious dog exposure against any possible liability that could arise.

Deductibles — Uses and Effects

Deductibles are specified in the bureau rating rules. They have undergone many changes since the first policies of this line were introduced. At first they were optional and no larger than $25 or $50. By the 1980s, $100 was the usual minimum, with options available up to $1,000.

A unique feature of the homeowners policy was the disappearing deductible. Most commonly used with an amount of $50, it provided that the insurer will pay nothing if the loss is $50 or less. For losses above $50, the company pays 111% of the amount above $50 up to $500. The policyholder's participation decreases as the loss increases. Losses of $500 or more are paid in full, with no deductible. The same principle was adopted later for a $100 disappearing deductible, with a multiple of 125% being used so that the deductible disappears at $500.

Disappearing deductibles became less desirable from the insurer's standpoint as inflation increased the size of the average claim. Furthermore, hurricanes or tornadoes have caused average losses well in excess of $500, so the deductible clause has been of little help in reducing the exposure of the carriers. As the facts became evident, there was a movement away from the disappearing deductibles and toward the adoption of flat deductibles, whereby the policyholder pays the same amount for every loss in excess of the deductibles, regardless of size. By the start of the 1980s, only a few states still offered the disappearing deductibles.

Current deductibles apply to all perils and all property under the basic parts of division I. They do not apply to any part of division II, which is the comprehensive personal liability portion of the policy nor to scheduled items under the personal article floater, in most cases.

Deductibles under personal package policies accomplish all the major objectives attributable to deductibles. They are selected by applicants who are anxious to reduce their premiums: as inflation increases the amounts of the losses, and such perils as crime increases the frequency, the premiums have increased to a noticeable degree. At the same time, the applicant who expects to have losses, or who intends to "get his premium back," will select low deductibles. Some producers encourage low deductibles in order to keep premiums higher (commissions are a percentage of the premium in most cases) or in order to render more frequent service in paying for losses. Other producers urge higher deductibles in order to reduce premiums and thus help their competitive position. Deductibles also help to avoid possible underwriting difficulties which may follow a loss frequency.

Underwriters prefer higher deductibles in most cases, since this maintains more of the true meaning of insurance: to pay for the loss which would distress the policyholder, not for every little occurrence. On good risks, underwriters realize that it is expensive for the company to cover small losses because the adjustment costs are out of proportion. Still, if an applicant is willing to pay the price, and if the cost is high enough to cover the expenses, the underwriter usually is willing to offer low deductibles.

Policies which present poor loss experience are a different matter from the standpoint of the underwriter who may feel that the frequency of small losses is too expensive for the company. At that point, a deductible, or a higher deductible, as an alternative to cancelling the policy may be insisted upon. Many small losses can be cured by proper deductibles, turning a problem insured into a profitable one. Examples of losses which may be cured in this fashion are theft losses, windstorm damage and claims for water damage from plumbing fixtures. On the other hand, some losses may easily become large losses the next time, such as grease fires in a kitchen, electrical short circuits or fires from smoking in bed. In these latter cases, the imposition of large deductibles will only reduce the premium; it will not help very much in case of total loss. Cancellation of the policy rather than imposition of underwriting deductibles is a better course of action under some circumstances.

Concurrency of Coverage

Concurrency of coverage is seldom a problem in personal package policies. In almost every case, the entire coverage is written in one company, so there is no need to be concerned about the policy forms used by various companies. However, some dwellings have such high values that underwriters will accept only a portion of the risk. In such cases, two package policies must be written, one in each of two companies. It is essential, in these cases, that these policies read exactly alike in order to be sure that the policyholder is not penalized after a loss. Concurrency of coverage is required in these cases, and this is another reason that most companies use the bureau forms. The situation is very similar to that which exists under fire policies, although less common in packages. Incidentally, it is generally considered to be poor practice to divide liability coverages between two companies, so the common practice is for one insured to exclude all of division II — liability from its policy, leaving the entire coverage for the CPL policy in one company.

The CPL coverage of the homeowners policy is identical with that issued by companies writing personal liability insurance. The same bureau forms are used by most companies. A few independent companies use their own CPL coverages, both in liability policies and packages, but these are quite similar to the bureau coverages in most cases.

Mortgagees play the same important role in packages as in fire. They are named on a large share of the personal package policies and have an influence on the term and conditions of the policies. At first slow to accept packages, all mortgagees now consider them as at least equal to a fire policy. Since most package policies are quite similar, most mortgagees accept all of them.

Coverages endorsed onto packages, such as the personal articles floater, are written on the forms used by the companies. Most of them are written on bureau forms, but some independent forms are used. Also some minor modifications are used to fit the coverages into the structure of the package.

RETENTION AND REINSURANCE

When a personal lines package policy application is accepted, the underwriter must be concerned with the amount of exposure retained. The underwriter must consider both the possibility of a large single loss and a multiple-risk catastrophe. These are the same problems a fire underwriter faces, because most of the package exposure is identical to that under fire policies.

Single risk exposures need more careful handling under a package policy than under a fire policy because of the many coverages that are automatically included in the package. It is not enough to consider the amount of insurance on the dwelling, although that figure is all that is needed for rating. The underwriter must also consider the other coverages which can be involved in the same loss. Since retention is based on the maximum potential loss at one location, the entire package exposure must be considered.

As an example, assume that a company has established $75,000 as the maximum exposure which it wishes to have at one location. The underwriter accepts a homeowners policy with $50,000 on the dwelling. It is conceivable that a total loss could occur under all coverages in one occurrence. These are the amounts of insurance under the Basic or Special Form — the most popular ones:

$ 50,000 on the dwelling building
5,000 on private structures (10%)
25,000 on unscheduled personal property (50%)
10,000 on additional living expense (20%)
$ 90,000 total

The underwriter, in this case, has accepted $15,000 more than his limit, even without any scheduled items or other added coverages. It is now necessary to make some arrangements to reduce the retention to $75,000. One possible arrangement is to accept only a portion of the risk, perhaps 50% and let the producer find another company to write the balance. Of course, the underwriter could accept $40,000 on the dwelling for a total exposure of $72,000, but this probably leaves too small an amount for any other company to take; a 50-50 split would be more common.

Another possibility for the underwriter is to accept the entire amount and reinsure the amount over $75,000. It is common to use the same reinsurance treaties and facilities for package policies as for the fire insurance written by the company. The underwriter may also have a surplus treaty or a facultative arrangement available, either one on a pro rata basis. If the fire reinsurance is on an excess basis, the package is probably covered under the same treaty. Whatever the arrangement, the package underwriter will usually have a reinsurance facility available to handle the large property exposures, unless the company has adopted the practice of accepting only portions of risks and letting producers place balances in other companies.

The liability section of the package policy presents few reinsurance problems. Policies may have higher limits than a company wishes to retain, but treaties almost always exist to handle the additional exposure. The danger of two or more policyholders being involved in a single loss is remote, but the excess reinsurance treaty usually covers this, too. This reinsurance, which may be in several layers, may be the same one used for property coverages of the package. It could also be the same one that is used for all liability insurance written by the company, or it could be a special treaty that is written for this particular exposure. In any event, the underwriter seldom needs to be concerned about reinsurance on the liability coverages of the policy.

Catastrophes may involve many package risks, the same as they can involve fire risks. Many of the coverages are similar, so large losses can occur under either type of policy form from such exposures as windstorm, hail, hurricane, catastrophic fires, or other catastrophes. Since many companies write both fire and package policies, the aggregate exposure must be considered. When a company attempts to limit its exposures to catastrophes, such as by setting a maximum limit in one city or area, it must include the total package exposure along with the fire insurance. Excess reinsurance is a necessary part of property underwriting, usually with several layers of reinsurance, and the same treaties ordinarily cover fire and package exposures. Although these are arranged by the home office staff, package underwriters should know the retentions and potential recoveries in order to evaluate business properly.

QUESTIONS FOR DISCUSSION

1. Explain briefly the differences between personal lines packages in these coverages:
   (a) property
   (b) liability
2. List some of the optional coverages which are available under a homeowners policy.
3. Would a risk which is not acceptable for one of the component coverages be acceptable for a package policy? Explain.
4. Are photographs used as frequently on package policies as on personal lines policies? Explain.
5. Describe the 2 basic methods of rating personal lines packages.
6. What are the purposes of deductibles on personal lines packages?

36

Commercial Lines Package Policies

Package policies are playing an increasingly important role in commercial lines. (Although true package policies were first written in personal lines, they followed soon after in commercial lines.) The first commercial packages were introduced in the late 1950s. In 1986, total premiums were more than $16 billion.[1]

For many years, the most common name for a commercial package policy was "Special Multi-Peril Policy" (SMP). This was the name used by ISO. However, the simplified-language commercial program of ISO dropped this special name. The modular concept provides that various forms can be combined without the use of particular names for each program. Some companies have used their own names for their programs, most of which tend to follow the SMP in overall concepts. The name "Commercial Package Policy" is now used to designate policies written in the multiple-line format, even if no special name appears on the policies themselves.

Commercial package rates frequently are very competitive. This practice, which could result in underwriting losses, has had an adverse effect on premiums. These policies were profitable in 1979, but results worsened during the next seven years. In 1985, the loss ratio improved for most companies, but was still a high 73.3%. About 72% of the 1985 premiums were written by the national agency companies; direct writers accounted for 12%, and the remaining 16% was written by regional and specialty companies.[2]

Commercial packages have been divisible policies almost entirely from their inception. There is so little homogeneity between the various types of risks, and so

---

1. "Review & Preview: Up from the Ashes," *Best's Review, Property/Casualty Insurance Edition,* Vol. 87, No. 9 (January, 1987) p. 87.

2. "Property Insurance Marketing — 1985," *Best's Review, Property/Casualty Insurance Edition,* Vol. 87, No. 7 (November, 1986), p. 24.

many rate differences within each type, that indivisible rating is not practical. However, indivisible policies have been used for a few defined classes such as gasoline service stations, retail stores, and apartments. These special policies are similar to homeowners policies in approach, with fixed relationships among the coverages and simplified rating. Otherwise, commercial packages are rated by determining the separate premiums for the component parts, applying a package discount to most of them, and adding together the net premiums.

A commercial package policy is designed to provide almost all of the insurance coverages needed by most businesspersons. Every policy must contain the basic coverages of fire and extended coverage on buildings (if owned) and contents (if the business is operated by the insured), and bodily injury and property damage liability for all general liability hazards covered by the policy. Optional coverages are available in fire, crime, glass, and liability lines.

Workers' compensation insurance is not included in commercial packages. Some commercial packages do not include automobile insurance, and the only bond type of coverage available is fidelity insurance under some crime coverages. However, many package policies now written do include automobile and various surety coverages. With these exceptions as noted, virtually every insurance coverage sold to commercial enterprises may be included in the package.

The first commercial packages were designed for those businesses that principally provided services — those *not* manufacturing, processing or merchandising. The first bureau program applied to motels, and then other service industries followed. As the concept spread, new programs were offered for different classes of risks. Eventually, all commercial policyholders became eligible for packages.

Modular policies have become more popular, using common policy conditions. The same forms can be used for policies with only one line (such as fire insurance) and complete package policies. Under this concept, the policies for various policyholders may look alike in general appearance, but a package rate modification (reduction) is offered only to those policies which contain *both* property and liability coverages.

Since the commercial package policy is divisible, there is no controlling section as is used on personal packages. Each section of a commercial package must stand on its own. The minimum rules of the separate coverages also apply under the package.

DESCRIPTION OF COVERAGES

Commercial package policies are quite uniform. Even the independent forms are different only in details, with the major features generally being the same. There are a few variations in forms used in some states, but again these are minor differences only.

Commercial package policies ordinarily contain four sections.

Section I — Property
Section II — Liability

Section III — Crime
Section IV — Boiler and Machinery

Sections I and II are mandatory for a rate reduced package, while Sections III and IV are optional. Section IV is the same as under a separate boiler and machinery policy with one exception: when a manufacturing risk is written, all fixed and unfired pressure vessels and piping must be insured if the coverage is written.

Basic Property Coverage

The basic coverages which are mandatory under the commercial package are these.

1. Building, if owned by the insured.
2. Business personal property, unless the building owner does not operate a business on the premises.
3. Improvements and betterments.
4. Newly acquired property, subject to limitations.
5. Trees, shrubs and plants, with limitations per item and per occurrence.
6. Replacement cost on the building, under specified conditions.

Basic Form Perils Covered

1. Fire and lightning.
2. Extended coverage (windstorm, hail, explosion, riot, riot attending a strike, civil commotion, aircraft, vehicles and smoke).
3. Vandalism and malicious mischief
4. Sprinkler Leakage
5. Sinkhole Collapse
6. Volcanic Action

Broad Form Perils

This is a named-peril policy covering all of the Basic Form perils plus the following:

1. Falling objects. Damage to the interior of the building, or property in the building, is covered only if the building first sustains damage to the exterior.
2. Weight of ice, snow or sleet. Excluded are lawns, trees, shrubs and plants.
3. Collapse. This refers to collapse of a building or a part thereof, but not settling, cracking, bulging or expansion.
4. Accidental discharge, leakage, or overflow of water from within a plumbing or heating system.
5. Breakage of glass which constitutes a part of the building.

Special Form Perils

Buildings and contents may be covered under an "all-risks" form. In general, this form covers all of the perils previously listed, plus unnamed perils. Actually, the exclusions are written carefully enough so that there are few perils which would be covered under this form and not under a broad form.

Optional Property and Perils

Programs vary by company, but many permit the addition of these coverages.

1. Replacement cost coverage on buildings and personal property.

2. Accounts receivable coverages.
3. Neon and outdoor sign coverage.
4. Various crime forms, such as blanket crime coverage, comprehensive crime coverage, mercantile robbery and safe burglary coverage, mercantile open stock burglary and theft coverage, storekeepers burglary and robbery coverage, broad form storekeepers coverage, and church theft coverage. Broad form personal theft may be purchased where applicable, such as by the owner or manager of a motel or apartment if that person resides on the premises.
5. Business income coverage.
6. Extra expense coverage.
7. Builder's risk coverage.
8. Glass coverage.

Basic Liability Coverage

Bodily injury and property damage liability coverage must be included for all hazards covered by the policy, except for the optional coverages. The minimum is a $100,000 single limit, or $100,000 aggregate where applicable.

Optional Liability Coverages

1. Premises medical payments.
2. Personal injury liability.
3. Advertising liability.
4. Employees' non-ownership liability for automobiles.

These are the basic and optional coverages generally available on commercial package policies. In addition, some independent policies include, at the applicant's option, full coverage for personal and commercial automobiles owned by the business.

Programs Available

In the early years of Commercial Package Policies, only certain classes of risks were eligible. Later, special programs were written for homogeneous risks, such as motels, apartments, offices, and institutions. These programs generally have been replaced by programs which fit all risks, subject to tailoring by underwriters.

The Business Owners Policy (BOP) remains as a separate, indivisible policy. Although it might later be abolished in favor of using modular forms for all commercial policies, it is a popular contract for writing small commercial risks because of its simplified rating and automatic coverage features. No coinsurance clause is used, and owned autos may not be added to this policy. The BOP is available in the simplified-language format from ISO.

Separate policy forms are used to insure Condominium associations and commercial condominium unit owners. Modifications are made to accommodate the specific nature of this type of ownership, such as coverage for property used to maintain or service the building for associations, and elimination of building coverage for unit owners.

Acceptable Risks

Commercial lines package policies are subject to specific rules on eligibility.

General rules applicable to all risks are specified in the manuals.

Insurers have their own rules about the types of risks they desire to write, of course. When the packages were first introduced, only relatively few risks were considered acceptable. The package discounts were justified partly on the basis of careful selection of risks, with only the superior risks in each class being acceptable. The programs were even limited to those few classes where it was felt rates were excessive for the class, and particularly for the better risks in those classes. The theory was that discounts could be given only to the superior risks in those few classes. Processing and manufacturing risks were certainly not considered to be preferred risks for packages, then.

The acceptance of commercial packages by producers and clients soon caused pressure on insurers to make more classes and more risks eligible. Today, virtually all classes are eligible under most programs.

Individual insurers have their own thoughts about acceptability for commercial package policies. Those that deviate on separate lines and attempt to select risks carefully are equally selective on packages; sometimes they are more selective because of the the package discounts. Most companies write the bureau programs at bureau rates, as they do on other commercial lines. These companies also tend to write most applicants who comply with the acceptability rules, but with somewhat more careful selection because of the discounts. Few insurers use surcharged rates and write less desirable risks. At the present stage of the development of packages, the general thinking is that if a risk is below standard, there is no reason to offer a package with its discounts; separate policies are written in most of these cases.

There is little difference between the programs on risks which companies consider acceptable. Generally, no program is more desirable than others. Some insurers prefer, as on separate lines, to write only smaller risks, with perhaps few or no manufacturing enterprises being considered acceptable. In some areas, certain programs are considered more or less desirable at any one time; examples are apartment houses and small retail stores. These differences tend to follow the experience of such risks under separate lines, and these change over the years. Thus, school and governmental property were preferred risks in the early 1960s because of their good experience, but they became undesirable in the late 1960s and early 1970s because of riots and civil unrest. When these factors became less of a problem, these classes returned to favor — only to develop new concerns with the advent of the "deep pocket" theories in the 1980's.

Unacceptable Risks

Commercial package policies are not subject to long unacceptable lists, other than those specified in the manual rules themselves. Underwriters, instead, consider every risk and evaluate each applicant on its own merits.

While it is easy to say that any risk unacceptable for any of the component coverages is unacceptable for the package, this is not true in many cases. The advantages of other lines sometimes outweigh the problems of one line. Hence, coverage package underwriters are more likely than most underwriters to consider each risk separately, and thus not to use unacceptable risks.

Some insurers do, of course, use unacceptable lists. Those that write at deviations are more likely to establish certain types of undesirable risks based upon their own experience. Typical lists would include the major features of the separate lines. From a fire standpoint, companies may consider as unacceptable, older buildings, isolated risks and vacant property. From a crime standpoint, unacceptable risks might be those located in hazardous areas, those with inadequate police protection, or those without adequate protective devices or controls. Liability problems could cause the list to include certain products, subsidiaries or contractual obligations.

The inclusion of theft coverages in packages has raised new concerns. Employee theft, particularly, needs careful underwriting, because theft by employees far exceeds the losses from burglary, robbery and shoplifting for merchants and manufacturers, according to reliable estimates. Applicants who do not practice proper controls may not be able to secure this coverage — or should not be able to do so, if proper underwriting is practiced.[3]

All insurers are unlikely to write applicants who have poor business reputation, inadequate maintenance of premises, poor housekeeping, personal instability, questionable legality of the business, inadequate record keeping, poor loss experience, insufficient insurance to value and unusual susceptibility to loss. Not all of these undesirable features may appear on unacceptable lists because some of them are difficult to define, but these are illustrative of the types of risks which would be unacceptable in most companies.

Another approach used by some insurers is to list those occupancies or types of risks which are unacceptable. Within each program, unacceptable risks might be listed. For example, in the mercantile program, such occupancies as camera shops, clothing stores, hobby shops, medical supply stores and photographic studios may be unacceptable. Sometimes certain risks are qualified — that is, they are considered as being unacceptable, unless burglar alarms (if crime coverage is written) or other protective devices are installed. These occupancies are based upon the experience and background of the underwriters.

In spite of long lists of potentially undesirable risks, the fact remains that most package underwriters are willing to consider almost any applicant who is acceptable by the rules. The problem factor or line may well be overshadowed by the many other coverages under the package policy. Substantial premiums can be developed under these policies, and these premiums can sometimes outweigh some of the problems which would be otherwise overwhelming on a single line of insurance. An underwriter cannot help but be impressed by the sizeable premiums. In commercial package policies, more than in most other lines, the old saying may often be true that "The perfume of the premium hides the odor of the risk."

Account handling is the key in commercial package policies. Many of them are

---

3. For an excellent discussion of this problem, see William H. Rodda, "Best's Underwriting Newsletter," Vol, 10, No. 17 (December, 1981).

rated and handled on an account basis. Underwriting should be on this same basis, too. Under this concept, unacceptable lists should be as short as possible. Underwriters should consider almost every applicant, weighing the total exposure against the total risk. It is immaterial that one line may be unprofitable; if the total policy is profitable, the account is acceptable and should be written. This is the secret of multiple-line underwriting, and it permits the writing of some applicants who are otherwise unacceptable for one particular line of insurance coverage.

There is, however, another important factor to consider. Many commercial package policies are quite complex, requiring vast amounts of knowledge in order to be underwritten properly. Few underwriters are that knowledgeable in fire, crime and liability lines, particularly when considering all the optional coverages available. Many insurers have solved this problem by using several underwriters on a commercial package policy, each an expert in one line. This permits better informed underwriting for one thing. Still, it is not multiple-line underwriting, and it almost prohibits account underwriting; no one specialist is willing to take a chance on the large losses which could occur on the line with a problem risk, even though the other lines may look good.

Insurers are still searching for the best solution to this dilemma. Many are using a multiple-line underwriter on the more simple package policies, giving help on problem coverages. They use several specialists to underwrite the separate lines on the more complex policies, with a supervisor or lead underwriter acting as coordinator and final decision-maker.

SECURING INFORMATION

Commercial package underwriters have access to all sources of information that are available on the component lines. They use these sources to determine eligibility and acceptability and to establish the correct rating. As with other policies, the application is the basic source of information.

Application

Most insurers require the producer to complete and submit an application, as in other lines. Most of the information requested on component lines is desired on the package application, although duplicate information is needed only once. A commercial package application is quite long because a great deal of information is needed for underwriting and rating.

Applications contain questions about the psychological and physical factors. Some questions deal with personal characteristics of the owner or manager. Most companies do not require a signature of the applicant and the application is not made a part of the policy, although the basic coverage and identifying information is reproduced on the front of the policy.

Some companies use separate applications for the different programs, while others combine them on one long application. There is no uniformity beyond the rating and coverage information, but the questions generally fit within these three categories.

1. Personal

2. Description of property, operations and exposures
3. Insurance information

The questions within each category generally follow the following pattern.

1. *Personal*
   - A. Full name of the applicant, including the business name, if any.
   - B. The structure of the firm, whether individual, partnership or corporation.
   - C. Business location and mailing address.
   - D. Stability factors, such as the age, marital status, citizenship, and home ownership of the applicant, and how long in this business.
2. *Description of Property, Operations and Exposures*
   - A. Location and description of all premises owned or used by the applicant.
   - B. The product handled by the applicant, along with a description of the processes used, material involved and type of equipment employed.
   - C. Fire information concerning construction, occupancy, protection and exposures.
   - D. Liability information about classifications of hazards as described in the manual, contractual obligations, details about subsidiaries and other liability exposures.
   - E. If crime coverages are written, information about protective devices, characteristics of the neighborhood, and other pertinent information. If safe burglary is covered, details about the safe are needed.
   - F. If glass coverage is desired, details of the glass, including size, description, location and class.
3. *Insurance Information*
   - A. The amount of insurance or limits of liability desired on each item of coverage, with specific details about each optional coverage desired.
   - B. Amount of deductibles desired, the coinsurance clause to be applicable, and any other required information as to limitations on coverage.
   - C. Proposed effective date.
   - D. Name and address of any mortgagee, loss payee, or additional interest.
   - E. Description of any other insurance on the property.
   - F. Details concerning losses of the types which would be covered under this policy, during the past three years.
   - G. Information about the previous carrier for each line covered under the policy; name of the company, type of coverage, amount of insurance or limits of liability, policy number and whether the policy was cancelled or nonrenewed by the company.

Inspection Reports

Commercial package underwriters use inspection reports to secure information in many cases, although other sources are more valuable for some risks. A good underwriter will use the source which is the most capable of furnishing the specific information required on each risk. Since package policies in commercial lines cover a multitude of exposures, differences will exist on the information needed.

When an inspection company is used, it usually is the same one used for other policies. Some of these companies are local while others are national in scope. An underwriter may find that some companies are better for one type of information, while others are more proficient in different directions.

Many large companies use their own personnel for inspections. When this is done, this task ordinarily is combined with that of furnishing loss prevention reports, as is described subsequently.

A major value of inspection reports is they furnish information on the character, reputation and moral aspects of the applicant. The inspectors for these companies are trained to develop this type of information from neighborhood informants, customers, suppliers and others. There are business applicants who appear to offer potential moral hazards, and inspection reports can furnish valuable information to underwriters concerning these matters.

Another important contribution of inspection reports is that they can verify the information of the application. An underwriter may wish to ascertain the values of property, the types of operations conducted or materials used or the liability exposures which exist. Some of this information can be gathered from other sources but much can be learned from inspection reports, and perhaps at less cost.

Inspection companies can also report on more technical engineering subjects or on financial data. On the other hand, the exposures under a commercial package policy often are so large that specialists are used in these fields, instead.

Loss Prevention

Loss prevention specialists are used by commercial package underwriters to furnish reports and to help prevent losses. These people who may be insurer employees or who may work for companies supplying this service, are the same ones used for separate insurance lines. Loss prevention specialists are particularly helpful in furnishing reports on the physical freatures large or complex risks since they are trained along these lines and can furnish more technical reports than those employees of inspection companies. These physical features may include a description of the building construction, the type of equipment used, the characteristics of the products handled and the types of operations performed. Such reports may include information on the adequacy of protective devices, recommendations for improvements in the risk, and comments concerning desirability of the risk.

These people also are helpful in preventing losses through their efforts in safety promotion. Their principal efforts in this field were limited initially to the operation of trucks and in workers' compensation hazards. Today, however, they are used in all lines, because present complex operations and broad coverages require loss control measures in order to minimize losses.

Financial Reporting Services

Commercial package underwriters use financial reporting services on many risks, perhaps most of them. Since fire lines form a major part of package policies, and since fire underwriters use these services on a majority of applicants, it is logical that most package risks are investigated fully from the financial standpoint. The broad coverages of many packages offer so many chances for fraudulent losses, or for losses resulting from financial instability, that the financial standing of risks becomes very important.

Companies furnishing financial reporting services publish books listing the financial rating and condition of most firms. In addition, special reports may be secured upon request, giving more details.

Bureau Reports

Fire rating bureaus publish information that is helpful to package underwriters as much as to commercial fire underwriters. The same problems exist under packages as under fire, so the same type of information is needed.

Fire rate material contains basic information about construction, exposures and protection. More detail is usually available through the reports on file with the bureau and furnished upon request. Maps are also available; an insurer which uses maps to record and identify its commercial fire risks also uses them for commercial packages. Maps are helpful in identifying specific characteristics of building construction and exposures, as well as in determining total exposures of the insurer within each block or area.

Experience of Other Insurers

Commercial package underwriters seldom exchange experience on packages themselves, but they may do so on the individual lines. If a previous insurer had written a commercial package policy, a new underwriter seldom would ask for experience. The coverages are too broad and the policies too complex and varied to permit an easy and relevant exchange of information.

But, many package policies are written to replace individual line policies. In these cases, the underwriters follow the same patterns as for the separate insurance lines. On crime coverages, a fairly free exchange is practiced, although the mechanics become too great a burden in some cases. Fire and other property lines are rather infrequently involved in exchanges because of the relatively low frequency of loss. Liability insurance experience is also seldom exchanged because of its complex and different coverages.

The net result is that a limited amount of information can be expected from prior insurers. Where this information is received, it is very helpful to underwriters, just as it is in separate insurance lines.

CLASSIFICATION AND RATING

Commercial package policies are generally rated by computing rates for each of the component parts and applying a package discount. Since these packages are divisible policies, each part is rated separately; no single package rate is used.

Section I (property) is rated according to the practice followed by the insurer on fire lines, and then a package discount is applied. First of all, the underwriter needs to identify the property to be insured, the perils to be covered, the time element coverages to be provided, and any miscellaneous coverages. The net annual rates for fire, extended coverage, and any other perils on buildings and personal property are determined, using the specific rates or rate tables of the fire underwriter, and applying coinsurance credits. Then the package discount is applied; it varies by program and is occasionally amended, but, generally, it amounts to about 15%.

Large risks may be acceptable for a dispersion credit plan which applies to section I. This is a special plan which affords substantial rate credits on the premium for fire, extended coverage, vandalism and malicious mischief, and sprinkler leakage. Credits are based on such factors as loss frequency, spread or dispersion of risks, expense savings, and the efficiency of management in preventing losses. Only risks with two or more locations are acceptable, with over $1,000 of annual premiums for the specified perils, and with the value of one location, other than the principal location, equaling at least $50,000 of 10% of the total value at all locations.

A separate application is used for this plan, and 90% or higher coinsurance is required on nonreporting forms.

Section II (liability) rates are given in the rate manuals. A table is provided for increased liability limits and increased medical payments coverages. These rates and increased limit tables may differ from those used in separate policies, depending upon the experience of the program. Any added coverages, such as personal injury or elevator collision, are rated by the company's regular rules, with no discount applicable.

Section III (crime) and IV (boiler and machinery) are rated by the company's rating practices for separate coverages.

Most programs are rated the same. The major discounts are given in the basic property coverages, which comprise the majority of premium in most acceptable risks. A worksheet is available to facilitate the rating; this is helpful because of the rather complex coverages included in the package.

Some differences exist among the programs used by different companies. However, the pattern is generally the same: determine the premium applicable for the separate lines, apply a package discount to most of them, and then add these net premiums together to get the package premium.

Interesting problems arise for those who promulgate the rates for commercial packages. Some programs are large enough to have substantial total premiums, but their experience cannot always establish their own rates. From a marketing standpoint, it is unrealistic to use package rates that are higher than the sum of the individual coverages. This situation could result from the analysis of actual experience, at least as long as a minority of the risks are written on packages. Even with an attempt to select the better risks for packages, the experience on them could be worse in any given period.

Because of these marketing problems, package credits generally are used. The intention is to adjust these credits, either up or down, depending upon the experience of the component lines. The difficulty with this approach is that it requires more detailed statistics and better methods of analyzing them, than have been available.

The solution has been to maintain a close relationship between the rating of the component lines and the package policies. When rates are adjusted in one, similar changes are made in the other. This avoids marketing complications, but it may result in rates for some packages which appear to be inadequate. Underwriters must compensate for such situations by selective underwriting, accepting only the best risks of each class if the rate level is too low.

POLICY FORMS

Standardized policy and forms are used by most insurers, although companies use independent forms. Even the independent policies generally follow the same type of format. This format is quite similar to that used for personal package policies.

Forms are used to tailor the coverages to fit the applicant. A general property form is used to cover the basic property coverages. A liability form is attached, although it is substantially the same for all programs. Then special forms for certain occupations, and for all optional coverages are attached. Some policies contain a multitude of forms for some risks, making the reading of the policy rather difficult. An alternative approach is used by some independent companies, with each occupancy program having its own policy and with the common options being a part of the policy. This approach makes the policy easier to read, but it increases costs substantially.

Warranties, coinsurance clauses, deductibles, and other policy conditions are added by endorsement to commercial package policies. These are the same as those used on the separate insurance lines. Few, if any, are prepared just for package policies, at the present stage of development. The complexities of commercial packages require many forms and endorsements. Many of these are printed for general use. Occasionally an underwriter will write endorsements to handle special circumstances. The modular concept, which has been developed more recently, provides that identical forms can be used on monoline and package policies.

After a slow start, deductibles have become quite common on commercial packages. In most states, mandatory deductibles are used on bureau forms, and many independent programs do the same. Sometimes deductibles apply only to specified perils, but the trend is toward deductibles that apply to all property perils; there are commonly known as "across-the-board" deductibles.

RETENTION AND REINSURANCE

All the retention problems of the separate lines also face the commercial package underwriter. There is no package reduction here; in fact, exposures may increase as more lines are added.

Line limits and block limits are the same for the package underwriter as the commercial fire underwriter. The exposures are the same, so an insurer has no justification for changing. The maximum retention at any one location, or within one block, must be the same. As a matter of fact, package underwriters and fire underwriters must cooperate closely to be sure that their combined totals do not exceed the limits established by the company.

The property exposure on a commercial package may exceed the line limit of the company, or may exceed the block limit. The underwriter who wishes to accept the package must be able to place part of the exposure elsewhere. The fire practice is followed on packages: two or more insurers share in the property exposure. This is an important reason for using standard policy forms, the same as for fire insurance.

Two different practices are followed when more than one company shares the property exposure. The first is for one company to issue the complete package policy but with its only retention on the section I property coverages, and for the other company to issue its policy covering only its share of the property coverages. The other practice is for the companies to share only in the basic property coverages, with all optional coverages remaining in the company which issues the package.

Some cases arise when it is not possible to have two or more companies issue policies. This occurs when a client insists upon one policy, or the producer does not have access to other companies that will accept a part of the exposure. Sometimes the problem exists in liability coverages, where it is not customary to share the exposure among primary insurers. In these cases, the package underwriter must write the entire risk and reinsure a portion with a reinsurer. With property coverages, this usually is done on a pro rata basis, under either a surplus treaty or a facultative arrangement, although excess of loss reinsurance is becoming more common. With liability coverages, the reinsurance is always on an excess of loss basis, either by a facultative placement or by obtaining a separate policy to cover the excess.

Catastrophe exposures are at least as great for package underwriters as for line underwriters. They even may be greater because of the totals of several lines, and because of the tendancy among package clients to purchase more optional or "fringe" coverages. Catastrophe reinsurance is written on an excess of loss basis. Although it is arranged by the home office staff the underwriter must know its general terms and limitations.

A commercial package underwriter must be as familiar with reinsurance problems, language, and arrangements as each of the underwriters of the component insurance lines. The commercial package underwriter must understand line limits, block limits, PML (probable maximum loss), per cent subject, liability excess reinsurance, and all other facets of property and liability reinsurance. This subject illustrates yet another of the problems in the attempt to use multiple-line underwriting on commercial package policies. Even if a multiple-line underwriter is able to learn acceptability, rating structure and policy forms for package policies, the company could become insolvent if retentions are not limited properly. Commercial reinsurance is quite complex, but it is vital to successful underwriting. The package underwriter might be unable to refer retention problems to line underwriters for guidance, merely because the existence of a problem is not recognized. Unless a company has multiple-line underwriters who are expert in all phases of underwriting, including retention and reinsurance, it is on more secure ground to use line underwriters for commercial package policies, with a committee or lead underwriter being responsible for coordination.

QUESTIONS FOR DISCUSSION

1. Are commercial package policies generally divisible or indivisible? Why?
2. What is the one type of insurance coverage needed by commercial enterprises which is not included in commercial packages?
3. List 5 optional property coverages, and 3 optional liability coverages, which may be included in commercial packages.
4. Explain why an underwriter might accept a commercial exposure on a package policy but reject the same exposure for a separate property or liability policy.
5. List 5 features which might cause an underwriter to reject an applicant for a commercial package policy.

37

Farm Package Policies

Farm risks were the last major group to be offered as package policies. When personal lines and commercial lines had been packaged, insurers then turned to farms. A few specialty companies moved rather quickly into the farm field, but it was into the 1980's before most companies entered this area.

One major problem has been the fact that farms are neither personal nor commercial; perhaps it would be more accurate to say that farms are both of a personal and commercial nature. The dwelling and its contents are virtually the same as for other dwellings which are considered personal lines. At the same time, agricultural equipment, barns, livestock, and farm operations are really commercial in scope. These differences did not cause much trouble in separate lines; each underwriter handled the farm exposures that were submitted, and it mattered little that some policies were in the personal lines field while others were of a commercial nature.

Package policies for farms required a consolidation of these various lines. The complexity of the risks and the number of options available almost required that divisible policies be issued. Thus, farm package policies more closely resemble commercial package policies than personal packages.

The name used by the bureau for its farm package policy is "farmowners-ranchowners policy."[1] Thus, the name is more closely akin to the homeowners policy of the personal line, again demonstrating the combination of the major lines in farm policies. Some companies have prepared their own policies for farms, and most of them use different titles for the policies. The large majority of insurers use the bureau farmowners-ranchowners policy.

The farmowners package is a combination of a personal lines fire policy on the farm dwelling, its garage, and its household personal property, plus coverage on the barns and other buildings which relate to the operation of the farm, the farm equipment and other personal property, and the farm liability coverage. A tenants policy is offered for those occupants who live in the farm dwelling but who do not own the

1. In 1987, ISO introduced a simplified language farm program which makes use of the modular format described in Chapter 13. For the most part, the only coverage changes made are to bring the farm coverages into conformity with current homeowners or commercial property provisions. A complete discussion of the ISO farm program may be found in the Farms tab of the Personal Lines Volume of the FC&S Bulletins.

buildings. Several combinations of coverage are available, somewhat like the homeowners policy. Some coverages are mandatory while others are optional, an arrangement which is more like a commercial package policy.

Farmowners Versus Homeowners Policy

The farmowners policy is similar to the homeowners policy, insofar as the dwelling and contents are concerned, with only a few major differences. The most important of these differences are as follows.

1. The dwelling owner is not required to live on the farm. A tenant may buy a farmowners policy to cover property and interests, just as the owner of the farm may obtain a farmowners policy to cover property and interests. The absentee owner may operate the farm, may contract the management to another person, or the tenant may actually operate it.
2. There is little or no extension of coverage to trees, shrubs and plants under the farm policy. Most vegetation would apply to the operation of the farm, and it would be difficult to delineate that which was grown for household purposes alone.
3. The deluxe (form 5) policy of the homeowners program is not written under the farmowners program of most companies.
4. Appurtenant private structures are not covered as an extension of the coverage on the dwelling. Each structure must be specifically scheduled, with a separate premium, under the farmowners policy.

DESCRIPTION OF COVERAGES

Although farm package policies are quite uniform throughout the states, some companies use independent policies which differ somewhat. However, the general pattern of coverages is the same.

Types of Policies

Four types of policies are issued. They differ only in the perils covered under the dwelling, private garage, household personal property, and additional living expense coverages. The coverages for farm property and liability are the same under all of the forms.

1. Basic Form. The peril of fire, lightning, extended coverage, vandalism and malicious mischief, and theft of personal property are covered under this form, the same as under the Basic Form of the homeowners policy.

2. Broad Form. The perils are the same as under a broad form fire policy. These are the fire perils under the basic form plus such perils as falling objects, collapse and freezing. Theft of personal property is also covered, so the form is very similar to a Broad Form policy.

3. Special Form. "All risk" coverage applies to the dwelling building, and Broad Form perils plus theft is used for personal property, as in the homeowners policy.

4. Tenants. The farmowners tenant form is similar to the tenant homeowners policy. Both cover the household personal property against the broad form perils, plus theft.

Coverages

Farmowners policies contain a number of coverages, similar to the construction of a homeowners policy. Coverages A through F are the property coverages, whether personal or farm. Coverage G through I contain the farm liability protection.

A. Dwellings. The farm dwelling is described the same as a dwelling under personal lines fires.

B. Unscheduled Family Personal Property. Personal property which appertains to the occupancy as a dwelling is covered under this item. The definitions and exclusions are similar to those of other policies; personal property which is usual or incidental to the operation of the farm is not covered here.

C. Additional Living Expense. The necessary increase in living expenses caused by an insured peril is covered. These are the family expenses, and are defined as in other forms. If the policyholder is a landlord, this coverage applies to the fair rental value of the dwelling or portion of the dwelling which is damaged by an insured peril.

D. Scheduled Farm Personal Property. Personal property which is usual *and* incidental to the operation of the farm is insured on a described basis under coverage D. Included are such property as grain, hay, machinery, farm vehicles and equipment, livestock, and farm records. Excluded are such types as fruit, bulbs, vegetables, tobacco, cotton, race horses, and the like. Also excluded are fences, windmills, automobiles and other vehicles principally designed for use on the roads. Crops in the open in stacks and shocks are covered only against damage by fire.

E. Unscheduled Farm Personal Property. The same types of personal property are covered as under coverage D. However, blanket protection is afforded without specific descriptions of properties. An 80% or higher Coinsurance clause applies, to encourage proper insurance to value. The minimum amount of coverage is $25,000.

F. Farm Buildings and Structures. Barns, silos, storage sheds, and other buildings which are used in the operations of the farm covered. Each must be described and insured separately. The perils available under coverages D, E and F are fire, extended coverage, vandalism and malicious mischief, and theft. Private structures appertaining to the farm dwelling may also be covered under this item since there is no automatic extension to them under the dwelling coverage. Additional farm dwellings may also be described and covered.

G. Farm Liability. Bodily injury and property damage liability is provided under a coverage which may be referred to as farmers personal liability, farmers comprehensive personal liability, or simply farm CPL coverage. It differs from the comprehensive personal liability coverage which is written in personal lines in only a few respects, although those few are important. Actually, this is a combination of a CPL policy and protection against the liability connected with farming premises and operations. The premises definition includes all of those owned, rented, or operated as a farm, and includes all residences on the premises and all farm structures. The exclusion of business pursuits does not apply to farming. Products liability is covered automatically. Excluded is property damage liability resulting from spraying or dusting from aircraft.

Custom farming is covered at no additional charge if it is incidental to the policyholder's farming activities. "Custom farming" refers to a farming operation performed by the policyholder for others under a contract or agreement and for a charge. It includes the maintenance, operation, and use of farm tractors, trailers, implements, draft animals and vehicles. It also covers the use, or furnishing, of sprays, dusts, poisons and fertilizers. If custom farming is not incidental to the operation of the farm, an additional premium, based on an audit, is required by most companies, or these operations may be excluded from the policy.

Fire legal liability is automatically included under coverage G, as it is in a dwelling package policy. This covers the insured premises or household furnishings, not owned by the policyholder, if damage is caused by fire, explosion, or smoke or smudge caused by the sudden, unusual, and faulty operation of any heating or cooking unit.

Employers liability is an important coverage for most farmers. It protects the liability of the policyholder for bodily injury to employees, whether they are domestic servants or farm laborers. The basic form includes residence employees who are engaged in domestic or household service on the farm; one or two employees are covered at no additional charge, but extra premium is required for more. An optional coverage applies to employer's liability and medical payments for farm employees, with an additional premium computed separately for full-time and part-time employees.

H. Medical Payments. As under the CPL policy, this coverage pays for the reasonable expenses incurred for necessary medical expenses of others. It does not apply to the insured or family, nor to farm laborers on the premises. An optional coverage may be added to cover the medical expenses of the policyholder and relatives if they are injured while engaged in work pertaining to the farming operations conducted on the premises. Included in the form are medical expenses of others who are on the premises because of a neighborly exchange of assistance. To qualify as a "neighborly exchange of assistance," the activities must be reciprocal, typical, and with no obligation on the part of the insured to pay any money.

Available as options under most farm package policies are livestock floaters and agricultural equipment floaters, both described in Chapter 28. Some policies even permit the writing of personal automobiles and farm trucks; where permitted, the rules and rates of the company generally apply, so no further discussion will be included in this chapter.

Limits of Coverage

Some of the limits of coverage under the farm package policy relate to the amount of insurance on the dwelling, somewhat like the homeowners policy. A number of minimum amounts, automatic extensions, and minimum amounts for rate discounts are specified in the rules. While there are some variations, the general pattern is this.

A. Dwelling. The minimum amount of insurance varies by the type of dwelling (depending upon quality and upkeep characteristics) from $12,000 to $20,000.

B. Family Personal Property. The limit is 50% of the amount on Coverage A, which parallels the limit under the homeowners policy. The amount may be increased for additional premium. Ten percent of this amount, or $1,000, whichever is the greater, may be applied away from the described premises, too. Since a tenant would not purchase coverage on the dwelling, the minimum amount on family personal property is $6,000.

C. Additional Living Expense. Ten percent of coverage A is the amount of insurance under this item, or 10% of the amount on family personal property under the tenants form. These amounts are less than under most homeowners forms, where the coverage is 10% under the Basic Form, 20% under the other complete policies, and 20% of the personal property amount for tenants.

D, E, F. Farm Personal Property, Farm Buildings. An owner-occupant has complete options on these coverages. An owner-occupant must purchase at least one of these: $25,000 on coverage D, $10,000 on coverage E, or $10,000 on coverage F. A tenant must purchase the same amounts on coverages D or E.

G. Farm Liability. The basic limit is $25,000, or sometimes $100,000. Higher limits are offered for additional premium.

H. Medical Payments. The automatic amount is $500 or $1,000 with higher amounts available for extra premium.

UNDERWRITING FACTORS

Eligible Risks

Farm package policies, like other packages, have specific eligibility rules: Not all risks are eligible. Those which are not, may secure separate lines of insurance, but not a farm package.

The basic eligibility rule is that the farm dwelling must contain only one or two family units which are used *exclusively* for dwelling purposes. Incidental office occupancy is permitted, just as under a personal lines fire policy. Vacant property is not eligible. A farm corporation is eligible if it is financially controlled by the named insured, either singly or in conjunction with another individual, such as a spouse or a relative.

Under the basic eligibility rules, a farm is not eligible if its principal purpose is to supply commodities for processing or manufacturing by the insured for sale to others. Examples are creameries, dairies or farms principally used to raise and race horses.

Occupancy rules are somewhat different from personal lines package policies. Under a farm package, the owner can live in the farm dwelling and either operate the farm or have it operated by managers. The dwelling can be occupied by a tenant who operates the farm, or by a tenant who has no relation to the farming operation. If the tenant pays rent for the privilege of operating the farm, the owner is not eligible for a farm package (but the tenant may purchase a tenants policy).

Farm package policies were first written only for the better risks, following the pattern established by other packages. Under the pressure of competition, some deterioration in this approach has taken place. However, companies writing farm packages have held more closely to the original intent than has been the case for other packages. Farm insurance remains somewhat of a specialty line, and those companies writing a substantial volume of it are quite careful to write packages only for superior risks. There are many coverages included in a farmowners policy, and the companies do not wish to give package discounts to those risks which are more likely to suffer losses.

Companies tend to write farm packages much as they write separate farm lines of insurance. Some specialty companies write a considerable volume of farm insurance, usually within the limits of one state or one geographic area. These companies select all risks carefully, and are even more restrictive for packages. Their acceptability list is fairly limited. Many other companies write farm insurance more as an accomodation line, whether for property or for liability insurance. They are somewhat less expert, in many cases, but they are cautious about writing packages. As a general rule, only the better farm risks are acceptable for a package.

Unacceptable Risks

Farm package policies resemble commercial packages more than personal packages in the approach to unacceptable risks. Long lists of those which are unacceptable are seldom used. Rather, underwriters tend to consider most risks and to evaluate each one on its merits.

Some of the sophistication of package underwriting seems to have been absorbed in the farm package, perhaps because it was the last to be developed. Risks unacceptable for one line are not necessarily unacceptable for a farmowners policy. A sizeable premium in other parts of the package may outweigh the deficiencies in one part.

Some unacceptable lists are used, of course. Those companies writing the farm package at a deviation from bureau rates are particularly inclined to publish lists of the risks which are not wanted. These lists include the worst of the features of the separate lines — those which ordinarily cannot be offset by other coverages.

In the farm dwelling category, the list contains those dwellings which are unacceptable for personal lines fire. The degree of fire protection is seldom a factor, for most farm risks are unprotected; a farm underwriter must accept this fact and depend upon the rates to measure this deficiency, or else the company will write very few farmowners policies. Other factors are used, and some of them are applied more strictly because of the lack of fire protection and building codes. Some of these unacceptable risks are the older homes, smaller homes, those with inferior construction and wiring, low-valued dwellings and those with poor maintenance.

Insurance to value is usually required on farm dwellings, with most underwriters insisting upon the usual percentages of actual cash value or replacement cost coverage, depending upon the policy. However, some farm underwriters take the opposite approach, refusing to accept full insurance to value. Their theory is that if a policyholder is uninsured for about one-third of the value, that person will take preventative measures to prevent losses which might escalate into large losses. Some underwriters even use the old clauses requiring the insured to be a participant in each loss, perhaps to the extent of one-fourth of the amount of the loss, but this clause is seldom used on farm packages. These different approaches still cause controversy, but most package underwriters write farm dwellings on the same basis as other dwellings, insisting upon adequate insurance to value.

Farm personal property, particularly farm machinery and tools, is generally handled the same as an agricultural equipment floater. Property which is kept in areas subject to flooding is unacceptable. Self-propelled machinery is not desirable when used for custom farming.

Farm buildings and structures are one of the major problem areas for farm package underwriters. Many of them are old and dilapidated. It is for this reason that unacceptable lists often prohibit coverage on those buildings having a value of less than a certain amount, such as $5,000.

Liability coverages seldom appear on unacceptable lists, although underwriters are concerned with those presenting an abnormal exposure to loss. Examples are farms permitting members of the public to pick fruit from trees on the farm, and farms permitting hunters to shoot game in the fields. Some companies prefer not to write farmers who engage in custom farming, or who hire a large number of farm workers.

In general, most companies consider, as unacceptable, those farms which are unprofitable, poorly maintained and run-down or those that have suffered an unusually high number of losses. Applicants who demonstrate a lack of responsibility or an interest in maintaining the property are unacceptable, too. Also, until all facts are explained, a farm is unacceptable if another insurer has cancelled or declined to renew a policy.

Farm package policies have been fairly profitable. As a result, the underwriting has not varied as much as under the personal lines package. Farm underwriting is somewhat specialized, and most companies have tended to use separate underwriters for farm risks, for many years. Thus, there has been no problem with multiple-line underwriting. Most farm underwriters were trained in most or all lines needed by a farmer, and it was a minor adjustment to underwrite packages. The general pattern is for a farm underwriter to handle the entire package, the same as under dwelling package policies. The similarity of these policies logically leads to this same handling; both present their major exposures in property lines, while liability exposures are relatively minor and uncomplicated. For the most part, farm packages generally are fairly simple, although some can be quite complex, while premiums are higher than for the typical homeowners policy, but less than for many commercial packages.

SECURING INFORMATION

A number of information sources are available to farm package underwriters. Most of these are the same as those available to other underwriters. Some of the information is used for rating purposes, but most is used for underwriting. As with other lines, the application is the primary source of data.

Application

A farm package underwriter uses a fairly complete application, since a large number of coverages are offered. Most of the questions are a repetition of those under separate lines, although duplication is avoided. Several pages are needed for most companies.

Most of the questions are concerned primarily with physical information, since most of the exposure is in property lines. Some questions, however, concern liability exposures and psychological factors.

The signature of the applicant is usually required. The identifying information is repeated on the face of the policy, but the application is not made a part of the policy. There is little uniformity among applications used by different companies, but most of them contain questions which could be grouped into three categories.

1. Personal
2. Description of property and operations
3. Insurance information

Most questions in each of the categories are along these lines.

1.*Personal*

A. Full name of the applicant, including the firm name of the farm, if any.
B. If the farm is operated by a firm, its structure: individual, partnership or corporation.
C. The location and mailing address. Location often must be described legally by lot and tract number, and for common purposes, by directions in relation to landmarks or other identification points.
D. Such stability factors as age, marital status, home ownership, length of time at this farm and number of years of experience at farming.

2.*Description of Property and Operations*

A. Acreage of the farm and the types of farming conducted, including details if any custom farming is done. Also, any business conducted on the premises, other than farming, must be described in detail.
B. Description of each building on the farm, whether insured or not. Included must be construction, age, type of roof, age of roof, size of building and use of the building.
C. Type of heating system and fuel used in each building.
D. Information about fire protection: rating of the area, and the distance to the nearest responding fire department and water source.
E. Information about police protection; exposures to forest or brush, whether there is a telephone on the premises and a year-round road and the distance to other residences.
F. Estimated total value of all household personal property, with a description of each item of jewelry and fur over $500.
G. If articles are to be scheduled under a personal articles floater, details concerning the age, condition, use and value of each article.
H. Estimated total value of each type of farm personal property, whether insured or not.
I. If an agricultural equipment floater is to be used, a description of all equipment for which coverage is requested, including manufacturer, serial number, year built, date purchased and cost. Also, details on where the equipment is stored when not in use and if it is ever loaned to others.
J. If a livestock floater is desired, a description of all livestock to be covered is required, with details on specified animals to be covered under a schedule and number of head of each type under blanket coverage. Also needed are the breed and value of animals, where they are kept, and where they are exhibited, if any.
K. Under liability coverages, information about any swimming pools on the farm, any boats owned and the number of employees hired.

3.*Insurance Information*

A. Type of policy requested.

B. Amount of insurance or limits of liability desired on each item of coverage, with specific details about each optional coverage desired.
C. The amount of any deductibles or special limitations desired.
D. Proposed effective date.
E. Name and address of any mortgagee, loss payee, or additional interest.
F. Description of any other insurance on the property.
G. Appraisals or bill of sale on all items to be scheduled.
H. Information about the previous insurer: name of the company, type of policy, amount of insurance and policy number.
I. Complete explanations if any policies which would apply to the coverages desired have ever been cancelled, declined or denied renewal.
J. Information about any previous losses in the past few years, usually three, of the types which would be covered by the policy.

Inspection Reports

Farm package underwriters use inspection reports somewhat less frequently than many other underwriters. The costs are greater because of the distance an inspector must travel, and more technical sources are often available. On the other hand, a large number of coverages are included in the policy, so more information is sometimes desired.

When they are used, inspection companies can give detailed reports about the operations and property on a farm. The same companies are used as for other lines, but the inspectors generally are specialized. Since many coverages may be written, a farm inspection form is used, containing details about all of the relevant factors, from a discussion of the moral habits of the applicant to a detailed description of all farm equipment.

Some of the information is secured only to verify the existence and condition of property which is insured. Other information may relate to the types of operations conducted, the liability exposures which exist, and the financial status of the applicant.

Photographs

Farm package underwriters use photographs more commonly than any other underwriters. A picture can convey so much more information than a verbal description, where a large farm is concerned, that photographs have long been required by many farm underwriters.

Producers are the main source of photographs, although special agents assist in this area. A producer of farm business often is accustomed to submitting pictures of each structure and piece of equipment which is covered. This saves the producer a considerable degree of written explanation, so it is of mutual benefit to producers and underwriters. When producers do not submit photographs, underwriters may request them from an insurance company.

Loss Prevention Reports

Loss prevention specialists often are used on farm package risks to furnish reports and to help prevent losses. Some of these people may be the same ones used on commercial risks or they may be specialized farm experts. They may be employees of the insurer or of a company that supplies these services.

Large, complex farming operations are particularly subject to those reports. A report may give a great deal of technical information to the underwriter. At the same time, the specialist may be able to recommend safety devices and practices, and to suggest safety programs, all of which may contribute to reduced losses.

Experience of Other Insurers

Farm package policies are similar to commercial packages in complexity, so it is not surprising that little exchange of information is practiced. It would be too troublesome to attempt to identify similar coverages.

When a reciprocal exchange of information can be arranged, such as on certain of the component insurance coverages, an underwriter can benefit. Package policies written to replace separate lines may be helped by prior experience, too.

CLASSIFICATION AND RATING

Farm package policies are classified and rated by combining component insurance coverages. In this respect, the policy is similar to a commercial package policy; the policy is divisible, composed of a number of coverages added together. Each part is rated separately, some package discounts are applied, and the sum is then the package premium.

Property coverages are rated by the rules and procedures followed by the company under separate lines. The property must be identified and classified. The perils and coverages must also be identified. The net annual rates are determined for each coverage, using the regular rate tables or procedures. A substantial package discount applies to the dwelling and family personal property portions (coverages A, B and C). Smaller discounts apply to the farm property under specified conditions.

Farm personal property may be rated either on a schedule or blanket basis. When a schedule is used, each type of property must be specified and rated according to the regular manuals. Insurance 100% to actual cash value is required. A package discount applies. Items not scheduled may be rated on a blanket basis, with 80% or higher coinsurance required. An average rate may be promulgated by the underwriter, or the highest rate applicable to any item is used, subject to a package discount. Some property may be scheduled while the balance is on a blanket basis, or all items may be either schedule or blanket rated. The only exception is that some items can be written only on a schedule basis; examples are fences, windmills, harvester combines, contents of poultry houses, cattle and crops in the open.

Liability coverages are rated from the farm comprehensive personal liability rate table. The approach is similar to that used in personal lines for CPL coverages, with a table for increased liability limits and higher medical payments limits. Rates also increase as the size of the farm increases, using large groupings; for example, the basic premium might apply up to five acres, the next layer include five to 80 acres, and so on. Custom farming is rated by applying a stated rate to each $100 of annual receipts from this source, usually excluding the first $750 or so. A small package discount usually applies to all liability coverages. Large risks are subject to premium modifications based on the actual experience of the risk, in some companies.

Coverages such as livestock floaters and agricultural equipment floaters are rated by the regular manual. Most companies apply a small package discount.

POLICY FORMS

Farm package policies are written on standardized forms by most companies. Some independent forms are used, most of them generally following the standard format. A few specialty companies use different approaches to the policy forms, with policies tailored and printed for specific types of risks.The policy forms promulgated by ISO are being made available in simplified language.

The standard format is similar to that used for personal and commercial packages. The policy back contains the typed policy identification, an inside page contains the wording of the standard fire insurance policy for the state, and common provisions are printed. Forms are attached to tailor the policy to the individual risk. One of the four policy types is applied by use of the proper form for section I: basic form, broad form, special form, or tenants form. The farm CPL form is attached, plus all of the special forms needed to add the various coverages desired by many farmers. A large number of forms are available to the underwriter for use on various risks. These forms cover most situations, so it is not common for an underwriter to prepare tailor-made endorsements. Deductibles are commonly used on most property coverages and their use is increasing steadily.

RETENTION AND REINSURANCE

Farm package insurance is somewhat similar to personal fire insurance as regards retention and reinsurance. Relatively low amounts of exposure are present in most risks, although some risks are fairly large. Occasionally a liability problem will arise, but not often.

From the standpoint of individual property coverages, the farm underwriter must consider the exposure to any one loss. Usually this means the highest valued building on the farm, including its contents. However, more than one building may be involved in a single loss. The underwriter must, therefore, consider the distances between buildings; the types of roof and construction; such means of spreading fire as dry grass or piles of straw; and property in the open which may be exposed by a building. Fire protection is often poor, so distance and the direction of the prevailing winds are important.

Each company specifies the maximum amount which it wishes to expose to one loss. The underwriter must determine if the largest probable loss will exceed that amount; in this respect, a farm package underwriter must learn to handle the probable maximum loss (PML) concept used by a commercial fire underwriter.

If the exposure to one loss exceeds the retention limit, the underwriter must take steps to control a maximum loss. A common practice is to share the coverage among several insurers, as is done in fire insurance. This practice is less common on farm packages than many other property lines, because a sizeable share of the exposure may be of inland marine coverages, not just fire. Where the coverage is fire, more than one company may share in the property coverages, just as in commercial packages.

An alternative is to use a reinsurance facility for a portion of the exposure. A pro rata surplus reinsurance treaty or facultative arrangement may be used; this is the most common practice. Some insurers use excess reinsurance to handle large property lines.

A farm package underwriter must be concerned about the catastrophe exposure, the same as other property underwriters. This is basically less of a problem than in most fire lines, because it is difficult to build a concentration of farm risks in one contiguous area. However, the multiple exposures on a large farm may present a catastrophe hazard for a tornado, hurricane, or windstorm, and more than one farm could be involved in one storm. The same treaties are used for farm package risks as for those is other property lines. As with the underwriters of those lines, the farm underwriter has little control over the specifications of the catastrophe reinsurance. However, all underwriters should be familiar with the retention and protection limits, and be guided accordingly in underwriting.

The liability portion of a farm package policy is a minor problem to underwriters, just as under a personal liability policy. The only concern is when the desired limits of liability exceed the retention of the insurer. In such cases, an automatic treaty ordinarily protects the exposure, on an excess basis. In some instances, such as when there are commercial exposures in conjunction with the farm and high limits are needed, a specific excess policy may be arranged to cover the higher limits. This is relatively rare, and reinsurance on the liability section of the policy is seldom a concern to the farm package underwriter.

SPECIAL PROBLEM

The number of farms in the United States is declining. There are now only about two million farms in this country. The total number of Americans living on farms has dropped to 5.3 million, which is 2.7% of the population. Most farms are considered small, and big operators continue to gain an ever-increasing share of production. Because of this, the median farm-family income is a quarter less than in non-farm families, and many farmers are being forced to find work elsewhere.[2]

These trends will obviously have an impact on the future of farm package policies, and farm underwriting.

---

2. "Is Farming on Way Out?" *Whittier Daily News,* May 11, 1986, p. 6.

QUESTIONS FOR DISCUSSION

1. Is a farm a personal or a commercial risk? Explain.
2. List the important differences between a homeowners policy and a farm package policy.
3. List the 3 types of farm package policies, and explain the differences.
4. What is "custom farming?" How is it insured under a farm package policy?
5. Explain the use, or lack of use, of photographs in the underwriting of farm package policies.

38

All Lines Package Policies

A true all lines package policy will contain at least life, property, and casualty coverages. Because of the inclusion of these varied lines, the policies almost certainly will be divisible.

No all lines package policies are written in the United States. State laws have prohibited a life insurance company from writing property and casualty lines, and a property-casualty insurer from writing life insurance in one package. However, former prohibitions on ownership have been lifted, and companies of each type have started, or acquired, companies of the other types. Today some of the giant life insurance companies own property-casualty companies, and vice versa.

These developments are breaking the traditional barriers between the two major lines of insurance: life insurance and property-casualty insurance. As the managements of more companies become involved in all lines, the pressure may increase for a true all lines policy. For this reason, every underwriter should be aware of the concept of all lines packaging.

HISTORICAL DEVELOPMENTS

For many years, state laws prohibited life insurance companies from writing and investing in property and casualty insurance.

Sound reasons seemed to lie behind these old laws. Since a life insurance company is in the position of a fiduciary, retaining and investing the funds of policyholders for many years, conservative investment practices were mandatory in order to avoid erosion or loss of the funds which had been entrusted to the care of the insurer. State legislators and regulatory officials were deeply concerned that the interests of widows and orphans be protected as much as possible.

Property and casualty companies, on the other hand, are subject to wide fluctuations and adverse trends. Hurricanes, tornadoes, fires from riots, earthquakes and other catastrophes can cause huge losses. An individual company could suffer extreme losses if its distribution of risks were wrong for the weather pattern in a period of time. Laws concerning liabilities and defenses can change rather quickly, resulting in substantial losses that cannot always be offset by increased premiums. Law suits can last for many years, requiring large reserves, with the ultimate settlement unknown for a long time. For these reasons, life insurers were prohibited from writing property-casualty insurance, or even from owning companies which wrote those lines.

These laws were changed because of pressure to supply a broad spectrum of insurance products to meet the needs of clients. The division between life and property/casualty is internal to the business. The public perceives exposures to loss, and seeks insurance to help in the handling of these losses. A producer who is well enough acquainted with a client to meet the property and casualty exposures should then be able to see the needs in a life insurance context.

Another reason for change was the realization that since most property-casualty were stable, sound enterprises, they should be good investments — and life insurers need high quality investments. It was not logical to permit a life company to invest a portion of its funds in a manufacturing or service organization, but not in a property-casualty insurance company. So long as the portion of the funds which were so invested were strictly controlled, the solvency of the life insurer should not be threatened, regardless of the fortunes of an insurance subsidiary.

The changes in the laws started about 1970. Previously, property/casualty insurers were permitted to own life insurance companies. Now life insurers were permitted to own property/casualty companies. Several of the large life companies soon formed or purchased subsidiaries to write property-casualty lines, under a holding arrangement, and a new era in insurance began.

The first steps of these subsidiaries were to reinsure large exposures. Capacity had become a problem in some lines; an example was aviation insurance, where the advent of the so-called jumbo jets brought about large concentrations of exposure. Some of the first forays into this field were reinsurance treaties on portions of the aviation exposure, followed quickly by general reinsurance of another company's catastrophe exposure, replacing a treaty formerly written by a professional reinsurer.

Soon, these subsidiaries of the life insurance companies started the direct writing of automobile and homeowners fields. Their sales were substantial, and their names appeared within a few years in the lists of the larger writers.

This entry by subsidiaries of the life companies into the mass lines of the property-casualty business holds great import for the future. Some life producers may not want to write property or casualty policies, but most of them will do so. Starting with automobile and homeowners policies, they will later expand into other personal lines and then into commercial lines.

At this time, it appears that the inroads of the life companies into the property-casualty field will increase, probably quite rapidly. This development may cause competitive problems for insurers and producers. Too, it will certainly increase the pressure for an all lines package policies.

PRINCIPLES OF ALL LINES PACKAGES

The principles which can apply to an all lines package policy can be developed from the information given in the preceding chapters.

1. Policies must be tailored to fit the needs of the applicants. As more coverages are added, there will be more prospects who are eligible for the package, and who may want it.

2. Early policies will be fairly simple. Perhaps a mortgage redemption life policy, which is a decreasing term policy, will be added to a homeowners policy. This is a logical combination and fits the needs of many applicants, although not all property owners have mortgages. Another step might be a retirement income policy combined with a homeowners and automobile policy. In the commercial field, early developments might be to add a partnership life policy to a commercial package policy; later, employee benefits (except for pension plans) could be combined with property and casualty coverages, perhaps on a retrospectively-rated policy.

3. A divisible policy will probably be used. The total insurance needs of applicants are so different that only limited opportunity for indivisible packages exists. One possibility for an indivisible policy is a homeowners policy containing a mortgage redemption policy with an amount that varies by the value of the dwelling. Perhaps various combinations can be developed and rated to fit the needs of a sizeable share of property owners; the proceeds from a term life policy can be used for any purpose, of course, so its face amount and term do not need to match the mortgage.

Beyond this simple combination, few opportunities for indivisible packages seem to exist. Most policies will be divisible with package discounts. In order to qualify as an all lines policy, it is likely that at least one policy must be included from each of the three major lines: life, property and casualty. (A multiple-line package policy, which includes both property and casualty lines, can satisfy this requirement when combined with a life policy.)

4. A single policy must be used, not just a marketing device of placing two or more policies in a jacket, combining the invoices, and calling a "package." On the other hand, there is no reason that two or more insurers cannot place their names on one policy, each specifying the portion which it insures. This technique was used as recently as the 1950s in automobile insurance because some companies were licensed only for liability coverages, while others wrote only property coverages. It was common for one to insure the bodily injury and property damage liability coverages, while the other insured against damage to the car itself, under comprehensive and collision coverages.

This same technique could be used on an all lines package policy. Actually, it appears that this device could be employed today for an all lines package, but apparently it is not being done. The reasons are probably these: heavy underwriting losses in many property and casualty lines; changing legislative climates regarding the liability system of automobile insurance and cancellation practices; a reluctance to expand too quickly into more package lines; and a lack of any demand from the market for such a policy.

UNDERWRITING PROBLEMS

Some of the problems that will face all lines package underwriters can be foreseen now, because most of them are merely extensions of problems facing current packages. They are not insurmountable, but they will be serious.

First, it must be recognized that the objectives of underwriting are the same, regardless of the line. A safe, profitable distribution of risks is desired in every case. However, the methods employed to meet those objectives are different by line, so some means must be found to bring about a common method of underwriting.

Life Versus Property-Casualty Insurance

There are several basic differences between life insurance and property-casualty insurance which are certain to have serious implications for package underwriters.

First, a life insurance policy may not be cancelled by the company. After it is written, the underwriter can never retire from the risk, no matter how much it deteriorates, so long as the policyowner wishes to keep the protection. Property and casualty underwriters traditionally have been able to cancel a policy at any time, with or without a reason. However, this picture has changed in recent years, too. First automobile, then fire, were subjected to laws which prohibited mid-term cancellations. Starting in 1970, some states even prohibited nonrenewals, thus requiring companies to guarantee renewals. The laws were different, but generally permitted nonrenewals under specified conditions, such as the loss of a drivers license by an insured. Thus, property-casualty underwriters are losing their rights to control policies, but they are still restricted much less than life underwriters.

Second, a life policy in incontestable after a stated period, usually two years. After the incontestable period, the underwriter cannot cancel the policy, even if there is proof that the applicant lied about such important information as medical history, or even intended at that time to commit suicide later. In contrast, a property-casualty underwriter may cancel a policy when it can be shown that fraud or deliberate misrepresentations were present, although in some states, the company must wait and nonrenew the policy. Even in states with guaranteed renewable laws, it usually is permissiblee to nonrenew a policy because of willful misrepresentation in the purchase of the coverage.

Third, a life insurance premium is fixed and cannot be increased by the underwriter. No matter how much the hazard is increased, the premium remains the same; the insured can change to a hazardous occupation or hobby, can suffer serious injuries or sickness, or can even threaten suicide, but the policy will continue without change. This is in sharp contrast to a property or casualty policy, where the rate may be increased every six or 12 months. Increases in hazards because of driving records, advancing age, or other reasons can be cause for increases in premiums under automobile or property policies, whether noncancellation laws are passed or not, so long as the regulatory requirements are met.

Fourth, nonforfeiture provisions are automatically contained in some life insurance policies. These provisions continue the coverage, in one manner or another, if the policyowner ceases to pay the premium. By using a reserve fund which has accumulated, the coverage may be continued without interruption for a period of time, or a reduced amount of insurance is paid up for the balance of the policy term.

Fifth, many life policies build reserves which the policy owner may use. The owner may borrow money against the reserve, at a reasonable rate of interest, or may even cancel the policy and receive a refund of the cash surrender value which may come close to the entire premium that has been paid.

Finally, in life insurance, the insured event is certain, i.e., the person who is insured by the policy will die. The uncertainty lies in when and how the insured will die (the "how" is important only in cases when additional death benefits are paid because of accidental death.) This is in sharp contrast to property and casualty insurance, where it is the desire of all concerned parties that the specified event will not occur, and it does so only rarely, in general.

These basic differences cause entirely different approaches to underwriting. A life underwriter is much more deliberate and cautious in accepting and rating a risk. Once a decision is made, the underwriter cannot cancel, contest (after a brief period), or raise rates on the policy. A life underwriter must be much more careful than a property or casualty underwriter, who can cancel or nonrenew in most cases, rescind or nonrenew in serious cases, and raise rates at regular intervals if the risk is retained.

Questions to Consider

How will an all lines package be underwritten, in view of these problems? One portion can never be cancelled; is the underwriter willing to remain forever on the property and casualty exposures? The policy will be divisible, so portions of it could be cancelled, but would it remain an all lines policy? What is the advantage of selling a package if it could be changed easily into just a life policy? By the same token, could part of the policy be challenged because of a misrepresentation while the balance remained unscathed? Will it be practical or desirable to increase a portion of the premium, perhaps to a prohibitive level, without destroying the benefit of the package by threatening to force the policyowner to cancel even the life insurance because the package premium is beyond reach.

These are some of the questions on the basic principles which must be answered before an all lines package can be issued.

Problems of a Mechanical Nature

In addition, there are problems of a more mechanical nature facing all lines package policies. Four of these are described below.

1. There will be an increased chance of a large loss resulting from a single occurrence. Just picture an automobile policy and a life policy combined into a single package written by one company. Then imagine a bad auto accident in which the insured, who was at fault and subsequently killed, also caused serious injury to the people in the other car, as well as to the insured's family. In addition to the liability payments, the medical payments to the family, and repairs to the car, the insurer would have to pay the life insurance proceeds to the survivors.

2. It will be difficult to correlate the underwriting of the component coverages of the package. The problems now faced by commercial package underwriters, when two or more line underwriters must agree on acceptability, will seem mild in comparison. The automobile or fire underwriter may be willing to take a chance on an applicant, but the life underwriter may not. Each will be looking at the available data differently because each has different problems. It will be almost impossible to find an all lines underwriter who will be able to handle all coverages. The only solution will be to use the committee approach, which has proved to be quite unsatisfactory in property and casualty packages.

3. Policy forms and rating structures will present real problems. How can a single package policy be written with some portions cancellable at the option of the underwriter, while others are incontestable after two years? The many problems involved in writing a package policy for all lines probably will help to delay development of such a policy. At the same time, rate and rate regulation will also be difficult to combine. Premium payment periods, the ability to adjust rates, and similar subjects will be obstacles in the preparation of an all line package.

4. The application is handled differently by various lines. In life insurance, the policy may be rerated or adjusted in amount during the contestable period, if any misstatements appear on the application. Even if they are inadvertent, a misstatement of age, health, or other pertinent factors will be cause for revision in the policy. To control this factor, the application is reproduced and made a part of the policy. Property and casualty underwriters generally do not have the authority to rerate policies because of misstatements of fact, so the application is not made a part of the policy in most lines. Under an all lines package policy, some adjustments will need to be made in these practices, at least by one group of underwriters.

THE ULTIMATE CONCEPT

Underwriters have dreamed for years about a policy which will insure against any contingency, other than business and investment losses. For a long time, the segregation of casualty and property lines prohibited such a policy. Now there are multiple-line package policies, but death benefits are not included, nor are the saving features of permanent life insurance.

The ultimate insurance policy will say to a person, in effect: "We insure you. We will replace or reimburse for anything that happens to you." If property is destroyed, it will be replaced, or cash given to permit replacement. If the insured is sued, defense will be given, and any adverse judgment will be paid. If unforeseen expenses are incurred because of fortuitous circumstances, whether in the home or in the business, reimbursement will be made. If the insured is disabled, income to the family and the business will be continued. If the insured should die while the policy is in force, payment will be made to the family, and to the business if the death would adversely affect its operation.

Exclusions would be at a minimum under this concept. Self-inflicted and deliberate acts would not be covered, at least during the initial period. Illegal acts would be excluded. Perhaps such catastrophic events as war and nuclear explosions would need to be excluded. Otherwise, the policy would cover all losses. Too, the contract would be noncancellable by the company. Every exposure would be covered. Naturally, the premium would be high, and a means of measuring the exposure for rating purpose would be needed.

Perhaps such a policy will never be developed because it has many problems. However, the insurance industry has moved closer to that goal, with its broad policies and package contracts. Developments have been particularly rapid since about 1950. One major stumbling block remains before insurers can attack the relatively minor but still troublesome problems of exclusions and limitations. That obstacle is the separation of life insurance from property and casualty insurance. This is why the prospect of an all lines package policy is so exciting to an underwriter. However, the all lines package policy, when it is developed, will be a giant step toward achievement of the ultimate concent, the all loss policy.

QUESTIONS FOR DISCUSSION

1. How does an all lines package policy differ from a personal or commercial package policy?
2. (a) Why are all lines package policies not written in the United States?
   (b) What are the reasons behind this situation?
3. What will be a major result, from a marketing standpoint, of the entry of life company subsidiaries into the property-casualty business?
4. Will all lines package policies be divisible or indivisible? Explain.
5. Give 4 basic differences between life insurance and property-casualty insurance which will affect underwriting.

INTRODUCTION TO PART VII

AUXILIARY DUTIES OF UNDERWRITERS

Most of the material in the preceding chapters of this book has concentrated on the underwriting of new applications. Mention was made occasionally about the handling of risks which developed problems after the insurance was written, but more references were to new business. This was deliberate. The primary duty of an underwriter is to select risks, and a large percentage of an underwriter's time is spent in handling new applications.

Underwriters also have other duties. Although requiring less total time, these other duties may be very important in the effort to achieve a profitable operation. Those duties are described in this part and are called "auxiliary duties," because they are performed in addition to the principal duty of underwriters and because they support the efforts of underwriters.

After an application is accepted by an underwriter, it is not necessarily perfect in performance forever after. Many problems can arise, problems that require the attention of an underwriter. Changes are made in policies, and losses occur which indicate that risks have changed. The underwriter may need to apply the same principles of decision-making as on new applications. Sometimes he or she may want to reevaluate the risk at the time that a potential problem appears, while at other times, to conduct a review when renewal is approaching. These two methods of underwriting policies after they are once accepted are explained in Chapters 39 and 40.

Other auxiliary duties performed by underwriters include the handling of assigned risks and involuntary pools which may be routine or complicated. They are certainly different from regular underwriting. The background and present status of this ever-changing field is discussed in Chapter 41.

Jumbo risks are a separate type of risk, requiring some different approaches. Ordinarily these risks require only a small portion of an underwriter's time, so they are classified here as falling under "auxiliary duties" and discussed in Chapter 42.

The preparation of reports is another important but not necessarily essential duty of underwriters. The types and purposes of the reports are explained in Chapter 43.

Finally, underwriters have an "auxillary duty" to coordinate their activities with other departments in the company. This coordination is not essential to underwriting; a risk could be accepted without regard to the sales, claims, or auditing services which might be needed. An underwriter could act as though this is solely the client's worry. However, the importance of providing good service to producers and clients alike is so important that the underwriter should never overlook it. It is an "auxiliary duty" only in the sense that it is not essential to the pure underwriting function. However, service is such a vital part of the work of every employee, and particularly of underwriters, that it must be considered as an important duty of underwriters. It is, therefore, discussed in Chapter 44.

39

Maintaining Policies in Force

Most of the discussion in the preceding chapters has been concerned with new applications. Another part of the underwriting process, and one that is just as important, is to handle policies after they are written. These policies in force will not always remain profitable, even if they are properly underwritten at inception. Insurance is not static. Risks change, conditions are altered and new factors are introduced. It is possible that a wrong action was selected by the new business underwriter, from among the alternatives available. These are the reasons that underwriting must be applied to policies in force in order to maintain them as profitable risks.

The principles of decision-making in underwriting were explained in Part II. The fourth principle, the one that follows the actual underwriting action, is to check results. It is followed by the fifth principle — taking corrective action. These steps can be taken only after policies have been in force long enough for results to be obtained. Policies in this situation are referred to as "policies in force," to differentiate them from new business policies. These are the policies upon which results can be checked and corrective action can be taken.

Several types of opportunities are given to underwriters to permit them to check results. These opportunities, on individual policies, arise when changes are made in policies, when losses are reported, and when reports are received from other departments in the company. There is another opportunity at the time of renewal. This entails a different approach, for a decision must be made to renew the coverage for another term, or to discontinue it. This subject is discussed in the next chapter.

On groups of policies, review programs may be used to check results. Each of these opportunities is discussed in a separate section of this chapter. They are followed by an explanation of some of the underwriting programs that may be used to check results on policies in force. The final section discusses some of the limitations that are placed on underwriters when they are planning to take corrective action.

POLICY CHANGES

Insurance policies are changed for a variety of reasons. Some policies may remain unchanged for years, while others are revised frequently. Each change has a potential effect on the desirability of the risk, so the underwriter will want to review the file and consider the necessity of taking action. Examples of the types of changes that may be made on various lines of insurance are these.

—Increase or decrease in amount of insurance.

—Addition or deletion of perils or coverages.

—Addition or substitution of vehicles.

—Change in, or addition of, locations.

—Increase or decrease in the number of employees.

—Change in the types of operations performed.

—Addition or deletion of protective devices.

—Addition or deletion of a mortgagee or other loss payee.

—Revisions in deductibles or other contract provisions.

Most of these changes may affect the desirability of the risk, although to some degree, a new risk is created with every change. Underwriters, therefore, will want to review most policies when changes are made to see if any new action is needed.

Acceptability of the risk may be impaired and may not qualify under the rules of the company. For example, the new liability limit may be higher than the company writes on that type of risk. A new location may have no fire or police protection and, therefore unacceptable by company rules; a risk may be acceptable for basic perils but unacceptable for broad coverages, such as earthquake or water damage perils.

Eligibility of the risk may be impaired, too. The new risk may be eligible, but the underwriter may find it unacceptable. A youthful driver who begins driving an automobile may not be acceptable to the underwriter. Higher burglary limits may put the risk into a category the underwriter does not want to keep. A commercial risk may be acceptable for basic liability coverages, but not acceptable for products liability coverages.

Not all changes are serious enough to warrant an underwriter's concern. Some types may be so innocuous that the underwriter will permit a clerk to make the change without so much as reference to the underwriter. For example, if one automobile is replaced by a newer model with similar characteristics and no change is made in the driving pattern, the transfer of coverage may be made by clerical personnel. Also, a change of name on a fire policy, stemming from a marriage or divorce, may not be of interest to an underwriter.

At the same time, the underwriter who finds the change itself as unimportant, finds the request as an opportunity to reevaluate the risk. Perhaps the automobile does not need to be checked, but the drivers are due for a verification of their driving records. The change of name may not be critical, but a reexamination of the building itself may be in order. Thus, policy changes may be made without referral to an underwriter, but care should be taken so that those risks that might need reevaluation are not handled in such a routine fashion that underwriting is overlooked. Policy changes afford an excellent opportunity for underwriting evaluation of policies in force, even if no action is needed.

Underwriting action of various types may result from a review of each policy change. The underwriting review will follow the decision-making principles which underlie all of the underwriting function. After receiving a request for the desired change, the underwriter will secure any additional information needed. Then the underwriter will develop alternatives, select from among them and take the necessary action. Some of the alternative courses of action are these.

• Accept the change, making any reclassification or rerating necessary. This is the most frequently followed alternative. It is preferred above all others, if the underwriter can select it without causing a degeneration of the risk.

• Make a counter-offer. The change may be acceptable under revised conditions. Deductibles may be required, one driver may have to be excluded, or a slightly more restricted form may be offered (for example, broad form instead of special form on a personal fire policy). Often a change that is unacceptable may be made acceptable by a minor revision.

• Refuse to make the change, if this is possible while still retaining the risk. The policyholder may desire a broader coverage, but the best that can be offered is limited coverage. Naturally, there is a possibility that the client will move the business elsewhere if the underwriter will not make the desired change. This is a chance the underwriter must take. It is a preferable course to cancelling the policy or accepting a change that will make the risk otherwise undesirable.

• Cancel the policy, if the change is an integral part of the risk. For example, a manufacturer seldom will change the product it has decided to make, merely to please the underwriter. If a store operator or homeowner moves to a new location, it is unlikely that either will return to the former location because the new location is unacceptable to an underwriter. In these cases, the underwriter has no choice but to cancel the policy.

LOSSES

Every insurance policy is subject to losses. If there were no chance of loss, insurance would not be purchased. On the other hand, an underwriter does not take action on a policy simply because a loss has occurred.

However, losses are an indication that a risk may have worsened because most policies do not have losses. Premiums are much too small to permit many losses without causing adverse underwriting results. When a loss is reported or paid, therefore, the file should be referred to the underwriter and an analysis made to see if a problem has developed.

Loss situations can consist of one or the other of two problems: *frequency* or *severity.*

Frequency deals with the occurrence of an unusually large number of losses. Many of them, even all of them, may be small, but they still should be of concern to an underwriter. For one thing, losses are expensive to adjust, in most lines, and loss adjustment expense is one the expense factors that must be held in line if competitive rates are to be maintained. Another problem is that the aggregate of even small losses can be a considerable drain, causing a net dollar loss on the policy. Most important from an underwriting standpoint is the fact that numerous small losses may indicate that a risk has deteriorated and that a large loss may occur at any time. Thus, the type of loss is important, when a frequency problem exists.

Severity deals with the size of the loss or losses that occur. The untrained underwriter or layman is badly shaken by a single large loss, feeling that something must have gone wrong in the selection process. The experienced underwriter knows that almost any loss has the potential for being large, and that the size of the loss often is beyond the control of the policyholder. Thus, when a large loss is reported, the underwriter should look into the circumstances to see if it was an unfortunate, isolated occurrence, or whether there are indications that a repetition is likely.

Either frequency or severity of losses may indicate that the desirability of the risk is affected. Hence, each time a loss is reported, the file should be reviewed by an underwriter to see if new underwriting action is needed.

Acceptability of the risk may be affected. Most lines have guides or specific rules which provide that a risk is unacceptable if it has incurred more than a stated number of losses within a certain time span. Personal auto is a notable example. A driver who has been involved in several accidents within a three-year period may not be acceptable. Such a driver may feel that this is no worse than the average, but the underwriter knows that 83% of drivers are accident-free in a three-year period, as was explained in the discussion on personal automobile insurance in Chapter 19. Policyholders in one line who have more than the average number of losses, or who have severe losses that indicate difficulties, may be unacceptable to underwriters. Not all losses indicate that a risk needs correction. Some losses are beyond the control of the insured and should not be charged. It is important, therefore, that each loss should be analyzed to determine if it indicates a problem or not.

Frequency is not too difficult to analyze. The underwriter should have an idea of the average frequency of losses, in order to determine if a particular risk is better or worse than average. Companies sometimes publish lists of average losses to guide underwriters. For example, a list may show that the average time between comprehensive claims on a personal automobile policy is seven years, and 10 years between collision claims. Similarly, the average personal fire policy holder may report only one fire claim in 15 years. When a risk develops a frequency higher than the average, some type of underwriting action may be needed.

Severity of loss is more difficult to analyze. If a severe loss is caused by the carelessness of the insured, and the same situation might be repeated, underwriting action is needed. If the loss is not controllable nor is likely to be repeated, the underwriter might take no action.

Frequency and severity may be analyzed together. In fact, each should be taken into account when analyzing either one. A frequency of small glass losses may indicate no problem, or at least one which is easily controlled. However, a frequency of small kitchen fires, or small smoking fires, may lead to the conclusion that only luck has prevented them from becoming large fires. The next one may be a total loss.

More extreme underwriting action is indicated in order to prevent a future severe loss. The type of loss is of primary importance to an underwriter, along with expectations for the future.

Although some losses are not necessarily the prelude to underwriting action, they do afford an opportunity for reviewing files. Some few types of losses, where no frequency is present, may not need referral to an underwriter, but most losses are referred to underwriting for analysis.

Underwriting action often is taken when losses indicate that a problem has arisen. (The action is taken on individual risks, although occasionally a group of policies with similar loss experience will be analyzed together.) The underwriter first needs to secure all necessary facts to determine why losses have occurred, and to help in arriving at alternative courses of action. After developing alternatives, the underwriter must select one and take action. These steps taken follow the principles laid out in a previous chapter.

Alternative Actions After Loss

Some of the alternatives that may be used, when losses are referred, are these.

Close the File Without Action. This is a commonly used alternative. Many policyholders who incur losses do not really have problems, upon careful evaluation. If no real problem exists, no action should be taken. Rather, the file should be closed until another circumstance brings it to the attention of the underwriter. This alternative should be selected, unless conditions indicate that a problem does in fact exist.

Remove a Coverage. Often one coverage or one peril will be the cause of the problem. The policyholder may be agreeable to removing the offender. Examples might be towing coverage on automobiles, vandalism or glass breakage on a fire policy, and theft from unattended automobiles on a crime policy. These are cases when frequency of loss is a problem. It is a help in "selling" this type of decision to the producer and policyholder to realize that a premium reduction will be made because of the deletion.

Apply Deductibles. A common alternative is to apply deductibles. If one is already on the policy, a larger deductible may be used. This alternative can be very effective when the problem is frequency of small losses. Glass breakage, windstorm damage and pilferage are examples of losses when deductibles may be used effectively. Sometimes a $25 deductible will be all that is needed, while at other times the type of loss may require a deductible of $100, $250, or even $1,000. Again, rate reductions are given, so the action is more palatable.

A request by the underwriter to use a deductible is self-policing. A policyholder who thinks it unlikely to have more losses will be glad to accept the deductible, with its lower premium. On the other hand, a policyholder who insists that a deductible cannot be tolerated is probably expecting to incur more losses. The underwriter in this latter case will not be anxious to retain such a risk.

Deductibles, like limitations of coverage, are a good alternative for another reason. A policyholder who does not wish to accept the restriction may choose to cancel the policy. From a political standpoint, it is better for the underwriter to be willing to write the policy according to the insurance company's terms, and for the insured to cancel if not satisfied. In any event, cancellation by the underwriter should be a last resort — other alternatives are preferable.

Deductibles, can mislead the underwriter who is unwary, however. A deductible is not a cure-all for every problem. The losses may be small, but they may be of a type which can produce large losses at any time. Fire losses from cooking and from smoking in bed are ideal examples. A number of losses may be quite small, well within the range of a deductible. However, any one of these losses may produce a fire which will totally destroy the premises, given the proper set of circumstances. In such a case, the underwriter will reduce the premium income by use of a deductible, but may still pay almost as much in the next loss.

Deductibles are an excellent control for the frequent, small losses which are the result of unfortunate circumstances and have little potential for large losses. But deductibles are of little or no benefit when losses are caused by carelessness, poor maintenance, or other moral or morale hazards.

An underwriter must realize that if an insurer elects to issue a policy which does not preclude small losses, it is not fair to blame the policyholder for collecting what the policy provides. Homeowners insurance is not designed to cover maintenance losses, but this is what can happen if no deductible, or a small deductible, is used. A better alternative to cancelling or nonrenewing a policy with a frequency of small claims is to offer high deductibles. This will still provide protection for the catastrophic losses, which is the original intent of the policies.

Cancel the Policy. If a loss pattern cannot be controlled in any other fashion, the only alternative is to cancel the policy. Where the loss picture is not severe, cancellation should normally be deferred until the expiration date, when the policy can be nonrenewed. However, where there appears to be a strong possibility that a large loss will occur before the expiration date, the policy should be cancelled as soon as possible, taking into account the notice requirements of the policy, any applicable laws, and the desirability of giving advance notification to the producer.

No precise rule can be given when to cancel and when to nonrenew a policy. The policy of the company is important. A general rule followed by most underwriters is that the policy will be held to renewal if the condition is not too severe and the time to expiration is not too long — perhaps three months or less. Each case must be handled on it own merits. But it must be kept in mind that cancellation laws also affect the decision on some lines.

INFORMATIVE REPORTS

An underwriter occasionally receives a report which indicates that a policy on the books needs a reevaluation. These reports may come from several sources. Each should be analyzed carefully. Some of the sources are these.

1. Producers. A producer may learn of information which may have an effect on the risk. When the producer sends it to the underwriter, it deserves careful consideration. Since producers generally are sales-minded, a report of adverse information indicates a potentially serious condition.
2. Loss prevention specialists. Some loss prevention reports are continuous, being made at intervals during the term of the policy. Other reports may be made at the inception

of the policy, and further information developed as the specialist discovers new facts. (Perhaps as the risk is being surveyed for another policy the loss prevention specialist may overhear derogatory information.) As with new reports, these reports are a reliable course of infomation.

3. Inspection companies. Some inspection companies, as well as clipping bureaus, forward information which is received after a report is written. Files might be kept open for a year or more, with new information being sent to the underwriter as it is received.
4. Claims adjusters. A claims adjuster may report unfavorable facts that are discovered during the handling of a claim. The loss itself may not be serious, but an adverse comment by an adjuster demands careful consideration.
5. Auditors. When an auditor encounters unfavorable facts during a checking of payrolls or other factors, this may be reported to the underwriter.

Underwriting action may be taken as a result of the information received from these sources. When a report is sent to an underwriter, he or she needs to evaluate the risk in light of the new facts. The underwriter will secure as much information as is needed, checking on the data for verification if this appears to be needed. New alternatives can then be developed, encompassing any of the types of underwriting action. A decision must be made and action taken if any change is indicated.

After evaluating the risk, the underwriter might continue this policy with no change, may apply changes in coverage, deductibles or other aspects of the risk, or may even decide to cancel or nonrenew the policy, if no other alternative is available.

Underwriters must overlook no opportunity to review policies in force. Any type of information, or any type of referral from internal activities may lead to a discovery of problems in policies. Underwriting action, therefore, may be needed in order to maintain policies on a profitable basis.

GROUPS OF POLICIES

Problems with policies in force may arise on groups of policies, as well as on individual policies. Underwriters may find it a necessity to review an entire group of policies, taking action on some or all of them. The same principles are followed as on individual policies, as explained in previous sections of this chapter, but there may be differences in the techniques used.

Examples

Various groups of policies may be reviewed because of unprofitable factors. Examples of some of the groups which an underwriter might review are these.

1. *All policies with certain coverages.* If a problem occurs under vandalism coverage for public property, as an example, the underwriter may wish to review all such policies carrying that coverage. Since some may not yet have suffered losses, they otherwise would not be discovered until a review is made following reported losses. This may be considered as a type of preventative underwriting: when a sizeable number of risks with certain characteristics suffer losses, all policies in that group may be reviewed inn the hope of preventing future losses.

2. *Policies with a certain frequency of loss.* A group of policies reporting a specified frequency of losses may need review in order to determine problems. One example is all automobile risks that have incurred three or more collision losses with in the past two years. Another example is a group of fire risks with two or more recent

windstorm losses. These policies could be discovered upon review of individual losses but they could escape underwriting review if the frequency is low. However, action might be indicated on the group as a whole.

3. *All policies within a class with severity problems.* Sometimes a group of policyholders will suffer unusually severe losses, such as doctors who have malpractice problems, or contractors who have severe claims because of poor work. In these cases, all policies in the group may have to be reviewed in order to identify those with similar characteristics which may also lead to severe losses if steps are not taken otherwise.

4. *Policies in a given area.* Underwriters occasionally realize that a loss ratio in one area is higher than in other areas. Unless other actions can be taken, such as increasing rates, it is necessary to act upon those policies, and underwriting corrections even may be taken on all policies in the area. Alternatively, all of the policies may be analyzed and action taken only upon those having unusual characteristics.

5. *Policies of a given producer.* Since statistics sometimes reveal that policies of one producer are unprofitable, the underwriter may find it desirable to review all of the policies of that producer. Perhaps corrective action eventually will be taken on all of these policies. More often, however, all of the policies will be reviewed, with action taken only upon those unprofitable ones or those that appear to present problems.

Underwriting desirability may be affected in the same fashion by unprofitable groups of policies as by individual policies. As a matter of fact, the cumulative effects of poor groups of policies can far exceed the losses from individual policies. For this reason, the underwriter must be aware of problems with groups of policies. The underwriter may find that one entire group is unacceptable, at least without some type of corrective action.

However, underwriting action on groups of policies must be taken on the individual risks which comprise the group. Even if the same action is taken on all policies in the group, an individual change must be made on each policy. Thus, while the problem may be present in the entire group, the action is taken on separate policies.

Moreover, group underwriting action must follow the same principles as are observed on separate policies, whether they are new or existing insureds. All pertinent information must be secured, then alternative courses of action have to be developed. Next, a decision must be made and action taken. Additionally, the problem policies in the group need to be identified, unless action is planned on the entire group of policies.

This underwriting process on groups of policies is called "reunderwriting." This term denotes a repeat of the entire underwriting process, applying the steps of decision-making to the group of policies. This term is not commonly used on separate policies that are referred because of policy changes or losses. Rather, it is used in identifying the process of reviewing a group of policies having some common characteristics. Reunderwriting seldom is a continuous process; more often, it is used infrequently as a means of correcting problems which appear to be insurmountable by other means.

Examples of Action Taken

Examples of the types of action which may be taken following a reunderwriting program are these.

Restrict Coverage. All policyholders in a group may be affected, such as a general problem involved in an area which experiences landslides or earthquakes. If the underwriter does not wish to continue insuring against either of those perils, he or she may either restrict or remove the coverage on all of the policies. Sometimes, only certain policies in the group need be restricted. An example are properties located on hillsides, for landslide coverage, or those constructed of brick or masonry, as regards earthquake insurance.

Apply Deductibles. All policies in the group may receive a deductible, if this is the most effective means of controlling the problem. Perhaps all risks in the group will receive a deductible on crime perils, or a deductible on comprehensive coverage of automobile policies. The problem may be more restricted, so deductibles need only apply to certain types of risks. Crime deductibles may be needed only on specified occupancies; or comprehensive deductibles may be applied only to certain types of automobiles or rate classes.

Rerate the Policies. If the problem appears to be one of an inadequate rate, a new classification system may be needed. A new rate class or territory might be developed, too. However, a change in classifications or rates is ordinarily applied to all policies in the group.

Cancel or Nonrenew. When no other alternative is available, the underwriter must cancel or nonrenew the policies. As with separate policies, this should be a last resort, when no other course of action is practical. Termination ordinarily applies to selected policies only. Once in a while, however, a group may present such a problem that no other course is available for the entire group. Climatic conditions may be too severe. Rate increases may be impossible to secure. Cancellation or nonrenewal of all policies in the group is unusual and undesirable generally, but it may be necessary on some occasions. Another underlying cause of this drastic action relates to the producer. If a specific producer employs poor selective practices, gives the company an adverse selection, or uses an inadequate rate on a group which the producer controls, there may be no other alternative but to terminate all of the policies. This severe action is used only as a last resort, but it is available if nothing else works.

UNDERWRITING PROGRAMS

A good underwriter makes specific plans that will help to maintain policies in force. In other words, the underwriter does not depend upon luck to bring to attention those risks that need attention. Typical of the underwriting programs which are used to help in this goal are these.

—Refer all policy changes. In any insurance operation, many changes will be referred to the underwriter for approval, giving an opportunity to reevaluate the entire risk. New locations, new drivers, added coverages, and similar changes are referred in almost every case.

The pressure for quick, efficient handling leads some companies to bypass the underwriter on certain changes. Reductions in coverage can be handled by a clerk, such as a change from one vehicle to another similar one, a routine change of name, a move to similar premises, and the like. The problem is that such handling by clerical personnel deprives the underwriter of the opportunity to look at the risk — to reappraise the desirability of the entire policy.

The underwriter, therefore, may decide to have all policy changes referred. This increases handling costs, but it may reduce losses. Certainly, it gives the underwriter an opportunity to evaluate the previous action and to take corrective steps if needed.

—Refer all losses. In a parallel to policy changes, some insurers economize by not referring all losses to an underwriter. The theory is that if there is no frequency, no severity and no fault, there is slight chance of underwriting action. Thus, isolated cases of small thefts, glass breakage, or similar losses are handled by clerks — being filed without referral to an underwriter.

Cautious underwriting, however, requires that all losses be referred to the underwriter. A clerk may not recognize a latent or potential problem which otherwise could be revealed by expert analysis. Furthermore, a referral of each loss increases the opportunities for an underwriter to reevaluate the risk. This is another chance to complete the underwriting process by checking the results of previous decisions and taking corrective action where needed.

—Adopt reunderwriting programs. An alert underwriter will watch for problems on groups of policies. When they arise, as they will periodically, reunderwriting programs should be instituted. Various types of programs may be used and, often, it helps to have tentative programs prepared in advance.

A reunderwriting program may include a review of all policies with certain coverages, all in a specific area, all of one producer, all with specified characteristics or any other groups. Combinations may be used, of course. For example, all personal automobile policies in one county, having two or more losses within the past three years, may be reviewed. If a producer is developing a poor loss ratio on certain coverages in a class, the policies with those coverages may be reunderwritten, too.

Reunderwriting programs may be conducted at any time. It is most common to review policies a short time before renewal, so that action can be taken on the renewal date. Cancallation laws on some lines, and public relations on all lines, encourage the application of underwriting action at the renewal date, rather than at mid-term. Many reunderwriting programs, therefore, are conducted in conjunction with, or in the place of, the underwriting of renewals. (The latter subject is discussed in the next chapter.)

—Secure more information. Any of these other programs may require underwriting decisions. These decisions must be based on facts, as with other underwriting. The underwriter who plans to institute reevaluation programs is wise to make specific provisions for the securing of more data. Separate budgets may be needed to accomodate the ordering of inspection reports, loss prevention reports, motor vehicle records or whatever is necessary.

After securing the desired information, the decision-making process must be followed. Alternatives must be developed, then a selection made and action taken. All of these steps should be routine for an underwriter who wishes to maintain the existing policies in a profitable condition.

LIMITATIONS ON UNDERWRITING

Underwriters cannot always take the most effective course of action. Alternatives may develop that will help to maintain the profitability of policies in force, but some of them may be impossible to implement. There are limitations placed on the actions of underwriters which restrict them from taking certain steps.

Some of these limitations are statutory or contractual in nature, while others are subtle or unenforceable, but present nevertheless. The most common limitations are these:

Noncancellation Laws or Regulations

Many states have laws prohibiting mid-term cancellation of certain policies. In other states, the same effect is achieved by regulations issued by the insurance department authorities. Personal automobile is the most frequent victim of these limitations. (Light commercial automobiles sometimes are included.) Starting in about 1970, fire and other lines were also brought under these laws in some states.

The usual noncancellation laws provide that no cancellation maybe effected by the company after the new business period, during the term of the policy, except for a few stated reasons. A "discovery period' or "new business period" is always included, providing that cancellation or declinations may be made for any reason. The usual period lasts 60 days after the effective date of the policy. During this period, the underwriter may secure information, make a decision and take action.

After the discovery period, the company cannot cancel except for specified reasons. State laws vary considerably, but the trend is toward fewer permissible reasons for cancellation. The most common ones are failure to pay the premium, revocation or suspension of the driver's license of the insured, misrepresentation or deceit in the application and an increase in the hazard. Some states add other reasons, such as frequency of convictions or accidents.

The trend is toward expanding noncancellation laws into other states and other lines of insurance. Most underwriters will feel these limitations in the future.

Noncancellation Provisions in Policies

Some personal automobile policies contain guarantees that the policies will not be cancelled for at least a stated period, usually two to five years. Specified exceptions are included, as under noncancellation laws.

These provisions generally are used only by companies with rate structures permitting surcharges for adverse factors, such as frequency of accidents or convictions. An underwriter would be severely handicapped if the company could not cancel and could not increase premiums to a tolerable level. Even with this protection, underwriters are limited by such clauses. Some risks are unprofitable at any price, and underwriters usually prefer to be able to cancel at least the worst risks.

These policy limitations were introduced as advertising materials. They furnished good copy for advertising for awhile. It appears that adoption of these limitations by many other companies in the future is quite unlikely. The first companies exploited the advertising advantage out of these plans; hence, future programs may have less impact. States laws have almost preempted the field of noncancellation, so company plans have less impact. In spite of these difficulties, some voluntary restrictions are being adopted by some companies.

Guaranteed Renewal Laws

Several states have enacted laws which not only prohibit cancellation but also require renewal. The early laws applied only to personal automobiles. Nonrenewal is permitted for stated reasons, such as nonpayment of premium, specified accident or conviction records, suspension or revocation of license, and the like. Advance notification of nonrenewal, if permitted, is required. Reductions in coverage are permitted, generally. The trend for the future is toward more of these laws which guarantee renewal, with expansion into other lines being almost inevitable.

A guaranteed renewal law puts pressure on underwriters to select risks with extreme care. A new business discovery period is provided, during which the underwriter may take action. After that, the company might remain on the risk for many years, regardless of how bad the losses become. The underwriter has only one safe course of action, other than to use a rating structure which secures adequare premium for poor risks: a very careful, complete evaluation of the risk before it is accepted. Strict selection practices, therefore, must be used with laws which restrict the underwriter's freedom of action.

Public and Legislative Pressures

Even in states and on lines where cancellation is permitted, it is becoming perilous for an underwriter to cancel a policy. A disgruntled policyholder can stir up trouble and be the instigator of restrictive legislation. The problem is even more acute if the underwriter cancelsd a block of policies, such as all those who are written by a specific unprofitable agent.

Pressure often is exerted through state departments of insurance, too. Legislators or the public may complain about an alleged unfair act, and pressure can be brought to bear to reverse the action, with the threat of legislation being held over the head of the underwriter.

A great dilemma faces the underwriter in such cases, particularly in those where the underwriter has reason to expect that pressure will be brought if action is taken. If the underwriter does nothing, the company probably will lose money on the risk, but if the underwriter takes action, this may bring wrath down upon the heads of company superiors. Most companies have an established policy to deal with such circumstances, and naturally it should be followed, but the general trend is to nonrenew, rather than cancel on most risks except, perhaps, the very worse cases.

The underwriter who ignores these pressures — especially when there have been no problems or any pressure — can cause great damage. If the underwriter persists in a course which disregards the feelings of the public and the legislators, this can cause restrictive laws to be passed. These laws, of course, hamper all underwriting, not just the guilty party. Each underwriter must, therefore, practice a degree of statesmanship in order to help the industry through these trying times.

Pressure From Producers

Underwriters face pressure from producers to retain policies on the books. Attempts to cancel poor risks may cause threats of retaliatory action, such as a producer's threat to stop placing business with the company. A much safer course with most producers is to nonrenew undesirable risks, rather than to cancel them since producers ordinarily find it easier to place a risk with another company at renewal date than during mid-term.

The type and degree of pressure depends upon the type of arrangement used with producers. Some producers may be able to exert more pressure than others. In every case relations are important because the inflow of business is vital. A good underwriter can convince the producer of the desirability of the proposed action, but the threat of pressure constitutes still another curb on the decisions of underwriters.

Threat of Loss of Other Business

A common restraint on underwriters is the existence of other policies in the company for the insured. If these other policies are profitable, the insured may threaten to move them to another company if one unprofitable policy is cancelled. Sometimes the threats are idle; many people do not want to lose a good policy or good rate merely to teach the underwriter a lesson. On the other hand, some people do just that. Hence, when there is related business, underwriting decisions must be weighed carefully.

In these circumstances, unlike some of the others, the underwriter is even restrained from reducing coverage or applying deductibles. A policyholder may become irritated over any action. This threat poses a very real problem to underwriters. It is a reason that action is not always taken on unprofitable policies. Most underwriters attempt to practice "account underwriting," taking the entire account into consideration. This means that if the profitable policies can carry the unprofitable ones, no action is needed. This concept often is overworked. One borderline policy may be cited as justification for keeping several unprofitable policies. An underwriter must be aware of the threat of loss of other business, and should attempt to underwrite on the basis of the entire account. At the same time, an underwriter must not let the existence of other policies blind him or her to the necessity for taking action in certain cases. The "account concept" sometimes is used as a convenient excuse for the avoidance of an unpopular decision.

Costs of Additional Handling

A different type of limitation on underwriting action is presented by the costs of doing business. It is expensive to have every change and every loss referred to an underwriter. It is even more expensive if the underwriter then decides to reduce coverage, apply deductibles or cancel the policy; these reduce income, as well as increase costs of handling transactions.

Profit of the company is the ultimate concern of the underwriter. If a particular type of referral or action is not economical, it should be avoided. While an underwriter may feel more comfortable in reviewing every activity on every policy and taking every possible action, all of this may cost more than the resulting savings.

Part of the problem is in measuring costs and results. While the expense of handling is easy to measure, the reduction in losses is difficult or impossible to measure accurately and the relationship seldom can be reduced to dollars and cents. Still the underwriter should try to determine each of these factors and to take the course that produces the greatest overall profit. This may include permitting clerical employees to handle certain routine changes and certain types of losses, without referring them to an underwriter. It may also include taking less action to reduce exposure in favor of continuing the present policy until renewal. When the renewal date is not too far off, and if all renewals are referred to an underwriter, these decisions, to miss referrals or avoid action, often are wise.

Reunderwriting programs also are expensive, but are sometimes necessary in order to correct a block of policies. Before such a program is started, however, careful review should be made to ascertain that the expected results will justify the expense.

In summary, an underwriter is not always permitted to take desired action. Even if the action is taken, an underwriter may find it more judicious to exercise restraint and should weigh carefully the probability of loss, the possible size of a loss, the ultimate consequences of taking action, and all related factors. All of these enter into the selection from the available alternatives. Finally, action must be taken that will accomplish the best results toward maintaining a profitable book of polices.

QUESTIONS FOR DISCUSSION

1. If underwriting of new applicants is performed properly, why should underwriters be concerned with further consideration later?
2. Give examples of the types of changes which may be made on policies, after they are written.
3. What underwriting actions may be taken after a loss is reported?
4. (a) List and describe 4 groups of policies which might be reviewed by an underwriter.

   (b) What underwriting action may be taken on groups of policies?
5. Explain 4 types of limitations which are imposed on underwriters and which may restrict their actions.

40

Underwriting Renewals

When a policy is approaching its renewal date, the underwriter has new opportunities for making decisions. Another term will be approximately the same as the first term of new business, but the underwriter now has the benefit of experience under the policy upon which to base a decision.

Casualty insurance is usually written on either a six-month or annual term. Fire insurance sometimes has a term of three years, but annual policies are most common. Even on three-year fire policies, almost all are payable annually, and the premium date can be used as a time for an underwriting evaluation, if desired. Most underwriters, however, consider renewal to be the time when one policy expires and another one needs to be issued, if the coverage is to continue.

Continuous policies are used by some companies. These policies do not expire, since they have no stated term. Coverage is continued by the payment of a premium amount, which may be adjusted at each billing period. The premium periods usually are for six months or one year, although shorter or longer periods may be used. Continuous policies generally are used when electronic billing machines are used to issue invoices, because a major benefit of this type of policy is the economy which can be realized by machine handling. This fact makes it more difficult to underwrite renewals, because the file is not actually taken from the drawer or file section and handled for renewal billing. The electronic machines automatically prepare the billing. Therefore, an underwriter who wishes to underwrite renewals must take positive steps to do so, such as obtaining a list of policies before renewal and gathering the files for those to be reviewed.

Some policies are term policies which are renewed by certificate. Related to them are those which can be renewed by a billing notice which, in itself, is a form of renewal extension; many different types are used. All are modifications of either term or continuous policies, often combining features of each. The important advantages of each group are these:

- Term policies. The contract may be amended at renewal; more limited contracts may be used, if these are the ones being issued on new business. Classifications may be changed and retention may be adjusted.
- Continuous policies. Economies can be achieved by preparing only an invoice at renewal, not a completely new policy.

The differences between term and continuous policies, as well as modifications of them, are of little concern to a desk underwriter. While there are important differences from a legal standpoint, as well as from the expense factor, the underwriting itself is almost entirely the same.

Underwriters use the word *renewal* to apply to all policies. Technically, a term policy expires and may be renewed. A continuous policy has a premium due date and must be cancelled if the underwriter does not wish to continue it. Renewal certificate policies generally expire and are renewed by certificate. From a practical standpoint, therefore, all policies are renewed or not renewed insofar as the underwriter is concerned.

RENEWAL PROCEDURES

The renewing of a policy is a mechanical function, so specific procedures need to be establised if underwriting review is desired. Continuous policies often are renewed by data processing methods, while the renewal of term policies can be accomplished by the mailing of a renewal policy from the clerical section. A few types of policies need new information on exposures and methods of computing premiums, but even these can escape the underwriting process if desired. Thus, renewal of an insurance policy does not necessarily involve underwriting.

However, underwriters for most lines consider the renewal to be an ideal opportunity for reevaluating the risk. In effect, a new contract period is starting and the underwriter should be aware of the conditions of the risk. But, while the underwriting of renewals is important, it is not automatic. The methods of referral are explained next, followed by the underwriting considerations and the steps taken in arriving at decisions.

Referral of Renewals

Underwriting cannot be applied to renewals, unless the file is referred to an underwriter well in advance of the expiration date. Different methods of referral are used on term and continuous policies, and the time element is important if proper underwriting is to be conducted.

Term policies. A term policy must be prepared and handled at renewal with the same detail as a new policy. In many lines, this means that rating information must be secured. Some companies also determine in advance if the renewal policy is desired by the producer or client. The policy must be taken from the files for these purposes well in advance of the expiration date.

The underwriter should require, as a part of renewal procedure, that the file be referred for any underwriting decisions. The time at which this is done will depend upon the handling of the line. If more information is to be secured, referral to the underwriter should be delayed until the facts are received. If no further requests for information are to be sent, the file should be referred to the underwriter before renewal procedures are started. In any case, referral should be made at a date which is early enough to permit the underwriter to secure any information desired, and to complete the underwriting process before the renewal policy must be mailed.

Continuous policies. Policies which are continued by the mailing of a premium billing or a renewal certificate seldom are handled by clerical employees. Most companies employing these types of policies have established automatic billing procedures, usually with computers. The policy files often remain undisturbed. Even if new information is needed, the computers may be able to handle the data without referral to a clerk who must secure the file.

Underwriting renewals on these policies is more of a problem because no one handles the file. There is no opportunity, therefore, to automatically refer policies to underwriters. As a result, policies may remain on the books for years with no reference to an underwriter. It is not safe to assume that these policies have no problems and thus need no underwriting review. Perhaps there have been no losses, or an insufficient frequency of losses to cause a referral to underwriting, but this does not mean that there are no underwriting problems. Acceptability rules change frequently. Policies which are acceptable today may be unacceptable next year. While these risks may not have suffered losses, there is an increased possibility of future losses, if the new rules are prepared correctly.

An underwriter who is concerned about this situation must take positive steps to review policies before renewal. Perhaps not all policies need to be reviewed, but only those with specified characteristics. As a matter of fact, the renewal time affords an excellent opportunity to reunderwrite groups of policies, as was explained in the previous chapter.

When an underwriter desires to review some or all policies of a class or type before renewal, procedures must be established to have these files referred. The method of establishing the procedure will vary by company. A list of all policies which are ready for renewal may be sent to the underwriter. More effective on most lines is a list of all policies with specific characteristics. The underwriter may request all of these policies to be taken from the file and referred, or the underwriter may review the list first and indicate those for review.

Many different handling procedures are possible. The important point is that an underwriter will not see these files at renewal, unless positive steps are taken to secure them. If this is not done, at least on a selective basis, the underwriter will have lost an excellent opportunity to review previous actions and to take any corrective steps needed.

SECURING INFORMATION

An underwriter cannot apply any judgment to renewal policies, unless more information can be secured than was available during the previous evaluation. There is no point in reviewing the same information because, logically, the same conclusion will be reached. This is true whether the policy was received during its term because of policy changes or losses, or whether the underwriter has not seen the file since the original decision on the new application.

Sources Available

A number of sources are available for securing information at the time of renewal. The most important are these.

—Producer. The producer may be able to secure valuable data for the underwriter. In fact, on policies written by producers who represent many companies, the policy may not be renewed unless the producer so requests. Such producers may prefer to place the coverage in another company for the next term. In these cases, the underwriter can take no final action on the renewal until he or she hears from the producer, although the underwriter may review the file and inform the producer if the policy can be renewed or if it must be placed elsewhere. In cases when the producer tells the underwriter that the client would like to renew the policy, the underwriter may insist upon certain current information being furnished by the producer. This may be in the form of a complete application, or it may be concerned with answers on a special renewal form or even answers to specific questions.

With other producers, the company automatically mails the renewal policy or continuation form. In such cases, the producer may be asked by the underwriter to furnish specific facts that will be helpful in underwriting the renewal. It is uncommon to use applications or forms for this purpose, although this could be done, and may be the practice on specific lines by some underwriters. The usual practice, however, is to ask for current information or answers to specific questions which the underwriter sends to the producer.

—Questionnaires. Some companies send questionnaires to their policyholders in advance of the renewal date, soliciting current information. The questions usually relate to rating factors only, but they may involve underwriting considerations. This type of direct questioning of the policholder generally is limited to those companies writing through employees or exclusive producers, and to the mass lines of personal automobile and fire. However, questionnaires could be used on any line by any company.

Since questionnaires frequently ask for rating information only, the answers may not be referred to an underwriter. However, good underwriting practices require that referrals be made of all items which might affect acceptability. There is no need for an underwriter to review answers which involve only rating, but care must be taken to identify those answers which also are of interest to underwriting. For example, the addition of a youthful driver on a family automobile policy may affect the rating and a rating clerk could handle the change. However, the underwriter may be concerned with the driving record of the youth and may want to review the file before renewal is offered.

—Policy records. Perhaps the most important source of information is the record shown in the policy file. An underwriter should consider the experience which has developed, before offering renewal.

Losses are the primary object of interest. If the underwriter finds that losses are too frequent or too severe, nonrenewal of the policy may be indicated. Changes made in the policy are also important; they may indicate instability and they do increase handling costs. At the same time, frequent changes may indicate a growing, expanding business, and an underwriter may be pleased to renew such risks. Even the payment record of the policyholder may be a factor; an insured who is slow to pay bills, and often makes partial payments only, may be in financial difficulties and thus be a questionable risk from an insurance standpoint.

Many of these factors are called to the attention of the underwriter as they occur. Losses and policy changes may all be referred, too. The value of reviewing the file at the time of renewal is twofold: (1) some referrals may have been overlooked or not referred to the underwriter, and (2) the entire picture of the risk can be reviewed, rather than a single transaction. While it is true that every referral should cause an underwriting review of the entire file, it is not always accomplished. The underwriter naturally is more interested in the details of the transaction; if a noncancellation law applies, the underwriter may not take the time to review the entire file because of a realization that the policy cannot be cancelled in any case. What the underwriter should do, of course, is to review the file and set it up for nonrenewal, if that is the decision, but this may not always be done.

For these reasons, most underwriters review the information in the policy file before offering renewal. The method and procedures used are different by line and by company, but in principle, policy information should be evaluated in advance of renewal.

DECISION-MAKING ON RENEWALS

The underwriting process of decision-making that is used on new business will also be used on renewals. In effect, the underwriter is evaluating the risk, and should follow the proper steps in arriving at a decision.

The first step is to secure information, as was explained previously. When the facts which are pertinent and available are received, the underwriter should develop alternative courses of action. These alternatives may include such steps as a renewal with no change, a revision in the contract or rate classification, an adjustment in the retention, or nonrenewal. All of the alternatives available on new business or policies in force are available on renewal.

A decision must be made at that point and action taken. As on new business, it is imperative that a decision be made. The renewal, or notice of nonrenewal, must be mailed by a specified date in advance of the expiration date. The exact number of days may vary by line of insurance and the processing system used, and it may be specified in a state law for noncancellation. The underwriter must know the deadline which applies. When that deadline arrives, a decision must be made and action taken even if certain desirable information has not yet been received. As on new business, the underwriter must act on the basis of the facts available. An underwriter does not enjoy the luxury of postponing the decision until every shred of available information has been received and analyzed.

After a policy is renewed, the underwriting process continues its cycle. Results should be checked by the methods described in the preceding chapter. Corrective action must be taken if it is indicated. If no intervening underwriting is performed, the process may be repeated when the next renewal is approaching.

In summary, underwriting renewals follows the same principles and the same general procedures as other underwriting. The goal remains the same: to write and renew as much profitable business as possible. The underwriter does not review renewals to see if any can be nonrenewed. Rather, the underwriter reviews them with the aim of renewing as many policies as possible on the same basis as before. When this is not a good move, a good underwriter attempts to find alternative means of renewing the policy, possibly with some adjustments which will indicate that the risk will be profitable. In any event, the policy will be nonrenewed only if no alternative means of renewing it can be found.

QUESTIONS FOR DISCUSSION

1. Why is the renewal of a policy considered to be a good opportunity for underwriting review?
2. Explain these alternative systems for handling the term of a policy, and give the underwriting problems of each:
   (a) Term policies
   (b) Continuous policies.
3. Describe the important sources of information which are available at the time of renewal.
4. How does renewal underwriting compare to the underwriting of new applicants?

41

Assigned Risks and Involuntary Pools

Insurance companies are required to accept some risks they otherwise would not accept voluntarily because laws in all states require the writing of specified lines on a mandatory basis. While underwriters have limited authority to take action on these risks, some authority usually is given. In any event, underwriters should be familiar with mandatory plans, even if they are given little control. As an integral part of the insurance business, underwriters should know of their existence and their general outlines, as well as how their daily decisions affect these plans.

Reasons for the adoption of these assigned risk plans are complex, and they are so inter-related that they are not clearly distinguishable. However, they are discussed under five headings: sociological, political, legal, insurance changes and competition.

SOCIOLOGICAL

Pressures have increased in recent years to require the furnishing of all rights and privileges to every person, regardless of race, age or economic status. Insurance is one of those rights which allegedly is denied to certain minority groups. The aim of sociologists is to assure that every person can purchase insurance if it is so desired. This is the aim, even though some of these persons are not insurable in the sense used by underwriters. Insurance is not to be denied because of poor driving records, physical impairments, poor condition of the property, lack of ability to read and write English and similar characteristics. The theoretical approach ordinarily permits declination of those risks which are truly not insurable or "not entitled, in good faith, to insurance." In practice, few risks may be declined.

Furthermore, price becomes an object of attack. It matters not that a trained underwriter feels that a surcharged rate is needed to avoid an underwriting loss on the policy or class. The statement is made that such handling creates groupings which are too small, thus violating the law of large numbers. This concept has been carried to the extreme of requiring an "affordable rate," presumably meaning a rate the applicant can afford to pay or perhaps desires to pay.

The application of these concepts to insurance can have only one result: the good risks subsidize the poor risks; or, to put it another way, the relatively well to do majority must subsidize the poorer minorities. In this way, sociological principles become intertwined with insurance principles.

POLITICAL

Minority pressure groups make their wishes known to legislators, too. This is the method by which the sociological principles can become implemented. Yielding to these pressures, state legislators enact laws which require the establishment of plans to assure that insurance coverages are available to everyone.

These laws can take many forms. They may require the establishment of a system of assigning distressed business to companies. They may force the creation of a pool to which every company must belong and write policies. Minority groups, low-economic groups, foreign-extraction groups, elderly citizen groups, or even groups of above-average homeowners in brush or windstorm areas — these are but examples of those who bring pressures upon the legislators. These groups often are organized and vocal. They are able to overrride the feelings of the majority when the latter are less deeply involved. These are the ingredients of legislation. The net result of political pressures are laws which require the furnishing of insurance to all applicants.

LEGAL

Involuntary plans are needed to carry out the express will of other laws. From a legal standpoint, some laws would be ineffective without these plans. The primary example is the passage of financial responsibility laws. These laws apply to a person who has become involved in an automobile accident resulting in bodily injuries or property damages in excess of a specified amount. Such person must then furnish evidence of an ability to respond and pay damages if requried to do so. Failing to provide such evidence, the driver's license may be revoked.[1] The limits may be $10/20/5, or $20/40/10, or even higher, and few people can meet the financial requirements without insurance.

The purpose of the financial responsiblity laws is to assure that most people carry

---

1. Even this requirement has been liberalized somewhat. In the case of *Bell vs. Burson, Director, Georgia Department of Public Safety, 1971 C.C.H. (Automobile) 7009,* The U.S. supreme court held that the license of an uninsured motorist involved in an accident could not be revoked for failure to show financial responsibility until the driver was shown to be at fault. A number of states have since amended their laws to provide that no license may be suspended until a hearing is given to determine if there is any possibility that judgment will be made against the uninsured motorist.

insurance, and most innocent victims will be reimbursed for their losses. This purpose cannot be accomplished if large segments of the population are unable to purchase insurance. It matters little if the inability to do so is attributable to the age, record, or condition of the applicant — which results in a denial of insurance by underwriters — or is the cause of premiums which are beyond the ability of the applicant to pay. In any case, if a person cannot secure insurance, the purpose of the financial responsibility law is avoided.

The solution to this dilemma is to enact more laws requiring every person to secure insurance. However, there are legal difficulties which involve such matters as denying freedom of contract, requiring concerted action and agreeing on price. The legal position is that the new law is necessary in order to carry out the purpose of the previous law.

INSURANCE CHANGES

In recent years, insurance has become vital to the average American family. As family and social structures change, insurance becomes more of a necessity and less of a luxury. The trend away from an independent rural existence to an inter-related urban life has resulted in a greater dependence on insurance. Close living conditions have caused more accidents, creating a desire for insurance to pay for the economic losses from those accidents.

All of these changes have made insurance more important to people. Thus, they are affected more strongly when access to insurance is denied them.

COMPETITION

The tremendous competition among insurers has led to rates which are inadequate for some risks. At the same time, refinement of rate classifications has been carried to such a degree in some lines that the rates for the poorer risks are almost prohibitively high. Rate regulation has played a part in developing inadequate rates, because insurance departments sometimes yield to political pressures and refuse to approve rate increases. The result of these activities is rate inadequacy and declination of certain risks because the rates are too low. Those who are rejected are likely to apply pressures to legislators to develop a means of providing insurance, and at a "reasonable" rate.

For these reasons, assigned risk plans (commonly referred to as automobile insurance plans) and involuntary pools are established. Ordinarily they are required by state laws, though at other times, they are required by order of a state insurance department, or they are the result of indirect pressures brought about by governmental agencies.

AUTOMOBILE INSURANCE PLANS

The earliest and largest of the plans are the automobile insurance plans. They were originally called "assigned risk plans" because the applicants are assigned to the companies. However, it was felt that a stigma attached to the name, so the names were changed to "automobile insurance plans."

These plans were originally designed only for personal automobile risks. Later, many plans expanded into commerical vehicles in order to accomodate the taxicab companies and truck risks which were finding it difficult to get insurance in the normal market.

The number of automobiles written in these plans varies with the market conditions in the voluntary market: up during a "hard" market, and down when "soft." Thus, in the late 1970's, 7.8% of the auto market in the United States was in the involuntary market, and the figures dropped to 5.9% in 1985. The five states with the highest shared-market premium volume accounted for nearly 75% of the writings in this market; they are, in order, New Jersey, Massachusetts, New York, South Carolina, and North Carolina.[2]

Historically, automobile insurance plans have been unprofitable. During the 10-year period of 1973 through 1982, the "shared market" (the newest term for these plans) caused an underwriting loss of nearly $5.8 billion. (In 1982 alone, the loss was over $1.1 billion.) In that 10-year period, New Jersey and Massachusetts together accounted for a loss of $3.4 billion, which is 59% of the total of all states.[3]

The procedures used by automobile insurance plans are fairly simple. Application is made through a producer to the plan's office. These offices exist for each state, since the laws are enacted by the states, although neighboring states sometimes combine their operations for purposes of economy. The plan's office then sends (or "assigns") risks to companies, in rotation. The company determines acceptability and rate classification, sends a rate quotation, and operates like a regular insurance operation after that. The company mails the policy, collects premiums, pays losses and performs all of the ordinary insurance duties.

These mandatory plans have been established by laws in each state in order to assure that every driver can meet the requirements of the financial responsiblity laws. The law establishes the basis for spreading the risks among companies, with the spread not precisely on the basis of other premiums because no pooling of results is required. Rather, each applicant is assigned to a company, in rotation, with the companies that write more business receiving more assignments.

This system works in personal automobile insurance because of the relative homogeneity of the risks. The worst risk which is acceptable under the plan is not much worse that the best risk forced into the plan. At least, this is true if limits of coverage are kept relatively low. The large volume of risks also tends to assure that the experience of each company is not too different from that of others.

Automobile insurance plans are governed by committees composed of representatives from insurance companies. Thus, within the framework of the laws, the administration is directed by the companies.

Although these plans have been unprofitable, it would be a mistake to assume

---

2. "AIPSO Facts 1985-86," Automobile Insurance Plans Service Office; Johnston, Rhode Island, pp 17, 27.

3. "1984-85 Property/Casualty Fact Book," Insurance Information Institute, 1984, p. 42.

that insurers have opposed them. Quite to the contrary, companies have urged their adoption because an assigned risk plan is the lesser of several evils. Legislatures, faced with a necessity of finding a means of assuring that the purposes of financial responsibility are met, may adopt one of several alternatives. One is compulsory insurance; companies generally oppose this route because of the tremendous enforcement problems and attendant expenses. Another is a state fund which writes insurance in competition with private companies; insurers oppose this solution because of the difficulty of competing with a nontaxpaying governmental agency and the historical tendency of state funds to expand their operations. Still another possibility is to adopt a different plan for spreading the risk as explained later in this chapter; these alternatives appear to be less desirable for automobile risks because of the administrative costs involved. The final solution, therefore, is the creation of an assigned risk plan which companies support as an alternative to the others.

Characteristics of Plans

Several types of operations have been used for automobile risk plans. They are known as Plan A, Plan B, Plan C and Modified Plan B.

Plan A — The original type of operation for automobile insurance plans has become know as Plan A. Applicants are offered only basic limits of liability insurance, those which comply with the financial responsibility laws of the respective states, along with uninsured motorists and medical payments coverages, when these are required by state laws.

Under Plan A, each company uses its own classification and rating structure. In addition, specified surcharges can be added for stated factors. The advantage of this system is the ease with which it can be handled by each company, since the basic rating structure is identical with that being used on regular business. The major disadvantage is the element of chance which becomes involved in the rating; a producer who submits several applications for coverage hopes that one of the applications is assigned to a company which uses deviated rates. This variable rating plan is politically unpopular because some assigned risks are forced to pay more than others who are similar, merely because of the luck of the assignment.

Plan B — This plan was devised to eliminate some of the undesirable features of Plan A. Policy provisions, classifications and rates are uniform for all companies. This means that every assigned risk under this plan pays the same premium as others with similar characteristics and coverages, regardless of the company to which they are assigned. Assignments and assessments are made on the basis of car-years for private passenger nonfleet risks and surcharges range anywhere from 10 to 150%. Other types of vehicles are subject to the individual rate filings of companies writing them.

Plan C — The limited coverages offered to assigned risks came under attack next. Pressures increased to offer the same coverages as were available to regular policyholders, particularly medical payments coverage and the physical damage coverages, and a method of paying premiums on installment rather than in advance.

Arguments pro and con were debated at length. In favor of expanding the coverages were those who claimed that most companies would not write these coverages for risks whose liability was written through the assigned risk plan. These risks, it was argued, were denied the added coverages simply because they were assigned risks. If they could get the coverages, they must pay exorbitant rates through substandard companies. Many people wanted these coverages, and some found them essential if they owed money on their cars. For these reasons, it was argued, the other coverages should be offered to every assigned risk.

The principal argument against the addition of more coverage for assigned risks was the desire to maintain the original purpose of the plans: to assure that every driver could secure insurance which would permit him or her to meet the requirements of the financial responsibility laws, thus protecting innocent victims of automobile accidents. Almost every automobile owner could purchase the material damage coverages if willing to pay the required premium. To make coverage available through the assigned risk plans would be to require other insureds to subsidize the poorer risks. This step, as well as the furnishing of these coverages to the few who were such poor risks that they could not obtain insurance at any price, was felt to be a completely different subject than the stated purpose of assigned risk plans.

Political pressures were brought to bear in favor of expanding acceptability and coverages. As a result, Plan C was developed and adopted in most states by 1980. Generally, companies are required to offer assigned risk applicants increased limits of liability, medical payments coverage (when liability insurance is also provided), comprehensive and collision coverages and a method of paying premiums on an installment basis. This plan requires the participation of insurers that only write the physical damage coverages, too. However, all of these additional and broader features are available only to applicants of private passenger nonfleet automobiles.

Modified Plan B — This plan includes essentially the same features as Plan C, but does not require the participation of insurers that write only the physical damage coverages. In other words, this plan is used when liability and physical damage coverages are to be written in one policy by one insurer. Those states that permit different insurers to write the liability and physical damage coverages generally are subject to Plan C.

Assignment Participation. In the early years of assigned risk plans, participation was based on the premium dollars of automobile insurance written. Under this system, a company writing at rates lower than the average received fewer assignments than a company writing at bureau or surcharged rates.

A change has since been made to base the participation — not upon premiums — but upon the number of automobile units insured by each company. While this method is felt to be more equitable by many, the position of a company obviously depends upon whether it writes at deviated, bureau or surcharged rates.

Credit for Voluntary Writings. A provision since adopted by most states encourages the voluntary writing of youthful driver risks. (This class, commonly called class 2, has a higher frequency of losses than other classes.) Companies commonly refused to write these risks, forcing them into the assigned risk plans. Many persons in the insurance industry felt that this was an unfortunate development which could alienate a large proportion of the future citizens of this country. Therefore, the "class 2 supplement" was an attempt to cure this problem. Each company gets credit against its participation in the assigned risk plan for the class 2 business which it reports as having written voluntarily. Credit is based on premium dollars, not on automobile units. Theoretically, this provision should cause most companies to write the less desirable, higher rated youthful drivers. As a matter of practice, there is serious doubt that many underwriters will accept such risks solely to get credit for voluntary writings. However, company policy may take this possibility into account, and thus some relief for the assignment may be realized.

Expanded Governing Committees. Proposals have been made to expand the governing committees of assigned risk plans. Most of the original plans used five members, generally selecting the larger companies. A mandatory spread among the companies that belong to the various trade associations was used. Pressures arose from various sources to expand the governing committee to include representatives of smaller companies, producer groups and the public. Some states have now made changes in the governing committees.

Underwriting Responsibilities

Automobile underwriters are given limited authority for handling assigned risk plans. As the acceptability requirements are reduced, less underwriting is required, but some is still permitted. A few characteristics may make applicants unacceptable. Underwriters must analyze each application to see if it is acceptable or not, under the rules of the applicable state plan.

Most plans provide that an annual policy will be issued to assigned risks, with two renewals permitted if the risk is still acceptable. Underwriters are given authority to decide if the risk is acceptable for renewal, within the limits specified in the plan. Furthermore, at the end of the three-year period, the underwriter may decide to renew the policy and thus gain credit for an assignment. The policy will be renewed if the risk appears to be average or better for assigned risks. If it is below average, the underwriter will inform the producer that the risk must be resubmitted to the plan for a new assignment. Thus, while risks are assigned to companies for handling, very little underwriting is permitted. Still, enough judgment must be exercised to remove the handling from merely a clerical function to one that should be handled by underwriters.

OTHER AUTOMOBILE PLANS

The disadvantages of the assignment procedure used by the Automobile Insurance Plans have led to the adoption of alternative plans in a few states.

Joint Underwriting Association

Under the assignment system, some insurers render service which is considered to be less than expected. Also, the fact that losses are not shared has caused some dissatisfaction on the part of insurers.

The JUA is one solution aimed at correcting these deficiencies. Losses are shared equally by placing all premiums and losses in the Association. Each insurer shares in the net result in proportion to its voluntary premium writings in the state.

Servicing of policies is conducted on behalf of the JUA by Servicing Carriers. Usually, several large companies are selected for this duty. They are paid a stated percentage of the premium to cover their expenses.

Uniform rates and policies are used. They only direct expenses of the Association are those required to apportion the results among the member companies.

Underwriters in the voluntary market are not involved with the JUA. Only those who underwrite for a Servicing Carrier are involved, and they must comply with the rules of the Assocation. Usually, very few risks may be refused coverage.

Direct Writing Pool

It is but a short step from a few Servicing Carriers, or perhaps just one, under a Joint Underwriting Association, to the establishment of a pool which handles all of the servicing. This avoids the occasional criticism of the efficiency of Servicing Carriers, and also sidesteps the question of the correctness of the fees paid for servicing the policies.

A Pool operates just like an insurance company. It issues the policies, collects the premiums, and pays losses. Its net profit or loss is distributed among all carriers in proportion to their voluntary premiums in the state.

This concept has not been adopted by any state for automobile insurance. It is used extensively in property insurance, as is explained in the next section.

Reinsurance Facility

The newest concept which has been adopted by a few states for automobile risks is the Reinsurance Facility.

Under this organization, each primary carrier is required to accept all, or virtually all, applicants. A few underwriting rules are permitted in some states, subject to the approval of the Insurance Commissioner. Otherwise, each applicant must be written.

Then the underwriter may cede some of the exposure to a Reinsurance Facility. Sometimes, all of a ceded risk must be reinsured. Under other programs, the underwriter may retain a portion of each risk. Ordinarily, an insurer may not cede in the aggregate more than a stated share, such as 30%, of the total automobile insurance written by that insurer.

The primary insurer services the risk completely. The premiums, losses, and loss adjustment expense are reported to the Facility for its share of each risk. The net profit or loss of the Facility is distributed to all insurers in the proportion to their voluntary premium writings in the state.

Under this approach, underwriters have little, if any, opportuntiy to approve or decline applicants. However, careful underwriting is needed to select those risks which are considered to have too high an exposure to loss, and to cede them to the Reinsurance Facility.

State Fund

Maryland established a state fund mechanism. Although private insurers do not participate directly in the fund, they are required by law to subsidize any losses from its operation, and may then charge the cost back against their own policyholders.

PROPERTY FAIR PLANS

Involuntary pools for property risks are much more recent, having developed only since the late 1960s. Most of them are called FAIR plans, and are designed to handle specific market problems. FAIR is an acronym for Fair Access to Insurance Requirments. The basic purpose of the FAIR plans is to provide a means of writing fire insurance on risks unable to secure coverage in the normal market because of riot expenses.

The first real evidence of a riot problem occurred in Watts, a portion of Los Angeles inhabited largely by minority racial groups, in 1965. A riot in the summer of that year caused insured losses which totaled almost $40 million. Newark, Detroit, and other cities suffered riots in the next few years, with insured losses equaling about $67 million in 1967 (1966 was fairly quiet), and $79 million in 1968.[4]

By 1968, many risks in the so-called urban core areas of most major cities were encountering difficulty in securing fire insurance. Underwriters were reluctant to write property which appeared to be subject to such unexpected catastrophes. Fire policies had insured against riot losses under the extended coverage endorsement for many years, with negligible losses from that peril. Accordingly, very little premium was allotted to the riot peril. Suddenly, losses in the millions were occurring with no end in sight, and companies became alarmed that high losses might deplete their surpluses. Their only course of action, therefore, seemed to be to stop writing insurance or to secure adequate reinsurance.

In desperation, the companies turned to the federal government for help, and Congress passed the Urban Property Protection and Reinsurance Act of 1968. Under this act, the government offered insurance against catastrophic riot losses. Most companies purchased this protection, although deductibles were substantial and initial premiums were high.

The companies were forced to pay much more than the riot reinsurance premiums, as they soon realized. One additional price was the requirement that each state must reimburse the federal government for a share of each riot payment made under the reinsurance program in that state, if the state wanted the companies to be able to purchase the reinsurance within that state. These state layers often were insured with the companies, placing a share of the burden back on them.

By far the greatest price was the requirement that each state establish a FAIR plan, if the companies were to qualify for riot reinsurance within the state. Hence, FAIR plans became the name used by most of the 28 plans (26 states, plus Washington D.C. and Puerto Rico) which werre established to write fire insurance for risks which were unable to secure insurance in the normal market, ostensibly because of the riot hazard. A basic provision of all plans was that no applicant would be denied coverage without an inspection and an explanation of the deficiencies which make

4. "I. I. I. Year-End Review," *Underwriters' Report,* (January 8, 1970), p. 17.

the risk ineligible. (The following discussion deals with the types of coverages written, the method of distributing the risks and the anticipated future of the FAIR plans.)

Coverages Written

The state FAIR plans differ in eligibility, as well as with the perils written.

Eligible Property. Most plans offer insurance for both personal and commercial risks. While farm property is excluded, manufacturing risks sometimes are eligible. Some plans write risks wherever located in the state, while others restrict eligibility to certain geographic areas.

Perils. Fire and extended coverage are required to be written on all risks. (The Federal Insurance Administration was given considerable authority under the act to specify minimum provisions of the plans, if they were to qualify the state for federal riot reinsurance.) Vandalism and malicious mischief was required later, while some states even offered other coverages, such as glass breakage. Pressures have grown for the offering of homeowners policies, and several states have required this in their FAIR plans. Crime insurance, added to some plans in 1971, is discussed in the next section of this chapter.

Distribution of Exposure

Several different methods of distributing the premium, losses and underwriting results are used. Some states started with one method and then changed to another. To understand this aspect of the problem, it is essential to differentiate between personal automobile and property risks. In personal automobile, as was explained in the previous section, risks are quite homogeneous; the best risks are not very different in exposure from the worst risks. Each policy can suffer a loss equal to the financial responsibility limits, but none can suffer larger losses (except where recent expansion has occurred). Property risks are comparatively heterogeneous. One risk may involve a $2,500 dwelling contents policy, the next a $75,000 dwelling and contents policy, and the next a $1,500,000 commercial policy. It would be grossly inequitable to assign these policies in rotation to participating companies.

Still another problem with fire insurance is the retention limit of companies. A company might retain only $25,000 at any one location, and its reinsurance treaties may exclude risks assumed under pool or assignment. Such a company obviously could not accept large commercial risks. In fact, few companies could accommodate the $1,500,000 policies which are eligible in most plans.

Recent Developments

The concern about riot losses decreased, with the end of the big-city riots in the late 1960's. Eventually, the federal government withdrew its riot reinsurance program because of low participation by the insurance companies. However, the FAIR Plans were then insuring a large number of properties, particularly in the inner cities, many of which would probably have difficulty in securing adequate insurance in the normal markets, except perhaps with surcharges. The state laws were soon changed to require the continuation of the FAIR Plans, and no indication exists that they will be phased out in the foreseeable future. Thus, these Plans became a classic example of a program which was established to meet a specific need, but which became permanent fixtures even though the original problem has long since disappeared.

In 1983, the FAIR Plans reported writings which totalled about $25.3 billion.[5]

OTHER PROPERTY POOLS

A number of other property pools are in existence; most of them are involuntary, but a few are voluntary. Examples of them are discussed briefly in this section.

"Voluntary pools" are those established by companies in order to achieve better loss control or a better spread of risk. Since their purpose is not sociological, they must be differentiated from the involuntary pools that are used to help solve social problems. These pools are discussed in Chapter 42, since they are designed primarily to handle jumbo risks.

The term "involuntary pools" is used to designate those pools that have been established by law or governmental decree and to which all companies of specified types must belong. These are pools which have been established under the guidance or pressure of insurance commissioners. (Some of these technically are voluntary, but most companies have felt that the pressure is so great that they have little choice.) Whenever the term "pool" is used in the balance of this chapter, it refers to involuntary pools.

Involuntary Property Pools

Examples of involuntary pools that have been established to write property lines include:

Florida Sinkhole Reinsurance Association. Certain areas of Florida are subject to land settlement because of "sinkholes," which are "subterranean voids created by the action of water on limestone or similar rock formations," to quote from the approved form used in Florida. Dwellings subject to direct loss by collapse from this peril must be offered this coverage by all property insurers in the state, which may then reinsure the exposure in the pool, to which all property companies writing in the state must belong. Provisions are made for uniform rates and deductibles, as well as maximum amounts that may be ceded to the pool.

Texas Catastrophe Insurance Association. Three hurricanes within the decade starting in 1962 caused devastation along the Gulf Coast in Texas. These losses caused a tightened market for all types of fire insurance in the counties which bordered on the Gulf of Mexico. In 1971, the state enacted legislation which created this association. It writes only windstorm, hurricane and tornado coverages, subject to special rates. Companies are permitted to exclude these perils from package policies, as well as from fire policies written with extended coverage. However, a credit is allowed for voluntary writing of the specified perils within the designated counties.

Similar Beach Plans have been established in other states in the hurricane areas, all in an attempt to make windstorm and hurricane coverages available to property owners in the beach or coastal areas who are unable to secure such insurance in the

5. "1984-85 Property/Casualty Fact Book," Insurance Information Institute, 1984, p. 45.

normal market. Practically all real and personal property located in designated beach areas are eligible in North Carolina, South Carolina, Georgia, Florida, Mississippi and Louisiana, as well as in Texas. All provide for sharing the catastrophe exposure among all companies operating in the state. The seven Beach Plans reported a total of $6.4 billion of insurance in force at the end of 1982.[6]

Brush Fire Pool. Certain areas in California are susceptible to catastrophic losses from brush fires. This brush, called chaparral, is highly volatile during the dry season, endangering homes built in the brush areas. Disastrous fires in the 1960s were followed by a restriction in the market for fire insurance in the brush areas. Special surcharges promulgated by the bureau were of little help from the standpoint of market availability. Legislation enacted in 1968 created a pool to write brush risks within the designated areas. This pool was begun only a few weeks before the FAIR plan to write risks in urban core areas was created. The two were combined, so the California FAIR Plans writes brush risks, as well as risks in urban areas.

Crime Insurance. In 1971, the federal goverment started to write, on direct basis, burglary and theft coverages in states where the Federal Insurance Administration had determined that a market problem existed. However, it did not write in those states where other arrangements had been made to assure market availability. Several states indicated a preference for handling these coverages themselves, so the FAIR plans were expanded to write crime coverage. The threat of federal writing remains, and the state plans must conform to the requirements of the federal government if the state plans are to remain the exclusive writers of these perils, along with the normal market, of course.

The federal crime program is similar to the federal flood program which started a year or so earlier. A servicing company is designated for each state. Rates are different from those used by the insurance industry; in crime insurance the federal government uses the term "affordable rates," with the inference that these may be inadequate but will be subsidized. Requirements for protective devices under crime insurance, and building codes under flood insurance, are part of the program. At the inception of the program, federal crime insurance was written in 10 states and the District of Columbia.

By the mid-1980's, the number of policies in the federal crime program had declined to such a low number that the Federal Insurance Administration recommended that the program be terminated. The proposal became involved in politics and Congress has kept the program alive by periodic extensions. If it is terminated, some states will probably adopt programs to handle this coverage, perhaps through the FAIR Plans.

THE ROLE OF UNDERWRITING

Where involuntary pools are in existence, a question always arises about the

---

6. "1984-85 Property/Casualty Fact Book," p. 45.

role of underwriting under regular policies. Underwriters must give thought about their relationship to the pools. The discussion in this section is not concerned with the underwriting of risks in the pools. Rather, this relates to the handling of risks which might be written in the pools, unless an underwriter accepts them as regular business.

Two different approaches can be used by underwriters. One considers that pools should be used as a last resort, and that underwriters should attempt to write every risk, even borderline risks in order to keep the volume of business in the pool at a minimum. The other approach is to assume that the company will get its share of all pool risks and this will avoid a concentration of losses, so every borderline risk should be declined and directed into the pool.

The first approach is the rugged individualistic approach. It will be used by those who feel that the insurance industry should handle its own problems without appeal to government. It assumes that a company should expect losses on a class of business, and that other companies will do likewise as the preferable alternative to governmental intervention.

The second approach is a more cautious one. It recognizes that some risks will be written by the pool in spite of the efforts of companies to write them in the normal market. This means that a company will have its share of those risks. Any additional risks which it writes voluntarily will increase the chance of a large loss in the event of a catastrophe or a loss. This approach leans toward writing only the best risks voluntarily and using the pool for others, on the theory that this is the reason the pool was created in the first place.

The decision between these alternatives ultimately is made by the management of each company, of course. Underwriters should be guided, in the absence of specific directives from management, by the principle of achieving a profitable distribution of risks. An underwriter should secure information which is available, and make a decision based upon the facts. From an underwriting standpoint, a substandard risk will not be accepted solely on the basis of its sociological problems. On the other hand, an underwriter should be aware that if the pool grows too fast, further political pressures are likely to be brought about.

"Dumping" is a term used to denote the cancellation of policies with the expectation that the risks will end up in a pool. Dumping is deplored by politicians and others who are concerned about the social implications of a large pool. Underwriters and other industry people also deplore dumping because it transfers to the pool those risks that should be written in the normal market; the problem is that most companies will not accept a borderline risk which has been cancelled by another company. The basic problem, therefore, is one of definition. No one will deny the right of an underwriter to cancel or nonrenew an individual risk which is causing loss problems; to expect otherwise is to end the right of insurance companies to operate at a profit. On the other hand, few would defend the practice of cancelling an entire block or class of policies, knowing that most or all will be written by no one but the pool. Most actual cases fall between these two extremes, so determining whether the action constitutes dumping or not depends upon the viewpoint of the individual.

The underwriting of risks, new applicants, or existing policies, which might be placed in pools, is another of the areas which cannot be specified with precision. The judgment factor, an essential part of underwriting, must enter into the decision. An underwriter will have little difficulty if aware of the principles of underwriting, including a necessary social consciousness and company policy on the subject.

The relationship of underwriters and pools in the property lines is still undergoing changes. It is essential that each underwriter be aware of the various factors involved, the types of pools which are available and the attitude of the company. Only in this manner can the company, the industry and the public be properly served.

QUESTIONS FOR DISCUSSION

1. Explain the sociological and political pressures that have led to the establishment of involuntary methods of writing insurance.
2. How does competition increase the need for some type of assigned risk plan?
3. Discuss the major criticisms of automobile assigned risk plans.
4. What are the differences between automobile and property lines which cause different mechanisms to be established for handling residual risks?
5. What are two approaches which underwriters can follow in handling risks which might be written in pools?

42

Underwriting Jumbo Risks

Different underwriting practices are used for large jumbo risks than for the regular risks ordinarily encountered. The underwriting principles are the same, but handling practices and approaches are somewhat different.

No standard definition of a jumbo risk is used in the industry. Perhaps the most common practice is to consider a risk to be jumbo if the total annual premium is $250,000 or more. These risks often are multistate or multinational in their operations. The terms "special account" or "national account" are commonly used.

Large, hard-to-place risks often are written by special markets, rather than in the ususal primary insurance companies. One category of these markets is called by several names: "surplus lines," "excess lines," and "non-admitted." Producers with special licenses are permitted to write risks in companies which are not admitted to do business in the state, as a means of maintaining a market for large, difficult or unusual risks, including those requiring or desiring broader coverages than are available in the admitted companies.[1] Another market category is the Exchanges formed in New York, Illinois, and Florida to write risks which might otherwise be written overseas in Lloyds of London or in other foreign markets. In the Exchanges, underwriting syndicates write as non-admitted insurers.[2] Still another category of these markets is comprised of "captive companies," which are owned by one or a group of non-insurance companies for the purpose of writing insurance for the parent and perhaps for others. All states permit these companies to write insurance, but the captives usually are based in such off-shore places as Bermuda and the Cayman Islands. As these captives expand, they can greatly affect the traditional patterns of commercial insurance.

---

1. For a more detailed discussion, see "Risk Management Manual," The Merritt Company, Vol. 2, p. 243.
2. "Risk Management Manual," Vol 2, p. 250.

Many insurance companies which write jumbo risks have established special risk departments to handle them, and underwriters in these separate departments are able to give more attention to the complex insurance needs of these large risks. At the same time, underwriters are relieved of other duties, and are often excused from meeting production requirements. The scope of underwriting duties is narrowed somewhat when a separate department is established for jumbo risks.

Almost all insurance requirements for jumbo risks are combined under the special risk department. Basic property and casualty lines are handled by these separate underwriters, too. Many companies exclude, from this handling, such lines as bonds, officers and directors liability, and employee benefit coverages, feeling that these are handled more effectively by specialists.

The underwriting practices of special risk departments are discussed in the next section of this chapter, followed by an explanation of some of the voluntary pools that are in use today.

UNDERWRITING PRACTICES

Three purposes of underwriting jumbo risks are present for every risk:

- To accept those risks that can reasonably be expected to produce a profit.
- To assist the producer in establishing a good insurance program for the client.
- To coordinate activities with other departments in the company as a means of providing proper service to these accounts.

No standard approach is used on jumbo risks. Coverages may be nonstandard, rates may be subject to negotiation, and commissions to producers are determined separately for each risk. Competition is a major factor, with extreme competitive pressures being present at each renewal. Additionally, the underwriter must be prepared to make concessions in rates, forms, commissions and every other aspect of the insurance.

While package policies may be used, they are of less value to jumbo risks than to smaller risks because large clients can obtain rate and coverage advantages normally associated with packages by using regular or tailormade policies. Possibly a more realistic approach is to think of jumbo risk underwriting as account underwriting. The underwriter views the entire account as he or she weighs the alternatives, and it is immaterial if a package policy is used or not.

Loss control is a major factor in writing and retaining a jumbo risk. The underwriter must work closely with the claim department in controlling losses, as well as with the loss control department. Together, these departments may be able to develop quality control or protective devices which will control losses. Since premiums are usually computed on some type of retrospective basis, loss control will result in lower premiums which, in turn, will improve the chances of retaining the account. At the same time, extra coordination is needed in the claim field, because some large risks insist that all claims must be paid; it is fatal to continuance of the account to deny a claim.

Different types of services are desired by jumbo risks. Some want more than others. Differences may be present in the loss prevention and inspection services, in the types of statistical reports furnished to the policyholder, and in the type of claims handling. Naturally, the premium will vary according to the type of service desired.

Underwriting jumbo lines is a specialized field. However, it is really a combination and adaptation of the underwriting practices used on separate lines. The principles of underwriting are unchanged. Company practices vary, with some desiring to write jumbo risks while others are not anxious to secure many of them. The most important consideration, for companies and underwriters alike, is that there is no magic in sheer size; a jumbo risk which is improperly underwritten can be unprofitable, the same as any other line. In fact, a large dollar loss can be incurred in a short time on a jumbo risk, so careful underwriting is essential.

Highly Protected Risks (HPR) form a particular class of business which is handled by special risk departments. A few companies, plus several insurer organizations, offer broad property coverages at reduced cost to the large firms having certain superior underwriting characteristics. These HPR clients are required to have effective loss control programs, and are subject to extremely selective underwriting.

VOLUNTARY POOLS

Jumbo risks often are written or handled by voluntary pools. In effect, these pools are the special lines, or large risk, departments of the member companies. This type of handling permits the concentration of expert underwriters and other specialists for handling jumbo accounts without the tremendous expense which otherwise would fall on each company if it were to establish its own department.

Two of the most important of these pools are:

Industrial Risk Insurers — The former Factory Insurance Association, a stock company pool, consolidated with the Oil Insurance Association in 1975 to form Industrial Risk Insurers. Now not limited to stock companies, it provides worldwide underwriting, claims, and loss prevention services for the approximately 45 member companies. Property insurance, both on fire and package policies, is written to include business income insurance and property under construction. Originally, IRI wrote only Highly Protected Risks (HRP), but now competes across the entire property market. The Association issues the policies, participates in loss control, and supervises loss adjustments, working directly with the producers.

IRM Insurance — Several of the direct-writing mutuals have combined for the purpose of writing property coverages on large risks. They write only superior industrial, mercantile, and institutional risks which are well-constructed and well-protected. They have developed a property policy which expands the "all-risk" concept for HPR clients, even to the point of including Boiler and Machinery exposures under the broad "all-risk" portion, rather than with separate own conditions and exclusions.

Other associations are in existence for specified lines. Aircraft pools have been formed to supply capacity for large risks and to permit member companies to enjoy the benefits of skilled specialists without incurring the expense necessary to establish their own departments. Other pools have been formed for oil-drilling and other problem classes.

Underwriters in companies do not handle these risks, in most cases. The underwriting is performed by the pools. In those cases where underwriters do process applications and share exposures through the pools, specific instructions ordinarily are given.

Pool risks may be part of an account handled by an underwriter. For this reason, underwriters must be aware of the general provisions of the pools in which their companies participate, so that they are able to take into consideration the pool aspect of each risk. All underwriters should consider all aspects of risks upon which they make decisions — this includes exposures placed through pools.

QUESTIONS FOR DISCUSSION

1. Why are special risk departments often used to handle jumbo risks?
2. State the 3 purposes of underwriting jumbo risks which are always present.
3. Why is the account concept a better approach than package policies for jumbo risks?
4. Why is loss control for jumbo risks an important factor for both the policyholder and the company?
5. Describe 2 voluntary pools which are used for jumbo risks.

43

Preparing Reports

An important auxiliary duty of underwriters involves preparing reports. Not every underwriter is involved in this duty; specialization may require this function to be performed only by specific underwriters, by supervisors, or by a staff department. Still, these reports are prepared by the underwriting department and they are used by underwriters. Therefore, every underwriter should be familiar with the types of reports which are prepared by the company.

Some reports are formal, highly structured documents. Statistics are accumulated automatically, with periodic reports being published on a predetermined schedule. The source of the information is the activity of desk underwriters. In some companies, underwriters keep a count of various types of transactions, supplying the raw data for the reports. In others, an automatic tabulation is made, either by clerical personnel or by electronic data processing equipment. Other reports are informal tabulations of specific items, prepared as a special source of information. These are usually produced from data collected manually.

The kinds of reports underwriters prepare are those which demonstrate the activities and results of underwriting. Many such reports are special, one-time analyses of particular subjects. It may be important to know, quickly, the composition of a sample of business by a particular characteristic, such as the age of all drivers of vehicles. Underwriters can develop such information within a short time, merely by a hand tabulation of one day's work. These reports are informal and not repetitive, and are designed to furnish information which can be used to solve a certain problem or answer a particular question. Underwriters commonly prepare these special reports. However, if only a simple tabulation is needed, clerical personnel could secure the information; an underwriter would then prepare the summary and evaluation.

Many underwriting reports are scheduled and formalized. They may be prepared monthly, annually or for any other period, and may be prepared by other departments, as well as by the underwriting department, depending upon the organization and size of the company. Some reports even may be prepared by the actuarial department, others by the claims department, and still others by the reinsurance department. A large company may have a separate statistical department which prepares all reports of this nature. Regardless of the source of these reports, they are mentioned in this chapter if they are of the type that measures underwriting results.

The scheduled reports prepared by the underwriting department seldom are prepared by line underwriters. Often, the figures are secured from clerical tabulations or computer print-outs. Then the reports themselves are prepared by staff personnel in the underwriting department or by supervisors. A frequent report requires the expenditure of considerable time, so most companies consign the preparation of it to other than a line underwriter. However, all underwriters may use any of these reports.

PURPOSES OF REPORTS

Reports prepared by underwriting departments may serve three purposes, although some reports serve more than one purpose. Each report, however, fulfills at least one purpose.

1. *Inform Management.* Results of past actions and trends for the future are of great importance to management. Underwriting reports are one source by which this information is given to the officers of the company. Results of past actions are indicated by statistical types of reports. The figures show what has happened. In addition, comments and evaluations by the underwriters will supplement the report and explain what has happened.

Trends for the future may be indicated by projections on charts, or may be shown in separate reports. Special comments are helpful when they are prepared carefully by underwriters. Many companies request an analysis of estimated results for the future. Underwriters can contribute to the knowledge of management by informed projections on the types of reports they prepare.

2. *Check Results.* Reports furnish an opportunity for accomplishing one of the important functions of underwriting, the checking of results. By analyzing reports, underwriters and managers can determine if underwriting is being performed properly. Indications are also given about the type of corrective action needed.

Statistical types of reports are used by underwriters for checking results, too. As various figures are reported and studied, a picture can be developed on the results of the actions that have been taken.

Charts and projections are used to indicate the expected results for the future. The need for corrective action will appear, and the reports and charts will show where the action is needed. By using reports properly, underwriters are able to measure their results quite accurately, and to see where they should be making corrections.

3. *Administration of the Department.* Supervisors and managers use reports as aids in the administration of the underwriting department. Some reports show the quality of the underwriting, while others are more of a quantitative measure.

The quality of underwriting is shown by reports which indicate the results of underwriting decisions. A manager can identify, by area and line, the places where good underwriting has been practiced, as well as the places where improvements are needed. With this information, areas can be pinpointed where more training and education are needed, where underwriters are performing well, and where weaknesses exist in personnel.

The quantity of underwriting is also shown by reports of certain types. Those are the ones which indicate the volume of transactions, the time between receipt of an application and its completion, and similar types. While quantity is not as critical as quality in underwriting, most companies find that a minimum volume of work can be maintained without any harm to quality. Expenses are important to every company, and a certain amount of production is necessary in order to control expenses. Underwriting managers, therefore, use reports to determine the number of transactions handled by the underwriting department. Thus, these reports are used by supervisory people in the underwriting department in the same fashion as in other departments, although with more emphasis on quality and less on quantity in the underwriting department.

TYPES OF REPORTS

Many different types of reports are prepared by underwriters. Each line of insurance has its own types of reports and each company has its own ideas about the types necessary.

One class of report is the spot-check, one-time report. There are so many types of these that no listing is possible. As examples, underwriters may analyze and report on the number of automobile applications showing no driving record for any driver; on the number of truck applications of risks hauling a certain kind of commodity; on the dwelling applications by age of dwelling; on the commercial crime applications where a specified kind of safe is present; and so forth. The same types of reports can be made for risks other than new applications, such as policies in force, policies reporting losses, policies in a given area, etc. The variety is limited only by the kinds of risks and exposures, by the problems and questions which may arise, and by the imagination of those who request the reports. Underwriters initiate some of these reports, while others are requested by other departments. There is really no limit to the types of one-time reports that can be prepared.

Formal reports are much more limited in scope. Each company has a certain number of reports prepared regularly. As mentioned before, some of these reports may actually be prepared by another department, but all may be prepared by underwriters, and all are underwriting types of reports. Although a great variance can exist on the exact reports used by any one company or any one line, the following are typical of all the types of underwriting reports generally used.

Frequency of Loss — A critical measurement of the effectiveness of underwriting is the frequency of loss, computed by the number of losses for a given number of policies in force. Financial reports include the effects of many other functions, but frequency of loss is largely under the control of underwriters.

Frequency of loss reports may be made for any line, but are credible only when there is substantial volume. These reports are of more value in lines such as personal automobile where the frequency is relatively higher than in fire insurance where a comparatively low frequency is common. They are also of more value on coverages where the underwriter has some control; for example, property damage liability frequency is more reliable than bodily injury liability frequency because the latter depends partly on the number of occupants of the other car — a factor the underwriter cannot foresee. Thus, frequency of loss reports are better for some lines than others, and can be divided by coverage and territory only when sufficient volume is developed to give meaning to the figures.

Reports on frequency of loss are used by underwriters and management to measure the effectiveness of underwriters and of underwriting programs. They give a relative measure among offices and territories. They are valuable only in comparison with previous reports, while fairly long periods (such as quarterly or longer) are needed in order to develop meaningful patterns. Frequency figures have definite limitations, but these reports are valuable tools of undewriting if the limitations are recognized.

Severity of Loss — The average amounts paid for claims measure the severity. Frequency and severity must be considered together in order to determine complete results.

As with frequency figures, severity statistics are meaningful only on lines with substantial volume. Averages are worthless with low-volume lines, so severity figures are used principally on personal automobile and other large lines.

The question is often raised about how much control an undewriter has over the severity of a loss. It is true that underwriting has less control than over frequency, and so the latter is used more often. However, the patterns of behavior an underwriter analyzes in making a decision on acceptability should give some indication of the expected severity. It is more than just chance, for example, that one driver of an automobile will cause no more than a bent fender while another will be involved in a head-on collision. Reports on severity of loss, therefore, are prepared and used by underwriters as one measure of the effectiveness of underwriting.

Decline and Cancellation Ratio — The activity of underwriters is measured, in part, by the action they take on unacceptable risks. The declinations of new business are related to the number of new applications to arrive at a decline ratio. Similarly, the cancellations of existing policies are related to the number of policies on the books to get a cancellation ratio.

Underwriters perform many functions other than declining and cancelling policies. Furthermore, the volume of declinations depends upon the quality of business submitted by producers. Thus, these ratios are not absolute in measuring the activity of underwriters.

On the other hand, a certain portion of applications will not be acceptable. The percentage is surprisingly uniform within a line, when allowances are made for territorial differences. The same is true of policies on the books which have deteriorated to the point where underwriting action is indicated. Thus, the efficiency and use of proper judgment of underwriters can be measured by analyzing these ratios.

However, care must be taken to use long enough periods of time to watch trends, more than immediate figures, and to modify the statistics by line of insurance. With these cautions, decline and cancellation ratios can give indications of the activity of underwriters.

Investigation Ratio — The number of investigation reports ordered can be compared with the number of new applications received to give an inspection ratio for new business. Similarly, although ordinarily less meaningful, an inspection ratio can be determined for policies in force.

Various types of inspection ratios may be prepared. An obvious distinction is by line of coverage. Another division can be by geographical territory or by producer. Separate ratios often are computed for reports by inspection companies, reports by loss prevention specialists, motor vehicle reports, financial rating reports, and others. It may be more meaningful to prepare separate ratios for each type of action, but the numbers often become so small that they are not credible, so combinations may be used.

Many companies set rough goals on the percentage of risks they expect to be investigated. While the ratio may vary by line and territory, it is quite uniform over a period of time. The ratio thus gives a fairly reliable indication of the action underwriters are taking.

Separate but related reports can indicate the results of the investigations. The percentage of new and relevant facts reported by each company may be reported; this is commonly called "protective information." Also, the action taken by underwriters following the receipt of inspections may be reported. Various types of reports may be prepared to show information that is helpful to underwriters.

Still other reports may compare the various types of investigative sources and the companies within each type. In this way, underwriters can determine which ones are the most effective. Long range results are better than monthly or quarterly figures, but trends may appear rather quickly. These reports also permit underwriters to point out deficiencies which are developing in the reports from companies, with the desire that corrective action may be taken.

It is obvious that various types of reports could be prepared showing different facts in relation to investigations. Not every company will use all of them, but most of the information is helpful to most underwriters.

Transactions Completed — The number of transactions completed by underwriters might be included in a report. The transactions may be by underwriters, by line, by type of transaction, or by other combinations.

These reports show only the quantity of work performed, not the quality; both are important in underwriting. If there is a choice, quality comes first. However, expense factors are important to insurance companies, and each employee is expected to produce a fair share of work. The number of transactions completed is an indication whether each underwriter is working efficiently or not.

Various types of reports may be produced. A numerical count is the simplest; trends can be determined by watching successive reports. Current figures can be computed as a percentage of previous figures, or in relation to the underwriting department as a whole to see how each underwriter is performing, and so forth. These reports help underwriters to see how they are doing, as well as in helping supervisors. If one underwriter is falling behind in transactions, there may be a need to seek better methods of performing duties, to change the type of transactions handled, or otherwise to find ways to improve productivity.

Loss Ratio — The traditional report for measuring underwriting performance is the loss ratio report. It relates premium to losses, indicating whether the "insurance" portion of the operation is profitable or not. (Expenses and investments are the principal other factors which must be added in order to determine the total results.)

Underwriters usually are held responsible for the loss ratio. However, as has been explained in other chapters, other departments also have a substantial influence on the loss ratio; the actuarial department ordinarily controls rates and the claims department actually pays the claims. Still underwriters are supposed to modify acceptability by the rate level and the claims approach which is used. For this reason, the loss ratio report is commonly used to measure the performance of underwriters.

Loss ratio reports may be prepared by underwriters or by other departments. It is purely a matter of figures in most cases, so a statistical department may be used for the actual preparation of the report. Underwriters, whether they prepare the report or not, may make changes in the type of report issued. Loss ratios may be computed on the basis of earned premium and incurred losses, or written premium and paid losses. (Underwriters may decide to remove from the report all losses in excess of a certain size, such as over $10,000, in order to avoid distortions by large losses or catastrophes.)

Loss ratio reports are used in many ways. The use to which they will be put has an influence on the type of report prepared. One example is to measure the profitability of an insurance line to see if changes are needed. Another is by state or local area, to see if rates or underwriting rules need to be revised. Still another is by producer, to measure the quality of risks being submitted and to ascertain if changes in authority or rules are indicated. The timing of publication of reports may also vary, depending upon the need for timely information, the credibility of the figures, and the labor needed to produce the report. Thus, a report by line and by state might be prepared monthly, one by a producer's total business on a quarterly basis, and one by each geographic area or by each line for a producer only on an annual basis.

In summary, reports of many types may be prepared. Those mentioned are illustrative only. The types actually used by a company will depend upon the needs of the company, the desires of management, the facilities available for preparation, and similar factors. Underwriters often request or prepare reports for their assistance in the analysis of their decisions.

QUESTIONS FOR DISCUSSION

1. What are the 3 purposes of reports prepared by underwriting departments?
2. Give examples of one-time reports used by underwriters.

3. (a) Describe "frequency of loss" and "severity of loss."
   (b) Which of these is a more critical measurement of underwriting effectiveness?
4. Of what value to an underwriter is a report of transactions completed?
5. (a) What is a "loss ratio"?
   (b) Which departments can influence the loss ratio?
   (c) How is a loss ratio used?

44

Coordination Of Underwriting

Underwriting is but one of the functions of the modern insurance company. It is essential for the efficient operation of the company that the underwriting department coordinate its activities with other departments and it is also essential to proper underwriting that every underwriter recognize the degree of coordination required.

A basic problem of insurance is the opposing viewpoints of the various departments of a company. Underwriters are in the middle of these differences, so they must recognize the relationship of these factors.

Rates, claims, and acceptability are inextricably entwined. If rates are so low that an inadequate margin is included for expected losses, acceptability must be tightened. If claims practices are more liberal than anticiapted, acceptability must be restricted; if liberal acceptability is practiced, claims settlement practices must be tightened in order to avoid rate inadequacy. The three major "insurance" departments, actuarial, claims, and underwriting are so closely related that a change in one must result in a change in another — if a proper balance is to be maintained.

The underwriting term "acceptability" translates to producers as "sales." When acceptability is tightened, sales are lost. Producers want liberal acceptability, low rates and liberal claims settlements. A producer who loses a risk to a competitor, often will critize the underwriting, rates or claims.

When some producers select applicants more carefully than others, they often are referred to as "good field underwriters." Such producers may receive better treatment from underwriters, in the sense that their applications are scrutinized less closely. This is a recognition that such producers are a help to the underwriter, performing a portion of the selection process.

Some producers also are able to wield considerable influence because of the size of their accounts. A large producer with a sizeable volume of premium is in a position to demand special consideration for clients of the agency. Sometimes this involves special forms, an unusual coverage, or simply the acceptance of a borderline risk. All of these cases are called "accommodation risks." They are handled in a fashion which accommodates a good producer. In return, the underwriter hopes to retain the good will of the producer and to secure more of the business. In fairness to the producers, it must be pointed out that they receive pressures from their clients, often with a threat to place all of the business elsewhere if a particular problem is not handled satisfactorily.

Other departments may also help underwriters. Producers can supply valuable information on individiual risks, coorindating their selection activities with those of the underwriters. Producers also can give information concerning market needs and the products of competitors. Claims adjuster can notify underwriters of problem situations they encounter on individual risks, as well as to furnish data to underwriters on trends in repair costs and legal decisions.

These situations indicate the necessity for coordination among the various departments. Their goals are not always the same; in fact, they may appear to be in opposition. In the long run, however, their objectives must be the same, but short-range goals and the methods of achieving them are in conflict, many times. The corporate objectives must be met, and the activities of each department must be coordinated toward that goal.

Two other types of coordination are described in the balance of this chapter. One concerns the need for coordinating the available services when acceptance of a risk is being considered. The other involves the coordination of staff underwriters with other departments in the performing of general functions which are important to the company.

COORDINATION FOR SERVICE

An underwriter must be concerned with more than the acceptability of a risk from the standpoint of the usual underwriting criteria. It must also be certain that service will be available to the risk. If it is not, the client will soon be dissatisfied and the producer will be unhappy. Even such underwriting requirements as periodic audits may not be met at later dates, if the client and producer decide to be uncooperative.

Three other functions must be coordinated in order to be certain that service is available: sales, claims and auditing. Each of these is explained on the basis of factors which may prevent the rendering of proper service.

Sales

A producer must furnish more service than merely writing the insurance. Policyholders may call at any time, or many times, while the policy is in force for advice, sympathy, help in making changes and reporting claims, and so forth. Most clients are close to the producer's office with no far-flung operations, so no great problems arise.

Some clients operate in many locations and require service at more than one place. For example, a distributor of manufactured goods may have warehouses in several states. Not always is it possible for the producer who is located near the main office to inspect each location and understand its problems.

But when producers have branches in a number of cities, they usually are able to furnish better service than a producer who has only one location. It is not necessarily true that a large producer organization can furnish better service than a small producer, but there is a better chance that this will be true. The underwriter should consider whether the producer is able to render proper service. (Some producers may not even have business in other states, causing problems if property is secured in another state.)

The size of the risk is not necessarily a relevant factor. Some very large risks employ specialists to handle the details, so the producer may need to contact only the home office. Other large risks may have few locations, so service is easy to supply. The greatest problems can occur with medium-sized risks which have a number of locations scattered over the country. An even greater problem exists when such risks are expanding, growing and acquiring new locations frequently.

Here, the underwriter must determine if the producer will be able to furnish satisfactory service, because both the underwriter and client are interested in ascertaining that when service is needed, the producer will be available.

Claims

The proof of a good insurance program is in the prompt, satisfactory settlement of claims. If a policyholder is dissatisfied with the claims activity, no underwriting effort at rates and coverages will keep the client from changing to another company.

Many insurance companies use their own claims department to handle claims. Unless adjusters are available in every section of the country, the underwriter should not accept a risk with locations in every state. Rather, the only risks which should be accepted are those with locations that can be serviced by the claims adjuster.

Other companies use claims companies or services. Even companies with their own claims department may employ outside adjusters for risks beyond their territory. In these cases, the location is not such an important factor. Still, the underwriter should coordinate activities with the claims department to be certain that help will be available if a claim is presented.

Again, the size of the risk is not the main factor. Rather, the distribution of the various locations is most important. Each location, no matter how small, may incur a claim and need help. It is one of the concerns of the underwriter to be certain that the client will be able to get that help when it is needed.

Auditing

Some risks require periodic audit in order to determine proper premiums. Since rating is an important part of underwriting, it is apparent that the underwriting function will suffer if the audits cannot be made.

Some insurance companies employ their own auditors, while others use outside firms. In either case, it is essential that an auditor is available to make the necessary audit. It is also essential that the proper books be available for audit. An applicant cannot be written under an audit type of policy if the books are kept so poorly that an audit is impossible, or if they are not made available to the insurance auditor. The management of the risk is important.

Size is not an important factor here. Large risks often are easier to audit than small risks because they keep better books. More crucial than size are the locations of books and the manner in which they are kept. Underwriters must coordinate their activities with those of the auditors to be certain that proper audits will be made as they are needed.

STAFF UNDERWRITING COORDINATION

Staff underwriters are assigned a multitude of duties, most of which involve coordination with other departments. The staff function is largely one of analysis and recommendation, so the actual implementation must involve other departments.

Some of the staff underwriting activity has been discussed in several preceding chapters. The following are the most important of these; both line and staff underwriting are involved in these, to varying degrees.

—Classification and rating. Staff underwriters work closely with the actuarial department in the preparation of classifications and rates. Staff underwriters may have the responsibility for the distribution of the rates.

—Policy forms. Staff underwriters cooperate with other departments in developing, maintaining, and revising policy backs, forms and endorsements. The physical handling may be assigned to the underwriting department or to another department. Close cooperation among the actuarial, legal, claims and underwriting departments is needed. The relationship with the legal department must be noted; since contracts are legal documents, the help of the legal department is essential. State laws and interpretation by state regulatory authorities must be also considered.

—Reinsurance. Staff underwriters are responsible for at least a portion of the preparation and dissemination of the reinsurance program of the company. Other departments are also involved, often including the reinsurance department, the accounting department and the claim department. The cooperation of several functions is needed to assure that an effective reinsurance program is prepared, and that it is applied properly.

—Acceptance of risks. Although line underwriters perform the actual acceptance or rejection of risks, staff underwriters prepare the outlines of the underwriting programs which guide these decisions. The analysis, promulgation, and dissemination of underwriting programs require cooperation with other departments. Actuarial, claims, statistical, and sales departments are primarily involved, along with underwriting. The experience is analyzed in many ways, such as by coverage, by territory, by class or by producer. Programs are prepared or amended with the intent of achieving underwriting profits without impeding the other objectives of the company. The distribution of new and revised programs to line underwriters, sales supervisors, and producers may be performed by staff underwriters or may be handled by another department.

Since other staff underwriting is unique to the staff function and these actions are a part of underwriting, they are described here.

—Education. Staff underwriters ordinarily prepare educational programs for underwriting and related personnel. Recommendations are made concerning the types of formal training and education which employees should pursue in order to improve themselves and their ability to perform their assigned duties.

Another aspect of education is in the work carried out by engineers and others whose duties include efforts at loss prevention. In these fields, employees are attempting to educate others on the most effective means of preventing losses. In property and casualty lines, these steps can include the installation of protective devices, such as sprinklers or burglar alarms, the use of non-skid materials on floors, regular sweeping schedules, and the like. Road patrols may be used for truck fleets. In workers' compensation insurance, safety programs, safety devices, and other steps are taken in an attempt to reduce industrial accidents and thus reduce insurance premiums, as well as to improve efficiency and morale. (Staff underwriters ordinarily work with engineers and others in the preparation and implementation of these programs.)

—Public relations. Staff underwriters often act as one of the public relations arms of the company. Underwriters serve on committees or boards of trade associations or other groups whose primary purpose is the improvement of public relations. Some of these orgainizations are the Insurance Information Institute, Western Insurance Information Service, the Insurance Institute for Highway Safety, the National Board of Fire underwriters, the American Insurance Association, the American Mutual Alliance, and the National Association of Independent Insurers. While these organizations differ in their goals, most of them attempt to present the insurance industry in a favorable light to the public, and to tell the industry's side of the insurance story. Many of the active workers in these groups are staff underwriters, too.

A similar type of organization is one whose primary goals deal with the prosecution of law-breakers, and then relate the story to the public on who ultimately pays for criminal and fraudulent losses. Two of the major organizations in this field are the National Automobile Theft Bureau and the Claims Bureau Advisory Committee of the American Insurance Association. Staff underwriters serve on the committees of these groups, helping to inform the public that they eventually pay for false and inflated claims through the higher rates which must be charged.

—Legislation. The legal department in a company ordinarily is charged with the responsibility of supporting or opposing legislation which is suggested or introduced in the state legislatures. There are so many ramifications of many bills that the help of specialists may often be required. Staff underwriters may be called upon to advise and recommend on subjects which involve underwriting. In fact, this may be one of the assigned duties of some staff underwriters. When a proposed bill, which appears to involve underwriting, is referred to the staff underwriter, he or she must analyze it and recommend a position for the company to take.

Many companies delegate at least a portion of the legislative activity to their trade associations. The latter maintain close liaison with legislators, so individual companies need not engage in extensive lobbying. Again, staff underwriters often sit in on the committees which determine the position of the association on specific subjects. Most companies continue to maintain some degree of surveillance of legislative activity, because they might wish to adopt a different course of action on some items than the position taken by the association.

Staff underwriters are called upon to perform these additional duties, as well as those specifically related to the underwriting function. Different companies may assign these duties to different levels or even to different departments, but they must be performed. While they are separate from the daily activities of line underwriters, they are essential to the company and must be performed, with staff underwriters often receiving these assignments.

QUESTIONS FOR DISCUSSION

1. Explain the relationship between rates, claims, and acceptability.
2. (a) Define a "good field underwriter."
   (b) Explain the role of producers in selecting risks.
3. How do auditors help underwriters?
4. Discuss 4 major activities of staff underwriters which relate closely to line underwriting.
5. Discuss 3 functions which are unique to the function of staff underwriting.

INTRODUCTION TO PART VIII

THE FUTURE OF UNDERWRITING

Underwriting has been an essential part of insurance for centuries, and the private insurance industry could not have grown and prospered without it. During this long period, underwriting has changed. It started as encompassing all insurance functions; underwriting was insurance in the early days. Then specialization developed as insurance grew, and today underwriters perform only a part of the insurance operation. Other departments have taken over many of the other insurance functions. Still, underwriters need to take these other operations into account, and underwriters also must perform miscellaneous duties that are not necessarily a part of the selection process.

Underwriting will continue to change in the future because the forces of change are strong. In fact, insurance is so deeply entwined in the social fabric that it will be affected by other changes and will itself change.

Underwriting cycles have had an increasing impact upon underwriting, as well as upon insurance in general. Underwriters need to understand the anatomy of these cycles, and must be aware of how the underwriting processes are affected by the various stages of the cycles. Chapter 45 explains underwriting cycles and their impact on underwriting.

Regulation by government is an ever-present, ever-changing factor in the insurance process and underwriting must adapt to regulation. Chapter 46 describes the present role of governmental regulation, its effect on underwriting and the trends for the future.

Clerical functions are an integral part of underwriting, too. They are also a matter of concern to some underwriters who fear that they will become glorified clerks as specialization and automation become more common. Chapter 47 describes some of the clerical functions performed by underwriters, and shows that the future holds the promise the underwriters will be relieved of the clerical functions so that they can spend more time for more decision-making.

Computers represent the epitome of automation. Their rapid development and amazing capacities have raised fears that they will replace the underwriter of tomorrow. Chapter 48 explains how computers serve underwriters — how underwriters use computers. Recent developments in the field of underwriting automation are discussed.

Chapter 49 explores the transfer of underwriting authority to specific producers as one method of achieving better company results.

Finally, Chapter 50 discusses the essential nature of underwriting. Various alternatives to underwriting have been proposed, but none can replace underwriters in the private insurance industry. The last chapter demonstrates that underwriting is basic to the concept of insurance. When all of the miscellaneous details are stripped away, it is seen that underwriting remains the very heart of private insurance. In the future, as in the past, private insurance will survive only if it is served by underwriting — trained, educated, experienced and dedicated underwriters.

45

Underwriting Cycles

Underwriting cycles are not new, but until recently, most underwriters paid little attention to them. The disastrous down-cycle of the early 1980s caught everyone's attention, and it was apparent that underwriters needed to understand the cycles if they were to perform their functions effectively.

For centuries, underwriting was quite predictable. Only the occasional catastrophes were unpredictable. Underwriting profits were realized regularly. Underwriters knew what to expect.

During the first half of the twentieth century, the same pattern continued. Then changes started to appear, slowly at first. Brief cycles of unprofitability were encountered. The social changes which swept across the world had an effect on underwriting, causing minor adjustments in approaches.

By 1980, the changes were so extreme that they completely revised underwriting practices. The impact was great both on experienced underwriters who had learned their trade by years of effort and on those who had studied the principles and practices of underwriting. The principles had not changed, but they certainly needed to be applied in different ways.

We are now aware that the game has changed. Old underwriting practices no longer fit. New practices must be learned. Underwriting, and underwriters, will not survive if they do not adapt to the new realities.

UNDERWRITING CYCLES

Underwriting cycles are composed of periods of underwriting profits or losses. An "up cycle" is a period when underwriting profits[1] are increasing and under-

1. An underwriting profit is realized when earned premium exceeds the total of losses and loss adjustment expense. It is the direct result of the underwriting function, and does not take into account expenses involved in the operation of the business, investment income, or taxes.

writing losses are decreasing. A "down cycle" is the opposite.

The principles of underwriting remain the same through all stages of the cycle. Underwriters need to know these principles in order to perform their function properly. In fact, a strong case could be made for the statement that underwriters can make adequate adjustments to the cycle *only* if they really understand the principles of underwriting.

Underwriting cycles generally are of a short duration. Each phase requires its own type of handling, and approaches which are proper in an up cycle are counterproductive in a down cycle. The problem for underwriters is that if they do not react quickly to changes, they will be making the wrong decisions in many cases. By the time an underwriter has realized what is happening and makes adjustments, the cycle may have started to turn in the other direction. This is not generally recognized because of the short period of time between the peaks and valleys of the cycle, but it was brought dramatically to everyone's attention during the extreme down cycle which started in 1979 and continued through 1985. Longer than any previous cycle, it lasted for seven years.

The only way to be able to adjust to the cycles properly is to know and apply the principles of underwriting. Not only are they constant and applicable at all stages, but they also help underwriters make the right decisions at all times.

Underwriters must first understand cycles before they can make adjustments. This is particularly true as the pattern of cycles appears to have changed, and the insurance industry is well into a new phase.

THE PATTERN OF UNDERWRITING CYCLES

For many years, the pattern of underwriting cycles was quite predictable. There was a period of two or three years of losses, during which underwriting and rate adjustments were made, and profitability returned. Soon, however, rates and acceptability were reduced to secure more of the profitable business, and after two or three years of profits, the cycle again turned downward.[2]

Exhibit 1 shows the pattern of 27 years from 1954 through 1980. The relative stability is quite apparent, although the swings tended to be a little farther from the zero line, particularly on the down side, during the later years of the period shown.

Although it was not recognized for several years, the down cycle which started in 1979 was destined to completely change the pattern. This was not seen at first because the industry was accustomed to cycles, and this one apperared to be just another down cycle. By the time it was recognized for what it was, many companies were

2. A Special Report in *Nation's Business* said this: "Since the end of World War II, property and caualty insurance companies have been on an economic roller coaster controlled by an amazingly predictable profit-and-loss cycle. For two or three years, the business makes a profit. A few years of losses follow. Then the same pattern begins all over again and runs its course of another six-year cycle. Give or take a year, that has been the scenario for 40 years." "Why the Buyers' Market in Insurance," *Nation's Business*, September 1982, p. 51.

EXHIBIT 1
UNDERWRITING GAINS/LOSSES AFTER POLICYHOLDERS' DIVIDENDS PROPERTY/CASUALTY INSURANCE BUSINESS 1954-1980

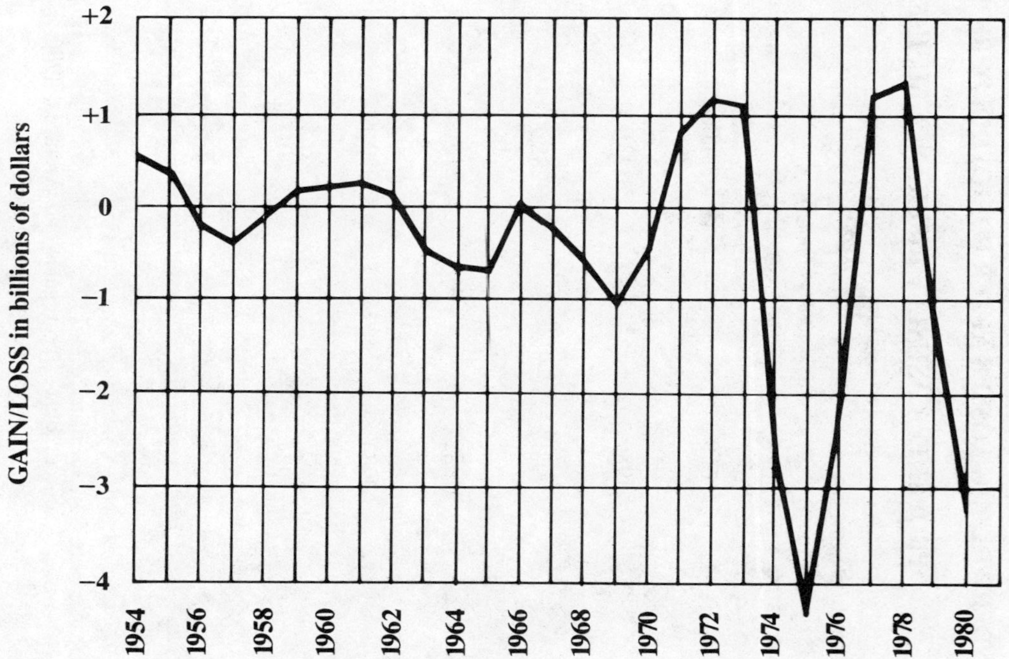

Source: Best's Aggregates & Averages

EXHIBIT 2

UNDERWRITING LOSSES AFTER POLICYHOLDERS' DIVIDENDS

PROPERTY/CASUALTY INSURANCE BUSINESS

1979-1985

(000's omitted)

1979	$ 1,301,000
1980	3,333,000
1981	6,288,000
1982	10,290,000
1983	12,930,000
1984	20,520,000
1985	24,560,000

Source: Best's Aggregates and Averages, 1986
All figures rounded

heading for trouble, and the insurance business was in turmoil.

Exhibit 2 shows the pattern of this downswing from 1979 through 1985.

The enormity of this down cycle is not apparent when these two separate charts are used. By combining them in Exhibit 3, the disaster of this period can be seen.

THE GREAT DOWN CYCLE

This 1979-1985 down cycle was analyzed many times by writers, panelists, and speakers. The causes of this unprecedented depression were explained, new names were created for the phenomenon, and the effects on insurance companies, producers, and clients were studied.

Causes

For the first two or three years of this cycle, observers assumed that the causes were the same as for earlier down cycles. The previous down cycle of 1972-1975 caused a reaction, which sometimes was referred to as the Turnaround of 1976-78. The efforts at turning the results around were primarily directed toward substantial increases in rates and a general tightening of acceptability, but there was also some reduction in the number of producers and in the lines of insurance which companies would write. These measures were applied on both commercial and personal lines, but primarily on the latter.

As a result of the turnaround efforts which started in 1976, the business returned to profitability in 1977 and 1978. When the results improved, the usual reaction occurred. Rates were reduced, more borderline applicants were accepted, and producers were again solicited to write more business.

The expected downturn followed. Observers felt that it was only a matter of a few years before the usual reaction set in, resulting in a reversal of the trend and a new up cycle. When this did not occur and results continued to deteriorate, it became obvious that conditions were different than they had ever been and that new explanations were needed.

A multitude of explanations emerged. While it is difficult to document all of these reasons, the most plausible appear to be these.

1. The supply of money available for risk-taking had increased substantially. Some of this money came from the oil-producing countries, principally in the Middle East, while some was attracted by the strong dollar which offered more stability than many foreign investments. Government-owned insurers from China and Brazil entered the market. A substantial portion of this new money was placed into reinsurance; this depressed the price of reinsurance, which was soon reflected in lower prices for primary insurance.

2. The demand for insurance was reduced. Captive insurance companies were formed by large corporations and industry associations. The tight insurance market following the 1973-75 down cycle, and the accompanying substantial increases in rates, caused businesses to look into the advantages of captive insurers. The tax structure encouraged this trend for a time. These captives wrote the insurance for their owners, and since the latter included some of the largest corporations, the reduction soon began to pinch the insurance companies which wrote coverages for these

corportions. Then, partly pushed by adverse tax rulings and partly by a desire to diversify, these captives began to write insurance and reinsurance in the regular marketplace, further reducing the premiums available to other insurers. For years, the licensing of captives was feasible only in such offshore locations as Bermuda and the Cayman Islands, but legislation in certain states, such as Vermont, encouraged their establishment in this country. As more and more captives were formed, the demand for insurance from the agency companies decreased. The law of supply and demand was working again: with a larger supply of money and no increase in the demand for insurance, the price dropped.

3. Less primary insurance was available. As insurance rates increased, large clients retained larger deductibles, or placed their protection in captives. Higher limits of coverage were insured on an excess basis, but this tended to leave insurance companies with the low-premium, high-exposure layers, hardly the best use of capital for primary companies. The writing of these layers required more expertise because of the relatively-low rates and the chances for large losses, but there was a deficiency of underwriters who were competent to handle these layers.

4. Takeovers of insurance companies by diversified companies caused a change in the approach to insurance by some insurers. Some of these acquisitions by noninsurance industrials apparently were intended to be tax shelters, although that was never stated as a goal. These conglomerates had an incentive to write insurance at a loss, taking advantage of the tax law to reduce pretax losses by tax credits. Independent insurance companies eventually exhausted these loss carryforwards and loss carrybacks, but conglomerates could generate taxable income elsewhere in the organization and continued to accumulate the sheltering deferrals. As a result, sound underwriting practices were abandoned in favor of price-cutting.[3]

5. Insurance companies had accumulated substantial tax credits which could be used to offset losses. Insurers could write business at rates which were guaranteed to result in losses, knowing that the losses would be offset by tax credits before the results were reflected in the bottom line of the financial reports.

6. High interest rates produced returns which could be used to offset underwriting losses. This became known as "cash flow underwriting": the deliberate acceptance of business at rates which were known to be inadequate, in order to secure cash for investments. An interest return of more than ten percent can permit an insurance company to increase surplus, even if moderate underwriting losses occur.

7. Claims reserves were established at inadequate levels. It is impossible to prove that this was a deliberate practice. The cause could have been a failure to foresee the increases in judgments which were awarded by the courts. Perhaps some company managements decided to gamble that the cash-flow underwriting cycle would end, and that rates would be sufficiently adequate to fund the deficiencies when they surfaced. Whatever the reason, inadequate reserves did increase the surplus shown

3. "Skinning the Cat," *Forbes*, April 22, 1985, p. 121.

EXHIBIT 3
UNDERWRITING GAINS/LOSSES AFTER POLICYHOLDERS' DIVIDENDS
PROPERTY/CASUALTY INSURANCE BUSINESS
1954-1985

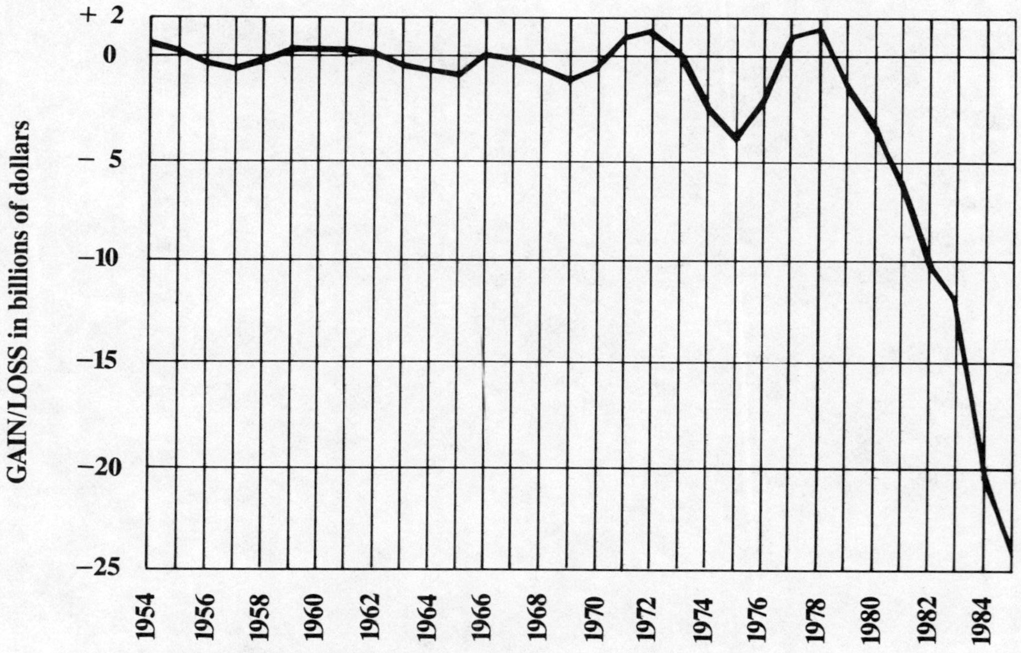

Source: Best's Aggregates & Averages

on financial statements, permitting insurers to write more business and still maintain a satisfactory ratio of surplus to written premiums.

8. A "soft market" was the natural consequence. Producers could secure insurance at rates which were competitive, and could often secure successively lower rates as more quotations were requested. Risk managers of larger customers were likewise able to secure rates which were lower each year, with no regard to losses.

9. All of these factors tended to interact. Higher interest rates tended to attract still more capital into a business which often held money for many years before it was needed as payment for claims. Management, which was urged to secure more cash for investment through insurance premiums, was inclined to distregard proper insurance principles in favor of a program designed to produce premiums, with complete disregard for the long range results of those actions.

Underwriting

The deeper the underwriting loss cycle descended, the more underwriting deteriorated. A basic principle of underwriting is that the premiums should be adequate to cover losses and expenses, and to produce a gain for the insurance company. Only by following this principle can underwriters assure the long-term profitability and growth of the companies.

Efforts were made by underwriters, during the early years of this down cycle, to secure rates which were reasonably adequate. On many applications, the proper rate cannot be determined with precision. Underwriters tended, during this period, to lean toward the low side of the range of rates which appeared to be proper, rather than using the middle, or most-likely-to-be-correct, rate. The applications of the basic principles of underwriting should result in the use of middle or higher rates, not low ones.

As the down pattern continued, underwriters needed to reduce rates even further in order to write business. Competitors were lowering rates and policies could not be written by underwriters who insisted upon quoting rates which were adequate or even close to adequate. During this period, such terms as "creative rating" and "innovative underwriting" were coined. These were merely euphemisms for "inadequate pricing"; apparently there was a desire to pretend that, somehow, underwriting principles had been suspended, and new principles had been discovered.

Insurance companies differed in the instructions which were given to underwriters. Top management, almost without exception, decried the cut-throat rating which was being practiced. Speeches and articles gave assurance that it was "the other companies" which were using inadequate rates; "our company" had no intention of engaging in such practices. Somehow the message became distorted by the time it reached the desks of underwriters. True, some companies tried to follow a pattern of rate adequacy and paid for this by losing a substantial share of the market. The causes of the rate problems were so complex and so deeply ingrained that no one company alone could follow a different course and emerge unscathed. This was not a time when underwriters could successfully "talk themselves out of a problem." No amount of breast beating or telling underwriters to use adequate rates could have an effect on the cycle.

Faced with a need to maintain market share, underwriters reduced rates as much as was needed to attract a proportionate number of clients. Some managers claimed, near the end of the cycle, that some of their underwriters had never learned how to underwrite; they had learned only how to reduce rates below those of their competitors. If this is true, it demonstrates the absolute necessity of extensive training of many underwriters, if insurers are to survive during future cycles.

As a matter of fact, as the up cycle got under way in 1985, examples surfaced where the underwriting was poorly handled. As one illustration, a medium-sized commercial account which was being offered to several companies found that each underwriter demanded different information, some of it quite irrelevant. It quickly became apparent that at least some of these underwriters did not really know what they were doing.

Some observers feel that one of the most significant internal factors which led to the extreme down cycle was the loss of control on pricing. The Insurance Services Office (ISO) and other rating organizations continued to promulgate rates which were adequate. However, many companies deviated downward from those rates in an effort to be competitive, particularly on commercial lines. As company managements decided that the bureau rates were not relevant anymore, this left "the 23-year-old underwriter out in Des Moines trying to figure out where you draw the line when that risk comes up for renewal and the agent says he's got another quote for 30 percent off the expiring rate. All of a sudden there's no benchmark in pricing anymore." The speaker who made that comment went on to say this: "As soon as top management let go of the reins on pricing in that way, all bets were off, and that's really what happened in commercial lines."[4]

THE UP CYCLE

Eventually, inevitably, the down cycle was reversed, and the next up cycle began. The beginnings were seen in late 1984, and were felt throughout the industry in 1985, although the rate increases and tightened acceptability standards were too late to prevent worsened statistical results in 1985.

Several reasons are given for the reversal.

1. The inadequate claims reserves eventually became evident. The cycle did not turn in time for increased premiums to offset maturing claims. State regulators uncovered evidences of inadequate reserves in some major companies and required increases. This strengthening of reserves had an immediate adverse impact on surplus, demanding that premiums be increased (or losses reduced through reduced writings) in order for the company to survive.

2. Tax credits eventually were exhausted. Without this buffer, losses dropped straight to the bottom line, reducing surplus. This had a severe psychological impact on management and also required corrective steps to avoid insolvency.

---

4. Peter Walker, quoted in "Need to Rebuild Underwriting Skills Stressed," *The National Underwriter*, December 21, 1984, p. 31.

3. Investors who had seen insurance as a good investment became disillusioned. They either withdrew their funds or demanded that insurers produce some return on the investments. This shift impacted reinsurers first, because of their international nature; when they started imposing substantial rate increases, this forced the primary carriers into such an unprofitable position that they were forced to start raising their rates. This situation spread through all reinsurers almost overnight, and was a critical factor in the turnaround which started in late 1984.

4. One of the factors which pushed the industry into the need for more premium was the losses from natural catastrophes which reached an all-time high during the first half of 1984. The record figures were roughly double the more typical first-half figures of almost $600 million in all but one of the previous five years.[5]

5. In 1984, the industry's net investment income was $17.6 billion. Since the underwriting loss was $21.3 billion, this left a net operating loss of $3.8 billion. The net operating loss may have marked the need for a turning point, as some experts had predicted would happen.[6]

There are good reasons to suspect that the old pattern of cycles will not return, with two or three profitable years followed by a like period of losses. The cycle which bottomed out in 1985 differed in several important respects from the previous cycles which turned after 1969 and 1975.

1. The underwriting loss was much greater in 1985, totalling 23 times as much as 1969, and almost six times as much in 1975.

2. Surplus dropped in each of these periods, but both of the previous declines were partially caused by the stock market. In 1985, the reduction in surplus was due to operating losses.

3. Personal lines had caused most of the problem in the previous periods, while commercial lines remained fairly profitable. That situation was reversed in 1985, with commercial lines generating astounding losses ($17,643,742) and personal lines being much less unprofitable ($7,096,258 underwriting loss).[7] Commerical lines take longer to reverse the results because they are not class-rated, and they have a longer tail (meaning that the losses tend to be reported later and then take longer to settle).

4. Reinsurers showed a relatively poorer result than the primary market, reversing the pattern of previous cycles. Their experience was so bad that it was stated in late 1986 that "of 130 firms that sold reinsurance in the United States in 1984, about 100 have left the business because they were not making any money."[8] This tighten-

---

5. "First-Half Catastrophe Losses at Record $1.32 Billion," *Smart's Insurance Bulletin*, July 18, 1984, p. 4.

6. "1984 Property/Casualty Results: An Updated Review," *Best's Insurance Management Reports*, April 8, 1985, p. 1.

7. "1985 Property/Casualty Results: An Updated Review and Preview," *Best's Insurance Management Reports*, April 7, 1986, p. 3. (000's omitted)

8. "Insurer Sees State Paying Victims for Some Losses," *Los Angeles Times*, October 21, 1986, Part I, p. 3.

ing of the reinsurance market would obviously have a negative impact on the ability of primary insurers to write business.

Because of these differences, the depth of the underwriting losses in the mid-1980s, and the fact that some of the basic causes of the decline are still in existence, the road to recovery from this seven-year down cycle will not be easy.

The steps which must be taken to start a new up cycle are the same in all cycles and are not difficult to determine.

1. Premiums must be brought into step with loss costs. How quickly this can be accomplished is a matter of debate. There are practical limits to the amount of increase which the market can absorb in any one year. Increases which are too large may generate buyer resistance and more captives. When rates have been depressed as much as they were by 1984, increases to an adequate level are difficult to achieve, and cannot be done overnight; in fact, they might drive good risks out of the market and result in adverse selection.

2. Underwriting must again be practiced. Selection must be tightened on many lines, and risk improvements required. Coverages may need to be restricted in some cases, with the broadest coverages not necessarily being offered to every prospect. Realistic deductibles may need to be imposed.

3. Claims reserving practices must result in adequate reserves. Unless this happens, the cycle will soon reverse itself.

THE ANATOMY OF CYCLES

Underwriting cycles have followed a fairly set pattern. Although the down cycle which started after 1978 was much more severe than the previous cycles, there is no reason to believe that the basic pattern will change.

Starting at the top of an up cycle, insurance companies are profitable. Because of the lag in completing financial statements, it may be some months before management realizes that a profitable period has arrived. As soon as the realization hits, steps are taken to secure more of the profitable business. Aggressive marketing programs are started. Underwriting positions are adjusted to accept and retain more prospects. Rates are reduced.

As the up cycle matures, underwriting standards are lowered still more, in an effort to write even more business. Soon the inevitable happens; losses increase, and underwriting profits disappear.

When management realizes that the business is no longer profitable (again after a time lag), defensive postures replace the aggressive positions. Rates are increased. Underwriting standards are tightened. Marketing concessions disappear, and some companies take drastic steps to reduce the number of producers.

These restrictive steps will result in profits, after a time, and the entire cycle can start over.

UNDERWRITING DURING CYCLES

Underwriting practices cannot be the same at all stages of the cycle. Management is looking for more business at one stage, and caring much more about profitability than production at another stage.

Underwriters are the key persons at all stages. Granted, management sets the direction and gives general instructions. It is how well those directions are carried out that determines if the company will be better than the average of all companies. Underwriters who know how to apply underwriting principles can keep their companies ahead of the competition at stages of the cycle.

As examples of how the principles can be applied by trained underwriters, consider three situations. In each of these, one of the basic steps is inoperative as the result of forces beyond the control of the underwriters.

1. **"Take all comers":** some states have passed laws which require insurers to provide coverage to every qualified person who applies; in auto insurance, this may mean every licensed driver. Underwriters cannot consider the acceptability. The coverage must be reduced or the price increased if underwriting losses are to be avoided. (In practice, most of these states have added another alternative: reinsure undesirable exposures in an industry pool, and use regular forms and rates, thus distributing the inevitable losses among all insurers. This illustrates that most principles can be legislated away, if the lawmakers do not care about the ultimate result.)

2. **Coverage specified by law:** many states require that some coverages be given in exactly the way the state stipulates. An example is Uninsured Motorist Coverage on auto policies; where the laws (often as interpreted by the courts) requiree stacking, intra-family liability, and other provisions which underwriters might prefer to exclude. Since underwriters cannot restrict the coverage, they must tighten the acceptability standards or increase rates, or both.

3. **Prices depressed by competition:** during the down cycle, many (or all) lines are subject to such severe price competition that underwriters cannot consider the adequacy of the premium. As previously explained, an underwriter attempting to secure a premium which could be expected to return a reasonable underwriting profit will be unable to write much business. The solution, by applying the principles, is to be certain that the applicants are acceptable at the specified coverages, and then to attempt to minimize the price deficiency. Underwriters need to realize that the rates will be inadequate, and while they should try to secure more premium, they must live with the inadequacy (unless it is so bad that the net premium is impossibly low).

The basic underwriting principles do not require a complete balancing of these three factors under all circumstances. To attempt to do so could result in a sizeable loss of business. Rather, a realistic balance should be achieved. When price is nonflexible, the other factors must be applied carefully to permit the writing of business without overwhelming underwriting losses. This is how the basic principles must be applied by underwriters who understand them.

Price should never be ignored, nor should underwriters resign themselves to feeling that nothing can be done about prices. On some lines, the net rate is computed by applying credits to the manual rate; the credits may be given for safety programs, management quality, advantageous locations, reduced exposures, employee selection practices, and similar criteria. Judgment is applied to the facts in order to determine the amount of the credit. When rate levels are depressed, underwriters need to apply credits with special care, being alert to the competitive needs but not reducing premiums more than is necessary. On those lines, constant attention is needed on both new business and renewals in order to maximize income but still remain competitive.

When a down-cycle starts to moderate, and competition begins to raise rates, underwriters must pay particular attention to these judgment factors in rates. If old practices are permitted to continue, net rates may well be considerably lower than is necessary to write the business. Underwriters must keep a close watch on the competitive situation, raising quoted rates as much as possible (without destroying the market), in order to help their companies recover from the down cycle. On those lines where rates are fixed but companies have a degree of latitude, such as by deviations, underwriters should recommend adjustments in the rates as quickly and extensively as is reasonably possible, again to increase the premiums to a more adequate level. On all lines, a time when the industry is starting to rebound from a down cycle can be one of the most critical periods for underwriters.

The five basic steps in the decision-making process of underwriting are explained in other chapters of this book. These are the steps which underwriters must follow through all of the cycles, if they are to make their expected contribution to the profitability and stability of their companies.

QUESTIONS FOR DISCUSSION

1. Explain how "underwriting profit" is realized.
2. List at least six causes of the 1979-1985 down cycle.
3. Does underwriting proficiency improve or decline during a down cycle? Explain, and contrast with other stages of a cycle.
4. Can the insurance industry expect future cycles, or will they be prevented? Explain the reasons for your answer.

46

Governmental Regulation

The future of underwriting will be greatly affected by governmental regulation, and underwriters will be limited in their freedom of action to a greater degree than ever before. Some of the limitations will seriously affect some of the basic underwriting decisions, too. Recent changes in regulation leave no doubt that the trend will continue. Both the federal and state governments are increasing their regulation of the insurance industry.

This trend toward more regulation appears to be a general movement in our society. (The deregulation during the early 1980s of specific industries, such as airlines and trucking, appears to be just a temporary reversal of the trend, and may well be changed back in the near future.) The relatively loose organization in economic and social fields is being replaced with a tighter organization at all levels. Insurance is an important element in these fields and inevitably faces more regulation. Since underwriting actions are subject to more control and closer scrutiny than ever before, underwriters must be aware of this trend if they are to understand why regulation is increasing, and how they can adjust to it. Recent changes in regulation at both the state and federal levels are discussed in this chapter, along with the types of limitations which are, and will be, placed on underwriting, and the effects of underwriting.

RECENT CHANGES IN REGULATION

Governmental regulation has expanded rapidly since 1944. In that year, the South Eastern Underwriters Association (S.E.U.A.) decision of the United States Supreme Court specified that insurance is subject to federal regulation. Public Law 15 was enacted soon afterward, giving the states an opportunity to regulate the insurance industry. Since then, regulation of the insurance industry has increased at both the state and federal levels.

State Regulation

All of the states grasped the opportunity presented by Congress and enacted regulatory laws. The most important of these were rate regulations, although the control of forms, deviations and other aspects of the business were included also.

Most states adopted the model rate legislation which was recommended by an 'All Industry'' committee. This approach assumed that "regulation" meant "prior approval" and the laws in most states required companies and bureaus to file all rates with the insurance department, and to receive approval before using them. A few states adopted "file and use" laws, which require filings to be made but permit the use of the rates, unless they are disapproved within a specified time, such as 30 days. A few other states provided for promulgation of the rates by the insurance department.

Only one major state (California) adopted an "open competition" or "no file" law. This law worked so well, particularly in view of the rate inadequacies which were partially caused by difficulties in securing approval of rate increases, that other states changed to this type of law in the late 1960s and the 1970s. By 1980, one state had no rate law, five required no filing of rates, 12 provided for file and use or use and file, and the remaining states used prior approval, or state-made rates. Some of these laws differ by line of insurance, but a substantial amount of insurance now has some type of "open rating", which means that no prior approval is needed.

There was hope that these changes would ease the severe market restrictions which allegedly were caused by inadequate rates. However, the desired improvement in market availability did not automatically follow in every state. Disillusionment caused some states to reverse themselves. It soon became apparent that more factors were involved than just the type of law. The administration of the law was important, along with the political climate, economic conditions, social changes and other complex factors. These other areas soon became targets for further regulation, and these other laws spread even to those states where competitive rate laws were working well.

Underwriting cycles in insurance can affect regulation. After a down cycle which causes large underwriting losses, companies raise rates and tighten acceptability requirements. This results in a "hard market," during which major segments of insurance buyers may have difficulty in purchasing insurance, or can buy it only at substantially increased prices. These groups then complain to legislators and regulators, and increased controls on insurance soon follow.[1]

Rate regulation at the state level has never been uniform for all lines. The pattern previously outlined applies to most lines. Workers' compensation laws are subject to prior approval in every state. On the other hand, some inland marine lines are unregulated in every state. Even in Texas, where the state board sets the rates, county mutuals are exempt from using those rates, thereby enabling them to maintain a market for substandard risks by charging higher rates. This has been so successful that

1. For a more detailed discussion, see Chapter 45.

some of the large nation-wide companies have acquired county mutuals in order to use nonboard rates for certain risks in Texas.

Most of the emphasis on state regulation has been on rates. Most states have regulated rates quite closely, but generally did not regulate underwriting or marketing. This situation led companies to place more emphasis on underwriting actions and marketing restrictions rather than on an accurate pricing structures which could supply the needs of the customers. The inflexibility of the prior rate approval laws, combined with the formalistic or politically-inspired insurance departments which tried to administer some of them, led to restrictions on writings. When attempts at reforms in the rate regulations failed to solve the problems, underwriting and marketing became the targets. (The limitations which were placed on underwriting are explained later in this chapter.)

Federal Regulation

The federal government has been involved in insurance for years. Some of the types of coverages sold by the United States government, or one of its agencies, are these:

1. War risk insurance
2. Crop insurance
3. Social security (old age and survivor's coverage)
4. Mortgage insurance
5. Foreign credit insurance
6. Flood insurance
7. Crime insurance

Generally, regulation of the private insurance industry has been left to the states. However, the movement of the federal government into the riot insurance field caused a type of federal regulation. The federal government offered riot reinsurance to companies with the requirement that they belong to state FAIR plans in states where the reinsurance was desired. The Department of Housing and Urban Development (HUD) then imposed restrictions and regulations on the FAIR plans. Certain coverages were mandatory, inspection requirements specified, statistics and results scrutinized carefully, and other regulations imposed. However, there are limits to the degree of federal regulation which the states will tolerate. In 1979, Congress passed the Holtzman Amendment which added new rate and organizational controls to the FAIR plans. Rather than accept these new controls, five of the 26 states having FAIR plans gave up the right to purchase federal riot reinsurance. The FAIR plans continued to operate, but under state control, not federal regulation. Eventually, the federal riot reinsurance program was discontinued, and all FAIR plans operated solely under state laws.

Another step by the federal government was to offer crime insurance on a direct basis, unless a state organization, like a FAIR plan, offered the coverage in states with market problems. Those states which elected to handle their own needs were subject to further regulation by HUD.

Periodic studies are conducted by Congress into the adequacy of state regulation. Threats are made that state regulation will be replaced by federal regulation.

The automobile problems, particularly of the fault concept, has led to such threats. Serious consideration has been given to repeal of Public Law 15 (the McCarran-Ferguson Act of 1945, which exempted insurance from the federal antitrust laws, if the states regulated the insurance business). The threat continues, but repeal is opposed by most segments of insurance industry, as well as by the states. A more likely development might be revisions in the law which would expand the control for the federal government in specific areas.

Two facts are obvious. One is that the insurance industry will be subject to more regulation in the future. The other is that present regulation comes from both the state and federal governments, and that the only question is which one shall predominate.

State regulation has weaknesses. It results in laws which are inconsistent, contradictory, and difficult to handle by companies operating in many states. It is local, sometimes provincial. Often it is inefficient, politically dominated, underfinanced, and saddled with excessive administrative expenses.

Federal regulation offers consistency and uniformity. At the same time, political pressures will remain, and bureaucratic controls will be at least as bad as those of the states. Federal regulation probably will tend toward less flexibility and thus less experimentation and innovation. Perhaps most serious is the trend toward centralization and strong federal control instead of local control; basic political and social issues are involved in this aspect of the problem.

A reasonable prediction is that federal regulation will increase. It may replace state regulation, or it may be an added regulation. There is little doubt that the tendency will be toward further restrictions on insurance operations.

Underwriters are not concerned greatly with the problem of state versus federal regulation. However, they are affected by regulations which restrict underwriting actions, whether imposed at the state or federal levels, since any regulation which limits the alternatives available to underwriters will have an effect on their performance of duties.

LIMITATIONS ON UNDERWRITING

While governmental regulation has limited underwriting in several ways, most of these limitations apply only to specified lines, but others are applicable to all lines. Every underwriter must be aware of these limitations which have been placed on actions. Furthermore, every underwriter *should* know the trends which are taking place, and the effect which actions will have on the future.

There are five separate classifications into which the limitations on underwriting may be placed:

1. Regulatory guidelines. Insurance commissioners in some states have established guidelines which have the effect of limiting the right of underwriters to cancel policies. Most of these guidelines have applied only to personal automobiles, although a few have been extended to other personal lines. The authority of the commissioner to enforce the guidelines varies among the states; most lean heavily on voluntary compliance. Cancellation guidelines have proved to be only a temporary expedient. Usually, they are soon replaced by laws which are enacted by the legislators.

Other types of guidelines are promulgated by regulatory officials, too. One of these is the prohibition of companies from refusing to write risks in the lower-economic levels; for example, a minimum amount of insurance under a homeowners package policy of $25,000. Another prohibits ceilings which are too restrictive, such as not writing any home with a value of more than $200,000. Still others tend to prohibit low retentions on commercial risks, such as $15,000 on a large market or restaurant, and on ineligible rules which appear to be illogical; illustrations are aluminum siding on homes, military risks for automobiles and schools for fire insurance.

Insurance commissioners usually try to discourage such practices by discussing the situation with individual companies. Occasionally they find it necessary, or more effective, to issue orders specifying the guidelines which companies are expected to comply.

2. Cancellation laws. Many states have enacted laws limiting the right of underwriters to cancel policies during the term. Each law is different, but the most important factors are as follows.

A. Personal autombile policies are most often involved; usually excluded are assigned risks, fleets of five or more automobiles, and vehicles owned or used by garages and service stations. Personal fire policies are involved in some states. Commercial vehicles and property are affected in some instances.
B. A "discovery period" is provided. This is the first period, usually about 60 days, within which the underwriter may conduct an investigation and discover facts about the risk. Cancellation is permitted during this period for any reason.
C. After the discovery period, cancellation is permitted only for specified reasons. Common provisions are nonpayment of premium, loss of driver's license of the insured, fraud or misrepresentation affecting the policy or the presentation of a claim, and a substantial increase in the hazard. Some states permit cancellation for more reasons than others, so each law must be analyzed separately. When cancellation is permitted, an advance notice must be given. Most states also require the underwriter to provide the insured with the reason for cancellation, either with the notice of cancellation or upon request.
D. Nonrenewal is permitted, sometimes with few restrictions. Too, a specified minimum advance notification is required, often with reasons being provided with the notice or on request.
E. The insured sometimes may appeal a cancellation or a nonrenewal, and provisions are established by law for hearings.

3. Nonrenewal laws. Some states have taken the additional step of requiring the underwriter to offer renewals of every policy, subject to specified exceptions. Personal automobile risks were the only line affected by these laws as they were enacted in the first states. The same type of exceptions are permitted as under the cancellation laws. Some states are less restrictive than others, permitting nonrenewal for a specified number of convictions or accidents over a recent period of time, among other reasons. The same type of notification, reason for action, and appeal provisions are used as under cancellation laws.

4. Nondiscrimination laws. Many states have enacted laws prohibiting cancellation or eligibility because of specified factors. These laws are in addition to the rating laws which long have prohibited unfair discrimination in rates without defining what is meant by that term.

State laws differ on the factors which apply. The most common are age, race, color, creed, nationality, sex and occupation. More recent laws have attempted to prohibit discrimination because of the geographical location of the risk, as well as for marital status, "sexual preference," criminal record, mental or physical disability, and moral character. Few, if any, states use all of these factors. It is more common to prohibit discrimination "solely because of the age of the applicant," for example. Underwriters may not refuse an applicant solely because the applicant is under 21 or over 65 years of age, in this example, but they may reject the application if the driving record also is poor. Nondiscrimination laws ordinarily are aimed at personal automobile risks. However, often they are written in such a way that they apply to other lines as well, particularly personal lines and sometimes commercial.

5. Regulation of risk investigation. A federal law contains specific requirements that underwriters must follow when investigating risks. Known as the "Fair Credit Reporting Act," it requires that the subject (applicant or policyholder) be notified in writing that an investigation is being ordered which may involve information concerning the character, general reputation, personal characteristics, and mode of living of the subject. The underwriter must disclose the nature and scope of the investigation, if requested by the subject. If underwriting action of any type is taken as a result of the investigation, the subject must be told of this, and given the name and address of the investigation company.

The intent of this legislation is to permit people to learn of any action that is being taken as a result of an investigation on the file of an investigation company. The subject may then learn what type of information is in the file; the law requires the investigation company to disclose the contents of the file. These steps give a person the opportunity to correct information which is false or misfiled. It is one of the "consumer protection" laws which has been enacted.

TRENDS TOWARD FUTURE RESTRICTIONS

No knowledgeable person is so naive as to assume that governmental restrictions on underwriting have run their course. It may be predicted with absolute safety that the future will bring more regulation and more restrictions. There are three major areas of concern to underwriters where further legislation is expected: cancellation and nonrenewal, discrimination, and the type of liability system used. Each of these deserves a brief look.

Cancellation and Nonrenewal

Cancellation laws are expected to expand until every state has limitations on the right of underwriters to cancel personal automobile risks. Expansion into other lines is also expected; first into personal fire and package lines, and possibly into other personal and commercial lines as well.

Nonrenewal laws will follow more slowly, but will continue to expand. They will follow the same pattern of insurance lines as cancellation laws. These laws are expected at the state level only, with little possibility of federal regulation in this area. As a result of this, the laws will differ greatly.

Discrimination

Nondiscrimination laws are also expected to expand. They will probably follow the same general pattern of insurance lines as cancellation laws, except that nondiscrimination laws may occasionally be applied to all property and casualty lines at the same time.

The federal government may regulate some types of discrimination. It is more likely, however, that state laws will be the major factor in this field. Again, this means that many differences will exist.

Automobile Compensation Plans

The attack on this type of liability system used by the insurance industry has centered on automobile risks. Various proposals have been made to change the liability system. These plans have had various names, such as automobile compensation plans, basic protection plans, first party protection plans, and no-fault insurance. The term "no-fault" is becoming the most common name for these various plans.

The intent of the proposed legislation is to change the automobile insurance policy from one which protects the liability of the policyholder to others, to one which pays the out-of-pocket economic loss of the policyholder and others in the car. It is alleged that the present tort system delays settlements, clogs the courts, pays too much for small injuries and too little for large injuries, and depends too much on the quality of the attorneys representing each party. Proponents of no-fault plans also hope for reductions in insurance premiums.

The principle of the automobile compensation plans is that each injured person collects from his or her own insurer, regardless of fault. This is, of course, the principle used for years under medical payments coverage, as well as for comprehensive and collision damage coverages to the automobile and workers' compensation insurance. So far as medical costs are concerned, these plans are an expanded, mandatory medical payments coverage, usually up to a stated amount. To this is added protection against loss of income at a fixed percentage of wages with a maximum amount stated, and a stated amount for "replacement services" to cover the costs of hiring help to perform the household duties ordinarily performed by the injured person. Some plans provide a schedule of payments for dismemberment and funeral expenses. Payment for "pain and suffering" is disallowed under some plans and is limited to a fixed percentage of medical costs in others. Arbitration of small claims ordinarily is required.

The principal opposition to these compensation plans comes from those who believe that persons should be responsible for their own acts. The old system of liability preserves this principle, albeit transferring most of the monetary penalty to an insurance company. This belief is so strong that most plans which have been proposed have retained the fault concept if injuries or "economic loss" exceed a stated amount, such as $3,000. The no-fault concept would apply below that amount, and the old liability concept above it. Experience proves that such a dollar "threshold" (above which a suit can be brought) could easily be breached in virtually every accident involving bodily injury. The newer approach has been to use a "verbal threshold," with suit permitted only in cases of "death, disfigurement, or serious impariment of a bodily function", or similar words. Studies have shown that insurance costs remain approximately the same under liability or no-fault laws, but the latter does provide more equitable payment to some victims of automobile accidents.

Various states, as well as the federal government began studying these concepts around 1970, and then efforts were made to enact legislation in almost every state. To date, 23 states have enacted some form of no-fault automobile insurance, but only 14 of them contained restrictions on the right to sue. The other nine merely mandated medical payments coverage with wage loss and substitute services coverage. Nevada became the first state to repeal a no-fault law.

Congress has considered adoption of a federal no-fault law. None has been enacted, but strong pressures were brought for federal "guidelines." Under these, any state which did not enact a law which met or exceeded the federal provisions, would have the federal rules imposed. As proposed, the federal standards were more severe than those of almost any state.

Most of the emphasis under the no-fault proposals has been on bodily injury. Only a few states have included property damage liability or material damage.

EFFECTS ON UNDERWRITING

These limitations imposed by governmental regulation cannot help but have an effect on underwriting. An underwriter finds alternative courses of action to be restricted, and also finds that actions cannot always be taken that appear to be the best from an underwriting standpoint.

Cancellation limitations, whether by guidelines or laws, seriously affect underwriters. Since an underwriter may not cancel a policy which produces poor experience, risks must be selected much more carefully. Any risk which has an exposure too great for the price charged for its group, must be declined. The only alternative is to find some other way to write the risk, such as by using deductibles, by restricting coverages or by reducing limits.

Guaranteed renewable laws are even worse from the standpoint of the underwriter. Not only must a poor risk be kept for the balance of the term, now it must be kept for years. Eligibility must be tightened still further. The temptation is to use very restrictive rules for eligibility, but the underwriter soon realizes that these may conflict with the production and other goals of the company.

Other types of regulatory guidelines can be tolerated, generally. Sometimes the rules hurt on a pet subject of an underwriter, but seldom are they unreasonable. An imagintive underwriter can usually find means of maintaining a profitable book of business. Perhaps tighter insurance to value limits are needed on low-valued homes, and higher deductibles on high-valued residences. Retentions often can be increased without endangering the profit picture. Some risks which appear on unacceptable lists may be acceptable after careful investigation and evaluation, perhaps with surcharges, deductibles, exclusions of problem portions of the risk, and similar actions. Since some risks may be susceptible to improvements which would then make them acceptable, underwriters may need to request more loss prevention reports.

Discriminatory practices may appear to be needed at times, but they must be stopped when laws are passed. A fire underwriter may know that most risks in a certain geographical area are poor risks because of overcrowding, code violations, slum conditions and absentee owners. The underwriter knows that there will be a few risks which are reasonably well-maintained and are acceptable, but the expense of finding those few does not warrant the result. However, the passage of a non-discrimination law means that now the underwriter must inspect all risks and write those which are acceptable. Those who pass the laws consider that each person whose home is properly maintained should be able to obtain insurance, and not have it denied merely because the home is located in a depressed area.

The same principle applies to automobile underwriters when they are considering age, sex and other factors. All underwriters can find the same means of complying with the laws.

Not to be overlooked, however, is that discrimination laws may increase expenses, and often do so. They should not affect the loss ratio, if underwriters follow the proper principles. Most regulators do not expect underwriters to write risks which offer a good chance of losing money. On the other hand, they expect that good risks will be written, regardless of factors which usually, but not always, cause problems.

Automobile compensation laws probably will have little effect on underwriting. These no-fault laws will change only a small part of the automobile policy, for they apply only to bodily injury, not to property damage liability, material damage coverages, or other coverages under the policy. One source states that "nearly two-thirds of the automobile insurance premium dollar is spent for car damage coverages, and more than 10 times as many people incur damages to their cars as incur personal injuries."[2] Even on the bodily injury coverages, few changes appear to be needed in the underwriting. As experience is gained, and the types of plans are observed, some minor modifications in underwriting practices may be needed.

In summary, underwriting will be affected by governmental regulation. No one expects underwriters to accept risks that are uninsurable, whether from physical or moral standpoints. On the other hand, the public is becoming more definite in stating that underwriters must accept all risks which can be accommodated within the pricing structure and capacity of the company. The emphasis is on eliminating what

---

2. Reported by the Independent Auto Damage Appraisers Association, *The Insurance Report,* Issue 31 (April, 1970).

is perceived to be unfair discrimination. If insurers do not fulfill that obligation, either mandatory insurance or government insurance will follow.

The problem is not with the risk which is good or the one which is poor; it is with the marginal risks. Marginal acceptability characteristics lead to declinations, in many cases. The underwriter who wishes to survive in the future must find a means of writing those risks. Risks should not be declined because the rate is too low, because surcharged rates might be used. Similarly, if the rate is too high, causing reinsurance concerns, improvements may be possible to reduce the rate. Deductibles, reduced expense factors, more reliable statistics and other tools must be used.

Underwriters need to be selective — that is their job. However, they should not be too selective. They must be willing to accept some "average" or "marginal" risks. They are permitted to use adequate rates, in most cases, and to tailor the coverages to fit the risks. However, they will not be permitted to "skim the cream" by accepting only the very best risks.

There is only one available tool by which a company can make money on the marginal risks and that is by depending upon the underwriters — provided those underwriters are informed, experienced, trained, educated and able to use sound underwriting judgment.

QUESTIONS FOR DISCUSSION

1. Is insurance regulated by the federal government or the states?
2. List 4 types of coverages sold by the federal government.
3. (a) What is the difference between cancellation and nonrenewal?
   (b) Which of these is more often limited by state laws?
4. Explain the effects on underwriting of limitations imposed by governmental regulations.

47

Clerical Functions

A number of clerical functions are performed by underwriters, as has been mentioned several times previously. While trends indicate that this will always be the case, fewer clerical functions will be assigned to underwriters in the future.

Recent trends, and the outlook for the future, show the following changes which affect the degree of clerical work performed by underwriters.

- *A greater number of classifications are being used in many lines.* As competition becomes more intense, the tendency is to use more classifications in order to attract the better risks within each group. This trend leads to more complicated classification, requiring more detailed assignment of rating factors.
- *A greater number of options are being made available.* More coverages are offered, more deductibles are given as alternatives, and more types of packages are prepared. These additions tend to complicate the writing of policies, needing detailed explanations by underwriters in order to assure the correct coverages are used.
- *Mechanization of the insurance industry requires more technical and detailed handling of files.* Someone must assign codes and numbers to many items, and a portion of this task falls upon underwriters.
- *Specialization leads to simplification of job duties.* The trend in this direction, in insurance as in other types of industry, leads to less complicated underwriting work and thus more clerical types of transactions.
- *Rate classes are substituted for underwriting in some situations.* At least, this is the attempt which is made by some companies. To the extent that rate classes are considered to replace underwriting, the task of underwriters will be to assign proper classifications rather than make decisions based on underwriting factors.

- *Governmental regulation prohibits the use of some subjective factors in underwriting.* As more dependence is placed on objective factors, the trend toward underwriting by facts instead of judgments will increase.
- *The growth of clerical functions in underwriting operations means that portions of the work may be performed by clerical employees.* This will relieve underwriters of many of the routine transactions. As a result, underwriters will spend more of their time performing judgment operations and making decisions.

The actual types of clerical functions performed by underwriters, and the outlook for the future are explained in this chapter, after a discussion of one other major trend which may reduce underwriting into a more clerical function: mass merchandisiing.

MASS MERCHANDISING

A possible development which may lead to a de-emphasis of underwriting is the trend toward mass marketing. Also known by such terms as "group auto" and "payroll deduction plans," mass marketing programs have been developing for several decades.

The rationale behind mass merchandising plans is that the factors which have caused an increase in group life and group health plans will have a similar effect on property and casualty lines. These factors are the advantages of payroll deduction, the contributions by employers, and the leveling of premiums by removing distinctions among the members of the group.

Many types of mass marketing plans are possible. Some may offer only payroll deductions with no other changes. Others reduce costs by lowering policy issuance expense and commissions to producers, both of these by the advantages of writing a sizable volume of risks in the group. Still others may involve contributions by employers, thus reducing the premiums to the individuals and tending to level all premiums to a common figure. Any combination of these items is possible.

Mass merchandising has developed slowly in property and casualty lines. The advantage of payroll deduction appears to have limited appeal to most people, if it is the only advantage offered. Employers appear to be reluctant to install plans which may lead to ever-increasing contributions by the employers — a tendency which seems to be inevitable. An averaging of rates is not satisfactory because those risks which can secure insurance for a lower rate than that offered to the group will go elsewhere. This will tend to increase the group rate until it approaches that of the highest rated risk. Employer contributions are needed to reduce the group rates to an amount which is equal to, or lower than, the lowest rate available to any member of the group, and employers are not anxious to start on a program of contributions. Until employer contributions are required by labor contracts, and tax deductions are permitted, mass merchandising plans probably will not increase rapidly.

Some states have prohibited mass marketing of property and casualty policies. The reason most often given is that a "fictitious fleet or group" is thus created, as respects automobile risks. Unfair discrimination among risks in the same class would result, it is alleged, and that is prohibited by the rate laws. Some producer groups have led the movement to prohibit mass merchandising programs. These state barriers probably will be removed as the savings develop in other areas under group auto and similar plans. Changes will be made slowly, and state laws or regulations or insurance departments will hinder the development of mass marketing plans in some states.

Slow, steady growth has marked mass merchandising plans in the early years. Most of them included only personal automobiles, but some included such other lines as personal package policies.

Some plans permit regular underwriting. Others deny underwriters some of the rights of selection and rejection of risks, or perhaps all of those rights. In the latter cases, employer contributions and level rates are used to produce profits, rather than depending upon underwriting. Most mass merchandising plans require more detail handling and less underwriting selectivity than separate policies. Thus, the growth of these plans will tend to increase the clerical functions performed by underwriters and reduce their judgment areas.

Present indications are that mass merchandising plans will not grow rapidly, and that they will never apply to more than a small proportion of the available risks. It appears unlikely that more than 20 or 30% of the personal automobile and personal package lines will be written under mass merchandising plans in the foreseeable future, and the penetration in other lines will be much less.

This trend, therefore, probably will have little effect on the clerical functions performed by underwriters and their application of judgment to individual risks, for many years to come.

CLERICAL DUTIES OF UNDERWRITERS

Many types of clerical functions may be performed by underwriters. The specific duties vary by line and by company. Examples of some types of clerical duties are these.

—*Assign Rate classes.* Since underwriters are required to determine the rate class in order to underwrite properly, it requires very little additional effort to indicate the proper rate classification on a file. Underwriters often enter the proper rate class, by number or letter, in a specified place on the application.

—*Specify Coverages.* The underwriter must indicate the coverages approved, and the deductibles required. It is easier to indicate the coverages on the application or a rating form than to instruct a clerk on the proper coverages.[1]

—*Order Inspections.* Underwriters determine whether inspections should be

1. In many companies, paper applications and rating forms are no longer used. Desk-top screens (cathode-ray tubes — CRTs) contain the information and permit underwriters and others to enter instructions directly into the computer. This is not a change as far as the duties to be performed are concerned, and does not increase or decrease the amount of clerical work performed by underwriters, so it is not specifically referenced in the text.

ordered. They decide upon the type of inspection, the company or inspector to use, and any special item to be checked. The same type of decision is made for loss prevention inspections, credit reports, motor vehicle reports, and the like. Some companies conclude that since the underwriter is making these decisions, he or she can easily indicate them on the proper forms. This clerical function of ordering a report often is performed by an underwriter.

—*Write Letters to Producers.* Much correspondence is passed between producers and underwriters. Some of it originates with producers, often requiring an answer from an underwriter. In other cases an underwriter may decide to ask a producer for specific information, or to transmit something of importance about the risk. The actual completion of a form or the writing of a message is a clerical function, but it is performed by the underwriter.

The logic behind the assignment of these clerical duties to an underwriter is that the underwriter has to determine the information. He or she could instruct a clerk to enter the rate class, specify the coverage, order the report, or write the note to a producer. However, often it takes no more effort to perform the task than to instruct a clerk on how to do it. It is just as easy to write the rate class on the application as to write instructions to a clerk. The note for an item to be inspected specifically might as well be written by the underwriter on the order form as on a note to a clerk. The memo to a producer is more exact if it is written by the underwriter rather than by a clerk from a rough indication on a piece of paper.

These clerical operations are not designed to be a burden to an underwriter, nor to relegate underwriting to a clerical role. The performance of these duties by an underwriter is a more efficient, accurate means of handling the information than for it to be conveyed to a clerk for handling. The duties in the past and the present of a clerical nature for underwriters, appear only in minor cases and only because this is the easiest, most accurate means of performing the function.

FUTURE OUTLOOK

It appears to be inevitable that more details will be required of those performing underwriting duties, and that the use of judgment factors will be reduced in the future. This does not mean that underwriters themselves will be required to perform more clerical functions. Rather, it indicates that these clerical duties will be transferred to others, tending to release underwriters for the performance of more true underwriting.

The handling of details will be assigned in greater quantity to clerical employees and machines. More details will be needed as rate classifications and options are expanded, and underwriters must assign or decide on these factors. However, underwriters will need, in increasing degrees, only to indicate by check marks or numerical entries the assignments or decisions. Clerks or machines then will handle the details from the point of these entries. This procedure will require less handling of details on the part of underwriters than has been the practice in the past.

Governmental regulations will prohibit some underwriting decisions based solely on such subjective factors as marital status and occupation. If these are the only factors which make a risk unacceptable, it cannot be declined. Risks with those characteristics do not need underwriting decisions; if every facet of a risk appears to be satisfactory, a clerk or computer can screen those risks and approve them. Currently, this type of handling applies primarily to the large mass lines of personal insurance, but will spread to some other lines as well, in the future.

Clerks and computers will assume more of the clerical duties and will handle the screening of risks on some lines. Perhaps a major contribution of employees who are not trained as underwriters will be to program computers and to enter into computers the data needed for the screening, issuance, and referral functions of these valuable machines. Underwriters will be relieved of many of the clerical duties, and will be able to handle applications more easily as the use of computer screens and entry capabilities becomes more common. Underwriters will then be permitted to spend more time on true underwriting matters.

This trend will enhance the position of underwriters, since they will spend less time on details, reversing a trend which has developed in the past few years on many lines. This will free them for analyzing risks and making decisions. After all, these are the functions for which underwriters are trained and which they do best. Hence, the prestige of underwriters, and the pleasure in performing decision-making tasks, will increase with this trend.

QUESTIONS FOR DISCUSSION

1. Name 4 changes which will affect the degree of clerical work performed by underwriters.
2. (a) Describe 2 types of mass merchandising plans.
   (b) Why is mass merchandising developing slowly in property and casualty insurance?
3. Describe 3 functions performed by underwriters which could be classified as clerical.
4. (a) Will the use of judgment factors be increased or reduced in the future?
   (b) Will these increase or reduce the importance of underwriting?

48

The Impact Of Computers

Computers are essential for insurance companies. They facilitate accounting and bookkeeping transactions, handle billings, issue policies, and perform many other valuable functions.

Underwriting has been impacted greatly by computers. The clerical functions performed by computers are related to underwriting. Even the decision-making process is affected by electronic data processing, and more developments are inevitable in the future.

Each of the five steps in the underwriting process is helped by computers, so it is logical to evaluate their impact through each of these steps.[1]

SECURE INFORMATION

Perhaps the principal asset of computers is in their ability to process information quickly and accurately. This fact can be used by underwriters to assist them in the gathering of information.

Automobile underwriting depends greatly on motor vehicle records (MVRs). Computers can order these reports, analyze their contents, and refer cases with potential problems. The vehicle identification number (VIN) can be used by a computer to establish the rating symbol and to create the description of the vehicle for the declaration page.

Commercial underwriters can secure financial information on applicants through a computer link-up, automatically giving this type of data which can be critical in the evaluation of risks. Company data from other policies or concerning the subject policy when a later review is being conducted, can be supplied quickly to

1. For a more detailed discussion of the operation of computers, and their uses in insurance, see G. William Glendenning and Robert B. Holtom, "Personal Lines Underwriting," Insurance Institute of America, 2nd Ed. (June, 1982), pp. 489-530.

underwriters.

Policy files, containing the background information so important to many decisions, are always available through the computer. No longer is a file "out," or misfiled, or illegible. All pertinent data is available at the same time to everyone needing the information.

DEVELOP ALTERNATIVES

The evaluation of the data takes place during this step in the underwriting process. It is the portion of the underwriting function which offers the most promise of cost savings, and is the most exciting in its prospects. Changes in the evaluation process can be described in a chronological pattern.

Traditional. For centuries, underwriters analyzed facts and developed alternatives in the same fashion. An application, usually written, was presented to the underwriter, who then analyzed the information. More information might be ordered by a letter or memorandum to the producer, an order form to an inspection company or Department of Motor Vehicles, a request to a loss control specialist, and so forth. Each piece of paper was carefully attached to the file, and reviewed before any future transaction was approved. The underwriter indicated all actions by written notation in the file.

Screening by Assistants. Late in the 1960s, some large companies adopted a screening process for personal lines, particularly automobile. An underwriting assistant (above a clerk in classification but below an underwriter) would review every incoming transaction, including new applications, requests for changes, and cases referred by claims personnel. The assistant would review the facts and compare them with a list previously prepared by underwriters, showing factors which were of concern. The screener was looking for risks which had one or more characteristics which were on the list of factors to consider. If such factors were found, the file was referred to an underwriter. If no factors were found, the transaction was approved, and the file was forwarded for processing. One company found that 75% of new private passenger automobile applications could be approved in this fashion, thus saving underwriters the time and trouble of reviewing applicants with no adverse characteristics to evaluate.[2]

Screening by Computer. It was a short step to transfer the screening to a computer. Since a screener was looking for specific items, the computer could likewise look for those items. The computer is fast, accurate, and economical. Computers do not forget, are not prejudiced, do not get headaches, do not daydream, and are consistent. A clerk could enter the pertinent data from an application into the system, and the computer program would accomplish the screening. Usually, the same "referral by exception" was used as with the people doing the screening; any risk which was an exception to the acceptable list would be referred. However, some companies developed a second system, called "referral by total point count." Under this

2. "P/C Automation Under Way," *Journal of Commmerce* (August 30, 1985), p. 8A.

method, underwriter would develop a point count for each item evaluated. The computer would add the points and refer the file if the total exceeded a specified number. An advantage of this method is that it is equally effective on renewals and policies in force. A disadvantage is that it is difficult to arrive at a proper level to refer cases with potential problems and still accept enough risks to be efficient.

This system, while an advance over screening by assistants, was usually limited to personal lines. However, at least one "underwriting by exception" program for commercial lines is now available.[3]

Screening, whether by people or by computers, is not underwriting, but it is part of the underwriting process. An underwriting decision was made to build the program, and the screening is an activity which relates to the selection of risks.

Artificial Intelligence. The newest development to date is the use of expert systems which use artificial intelligence. One article defined it this way: "An expert system is an AI (artificial intelligence) program that captures in computer code the knowledge and informal rules of thumb used by a particular human expert to solve a particular problem."[4] In its underwriting application, qualified underwriters painstakingly develop every step and every item of information used in the evaluation process, and then computer technicians translate this into a computer language and into a software program.

Underwriting professionals have a vast amount of acquired knowledge. Commercial lines rely heavily on this expertise. However, it is time-consuming to apply that knowledge to complex applications, and market pressures often require quick decisions, many times with information which is less than complete. The advent of "superchips" (computer memory chips with fantastic speed and capacity) permits the development of programs which build underwriting expertise into computer programs.

Computer experts need to identify each step in the underwriting process, and to ask proper questions. Then they can construct a program which will enable the computer to analyze the data and to secure other information as needed. "The most difficult task associated with knowledge engineering," one expert stated, "is to determine an adequate structure for the knowledge base."[5]

An expert system greatly increases the knowledge base of underwriters. It acts like a panel of experts who can lead an underwriter to the right questions and sources. By guiding the underwriter through the necessary steps, and identifying the information which is needed, the computer program can improve the quality of the decision making. Consistency will also improve, as will productivity.

Commercial lines will particularly benefit from these expert systems, but their use in personal lines will help junior personnel deliver better results.

---

3. "Duns Offers Automated Guide for Assessing Risks," *Underwriters Report* (May 16, 1985), p. 6.
4. "How to Clone an Expert," *Time* (September 2, 1985), p. 44.
5. David Shpillberg, "One Giant Step for Insurers," *Best's Review, Property/Casualty Insurance Edition,* Vol. 87, No. 1 (May, 1986), p. 54.

DECIDE AND TAKE ACTION

After the decision-making process is completed, the underwriter needs to make a decision, and to take action to implement that decision. Computers can help in these functions, also.

Decisions are easier to make when the facts are clearly displayed. The computer programs explained above can help in this regard. As stated previously, even the screening by an assistant can result in a decision to accept a new application in about 75% of the cases.

Taking action requires issuance of the policy if the application is accepted. Computers are used almost exclusively by most companies to issue policies. The information identifying the policyholder, the coverage, and the premium is printed by the computer on the declaration page. (References in this book to "typing" include computer printing as well as typewriting, which is still used to some extent.)

Rates must also be applied, and computers are helpful here, too. Insurers who develop their own rates can program them into a computer for ease of rating. ISO has made its advisory rates for commercial auto and general liability available on magnetic tape for interface to an insurer's automatic rating system.

Policy forms are needed for issuance. These, also, may be produced by computers, and stored for future reference. ISO forms are being made available for computer use.

CHECK RESULTS

An important part of the underwriting process is to check the results of past actions. The starting point in this step is to secure reports showing loss experience by line, territory, rate class, producer, or other factor. Sometimes an underwriter will want to review all policies with certain characteristics.

Computers are of tremendous help at this stage. They usually are programmed to produce regular reports of specified types. With special programming, they can give information on any factor which is coded into the computer, and in almost any combination or format. Computers make the checking or results a much more effective process than existed previously.

Another valuable contribution of computers is to refer cases on which action is needed, according to pre-determined data or circumstances. For example, a youth who has not yet attained driving age may become a problem when the date is reached, or at least might cause a re-rating of the policy. The computer can refer the file to an underwriter on that date, and since state laws differ on driving age, a special table can be used in the computer to make the referral at the right time. Another example is when a file is set, mid-term, for nonrenewal; it is critical that action be initiated on the proper date.

MAKE CORRECTIONS

The last step in the underwriting process is the making of corrections. These actions can include cancellation, nonrenewal, or changes in policies.

The speed and ease of making changes or taking action by means of a computer illustrate still another benefit from this powerful tool. The file is never "out," state laws concerning notice of action cannot be overlooked, and the proper copies of transactions are always made. In these situations, as in so many others, computers are valuable allies of underwriters.

QUESTIONS FOR DISCUSSION

1. Explain how computers can assist underwriters in securing information.
2. What are the two methods by which applications have been screened, and how are they similar?
3. Explain the two systems used to refer applications.
4. Explain the use of "artificial intelligence" in the underwriting process.
5. In what ways can computers assist underwriters in checking results?

49

Producers' Underwriting Authority

Insurance companies suffered tremendous losses during the soft market of the early 1980s. Insolvencies, actual and threatened, reach all-time highs. Now, new technologies and new legal standards require more informed decisions. Underwriters of the future will need to be market-oriented, as well as being technical experts. The most successful companies will be those which work with their producers as problem solvers. One of the methods of achieving better results may be to establish new procedures whereby underwriting authority may be transferred to specific producers. This is already being tried by some companies with large or specialty brokers and seems to be spreading to medium-sized generalist producers.

REASONS FOR CHANGING

Several reasons have been given for this transfer of underwriting authority.

Avoid Duplication of Effort

Under the traditional system, the producer selects the applicant, inspects the property, completes an application, and checks the completed policy for accuracy. The insurer also selects from the application, may conduct an inspection, issues the policy, and checks the policy before mailing. Some of the steps can be eliminated if the producer underwrites and issues the policy. The economies which are achieved can be reflected in a lower expense factor, which can result in lower rates and a better competitive position.

Give Faster Service

The traditional system requires mailing and handling time between the producer and the company office. This time can be reduced if the producer underwrites and issues the policy. When a rush delivery is needed, it can be accommodated more easily in the producer's office. This improves the prestige and image of the producer.

Achieve Flexibility

Producers sometimes can gain a sales advantage by being flexible in acceptability, contract terms, or pricing. When the underwriting, rating, and issue are controlled by the producer, this advantage can be gained when needed.

Use Experience of Producers

Experienced producers who have profit-sharing agreements (loss-ratio bonuses) with insurers have learned which types of applicants are more likely to incur losses. A good producer of this type will avoid such applicants. This knowledge, along with a personal acquaintance with applicants and the territory, can develop a good underwriting background. When compared with an underwriter trainee in the company, who may have only a few months' experience, such a producer may possess superior knowledge of the underwriting process.

Recognize that Most Applicants are Accepted

It is a fact that most applicants for any of the common lines of insurance are accepted on the basis of standard rating and contracts. Producers can more efficiently underwrite and issue those policies, which may constitute some 80 percent of the total number of applicants, and refer the other 20 percent to the company underwriters. This is particularly true on personal lines and smaller commercial lines policies. Since insurance companies trust some producers, accepting most of their submissions, they can formalize this relationship by granting authority to the producer to underwrite and issue the business.

Increase the Volume from a Producer

Insurance companies which deal with the American Agency system are constantly competing with other companies for a large volume of business from the better producers. The company which can find a means of attracting more of that business will grow faster than others. The granting of authority to underwrite and issue policies is seen by some insurers as one of those steps which can lead to increased volume from good producers.

ORGANIZATION OF PRODUCER-UNDERWRITER SECTIONS

The usual organization will involve the establishment of a separate section in the producers' offices. The section will contain underwriters, raters, and typists, as well as other clerical workers.

An underwriting section in a producer's office will be treated as a branch office by the company. When underwriting rules or guidelines are changed, the information must be conveyed to all underwriters, including those in producers' offices.

Obviously, this type of program can be used only in larger producer offices. Small offices cannot afford to set up a separate section, with several workers at a minimum.

EVALUATION OF PROGRAM

It is absolutely essential to the success of this type of program that all underwriting principles be followed. These principles are the same regardless of where the underwriters are located. There is no basic reason why underwriters cannot be located in a producer's office, provided proper separation of duties is arranged.

Independence of the underwriting section is essential to the success of this type of program. Underwriters can make exceptions for producers; this is a common practice now. If the underwriters are located in the producers' offices, they must be independent of the influence of the producers, making exceptions only on the basis of sound underwriting decisions. The independence is possible only if the owner of the agency establishes separate sections for sales and underwriting, each reporting only to the owner, who makes decisions by balancing both commissions and profit-sharing arrangements. This is the weakest link in this program; if it cannot be achieved, the arrangement will ultimately fail.

However, if complete independence is established, some of the reasons for this program lose their importance. Salespersons must complete applications and submit them to the underwriters. The principal savings, then, are in the mailing costs and mailing time. The ability of underwriters to be flexible and to apply their training and experience is lost if the decisions are made on the basis of marketing, and only if this independence is retained will the program succeed.

As stated above, perhaps 80 percent of the applicants in some lines can be accepted without much use of decision-making abilities. The secret of successful underwriting is not only to make proper decisions on the remaining 20 percent, but also in identifying which of the applicants fall within that 20 percent. If it were an automatic operation to separate applicants into the 80 percent or 20 percent groups, all insurers would let their producers issue policies to those in the 80 percent category. The problem is that the person who is separating the applicants might not know which ones to place in each group. This, of course, is the core of underwriting, the key to the separation between salespersons and trained underwriters. In order to be effective, the underwriters in producers' offices must be properly trained as underwriters, and will be no more effective during their first few months in the position than the newer underwriter in a company office. This, also, is a factor which could cause these programs to fail.

CONCLUSION

If the purpose of establishing an underwriting section in a producer's office is to achieve more sales from the producer, it is likely that the underwriting process, and the need for independence of action, will be secondary to sales. The result, over a period of time, will be adverse underwriting experience. Sales and underwriting must remain equal and separate in order for such a program to be successful. If sales dominates, underwriting will suffer.

If the purpose is to bring the underwriting closer to the customer, and if underwriting principles are followed, this type of program could be successful. In effect, this would be an extension of a trend toward establishing branch offices which are closer to the clients than a regional office or the home office.

Underwriting can be performed under many circumstances. There is no inherent reason why it cannot be done in the office of a producer, if the producer is large enough to separate sales and the underwriting function into different sections. But if the principles of underwriting are lost in the process, the ultimate result will be disaster.

QUESTIONS FOR DISCUSSION

1. Why are insurance companies working with plans to expand the underwriting authority of producers? Give at least four reasons.
2. Explain why a program of expanded authority for producers will be limited to larger producer offices, rather than small offices.
3. Is complete independence of a producer's undewriting program desirable? Why? Is it realistic?
4. What will happen if the underwriting section in a producer's office becomes secondary to the sales function?

50

The Essential Nature Of Underwriting

Recent trends in the United States have changed the position of underwriters in insurance companies; the stature of underwriters has increased. At the same time, more problems have arisen than ever before.

The stature of underwriters has been affected by two major factors; increased competition is the first. As companies compete for desirable business, the edge may go to the company with the best underwriters. A knowledgeable underwriter can help the producer and client. An imaginative underwriter can suggest a new approach which better suits the needs of the applicant. A clever underwriter can find or develop premium saving courses of action benefiting all parties. The keen competition of today calls for good underwriters. The other factor affecting the stature of underwriters deals with the shrinkage of profit margins. It has become increasingly difficult to achieve profits on many lines. The difference between profit and loss may lie in small items or minute changes. An underwriter can help achieve profits by selecting risks more carefully, by analyzing trends and new conditions, by taking action promptly, by applying deductibles or other corrective action when the first need for it appears, and in many other ways. These actions by underwriters can change a loss condition to a profitable condition.

These factors apply in both up and down cycles. In an up cycle, insurers want to write more business, and underwriters are valuable in developing new approaches to rating, coverages, and acceptability. In a down cycle, losses are increasing, and it becomes critical to having underwriters who can cut costs and weed out the undesirable risks, without jeopardizing market share.

As a result of these factors, the importance and prestige of underwriting has increased in recent years. Company officials are more aware now that good underwriting can make a substantial contribution to profits — perhaps a critical contribution.

Ironically, underwriters have been confronted with more problems, even as their value is recognized. These problems seem to be general among all underwriters. They are not unique, however, for other businesses are faced with somewhat the same problems.

Pressures have increased, comprising a major problem. Pressures on time have a particular effect upon underwriters, because underwriting requires time to think and make a decision. When time and productivity become problems, this increases the need for training and education in order to be able to make correct decisions more promptly. Pressures on costs are also increasing and are related to other pressures. Expenses are often the difference between net profit or loss, and underwriting expenses are scrutinized, as are those of other departments. If a cost squeeze limits the volume of investigation reports an underwriter can order, action must be taken based upon the limited information available. Again, training and education help when a decision is made on information which is incomplete.

Another problem is with the rapid technological change that is taking place today. New products, new operations, even new concepts are introduced almost every day. The underwriter must keep abreast of these changes in order to act in a knowledgeable fashion. Experience over many years is helpful in mastering underwriting techniques, but it may be inadequate in analyzing applications.

Still another problem lies in the area of developing underwriting talent. Supervisors and managers feel the pressure to a greater degree, but line underwriters who like to help others develop, can also feel the need for better employees. A person can perform better work, ordinarily, when co-workers are talented and capable. In underwriting, recruiting of new employees has suffered in recent years, as many college graduates have turned toward occupations which appear to be more glamorous. Related to this problem is the difficulty other businesses may have in securing good workers. The underwriting job is more difficult if inpsection companies cannot get good workers, if motor vehicle reporting companies cannot keep trained clerks, and if repair shops cannot hire good mechanics. Current problems of hiring dependable, dedicated employees extend to many businesses, and underwriters suffer in numerous ways from these difficulties.

Underwriting is in a state of change. Its stature is increasing, but its problems are growing at the same time. The next section views one type of solution: the use of alternatives to underwriting and analyzes possibilities of these alternatives, along with the basic meaning of underwriting to insurers. And, finally, a glimpse of the future of underwriting.

ALTERNATIVES TO UNDERWRITING

Various people have suggested that alternatives be developed under which underwriting is not needed. They point to the pressures on time and cost, the technological changes which render yesterday's underwriter obsolete unless brought up to date, and the difficulty in securing good new underwriters. They suggest that the concept of underwriting is ready to be replaced by another method of handling the risks.

Five of these alternatives are discussed next.

1. Adopt sophisticated rate programs. This concept evisions a complex, sophisticated rate structure under which each risk would be charged its proper rate. There would be no need to decline or cancel risks, because each risk will be profitable at its rate. The argument used here is that virtually every risk can find a market today. Various rate levels are used by different companies, so the only problem is to find the right company. Even those unable to find a market could be rated and should have access to insurance. Since every risk has a proper rate, and almost every one is now written by someone, the solution is to require every insurer to use proper rates and write all applicants. Everyone would pay the correct premium and no underwriters would be needed.

2. Adopt a flat rate system. This concept is the opposite of the previous one described. Every applicant would pay the same rate. The rate would be an average among present rates, so the total premium would be unchanged. Essential to this concept is the provision that every risk which applies for coverage would be accepted. No company could decline a risk. The market problem would be solved, and rate discrimination would end. Every applicant could buy insurance at the same rate, and no underwriters would be needed.

3. Permit producers to select risks. The idea here is that the producer knows the applicant better than any desk underwriter sitting in an office. The producer has the same interest in a profitable operation as the underwriter, because the competitive rate level depends upon the agency's own experience. The principle is that the producer would perform the duties of the underwriter. The only change needed is to give absolute authority to the producer.

4. Program computers to select risks. This concept was discussed in a previous chapter. It provides for a program in the computer, by which the policy data are processed by the computer and either a policy issued or a declination notice issued.

5. Write groups with no right of selection. Some group policies already written carry the provision that the company will neither reject nor cancel a member of the group. This is the same principle as is used for group life and health insurance. This concept was discussed in Chapter 46. If all risks were written under group policies when the company had no right of selection, there would be no need for underwriters.

THE NECESSITY OF UNDERWRITING

Underwriting has been a key element in private insurance since its inception. Through many years, insurance has depended upon underwriting. This basic relationship cannot be changed by latter-day social planners, do-gooders, and others who seem bent upon replacing a strong, reliable bulwark of protection with ill-conceived, irreversible concepts which would not operate without the massive contributions of government, and ultimately controlled by that government.

Unworkable Alternatives to Underwriting

These are several reasons why alternative proposals to underwriting will not work under private insurance.

Sophisticated Rate. Confusion, argument, and increased expenses would follow adoption of a sophisticated rate system with "proper" rates for each risk. Actuarial science is not precise enough to determine the correct rate for each risk, so underwriters would still be needed to select those where the rate appears to be most favorable. Changed conditions can be met more quickly by underwriting action than by cumbersome rate adjustment which will always lag behind experience.

Some applicants will feel that they cannot afford their proper rate. They will be uninsured, increasing the social and political problems. Underwriting will continue under this system, if a company wants to have a better chance of making a profit. At the same time, political pressures will increase. There are some analysts who feel that many of today's insurance problems have been caused by the semi-sophisticated rating structures now used. More highly sophisticated rating systems would increase the problems from all sides.

Flat Rates. No system of flat rates would work without compulsion. If all automobile risks were required to be written at the same rate, underwriters would accept only those whose experience was expected to be the best. Average rates mean that some risks pay more than their experience justifies, while others pay less. The latter group could not secure insurance unless laws were passed which required companies to accept every applicant. Even then, alert companies would devise means of discouraging certain risks from applying, so extensive regulatory machinery would be needed.

The regulation which would necessarily accompany a flat rate system would change insurance from a private enterprise to an arm of government. If this did not happen, underwriting would be used to select the best risks, and the system would collapse. If it does happen, government will have taken over the insurance business. It is highly doubtful that the public would permit such a happening; it is also doubtful that the majority of risks with relatively good experience are interested in having their rates increased in order to reduce costs for those with poor experience.

The insurance industry is built on the principle of rate differentials which reflect differences in experience. Underwriters are an essential element of that system. If flat rates are used, the insurance industry will be finished, after centuries of providing good protection under all types of conditions.

Producers. The very existence of underwriters today provides the answer to those who suggest that producers can perform underwriting duties. If producers could do this, underwriters would have nothing to do, and economy-minded companies soon would release all of them.

In actuality, underwriters are needed to help in the selection process. Producers perform some selection duties, of course, and their preliminary screening is helpful. Those that underwriters must reject, or adjust on coverage or rates, are few in percentage but large in effect on company results. There is no reason to expect that producers would act differently if there were no underwriters. A look at the financial results of most companies in recent years indicates that there is little margin for further losses, and this has been the result of careful handling by underwriters, in addition to screening by producers.

Some modification of this position has been taken, as was described in the previous chapter. Companies are experimenting with underwriting sections in the offices of some large producers, and it appears that this will be successful. However, it must be emphasized that these programs involve only a shift in the location of underwriters, from company offices to producer offices. Separate underwriting sections in the producer offices must be maintained if this approach is to be successful. No present known program authorizes the producers who are sales persons to perform the underwriting function. These people are not trained to look at situations with the approach used by underwriters. They have neither access to sources of information nor the time to analyze situtations and trends. The sales section of a producer's office is essential in producing business. The underwriting section of a producer's office, where used, is a clearly separate function.

Computers. To some extent, computers are performing certain underwriting functions, as was explained in a prevous chapter. However, only screening types of processes are performed by these machines. While computers are becoming more helpful and sophisticated, they cannot match the capability of an underwriter's brain in evaluating and selecting applicants for insurance.

At the present state of development, computers can screen applicants and accept the "clean risks" on certain personal lines. Underwriters are still needed to evaluate both the questionable risks on those personal lines, and all applications on the other lines. In view of the rapid development of sophisticated computers, the day may come when computers can perform the underwriting function, at least on some lines. Until then, they are not an alternative to underwriting.

Groups. The trend toward more group writings of property and casualty coverages is inevitable. Many of these groups will permit selection by underwriters. Others will require that all members of the group must be accepted if they apply. The future is not clear, but probably both types will increase.

Underwriters will not be needed to handle those groups where selection is prohibited. This will be only a portion of group policies and all group policies will be in the minority of total business in the foreseeable future. The need for underwriters might reduce slightly, but it will be many years before any impact is noticeable. Underwriters will still be needed for the majority of the business.

UNDERWRITING IN THE FUTURE

The future of underwriting is inextricably related to the future of the private insurance industry. Underwriting will not be needed if insurance is written by a governmental agency. On the other hand, underwriting is the very heart of private insurance, and the latter cannot survive without underwriting.

Changes in recent years have made it difficult for underwriters to perform their duties properly. Rate flexibility was lost in many states because of political problems. Underwriters could not adjust rates, so they were restricted in their alternatives.

More recently, competitive rate laws have spread, causing rate regulation to be less rigid in some states. The situation has created new opportunities for underwriters.

Imagination can be used, and risks which were formerly unacceptable may be written if rate adequacy can be achieved.

At the same time, new challenges have been presented to underwriters. Non-cancellation and guaranteed renewable laws restrict the right of action on risks that develop problems. Laws which prohibit selection on such factors as age or sex will further restrict underwriting — these conditions, and others which develop, offer new challenges to underwriters.

Through it all, underwriters have carried on a vital function. Companies generally make profits, although the margin often is slim, and sometimes disappears temporarily on some lines. Private insurance has survived many challenges, and underwriters have played a strong role in that survival.

Underwriters perform many functions as has been explained in previous chapters. An underwriter may classify risks, prepare and apply rates, write policies and endorsements, arrange for reinsurance, advise on questionable claims, ascertain that necessary services are available, prepare reports, handle assigned risks and involuntary pools and participate in many other important activities.

Important as these activities are, they are subsidiary to the main function of underwriting. They could all be removed and underwriters still could perform their basic function of evaluating and selecting risks. This is the activity that is so essential to the entire insurance mechanism. This is the very heart of the private insurance industry.

Training, education, and experience are all valuable in the development of underwriters. Many types of underwriters are needed: specialists and generalists, line and staff. The industry needs desk underwriters, supervisors, managers and executives. All of these people have opportunities to develop and earn promotions in underwriting and in other departments. The future of underwriting is bright for those who are willing to devote their time and efforts toward becoming capable underwriters.

The future of the private insurance industry is equally bright. Capable, well-trained people will enable it to survive and grow in the face of all obstacles. So long as the private sector survives, underwriters will be needed. In fact, a significant share of the growth and survival will be contributed by those whose predecessors started insurance, and who are so vital to its operation — the underwriters.

QUESTIONS FOR DISCUSSION

1. How has underwriting been affected by competition and shrinking profit margins?
2. Explain 3 problems which have faced underwriters in recent years.
3. (a) List and discuss 4 alternatives to underwriting which have been suggested.
   (b) Explain why these alternatives are not workable.

GLOSSARY OF INSURANCE TERMS

Acceptable Risk. An individual exposure or property upon which an underwriter agrees to write insurance.

Acceptance. An agreement to the offer or application of another so that a contract is concluded and the parties are bound.

Accident. An act that is unforeseen and unintentional.

Accommodation Linc. An acceptance of an otherwise unacceptable risk which is made in order to curry favor with a particular producer.

Account. An insured, including all of the policies of the insured.

Acquisition Cost. The cost to the company of getting business; ordinarily includes only commission to producer, but may include sales and other expenses.

Actual Cash Value. Worth of property, ordinarily defined as replacement cost less depreciation and obsolescence, if any. In some states, it is market value.

Actuary. A person who develops rates for insurance by mathematical means.

Additional Living Expense. Cost to maintain, as nearly as practicable, the normal living conditions of the insured in spite of damage to the property.

Adjuster. A person who determines if a claim is to be paid and if so, in what amount; often called a "claims adjuster."

Adverse Selection. The acceptance of risks which have an exposure to loss that is greater than the average.

Agent. A producer who represents one or more insurance companies when writing insurance.

Anniversary Date. The date each year upon which the policy was originally made effective.

Applicant. A person who requests the insurance.

Application. The form upon which the applicant submits a request.

Arson. The deliberate, wilful burning of property.

Assignment. The transfer of an insurance policy from one person to another.

Assured. Same as "insured." The term "assured" is an older term which is now used only in a few lines in the United States, although it is more common in Great Britain.

Audit. The act of inspecting the books of the insured to determine the actual exposures which existed during a specified period of time, in order to develop the proper premium.

Average Clause. See "coinsurance clause." These two are virtually the same in practice, although technical differences exist.

Bailee. A person who has temporary possession of the property of another for specific, lawful purposes.

Bind. The act of making insurance coverage effective.

Binder. An agreement to furnish protection until an insurance policy can be issued; also called a binding slip.

Blanket Coverage. An insurance contract which protects more than one item of property or type of hazard without specifically describing each item or hazard.

Bodily Injury Liability. The obligation imposed by law upon one person for injury to, or death of, another person, caused by the negligence of the first person.

Borderline Risk. A risk which is barely acceptable and thus not really desirable.

Broad Form. An insurance coverage which includes more than basic coverages. May be used in many lines, but is more common in fire insurance to denote a specific coverage which includes more perils than fire and extended coverage.

Broker. A producer who represents the applicant when writing insurance.

Bureau. A nonprofit organization of insurance companies formed to promulgate rates, rules, and forms for the use of its member and subscriber companies.

Burglary. The felonious taking of money or property by breaking into, or out of, the premises of another.

Business Interruption Insurance. Coverage which is designed to reimburse a business property owner for specified fixed costs and profits resulting from damage caused by an insured peril; also called "Use and Occupancy" (U and O) or "Loss of Business Income."

Cancellation. Act of terminating an insurance policy before its expiration date, either by the policyholder or by the company.

Carrier. An insurance company.

Casualty Insurance. The group of coverages which includes insurance against liability claims and almost all other types except fire, marine and life.

Cede. Act of transferring all or a portion of a risk to a reinsurer.

Civil Commotion. An uprising of a group of people in a disorderly fashion.

Claim. The amount due, or alleged to be due, under an insurance policy following the occurrence against which the coverage protects.

Claims Adjuster. See "Adjuster."

Class of Insurance. One of the two major classes or groups of insurance: Property and Casualty.

Clause. A provision in a policy or endorsement.

Client. A person who depends upon a producer to obtain insurance coverage and advice.

Coinsurance Clause. A provision in a policy by which the insured agrees to maintain at least the specified percentage of insurance to value, and by which the insured agrees to share in a portion of each loss if the amount is not maintained; see also "Average Clause."

Collision. Violent contact between two or more objects.

Commercial Lines. The lines of insurance applicable to business establishments.

Company. See "Insurance Company."

Comprehensive. A general term which includes all coverages or all perils except those specifically excluded. Used specifically to refer to the coverage under an automobile policy insuring the vehicle owner against damage by perils other than collision.

Concurrency. A requirement that all policies applying to a single risk contain exactly the same provisions; if they do not, the insured may not be able to collect from some insurers for the share of the loss which they otherwise would pay.

Contents. Personal property in a building or appertaining to a building.

Contract. A legal document.

Coverage. Protection provided by a policy against the results of the described perils.

Daily. Same as "Declaration Page."

Declaration Page. A separate sheet of paper containing typed information about the individual risk and the coverage afforded; it is attached to a policy back to form a complete policy. Also called "dec," "face sheet," or "daily."

Decline. Refusal to write a policy. Cancellation of a new application is called a declination, even if the technical act is one of cancellation with advance notice.

Deductible Clause. A policy provision that the insurer will pay only that amount of any loss which is in excess of a specified amount. May be either (1) a specified dollar amount, or (2) a specified percentage of the loss or of the value of the property.

Depreciation. A decline in value caused by the effects of age, wear and tear, use, weather and similar factors.

Diminishing Deductible. A type of deductible under which the amount of the deductible reduces as the loss increases, and disappears completely above a stipulated amount of loss.

Disappearing Deductible. Same as "Diminishing Deductible."

Discovery Period. The initial period of a policy term during which the underwriter may take action for any reason, and after which the policy may be cancelled only for specific reasons under the applicable noncancellation law.

Discrimination. The act of applying different rules or rates to individual risks. Fair discrimination is the heart of insurance rating, for it applies rates which differ by measurable factors. Unfair discrimination generally is prohibited, for it is the practice of applying different rates to risks which are identical in measurable factors.

Distribution Clause. Provision in a property policy that spreads a blanket amount of insurance to the various subjects of insurance in the proportion that the value of each bears to the total value.

Dividend. A portion of the premium distributed to the policyholder at the expiration of the policy term as a refund of the amount not needed to pay that policyholder's share of the losses and expenses.

Earned Premium. Portion of the premium which the company may retain because it has furnished the agreed protection for the period of time involved.

E.C. or E.C.E.. Abbreviation for "Extended Coverage Endorsement."

Effective Date. Date coverage begins.

Eligible Risk. A risk which is in a category the company wishes to write and is not listed as being ineligible.

Employer's Liability. The responsibility of an employer to reimburse an injured employee for accidents occurring in the course of employment.

Endorsement. A form attached to a policy in order to modify its terms.

Equipment. Property which is attached to other property (as a radio is equipment on an automobile) or which is used for the service of a business (as the jigs and dies are equipment of a machine shop).

Excess Insurance. A policy which pays only after a loss exceeds the limits of underlying insurance or the insured's retention.

Exclusion. Policy provision removing coverage for specified property, perils or events.

Expiration Date. Date when a policy terminates by its provisions.

Exposure. In property insurance, the neighboring premises which may cause loss to the property because of perils or losses in them. In all lines of insurance, the amount of loss the company could conceivably pay under the terms of the policy.

Extended Coverage Endorsement. Form attached to a fire policy adding the perils of windstorm, hail, explosion, riot, riot attending a strike, aircraft, vehicles and smoke.

Extra Expense Insurance. Coverage for the additional costs an insured must incur in order to continue operating the business after damage to property by an insured peril.

Face Sheet. Same as "Declaration Page."

Financial Responsibility Law. A law requiring motorists to furnish proof that they could satisfy a judgment up to a specified amount, the proof of which must be furnished following an accident of a stated amount in order to avoid suspension of their drivers' licenses.

Fire Insurance. Protection against loss to real or personal property by the perils of fire, lightning and removal.

Fixtures. Personal property affixed semi-permanently to real property, such as counters, shelves, and display cases.

Flat Deductible. Same as "Deductible." A flat deductible applies regardless of the size of the loss, unlike a diminishing deductible. When the unmodified word deductible is used, it means a flat deductible.

Floater Policy. Coverage on movable property, ordinarily on an all risks basis and at any location where the property is taken.

Form. A sheet attached to a policy in order to modify or complete coverage.

Franchise Clause or Franchise Deductible. Operates like a deductible except that if the loss exceeds a stipulated amount, the deductible disappears completely and the loss is paid in full.

Full Coverage. A policy that has no deductible.

Group of Insurance. See "Class of Insurance."

Hazard. A condition which increases the likelihood of loss.

Heterogeneous. Risks composed of unlike elements or parts; different; dissimilar.

Homogeneous. Risks composed of similar elements or parts; of uniform character or nature throughout; alike.

Hull Insurance. Coverage on a ship or airplane, protecting against loss by damage to the vessel itself.

Improvements and Betterments. Additions or alterations made by a tenant to real property, at the tenant's expense, which become a permanent part of the real property.

Ineligible Risk. A risk in a category the company does not wish to write.

Inland Marine Insurance. The group of coverages which insure property not of an ocean-going type, usually with a degree of mobility or transportation involved, or related to transportation or communications.

Insurable Interest. A condition under which the policyholder would suffer a monetary loss if specified events should occur.

Insurance. A contractual arrangement under which one party agrees to indemnify another against loss or damage arising from an unknown event for a certain sum (premium).

Insurance Carrier. The entity which agrees to provide the indemnity to another in the event of loss.

Insurance Commissioner. State official who is charged with the regulation of insurance companies within the state. Other titles are used in some states, such as "Superintendent of Insurance."

Insurance Company. A commonly used term to denote any insurer, although the latter need not be an actual "company."

Insurance Policy. Written contract of insurance.

Insured. Party to be indemnified by the insurer in the event of loss or damage.

Insurer. Insurance carrier.

Judicial Hazard. Same as "Legal Hazard."

Lapse. The termination of a policy because of nonpayment of renewal premium by the insured.

Larceny. The unlawful taking of the property of others by stealth.

Law of Large Numbers. The mathematical premise which states that the degree of uncertainty is reduced as the number of events increases. Insurance is built upon this premise, permitting forecasts of loss certainty in a large group of similar risks.

Lease. A contract giving permission for the use of land and structures on the land for a specified period of time.

Legal Hazard. An increase in the likelihood that a loss will occur because of court actions or the passage of laws.

Legal Liability. Duty imposed by law or contract making a person responsible for negligent acts of that person.

Lessee. Person to whom a lease is granted; often called a tenant.

Leasor. Person granting a lease; often called a landlord.

Liability Insurance. Protection against loss because of the claims of others arising out of real or alleged acts of the insured.

Limit of Liability. Maximum amount the insurer will pay in the event of a loss that is covered under the policy.

Lines. Types of policies or business a company writes, such as fire lines, commercial lines, or personal lines; also is used to designate a specific account or exposure.

Line Underwriter. An underwriter who actually performs the selection process on individual risks.

Lloyds of London. A clearinghouse for the placement of insurance and reinsurance.

Loss. Valid claim for recovery under a policy.

Loss Ratio. The proporation that losses bear to premiums during a specific period.

Marine Insurance. Coverage for ocean-going vessels and cargo, as well as related liabilities; often called Ocean Marine or Wet Marine to differentiate it from Inland Marine.

Material Damage. Used synonymously with "Physical Damage" to refer to damage to a vehicle under fire, theft, comprehensive and collision coverages.

Medical Payments. Sums paid to or on behalf of the insured for medical, surgical, ambulance, hospital, and similar expenses made necessary by an insured injury.

Minimum Premium. The least amount of money for which a company will issue a policy.

Misrepresentation. A deliberate misstatement of material facts.

Moral Hazard. An increase in the likelihood that a loss will occur because of personal acts of the insured or another person which would cause losses.

Morale Hazard. An increase in the likelihood that a loss will occur because of an insured's carelessness or indifference to loss.

Mortgage. A document under which a lender retains a residual interest in property if the loan is in default; generally used by insurers to apply to all similar secured conveyances of title, such as trust deeds.

Mortgage Clause. A policy provision containing an agreement to notify the mortgage holder of changes in the policy, to have the mortgagee's rights unaffected by acts or omissions of the insured, and to have every loss payable to the mortgagee as its interest may appear.

Multiple-Line Insurance. A combination in one policy of coverage from each of the two major groups: Property and Casualty.

Mutual Insurance Company. An insurer which is owned by the policyholders.

Named Insured. The person who is named in the policy; one who seeks protection.

Negligence. An act of commission or omission in which there is failure to use the ordinary care a prudent person would use under the circumstances.

Net Retention. Same as "Retention."

Nonbinder Risk. A risk which is in a category for which authority to bind the coverage has not been given to the producer.

Nonrenew. Refusal to extend insurance beyond the expiration date.

Occupancy. The type of use to which a specific property is placed.

Occurrence. An unexpected or unintended event.

Partial Loss. Damage to property which either is less than the amount of insurance or less than the total value of the property.

Party. One of the persons participating in a contract or legal action.

Peril. Cause of loss.

Personal Lines. Classes of insurance applicable to individuals rather than businesses.

Personal Property. All property that is not real property — that is, not affixed to the realty.

Physical Damage. See "Material Damage."

Physical Hazard. The increase in the likelihood that a loss will occur because of features in the construction, maintenance, use or condition of the property itself.

Policy. The written contract of insurance. Also used to refer to a settled course of action or method of operation which has been adopted by management.

Policy Back. Same as "Policy" except that "policy" usually refers to the complete contract while "policy back" often is used to refer to the printed provisions of the policy to which a face sheet or declaration page is attached.

Policyholder. Same as "Insured."

Policy Limit. Same as "Limit of Liability," or "Amount of Insurance."

Policy Term or Policy Period. The length of time during which coverage is in force extending from the effective date until the expiration date or renewal date.

Pool. An organization made up of a group of companies that join voluntarily or involuntarily in order to supply insurance to one or more persons or businesses.

Preferred Risk. An individual risk for which a company desires to write insurance, considering the risk to be better than average.

Premium. Sum or consideration given for insurance protection.

Producer. A person who sells insurance.

Producer's Report. A form, usually part of the application, that is completed by the producer as a means of furnishing desired information to the underwriter concerning a specific risk.

Profit. Amount of money a company may retain after paying all losses, expenses and taxes.

Prohibited Risk. A risk in a category a company does not wish to write; it may not be bound by a producer nor (in most cases) by an underwriter below the management level.

Property Damage Liability. The obligation imposed by law upon a person for damage caused by negligence of that person to the property of another.

Property Insurance. A general term ordinarily including fire insurance and inland marine insurance; covers loss to the property of the insured as contrasted with liability coverage.

Prorata Cancellation. Termination of a policy before its expiration date under which a refund of premium is made to the insured in proportion to the time that the coverage had been in force.

Protection. Same as "Coverage."

Rate. Factor used to determine the premium for a policy.

Rating Bureau. A nonprofit organization of insurance companies formed to promulgate rates for its members and subscribers.

Real Property. Buildings and other fixed properties attached to the land or realty.

Realty. Generally used to mean land; may also mean real estate, including both land and real property attached to it.

Reciprocal. An insurer whose members exchange insurance contracts with one another and appoint an attorney-in-fact to manage the operation; also called an "inter-insurance exchange."

Reinsurance. The assumption by an insurer, called a reinsurer, of all or part of the risk of loss of another insurer, known as the ceding company.

Renew. Acceptance of a risk for another term following the expiration of renewal date.

Rescind. Cancellation of a policy as of its effective date.

Retention. Amount of risk retained by a company when a portion is ceded to a reinsurer, or retained by a policyholder and not insured.

Reunderwriting. Review of an individual risk after it has been in force to determine if it is still acceptable.

Rider. Same as "Endorsement."

Riot. A disturbance caused by three or more persons who assist one another in attempts to disrupt legal processes of order.

Risk. The subject matter of insurance; the insured property or exposure. Also used to denote uncertainty about financial loss.

Robbery. The felonious taking of property by violence or the threat of violence.

Schedule Policy. One covering only the specified and described property or perils, as contrasted with blanket coverage.

Short Rate Cancellation. The termination of a policy before its expiration date under conditions permitting the company to refund to the insured less than a proportion to the time that the coverage has been in force, in order to help cover the expense of writing the insurance.

Solicitors. Persons who are licensed as such, and are employed by agents or brokers to assist in selling insurance.

Special Form. A dwelling coverage which is added to a fire policy to provide all risks coverage, subject to stated exclusions and limitations.

Sprinkler Leakage Insurance. Coverage against loss resulting from the accidental discharge of water from a sprinkler system, due to a fault in the system.

Staff Underwriter. An underwriter who performs such staff functions as research, rule preparation, analyses of problems by class or area, audit and advice.

Standard Risk. An individual risk with average characteristics and loss probabilities, neither better than average (preferred) nor worse than average (substandard).

Stock Company. An insurer owned by stockholders.

Subject. The object to which the perils can cause loss. Also used to denote exposure to loss, as "amount subject to one loss."

Substandard Risk. An individual risk for which most companies do not desire to write insurance — considering the risk to be worse than average.

Surplus. The excess of assets over liabilities.

Term. The period for which a policy is issued.

Theft. Felonious taking of property.

Total Loss. Complete destruction of property. Also used to describe the destruction of property to such a degree that repairs would exceed the value of the property; often this is called a "constructive total loss."

U.M.. Abbreviation for "Uninsured Motorists Coverage."

U.I.M. Abbreviation for "Underinsured Motorists Coverage."

Underwriter. A person who is engaged in the process of underwriting. Sometimes is also used to denote any person who is involved in the insurance function except insureds; this may include a producer, a claims adjuster and an employee of an insurance company.

Underwriting. The process of securing and analyzing information, and making decisions to accept or reject risks. Includes the evaluation, selection, classification and rating of those risks accepted.

Underwriting Profit or Loss. The net increase or decrease in the surplus of the company resulting from the insurance function as distinguished from the investment function. It is computed by deducting from premium such expenses as losses, claims adjustment expenses, commissions, overhead expense and bureau fees, but not taxes.

Underinsured Motorists Coverage (U.I.M.). Protection under an automobile liability policy against a loss by failure to collect in full from a negligent party whose liability limits are insufficient to cover the entire loss. The insured's own policy pays the amount of loss above the limits of the other policy, but only if the other party is liable, and only up to the limits of the insured's policy.

Uninsured Motorists Coverage (U.M.). Protection under an automobile liability policy against a loss caused by failure to collect from a negligent party who is not insured. The insured's own policy pays instead of the uninsured motorist, but only if the latter is liable.

Use and Occupancy Insurance (U and O). See "Business Interruption Insurance."

Vandalism. Willful or malicious destruction or deferment of property of others.

Warranty. A pledge or promise that something is what it is represented to be.

Index

A

B

D

E

F

G

J

K

L

M

P

Physical hazard, 17, 223-234
defined, 687

Q

R

S

T

U